W9-BXH-351

FrontPage® 2002
Bible

FrontPage® 2002 Bible

David Elderbrock and David Karlins

Hungry Minds™

Best-Selling Books • Digital Downloads • e-Books • Answer Networks • e-Newsletters • Branded Web Sites • e-Learning

New York, NY ✦ Cleveland, OH ✦ Indianapolis, IN

ST. PHILIP'S COLLEGE LIBRARY

TK
5105.8885
.M53
E433
2001

FrontPage® 2002 Bible

Published by

Hungry Minds, Inc.
909 Third Avenue
New York, NY 10022
www.hungryminds.com

Copyright © 2001 Hungry Minds, Inc. All rights reserved. No part of this book, including interior design, cover design, and icons, may be reproduced or transmitted in any form, by any means (electronic, photocopying, recording, or otherwise) without the prior written permission of the publisher.

Library of Congress Control Number: 2001091981

ISBN: 0-7645-3582-X

Printed in the United States of America

10 9 8 7 6 5 4 3 2 1

1B/ST/QX/QR/IN

Distributed in the United States by Hungry Minds, Inc.

Distributed by CDG Books Canada Inc. for Canada; by Transworld Publishers Limited in the United Kingdom; by IDG Norge Books for Norway; by IDG Sweden Books for Sweden; by IDG Books Australia Publishing Corporation Pty. Ltd. for Australia and New Zealand; by TransQuest Publishers Pte Ltd. for Singapore, Malaysia, Thailand, Indonesia, and Hong Kong; by Gotop Information Inc. for Taiwan; by ICG Muse, Inc. for Japan; by Intersoft for South Africa; by Eyrolles for France; by International Thomson Publishing for Germany, Austria, and Switzerland; by Distribuidora Cuspide for Argentina; by LR International for Brazil; by Galileo Libros for Chile; by Ediciones ZETA S.C.R. Ltda. for Peru; by WS Computer Publishing Corporation, Inc., for the Philippines; by Contemporanea de Ediciones for Venezuela; by Express Computer Distributors for the Caribbean and West Indies; by Micronesia Media Distributor, Inc. for Micronesia; by Chips Computadoras S.A. de C.V. for Mexico; by Editorial Norma de Panama S.A. for Panama; by American Bookshops for Finland.

For general information on Hungry Minds' products and services please contact our Customer Care department within the U.S. at 800-762-2974, outside the U.S. at 317-572-3993 or fax 317-572-4002.

For sales inquiries and reseller information, including discounts, premium and bulk quantity sales, and foreign-language translations, please contact our Customer Care department at 800-434-3422, fax 317-572-4002 or write to Hungry Minds, Inc., Attn: Customer Care Department, 10475 Crosspoint Boulevard, Indianapolis, IN 46256.

For information on licensing foreign or domestic rights, please contact our Sub-Rights Customer Care department at 212-884-5000.

For information on using Hungry Minds' products and services in the classroom or for ordering examination copies, please contact our Educational Sales department at 800-434-2086 or fax 317-572-4005.

For press review copies, author interviews, or other publicity information, please contact our Public Relations department at 317-572-3168 or fax 317-572-4168.

For authorization to photocopy items for corporate, personal, or educational use, please contact Copyright Clearance Center, 222 Rosewood Drive, Danvers, MA 01923, or fax 978-750-4470.

LIMIT OF LIABILITY/DISCLAIMER OF WARRANTY: THE PUBLISHER AND AUTHOR HAVE USED THEIR BEST EFFORTS IN PREPARING THIS BOOK. THE PUBLISHER AND AUTHOR MAKE NO REPRESENTATIONS OR WARRANTIES WITH RESPECT TO THE ACCURACY OR COMPLETENESS OF THE CONTENTS OF THIS BOOK AND SPECIFICALLY DISCLAIM ANY IMPLIED WARRANTIES OF MERCHANTABILITY OR FITNESS FOR A PARTICULAR PURPOSE. THERE ARE NO WARRANTIES WHICH EXTEND BEYOND THE DESCRIPTIONS CONTAINED IN THIS PARAGRAPH. NO WARRANTY MAY BE CREATED OR EXTENDED BY SALES REPRESENTATIVES OR WRITTEN SALES MATERIALS. THE ACCURACY AND COMPLETENESS OF THE INFORMATION PROVIDED HEREIN AND THE OPINIONS STATED HEREIN ARE NOT GUARANTEED OR WARRANTED TO PRODUCE ANY PARTICULAR RESULTS, AND THE ADVICE AND STRATEGIES CONTAINED HEREIN MAY NOT BE SUITABLE FOR EVERY INDIVIDUAL. NEITHER THE PUBLISHER NOR AUTHOR SHALL BE LIABLE FOR ANY LOSS OF PROFIT OR ANY OTHER COMMERCIAL DAMAGES, INCLUDING BUT NOT LIMITED TO SPECIAL, INCIDENTAL, CONSEQUENTIAL, OR OTHER DAMAGES.

Trademarks: FrontPage is a registered trademark or trademark of Microsoft Corporation. All other trademarks are property of their respective owners. Hungry Minds, Inc., is not associated with any product or vendor mentioned in this book.

Hungry Minds is a trademark of Hungry Minds, Inc.

About the Authors

David Elderbrock has worked as a technical consultant and Web application developer. He got his start as an Internet developer at the University of California, Berkeley, where he helped design an online reading and composition database for writing instructors while finishing a PhD in English. Since 1995 he has worked with dot-com startups, small businesses, and large corporations to help them create and manage online applications to facilitate communication, knowledge sharing, and learning. He is the principal author of *Building Successful Internet Businesses* and a contributing author of *Producing Web Hits*, both published by Hungry Minds (formerly IDG Books Worldwide). David is founder and principal of Literate Technologies, LLC, located in Madison, Wisconsin.

David Karlins is a FrontPage Web designer, consultant, teacher, and the author or co-author of several FrontPage books. David designs Web sites for the art, music, and theater communities, and his ppinet.com Web site provides resources for FrontPage Web developers. In addition to *Microsoft FrontPage Bible*, David Karlins's recent books include *Create FrontPage Web Pages in a Weekend, Teach Yourself FrontPage 98 in a Week, MCSD: Designing & Implementing Web Sites with Microsoft FrontPage* (MCSD Exam 70-055), *FrontPage 2002 Virtual Classroom*, and *The Complete Idiot's Guide to Flash 5*.

Credits

Acquisitions Editor
Carol Sheehan

Project Editor
Gus A. Miklos

Development Editors
Gus A. Miklos
Andy Marinkovich

Technical Editor
Christopher DiMaano

Copy Editors
Luann Rouff
Maarten Reilingh

Editorial Manager
Colleen Totz

Project Coordinator
Dale White

Graphics and Production Specialists
Joyce Haughey
Jill Piscitelli
Brian Torwelle
Julie Trippetti
Jeremey Unger
Erin Zeltner

Quality Control Technician
Carl Pierce

Proofreader
Laura L. Bowman

Indexing
TECHBOOKS Production Services

As always, to Tamar, Eric, and Evan. —David Elderbrock

To everyone on the planet with a message to share. —David Karlins

Preface

Today the Internet has become a ubiquitous part of our everyday lives, both at work and at home. Even the recent bursting of the bubble of Internet optimism is less a sign of disillusionment with Internet technology than it is a substitution of an initial, giddy enthusiasm with serious reckonings over how best to use the new technologies that have sprung up in the past five years. The Internet is here to stay (at least until the next technological revolution comes along) — only now with rules.

Part of what this means is that an increasing number of people, with a broad spectrum of needs and technical abilities, continue to be called upon to create and maintain Web-based content and information. By and large, these people will not be experts in HTML or any of the other members of the ML family (DHTML, XHTML, XML, WML, and so forth). They will be people who, for reasons of business or personal interest, want to use the Web as a medium with which to communicate. FrontPage 2002 is designed for these people, technical and nontechnical alike.

FrontPage, now in its fifth revision (by our count) since Microsoft first acquired the product, is a remarkably easy-to-use tool for creating Web pages and organizing and managing Web sites. First added to the Microsoft Office suite in the previous version, FrontPage continues to serve as a point of integration between the traditional desktop communication and productivity tools and the Web. With FrontPage, Web-page authoring has grown up and joined the mainstream.

Who Will Want to Read This Book

This book explores FrontPage and the multifarious Web technologies that serve as its underpinnings with the full spectrum of users in mind. For all readers, novice and expert alike, *FrontPage 2002 Bible* is good, solid information presented in readable doses. It recognizes the serious nature of Web publishing yet strives (thankfully, we think) to retain the sense of fun — and occasional good-natured irreverence — that has characterized the Web since its inception. We believe that FrontPage is an excellent tool for a variety of Web design and development tasks. We are not afraid to caution readers about some of its shortcomings, however, and even more valuably to suggest ways to work around these deficiencies (at least until they are fixed in the next version of the product).

More precisely, this book attempts to address three specific (if overlapping) audiences:

✦ **For the novice Web-page author:** *FrontPage 2002 Bible* offers plenty of carefully explained, step-by-step examples and tutorials. It is ideal for anyone who wants to create high-quality Webs without focusing on the technical side, whether you're planning to concoct your own personal Web site or have been tasked with adding content to your company's intranet.

✦ **For intranet content teams:** Microsoft has been proactive in revising all of its Office tools with the corporate project team in mind. FrontPage, particularly, has a number of features designed for Web project teams that need to coordinate the work of content editors, graphic designers, and programmers. This book offers sage advice on how to get the work done quickly, while ensuring quality results.

✦ **For professional developers:** *FrontPage 2002 Bible* pushes and prods FrontPage users at every turn to take the application as far as it can go. This book is for developers fluent in the ways of the Web, looking for the tools to become more productive and to expand their repertoire of technical expertise.

How This Book Is Organized

FrontPage 2002 Bible retains the fundamental wit and wisdom that are hallmarks of its earlier versions. It has, of course, been revised to highlight new and altered features in FrontPage, and several sections have been added to cover advanced topics in even more depth. We have taken special care to address issues brought to our attention by readers of the previous editions. Here are some of the highlights in this edition:

✦ **Expanded coverage of Web databases:** Largely in response to the number of reader queries received on this topic, we have added a second chapter on FrontPage database applications. Together the two chapters cover all the basics of using FrontPage to connect to databases — and then take you well beyond that.

✦ **Detailed examples of working with Flash, JavaScript, DHTML, and other Web technologies:** Although you can create lots of sophisticated effects with nothing more than FrontPage, this book also shows how to use FrontPage in conjunction with some of the most popular Web multimedia applications and programming technologies.

✦ **Full coverage of Microsoft's new SharePoint technology:** The replacement for Office Web Server, SharePoint Webs provide a quick and simple way to create team-oriented Web services without months of custom development.

✦ **Tips for navigating the jungle of Web technologies:** As the Web grows ever more sophisticated, the multiplicity of technologies and the products that support or don't support them becomes ever more complicated. FrontPage, although helpful in some ways in this respect, shows a decided bias toward the Microsoft way of Web development. This book strives to provide a more general perspective — alerting you to pitfalls and helping you build sites compatible with all environments.

Whatever your level of interest, you can use the book as a cover-to-cover tutorial, beginning with the basics and proceeding to the advanced stages of FrontPage 2002 and beyond. Or, you can use this book as a reference, dipping into it topic by topic as you deem necessary.

Following is a brief synopsis of what you'll find in the pages of this book.

Part I: FrontPage Essentials

The first chapter, "Getting Started with FrontPage," provides a quick-start tour of FrontPage 2002, taking you through the basic steps of creating a personal Web. Only one chapter into the book, and already you've created your own Web site! Chapter 2, "Working with FrontPage Web Sites," provides an overview of FrontPage's tools for creating, organizing, and maintaining Web sites. Chapter 3, "Publishing and Maintaining FrontPage Web Sites," examines the ins and outs of publishing your FrontPage content, while Chapter 4, "Integrating FrontPage with Office Applications," shows how you can use FrontPage in conjunction with other Office products, such as Word, Excel, and PowerPoint.

Part II: Designing Web Pages

In Part II, we focus on the details of designing Web pages in FrontPage. Chapter 5, "Page and Text Formatting," looks at the practical details of text-formatting issues. Chapter 6, "Working with Layout: Tables and Layers," shows a number of techniques for defining the layout of your page. Chapter 7, "Designing Pages with Shared Borders and Frames," examines ways to divide the layout of your page into defined regions. The last chapter in this section, "HTML Editing," shows how you can use FrontPage to get under the hood of your Web pages and edit the HTML directly.

Part III: Organizing FrontPage Webs

In Part III, we move from page-level issues to site-level issues. This section examines ways to design and organize your site to produce consistent, inviting Web sites. Chapter 9, "Building Navigational Elements," focuses on ways to create the system of buttons and hyperlinks you use to guide your users around your site. Chapter 10, "Using FrontPage Themes," shows how you can give your entire site a professional and consistent look and feel with a few simple clicks, with a focus on creating your own unique theme design. Chapter 11, "Working with Styles and Style Sheets," discusses FrontPage's support for the Web standard Cascading Style Sheets (CSS) as a supplement or alternative to themes.

Part IV: Working with Pictures, Animation, and Multimedia

Part IV provides thorough coverage of a wide range of elements that you can add to your FrontPage Web pages to give them dynamic visual appeal. Chapter 12, "Using Pictures," digs into the details of working with graphic images and multimedia content in FrontPage, including embedding video and sound files. Chapter 13, "Using Animation Effects," covers FrontPage's built-in DHTML capabilities. Chapter 14, "Adding FrontPage Components," reviews all of the ready-to-run Web components included in FrontPage. Chapter 15, "Embedding Components," looks at a variety of advanced components — plug-ins, ActiveX controls, and Java applets — that you can add to your pages and configure in FrontPage.

Part V: Activating Web Pages

Part V explores the many ways FrontPage 2002 makes it possible to provide an interactive user experience. Chapter 16, "Designing Forms," the first of two chapters on forms, focuses on designing and creating HTML forms. Chapter 17, "Activating Forms," builds on the previous chapter by showing how to handle the input submitted by users via your forms. At this point in the book, we turn our attention to a number of advanced topics, beginning with Chapter 18, "Client-side Scripting," which shows how to add JavaScript and DHTML to your Web pages. Chapter 19, "Server-side Programming," focuses on CGI and ASP programming issues.

Part VI: Connecting Databases to the Web

Part VI is devoted to the issue of connecting your Web pages to a database. The first of two chapters on this topic, Chapter 20, covers FrontPage's basic support for creating views of database content using the Database Region Wizard. Chapter 21 shows how to create a full-fledged Web-based database application, starting with the newly added Database Interface Wizard, and then filling in a number of pieces that this wizard does not supply.

Part VII: Advanced Topics

The last part of the book examines a number of issues relating to managing and publishing your Web project and administering your Web site. In Chapter 22, we discuss the ins and outs of customizing the FrontPage environment to suit your purposes. Chapter 23 takes up server administration issues related to FrontPage and provides in-depth explanations of working with the FrontPage Server Extensions. Chapter 24 describes the exciting new SharePoint technology for developing team-oriented Web services and how FrontPage fits into this picture.

Conventions Used in This Book

FrontPage 2002 Bible uses a simple notational style. All listings, filenames, function names, variable names, and keywords are typeset in a `monospace font` for ease of reading. The first occurrences of new terms and concepts are in *italic*. Text you are directed to type is in **boldface.**

Each chapter starts with a short list of all the neat things that you'll learn in that chapter. The summary at the end of the chapter tells you a bit more about what the chapter covered.

Following the time-honored tradition of the Hungry Minds *Bible* series, we use icons to help you quickly pinpoint useful information. Following are the icons used in this edition:

The Note icon marks a general interesting fact — something that we thought you'd like to know.

The Tip icon marks things that you can do to make your job easier.

The Caution icon highlights potential pitfalls. With this icon, we're telling you: "Watch out! This could produce unexpected and/or undesirable results!"

The New Feature icon calls special attention to additions and changes to FrontPage 2002.

Sidebars

We use sidebars throughout the book to highlight interesting, noncritical information. Sidebars explain concepts you may not have encountered before or give a little insight into a related topic. If you're in a hurry, you can safely skip the sidebars. On the other hand, if you find yourself flipping through the book looking for interesting information, reading the sidebars is a good idea.

About the Book's Web Site

FrontPage 2002 Bible contains a wealth of examples to illustrate the numerous Web development concepts and techniques discussed in its pages. In order to make it as easy as possible to obtain copies of these example files, Hungry Minds has set up a Web site for downloading these files. To access the Web site, point your browser to http://www.hungryminds.com/extras/076453582x and follow the links. Examples have been organized by chapter for easier reference.

In addition, the authors maintain a separate support site at www.ppinet.com, where you can always find related data files, updates, a discussion forum, and FrontPage resources.

Reach Out

The publisher would like your feedback. After you have had a chance to use this book, send any feedback to my2cents@hungryminds.com. Please include the book's ISBN and/or title in the subject line so that your comments reach the right people.

You can also share feedback directly with the authors at www.ppinet.com.

Acknowledgments

This is now the third edition of *FrontPage Bible*, and, again, I would like to thank the folks at Hungry Minds (formerly IDG Books Worldwide) for giving me the opportunity to revise and update the content for the latest release of Microsoft's FrontPage. Revising a software book in step with the development of a new product is always a roller-coaster experience. A number of people at Hungry Minds have helped to keep things on track with the seat belts fastened. I would like to thank acquisitions editor Carol Sheehan for her efforts in managing the editorial process. I am also indebted to project editor Gus Miklos and technical editor Christopher DiMaano, who helped ensure that this book is editorially sound and technically accurate, respectively. Most especially, I owe a special thanks to my co-author, David Karlins, whose efforts to ensure that this is the best FrontPage book in print are unflagging. — *David Elderbrock*

I'd like to recognize the contributions of hundreds of readers around the world who have submitted suggestions, constructive criticisms, discoveries, and insights at the FrontPage Forum (www.ppinet.com). They deserve important credit for the content and approach of this book. Thanks also to David Pfeiffer at DPA Software (FrontLook), Ali Ketchum at LaGarde, Inc. (StoreFront), Sandra Chafin at Webs Unlimited (J-Bots), and Colwin Chan at Ulead (GIF Animator) for assistance with FrontPage add-in documentation. Photo, art, and site content credits: Jason West, Andrea Bozeman, Evanna, Jose Avila, Elvira Avila, Sasha Karlins, and Happily Dugless (happilydugless@musician.org).

Finally, in working on the third edition of this book, I've come to appreciate even more the unique contributions of my co-author, David Elderbrock. Nobody does a better job of solving the mysteries of FrontPage database management and other advanced-level FrontPage Web design challenges. — *David Karlins*

Contents at a Glance

Contents

FrontPage Essentials

Getting Started with FrontPage

CHAPTER

1

♦   ♦   ♦   ♦

In This Chapter

Introducing FrontPage
2002

A quick tour of
FrontPage

Designing and
managing a Web site

Editing Web pages

♦   ♦   ♦   ♦

Getting Started with FrontPage 2002

FrontPage 2002 is both a powerful tool for creating sophisticated
Web sites, and fairly easy to use. This means that you'll probably
feel at home in FrontPage right away, and it also means that
many important FrontPage features won't be so obvious to you.

FrontPage is actually a combination of many different elements.
FrontPage's Page view provides an easy, intuitive way to edit
and format Web pages. Other views provide complex options for
managing the large sets of files used in a Web site. In addition,
FrontPage comes with built-in tools that generate animation
(moving graphics), interactivity (objects that respond to
visitor's actions), and even online data collection and data
management.

In this book, we'll explore the full depth and breadth of
FrontPage. We assume that you want to squeeze the most out
of FrontPage, and we'll help you do that. We also assume that
you're not necessarily a programmer or Web technician, so
we'll break down even high-powered features like animation,
media, and Web database management into bite-sized pieces.

If you are in a hurry to create a Web site, start here. The
chapters that follow expand on and add to the concepts
introduced in this chapter. You can use the rest of this book
as a reference, looking up features as you need them. You can
also work your way through the book section by section,
explore the tutorials along the way, and acquire a complete
set of skills for creating and managing FrontPage Web sites.
This chapter moves quickly through all the essentials

ST. PHILIP'S COLLEGE LIBRARY

necessary to create a Web site in FrontPage 2002. If you're already familiar with Web design and Web page editing, this first chapter will provide a quick roadmap to follow to apply your skills to FrontPage 2002. If you're brand new to Web design, this chapter is a good introduction and starting point.

Before diving into the nuts and bolts of creating a Web site, the next section briefly defines some of the basic elements with which you will be working.

FrontPage Webs, Web Sites, and Web Pages

From the vantage point of a Web designer, when you create a Web site, you work on two basic levels: Web design and page design. Unless your Web site is simply one page, you have two related jobs. You need to design a Web structure that visitors can use to navigate from page to page, and you need to design the Web pages themselves. To use an analogy from architecture, your job is to design both a building (your site) and individual rooms or offices (your pages).

The streamlined interface in FrontPage 2002 makes all of this very intuitive. You can easily jump to views that enable you to see an overview of your entire Web site. You can also zoom in to an individual page, and edit the content and look of that page.

Although the FrontPage interface enables you to shift back and forth seamlessly between Page view and Site view, having a basic sense of what's happening "under the hood" will help you while you put your Web site together.

FrontPage Webs and Web sites

FrontPage Webs are organized collections of files that are associated with a Web site. Unless they are very simple, one-page sites, most Web sites are composed of many Web pages, and almost every Web site (even a one-page site) will have many files — HTML Web pages, media files, images, and so on. To visit a Web site, you enter a Web site address, known as a *Uniform Resource Locator (URL)*, into the browser. The Web site is located by the browser and displayed.

Just to complicate things, FrontPage has its own use of the term Web. A Web, in FrontPage's lexicon, is a set of Web pages and associated files organized in a single folder or directory structure. In general, your FrontPage Web is your Web site, although multiple FrontPage Webs can be created on the same Web site. That is because FrontPage uses the term Web to refer to the folder or directory structures that hold Web site files. More than one of these Webs can be attached to a single URL or Web site.

The practical implication of all this is that the first step in creating a Web site in FrontPage is to define a FrontPage Web. This chapter jumps right into that process, but let's first take a quick look at the other main elements of Web sites.

ST. PHILIPS COLLEGE LIBRARY

In most cases, a FrontPage Web and a Web site are the same thing. The two terms describe what is going on from different perspectives — Web site being the external appearance, and FrontPage Web being the underlying file structure. Unless it is necessary to make a distinction, this book refers to FrontPage Webs as Web sites.

Web pages

Web pages differ from other documents in that they are designed to be interpreted by Web browsers. Microsoft Internet Explorer (IE) and Netscape Navigator take text, graphics, and even interactive elements, such as input forms, sound, and video, and enable them to be accessed by visitors to your Web site.

Web browsers interpret and display Web page content by reading Hypertext Markup Language (HTML). FrontPage shields you from having to learn HTML, by translating the menu options that you select into HTML code. If you prefer to do your own HTML coding see Chapter 8.

Not only does FrontPage translate your commands into HTML, it also generates programming scripts in other languages, enabling you to add content such as search boxes, input forms, interactive responses to visitors, and sound and video.

FrontPage server extensions

Let's start with a quick quiz (don't worry, nobody flunks!):

FrontPage Server extensions are

a) The most powerful component of FrontPage

b) The most mystifying element of FrontPage

c) The most frustrating part of FrontPage

d) The part of FrontPage that simplifies complex tasks such as collecting data, which you just can't do with any comparable program

e) All of the above

The answer is . . . e! FrontPage server extensions enable the most powerful elements of FrontPage to work. Among the FrontPage features that require server extensions are the following:

✦ Collecting form data

✦ Presenting database content

✦ Assigning Categories to Web pages (useful in defining search engines)

✦ Style sheet links (for assigning formatting to multiple pages)

✦ Confirmation fields for input forms

✦ Online discussion forums

✦ Hit counters

✦ Search forms (for your site)

You can look at this list in two ways. On the one hand, it is an impressive list of features that are not generally available (for example, with Dreamweaver or GoLive). On the other hand, these features *don't work unless you publish your Web to a server with FrontPage extensions.*

Confusion about the necessity and role of FrontPage server extensions can lead to quite a bit of frustration if not understood. Therefore, let's take a brief look at what FrontPage server extensions are, where you get them, and how they work. FrontPage server extensions are files that are installed not on your personal PC, but on the server on which your Web site is hosted. Technically, you can have a Web server on your own PC. However, it is more likely that your server software is going to be located on a remote computer connected by an office intranet or the Internet. FrontPage makes it easy to publish your Web site from your own PC to a server, a process described in detail in Chapter 3. The short story is that your server administrator provides you with a URL, a user name, and a password. With that information, you set up a link to transfer files from your local development computer to a Web server.

> **Note**
>
> Client? Server? A Web *server* is the computer that hosts a Web site and the associated software. The *client* is another way of talking about the computer and browser software used by a visitor to view and interact with your Web site. Do all Web servers have FrontPage extensions? No, but millions do. Office intranets created using the Microsoft Windows 2000 operating system come with FrontPage server extensions (although installing them is an option for the server administrator). In addition, thousands of commercial Web site providers that offer FrontPage extensions are competing for your Web-hosting dollars. Some of these providers will set you up with a fully FrontPage-enabled Web site for less than $100 per year.

If you are going to develop a Web site in FrontPage, it probably doesn't make sense to do so unless you plan to publish your site to a server with FrontPage extensions. FrontPage extensions enable approximately 20 percent of the features in FrontPage, and they are among the most powerful and valuable features.

The biggest drawback in this whole scenario is that until you publish your Web to a server, you won't be able to test features such as input forms, search boxes, and other elements of your Web site.

Previous iterations of FrontPage and Office included a stripped-down version of a FrontPage–enabled server called the *Personal Web Server* (*PWS*). Chapter 4 examines the role of PWS in more detail; unfortunately, as of FrontPage 2002, there is no version of the Personal Web Server available for Windows 95, Windows 98, or Windows ME that supports the most recent FrontPage Extensions. In short, if you are developing a site using any of these Microsoft operating systems, you will need to publish your site to a remote server before you can test many of the features you include in your Web site. Developers who have Windows 2000 on their local computers can install a local server that does support FrontPage 2002 server extensions.

Again, we'll explore all this, including your options for publishing to FrontPage servers, in Chapter 3.

Note   The simplest, and most universally available, option for publishing Webs to FrontPage–enabled servers is to contract with one of the many Web-hosting companies that provide FrontPage extension server sites.

As if all this weren't complicated enough, new features in FrontPage 2002 require Web servers with FrontPage 2002 extensions. Most FP 2002 features work on sites published to servers with FP 2000 extensions, but a few don't. That's because some *new* features of FrontPage 2002 won't work if your Web site is published to a server with extension files from FrontPage 2000.

Using FrontPage 2002 extensions can cause headaches for Web server administrators (and you folks can jump to Chapter 23 for help). You can avoid worrying about any of it, however, by simply contracting with a Web provider that has FrontPage 2002 extensions as part of its Web-hosting package.

What's New in FrontPage 2002?

There's more new to FrontPage 2002 than meets the eye. At first glance, users of previous editions (especially FP 2K) will notice that the basic layout of views and toolbars has not changed dramatically, which is nice for those of us who invested time learning our way around FP 2002's older sibling.

New elements in FP 2002 range from little fixes to rather substantial new features. Table 1-1 describes the most impressive ones, and organizes them in main areas.

Table 1-1	
FrontPage 2002 New Features	
New Feature	**Description**
Database Features	The Database Interface Wizard enables you to generate an online database that collects data, displays it (including using queries), and (this is the new part) enables visitors to add and edit records online. We clamored for just such additional built-in functionality in FrontPage databases, and we got a significant improvement. Another cool new feature is the upload Browse button you can add to database forms, enabling visitors to navigate to a file on their system for uploading to the server. You can also create customizable image buttons. (See Chapter 19.)

Continued

Table 1-1 *(continued)*	
New Feature	**Description**
Shared Borders	Improved capability to format shared borders. (See Chapter 7.)
Reports	New reports include usage analyses to identify where your visitors are coming from, what browsers they are using, and other information. (See Chapter 14.)
Top 10 Lists	Related to new reports, these are Top 10 Lists that can be added to sites, telling visitors about themselves, including sites they are coming from. (See Chapter 14.)
Link Bars	FrontPage's generated navigation bars have been made more customizable in the form of link bars. These are a welcome relief to the constraint of using one navigational logic throughout a Web site, and a more complex way to include automated links. (See Chapter 9.)
Improved Publishing	FrontPage has finally given us more control over how much of a site we publish to a server. (See Chapter 3.)
New Themes	FrontPage 2002 has added a dozen or so new themes. Real theme lovers will continue to explore the add-ins provided by FrontLook. (See Appendix D.)
Drawing Tools	The most questionable addition to FrontPage is the inclusion of WordArt and Drawing tools that work okay in PowerPoint and Word, but aren't really appropriate for Web design. These features will likely be improved in the next version of FrontPage. (See Chapter 12.)
Remove Underlining from Links	FrontPage has tweaked page formatting and style features. Most noticeably, you can use the Underline icon in the Formatting toolbar to remove underlining from text links. (See Chapter 11.)
Internal Frames	Internal (embedded) frames are a cool way to display content within a Web page — anywhere on the page. (See Chapter 7.)
Better Table Editing	FrontPage tables now include automatic formatting features, including AutoFit to Contents (to adjust column widths) and AutoFormat (to apply pre-set formatting). Other new table features include commands to split a table and automatic data fill features. (See Chapter 6.)
Photo Galleries	FrontPage includes a new feature that uses a rather complex combination of tables and JavaScript to enable you to automatically generate a display for a collection of photos — displaying them as thumbnails, and creating links to full-sized pictures. (See Chapter 12.)

New Feature	Description
SharePoint/ Intranet Tools	Office XP ships with a pre-fabricated intranet component called SharePoint. You can use FrontPage to alter and customize the SharePoint interface. In addition, some of the intranet objects included with SharePoint — such as lists and libraries — can be embedded in any FrontPage Web site. (See Chapter 24.)

A Quick Tour of FrontPage

When you open FrontPage 2002, you see a Views list on the left side of the screen, which is where you select from many different ways to look at the files you create in FrontPage. On the right side of the screen is a big open space, which is your workspace.

FrontPage views are generally divided into those that let you organize your whole Web site, and Page view, which is where you design the content of specific pages.

FrontPage 2002, like other Office XP applications, opens with a Task Pane displayed on the right side of the FrontPage window. Here, you'll find quick links to jump to frequently used features in FrontPage.

The FrontPage Task Pane

The drop-down arrow at the top of the Task Pane toggles between displaying the standard Task Pane (with links to create new pages and Webs), a Clipboard display, and a help search box. The drop-down list is displayed in Figure 1-1.

Figure 1-1: The Task Pane has three different functions: a quick way to create new files, a Clipboard viewer, and a help search box.

The standard Task Pane is a nice way to quickly open a new Web page. The specific tasks displayed in the FrontPage Task Pane depend on your work history. For example, recently opened Web pages are displayed as quick links.

The Clipboard pane is a helpful way to grab recently copied or cut objects. The Search pane is an easy way to rummage through a Web site to locate pages with select text.

All of the features available in the Task Pane are also available from the FrontPage menu, and many are available from buttons on various taskbars. In other words, the Task Pane duplicates features found elsewhere in FrontPage, and it takes up a lot of space. You'll probably find yourself using its handy links when you first start using FrontPage, but closing it for good as you learn your way around the available views and toolbars.

FrontPage views

Before you start creating Web pages and organizing them into a Web site, you can introduce yourself to the following different views in FrontPage 2002:

✦ **Page view:** If you are responsible for the content of a Web site, you will probably spend much of your time in Page view, which is where you edit individual Web pages. Figure 1-2 shows FrontPage's Page view. You can view or hide a list of your files by selecting View ⇨ Folder List from the menu.

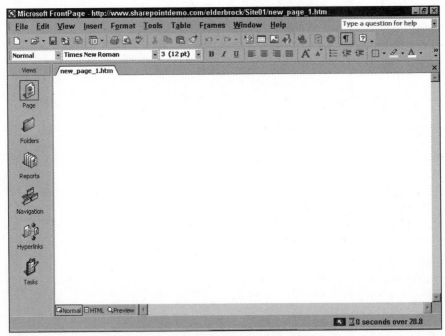

Figure 1-2: Use FrontPage's Page view to design your Web pages.

✦ **Folders view:** This is a directory of the files that you create in FrontPage. FrontPage creates two empty folders (_private and images) when you open a new Web site. When you save a Web page, or any other element of your Web site, you'll see files listed in this view.

✦ **Reports view:** FrontPage can generate reports that assess the status of your Web site. The default view that appears when you click the Reports icon in the View bar displays a summary of the different reports available. You can view any particular report by double-clicking it in the Site Summary spreadsheet, or by selecting a report from the View Reports submenu.

✦ **Navigation view:** This view enables you to organize all of your different Web page files into an integrated Web site, and to define navigational links between pages.

✦ **Hyperlinks view:** Hyperlinks (or links, for short) are text or graphics that, when clicked, connect a visitor to another Web page within, or outside of, your Web site. Links can become corrupted or outdated when Web pages change, and this view checks them for you.

✦ **Tasks view:** FrontPage enables several members of a Web design team (or an individual Web designer) to create lists of things to do. Tasks can be assigned to different team members, who in turn can check off their progress as the Web is completed.

Creating a Web site

Because Web sites are collections of Web pages, you can start either by designing the site structure or by creating the page content. If, for example, you are designing a site that will include many Web pages created in other Office 2002 applications, you may not need to do much with page content, and your entire task may be orchestrating and organizing all of these pages into a Web site. In another scenario, you may be creating the entire Web site, including its content, from scratch.

In either scenario, your first task is to create a FrontPage Web, the underlying structure that holds together, coordinates, and manages all the files in your Web site.

Note　You may be tempted to start designing a Web page without first defining a Web site. This is a bad idea. Unless you are in a position to make a conscious decision to circumvent FrontPage's Web structure, stick with Web design. The only situation in which you would ever have a reason to create Web pages without creating a Web structure first is if you aren't going to use FrontPage to publish your Web to a server.

When you select File ⇨ New from the FrontPage menu, you'll see the New Page or Web Task Pane, as shown in Figure 1-3.

Figure 1-3: The New Page or Web Task Pane

Your first decision is whether to create a new Web from scratch or to get help and save time by using a Web template.

In either case, you'll be choosing from the links under the New From Template heading in the New Page or Web Task Pane. If you want to create your own Web from scratch, choose Empty Web. Alternatively, you can choose from the set of preconfigured Web templates. Each of these templates includes Web sites with formatted pages, navigation links, and some beginning page content or page content advice.

Choosing a Web template

FrontPage includes the following templates for generating Web sites:

- ✦ **One Page Web:** A new Web with a single blank page
- ✦ **Corporate Presence Web:** A complex Web with dozens of pages that can be converted into a Web site for a corporation
- ✦ **Customer Support Web:** A Web site that includes input forms for customer questions and feedback
- ✦ **Database Interface Web:** Generates an online database with input forms to collect data, queries to present data, and forms to enable visitors to edit the database content
- ✦ **Discussion Web Wizard:** A wizard that leads you step by step through the process of creating a Web site in which visitors can post questions and get answers

✦ **Empty Web:** A Web site without pages

✦ **Import Web Wizard:** A wizard that leads you through the process of assembling a Web from pages created outside of FrontPage

✦ **Personal Web:** A nifty little four-page Web site that works well for sharing your interests

✦ **Project Web:** A specialized Web site template for project managers only

✦ **SharePoint Team Web:** Generates an intranet portal with a schedule, a documents library (to which participants can upload files), links, and other office intranet goodies

The Web Site Templates list is shown in Figure 1-4.

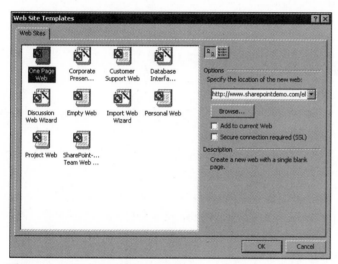

Figure 1-4: Web template options

Some of these templates are quite complex, and require a fairly high level of experience with FrontPage in order to customize. The Corporate Presence Web, the Customer Support Web, the Discussion Web Wizard, and the Project Web include many components that won't work unless you have saved your site to a Web server with FrontPage extensions (the Personal Web Server will work). Moreover, the SharePoint Team Web requires still more server extensions — the SharePoint extensions. The Empty Web, One Page Web, and Personal Web work well without FrontPage extensions on a Web server.

After you select a template, your next decision is where to save your Web.

Where to save your new Web

As mentioned earlier, you have two basic options in creating a Web. One, you can create your Web on a Web server that is accessible to the Internet or an intranet. Two, you can create your Web on a local computer drive (your hard drive). Webs saved to your hard drive do not all have the advanced features available in FrontPage, such as the capability to collect data from input forms. Nor can they, of course, be visited by anyone else. You can, however, use your local drive to design a Web, and then publish it to a Web server when one becomes available.

Saving to a folder on your hard drive

To create your Web on your local hard drive, enter a drive and folder location in the drop-down box labeled "Specify the location of the new web" on the right side of the Web Site Templates dialog box. For example, in Figure 1-5, the folder is defined as `C:\FrontPage Web Sites`.

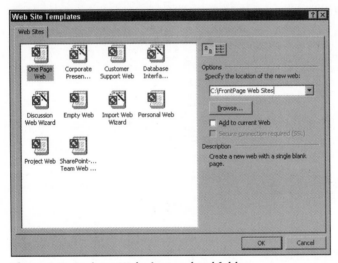

Figure 1-5: Saving a Web site to a local folder

After you select a template, you can click the OK button to generate a local Web for your FrontPage Web site.

Saving to an intranet or Internet Web server

If you have access to an Internet or intranet Web server, you can publish your Web there. You need a URL (site address) from your Web administrator, and you need to be connected to the Internet or your intranet. Establishing these connections is the job of your Internet Service Provider (ISP) or your local intranet administrator. They should provide you with the URL address to which you are publishing, and a password.

Selecting a Location for Your Web Site

If you have just unwrapped your copy of FrontPage and installed it, this discussion of where to save your Web site may seem a bit daunting. However, after you complete the process of deciding where you are going to save your Web site, you don't have to make that decision again. In addition, you can easily change the location of your Web site. As long as you've chosen one of the options previously discussed for saving your Web site, you can automatically publish your Web site to the Internet or an intranet, and FrontPage will handle all your file transfers automatically.

You *can* bypass the entire process of selecting a Web site location by choosing File ➪ New ➪ Page instead of File ➪ New ➪ Web when you start to create new Web pages. If you do that, you can still create individual Web pages, but you lose much of FrontPage's power to manage all of your files and transfer them from one Web location to another.

If you're just starting out with FrontPage, save your Web to a local folder on your computer. Later, you can explore options for obtaining server space from a Web server provider.

On the other hand, if you need your site on the World Wide Web *now*, you can contract more or less instantly with a Web server provider. You can find an updated list of some in the FrontPage resources area of `www.ppinet.com`. These providers will help you grab a domain name and sign you up for the Web space and features you need.

If you have a Web server, enter the URL of the Web address in the drop-down box labeled "Specify the location of the new web" in the Web Site Templates dialog box. After you select a template and click OK, you'll be connected to your Web server and prompted to enter a user name and password.

An additional option is to install a Web server on your local computer. We'll explore that option in Chapter 3.

Defining a home page

After you generate a Web, the next step in designing your Web site is to create a home page. All templates (except the Empty Web template) generate a home page for you.

Note

A home page is the page that opens when a visitor goes to your URL with their browser. FrontPage templates usually assign the filename `Default.htm` to the generated home page, but home pages can also be named `Default.html`, `Index.htm`, `Index.html`, or either `Index` or `Default` with an `.asp` filename extension. Because FrontPage is generating the page for you, and assigning a filename, you don't need to know or worry about page-naming rules, just note the page FrontPage creates.

If you used the Personal Web template or the One Page Web, your Web opens with a home page. Figure 1-6 shows a new Web generated by the One Page Web template, with a lonely-looking home page in the middle of Navigation view.

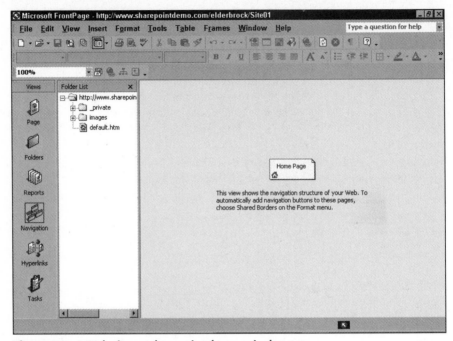

Figure 1-6: A Web site can be as simple as a single page.

If you created your new Web from the Empty Web template, you can click the New Page button in the FrontPage toolbar to create a new page. The first page that you create will be your home page.

Adding pages to your Web site

You can add Web pages to your Web site in Navigation view by clicking the New Page button in the toolbar. As you click the New Page button, new pages appear as "child" pages of the home page.

If you click one of your child pages and then click the New Page button, the new pages become child pages of child pages. You can construct many levels of Web pages in this manner. Figure 1-7 shows a Web site with three levels of pages.

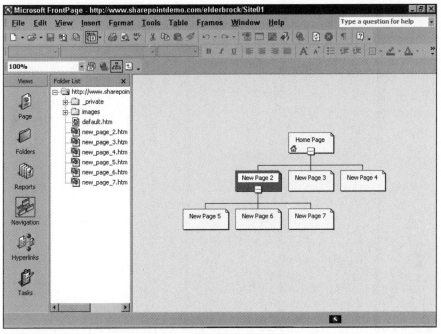

Figure 1-7: You can chart out your Web site in Navigation view.

Web structure strategies

As you design your Web site structure, put yourself in the shoes of someone visiting your Web site. One convention used by many Web site designers (and programmers of all types) is to present visitors with between three and five options at each level of the Web site. Therefore, for example, you might welcome visitors to your site at your home page, and present them with three options. Each of those options might have three, four, or five sub-options.

Web design strategies are explored in much more detail in Chapter 2, and navigation options are discussed in depth in Chapter 9. For now, remember that your Web site can run many levels, but in general, you should limit the number of pages at each level of the site to between three and five.

After you define a Web structure, you can easily change it. Just click and drag a page in Navigation view to move it to another location or level in the flowchart. Figure 1-8 shows a page being moved.

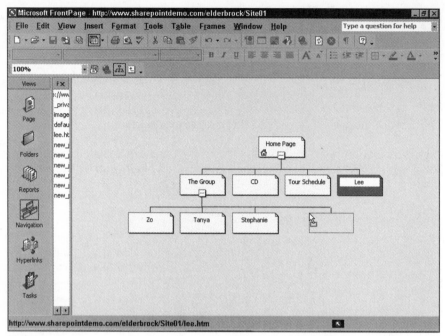

Figure 1-8: You can rearrange pages in Navigation view by clicking and dragging.

You can delete pages from your Web by right-clicking them in Navigation view and selecting Delete from the context menu. You will be prompted to delete the pages either from the navigation structure, or from the Web site. If you elect to delete a page from your Web site, it's gone for good. If your site is large, you can use the horizontal or vertical scroll bars to navigate within it.

You can collapse any section of Navigation view by clicking the minus symbol (-) on parent pages, to display only the parent page for that section of the Web. To expand the flowchart, click the plus sign (+) under a parent page.

Page titles and filenames

Web pages have both titles and filenames. The filename is used internally for FrontPage to organize the Web. The title is the "public" name of the Web page, and is displayed in the visitor's browser when the Web page is opened.

New pages are generated with filenames that have titles such as New Page 6. You will want to change the titles for these pages to something more descriptive and creative, as these will appear in the title bar of your visitor's browser.

Changing page titles

To change the page title in Navigation view, right-click a page in the flowchart and select Rename from the context menu. Type a new name and press Enter.

> **Tip**   A quick trick for renaming many pages is to use the Tab key to jump from one page to the other, which automatically enables you to rename pages. You can also change a page title by slowly double-clicking the page in Navigation view, or by clicking the page once and pressing the F2 function key.

Page titles are not restricted to eight characters, and can include spaces. However, you don't want to make them so long that they don't fit in your visitor's browser window.

Changing page filenames

Although page names do not appear in browser title bars or as generated navigation links, you still may want to rename them. One good reason is so that when you edit pages and keep track of files, you can associate a page filename with a page title.

As you generate new pages in Navigation view, they appear as HTML files in the Folder list on the left side of the Navigation view window. For now, the safest way to name a Web page is with an eight-character filename, with no spaces or non-ASCII characters, and with a filename extension of `.htm`. You can assign a new filename to a Web page by right-clicking the filename in the Folder list on the left side of the FrontPage window, and selecting Rename from the context menu. Type a new filename (don't forget the `.htm` filename extension) and press Enter to change the filename.

> **Tip**   Sometimes, matching a filename with a page title can be difficult. After you rename your page titles in the flowchart area of Navigation view, your page filenames in Folder view will not match those titles. The solution is to right-click a page in the Folder list and select Find in Navigation from the context menu. The page associated with the file will be selected in Navigation view.

Adding global Web site elements

Two global elements exist in designing a Web site: navigational structure, and look and feel. These elements work together to create the overall flow and ambiance of your site. Think of an engineer and an interior decorator working together to make a building habitable.

You design the flow of your Web site by moving pages around in Navigation view. Unless you are aiming for the ultra-minimalist look, you will want to define a global atmosphere for your site. You do that by assigning global elements such as a global color scheme, global graphic elements, global text fonts, and global page backgrounds.

You can define and assign these global design elements by assigning a *theme*. FrontPage comes with a large selection of themes, each of which includes attributes such as fonts, colors, and icons. FrontPage supplies over a dozen themes. Additionally, by selecting or deselecting options such as vivid colors or a background picture, you can define several variations on each theme. Furthermore, you learn how to create your own custom themes in Chapter 10. In the following sections, you'll learn how to implement the themes that come with FrontPage, starting with a discussion of how to select a site theme.

Selecting a site theme

Each theme is a group of elements that can be applied to every page in a Web site. You can remove a theme from a page, or even use different themes for different pages in a Web site. The purpose of selecting and applying a theme, however, is to use the same colors, icons, and other attributes throughout a site, to give the site a unique and consistent atmosphere.

To assign a theme, follow these steps:

1. With your Web open, select Format ➪ Theme from the FrontPage menu. You can do this from any view.

2. To apply your theme to all pages in your site, click the All Pages radio button. Alternatively, if you have selected a single page (or pages) in Folder, Page, or Navigation view, you can click the selected page(s) radio button to apply the theme to only the selected page(s).

3. Click one of the themes in the list on the left side of the Themes dialog box. A preview of the theme is displayed in the Sample of Theme area on the right side of the dialog box. Use the checkboxes on the left to experiment with Vivid Colors, Active Graphics, or a Background Picture, as shown in Figure 1-9.

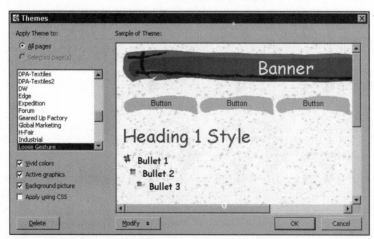

Figure 1-9: Themes provide color schemes, navigational icons, fonts, and colors.

4. When you settle on just the right theme to suit your image, click the OK button to apply the theme to your Web site (or selected pages).

You can sneak a peek at your Web pages now by double-clicking a page in Navigation view to open it in Page view. However, you will better appreciate the impact of themes after you add shared borders, covered in the next section.

Note Themes collect many elements of global page design, two of which are font and paragraph attributes. These attributes can also be applied through inline formatting or Cascading Style Sheets. (Style Sheets are covered in Chapter 11.)

Adding shared borders

Along with themes, you can apply universal characteristics to all pages in your Web site by applying shared borders. These shared borders are often used, at least in part, as navigational tools.

To apply shared borders to your Web site, follow these steps:

1. Select Format ➪ Shared Borders from the FrontPage menu (you can be in any view). The Shared Borders dialog box appears, as shown in Figure 1-10.

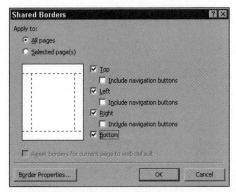

Figure 1-10: You can define up to four shared borders for a Web site.

2. Select the All Pages radio button to apply the shared borders to the entire Web, or select the Selected Pages radio button to apply shared borders only to selected pages.

3. Select any combination of top and left shared borders that are the most widely used. Start experimenting by selecting them. Later, you can deselect one or both of these shared borders and apply bottom or even right shared borders.

Note   Most page designers put navigational guides at the top, left, or bottom of a Web page, and avoid right-side shared borders. The right side of a Web page is sometimes outside of the browser window and can be viewed only if a visitor uses the horizontal scroll bar.

   4. If you select top and/or left shared borders, you can select the Include Navigation Buttons checkboxes for one or both of these shared borders.

   5. After you select your shared borders, click the OK button.

Viewing Your Pages

Even if you have not placed any specific content on individual Web pages, you can generate many Web elements simply by applying themes and shared borders. Moreover, if you used a template, such as the Personal Web template, to generate your pages, you have some comment text and other page elements.

To see how your Web site is shaping up, you can examine it in four ways:

   ✦ Page view, Normal tab

   ✦ Page view, HTML tab

   ✦ Page view, Preview tab

   ✦ A Web browser (such as Microsoft Internet Explorer or Netscape Navigator)

You can examine any page in Page view by double-clicking that page in the Folder list or in Navigation view. Page view is where you edit and view individual Web pages.

Normal tab

The Normal tab in Page view displays Web pages in a manner similar to how they will appear in a Web browser (see Figure 1-11). The Normal tab also displays page elements that don't appear in a browser, such as comment text (also referred to as purple text), dotted lines to demarcate shared borders, and other editing marks.

The Normal tab is discussed again shortly, because this is where you edit the content of Web pages.

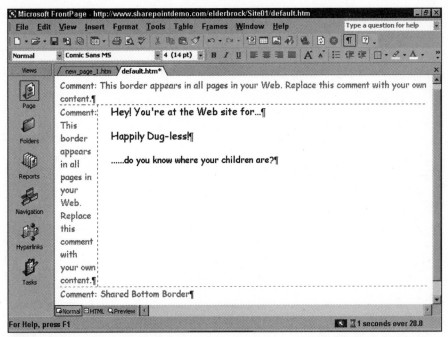

Figure 1-11: Comments and shared border dividers are visible in the Normal tab of Page view.

HTML tab

You can see the HTML code that is generated by FrontPage for your Web page by clicking the HTML tab in Page view. If you are an HTML coder, feel free to edit the HTML code in this view. If not, you can simply admire the fact that you generated all of this code without knowing HTML, or you can study the generated code and use it to teach yourself some HTML. Figure 1-12 shows the HTML tab of Page view.

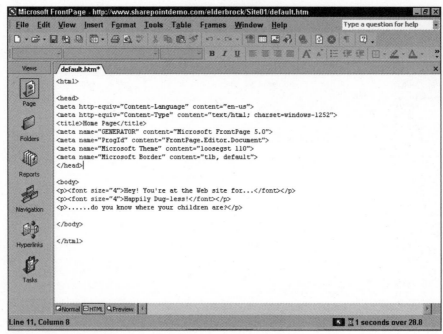

Figure 1-12: The HTML tab is a full-fledged HTML editor.

Preview tab

The Preview tab in Page view displays your Web page closer to the way that it will look in a browser (compared to how it is displayed in the Normal tab). Elements such as comment text and shared border dividers don't display in the Preview tab. However, you cannot edit in Preview tab. Figure 1-13 shows a Web page displayed in the Preview tab of Page view.

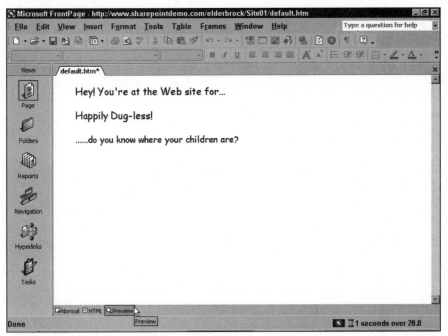

Figure 1-13: The Preview tab approximates the appearance of a Web page in a Web browser.

Previewing in a browser

The Preview tab roughly approximates how a Web page looks in a browser, but nothing can substitute for actually testing your pages by looking at them in Internet Explorer and/or Netscape Navigator.

Different browsers interpret Web attributes differently. In addition, different screen resolutions display Web pages differently. You should periodically preview your Web pages in both Netscape Navigator and Internet Explorer. It may be a good strategy to keep an older version of one of these browsers installed on your computer, so that you also can see how your Web pages look in those browsers.

To preview your Web page in a browser, select File ➪ Preview in Browser. The Preview in Browser dialog box enables you to select from any browser installed on your computer, and any screen resolution supported by your system.

Before continuing, in this chapter, to explore the process of editing and formatting page content, you may want to experiment with the following tutorial to sharpen your Web design skills.

Tutorial 1-1: Creating a personal Web site

1. Launch FrontPage 2002. Select File ➪ New ➪ Page or Web to open the New Page or Web Task Pane.

2. Click Web Site Templates in the Task Pane, and enter a location for your Web in the "Specify the location of the new web" drop-down list. This location can be a Web server or a file folder.

3. Click Personal Web in the Web Sites list, and click the OK button in the Web Site Templates dialog box.

4. Click the Navigation icon in the View bar to see your Web site in Navigation view. Click the Favorites page in Navigation view, and then click the New Page tool in the toolbar three times to create three child pages connected to the Favorites page.

5. Right-click the first (farthest to the left) of the new pages in Navigation view and select Rename from the context menu. Change the page title to People. Press the Tab key and rename the next page Places. Press Tab again and rename the third page Things.

6. Click and drag in Navigation view to move the three new pages so that they become child pages of the Interests page, as shown in Figure 1-14.

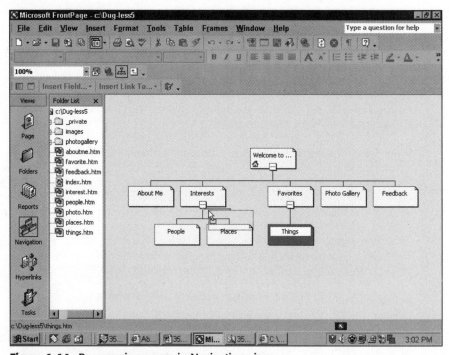

Figure 1-14: Rearranging pages in Navigation view

7. Select Format ➪ Theme. Select one of the themes from the list by previewing the list of themes in the Sample of Theme area of the Themes dialog box. When you find a theme that you like, experiment with the three available formatting checkboxes in the dialog box. (The Apply Using CSS checkbox does not affect formatting — we explore this option in Chapter 11.) After you choose a theme and select options that you like, click the OK button in the Themes dialog box.

8. Select Format ➪ Shared Borders and note the default settings that are associated with your theme. Close the Shared Borders dialog box.

9. Double-click the home page in Navigation view to open that page in Page view. Note the elements placed on your page by the theme and shared borders. Click the HTML tab to see the HTML code that you generated.

10. If you have a browser installed on your computer, select File ➪ Preview in Browser and then double-click one of your installed browsers. Test your Web site in your browser by clicking underlined links in the navigation bars to move from page to page (see Figure 1-15).

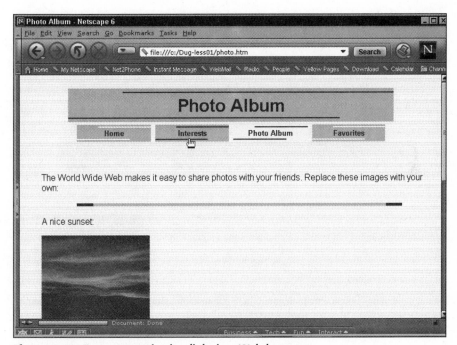

Figure 1-15: Test your navigation links in a Web browser.

11. Select File ➪ Close Web to close your entire Web, including all the page files. You can delete this Web if you want to by selecting File ➪ Open Web, right-clicking a Web file, and selecting Delete from the context menu.

Editing Pages in Page View

Chapter 5 is devoted entirely to an in-depth exploration of adding, editing, and formatting text in Page view. However, you can start here by entering and formatting text, and adding graphics. Because most of the work of designing Web pages and controlling Web page content takes place in Page view, you could say that the bulk of this book is about working in Page view. This first chapter can only scratch the surface of designing pages, but you don't really need to know much about Page view to edit and format text, and to add pictures.

You'll find that Page view is very much like a word processor or desktop publishing program—or even a presentation program, such as PowerPoint. You enter, edit, and format text much as you would in any text-editing program.

You can also insert, move, format, and edit graphics. All of this is explored in more detail in Chapter 12, but you can begin to work and edit in Page view without detailed preparation.

A look at Page view

You can open an existing Web page in Page view by double-clicking it in any other view, including Navigation view. The tools in the Standard and Formatting toolbars at the top of the Page view window provide quick access to the most frequently used page editing and formatting features. The Standard toolbar is shown in Figure 1-16.

Figure 1-16: The Page view Standard toolbar

Here is a quick explanation of each button (from left to right) in the Page view Standard toolbar:

- ✦ **The New drop-down list/button is set to Page by default:** At that setting, it creates a new Web page.

- ✦ **The Open drop-down list/button defaults to File:** Accesses the Open Files dialog box to open existing Web pages

- ✦ **Save:** Saves the open Web page

- ✦ **Search:** Opens the Search pane to search your Web site

- ✦ **Publish Web:** Publishes your Web site from your local computer to an intranet or Internet location

✦ **Toggle Pane:** Use this drop-down list/button to choose either Folder List (to display a list of folders and files associated with your Web site) or Navigation pane (to display a flowchart of your pages based on navigational links).

✦ **Print:** Sends your Web pages to your printer

✦ **Preview in Browser:** Displays your Web page in your default Web browser

✦ **Spelling:** Checks your Web page for spelling errors

✦ **Cut:** Cuts selected text or objects and saves them in the Clipboard

✦ **Copy:** Copies selected text or objects and saves them in the Clipboard

✦ **Paste:** Pastes contents of the Clipboard at the insertion point

✦ **Format Painter:** Copies a selected format to apply with the (paintbrush) format cursor

✦ **Undo:** Undoes your last command or keystroke

✦ **Redo:** Cancels your latest Undo action

✦ **Web Component:** Opens the Insert Web Component dialog box, where about half the features of FrontPage are crammed somewhat uncomfortably into a single dialog box

✦ **Insert Table:** Opens the Insert Table grid

✦ **Insert Picture from File:** Opens the Picture dialog box

✦ **Drawing:** Activates the Drawing toolbar, which enables you to draw WordArt and Microsoft Office drawing objects

✦ **Insert Hyperlink:** Opens the Create Hyperlink dialog box to define or edit a link to another Web page or a location on a Web page

✦ **Refresh:** Reformats the page based on the last saved version

✦ **Stop:** Stops refreshing a page

✦ **Show All:** Shows paragraph and line breaks, image anchors, and other elements that do not display in a browser window

✦ **Help Tool:** Opens the Microsoft FrontPage help window, with a variety of options for looking up information

Most of your Web page text formatting is controlled from the Formatting toolbar in Page view. You can see the Formatting toolbar in Figure 1-17.

Figure 1-17: Page view's formatting tools act a bit differently than those in Word.

Here is a quick description of each tool (from left to right) in the Formatting toolbar:

- ✦ **Style:** The styles in the list are HTML styles, and can't be edited in the same way that you edit styles in programs such as Microsoft Word. You can assign formatting without worrying about what HTML style is assigned to text. Styles are discussed in detail in Chapter 11.

- ✦ **Font:** Drop-down list from which you can assign fonts to selected text

- ✦ **Font Size:** Drop-down list from which you can assign font size to selected text. The selection of sizes is constrained by those available in HTML.

- ✦ **Bold:** Assigns boldface to selected text

- ✦ **Italic:** Assigns italics to selected text

- ✦ **Underline:** Underlines selected text

- ✦ **Align Left:** Left-aligns selected paragraph(s)

- ✦ **Center:** Centers selected paragraph(s)

- ✦ **Align Right:** Right-aligns selected paragraph(s)

- ✦ **Justify:** Aligns text left and right (full justification)

- ✦ **Increase Font Size:** Drop-down list from which you can increase font size to selected text.

- ✦ **Decrease Font Size:** Drop-down list from which you can decrease font size to selected text.

- ✦ **Numbering:** Assigns sequential numbering to selected paragraphs

- ✦ **Bullets:** Assigns indenting and bullets to selected paragraphs

- ✦ **Decrease Indent:** Moves selected paragraphs to the right (undoes indenting)

- ✦ **Increase Indent:** Indents entire selected paragraph(s)

- ✦ **Outside Borders:** Defines borders around selected text and/or objects

- ✦ **Highlight Color:** Adds a background highlight to selected text

- ✦ **Font Color:** Assigns colors to selected text

Editing text

You can type anywhere on a page in Page view to add text. You'll find that all standard text-editing and navigation techniques used in other Windows applications can be used to edit text in Page view. FrontPage also provides spell checking as you type, underlining words not found in its dictionary in wavy red lines, so that you can correct spelling as you go. You can find detailed coverage of text editing in Chapter 5, but for now, you can add and edit text by typing and deleting.

If you enter or edit text in a shared border (they are separated from the page by dotted lines in Page view), you affect the way that shared border appears on each page of your Web site. Shared borders are explored in detail in Chapter 7.

As you enter text on your Web pages, click the Save tool in the toolbar to save your changes. Changes to a Web are saved by saving individual pages (you don't "Save" a Web, you save pages in it to update files).

Formatting text

The tools in the Formatting toolbar can be used to apply formatting to selected text. For example, you can select text, click the down arrow next to the Font Color button, and select a font color to apply to selected text from the palette, as shown in Figure 1-18.

Figure 1-18: Assigning font color

Adding images

You have several ways to quickly add images to a Web page in Page view:

✦ Copy and paste images through the Clipboard.

✦ Insert an image from a file on your local drive or from the Internet.

✦ Use FrontPage's nice collection of clip art.

✦ Scan an image directly into FrontPage.

To insert clip art, follow these steps:

1. Choose Insert ➪ Picture ➪ Clip Art from the menu. The Clip Art Task Pane opens.

2. Enter a word in the Search Text field of the pane, and choose from your installed collections of clip art and media types in the Other Search Options area of the Task Pane (or simply accept the defaults, which search all collections for all media).

3. Click a clip art category to see a list of available pictures.

4. Click a picture that you want to insert, and select the Insert Clip button from the drop-down list, as shown in Figure 1-19.

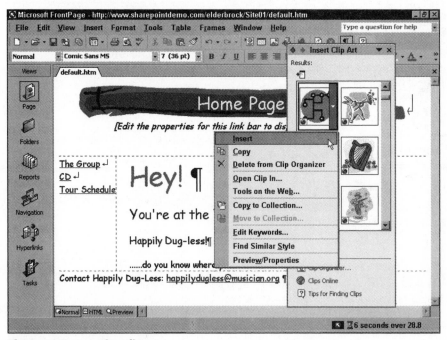

Figure 1-19: Inserting clip art

You can insert a graphic file in much the same way: use the menu, or more quickly use the Insert Picture button, following these steps:

1. Click the Insert Picture from File button in the Standard toolbar.

2. Click the Select a File from Your Computer button in the lower-right corner of the Picture dialog box.

3. In the Select File dialog box, navigate to the folder with your image file and double-click the file to insert that image in your Web page.

Flowing text around images

You can do many things to edit image properties in FrontPage's Page view. You'll explore using pictures in detail in Chapter 12, but let's look at one of the most useful features: the capability to flow text around a graphic image.

To flow text around a graphic, right-click the graphic and select Picture Properties from the context menu. Click the Appearance tab in the dialog box and select Right or Left from the Alignment drop-down menu. Click OK, and your picture is set to have text flow around it, as shown in Figure 1-20.

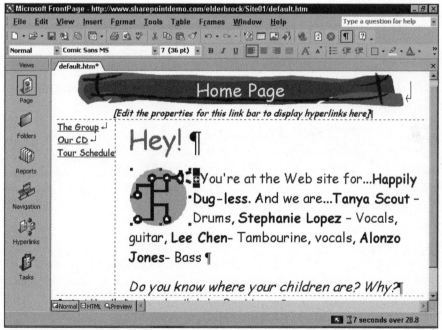

Figure 1-20: Flowing text around a picture

Making images transparent

Another useful graphic feature in FrontPage 2002 is the capability to assign transparency to one color in an image. To do that, click the image. When you do, the Picture toolbar, covered in detail in Chapter 12, appears on the bottom of the page. Each of the Picture toolbar's buttons is a powerful editing tool.

To assign transparency, click the Set Transparency Color tool in the Picture toolbar, and point the Transparency cursor at the color in your image that you want to make invisible. Figure 1-21 shows the Transparency tool aimed at a background color.

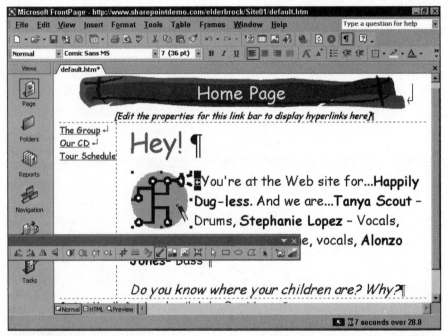

Figure 1-21: You can assign transparency to make one color in a picture disappear, revealing the page background.

Saving images

After you place a picture in a Web page, you can save that picture as an embedded image by saving the page. As you save a page with a new (or edited) image file, the Save Embedded Files dialog box appears. Here, you are prompted to save the image as well, as shown in Figure 1-22.

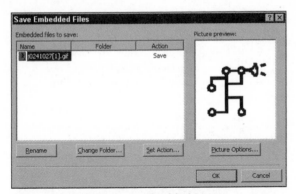

Figure 1-22: Saving an embedded image

As you save your page and its embedded graphic files, those graphic files are converted to a Web-compatible graphics format and saved to your FrontPage Web.

The following tutorial walks you through the process of creating and editing a Web page in a Web site.

Tutorial 1-2: Editing a Web page

1. Open a Web page from an existing Web (the Web you created in Tutorial 1-1 will work fine).

2. Click Navigation view in the View bar on the left side of the window, and double-click the home page in either Folder view or Navigation view to open the home page in Page view.

3. Click the page to set the insertion point at the top of the page, and type **Welcome to Our Web Site**.

4. Press the Enter key and type a paragraph describing what a visitor will find at your Web site.

5. Press Enter again and type three new, short paragraphs. Your Web page should look something like the one shown in Figure 1-23.

6. Click and drag to select the text in the three short paragraphs that you typed, and then click the Bullets button in the Formatting toolbar.

7. Click and drag to select the first line of text at the top of your page. Pull down the Font drop-down list and select Arial. Pull down the Font Size drop-down list and select 36 point. Click the Bold button in the Formatting toolbar. Use the Font Color drop-down list/button to select red, as shown in Figure 1-24.

8. Press Ctrl+End to move to the bottom of your Web page, and chose Insert ➪ Picture ➪ Clip Art.

9. Enter a word in the Search Text box of the Insert Clip Art pane, and click Search. Click one of the resulting images, and then click the Insert Clip button in the drop-down list next to the image. With your picture selected, click the Align Left button in the Formatting toolbar.

10. Press Ctrl+End again to move to the bottom of your Web page, and type **Visit Microsoft at www.microsoft.com**. Press the spacebar to convert this to a hyperlink.

11. Click the HTML tab to see the HTML code that you have generated.

12. Click the Save button. You'll be prompted to save the clip art image that you embedded in your Web page. Click OK in the Save Embedded Files dialog box.

13. Select File ➪ Preview in Browser and then double-click an installed browser on your computer. If you are connected to the Internet, you can test your link to www.microsoft.com.

14. Select File ➪ Close Web.

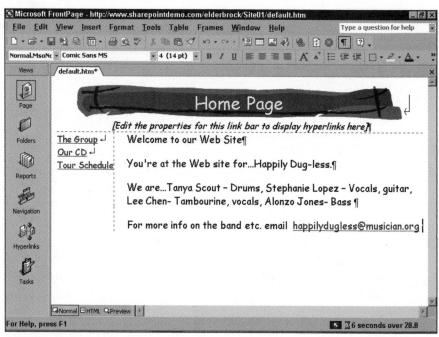

Figure 1-23: Entering text in a Web page

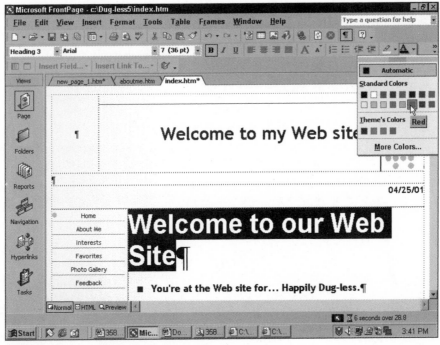

Figure 1-24: Formatting Web page text

Summary

The first step in creating Web pages with FrontPage is to create a *FrontPage Web*. This way, all your files will be organized, connected to each other, and ready to publish to a Web server. FrontPage Webs can be created on your local computer hard drive, or on a *Web server*—a remote computer that makes your site accessible to others.

You can speed up the process of creating a full-featured Web site by using one of the FrontPage Web templates. Or, you can start from scratch with an Empty Web template.

The first page you create in your site is the *home* page. FrontPage will usually assign a filename of `default.htm` to this page. You can create a navigational structure for your site in Navigation view. This navigation structure is used by FrontPage to automatically create links to your pages when you assign a *theme* to your page. Themes also apply formatting like color schemes, fonts, and navigation icons to your site.

Finally, when your Web site and navigation structure are in place, you can add, edit, and format page content in Page view.

With that, you've got a Web site! From here on, we'll explore how to add additional features, and polish your site to make it more accessible, more interactive, and more entertaining.

✦　　✦　　✦

Working with FrontPage Web Sites

In Chapter 1, you learned to create a Web site with linked pages. You applied themes and shared borders to give your site a sense of consistency and to enable visitors to navigate it. This chapter describes in more detail the process of designing and adding content to a Web site.

Web Design Strategies

Web pages and Web sites have something of a chicken and egg relationship: no real answer exists as to which comes first when you design a Web site. As discussed in Chapter 1, you can create Web page content first and then organize the pages together into a Web site. Alternatively, you can design a Web site and then plug in page content. With either approach, however, your site design creates the framework for the display of all the content that you provide.

Why start with site design?

Theoretically, you could create a Web site that consisted of a single page. If your Web site has much content at all, however, this approach presents both technical and aesthetic problems. The page would take unnecessarily long to download in your visitors' browsers, and they would have to wait for information to download that they didn't even want to access. Aesthetically, visitors would have difficulty finding and digesting information at your site. For these reasons, Web sites generally modularize information into many small pages. In addition, generally, many small, quick-loading pages with digestible bites of information are more helpful than a few long, slow-loading pages that mix together different kinds of information.

You face two main strategic decisions when you design your Web site:

✦ What kind of navigational strategy do you want to provide for visitors? What options for jumping to other pages in the site do you want to make available at each page?

✦ What kind of visual theme do you want to apply to your site? Consistent visual elements — such as color schemes, navigational icons, page backgrounds, and fonts — provide coherence to your site and are part of the message that you project to visitors.

After an architect designs a building and the beams are welded into place, the building can't easily be changed from a 48-story skyscraper to a sprawling, two-story campus. Luckily for Web designers, things are more flexible in cyberspace. You can modify the structure and design of a Web site fairly easily in FrontPage. You still need to make some initial decisions, however, as to how to lay out your site. One of the strengths of FrontPage 2002 is the capability it provides to change universally both the layout and design of an entire Web site. Chapter 1 explored the basic process of organizing a site in Navigation view and assigning themes. The next section investigates strategies for organizing your site structure.

Defining navigational links

Following are the two basic design approaches to laying out your Web site:

✦ **Linear design:** This approach takes visitors through your site in a straight line.

✦ **Hierarchical design:** This approach presents visitors with layers of options.

Figure 2-1 shows a Web site laid out in a linear design.

Most Web sites are organized in some version of a hierarchical structure, but both design strategies can be useful, depending on the kind of presentation you are preparing for visitors. The important thing is to make conscious decisions regarding which kind of approach you want to take to your Web site design, and then stick to that approach. By doing so, visitors will feel comfortable at your site, and will be able to jump intuitively to the information that they want. By making conscious decisions about Web navigation strategy, a Web designer can frame the kinds of options available to visitors in conformity with the mission of the site. For example, if your goal is to introduce every product and service that your company provides, the linear structure illustrated in Figure 2-1 channels visitors into a tour of those products and services.

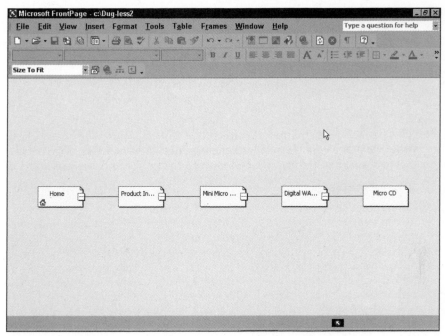

Figure 2-1: A linear Web site design marches visitors straight through your site.

Orchestrating a linear flow in your Web site involves laying out your pages in Navigation view, and then assigning appropriate link bars in Web pages.

To create a Web site that provides a linear flow, start by either creating a new Web site or opening an existing one. You can review the section "Creating a Web site" in Chapter 1, if necessary, for all the information that you need.

With your Web site open, click and drag in Navigation view to arrange your Web pages in one or more lines. Selecting or deselecting the Folder list from the View menu shows (or hides) a list of Web pages in your site. If you have Web pages that are not connected to the navigational flow, you can drag them from the Folder list into the Navigation window, as shown in Figure 2-2.

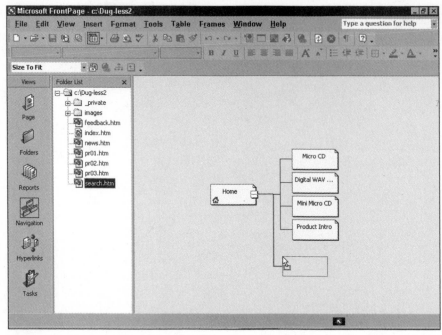

Figure 2-2: You can drag Web pages from the Folder list into the Navigation window.

With your site design defined in Navigation view, you can define link bars in your Web pages that apply the navigational structure in the form of navigational links. That process is explained in the next section, "Defining Link Bars in Shared Borders."

If you define a Web site with a long linear flow of pages, your site may be easier to view horizontally instead of vertically. To rotate the display of your Navigation view flowchart, right-click in the Navigation area and select Rotate from the context menu.

Hierarchical Web structures are used more frequently than linear site designs. Hierarchical structures enable visitors to make their own decisions about which pages they want to see, and in what order. Furthermore, hierarchical structures can be used to organize Web pages into groups, each with its own level of detail, as shown in Figure 2-3.

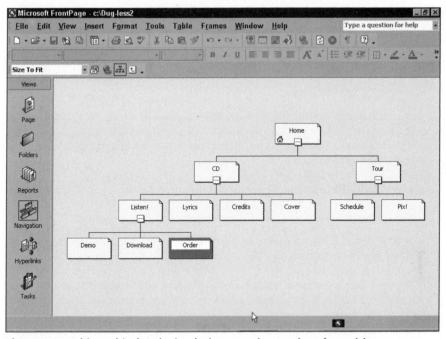

Figure 2-3: A hierarchical Web site design organizes options for a visitor.

A visitor who is interested only in CD products can navigate to the CD "branch" of the Web site and choose between the various CD options (listen, lyrics, credits, cover), without being distracted by other options.

Defining Link Bars in Shared Borders

After you lay out your site in Navigation view, you can define the link bars for each page. Link bars can be inserted at any location in a Web page, but they are normally inserted in shared borders, a special type of Web page that appears on every Web page. Shared borders can be attached to the top, bottom, left, or right side of a Web page. Therefore, theoretically, you can define four link bars in your Web site that will appear on every page in the site.

Four link bars would clutter up a Web site, but providing navigation options at the top, bottom, and left (or right) side of a page may be appropriate in some cases.

Each link bar in a shared border generates links, depending on the logic that you define for that particular bar. For example, if you lay out your Web site in a linear structure, you can generate Next and Back buttons to help visitors travel from the beginning to the end of your page sequence. Similarly, if you design your site with a hierarchical structure, you have several options for enabling visitors to jump to parent and child pages.

Tip Shared borders are not required in order to place link bars on a particular page. You can place link bars in the body of a Web page. However, using shared borders with link bars is a method by which you can create a navigational system for your entire Web site.

To assign shared borders to a Web site, follow these steps:

1. In any view, select Format ➪ Shared Borders from the menu.

2. In the Shared Borders dialog box, select the All Pages radio button to assign shared borders to every page in your Web site.

Note After you define a shared borders design for your entire Web site, you can disable the shared border(s) for specific pages by selecting a page and using the Current Page radio button.

To insert a link bar in a shared border, follow these steps:

1. Open any Web page in a Web site to which you have added at least one shared border.

2. Click in a shared border.

3. Select Insert ➪ Navigation. In the Insert Web Component dialog box, click Bar Based on Navigation Structure in the Choose a Bar Type area.

Note For a full exploration of the other navigation options in the Web Component dialog box, see Chapter 9.

4. Click the Next button in the Insert Web Component dialog box, and use the vertical scroll bar to explore the various styles of available link bars. Select one and click Next.

5. In the final window of this Wizard, choose either a vertical or a horizontal layout for your link bar and click Finish. You're not really finished — now you're ready to define the logic that will determine how FrontPage generates links.

6. In the Link Bar Properties dialog box, select one of the six radio buttons in the Hyperlinks to Add to Page area at the top of the dialog box. Use the Additional Pages checkboxes to add a link to the home page on every page, and/or a link to the Parent Page on every page. The Link Bar Properties dialog box is shown in Figure 2-4.

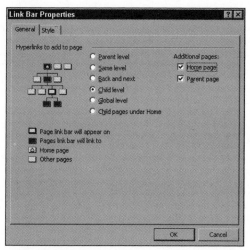

Figure 2-4: The Link Bar Properties dialog box provides six navigation options for your Web site.

7. You can revisit or revise the style choices you made for your link bar by clicking the Style tab in the Link Bar Properties dialog box. In addition to (re)choosing a bar style and orientation (vertical or horizontal), you can also use checkboxes to add vivid colors (for example, a different color scheme based on, but more extreme than, the one associated with your theme) or Active Graphics (graphical navigation buttons that react when a visitor hovers over them with his or her mouse cursor).

Navigation Options

The six radio buttons at the top of the Link Bar Properties dialog box basically break down into two different navigational strategies. The Same Level option and the Back and Next option enable visitors to navigate along a single row in the Navigation view, for a linear navigational approach. The difference between these options is that Same Level enables a visitor to jump to any page in a row, whereas Back and Next offers only two options, the pages to the right and left of a page in the Navigation view flowchart.

The other radio buttons offer variations on a hierarchical scheme. The most utilitarian hierarchical option is probably the Child Level radio button, along with the Home Page and Parent Page checkboxes. This combination of selections in the Link Bar Properties dialog box enables visitors to navigate up or down at any time, and always provides a link to the home page.

As you experiment with different navigational options, they are illustrated in the flowchart to the left of the radio buttons.

After you assign link bars to your shared borders, save the page in which you edited the links, and then select File ➪ Preview in Browser to test the links in your browser.

Customizing links

Automatically generated navigational links have a great advantage, which is also their shortcoming: They apply the same logic to every single page. If you define a link to child pages in your link bar, every page (that has a child page) will have a link to that page. In that sense, link bars cannot be customized for particular pages.

However, other options are available that give you much more specific control over what links are available from your Web pages. Those options are introduced next.

Adding links to page content

You can insert a link (or *hyperlink*, as FrontPage calls them) anywhere in a Web page. You can either type the URL to which you are creating a link, or assign a link to an existing object, such as text or a graphic image.

To include a link, simply type the URL (or e-mail address) in the Web page. Press Enter to create a paragraph break, Ctrl+Enter to create a line break, or use a punctuation key followed by the spacebar. Your URL address is automatically transformed into a link.

To assign a link to existing text (or to a picture), select the text (or picture) and click the Hyperlink button in the toolbar. The Hyperlink dialog box appears. Double-click a Web page in your Web, or enter a URL address outside of your Web in the URL drop-down list. Then, click OK to assign the link.

Adding links to a shared border

Shared borders can include generated link bars, but they can also be edited to include other text or links.

Besides the links generated by link bars, you can add your own, specific links to a Web site or to any page. For example, you may want to include a link to a special page in your Web site from any page in the site. If that special page is your home page, you can do this by selecting the Home Page checkbox in the Link Bar Properties dialog box. If it isn't your home page, you can still add the link to a link bar.

Figure 2-5 shows a link to the "Buy Our CD Right Now" link in the left shared border. This link was not generated by a link bar, it is a regular link created in the shared border, and will appear on every page in which the shared border is embedded.

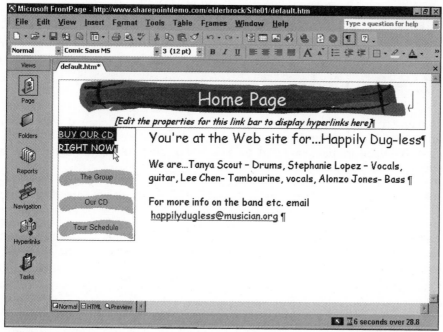

Figure 2-5: Custom links can be inserted into shared borders or into page content.

Adding link bars to page content

A final option for customizing links is to insert a link bar directly into the content of a page. Although this isn't a widely used feature in FrontPage 2002, it has some valuable uses. For example, a link bar with links to child pages can function as a miniature table of contents in a Web page.

Remember foremost that link bars inserted into page content appear only on the page in which they are inserted, whereas link bars placed in shared borders appear on every page to which a shared border has been applied.

Deleting pages from link bars

You can delete a page from the navigation structure by clicking the page in Navigation view and pressing the Delete key. The Delete Page dialog box appears, as shown in Figure 2-6.

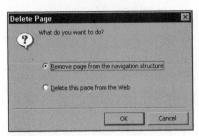

Figure 2-6: You can delete a page from link bars or completely remove it from your Web site.

The Delete Page dialog box has two options:

✦ **Remove this page from navigation structure:** This option doesn't delete the page from your Web site, but removes any link to this page from automatically generated link bars.

✦ **Delete this page from the Web:** This option deletes the page and its contents from the Web site. This is a more drastic option and should be exercised with care, because after you delete a page from your Web site, it cannot be restored.

Changing navigation labels

Navigation labels for generated link bars are based on page titles. Other generated navigation links (such as Home or Back) can be customized for your Web site.

You can redefine the labels that FrontPage generates for the home page, for moving up a page in a Web structure, and for Back and Next labels (used with a linear site design). To change label names, follow these steps:

1. Select Tools ➪ Web Settings and click the Navigation tab in the Web Settings dialog box. The tab is shown in Figure 2-7.

2. Enter new label names for any of the four generated titles. For example, you can change the label assigned to a link to the previous page in a layout from "Back" (the default) to "Previous." (You could also use something like "See previous slide.")

3. After you change the generated label text, click OK. (Clicking OK in the Web Settings dialog box updates links in an existing site.)

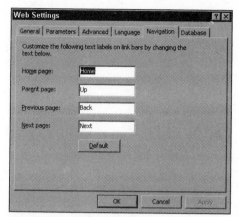

Figure 2-7: You can rename the labels generated in link bars.

Importing an Existing Web Site

You can organize existing collections of files into FrontPage Webs by using the Import Wizard, which imports files from two sources:

✦ An existing Web site that is not a FrontPage Web

✦ A folder on your local drive or network

After you import files, you can work with them as you would any FrontPage Web, organizing them in Navigation view, and adding themes, shared borders, link bars, and so on.

Importing files into a Web

To import files into a new Web, follow these steps:

1. Select File ➪ Import. The Import dialog box appears.

2. Click the Add File button to add a file (or selected files) to your site, or the Add Folder button to add one or more folders.

3. In the Open File dialog box, navigate to the file(s) or folder(s) you wish to import. You can use Shift+Click or Ctrl+Click to select more than one folder or file. Click the Open button to add selected file(s) or folder(s) to the Import list.

4. Click OK in the Import dialog box to add files to your site.

Importing a Web site into a FrontPage Web

To import an existing Web site into a FrontPage Web, follow these steps:

1. Select File ➪ Import.

2. Click the From Web button. The Import Web Wizard opens, as shown in Figure 2-8.

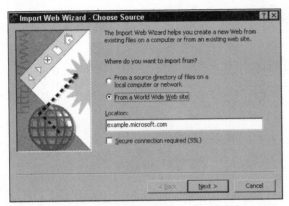

Figure 2-8: FrontPage provides a wizard to integrate existing objects into a new Web.

3. At this point, you have two options:

   - Choose "From a Source Directory of Files on a Local Computer or Network" to import a folder from your local system.
   - Click the "From a Worldwide Web Site" radio button and enter the URL for your Web page in the Location dialog box.

   Click Next.

4. The Edit File List dialog box allows you to deselect files you don't wish to import from the selected Web or folder. Click on files to exclude from importing (use Shift+Click or Ctrl+Click to select multiple files), and click the Exclude button to remove them from the list of files to import. Click Next.

If you are importing a Web or folder from the World Wide Web, you'll see the Choose Download Amount dialog box as part of the download wizard. The Choose Download Amount dialog box enables you to restrict the amount of disk space and files that you download. You can limit how deep into a Web site's structure the Import Web Wizard probes by checking the Limit to This Page Plus checkbox and selecting a number of levels from the Levels Below spin box. You can limit the size of files imported by checking the Limit To checkbox and entering a maximum file size for imported files. Finally, you can limit the types of files to text and graphics, thereby avoiding the long download times required for, say, a 20MB digitized file. The options in this dialog box protect you against filling your entire hard drive with files from a Web site of undetermined size.

5. Click Finish to close the wizard and to add the selected files to your site.

Using Web Templates and Wizards

In FrontPage terminology, a Web template is a set of predesigned Web pages collected into a single Web. In many cases, sample text is supplied, or comment text is used to provide assistance in adding content to the Web. In Chapter 1, you used the Personal Web template to create the basic structure for a Web site.

A wizard is similar to a template, only smarter. Rather than create a Web with all generic content, the Corporate Presence and Discussion Web Wizards first ask you to answer some probing questions, such as "What is your name?" They also ask you what kinds of Web pages you want to include in your Web site. Those wizards then place your answers in the appropriate spots in the template. When you first open a Web that is generated by one of these two wizards, it is already filled with customized content based on your answers. This feature can save you time, although you are likely to want to customize the pages to your liking.

Some of the available templates briefly described in the section "Choosing a Web Template" in Chapter 1 are explored in more depth in the following sections.

Shared Borders — Plus and Minus

Love 'em or hate 'em, shared borders with link bars are a defining element of FrontPage Web sites. They are incredibly convenient — you can generate distinct and somewhat intelligent links on every page in your site in seconds by having FrontPage generate link bars in shared borders. Compared to the tedium of manually creating, changing, and updating navigation areas of Web pages by hand, shared borders with link bars are a godsend.

The downside? Link bars in FrontPage tend to give your Web sites that somewhat institutional look that tells the world you created your site in FrontPage instead of handcrafting every page.

Is there a way to get the best of both worlds? Our design approach often utilizes the productivity of shared borders and link bars, but disguises their use by customizing themes and assigning unique properties to shared borders. You'll explore ways in which you can spruce up the look of shared borders in Chapter 7 and custom themes in Chapter 10.

One Page Web

Because the One Page Web template creates only a single Web page, you may wonder why you should bother using it. Actually, the One Page Web handles several important tasks that save time in generating a Web site. A Web folder is created on your server, ensuring that all of your files will be properly managed by FrontPage. This template also creates a Web page, with the filename `Default.htm` and the page title Home Page (for a full discussion of page names and titles, see the section "Page titles and filenames" in Chapter 1).

The One Page Web template also generates two subfolders in your Web site: `_private` and `images`. The `images` folder can be used to organize picture files for your site and the `_private` folder can be used to store pages and other files that you don't want identified by searches or linked in link bars.

If your project is to develop a Web site from scratch, the One Page Web is a quick way to get started.

Using the Corporate Presence Web Wizard

The Corporate Presence Web Wizard is a basic site for communicating information about a company. This is the most elaborate wizard included with FrontPage. The first dialog box in the wizard, shown in Figure 2-9, asks you which main pages you want to include in your Web site.

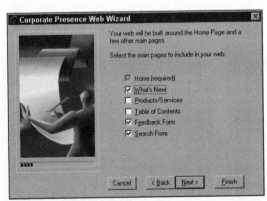

Figure 2-9: The Corporate Presence Web Wizard generates up to six main pages.

The pages available from the Corporate Presence Web Wizard are as follows:

✦ **Home:** Not optional, because it anchors all the navigational links in the site.

✦ **What's New:** Lists links to other pages. If you select this checkbox, the wizard later provides a list of linked articles that you can generate.

✦ **Products/Services:** Can have any number of links to both products and services. If you select this checkbox, you later are asked how many products pages and how many services pages to generate, and what information you want on those pages. Some of these generated pages include input forms that collect data from visitors. The results of these forms are saved in files that are stored in the _private folder.

✦ **Table of Contents:** Generates a table of contents for the site on a separate page.

✦ **Feedback Form:** Generates a Web page with an input form that collects feedback from visitors. The data submitted to this form is collected in a file called inforeq.txt (located in the _private folder). Double-click that file in Folders view to display information in your word processor.

✦ **Search Form:** Creates a search form page that allows visitors to search *your site* (not the Internet) for words or phrases.

After you select the pages you want to include in your Web site, the wizard prompts you for information related to generating those pages. When you complete the wizard, you are asked whether you want to see the Tasks view after your site is generated. Select Yes to see a list of remaining tasks that you need to perform to complete your Web site.

Customer Support Web

The Customer Support Web template generates ten main Web pages in a navigational flow, as well as additional Web pages that are used to supplement those pages. The pages in the Navigation view generated by this template are as follows:

✦ **Customer Support Web:** Home page—welcomes visitors to the support site and has links to other pages.

✦ **Contact Us:** Creates a table with e-mail, phone, and Web site URL links.

✦ **Search:** Includes a search box that visitors can use to find information at your site.

✦ **What's New:** A list of links to pages with update documentation. To make these links functional, you need to edit their content, right-click them, select Hyperlink Properties from the context menu, and link them to actual pages that you create.

✦ **Products:** A page with links to support pages by product–so you can support more than one product at your site.

✦ **FAQ (Frequently Asked Questions):** Includes a list of six questions, with links to bookmarked answers in the body of the page. Bookmarks are discussed in "Inserting bookmarks," later in this chapter. You need to edit the questions and answers.

✦ **Service Request:** Provides a form for clients to fill out to receive help with a specific problem.

✦ **Suggestions:** This is also mainly composed of an input form. Data entered into this form can be viewed by opening the Feedback.htm file.

✦ **Catalogs/Manuals:** Used to enable visitors to link to an FTP (File Transfer Protocol) download site. If you have files at an FTP site, you can edit the links at this page to send visitors to those files.

✦ **Support Forum:** Links to a threaded discussion group, where visitors can post comments or questions, and respond to posted articles.

Note   Some of the pages in this template create input forms that collect and process data. Creating forms is discussed in detail in Chapter 16, and managing form input is explored in depth in Chapter 17.

Using the Database Interface Web Wizard

The Database Interface Web Wizard generates a site with input forms, reports, and queries. A typical site generated by the DIW, with all options selected, creates an Access database at your Web server, and includes the following:

✦ A submission form for visitors to enter data

✦ A results page that displays content from your database

✦ A Database Editor section — pages that enable visitors to view, add, delete, and update records in your database using a Web browser

For a full exploration of FrontPage database features, see Chapter 20.

Discussion Web Wizard

The Discussion Web Wizard generates a fully threaded, searchable discussion group, like the one shown in Figure 2-10.

Empty Web

The Empty Web template generates a Web folder and _private and images sub-folders, just like the One Page Web template. The difference is that the Empty Web template doesn't generate a home page.

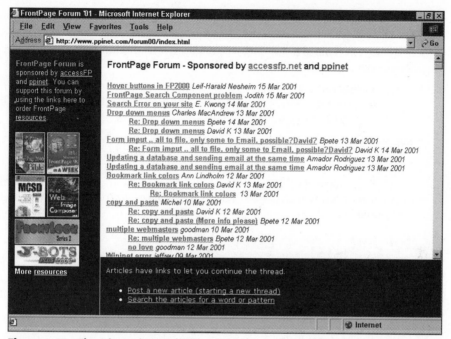

Figure 2-10: The Discussion Web Wizard creates an interactive, threaded discussion forum.

Import Web Wizard

The Import Web Wizard is generated when you select File ➪ Import. For a discussion of how this works, refer to "Importing an Existing Web Site," earlier in this chapter.

Personal Web

The Personal Web template generates a Web site with a home page and five other pages: About Me, Interests, Favorites, Photo Gallery, and Feedback.

Project Web

The Project Web template generates a Web site specifically designed for displaying project-management information. The template generates six linked pages in Navigation view, some of which are connected to additional pages that don't display in Navigation view. The six accessible pages are as follows:

✦ **Members:** Lists team personnel and provides hyperlinks to their e-mail addresses.

✦ **Schedule:** Posts tasks due this week and next week, and lists project milestones (important nodal points in the project).

✦ **Archive:** Includes hyperlinks to documents created by project members, to software programs, and to other elements of the project.

✦ **Search:** Includes a search box.

✦ **Discussions:** Includes links to two threaded discussion groups that are generated by the Project Web template: the Requirements Discussion and the Knowledge Base.

✦ **Contact Information:** A page where you can enter your e-mail address.

SharePoint Team Web

The SharePoint Based Team Web site is a ready-to-use, editable intranet site portal that enables your department, organization, or group to share files and information. SharePoint is included in Office XP, and it requires that the SharePoint server files be installed on your intranet server. For a full exploration of SharePoint, see Chapter 24.

Tutorial 2-1: Generating a Web site using the Corporate Presence Web Wizard

In the following tutorial, you will use the Corporate Presence Web Wizard to generate a Web site.

1. Select File ⇨ New ⇨ Page or Web from the FrontPage menu.

2. In the Task Pane, click the Web Site Templates link.

3. In the Web Site Templates dialog box, enter a location and name for your Web in the "Specify the location of the new web" drop-down list.

4. Double-click the Corporate Presence Web icon in the dialog box.

5. Read the first wizard option box and click Next.

6. In addition to the Home Page, select the What's New, Feedback Form, and Search Form checkboxes. Click Next.

7. From the list of topics to appear on your home page, select all four checkboxes and click Next.

8. From the list of topics for the What's New page, select all three checkboxes and click Next.

9. From the list of options for the Feedback Form, select all seven checkboxes and click Next.

10. For the Feedback Form format, select the option labeled "No, use web page format." This displays input data in a Web page. Click Next.

11. In the dialog box that asks what should appear on the top and bottom of each page, choose all the checkboxes except Your Company's Logo, and click Next.

12. In the Construction Icon options box, select the No radio button to omit the Under Construction icon from your pages. Click Next.

13. In the dialog box that collects information about your company, fill in the three fields and click Next.

14. In the dialog box that collects information about your phone numbers and e-mail addresses, fill in the four fields and click Next.

15. Click the Choose Web Theme button and select the Straight Edge Theme from the Choose Theme dialog box. Click OK and then click Next.

16. In the final dialog box, leave the one checkbox selected to show Tasks view after your Web is generated. Click Finish.

17. In Tasks view, right-click the first task, Customize Home Page, and select Start Task from the context menu.

18. Click and drag to select the comment text, and then replace it with text of your own.

19. Close the page, saving your changes. You are prompted to mark this task as completed. Click Yes in the dialog box.

20. Return to Tasks view and complete the remaining tasks by replacing comment text with your own text.

21. Open the Home Page in Page view. Select File ⇨ Preview in Browser to see your Web site in your browser.

22. Inspect your home page in your browser. Test the link to the Feedback page at the top of the page.

23. Fill in the fields in the Feedback form, as shown in Figure 2-11.

24. After you fill in the form, click the Submit Feedback button. Then, click the Return to Form link in the Form Confirmation page.

25. Return to FrontPage and view your site in Folders view. Double-click the _private folder to view files in that folder. Double-click the file Inforeq.htm to open that file in Page view. Examine the input that you collected.

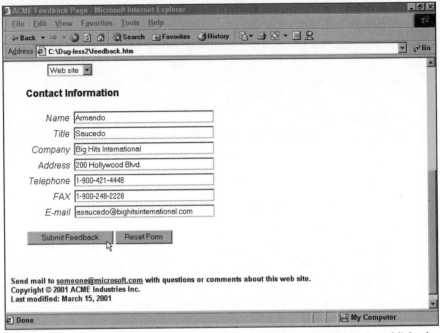

Figure 2-11: You can test the Feedback form in a browser if your site is published to a Web server with FrontPage extensions.

Note   Input forms work only when your Web is saved to a server with FrontPage extensions. For a discussion of server options, see Chapter 3.

26. Select File ➪ Close Web to close your Web after you finish experimenting with it. You can delete this Web by selecting File ➪ Open Web, right-clicking the Web, and then selecting Delete from the context menu.

Creating Basic Web Page Content

After you lay out the basic structure of your Web, you are ready to fill in page content, which includes text and many other components, such as pictures. Chapter 5 explores in detail the editing and formatting of text; Chapter 12 covers inserting pictures. Other advanced elements are covered in the remaining chapters of this book. In fact, for the most part, the rest of this book is about how to place content on your Web pages.

In addition to text and pictures, FrontPage has many powerful elements, called Web components (examined in detail in Chapter 14). They range from search boxes to time stamps to hit counters. This section briefly looks at editing Web page text, and then examines some other basic elements of Web page content: breaks, horizontal lines, comments, and bookmarks.

Editing Web page text

Entering and editing Web page text is very intuitive: click and type. You'll find most of the luxuries of a modern word processor, including red, squiggly underlining of words that are not found in the dictionary. Other editing help includes the following:

✦ **Format Painter:** Select text, click the Format Painter tool, and then click new text to apply the formatting of the original text to the target text.

✦ **Thesaurus:** Select a word and then choose Tools ➪ Thesaurus to see a list of synonyms. Find a good one in the Replace with Synonym list and click the Replace button.

✦ **Edit, Find and Edit Replace:** Find text strings, with the option of designating replacement text. The Find and Replace dialog boxes don't have the option of locating (or changing) special characters, such as hard line returns, tabs, or paragraphs.

✦ **Tab key:** Use it (or the spacebar) to insert additional spacing between words.

Inserting breaks

The Break Properties dialog box enables you to insert a forced line break (as opposed to a paragraph mark). To create a forced line break, select Insert ➪ Break. The Break Properties dialog box appears, as shown in Figure 2-12.

Figure 2-12: You can force line breaks with the Break Properties dialog box.

To create a forced line break (within the same paragraph), click the Normal Line Break radio button and then click OK. Use the Clear Left Margin, Clear Right Margin, or Clear Both Margins radio button to move the next line past any pictures, so that the left or right margin or both margins are cleared to the margin.

To toggle on and off forced line break symbols (nonprinting), click the Show All button in the Standard toolbar.

Tip   An easy way to add a line break is to press Shift+Enter.

Adding horizontal lines

Before modern browsers and faster modems were able to interpret and download graphics quickly, older browsers recognized a graphic element called *horizontal lines*. New browsers still interpret these lines, and you can insert them as dividers between text or graphics. Select Insert ➪ Horizontal Line to place a horizontal line at your cursor point (no need to press Enter first).

Note   Default horizontal lines are simply plain, black lines. FrontPage themes, however, provide customized lines that match the theme colors.

Placing comments

Comment text is visible in Page view, but doesn't appear in a browser window. As such, it is helpful for placing notes to yourself or a collaborator. For example, two Web developers can use comments to leave each other messages about work that remains on a page.

To insert a comment, follow these steps:

1. Click to place your insertion point where the comment will appear in Page view.
2. Select Insert ➪ Comment.
3. Type text in the Comment window, as shown in Figure 2-13.
4. Click OK.

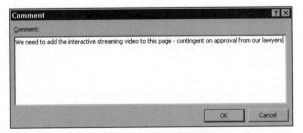

Figure 2-13: Comment text is not visible in a browser — unless the source HTML code is examined.

Note Although comment text doesn't appear in a browser, it does appear if a visitor selects the View ⇨ Source command in IE or the View ⇨ Page Source command in Netscape Navigator. When the underlying HTML code behind a Web page is displayed, comment text is surrounded by the code

```
<!--Webbot bot="PurpleText" PREVIEW="xxx" -->
```

where *xxx* is the comment text.

Therefore, don't put anything in comment text that you don't want the world to read!

You can double-click comment text to edit it. Comment text can be formatted like normal text, by selecting it and applying formatting attributes such as font color and size. However, formatting must be applied to an entire comment; you cannot apply separate formatting to parts of a comment.

Inserting symbols

Symbols include characters such as ã, ª, or   that aren't available in normal keyboard keys. These symbols can be interpreted by most browsers.

To insert a symbol, follow these steps:

1. Place your cursor at the insertion point where the symbol will appear.
2. Choose Insert ⇨ Symbol.
3. From the Symbol dialog box, double-click the symbol that you want to insert.
4. Click Close in the Symbol dialog box.

Inserting bookmarks

Bookmarks are locators in a Web page that can be the target of a hyperlink. Bookmarks can be used for navigation within a page, or as a locator for a link to a page.

To insert a bookmark in a page, follow these steps:

1. Click to place your insertion point on the page, or select text.
2. Select Insert ⇨ Bookmark from the menu.

3. If you selected text in Step 1, that text appears as the default bookmark name, as shown in Figure 2-14. If not, the Bookmark Name text box will be empty in the Bookmark dialog box, and you can enter a bookmark name. To avoid problems with older browsers, it is best to restrict the bookmark name to eight characters or less, with no spaces or punctuation.

4. Click OK to place the bookmark. If you assigned the bookmark to text, that text appears in Page view with a dotted line beneath it. If you assigned the bookmark to a blank space on your page, it appears as a small flag.

Figure 2-14: Bookmarks serve as targets for links within a page.

Bookmarks can be edited (or cleared) by right-clicking the bookmark, selecting Bookmark Properties, and then editing the properties in the Bookmark dialog box.

To create a link to a bookmark, follow these steps:

1. Select text (or a picture) that will be linked to the bookmark.

2. Click the Insert Hyperlinks button. The Hyperlinks dialog box opens.

3. If you are linking to a bookmark on another Web page, enter that page in the URL box. If you are linking to a bookmark on the open page, you can leave that box blank.

4. From the Bookmark drop-down list, select the bookmark that is the target of your link.

5. The bookmark link target appears in the URL box, with the bookmark preceded by a pound sign (#).

6. Click OK. You can test your link in the Preview tab either by previewing your page in a browser or by holding down the Ctrl key and clicking the link in the Normal tab of Page view.

Using Page Templates

FrontPage 2002 comes with *page* templates, in addition to the *Web* templates explored earlier in this chapter. These page templates are of three types: General, Frames, and Style Sheets. Frames are covered in Chapter 7. Style Sheets are covered in Chapter 11. The options in the General tab of the New dialog box are explored here.

To utilize a page template, select File ➪ New ➪ Page or Web. Click Page Templates in the Task Pane. The Page Templates dialog box appears. You can preview a page template by clicking (don't double-click!) on it and viewing a sample of the page in the Preview area, as shown in Figure 2-15.

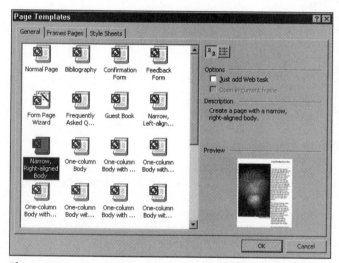

Figure 2-15: You can check out page templates before you generate a new page.

Some page templates are taken from the pages generated by Web templates. These include the Feedback Form page, the Form Page Wizard (that generates input forms), the Table of Contents page, and the User Registration page. You were introduced to some of these pages earlier in the chapter in the section "Using Web Templates and Wizards."

Other pages include sample graphics and content. Many of these pages are laid out in columns; these pages use tables. Using a table as a layout tool is covered in Chapter 6.

Use page templates as starting points for your own page content.

Other Views

Up to now, the focus has been on Navigation view and Page view. These are the two most powerful views in FrontPage. Navigation view displays and controls Web structure, while Page view is used to edit individual pages.

Four other choices are available from the Views bar:

✦ Folders view

✦ Reports view

✦ Hyperlinks view

✦ Tasks view

All four of these views, described next, complement Navigation view as a way to manage your entire Web site.

Folders view

Folders view works like Windows Explorer, enabling you to view all of your files in folders. As in Windows Explorer, you can create a subfolder in your currently selected folder, by choosing File ➪ New ➪ Folder.

When a FrontPage Web is generated, some folders are created that hold files that only "advanced" users are supposed to know about. These folders include the following:

✦ _borders: Holds pages that serve as shared borders.

✦ _fpclass: Holds Java classes. These are files used for objects such as FrontPage-generated Hover buttons (see Chapter 14 for more on FrontPage components).

✦ _overlay: Holds graphic images used with theme elements.

✦ _themes: Holds files used with themes.

In addition to these generated folders, other folders can be created when you apply advanced features in FrontPage, or use add-in programs sold by third-party vendors that attach additional features to FrontPage 2002.

To see these "advanced-level" hidden files, select Tools ➪ Web Settings, and click the Advanced tab in the Web Settings dialog box. Select the Show Hidden Files and Folders checkbox to display hidden files, as shown in Figure 2-16.

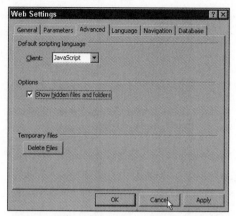

Figure 2-16: Hidden files include elements of themes, and embedded shared border pages.

With hidden files displayed, you can open shared border pages (`Left.htm`, `Right.htm`, `Top.htm`, or `Bottom.htm`) and edit them as you would any other page.

Reports view

Reports view provides a list of many useful statistics in your Web site. Additional reports update you on the status of navigational links, slow pages, and new files. You can select a report by choosing View ➪ Reports, and then selecting one of the available reports.

The following list describes each of the reports and how you can use them:

✦ **Site Summary:** Gives you an overview of your site. The rows in the Site Summary view are themselves links to other views. One of the most useful things about the Site Summary view is that you can get a quick idea of the size of your Web site, which is helpful when you look for server space for your site.

✦ **All Files:** Displays detailed information about each file in your Web site.

✦ **Recently Added Files, Recently Changed Files, and Older Files:** Display files that are defined by selecting Tools ➪ Options and selecting the Reports View tab, as shown in Figure 2-17. Slow pages are calculated based on the modem speed that you enter in the Assume Connection Speed Of spin box.

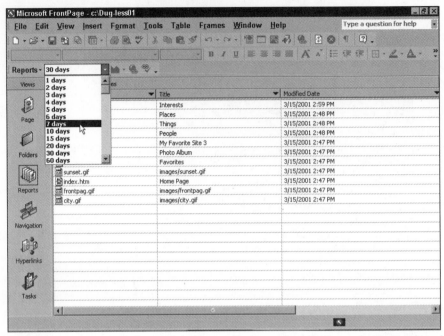

Figure 2-17: You can define which files to display as Recent, Recently Changed, and Older.

✦ **Unlinked Files:** Shows files in your Web site to which no links exist. These stranded Web pages are sometimes called *orphan pages*.

✦ **Slow Pages:** Displays a list of files that download too slowly, based on the time you define in the Report Setting drop-down list in the Reporting toolbar.

✦ **Broken Hyperlinks:** Shows hyperlinks in your Web site that are either invalid or untested. You can right-click one of these untested hyperlinks and choose Verify from the context menu to test the link. If the link is to an Internet or intranet site, you must be logged on to the Internet or your intranet to test the link.

✦ **Component Errors:** Tests FrontPage components (covered in Chapter 14) for errors.

✦ **Review Status and Assigned To:** Used for workgroups collaborating on a Web site. The Review Status report enables you to log pages that need to be reviewed, and track whether pages have been reviewed. The Assigned To report is similar to the Review Status report, but tracks who is assigned to which page.

✦ **Categories:** Sorts components of your Web site by type, such as .jpeg images, .html pages, .gif files, .class Java files, and so on.

✦ **Publish Status:** Lists which pages have been published to your Web (and which haven't).

Hyperlinks view

Hyperlinks view displays all links leading into a Web page from other pages in the site, and all links out of a selected page. First, choose Hyperlinks view from the Views bar, and then click a Web page in the Folders list.

Figure 2-18 shows a page in Hyperlinks view, with links coming in and going out.

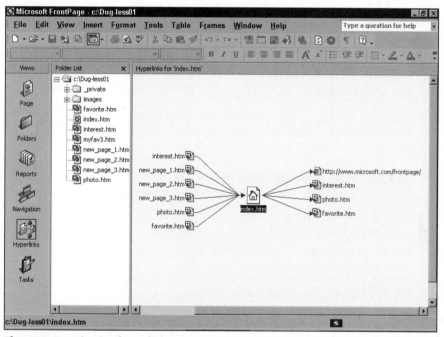

Figure 2-18: Viewing hyperlinks

Tip   If you are trying to track and test every hyperlink in a page or on your Web site, the Broken Hyperlinks report discussed in the previous section of this chapter is much more efficient than looking for broken links in Hyperlinks view. Use this view only if you need to examine in detail all links in and out of a page. For example, before deleting a page, you can use this view to identify the Web pages with links to the page.

You can modify Hyperlinks view to do the following:

✦ **Show page titles:** Right-click in Hyperlinks view and select Show Page Titles from the context menu to display page titles instead of filenames. Repeat the process to deselect page title display.

✦ **Hyperlinks to Pictures:** Right-click in Hyperlinks view and select Hyperlinks to Pictures from the context menu to display links that lead to graphics files. You can toggle off picture links in the same way.

✦ **Repeated Hyperlinks:** To display multiple hyperlinks with the same target URL, right-click in Hyperlinks view and select Repeated Hyperlinks from the context menu. Repeat the process to deselect this option, to turn it off.

Tasks view

Tasks view contains a list of "things to do." Tasks are added to the Tasks view list by wizards that generate Webs, or you can add them yourself.

To add a task, follow these steps:

1. Select Tasks from the Views bar.

2. Select File ➪ New ➪ Task, or right-click in Tasks view and select Add Task from the context menu. The New Task dialog box opens, as shown in Figure 2-19.

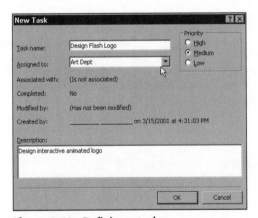

Figure 2-19: Defining a task

3. Enter a task name and a description. You also can modify the Assigned To box. Select one of the three priority radio buttons to assign a relative level of urgency to the task.

4. Click OK. The task appears in the task list.

Tasks that are created with a page open have that page associated with them. These tasks can be started by right-clicking the task in Tasks view and selecting Start Task from the context menu.

The context menu that opens when you right-click a task can be used to edit, mark as completed, or delete any task. However, only those tasks that were created with a page open (or generated from a wizard) can be started by right-clicking.

Global Site Editing

Most of the work that you do to edit the content of your Web site takes place in Page view, and is done on a page-by-page basis. However, some editing tools in FrontPage work across an entire Web. This section looks at two of these tools: spell checking, and search and replace.

Spell checking your entire site

To spell check your whole Web site, select Tools ➪ Spelling from a view other than Page view.

Note If you select Tools ➪ Spelling in Page view, or click the Spelling tool in the Standard toolbar, you spell check *only your open page.* When you select the Spelling dialog box (in a view other than Page view), the dialog box has two radio buttons: Selected Page(s) and Entire Web. To spell check your entire Web site, use the Entire Web option.

You can also select the checkbox labeled Add a Task for Each Page with Misspellings. This creates a list of pages that need their spelling checked. After you select these options, click the Start button to begin checking your spelling.

FrontPage checks all of your pages for spelling errors and then creates a list in the Spelling dialog box, as shown in Figure 2-20.

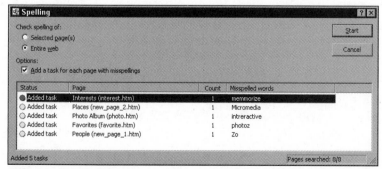

Figure 2-20: Checking an entire Web site generates a list of pages with spelling mistakes.

If you selected the Add a Task option, you can click the Add Task button to add the marked pages to your task list. If you would rather correct your spelling immediately, double-click the page in the list in the site Spelling dialog box to check spelling on that page.

Replacing text throughout a site

To replace text throughout a site, select Edit ➪ Replace in any view. In the Replace dialog box, enter the text to find in the Find What text box, and specify replacement text in the Replace With text box. The Replace dialog box includes the following options:

✦ Click the All Pages radio button to replace in every page

Note   The Direction drop-down menu defines the direction in which the replacing tool moves through Web pages. But it is only active when you are editing the current page, and is not active when you replace throughout your whole site.

✦ The Match Whole Word Only and Match Case checkbox options work like the Replace dialog box in Word or other Office applications.

✦ The Find in HTML checkbox enables you to search and replace HTML code.

After you define your replace options, if you are replacing text in an entire Web, click the Find in Web button. FrontPage will generate a list of pages at the bottom of the Replace dialog box with the text to be replaced. Double-click a page to make the changes in that page. Alternatively, click the Add Task button to add the task to your task list.

Tutorial 2-2: Editing Web page content

In the following tutorial, you will experiment with adding content to a Web page.

1. With a FrontPage Web open, choose Navigation view from the View bar.

2. In Navigation view, double-click the home page to open it in Page view.

3. Type **Welcome to my Web site** at the top of your home page and press Enter.

4. Click and drag to select the text that you typed. Select Arial Black from the Font drop-down list; 24 point from the Font Size list; Italics; Center; and Red, from the Font Color palette.

5. Click at the end of the text and select Insert ➪ Horizontal Line.

6. Under the horizontal line, select Insert ➪ Symbol and double-click the © symbol. Click Close. Type your name after the copyright symbol.

7. Select Insert ➪ Break, and with the Normal Line Break radio button selected, click OK to create a forced line break.

8. Select Insert ➪ Comment, and in the Comment window, type **This page needs to be finished!** Click OK.

9. Double-click the word "Welcome" and select Insert ➪ Bookmark. Click OK in the Bookmark dialog box.

10. Click to place your insertion point after the comment text. Press Enter 12 times and then type **Go to top**.

11. Double-click to select the word "top," and then click the Hyperlink button in the toolbar. Pull down the Bookmark list and select Welcome. Click OK.

12. Select File ➪ New ➪ Task, and enter **Add Content** in the Task Name text box. Click OK.

13. Click the Save button to save changes to the Web page.

14. Select View ➪ Reports to get an overview of your (rather small) Web site. How much server space would you need for this Web site? (Hint: Look at the All Files row of the report.)

15. Select Hyperlinks view. Right-click and select Hyperlinks Inside Page from the context menu. The links illustrate the bookmark link in the page.

16. Click the Tasks view. Right-click the task and select Start Task from the context menu. Add some text to your page and save it. Select Yes in the dialog box when prompted to mark the page as a completed task.

Summary

In designing your Web site, start by placing yourself in the shoes of a visitor. What information do you want to present right on the home page? What options do you want to make available from the home page? You can translate your vision into a real site design in FrontPage's Navigation view–where you drag pages into a flowchart.

FrontPage will generate automatic links on pages based on your Navigation view structure. These links are created in *Link bars*, which can be placed on pages, or in *shared borders* that are embedded in each page in your Web site (or most pages).

Once you design a site in FrontPage, you can use the Import tools to add other files from your computer or from the Internet. Or, you can integrate an already existing site into your FrontPage Web site.

FrontPage makes it fast and easy to create complex Web sites using templates, including an instant Corporate Presence Web, a Customer Support Web, and even an instant online database.

Creating page content is very similar to editing text in Microsoft Word. Additional page components like line breaks, symbols, and horizontal lines are available as well.

Once you have created a FrontPage Web site, global site editing tools are available including spell checking and site-wide search and replace.

✦   ✦   ✦

Publishing and Maintaining Web Sites

In the first two chapters, you used FrontPage to design dazzling Web pages to amaze your friends, your customers, even your boss (!); and you learned how to use FrontPage to organize those pages into a coherent Web site. Now you are ready to unleash your creation on the world—this chapter tells you how. In this chapter, you learn how to perform two important Web-related tasks: publishing your site and maintaining your site content.

New Feature

FrontPage 2000 first introduced the capability of "selectively" publishing pages to a web. FrontPage 2002 provides even more publishing options, and the process is much simpler and more flexible. FrontPage 2002 has also added a publishing log to help you keep track of your changes. In addition, FrontPage 2002 makes it easier to publish your web pages to a non-FrontPage-enabled Web server.

Publishing Considerations

When FrontPage refers to "publishing" your web site or selected pages within your site, it is using the term in a somewhat specialized way. In FrontPage, you do not necessarily have to publish your Web pages in order to make them public. If you open a Web in FrontPage that is already publicly accessible and make changes directly to its Web pages, those changes are immediately visible to viewers. In essence, your changes are automatically published.

In FrontPage, the term *publishing* refers specifically to the process you use to copy one or more Web pages from one location to another. Typically, this means publishing the Web page from a development, or staging, area that is off-limits to the general public to a production Web server. However, FrontPage's publishing process can also be used to make a backup copy of a live Web site.

Tip   The techniques described in this chapter to publish a Web site can also be used to make backup or archive copies of a Web.

In general, think of publishing in FrontPage as "smart copying"—when you publish pages in FrontPage, you are copying files from one location to another in a manner that enables FrontPage to do several things: to keep track of the changes you are making, to make any necessary adjustments to links and so forth, and to ensure that your Web site works correctly in its new location.

Note   You may have noticed that the FrontPage file menu also contains an Export option, which sounds like it could be used to make a copy of a Web as well (after all, you can import a whole set of files *into* FrontPage, right?). Well, for better or worse, Export is a one-page-at-a-time operation. If you try to select multiple pages, you will find that the Export option is no longer available. Therefore, if you want to copy a bunch of files from one place to another—you want to publish them.

How you set up your own publishing process depends on your circumstances. If you are designing your own personal site, you may simply open your Web in FrontPage and make changes directly to the live site. If you happen to misspell a word, or accidentally make the background black when you meant it to be beige, you can just change it back. Using the Preview tab, you can even catch mistakes before you save them for the entire world to see.

Still, the instant publishing model is probably best used by people who don't have to answer to anyone, who get a warm, tingly feeling from taking risks, and who are willing to subject their audience to an ugly error now and then in the interest of simplifying their own lives. If you recognize yourself in the foregoing description, you can stop reading now and go on to the next section of this chapter—you will never need to use the FrontPage publishing features. Otherwise, you should probably forge ahead.

Publishing scenarios

Once you have determined that you want to use a publishing model, give some thought to the particulars of your situation. The following sections describe some typical publishing scenarios.

Develop locally, publish remotely

If you are creating your own site, and have sole responsibility for creating and approving the content, the best scenario is to maintain a local, "development" version of your site. From here, you can make changes, and test and preview them before you publish changes to your "live" server, which in most cases will be hosted. This approach is especially useful if you are operating over a relatively slow dial-up connection, as it enables you to make changes offline and then dial-up to publish your changes all at once.

If you are working on your own, you may want to set up a Web server on your local system — Microsoft still has available a Personal Web Server (PWS) that was originally designed for users of Windows NT Workstation or for the Windows desktop operating systems (Windows 95/98).

You can also save the local version of your site directly to disk without the assistance of a Web server, although in this scenario you may not be able to test all functionality locally.

If you are working in a networked environment, perhaps on your corporate intranet, you can use the same model, although in this case both the development, or *staging* server as it is sometimes called, and the *production* server may simply be on the network. They may even be set up as separate virtual sites on the same Web server. The important thing is to have two separate instances of your site — one where you make and test changes, and one where you publish changes once they have been tested and approved.

Publishing to a Disk-Based Web

Publishing to a disk-based Web is FrontPage lingo for making a copy of an existing Web directly to a local or networked hard drive. Why would you want to do this? The following are some possibilities:

* To have a backup of your Web site

* To make a version of your Web site that you can show to others without being connected to a Web server

* To create a version of your live Web that you can use to test updates before republishing them

The process of publishing a disk-based Web is the same as for other publishing operations:

1. Open in FrontPage the Web that you want to publish.

2. Select File ➪ Publish Web from the menu bar.

3. Click the Browse button and identify the location on your local file system where you want to publish the Web.

4. Click OK to return to the Publishing dialog box. Click OK again to proceed with the publishing operation.

Any functionality in your Web site that requires a Web server and/or the FrontPage Server Extensions will not work in this disk-based Web. (For details about what functions require the server extensions, see Appendix A.)

Use multiple workgroups and publish to a single server

If you are creating a site with a team of developers, you need to give some thought to how you will divide the task of updating pages without accidentally overwriting someone else's changes. One approach is to use the check-in/check-out functionality of FrontPage to ensure that only one person at a time edits a file. However, this model requires that you check out a fresh copy of a page from a central location each time you want to edit it.

Another alternative is to divide your Web into multiple subwebs and assign an individual to each section. This method enables each person to maintain a local copy of the portion of the Web they are responsible for. In general, this method works best in situations where the content of each subweb is relatively self-contained — too much cross-linking can complicate the picture. If you are working in a team development environment, be sure to check out Microsoft's new SharePoint Team Services, described in Chapter 24.

Create a local copy of your Web

This approach is not so much a different publishing scenario as it is another use for FrontPage's publishing tool. In addition to using FrontPage to copy updated pages from staging areas to live servers, you can also use it to publish a backup or archived version of your live site to an offline location. You can also use this method if you want to create a portable, demo version of your site that you can show to people offline.

Selecting a Web Presence Provider

Before you can publish your Web site, of course, you need a place to put it. If you already have a site set up, you can leap ahead to the next section, which describes how to publish your pages in FrontPage. If you are looking for some advice about how to find a home for your site, read on.

First some definitions. In the beginning, the only Internet connectivity providers were Internet Access Providers (IAPs), more commonly known as Internet Service Providers (ISPs). An ISP primarily offers its customers connectivity to the Internet. Most ISP accounts come with e-mail, including some amount of online storage space for e-mail messages. Increasingly, ISPs also offer their customers other kinds of space, principally Web site space (and sometimes storage for anonymous FTP, as well). Typically, however, ISPs (with notable exceptions) are primarily in the connectivity business. They aren't as strong in the area of providing support and development services for business-oriented customers.

Enter a new breed of provider, the Web hosting company (sometimes called Web Presence Providers). These folks don't deal in providing Internet access for you. Instead, they focus on providing a safe and easily accessible home for your Web site on the Internet. In principle, this focus means that they can provide more expertise in the area of Web development, but they assume that you can find your own access to the Internet elsewhere.

Of course, the divisions are not always clear-cut. Many ISPs offer Web hosting services. Some companies that focus on Web hosting also offer various forms of access, although frequently they have simply partnered with a traditional ISP to provide this access. In general, you are likely to get a better deal by combining your dial-up and Web hosting with the same company, but support may not be equally strong in both connectivity issues and Web site hosting.

So what do you do? Chances are, if you are planning to create a Web site, you probably have looked into the issue of where to put the site — before you get ready to click that Publish button. Just for the sake of argument, though, let's suppose you haven't. Maybe you just figured, Hey, I'll click that old Publish button and something will come to me... Well, it's your lucky day, because Microsoft, in its infinite wisdom, put a button on the Publishing dialog box that links directly to a searchable database of FrontPage-enabled Web hosting services, or Web Presence Providers (WPP).

Using Microsoft's list of providers

Microsoft maintains a list of Web hosting providers who support FrontPage. As noted later in this chapter in the discussion of the FrontPage Server Extensions, you do not necessarily need to use a provider who supports FrontPage in order to use FrontPage to edit your Web pages. However, it is becoming increasingly difficult to find a provider who does *not* offer FrontPage support; therefore, if you have a choice, there is really no reason not to select a FrontPage-supported host.

To access Microsoft's list of providers, select File ⇨ Publish Web and click the "Click here to learn more" link in the Publish Destination dialog box. This opens the Microsoft Web page entitled "Locate a Web Presence Provider," which enables you to search for FrontPage-friendly providers, as illustrated in Figure 3-1. (Note that as of this writing, the URL for this page is
`http://www.microsoftwpp.com/wppsearch/`.)

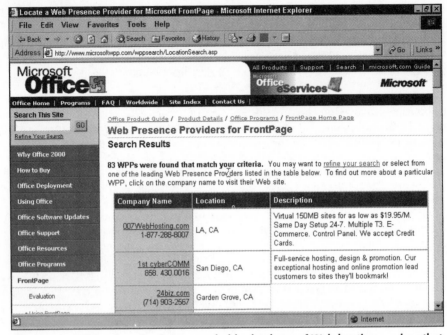

Figure 3-1: Microsoft maintains a searchable database of Web hosting services that support FrontPage.

The Microsoft search enables you to locate a Web hosting provider by name, location (by state or area code), or by additional services (such as Office server extensions, Active Server Pages, streaming audio/video, or Visual Studio/Interdev). This is convenient, but there are several limitations with this approach:

✦ Microsoft's database is clearly not exhaustive.

✦ In most cases, it is unnecessary to select a *local* hosting provider — does it really matter whether the provider is in your area code or state?

✦ Although finding a FrontPage supporting host is important, it is not the most important consideration when selecting a provider. Moreover, surprisingly enough, the additional services Microsoft focuses on all happen to be other Microsoft technologies. Although the descriptions of services provide good information, there is no way to search this database by pricing, for instance, or to find out which providers have a reputation for reliable service and/or customer support.

Other sources of information

If you are hunting for a hosting provider, one of the best ways to find a reliable source is to ask anyone and everyone you know for their recommendations. In general, people are open to sharing their feelings about their service providers (although this method is more likely to elicit a list of hosts to avoid like the plague than ones you might want to select). The key point is to focus on finding a highly regarded host provider, as this provider will most likely support FrontPage, rather than simply trying to wade through a long list of providers who advertise their FrontPage support.

If you already have an Internet Service Provider (ISP) that provides you with a dial-up account to the Internet, you might want to find out whether it provides Web site presence as part of that account and, if so, whether it supports FrontPage. An increasing number of ISPs do, although they may not have made it onto Microsoft's list.

There are also numerous online directories (Yahoo! lists 34) of Web hosting providers. These offer a range of search options and reviews, and can help give you a sense of your options. Be sure to check out several of these, however, and to take their "reviews" with a healthy grain of salt. Many of these sites are supported through the paid advertising of one or more of the providers they are ostensibly reviewing.

A wide range of services and prices are available, so be sure to check out your options carefully. Once you have a short list of possibilities, ask any WPP you are considering to provide you with a list of references you can check directly, and ask those references how satisfied they are with the service. Here are some additional considerations:

✦ **Features and pricing:** Do you need dial-up access in addition to Web hosting? Do you need e-mail? Programming and/or database support? Do you plan to use streaming multimedia in your site? Do you have specific requirements regarding usage reporting? All of these are available, but compare packages carefully—prices and services vary considerably. These days, you can get a fairly decent hosting package for under $20 a month—you can even find some reasonably good free hosting sites (see the following section). Currently, for around $50-$100 a month, you can get an e-commerce–enabled site with plenty of bells and whistles.

✦ **Support:** If you plan to use FrontPage exclusively, one of your main considerations is the level of FrontPage support provided. Options in the support category range from no support (the FrontPage extension is installed for you, but you are on your own) to extensive (and expensive) on-site training options. A survey of Web sites also indicates a range of commitment to and expertise with FrontPage. Many providers have added FrontPage Server Extensions because of customer demand, but they are not providing technical support for FrontPage. The list of providers with qualified, experienced support and technical staff to assist you with FrontPage questions is much smaller. Be wary of the site that touts their "support" for FrontPage, when in fact all they mean is that you can use FrontPage to create your pages and then use FTP to publish them. Make certain the site specifies that they are running the FrontPage Server Extensions, and be clear about which versions are available.

✦ **Reliability:** Ideally, you want to know two things: Does the provider keep its servers up and running and do they keep them running efficiently (as opposed to bogging them down by overloading too many customers on the same server). This is sometimes difficult to judge until its too late, but good providers should be able to supply statistics showing their uptimes — which should be well over 99% — and also share with you their policies concerning server loads. Many, unfortunately, simply prescribe a limited number of customers on a server, which does you no good if some of your server neighbors happen to be bandwidth or CPU hogs. If you are willing to pay the premium, you can find providers who offer the option of space on a less crowded server.

Free Web hosting

The number of sites offering free Web hosting has been growing rapidly in the past couple of years. Some of these operate on a business model that enables you to put up some Web pages in exchange for their right to add banner ads to the pages. Most have their own, simplified means of enabling you to create and edit pages, but some of these sites are beginning to support FrontPage as well. If you are interested in free hosting options, check out the following sites, which provide directories and reviews:

✦ `www.clickherefree.com`: Includes a good, searchable database of free Web hosting options.

✦ `www.100best-free-web-space.com`: Offers "Top 10" lists and informative reviews.

✦ `www.free-web-space-page.com`: Also offers useful review information.

Publishing a Web Site

This section walks you through the basic process of publishing a Web in FrontPage. It also describes how you publish your Web to a Web server that does not directly offer support for FrontPage. In the next section, you will examine the various ways in which FrontPage enables you to control the publishing process and selectively include or exclude pages from that process.

Publishing to a Web server with FrontPage extensions (via HTTP)

In order to publish to a Web server, you need to know the location (either domain name or IP address) of the Web server; and you need to be ready to supply a user name and password if the server has controlled access.

First, open the Web containing the site or page(s) you want to publish.

Note In FrontPage 2002, you do not need to define which pages you want to publish before you start the publishing process.

Select File ➪ Publish Web. If you have not published your pages before, FrontPage opens the Publish Destination dialog box, as shown in Figure 3-2. If you have published before, FrontPage automatically opens the site you published to most recently (you can change this location if you like, as described next). If you have unsaved pages in the current Web, FrontPage will ask you if you want to save these pages before publishing.

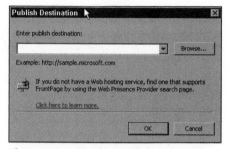

Figure 3-2: Use the Publish Destination dialog box to identify the site to which you are publishing your Web pages.

If you have published to this location before, you can select the destination from the drop-down list. If not, type the name, IP address, or the destination site or click the Browse button to locate the destination using the New Publish Location dialog box, as indicated in Figure 3-3.

If the destination you select requires it, you may be prompted to provide a user name and password before accessing the site to make updates.

Once you are successfully logged in to the destination site, FrontPage displays the Publish Web dialog box, shown in Figure 3-4, which shows the files in the source Web (the one from which you will be publishing files).

Tip After the first time you identify the destination location, FrontPage will automatically reopen the same destination. Use the Change button to change the destination.

You can perform several operations from this dialog box:

✦ **Change the destination location:** The "to" field at the top of this dialog box displays the currently selected destination. Click the Change button to enter a different destination, using the Publish Destination dialog box previously described.

✦ **Explore files in the dialog box:** Use this dialog box just as you would Windows Explorer to view folders and files. You can rename files. You can even delete files from the source Web by selecting one or more files and clicking the Delete button in the upper right corner above the file listing. This dialog box is primarily useful for selectively identifying files for publishing, a topic covered in the next section.

✦ **Sort files using the column tabs:** Click on a column tab (Name, Status, Author, Modified, Size) to sort files using that column. Click a second time to sort in the opposite order. Click and drag an edge of the column header to change its size (just as you would in a spreadsheet). Notice that you may have to scroll horizontally to see all of the columns. Alternately, click and drag the lower right corner of the dialog box to expand it.

✦ **Include subwebs:** By default, this checkbox is unchecked. Check it to view subwebs and include them in the publishing process.

✦ **Access the Publishing Options tab:** The Publishing options tab is accessible from the main FrontPage menu by selecting Tools ➪ Options. Click the Options button in this dialog box to open the same tab.

✦ **View destination files:** Click the Show button to expand the dialog box to show the directory structure of the destination Web site (see Figure 3-5). You can navigate this directory as described previously for the source Web site. Click the Hide button to show only the source files.

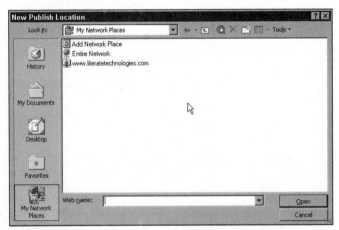

Figure 3-3: You can locate a publishing destination using My Network Places in Windows 2000 (or Web Folders in Windows 98/NT).

Figure 3-4: The Publish Web dialog box shows the location of your source files.

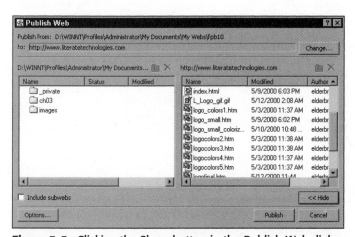

Figure 3-5: Clicking the Show button in the Publish Web dialog box shows you the directory structure of the target destination site, as well as the source location.

A word of caution about showing both source and destination: You might think that you could publish selected pages from the currently displayed source directory to the currently selected destination directory. This is typical behavior, for example, in many graphical FTP programs. However, this is not how the Publish Web dialog box works. Pages are always published in the same hierarchical structure found in the source Web site. If FrontPage doesn't find the same structure, it will re-create it. If this is a problem, one way around it is to open a specific subweb within the Web as the destination using the Publish Destination dialog box . If you identify a folder rather than a subweb, however, FrontPage prompts you to convert the folder to a subweb, which may not be what you want to do. Your other alternative is to drag and drop files from one location to the other, as described next.

When you are ready to publish your site, click the Publish button to begin the publishing process. FrontPage displays a dialog box indicating the status. You can also follow the status in the status bar in the bottom left corner of the main FrontPage window. FrontPage publishes your Web pages in the background so you can continue with other tasks while it is working. When it has completed its task, FrontPage displays a confirmation message like the one shown in Figure 3-6. If you like, you can click the link to the published site and review your handiwork, or access the publishing log (discussed in "Accessing the Publishing Log" later in this chapter "") to ensure that everything went as intended.

Figure 3-6: FrontPage displays helpful messages as it publishes your files.

Publishing to a Web server without FrontPage extensions (via FTP)

If you are publishing to a Web server that does not have the FrontPage Server Extensions installed (see the sidebar in this section for details), you can use FTP to publish your pages. In FrontPage 2002, the procedure you use to publish pages in this manner is virtually the same as the method described in the previous section for publishing your site to a server that supports FrontPage. Here are the details:

First, open the Web site from which you plan to publish. Select File ➪ Publish Web and identify the FTP destination location in the New Publish Location dialog box. You can do this either by typing the location directly into the destination field or by clicking the Browse button and selecting an FTP Location as shown in Figure 3-7. Select Add/Modify FTP Location to add a new location to the list of available sites. You will most likely need to supply a valid user name and password in addition to the site location (domain name or IP address).

Once you are logged into the FTP location, navigate if necessary to the directory where you want to publish the files (note that when publishing to a non-FrontPage-enabled Web server, the files will be copied to the directory you select).

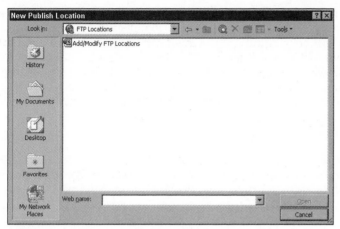

Figure 3-7: When publishing your site to a non-FrontPage-enabled Web server, you can use FTP.

Click the Publish button in the Publish Web dialog box to publish the designated pages. If pages on the destination site do not match those in the source, FrontPage asks you if you want to delete the nonmatching files and synchronize the two locations.

Publishing to a disk-based Web

You can also publish files to a file system location, or what FrontPage refers to as a *disk-based Web*. This enables you to make a local backup copy of a Web, which is not, strictly speak, publishing, as most people will not be able to access the files from your local file system, but who are we to quibble over semantics here?

Can I Publish Web Pages with Windows Explorer?

The answer to this question is yes, but why would you want to? In earlier versions of FrontPage, trying to copy files via the file system (i.e., using Windows Explorer) was a bad idea because FrontPage didn't realize that you made a change. More recent versions of FrontPage have gotten smarter about this, but you are still more likely to confuse FrontPage this way. In Windows 2000, you could conceivably even open a remote Web site using My Network Places in Explorer and copy files that way. But, again, doing this is prone to confusing FrontPage and, frankly, the Explorer interface is not as convenient for copying files from a source to destination as the new FrontPage 2002 features. Our advice is to stick to FrontPage for performing any file operations that involve FrontPage in some way.

You publish the currently open Web to a file system location by using the Browse button in the Publishing Destination dialog box. If you identify a location that does not contain a FrontPage Web, FrontPage will ask if you want to create a Web at this location. This is FrontPage's way of asking if it can add the configuration files its needs to keep track of your Web pages. Click OK to allow FrontPage to copy the necessary files to this directory (note that this does not automatically make the published files publicly accessible). Click the Publish button to publish designated pages to this location. FrontPage prompts you if the destination does not support some features of the source Web.

If the server you are using does not have FrontPage Server Extensions installed, you will not be able to open the Web directly. However, if the server does have the Extensions installed, how do you know what version it is using? Select Tools ➪ Web Settings and look at the FrontPage Server Extensions version listed in the General tab (see Figure 3-8). 3.x refers to FrontPage 98 extensions, 4.x to FrontPage 2000, and 5.x to FrontPage 2002. (For details on the FrontPage Server Extensions, refer to Chapter 23.)

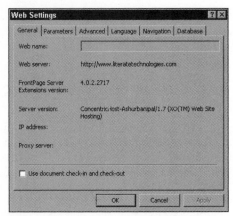

Figure 3-8: You can use Web Settings to determine which version of FrontPage Server Extensions are on your Web server.

Controlling the Publishing Process

When you click the Publish button, as described in the previous section, FrontPage publishes all the pages you have marked for publishing. This section describes the various ways in which you can define and control the publishing process by selectively including or excluding pages to publish. It also describes several methods for publishing pages interactively, rather than using the Publish button.

Using the Publish Web dialog box

If you like postponing your decisions until the last minute, you will really appreciate the new feature in FrontPage 2002 that enables you to selectively mark files for publishing using the Publish Web dialog box after you have opened the publishing destination. You do this by manually updating the publishing status of the files, as described in the next section.

Changing the publishing status of files

The publishing status of a file indicates whether it should be published or not published. It can also indicate whether a file has been updated and therefore needs to be published. When you open the Publish Web dialog box (by selecting File ⇨ Publish Web and selecting a destination), notice the icons to the left of the filenames. If you have not yet published your Web pages and you have not changed their publishing status, you should see a small green checkmark next to each filename. This indicates that the file is ready to be published. You can confirm this by checking the status of these files, which should say "Publish," as shown in Figure 3-9. Once you have published a page, the green checkmark icon disappears and the file's status is changed to "Up to date" until you make another change to the file.

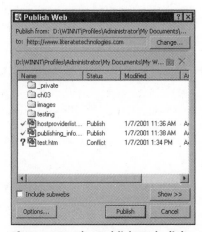

Figure 3-9: The Publish Web dialog box indicates the publishing status of files.

If you do not want to publish a page as part of the normal publishing process (i.e., when you click the Publish button), you can selectively mark files that you don't want to publish. To do this from within the Publish Web dialog box, select the file or files you want to mark, and click on them with the right mouse button, as shown in Figure 3-10. These files are then marked with the Don't Publish icon, an X in a red circle, and the status of the file is changed to Don't publish. To change the status back, simply select the files and again select the Don't Publish option, which should be checked in the option menu before you do this.

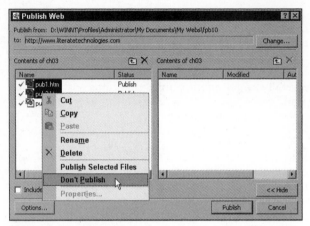

Figure 3-10: You can select one or more files that you do not want to publish using the Don't Publish option in the Publish Web dialog box.

Selective publishing

The Don't Publish option is handy if, for instance, you have created a draft copy of a Web page that you don't want to show to the world. But what do you do if your Web site contains three hundred (or three thousand) Web pages and you want to update five of them? Obviously, marking all of the files Don't Publish is not a very efficient way to do this. For this purpose, you can use FrontPage's capability to publish a selected number of files.

To use this feature in the Publish Web dialog box, select the file or files you want to publish, click on them with the right mouse button and select Publish Selected Files.   The selected pages are immediately published to the designated destination and their status updated.

Tip   Another way to control the publishing process is to convert a folder into a subweb and then make sure that the Include Subweb checkbox is unchecked.

Drag and drop publishing

In previous incarnations of FrontPage, the publishing features left a little bit to be desired in terms of their flexibility and ease of use. Microsoft seems to have compensated for that in FrontPage 2002 by providing more ways to publish your pages than you probably care to remember (in practice, you will probably find the method you like best and forget the rest). Therefore, if you don't like the right mouse click method described in the preceding section, you can also selectively publish pages by dragging them from their source location window and dropping them in the destination location window. Note that you will need to show the destination file directory first by clicking the Show button in the Publish Web dialog box if it is not already visible.

Besides being easy, the drag and drop method has one other potential advantage over other means of publishing—you can copy a file anywhere in the destination file system. The other methods of publishing publish files only to a parallel location on the remote server.

Caution   Be forewarned if you use the drag and drop technique to publish your files: FrontPage will not recognized the file as having been published. That is, it will not change its publishing status and it will not generate records in the publishing log if you copy it somewhere other than its parallel location. More critically, it will not update links appropriately, so use this function with caution.

Synchronizing deleted files

If you delete from the source location a file that you previously published, FrontPage will prompt you regarding that file the next time you perform a publish operation using the Publish button (note that it will not do this if you use one of the selective publishing operations just described). You can keep the file on the destination if you like, or delete it. In FrontPage 2002, this method of deleting files works even if you are using FTP to publish your pages to a non-FrontPage-enabled Web server.

Using FrontPage's Folder view

The selective publishing methods just described enable you to identify the publishing destination first and then decide what to publish. You can also work in the opposite order by first identifying the files you want to publish (or not publish) and then selecting a destination. You do this using FrontPage's Folder view (or the Folder list in any of the views that permit the Folder list.). The methods are very similar to those previously described, so they are covered briefly here—check the preceding section for more detail.

To mark selected pages so that they will not be published, first switch to Folder view by clicking the Folder View icon in the Views bar (if it is not visible, select View ➪ Views Bar from the menu list). Alternately, use the Folder list if you are in Page, Navigation, or Hyperlinks view (if the Folder list is not visible in one of these views, select View ➪ Folder List from the menu list). Select the file or files you want to mark, click on them with the right mouse button, and select Don't Publish. As indicated in Figure 3-11, the File icon changes to show the X in a red circle, indicating a page that is not to be published. Now, the next time you initiate the publishing process, the marked pages will not be published. (Note that if these pages have been previously published, they will not be deleted, they will simply remain unchanged.)

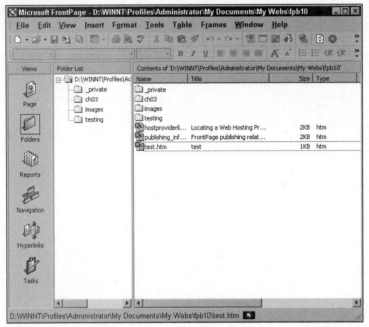

Figure 3-11: In Folder view, you can mark files you don't want to publish.

You can also use a file's Properties tab to set (or view) its publishing status. Select a file, right-click, and select Properties from the options menu. Select the Workgroup tab and check or uncheck the checkbox that says "Exclude this file when publishing the rest of the Web" (see Figure 3-12). This is a vestige from earlier versions of FrontPage and clearly more cumbersome to use than the Don't Publish drop-down menu option.

To publish selected pages only, select the file or files you want to publish, click with the right mouse button, and select Publish Selected Files. This open the Publishing Destination dialog box and initiates the publishing process described earlier, by-passing the interactive Publish Web dialog box.

You can also copy files to a destination Web from the Folder view using drag and drop. To do this, first open both the source and destination Webs in FrontPage. The hard part is maneuvering the windows of the two open Webs such that you can select the pages from the source Web and drag and drop them to the destination location. If small monitor size makes this difficult, try using copy and paste operations instead. You can also make more room for yourself by hiding the Views bar from each window, as illustrated in Figure 3-13. As noted earlier, using these basic copy operations for publishing will not update the publishing status of files.

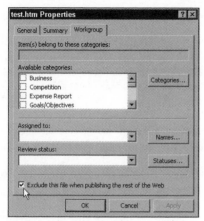

Figure 3-12: Another way to mark a file you don't want published is to select it in the Workgroup tab of its Properties dialog box.

Figure 3-13: You can drag and drop selected files from one Web to another, provided you have room to open both windows on your monitor.

Selective publishing using FrontPage's Reports view

The final place where you can set the publishing status of files is in the Publish Status report. The chief advantage offered by this interface is the capability to sort all files by their publishing status, so if you are managing a large number of files at a time, you may find this useful. For normal, day-to-day use, the preceding methods are probably more convenient.

To use the Publish Status report, select View ⇨ Reports ⇨ Workflow ⇨ Publish Status or open the Reports toolbar and use its drop-down menu, organized in the same hierarchy. The Publish Status report lists all files along with their basic file information, as well as their publishing and review status. (We discuss all reports in more detail in the section, "Using Web Site Reports.")

Caution   This report does not appear in the Site Summary list of reports, so it does not work to click Reports view to try to find it.

From this report, you can use the same methods of marking and publishing files described earlier. Select the files you want to work with, click with the right mouse button, and select Don't Publish to mark files you want to exclude from publishing, or select Publish Selected Files to initiate the publishing operation on the selected files.

Alternately, you can sort and set the publishing status of files using the Publishing Status column of this report. To sort by publishing status, simply click the Publishing Status column header. Figure 3-14 shows a sorted list of files. If you want to filter pages — for instance, to view only pages marked "Don't Publish," — click the drop-down arrow in the Publishing Status column header, and select Don't Publish. To return to viewing all files, repeat the process, selecting All. See "Using Web Site Reports" later in this chapter for more details about using reports.

Note   Double-clicking on a file in this report list will open the file in Page view — which is fine if that is what you want to do, but mildly disconcerting if it happens inadvertently.

The Publish Tab

The Publish tab of the Options dialog box contains additional publishing options you can control (although, to be honest, they are not options that you are likely to use in most cases). You access this tab via the FrontPage menus by selecting Tools ⇨ Options and selecting the Publish tab. The options available from this tab, shown in Figure 3-15, are divided into two sections: General and Logging.

The General section contains two options: Publish and Changes. Under the Publish option, you can elect to publish as follows:

✦ Changed pages only (the default)

✦ All pages, overwriting pages already on destination

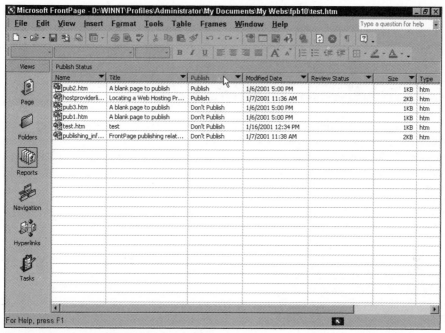

Figure 3-14: The Publish Status report enables you to sort files by their publishing status.

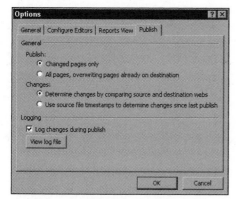

Figure 3-15: The Options Publish tab.

If you want to guarantee that the source and destination Webs are identical, you can select the option to overwrite all pre-existing pages.

The second option, Changes, has the following options:

✦ Determine changes by comparing source and destination webs (the default)

✦ Use source file time stamps to determine changes since last publish

If you elect to use the source file's time stamp as the measure of whether it changed since the last time you published, any file with a time stamp more recent than the time of the last publishing will be updated on the destination server.

Accessing the Publishing Log

Perhaps the most useful option on the Publish tab is the Logging option. Check the "Log changes during publish" checkbox to have FrontPage keep a record of your publishing history. You can also access the log file from this dialog box by clicking the View Log File button. If the View Log File button is grayed out. (inaccessible), it means you have not yet performed an action that would have generated a log file.

Caution   Keep in mind that only publishing operations conducted using the Publish button of the Publish Web dialog box will log results.

The publish log, a sample of which is shown in Figure 3-16, is an HTML page that lists information about the most recent publishing event. Information recorded includes the following:

✦ Publishing start and finish times

✦ File (or folder) creations

✦ File (or folder) copies

✦ File (or folder) renames

✦ File (or folder) deletions

✦ Confirmations and warnings

You can use the drop-down menu to filter the log file results to show any or all of these items.

Note   You can also access the log file after performing a publishing operation by clicking the "Click here to view your publish log file" link on the Publishing confirmation message box.

Using Web Site Reports

First introduced in FrontPage 2000, Web reports provide ready access to a wide variety of useful information about your Web site. Both before and after you publish changes to your site, you can use Web reports to help you keep track of your Web pages, to identify and help you correct problems, and to manage the maintenance process.

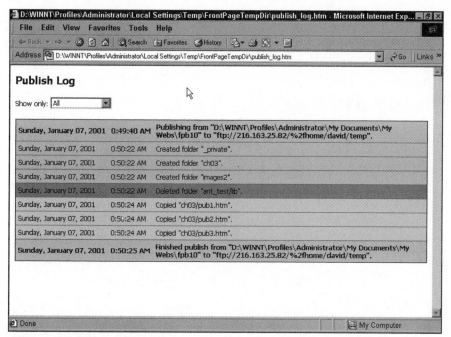

Figure 3-16: A sample publish log

You can navigate through the reports in several ways. Click Reports in the View list to view the Site Summary report. Double-clicking a hyperlinked summary item in the Site Summary report takes you to the detailed report for that item. Alternately, select View ➪ Reports from the menu bar and locate the report you want. You can also view the Reports toolbar by selecting View ➪ Toolbars ➪ Reports and then selecting a report from the Reports drop-down menu on the toolbar. In addition to the list of repots, this toolbar, contains several other useful items:

✦ **Report settings:** A drop-down list of setting options for reports that use them (for example, Older Files, Recently Add and Recently Changed Files, and Slow Pages).

✦ **Usage chart:** Creates a graphical view from any of the detailed usage reports.

✦ **Edit Hyperlink:** Opens the Edit Hyperlink dialog box for the selected hyperlink (in the Broken Hyperlinks report).

✦ **Verify Hyperlinks:** Calls the Verify Hyperlinks function.

New Feature

FrontPage 2002 features a number of Usage reports that enable you to get instant data about the visitors to your site. You will need a Web server with the latest version of the FrontPage Server Extensions installed to take advantage of this feature.

Reports are now organized in categories both in the View ➪ Reports menu and on
**New
Feature** the Reports toolbar. Not a major technical breakthrough, but arguably a clearer
way to organize reports.

Site Summary

The Site Summary report, shown in Figure 3-17, gives you a high-level overview of
the health and status of your Web. For each summary item, this report indicates the
report name, a count of the number of items included in the report, a file size total
where relevant, and a description. Many, but not all, items have a detail page. To
see the details for an item in the Site Summary report, click the hyperlinked line in
question.

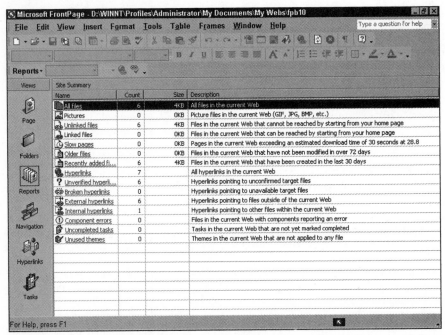

Figure 3-17: The Site Summary report, with the Reports toolbar in the upper left corner

Tip   Not all of the available reports have links from Site Summary. To access these, you
must use either the View ➪ Reports listing or the identical list on the Reports toolbar.

Table 3-1 lists the Site Summary line items and a brief description of each. Those
items with an asterisk have a detailed report, described in the next section.

Table 3-1
Site Summary Report Items

Report Items	Description
All Files*	Indicates the total number of files in your Web and their total file size
Pictures	Indicates the number of graphics in your Web and their total file size
Unlinked Files*	Indicates the number of orphaned files in your Web
Linked Files	Indicates the number of files that are referenced by one or more pages in your Web
Slow Pages*	Estimates the page download time, based on the total number and size of the files associated with the page. The summary indicates the number of *slow* pages, based on a designated download time.
Older Files*	Indicates the number of pages that have not been changed since a designated date
Recently Added Files*	Indicates the number of new pages added since a designated time. (The time designated for recent files is independent of the time designated for older files.)
Hyperlinks*	The total number of hyperlinks, consisting of the four types of hyperlinks described in the next set of report items
Unverified Hyperlinks*	The number of hyperlinks that have not been checked
Broken Hyperlinks*	The number of hyperlinks that do not go to a valid URL
External Hyperlinks*	Valid URLs to external sites
Internal Hyperlinks*	Valid internal URLs
Component Errors*	The number of FrontPage components you are using in your pages that are not functioning correctly
Uncompleted Tasks*	Indicates any tasks in the task list that still need to be done. Double-clicking this item opens Tasks view.
Unused Themes*	Lists any themes that have been added to the Web and then abandoned. Double-clicking this item causes FrontPage to attempt to remove any existing themes that are not in use.

Working with reports

All of the reports have some basic features in common. Although some functionality varies depending on the context, in most you can

✦ Double-click a filename to open it. You can also usually access all of the normal file property options by right-clicking on the filename in the list.

✦ Click on any column header in a report to re-sort the report on the information in that column; clicking a second time reverses the order of the sort.

✦ Drag the edge of a column to expand or shrink it.

✦ Drag the column header to reorder the columns.

✦ Filter report results using the pull-down menus in each column. Click the downward arrow in the column header to reveal a drop-down a menu containing the options: All (the default), Custom, and a list of the specific items currently in the list. In cases where blank values are allowed, you will also see Blank and Non-blank as filter options.

Selecting Custom enables you to define a custom filter formula with either one or two criteria using the Custom AutoFilter dialog box, shown in Figure 3-18. Use the following steps to create a custom filter:

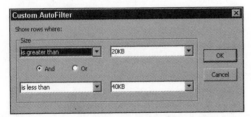

Figure 3-18: The Custom AutoFilter dialog box

1. Select an operator rule for the column from the first drop-down list.

2. Select or type in a value for the operator to match.

3. If you want to add a second filter criterion, first select And or Or to indicate how the two criteria should be related. (And signifies that both criteria must be met by all matches; Or indicates matches on at least one of the criteria.)

4. Select the operator and value for the second criteria.

Finally, you can right-click the title bar of a report to call up an options menu, as shown in Figure 3-19, with the following options: New Page, Copy Report, Paste (if relevant), Remove Filters (assuming filters are in effect), and Web Settings, a link to the dialog box of that name (found under the Tools menu). Of these, the most interesting is the Copy Report option. Selecting this option creates a copy of the current report, which you can paste into another Office document (such as Word or Excel) or even into an HTML page.

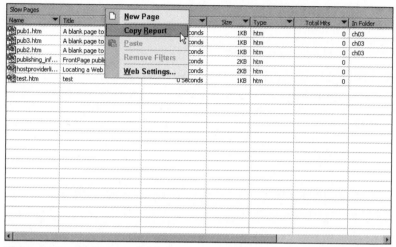

Figure 3-19: Options available from reports when you right-click on the report's title bar

Detailed reports

FrontPage 2002 includes over a dozen detailed reports that you can use to view information about the contents of your Web. In most cases, you can sort reports and even make changes to report items from within the report itself. Thus, the report serves as a powerful Find feature for problems when you are first preparing to publish or when you are doing periodic maintenance reviews of your site.

Following is a list of the reports, with its name and a brief description::

Note Reports have been organized as they appear on the Reports toolbar listing.

Files reports

✦ **All Files:** Provides details for the All Files summary item. It includes for each file the following: Name, Title, In Folder, Size, Type, Modified Date, Modified By, Total Hits, and Comments. You can change the filename and its title, and add comments from this list. This is a great place to check your page titles for consistency, by the way, because you can see all of your titles simultaneously.

✦ **Recently Added Files:** Lists all files added within a definable date range. It includes for each file the following: Name, Title, Created Date, Modified By, Size, Type, Total Hits, and In Folder. You can edit Name and Title. Use the Report Settings menu to define the data range. You can also configure the date that defines recent files in the Reports View tab of the Options menu or in the Reports toolbar.

Tip

If you want to define a custom date range not available in the Report Settings menu, you can set it in the Reports tab of the Options menu or you can set a custom filter on the Modified Date field.

✦ **Recently Changed Files:** Lists all files added within a definable date range. It includes the following: Name, Title, Modified Date, Modified By, Size, Type, and In Folder. You can edit Name and Title. Use the Report Settings menu to define the data range. You can also configure the date that defines recent files in the Reports View tab of the Options menu or in the Reports toolbar. Figure 3-20 shows an example report of recently changed files.

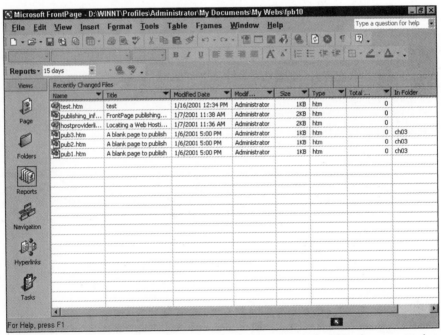

Figure 3-20: A sample report showing a list of files changed within the past 15 days

✦ **Older Files:** Provides details for the Older Files summary item. It includes the following: Name, Title, Modified Date, Modified By, Size, Type, Total Hits, and In Folder. You can edit Name and Title. Use the Report Settings menu to define the data range. You can also configure the date that defines recent files in the Reports View tab of the Options menu or in the Reports toolbar.

Problems reports

✦ **Unlinked Files:** Provides details for the Unlinked Files summary item. An unlinked file is any file that cannot be accessed by following links beginning with the home page. This report includes the following: Name, Title, Modified Date, Modified By, Type, Total Hits, and In Folder. You can edit Name and Title.

✦ **Slow Pages:** Provides details for the Slow Files summary item. It includes the following: Name, Title, Download Time, Size, Type, In Folder, and Modified Date. You can edit Name and Title. You can define a slow page in the Reports View tab of the Options menu or in the Reports toolbar. Note that download times are calculated based on the "Assume Connection Speed of" option in the Reports View tab of the Options dialog box.

✦ **Broken Hyperlinks:** Provides file details for the Broken Link summary item. It includes the following: Status, Hyperlink, In Page, Page Title, and Modified By. You cannot edit fields. Double-click a file to open the Edit Hyperlink dialog box (see Figure 3-21). Right-clicking on a file in this report brings up a set of options specific to fixing the hyperlinks: Edit Hyperlink, Edit Page, Verify Hyperlink (the selected link), and Show All Hyperlinks (including nonbroken ones), in addition to the standard options: Copy Report, Remove Filter, and Web Settings. More details about fixing broken hyperlinks are provided in the next section.

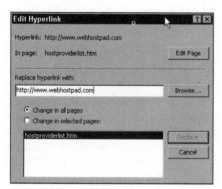

Figure 3-21: The Edit Hyperlink dialog box

✦ **Component Errors:** Provides file details for the Component Errors summary item. It includes the following: Name, Title, Errors, Type, and In Folder. You cannot edit fields.

Workflow reports

✦ **Review Status:** Lists review information for each file in the Web. You can also use this report to modify review information. It includes the following: Name, Title, Review Status, Assigned To, Review Date, Reviewed By, Expiration Date, Type, and In Folder. You can edit Name, Title, Review Status, Expiration Date and Assigned To.

✦ **Assigned To:** Lists details about page assignments for each file in the Web. You can also use this report to modify assignment information. It includes the following: Name, Title, Assigned To, Assigned Date, Assigned By, Comments, Type, and In Folder. You can edit Name, Title, Assigned To, and Comments. Double-click a file to open it.

✦ **Categories:** Lists category details about each file in the Web. It includes the following Name, Title, Category, Type, and In Folder. You can't edit Category information in this report. You can use the Reports toolbar to filter the report on a specific category.

✦ **Publish Status:** Lists publishing details for each file in the Web. It also enables you to enable or disable publishing for a file. It includes the following: Name, Title, Publish, Modified Date, Review Status, Size, Type, and In Folder. You can edit Name, Title, Review Status, and Publish.

✦ **Checkout Status:** Available only if you have enabled source control for the current Web. (See the next section for details on enabling and using FrontPage's built-in source control). It includes the following: Name, Title, Checked Out By, Version, Locked Date, Type, and In Folder. You can edit Name and Title only.

Usage reports

New in FrontPage 2002, the usage reports provide instant information about who is visiting your site, when they visit, and which pages they are viewing. They also provide useful information about your visitors — the browsers they are using, where they are coming from, and what, if any, search engine terms they typed to locate your site. All of this information is helpful in planning both the marketing and further development of your site.

Note To say that they provide "instant" information is a bit misleading. You can get the information instantly, but the usage data being analyzed is going to be historical. You can configure your web server to update usage information on a daily, weekly, or monthly basis. You will be looking at data that does not represent an up to the minute analysis of activity on your site.

Note In order to view usage information, your site must be (1) hosted on an web server running the 2002 FrontPage Server Extensions, (2) the server must be configured to collect usage data, and (3) your Web must be the root web (in other words, usage analysis does not work on subwebs).

Table 3-2 lists the items reported in the Usage Summary Report. Items. Detailed version for each of these items is available either by clicking the hyperlinked name of the report or by selecting the appropriate detailed summary report name from the Reports menu.

Table 3-2
Usage Summary Report Items

Report Items	Description
Date of first data	Usage data is analyzed starting with this date
Date last updated	The last date for which usage data is analyzed
Total visits	The number of pages viewed from external sources
Total page hits	The total number of pages requested
Total bytes downloaded	Total size of all files requested
Current visits	Number of visits in the most recent month
Current page hits	Number of page hits in the most recent month
Current bytes downloaded	Size of files requested in the most recent month
Top referrer	Web page from which users entered your site most often during the most recent month
Top referring domain	Domain from which users entered your site most often during the most recent month
Top web browser	Most frequently used browser by visitors during the most recent month
Top operating system	Most frequently used computer operating system by visitors during the most recent month
Top search terms	Most frequently use search items by visitors during the most recent month
Top user	Most frequent user during the most recent month

Setting Reports view options

To configure various Reports view options, select Tools ➪ Options and choose the Reports View tab (see Figure 3-22). Options you can configure include the following:

✦ **Recent Files:** Indicate how many days a file should be considered recent.

✦ **Older Files:** Indicate how many days before a file should be considered old.

✦ **Slow Pages:** Indicate download time to define a slow page.

✦ **Connection Speed:** Select a download connection speed for use in calculating download times.

✦ **Display Gridlines:** You can show or hide lines in your reports — for the design-conscious report reader.

✦ **Usage:** Number of months shown.

✦ **Usage charts:** You can elect to include these in saved usage reports or not, as you prefer.

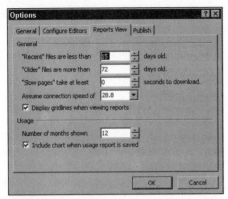

Figure 3-22: The Reports View tab of the Options dialog box

Performing Site Maintenance

Having access to the Site reports is very convenient, but the reports are only as good as the use you make of them. This section describes some of the common maintenance tasks you can perform with the help of FrontPage.

Maintenance tasks

In the last three or four years, the quantity of Web development talent and expertise has grown exponentially, in step with the feverish pace of increasingly sophisticated Web projects. Whereas a few years ago a single person could have been counted on to design, develop, and maintain a typical Web site, now it takes a full team of people. Larger, more complex projects also require more sophisticated tools to help keep them running smoothly. FrontPage is designed to serve the needs of everything from small-business Web site development to large, coordinated projects in multi-department corporations.

FrontPage 2002 includes the following utilities to help development teams collaborate effectively:

✦ **Tasks View:** Enables groups to assign and monitor tasks.

✦ **Workgroup Categories:** Enables groups to divide tasks into logical groupings.

✦ **Review Status:** Enables you to track pages and content files through the stages of publication.

✦ **Source Control:** Protects files from accidental overwriting in a multi-user environment.

✦ **Project Web Template**: A FrontPage Web for communicating among team members.

Many of the tools FrontPage includes for managing Web development can also be used to organize site maintenance tasks. The following sections describe these features in more detail.

Working with categories

You can use workgroup categories to classify your files in groups. After you categorize your files, you can use the categories to manage your files or to insert a list of filenames of a given category into a Web page.

Assigning categories to a file

You can assign a category to a file when the file is open or closed. If the file is open, right-click anywhere on the open page in Page view and select Properties from the options menu. Click the Workgroups tab and select one or more categories from the Available Categories list. To select a category, click the checkbox. To deselect a category, uncheck it.

If the file is closed, right-click the File icon in Folders view and select Properties from the options menu. Click the Workgroups tab and select one or more categories from the Available Categories list. You can set the categories for several files simultaneously by selecting the files in Folders view and proceeding as you would for a single file.

Viewing pages by category

You can view your files by category by using the Categories report. Switch to Reports view and select Categories from the Reports toolbar. By default, the Categories reports lists files in all categories. To view files for a particular category only, select the category from the Reports toolbar. You cannot edit categories directly in this report. However, you can right-click one or more files to edit categories, as previously described.

Modifying the Master Category List

FrontPage 2002 comes with several preset categories. You can modify this list to suit your purposes. To modify the Master Category List, right-click a file in Folders view and select Properties. Select the Workgroup tab and click the Categories button. In the Master Category List, shown in Figure 3-23, type a new name in the New Category field and click the Add button. To delete an existing category, select it from the list and click the Delete button.

Figure 3-23: The Master Category List is found in the Properties Workgroup tab.

Inserting categories into a Web page

After you categorize your files, you can add a list of pages of a particular category to a Web page. For example, suppose you have several pages describing the various products that your company sells. You have added each page to the Products category. To add a list of product pages to a Web page, follow these steps:

1. Open the Web page where you want the list to appear.

2. Select Insert ➪ Web Component ➪ Table of Contents and choose "Based on Page Category" from the table of contents options.

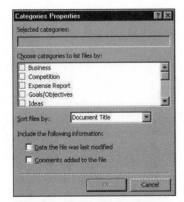

Figure 3-24: Insert a category into a Web page using the Categories Properties dialog box.

3. In the Categories Properties dialog box, as shown in Figure 3-24, select one or more categories to include in the list by checking available categories in the list labeled Choose Categories to list files by.

4. Optionally, select a sort method, either alphabetically by title or by modification date.

5. Optionally, select to include the file modification date and/or comments.

6. Click OK to insert the Categories component into the page.

This component updates dynamically any time that you add a new page to one of the selected categories in this list.

Assigning tasks to individuals or workgroups

FrontPage Tasks view is where you can keep track of the work that needs to be completed on your Web. This feature is neither a full-blown project management tool nor an incident tracking system. For average needs, however, it provides a convenient way to record and keep track of project tasks that need to be completed. You can use Tasks view to identify tasks, assign tasks, prioritize tasks, and update the status of tasks.

Creating a task

Several of the page-checking utilities described in this chapter — for example, the spell checker and the link checker — have the capability to create tasks automatically based on any errors that they detect. In addition to these mechanisms, you can add tasks manually, either associated with a particular page or just as a general-purpose task.

To create a general-purpose task, follow these steps:

1. From Folders view or Hyperlinks view, select File ➪ New ➪ Task to open the New Task dialog box, shown in Figure 3-25. Alternatively, from Tasks view, you can right-click the tasks list and select New Task from the option menu.

2. In the New Task dialog box, give the task a name, assign it a priority (high, medium, or low), and assign the task to an authorized user, using the drop-down menu. Optionally, add a descriptive comment to explain the task.

To add a task and associate it with a particular file, follow these steps:

1. In either Folders view or Page view, select the file to which you want to add a task. You can do this either by opening the file and selecting Edit ➪ Task ➪ Add Task or by right-clicking a filename in Folders view and selecting Add Task from the option menu.

2. Complete the dialog box as described in Step 2 in the preceding list. Note that the selected filename is identified in the Associated With field in the dialog box. This item can't be edited.

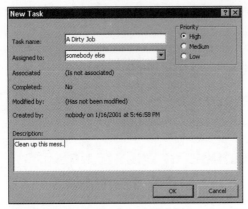

Figure 3-25: The New Task dialog box—
showing a general purpose task

Viewing and sorting tasks

To view current tasks, switch to Tasks view (a sample set of tasks is illustrated in
Figure 3-26). You can adjust column widths and sort the task list for any of the available columns by clicking the column name. For example, to sort tasks by priority,
click the Priority column heading. To reverse-sort the same field, click the column
heading a second time.

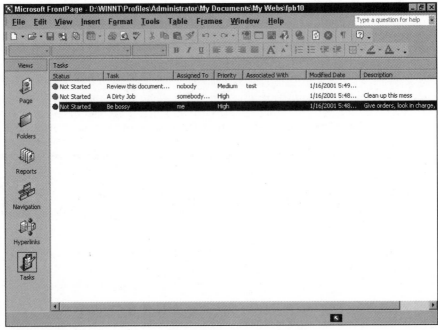

Figure 3-26: A list of newly created tasks

Modifying tasks

You can make changes to task details by using the Task Detail dialog box. To view task details, double-click a task. This displays the Task Detail dialog box, which is identical to the New Task dialog box. Alternatively, right-click the task and select the Edit Task item.

In addition, you can edit any of the fields in the Task Detail dialog box directly in the Tasks view list. This includes the Task Name, Assigned To, Priority, and Description fields. To edit a field, select the field value and then either type a new value or select a new value from the menu of available options.

To delete a task, right-click the task and select Delete from the option menu.

Starting tasks

If a task is associated with a particular file or Web page, you can use Tasks view to start the task. In Tasks view, right-click the task that you want to perform and select Start Task from the option menu. Alternatively, select the task and choose Edit ➪ Task ➪ Start. And in case that isn't enough options for you, you can double-click the task to open its Edit dialog box and then click the Start Task button. Note that tasks not associated with any page have the Start Task feature disabled.

Completing tasks

Sooner or later, all good tasks must be completed. After you complete a task, you should mark it as completed. To mark a task completed, right-click the task in Tasks view and select Mark as Completed from the option menu. Alternatively, select the task and then choose Edit ➪ Task ➪ Mark as Complete.

Tasks that have been completed can be removed from the list of Tasks that you view. To hide completed tasks, right-click inside the Tasks view window. If Show Task History is checked, all completed tasks will be displayed in Tasks view. To remove completed tasks from view, select Show Task History to uncheck this option. Alternatively, select Edit ➪ Task ➪ Show Task history and check or uncheck in the same fashion.

Using check-in/check-out source control

FrontPage 2002 includes a simple means of checking files in and out. You can use this feature to prevent two people from making changes to the same file and canceling out each other's work.

To use FrontPage's built-in source control, you must first enable it. To enable source control, you must have administrative-level privileges. Select Tools ➪ Web Settings and check "Use document check-in and check-out" on the General tab (see

Figure 3-27). If you enable check-in/out on an existing Web, FrontPage will need to recalculate the Web. Once it is finished, it places a small green dot next to each file, indicating that it is currently checked-in.

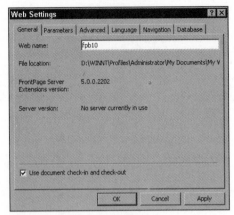

Figure 3-27: To enable check-in, select the check-in checkbox.

Checking out a file

To check out a file means to open it so that only you can make changes until you check it back in. When you have source control enabled, only one person can make changes to a file at a time. When you check out a file, others can view the file but they cannot modify it. Another side effect of enabling check-in/check-out is that the properties of files can only be changed when the files are checked out. You cannot change the categories for a file, or its review status or its "assigned to" designation unless you have first checked out the file.

To check out a file, switch to Folders view and right-click the file that you want to edit. Select Check Out from the option menu. Doing so marks that file with a little lock icon, indicating that you have checked it out. Note that selecting this option does not automatically open the file for you.

If you attempt to open a file in the normal fashion, FrontPage alerts you that the file is under source control, and asks whether you want to check out the file. If you click Yes, FrontPage marks the page with the checked-out icon and opens it for you to edit. If you click No, FrontPage opens the file without checking it out to you.

Tip   In most cases you should check out a file before attempting to edit it. This is the best way to ensure that your changes are recorded correctly.

Checking in a file

When you are done editing, you must check in a file that you have checked out. First, save any changes that you have made to the file. Right-click the file in Folders view and select Check In from the options menu. This releases the file for another user to edit.

Caution   It is possible (quite easy, actually) to close a file that you are done working with without checking it back in. If you forget, no one else will be able to edit the file.

Viewing checkout status

When you enable source control on your Web, all files are marked to indicate their checkout status. Files with a small green bullet next to them are available for checkout. Files with a red check next to them are checked out to you. Files with a lock icon next to them have been checked out to another user.

To view detailed information on the checkout status of files, switch to Reports view and select the Checkout Status report, illustrated in Figure 3-28.

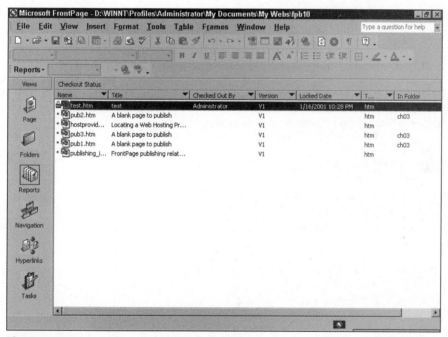

Figure 3-28: A sample Checkout Status report

The built-in source control has a few oddities. As noted above, even with source control enabled, you can open and edit a file without checking it out. Similarly, you can create and save a new page and continue to edit it without having it checked out. You can delete a file whether it is checked out or not. You can check out a file and then check it back in and still continue to make changes. In general, the best policy is always to begin by checking out any file you plan to edit and to check in any files you have finished editing.

Using review status

In addition to categories, development teams can assign a review status to their files as a way of tracking files through the development process. When changes have been made to the files, they can be marked to indicate that they require review. When they have been reviewed, their status can be changed to reflect whether they have been approved or sent back for more changes. (If you need a more sophisticated workflow, see the discussion of SharePoint Team Services in Chapter 24).

Setting the review status

Assuming that you do not have check-in/check-out enabled, you can set the review status of a file in one of three ways:

✦ When the file is open

✦ When the file is closed

✦ From the Review Status report

If the file is open, right-click anywhere on the open page in Page view and select Properties from the options menu. Click the Workgroup tab and select a review status code from the available menu, as shown in Figure 3-29.

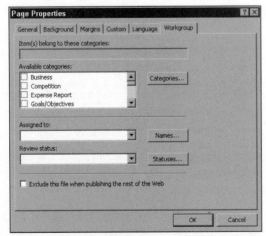

Figure 3-29: The Workgroup tab of the Page Properties dialog box, opened while editing a file

If the file is closed, right-click the File icon in Folders view and select Properties from the options menu. Click the Workgroup tab and select a review status code from the menu of available options. To set the review status code for several files simultaneously, select the files in Folders view and proceed as you would for a single file.

You can also set review status codes for one or more files by using the Review Status report. Switch to Reports view and select the Review Status report from the Reports toolbar. Click the Review Status field of a given file and then select a review status code from the list of available options.

You can add a new review status code from the Review Status report. However, to edit or remove codes, you must use the Review Status Master List, described next.

Modifying the Review Status Master List

By default, FrontPage includes a list of three review status codes: Approved, Denied, and Pending Review. You can modify this list to suit your purposes. To modify the Review Status list, right-click a file in Folders view and select Properties. Select the Workgroup tab and click the Statuses button. In the Review Status Master List, shown in Figure 3-30, type a new name in the New Review Status field and click the Add button. To delete an existing review status code, select it from the list and click the Delete button.

Figure 3-30: Modifying the Review Status Master List

Performing site maintenance tasks

It is tempting, once you have successfully created your Web site, to stand back and admire your handiwork. But don't rest on your laurels for too long. If you want your site to remain vital, you will need to keep it updated and in good working order. This section describes the capabilities FrontPage provides to help take some of the drudgery out of web site maintenance.

Keeping files up-to-date

In the rapidly changing Web environment, one of the worst things that can happen to your Web pages is that they develop the dreaded *page rot*. Page rot is what happens to pages that have not been updated and clearly represent stale, out-of-date information. If you choose, you can use FrontPage to help you institute a plan for ensuring that pages are regularly reviewed and updated if necessary to prevent page rotting. Here is the basic picture:

1. Set up the Older Files report to show all files that have not been changed for whatever period of time you like; let's say 30 days.

2. Whenever a file shows up on the Older Files list, you right-click it and set its review properties to Review Pending; and set the Assigned To field to the appropriate person who should review the pages.

3. Presumably that person's job will entail periodically checking for these files by opening the Assigned To report and filtering the list to find all of the files assigned to them. (If you like, you can also add a task to the task list as a double reminder and as a way of verifying that the review was completed.)

4. The reviewer's job, of course, is to look at the file and assess whether any changes need to be made to the file. If so, an appropriate process should be defined to get the page information up-to-date. If the file is still relevant, the reviewer can resave the page without making any changes, effectively updating its Last Modified Date, so that it will not come up for review for another 30 days. Reviewers also need to update the file's review status.

Setting an expiration date

Another approach to ensuring that a page doesn't rot is to assign an expiration date to it.

To assign an expiration date to a file, select the Review Status report and click the Expiration Date field for the file. This opens a dialog box with its calendar widget open, as shown in Figure 3-31. You can set an expiration date or simply mark the file Expired.

Slow pages

Even worse than page rot are those pages that take so long to load that the user (whose attention span is estimated to be something shy of 8 seconds) decides to go to another site instead. To prevent this from happening, you should take care to identify and deal with pages that are slow to load. Typical causes of slow pages include the following:

✦ **Eye candy:** The less than complimentary term for design elements — it used to be GIF animations, these days it tends to be Flash — which look very nice but don't really add any "nutritional" value to your site. As with any diet, moderation is the key. A small quantity of such elements is reasonable, but avoid overload.

✦ **Embedded components:** It is very easy to add lots of widgets to your site in the form of components; these, too, can be very fun and elicit "oohs" and "aahs" from your users on T1 lines, but be careful that you are not prompting other noises from your dial-up users.

✦ **HTML bloat:** Sadly enough, Office can frequently be the cause of this problem, as it has a nasty habit of adding a large amount of unnecessary HTML, and more recently, XML, to files you convert from one format to another. This is usually a less noticeable problem than either too many large graphics or embedded components, because here we are talking about text characters, which typically require very little storage space. However, we have seen files as large as 40K, which, when the excess tagging was removed, were more like 10k—a pretty big difference without having to make any sacrifices in the appearance of the page. Therefore, keep an eye on your HTML (for details on how, see Chapter 8).

To identify potential offending pages, use the Slow Page report previously described.

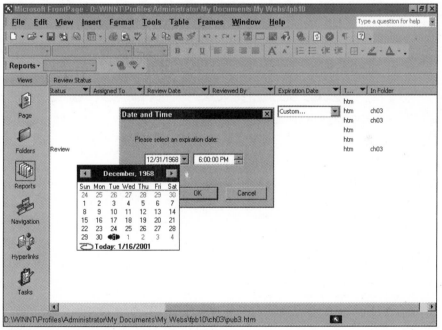

Figure 3-31: Setting a file's expiration date

Verifying and correcting hyperlinks

Using FrontPage to insert hyperlinks can vastly decrease the number of broken or invalid links in your Web pages. However, you still might create a link to a non-existent Web page, either on your own Web or elsewhere on the Internet. In addition, external links that are valid today may be non-existent tomorrow, so rechecking your external links periodically is a good practice. Moreover, if you think users are intolerant when it comes to page rot or slow loading pages, try dealing with users who have been clicking repeatedly on your broken link. Fortunately, FrontPage can track down and list invalid hyperlinks, making it easy to correct or eliminate them from your Web pages.

Checking hyperlinks

To view the number of broken hyperlinks in your Web, follow these steps:

1. Open the Web in FrontPage.

2. Select Reports from the View menu.

3. To see summary information on the number of links in your Web, select the Site Summary report. This report lists the total number of hyperlinks, unverified hyperlinks (links that FrontPage hasn't yet checked), broken hyperlinks, external hyperlinks, and internal hyperlinks (see Figure 3-32).

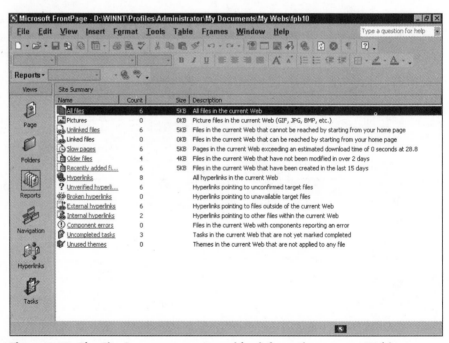

Figure 3-32: The Site Summary report provides information on your Web's hyperlinks.

4. To see a detailed list of broken hyperlinks, double-click the Broken Hyperlinks count in the Count column of the Site Summary report, or select the Broken Hyperlinks report from the Reports toolbar. A sample report is shown in Figure 3-33.

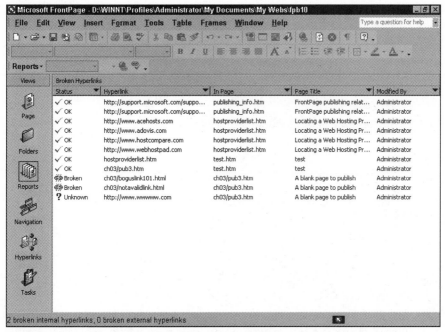

Figure 3-33: Detailed list of broken hyperlinks from the Site Summary report

To recheck any unverified links, right-click on the files in the Broken Hyperlinks report and select Verify Hyperlinks. If you select one or more files, FrontPage assumes you want to verify only those files. To verify all files, right-click on the title bar of the report. (If this command is inaccessible, it means that you do not currently have any unverified links.) FrontPage will display the Verify Hyperlinks dialog box, which enables you to specify whether you want to verify all files or just selected files. Alternately, you can select Tools ⇨ Recalculate Hyperlinks, which performs a number of tasks, one of which is re-verifying hyperlinks. Note that if you have a large number of external links, FrontPage may take several minutes to verify those links.

Note   You must be connected to the Internet for FrontPage to verify any external hyperlinks.

Editing invalid hyperlinks

After you identify broken links, you likely will want to fix them (at least we hope so). From the Broken Hyperlinks report, you can choose one of the following methods of dealing with broken links:

✦ To edit the hyperlink, double-click the list item, which opens the Edit Hyperlink dialog box, shown in Figure 3-34. Use this dialog box to change the hyperlink for the selected page or for all pages containing the same URL reference. Click the Edit Page button to open the selected page for editing.

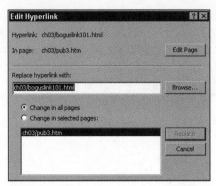

Figure 3-34: Use the Edit Hyperlink dialog box to fix broken and unverified links.

Note   You can't remove a hyperlink from the Edit Hyperlink dialog box. To remove a hyperlink, open the page and remove the hyperlink using the standard page editing tools.

✦ To edit the page containing the hyperlink, right-click the item in the Broken Hyperlinks report and select the Edit Page option from the option menu.

✦ To add the broken hyperlink to the Task List, right-click the item in the Broken Hyperlinks report and select Add Task from the option menu.

Dealing with unlinked files

In the Web publishing world, an *orphaned* file is one that has no references to it from other files. In other words, no other pages in the Web contain a link to the orphaned file. Typically, orphaned files are unused, forgotten files that you can safely remove from your Web. (Of course, sometimes you may have good reasons for having a file that is accessible on your Web server but not directly linked to from any other files). FrontPage considers a page *unlinked* if it is not possible to navigate to the page via hyperlinks from your home page. (For instance, if you have an unlinked page that has links to other pages, those pages would also be considered unlinked, even though in point of fact they are linked to a page.)

To find and remove unlinked files, follow these steps:

1. Switch to Reports view.

2. Select unlinked files from the Reports toolbar. If the Reports toolbar is not available, select View ➪ Toolbars ➪ Reports to show it.

3. To delete a file in the list of unlinked files, right-click the file and select Delete from the option menu.

Component errors

If you are using FrontPage components in your Webs, you can produce a report that lists any files that contain components with errors. The procedure for locating and correcting nonfunctioning components is very similar to the one described in the previous section for validating hyperlinks.

Checking components

To view the number of components with errors in your Web, follow these steps:

1. Open the Web in FrontPage.

2. Select Reports from the View menu.

3. To see summary information on the number of component errors, select the Site Summary report. This report lists the total number of errors.

4. If you have component errors, you can double-click the summary item to view a detailed list of the files containing components with errors. Alternatively, select Component Errors from the Reports toolbar to view this detailed report.

Editing nonfunctioning components

From the Component Errors report, you can work with broken components in one of two ways:

✦ Double-click an item in the report list to open the page and edit the component.

✦ To add the broken component to the task list, right-click the item and select Add Task from the option menu.

Summary

In this chapter, you learned what it means to publish your FrontPage Webs, how to do it, and how to find a hosting provider who can give you a place to do it. You examined a variety of ways to control the publishing process. You learned about the wide variety of FrontPage reports that you can use to manage files, detect and repair problems, manage your development workflow, and keep track of usage on your Web. These reports serve as the foundation of good site maintenance, and you have explored a number of ways to use these reports to help you keep your published Web site running smoothly and efficiently.

This chapter marks the end of the basic introduction to FrontPage. At this point you know how to create and edit web pages, manage a Web site, and publish and maintain your pages. Now you are ready to dig into FrontPage's wed development capabilities. In Part II, we explore the finer points of using FrontPage to design and layout your Web pages.

A Plug for Validating HTML

Do it. To validate HTML means to check that all of your HTML code is written as directed by a certain HTML standard, such as HTML 2.0, HTML 3.2, or HTML 4.0. Although you can use the HTML Source and Compatibility tabs on the Page Options dialog box to control your HTML output, FrontPage 2002 does not include any direct means of validating HTML. If you want to validate your HTML, you must use an external tool. (See Chapter 8 for details.)

✦   ✦   ✦

Integrating FrontPage with Office Applications

Suppose that you have documents in Word, illustrations in PowerPoint, a brochure in Publisher, and a table in Excel, and you need to integrate them all into your Web site. This chapter shows you how to do just that. Along with integrating Office content into FrontPage Webs, you can ship FrontPage content back to Office. For example, you can dump your FrontPage reports into Excel to analyze your database of site files, or export collected FrontPage data to a Word mail-merge file.

Finally, Office XP users can directly open spreadsheets and PivotTables in your site right in their Web browsers.

In Figure 4-1, for example, a visitor is calculating values in a spreadsheet embedded in a Web page.

From Office to FrontPage

All Office XP applications have their own distinct methods for converting documents to Web pages. Excel automatically generates Web sites that look like spreadsheets. Publisher creates Web site folders full of files, with a separate Web page for each page of a publication. PowerPoint Web sites look like slideshows; and Word, too, generates Web sites.

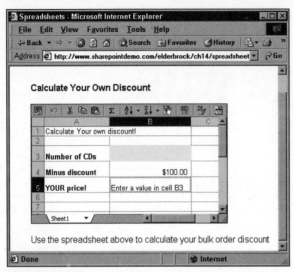

Figure 4-1: You can provide interactivity for visitors by using an Office XP spreadsheet Web component.

That's all fine for people using those programs who aren't demanding the capability to fine-tune their Web page display. However, as a FrontPage-empowered Web designer, you may want to select elements from Office applications to integrate into a Web site of your own design.

Importing Web components from Office applications requires an understanding of how they generate Web sites, where they stash the Web files, and how you can work around some of the automation routines to import just what you want into your Web site.

Moving from Word to FrontPage

Actually, you have several ways to move text from a Word file into a FrontPage Web site. The quickest way is to copy text, although even this option presents several alternatives that affect how the text format is translated to your Web page.

Other options include saving the file as a text file or saving it as HTML. Each method has its advantages and drawbacks, which are explored in this section.

Note   Most of the different ways of integrating Office documents into Webs involves using the Import dialog box, which is discussed in the section "Importing Files into Webs."

Attaching text files to a Web site

If your Web design responsibilities include integrating many documents into a Web site, you will very likely want to import large blocks of text from Word (or another word processor) into FrontPage Web pages.

You have many options available for integrating word processing files into a Web site. If you are presenting documents that don't need any formatting or Web design features, you can simply save your documents as text (.txt) files and import them into your Web site.

One drawback of using .txt file format is that when visitors see this text on a Web page, it will be displayed in long lines, without text wrapping. You can easily import a Word file in FrontPage. Open a page and choose Insert ➪ File. From the Files of Type drop-down list, choose Word from the list of file type options. Select a Word file, as shown in Figure 4-2. FrontPage will convert the Word file as it is imported.

 Tip The Word-to-FrontPage converter is a feature that is not installed in Office XP by default, so have your Office CD handy when you select this option for the first time.

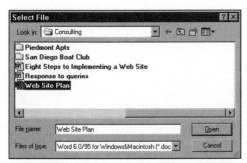

Figure 4-2: Inserting Word files in your Web site is a no-frills way to make a document available to visitors.

How Word creates HTML files

You can save Word files as HTML. Word 2002's File ➪ Save as Web Page option converts an open document to an HTML file (or, in some cases, to several files, including image files). How good are the results? The resulting files often take some work to restore formatting and images. Publisher 2002 does a cleaner job of converting document files to Web pages. If you want to do complex page layout outside of FrontPage, Publisher is a better choice than Word. However, if you want to convert a 50-page Word document to a Web site, the Save as HTML option accomplishes the job in a hurry. In addition, you can, of course, touch up the formatting in FrontPage Page view.

If you do save a Word file as HTML, the best way to work with it in FrontPage is to *import* the HTML file (created by Word). Even after you import the file, however, FrontPage will still identify this imported file as a Word file, and when you double-click on the file in Folder or Navigation view, FrontPage launches Word again. To avoid having your file open in Word, right-click on the file and choose Open With from the context menu. Then, select *FrontPage* (instead of Word) to edit the file in FrontPage.

Word saves complex documents by generating several files. For example, long document footers have separate files generated for the footer(s). Similarly, separate files are generated for embedded image files. Word creates a new folder when these files are generated, to keep them all together. In that case, when you import a Word file that has been saved to HTML, you import the entire folder. As you do, FrontPage retains the folder paths between the imported page and linked images.

Copying and pasting text into Web pages

The easiest way to get word processing documents into FrontPage Web pages is simply to copy and paste the text. First, copy all or part of a document into the Clipboard. Then, open a page in FrontPage 2002 Page view and select Edit ➪ Paste Special. The Convert Text dialog box appears, as shown in Figure 4-3.

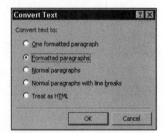

Figure 4-3: You have several options for pasting copied text into a Web page.

The following are the paste options:

✦ **One formatted paragraph:** Converts the text to one paragraph, replacing paragraph marks in the copied text with forced line breaks.

✦ **Formatted paragraphs:** Copies the text, preserving formatting and paragraphs.

Note

The difference between One Formatted Paragraph and Formatted *Paragraphs* is that the One Formatted Paragraph option converts the copied text to a single paragraph.

✦ **Normal paragraphs:** Copies the text, converting it to the Normal style defined for your Web site. If you assigned a theme with a defined Normal style, or if you defined a Normal style yourself, those attributes are assigned to the copied text.

✦ **Normal paragraphs with line breaks:** Converts copied text to Normal style (like the preceding option), but substitutes forced line breaks for paragraph breaks.

✦ **Treat as HTML:** Interprets any HTML code within copied text. *You are unlikely to use this option for imported Word text, unless you include HTML tags in your text.*

Note   Use the Treat as HTML option when you copy HTML code into a FrontPage Web page.

Creating Web sites from Publisher files

Microsoft Publisher follows its own rules when it generates Web sites. Those sites are fine, but they don't integrate well into FrontPage.

When you save a Publisher 2002 publication as a Web page, a new folder with multiple files is created. Publisher creates a new Web page for each page in your publication, and saves all of them to a folder. Therefore, when you save a Publisher publication as a Web site, you actually create and save to a folder, not to individual files.

To save your publication as a Web site in Publisher, select File ➪ Save as Web Page. You need to do this even if you saved your file prior to converting it to Web pages. The Save as Web Page dialog box prompts you to select a folder to which your many Web site files will be saved. The Save as Web Page dialog box prompts you for a file folder, not a filename. Be careful to save only one single set of Web files in a folder.

Publisher and FrontPage: An Insider's Perspective

As a Microsoft technical engineer confided to us, "We do not advertise any capability of being able to take Publisher .htm files to FrontPage or any other editor, and being able to have a lot of fidelity with them.

"As for sites, FrontPage and Publisher are very different. FrontPage uses a different naming convention and is able to upload only items with changes. Publisher uploads the entire site every time and uses arbitrary names (such as Img0001.gif instead of clown.gif). And after editing a page and re-publishing it, img0001.gif may actually be a different image altogether than it was the previous time you uploaded it.

"I would not say that Publisher Web pages can now be edited in FrontPage with any sense of fidelity or consistency. But then, it is not designed to do that. It is designed to be created in Publisher and be edited in Publisher."

Note   Publisher converts all embedded pictures into `.gif` format and stores them in the folder generated for your saved Web site. Because not all images save well as `.gif` files, you can substitute `.jpeg` files when necessary in FrontPage's Page view.

What, then, is the best workaround if you have to convert Publisher files into FrontPage Webs? Our suggestion is to obtain the original text and image files and, if necessary, copy and paste them into FrontPage.

Sending Excel objects to FrontPage

Excel offers three options for sending spreadsheets and charts to FrontPage Web pages:

✦ Use copy and paste to transfer selected cells or charts to a Web page.

✦ Save selected cells, sheets, or charts as Web pages.

✦ Save an entire worksheet, including all tabs, as a set of Web files.

Copying and pasting works fine for quick and dirty transferring of cells into a FrontPage table. Copying charts works fine—you simply transfer the chart into Page view as a picture that can be edited or formatted using all of FrontPage's picture formatting tools. For example, you can copy a chart into FrontPage, assign a transparent background, save it as a `.gif` file, and make it into an image map with linked hotspots. For a full discussion of all of these picture editing features, see Chapter 12.

To preserve cell formatting or to convert your entire spreadsheet (either one tab or all of them) into a Web site, you can save your spreadsheet to an HTML file.

Copying tables into FrontPage

The quick and easy way to move a table into FrontPage is to copy the cells in Excel and paste them into an open Web page in FrontPage. Copying and pasting cells preserves most formatting, including font color, font size, alignment, shading, and border formatting. In addition, you can always use FrontPage's own table formatting to restore or add table and cell formatting. Figure 4-4 shows a table from Excel moved into a FrontPage Web page.

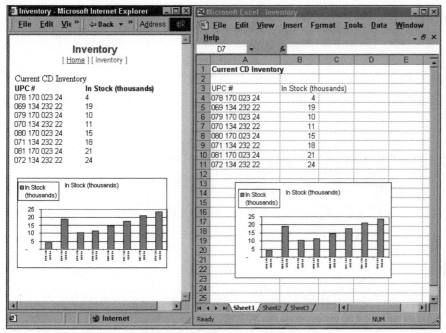

Figure 4-4: Charts copy and paste well in Office XP between Excel 2002 and FrontPage 2002.

Exporting Excel sheets as HTML pages

You can send either a selected range of cells or an entire workbook to a Web page in Excel by selecting File ⇨ Save as Web Page from the Excel menu. If you first select the cells that you want to convert, you can use the Selection Chart radio button in the Save As dialog box, as shown in Figure 4-5.

Figure 4-5: You can send convert a selected range of cells into a chart with the Select Chart option.

In the Save As dialog box, click the Selection: Chart button, choose a filename and destination folder, and then click Save.

The Add Interactivity checkbox in the Save As dialog box creates a page with an Office spreadsheet. For an explanation of how these interactive spreadsheets work in a Web page, see "Adding Office spreadsheets," later in this chapter.

Sending charts to FrontPage

You can copy Excel charts into FrontPage Web pages through the Clipboard. The results have improved with Office XP — in our experiments, copied charts came into FrontPage as nice, clean embedded .gif images. When you save your page, you'll be prompted to save the chart as well.

Another option is to save a selected chart as an HTML page in Excel.

To save a chart as an HTML page, follow these steps:

1. Open the Excel workbook and select the chart that you want to save.

2. Select File ➪ Save as Web Page. The Save As dialog box appears.

3. Click the Selection: Chart option button in the dialog box.

4. Select a folder in the Save In box to which you want to save your file.

5. Enter a filename for your chart in the File Name box, and click Save.

You can now import the HTML file into your FrontPage Web, and use it in Web pages.

Saving Excel workbooks as folders

You can convert an Excel workbook with two or more tabs into a set of Web files. When you do, Excel simulates a tabbed workbook that can be used to create a familiar format for Web visitors who are used to looking up information in spreadsheets, as shown in Figure 4-6.

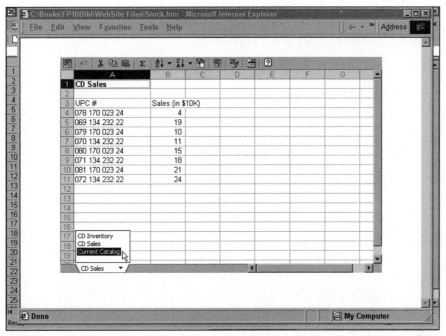

Figure 4-6: Excel can be used to generate framed Web pages that look like workbooks.

To generate an Excel-based Web folder, follow these steps:

1. Open an Excel workbook with multiple tabs.

2. Select File ⇨ Save as Web Page.

3. Select the Entire Workbook option button.

4. Navigate to the folder to which you want to save the generated Web files. Select Save to save the entire workbook, or select Publish to save selected elements of the workbook.

As you save or publish your workbook as a Web "page," a set of files is generated in a separate folder, which uses the name of your file followed by an underscore and the word "files." For example, if you save a workbook called Scores as a Web "page," a folder is created called Scores_files. That folder includes several files required for a Web site that is based on your file. In addition, an .htm file is created in the parent directory (the one to which you saved your file in the Save As dialog box), with the name of the file (for example, Scores.htm).

When you import this generated Excel Web into FrontPage, you need both the .htm file generated in the folder that you specify in the Save As dialog box and all the files in the additional (_files) folder.

From PowerPoint to FrontPage

PowerPoint in Office XP converts slideshows to HTML pages when you select File ⇨ Save as Web Page. As with Excel, a whole batch of files, including HTML and image files, is generated when you do this conversion. In fact, rather than saving a "file" to a "page," you save many files to a folder filled with Web pages and other files.

The folders generated by PowerPoint don't mesh well with FrontPage Web sites. Basically, PowerPoint gives you a highly specialized Web site with complex page designs and links. Use PowerPoint's Publish as Web Page option, shown in Figure 4-7, if you want a seamless slideshow on your Web site.

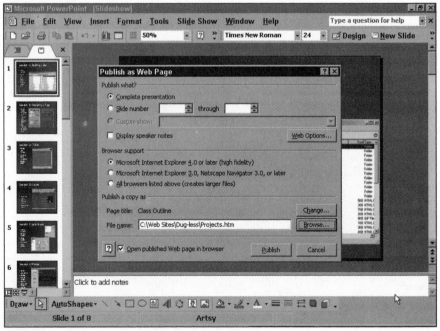

Figure 4-7: PowerPoint can generate Web pages.

Converting slides to Web pages

You don't have to convert an entire PowerPoint slideshow to a Web site. If you want only a single slide, you can save that slide as a .gif or .jpg (or .png) image. These picture files can then be added to a Web page just like any other image from a file.

To save a single slide as an image file, follow these steps:

1. Open the slideshow and the slide that you want to convert to a graphic file.

2. With the slide in view, select File ⇨ Save As. The Save As dialog box opens.

3. From the Save as Type drop-down list, select an image file format, such as .jpeg or .gif.

4. Navigate to a file folder and enter a filename in the File Name box.

5. Click the Save button.

6. When prompted with a dialog box that asks if you want to export every slide in the presentation, click No. You will save only the slide that you are viewing.

Note Although PowerPoint can export PNG files and FrontPage can display them, not all browsers support the PNG file type.

Integrating a slideshow into FrontPage

Our favorite Office-to-FrontPage option is converting PowerPoint slideshows into FrontPage Webs. The result is a JavaScript-driven online slideshow with expanding outlines and a full set of navigation buttons that enable you to jump around in your slideshow. Figure 4-8 shows a PowerPoint slideshow dumped into FrontPage.

To convert a slideshow into a Web-based slideshow, choose File ⇨ Save as Web Page, and click Publish (not Save).

In the Publish as Web Page dialog box (Office XP really means Publish as Web *Site* dialog box), select the slides you wish to export to your new Web folder. Additional options enable you to include (or exclude) speaker notes. The three option buttons in the Browser Support area allow you to choose the generation of browsers for which you will generate Web pages.

Note Generally, it won't harm anything to select Microsoft Internet Explorer 4.0 or later. This option will embed some features (such as expanding outlines) that are not recognized by older browsers. Viewers using older browsers, however, will still see the content of your slideshow.

After you select options in the Publish as Web Page dialog box, click the Publish button. A set of HTML and image files will be generated. These files can be imported into a FrontPage Web.

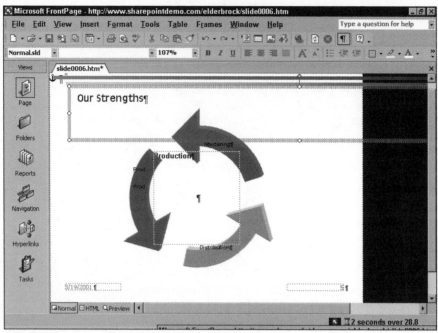

Figure 4-8: PowerPoint can generate automated online slideshows.

Importing Files into Webs

Each of the applications in Office XP that have been examined thus far can be used to generate HTML files, and other Web files as well. You can use FrontPage's Import menu to integrate these generated Web pages or Web sites into FrontPage.

In many cases, when you import a file from Word, Excel, or PowerPoint, it is necessary to convert the original file into a whole folder full of Web files. The folder will likely include image files, but may also include scripts necessary to convert a slideshow, for example, into a Web site. To import an entire folder, you can use the Folder option in the Import dialog box.

To import a file or folder with Office Web files into FrontPage, follow these steps:

1. With a Web already created, select File ➪ Import. The Import dialog box appears.

2. Click the Add File button to import one or more files, or click the Add Folder button to import an entire folder with files.

Note   If you import a folder, that folder becomes a folder in your FrontPage Web, and the files within it are kept together in the folder.

3. You can use the Add File and/or the Add Folder buttons as often as you want, until you have selected all the files and/or folders that you want to import.

4. After you select your files, click OK in the Import dialog box to copy files to your Web server or FrontPage Web folder.

If you are creating a new Web site from files generated by an Office XP application, you can select File ➪ New ➪ Web and double-click the Import Web Wizard in the New dialog box.

The Import Web Wizard walks you through the process of selecting a folder to import. You can also use the Import dialog box to add files to a Web generated from imported files.

Tutorial 4-1 requires a minimal knowledge of Word and Excel. If you can create a simple document in Word and a small spreadsheet and graph in Excel, you can test the ability of FrontPage to integrate these files into a Web site.

Tutorial 4-1: Importing Word and Excel files into a Web site

Here are the steps to bring Word and Excel files into your Web site.

1. Create a document in Word with text at the top of the page that says "Welcome to My Web Site." Add a line of text with your name.

2. Assign a Heading 1 style to the top line of text, and a Heading 2 style to your name.

3. Add a paragraph of text below your name. Assign formatting to the text, such as boldface, italic, font styles, and colors. Center all the text.

4. Select File ➪ Save as Web Page. Create a new folder called Web Files, and name the file index. Click Save.

5. Create a new Excel workbook. In cell A1, enter **Visitors this year**. In cells A2, A3, and A4, enter January, February, and March, respectively. In cells B2, B3, and B4, enter numbers.

6. Click and drag to select cells A2 through B4 and click the Chart Wizard button in the toolbar. In the first Chart Wizard dialog box, click Finish to accept the default chart settings.

7. Leave Excel open. In FrontPage, select File ➪ New ➪ Web. Enter a filename for your Web in the "Specify the location of the new web" box of the New dialog box.

8. Double-click the Import Web Wizard icon in the New dialog box.

9. Select the From a Source Directory of Files option button in the Import Web Wizard dialog box.

10. Click the Browse button and navigate to the folder in which you saved your Word file (`Index.htm`). Click OK in the Browse for Folder dialog box.

11. Click Next. The Add File to Import List dialog box displays all the files in the folder, as shown in Figure 4-9. Click Next, and then click Finish.

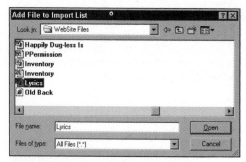

Figure 4-9: Selecting files to import

12. Switch to Navigation view. Your imported Word file has become your home page. Right-click on it and choose Open With from the context menu, and then select FrontPage in the Open with Editor dialog box to open the page in Page view.

Caution Double clicking on the icon in Navigation view opens up the document in Word rather than in FrontPage Page view.

13. Switch back to Excel. Select the chart and choose Edit ➪ Copy.

14. Switch to FrontPage and, in Page view, click to set the insertion point in your open Web page. Select Edit ➪ Paste to insert the cells.

15. Save the Web page. The embedded chart will be saved as an image file.

The copied spreadsheet cells become a table in FrontPage. Working with tables is explored in Chapter 6. The copied chart becomes an embedded image file, a topic explored in depth in Chapter 12.

Adding Office Web Components to Web Pages

Spreadsheets, PivotTables, and graphs can be added to FrontPage Web pages as interactive elements. Visitors who have Office XP installed on their systems can come to your Web site, enter data in a table, make calculations, and watch a graph display their input. Visitors who don't have Office XP can still download viewers that enable them to interact with your spreadsheets, charts, and PivotTables.

You can place interactive PivotTables in Web pages. PivotTables summarize information from spreadsheet or database tables and are somewhat complex. If, however, your visitors want to synthesize data from a database live at your Web site, you can provide the tools to do that.

Adding Office spreadsheets

You can use an interactive spreadsheet element that enables visitors to your Web site to make all kinds of calculations. For example, you can create a worksheet on which a visitor can calculate the cost of his or her purchase, including sales tax. You can protect some cells and leave others open for visitor input.

To place a spreadsheet on your Web page, follow these steps:

1. Open a Web page.

2. Select Insert ➪ Web Component ➪ Spreadsheets and Charts, and click Office Spreadsheet.

3. Click Finish to generate the spreadsheet.

4. Click and drag on side or corner handles to resize the spreadsheet, as shown in Figure 4-10.

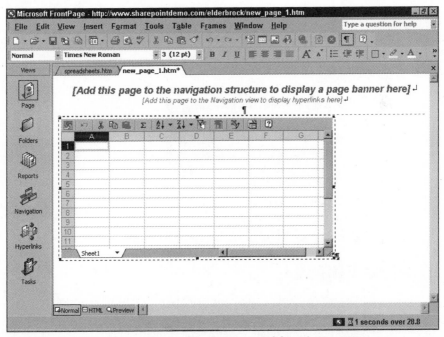

Figure 4-10: It's easy to embed and resize a spreadsheet in FrontPage.

Formatting Embedded Spreadsheets

Formatting, cell protection, and other display and function properties for embedded spreadsheet components are controlled by a combination of ActiveX control properties and spreadsheet properties. There is no particular rhyme or reason as to which options are controlled where. Some options can be defined in either dialog box, and some options (such as chart and cell protection) require attributes from both dialog boxes.

Let's face it—embedded spreadsheets are not the most frequently used feature of FrontPage, and Microsoft hasn't paid the same level of attention to organizing their use that was devoted to more popular features. If you persevere through both spreadsheet and ActiveX control properties, you can indeed create an interactive spreadsheet on your Web page.

We've divided the process of formatting an embedded spreadsheet into two sections: defining ActiveX control properties and defining spreadsheet properties.

Defining ActiveX control properties for a spreadsheet

Some attributes of your spreadsheet can be controlled in the ActiveX Control Properties dialog box. These properties include alignment (such as left or right), borders, and spacing around the spreadsheet.

To define ActiveX control properties, follow these steps:

1. Right-click the spreadsheet and choose ActiveX Control Properties. The ActiveX Control Properties dialog box is shown in Figure 4-11.

Figure 4-11: Use the ActiveX Control Properties dialog box to define how your spreadsheet will be displayed.

2. Use the dialog box to define any of the following attributes:

- In the Workbook tab, specify the spreadsheet name: A name is required if you plan to link the spreadsheet to a chart (see "Adding Office charts," later in this chapter). You can also name sheets within the worksheet in this area. Use the checkboxes in the Show/Hide area to display (or hide) scroll bars, a sheet selector tab area, and a toolbar. Finally, choose one of the radio buttons to set calculations to automatic or manual (you will probably want your spreadsheet to calculate formulas automatically).

Note
You aren't likely to need the options in the Format or Formula tabs of the ActiveX Control Properties dialog box. You can create formulas and define most formatting in the spreadsheet.

- In the Sheet tab, you can search your spreadsheet or use checkboxes to define how sheets are displayed.

- The Import tab is used to import an existing XML file, and the Data Source tab is used to connect your spreadsheet to an existing database. (See Chapter 21 for a full exploration of integrating databases into FrontPage.)

- The **Object Tag** tab ("tag" refers to the ActiveX control properties) defines the width and height, alignment, and spacing around your spreadsheet. The Width and Height boxes are an alternative way to size the spreadsheet (you can also resize in Page view by clicking and dragging sizing handles). The relevant options in the Alignment drop-down list are Left or Right. Use them to let text flow around the spreadsheet. Border thickness defines the width of a border around the spreadsheet. The HTML box defines a message, and URL displays if a visitor's browser doesn't support interactive spreadsheets. The default HTML informs visitors that they need a viewer to use this feature.

- The Advanced tab has some useful features, including the Autofit Spreadsheet checkbox, which enables you to define your spreadsheet as a fixed percentage of the browser window's width.

- The Protection tab enables you to define what editing features are accessible to visitors, including the capability to enter data in cells. You can modify the protection you define in the ActiveX Control Properties dialog box in the Spreadsheet Properties dialog box.

3. After you define properties, click Apply in the dialog box.

An embedded spreadsheet is shown in Figure 4-12.

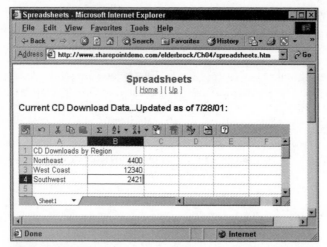

Figure 4-12: This interactive spreadsheet can be edited both in FrontPage and in a Web browser.

Defining spreadsheet properties

You can enter text, values, and formulas the same way that you do in Excel. Many other Excel functions are also available, using the Commands and Options dialog box. Some, but not all, of these property controls can be made available for visitors. For example, visitors can be allowed to enter data into cells and change cell formatting, but visitors cannot be given access to features such as Protection (a feature that defines which cells, if any, a visitor can change).

Figure 4-13 shows the Commands and Options dialog box as it appears to visitors using Internet Explorer 5.5 and later.

The Format, Formula, Sheet, and Workbook sections of the Commands and Options dialog box are available in browser windows *provided that Commands and Options were enabled in the Protection tab of the ActiveX Control Properties dialog box.* Therefore, these features are defined not only by the page author (you), but also by visitors who work on the spreadsheet at your Web page.

A detailed description of all the features of the Commands and Options dialog box would really require a book about Microsoft Excel, but here is a quick overview of the features available in each tab:

✦ The Cell Lock/Unlock Cells button in the Format tab enables you to disable protection from selected cells. This feature is not available for visitors. The rest of the Format tab has a fairly full-featured Formatting toolbar for defining font type, style, size, and color. Other boxes in this section refine cell display. Of particular usefulness is the Number Format drop-down list, which includes currency and date formats.

✦ The Formula tab is redundant, as formulas are normally defined in cells.

✦ The Sheet, Workbook, Advanced, Import, and Data Source tabs duplicate the same tab settings in the ActiveX Control Properties dialog box.

For an example of defining a spreadsheet Web component, see Tutorial 4-2 at the end of this chapter.

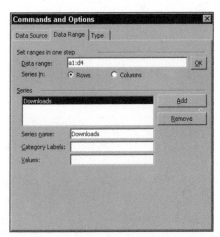

Figure 4-13: Most of the formatting attributes available in Excel are stashed in the Commands and Options dialog box, which can be made available to visitors who have Office XP on their computers.

For all practical purposes, you must publish your Web to a server with FrontPage 2002 or FrontPage 2000 extensions in order to link an embedded spreadsheet to an embedded chart.

FrontPage will manage the process of connecting your data and your chart, as long as you confine your work to a FrontPage extension site.

Adding Office charts

You can generate Office charts in FrontPage using three sources of data: a spreadsheet on the Web page, data you enter specifically to be charted, or data from a server database.

For an exploration of connecting to Web server databases, see Chapter 20.

Here, we'll focus on Office charts that are linked to embedded spreadsheets in FrontPage. These charts can interactively display spreadsheet content, enabling visitors who change data in your spreadsheet to see the new data charted on the Web page.

To link a chart to a spreadsheet, follow these steps:

1. Start by creating an embedded spreadsheet in a Web page (see instructions in the previous section). Be sure to name the sheet (in the Object Tag tab of the ActiveX Control Properties dialog box, which you can access by right-clicking on your selected chart).

2. Next, insert a chart. This can be done right next to the spreadsheet if you wish (as illustrated in Figure 4-14). To insert the chart, select Insert ⇨ Web Component ⇨ Spreadsheets and Charts ⇨ Office Chart. Click Finish. The Commands and Options dialog box appears.

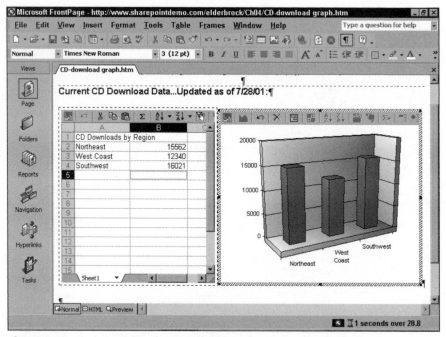

Figure 4-14: An interactive chart can be placed next to a spreadsheet.

3. In Area 1 of the Commands and Options dialog box, you have three options for a data source for your chart:

   • Choose the Data Typed into a Data Sheet option button to enter data to be charted.

- Click the Data from a Database Table or Query option button to define a connection to an online database.

- Click the Data from the Following Web Page Item option button to chart data from an existing embedded spreadsheet. If you choose this option, you can select from a displayed list of embedded spreadsheets. Use the Range button to define a graphing range (in the form of A1:D4, for example, to graph cells A1 through D4). You can name the range (the range name is defined in Excel).

4. Choose a chart type. Click outside the dialog box to display the chart.

Changing chart properties

You can resize a chart by selecting it and using the side or corner handles to change the size. Other chart properties are defined in the ActiveX Control Properties dialog box.

To change chart properties using the ActiveX Control Properties dialog box, follow these steps:

1. Right-click in the chart and select ActiveX Control Properties from the context menu.

2. Use the options available in the different tabs of the ActiveX Control Properties dialog box to change chart format or data. For example, use the Data Range area in the Data Range tab to redefine the data to chart, as shown in Figure 4-15.

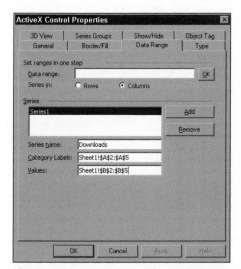

Figure 4-15: You can use the ActiveX Control Properties dialog box to redefine different elements of a chart.

Note   Available chart options will vary depending on the type of chart and the data source.

Controlling charts using the chart menu

If you elect to display the toolbar (in the Show/Hide tab of the ActiveX Control Properties dialog box), an active toolbar is associated with an embedded chart. The features you controlled in the ActiveX Control Properties dialog box are now controlled by toolbar icons, some of which are made available to visitors.

The active elements of the chart toolbar that are available in FrontPage in the toolbar are shown in Figure 4-16.

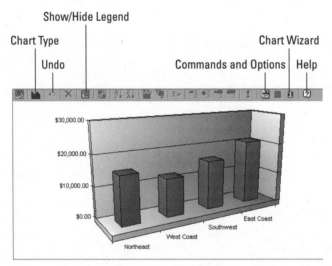

Figure 4-16: Visitors can control calculation, sorting, and formatting.

After you create a linked chart, you — or visitors — can enter data in the spreadsheet and see it graphed in the chart. Figure 4-17 shows a chart working interactively in a browser.

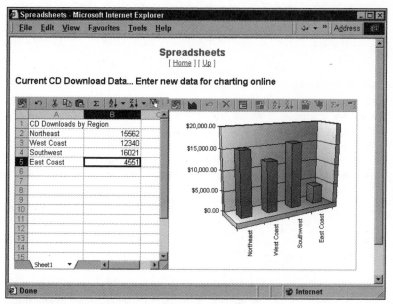

Figure 4-17: Graphing interactively in a browser

Presenting a database table in a Web spreadsheet

If you have an Access (or another) database at your Web server, you can present the contents of a table in that database in a spreadsheet. This first requires that you know how to import or create a database on your Web site—something you learn in Chapter 20. Very briefly, this can be accomplished by simply importing an existing database file (Access is the most hassle-free) into your Web using the File ➪ Import menu command. Then, click the Add File button in the Import dialog box, and navigate to your database file. After you select the database and click OK, follow the prompts to create an online version of your database.

Alternately, if you want to experiment with connecting a database to a spreadsheet before you are ready to create an online database, you can use the sample database that comes with FrontPage.

With a database imported into FrontPage (or using the sample database), follow these steps to display the content of that database in a Spreadsheet Web component:

1. Open a new page in FrontPage. You will use this page to display the database records in a database region.

2. Choose Insert ➪ Database ➪ Results.

3. If you have an imported (or FrontPage-generated) database, click Use an Existing Database Connection and choose your installed database from the Use an Existing Database Connection drop-down list. Alternately, click the Use a Sample Database Connection (Northwind) radio button.

Note We explore the Use a New Database Connection option in Chapter 20. In this step-by-step set of instructions, we'll zip past many database options, focusing instead on just creating a simple database region on which to base a spreadsheet. The "rest of the story" is found in Chapter 20.

4. Click Next. In the Step 2 Wizard dialog box, choose a table from the Record Source drop-down list. Choose a table to display in your Web page database region.

5. Click Next. Accept the defaults in the Step 3 and Step 4 Wizard dialog boxes by clicking Next. In the Step 5 Wizard dialog box, choose the Display All Records Together option button. Click Finish to generate a database region displaying the data from your database. A database region is shown in Figure 4-18.

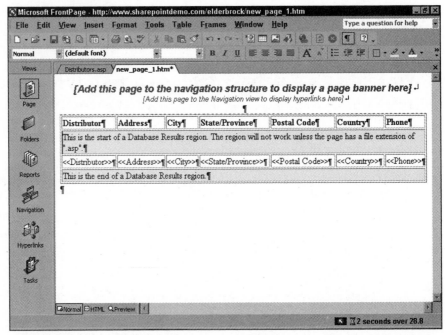

Figure 4-18: This database region presents data that can be displayed in a linked spreadsheet.

Note   You can generate a database region only if you are connected to a Web server with FrontPage extensions. In addition, you won't see the actual data until you preview your page in a Web browser.

6. Now it's time to save the page with the database region as an .asp file page, and then use it as a base for spreadsheet data. Start by choosing File ⇨ Save As, and choose Active Server Pages from the Save As Type drop-down list in the Save As dialog box. Give the .asp file a name in the File Name box, and click OK.

Note   In this example, because we started with a blank page, FrontPage assigns an ASP filename extension by default. However, that doesn't always happen if the page isn't blank, so we'll make a point of consciously assigning ASP file format to this page.

7. Create a new Web page (or open an existing one), and choose Insert ⇨ Web Component ⇨ Spreadsheets and Charts. Click Office Spreadsheet in the Choose a Control list of the Insert Web Component dialog box.

8. Click Finish to generate a spreadsheet. In the spreadsheet component, click the Commands and Options icon to open the Commands and Options dialog box.

9. In the Import tab of the Commands and Options dialog box, choose HTML from the Data Type drop-down list, and enter the URL for your page (the one you saved in Step 6), as shown in Figure 4-19.

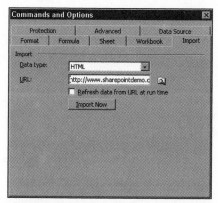

Figure 4-19: This spreadsheet component has been associated with a Web page with a database region.

Note It seems to work better to enter the absolute URL (i.e., the entire URL, including `http://www`).

10. To continually update the spreadsheet, click the Refresh Data from URL at Run Time checkbox.

11. Click Import Now. The spreadsheet will display the content of the associated database region.

Creating Office PivotTables

Of the three interactive Office Web components that you can use in a Web page, PivotTables are the most complex. PivotTables themselves are fairly complicated. A full discussion of PivotTables is quite a bit beyond the scope of this discussion, but in short, PivotTables summarize data from a table. Therefore, for example, if you have a list of 500 orders for 12 products, and the dates the orders were placed, a PivotTable could summarize how many orders had been placed for each of the 12 products. Or, the PivotTable could be used to total how many orders had been placed each day.

Assuming that you and your visitors are comfortable designing and manipulating fields in a PivotTable, you can create an interactive PivotTable that summarizes data in an Excel file or Access database table.

Connecting a PivotTable to an Excel data source

Steve Martin used to do a comedy routine around the theme of "how to make a million dollars and not pay *any* taxes." Part of the joke was that his starting point was "go get a million dollars," and then he would fill you in on the rest. The relevance here is that PivotTables are a rather complex art, and an advanced spreadsheet skill. If you're *already* comfortable with them, we can show you how to plug them in to a FrontPage Web site.

Note One of the clearest explanations of Excel PivotTables is found in the *Office 2000 Bible*, by Ed Willet, David Crowder, and Rhonda Crowder, published by Hungry Minds (formerly IDG Books Worldwide).

Even if you are comfortable with PivotTables, connecting a PivotTable to an Excel data source is not a simple process, but we will walk you through it step by step. The basic process involves first connecting an existing Excel file to your site as a recognized Web database, and then generating a PivotTable from a named range in that file.

To generate an interactive online PivotTable from an Excel spreadsheet, follow these steps:

1. Create or open in Excel a worksheet that has the information you want to summarize in your PivotTable.

2. Select the data and then choose Insert ⇨ Name ⇨ Define.

3. Assign a range name (for example, "Data"). You may want to jot down the range name, because you'll need it again in a later step.

4. Save the Excel file and note the filename and folder to which it is saved.

5. In Page view, open the FrontPage Web page in which you will insert the PivotTable.

6. Select Insert ⇨ Web Component ⇨ Spreadsheets and Charts. Choose Office PivotTable, and click Finish. A blank PivotTable appears in Page view.

7. Click the Commands and Options button (the only active button in the PivotTable toolbar) to open the Commands and Options dialog box, shown in Figure 4-20.

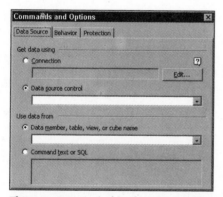

Figure 4-20: Buried in the PivotTable Commands and Options dialog box are the elements needed to connect your PivotTable to a data source.

8. Choose the Data Source tab in the Commands and Options dialog box. Click the Connection radio button, and then click the Edit button. The Select Data Source dialog box appears, as shown in Figure 4-21.

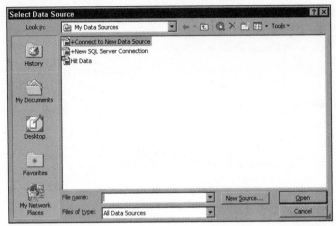

Figure 4-21: Choosing an Excel file to link to your Web PivotTable

9. Click the New Source button. You are about to connect your Excel file with your Web site. The Data Connection Wizard opens to walk you through that process.

10. Choose ODBC DSN as your database source. Click Next.

Note For a discussion of different types of Web database sources, see Chapter 20.

11. Choose Excel files as your data source, and click Next.

12. Navigate to your Excel Workbook in the Select Workbook dialog box. Choose your Excel file and click Next.

13. The Data Connection Wizard displays available named ranges (also referred to for these purposes as "tables") in your selected spreadsheet. Select one of these tables and click Next.

14. In the final Wizard window, enter a description and keywords to help identify and locate the PivotTable. These are optional. After you enter a description and keywords, click Finish. You will be returned to the Select Data Source dialog box, where your newly defined database connection (to your spreadsheet) is now one of the connection options. Click Open to connect your selected spreadsheet to the PivotTable.

15. Your PivotTable is now connected to your spreadsheet, and ready to have fields added. Click the Field List icon in the PivotTable toolbar to display field names, as shown in Figure 4-22.

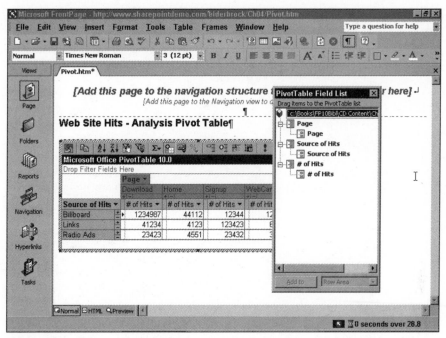

Figure 4-22: Once your PivotTable is connected to a data source, you can add fields.

Note For a brief step-by-step explanation of how to put fields into a PivotTable, see the section "Adding fields to a PivotTable" later in this chapter.

16. Drag fields into place in your PivotTable.

17. Save your page. Your PivotTable is now ready to be both accessed by visitors to your Web site and utilized to synthesize table data, as shown in Figure 4-23.

Defining a PivotTable

After telling you that PivotTable concepts were beyond the scope of this book, we'll try to provide a quick summary of how to put one together:

After your PivotTable control is connected to an Excel data source, you can use the Field List button in the PivotTable toolbar to add fields to the PivotTable displayed. Every PivotTable requires at least one Row or Column field, and at least one Total or Detail Field.

The basic concept is to summarize data by sorting it into categories. For example, if you wrote books for a dozen publishers over the past four years, you could produce a PivotTable listing how many books you wrote for each publisher each year, by making Year the column field, Publisher the Row field, and Books Written the Detail field.

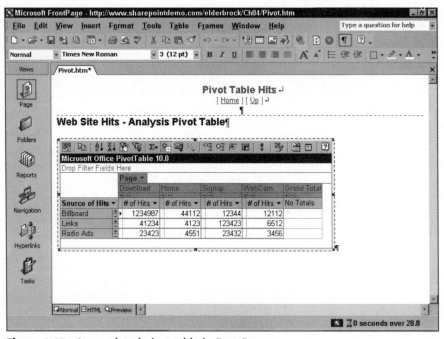

Figure 4-23: A completed pivot table in FrontPage

Adding fields to a PivotTable

To add fields to a PivotTable, follow these steps:

1. Click the Field List button in the PivotTable toolbar to display a list of fields in your database.

2. Drag one of the fields into the Drop Column Fields Here area of the PivotTable, and drag one field into the Drop Row Fields Here area, as shown in Figure 4-24.

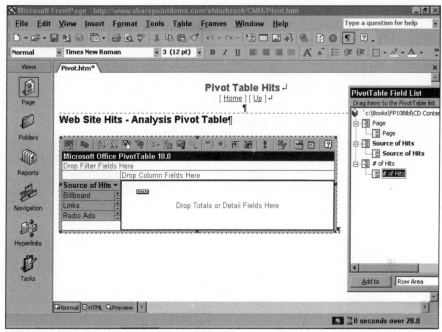

Figure 4-24: Adding fields to a PivotTable

3. You must have at least one field in the Detail area (in the middle of the PivotTable), so drag a field from the Field list into the middle of the PivotTable.

Note

The field in the Detail area normally displays values. These values can be summed, counted, or have other calculations performed on them, as you will see in a few steps.

4. You can drag a field into the Drop Filter Fields Here area at the top of the PivotTable to create a filtering drop-down list that will control what is displayed in the entire PivotTable. This field is optional and simply provides a higher level of filtering in addition to the options you already have in the PivotTable.

5. After you define your PivotTable, close the PivotTable Field List dialog box. Note that each field has a drop-down list associated with it. Use the checkboxes in these drop-down lists to filter your PivotTable results, as shown in Figure 4-25.

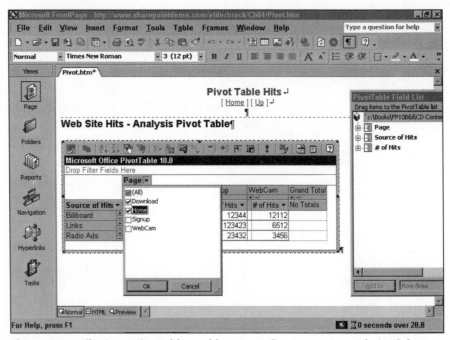

Figure 4-25: Filtering a PivotTable enables you to fine-tune your analysis of data.

6. You can remove fields by right-clicking them and selecting Remove Field from the context menu.

7. To calculate (count, sum, find maximum or minimum value), right-click a field in the Detail area and select AutoCalc. Then choose from calculation options such as sum, count, or average.

8. You can turn subtotaling on or off for fields where it applies by right-clicking on a field in the PivotTable and selecting or deselecting Subtotal from the context menu.

Formatting and calculating PivotTable data

After you define your PivotTable, save your Web page and preview it in Internet Explorer to test it. Figure 4-26 shows an interactive PivotTable in Internet Explorer.

In FrontPage, you can format, calculate, and sort PivotTable data by using the PivotTable toolbar, by right-clicking and choosing context menu options, or by using the Commands and Options button in the PivotTable toolbar to open the Commands and Options dialog box.

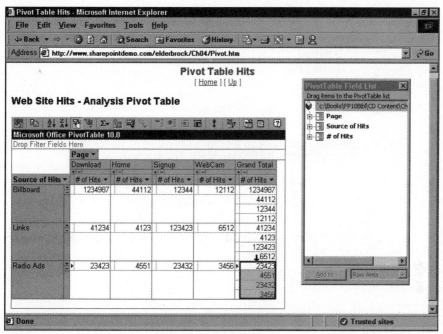

Figure 4-26: Visitors can do their own synthesis of your data with a PivotTable in Internet Explorer — as long as they have Office XP installed.

Some, but not all, of these filtering, sorting, formatting, and calculating features are available for visitors when they work with the PivotTable in a Web site. You can control table protection using the ActiveX dialog box associated with your PivotTable. This process is the same as for the ActiveX dialog box associated with a spreadsheet, which we explored earlier in this chapter.

Tutorial 4-2: Implementing an Office spreadsheet Web component

In this tutorial, you'll add a spreadsheet to a Web page.

1. Open an existing FrontPage Web or create a new one. Open a Web page in Page view.

2. Enter the title **See How Much of Your Time You Spend Commuting** on the page, and then press Enter.

3. Select Insert ➪ Web Component ➪ Spreadsheets and Charts, and choose Office Spreadsheet. Click Finish.

4. Click in cell A1 of the spreadsheet and enter **How many hours do you spend commuting?** Press Enter.

5. In cell A3 of the spreadsheet, enter **=A2/24**.

6. Click the Commands and Options button in the spreadsheet. In the Format tab, select Percent from the Number Format drop-down list.

7. Click in cell A2. In the Format tab of the Commands and Options dialog box, deselect the Lock Cells icon.

8. In the Protection tab of the Commands and Options dialog box, select Protect Active Sheet.

9. Save the file, and preview it in Internet Explorer.

10. While testing the spreadsheet in Internet Explorer, attempt to enter text in cell A1. Try to enter a number in cell A3. You should see a warning like the one shown on the bottom of the screen in Figure 4-27.

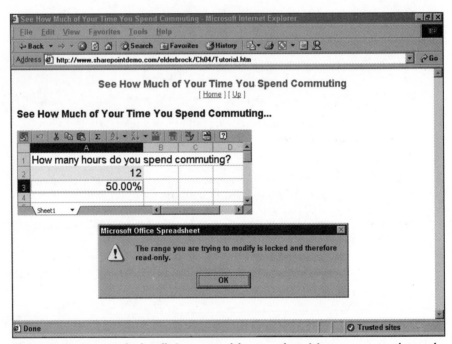

Figure 4-27: You can lock cells in a spreadsheet so that visitors can enter data only in cells that you designate to accept input.

From FrontPage to Office XP

The discussion thus far has focused on how to create Web page content in Office and transfer it into FrontPage Web pages. You can also collect information in FrontPage and send it to text or spreadsheet files that will be stored at your Web server.

Collecting data from input forms requires some advanced FrontPage skills that are covered in Chapter 17. This section takes only a quick look at input forms from the perspective of collecting data that can be used in a spreadsheet or text file.

Even before you examine how to create your own custom input forms, you can begin to experiment with the Feedback Form page template, which contains a pre-made input form.

Sending data to Word mail-merge files

You can create an input form by using the page template with an input form (using the Feedback Form page template, for example). With a Web open, select File ⇨ New ⇨ Page, and double-click one of the templates with an input form. The input forms are filled with different text and input fields and are surrounded by a dashed line.

To create an input form that sends data to a .doc file, follow these steps:

1. With a form on your page, right-click anywhere in the form (within the dashed lines) and select Form Properties from the context menu. The Form Properties dialog box appears.

2. Click the Send To option button and enter a filename with a .doc filename extension (for example, `maillist.doc`).

3. After you name the target file (the .doc filename extension is important), click the Options button in the dialog box and pull down the File Format list. Choose Text Database Using Tab As a Separator, as shown in Figure 4-28.

Note   Make sure you retain the .doc filename extension. FrontPage will try to change your filename extension to `.txt` when you choose the Text Database Using Tab As a Separator format.

4. Click OK.

5. Save your Web page.

You can test your input form by clicking the Preview in Browser button and entering information in the input form. After you do, click the Submit button.

You will see your .doc file in Folder view (you may have to press the F5 function key to refresh the Folder view). As data is saved to your .doc file, you can open the file in Word by double-clicking it. With fields separated by tabs, you can use this file as a mail-merge data file in Word.

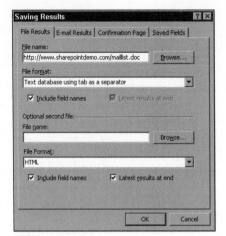

Figure 4-28: Sending input to a Word file

Sending data to Excel

You can save data to files that will open in Excel by using the same procedure previously outlined for saving to a Word file. The only difference is that your filename should have an .xls extension (for example, Feedback.xls). When you save tab-delimited text to an Excel file, you can open that file in Excel by double-clicking it.

Sending reports to Excel

With FrontPage 2002 you can save reports as HTML files, and then open them in Excel for printing, graphing, sorting, or other analysis.

To save a report as an HTML page, view the report (select View ➪ Reports and choose any report except for Summary). With the Report in view, choose File ➪ Save As, and save the file as an HTML file to any folder on your Web site or your local computer.

Note   When you save your report, use an .htm filename extension.

Excel 2002 will open these HTML files for analysis, as shown in Figure 4-29.

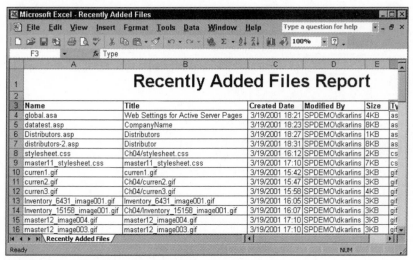

Figure 4-29: Viewing a FrontPage site report in Excel

You can save any report as an HTML file *except* the Site Summary report. Unfortunately, you can't even copy and paste the cells from the Site Summary report into a spreadsheet.

Summary

With Office XP, Microsoft has continued to smooth the integration between FrontPage and other Office applications. You can easily integrate Word documents, Excel spreadsheets, and PowerPoint presentations into your FrontPage Web.

FrontPage also can be used to create special components that allow you to put a little bit of Excel into your Web pages. These components display active, working spreadsheets, dynamically linked graphs, and even complex pivot tables in a Web browser.

Finally, you can export elements of a FrontPage Web into other office applications. One particularly useful example of this is sending FrontPage reports to Excel, where you can sort, calculate, or even graph information about your Web site.

✦   ✦   ✦

Designing Web Pages

Page and Text Formatting

In previous chapters, you learned how easy it is to design an entire Web site by using FrontPage's Navigation view. Page relationships can be defined; shared borders with navigation bars can be assigned; and themes can be applied. All that site design, however, still leaves you with the critical task of adding text content to your Web page. In this chapter, you'll learn how to add text to your Web page and how to edit and format Web page text.

Designing Web Pages in Page View

The specific content of distinct Web pages is controlled in Page view. This is where you will spend most of your FrontPage time. In Page view, you can add, edit, and format the actual content of your Web pages. You can also create new pages directly in Page view. These pages will not be automatically linked to your Web site and won't have navigation bars included. You can, however, toggle between Page and Navigation view to create page content, and then link new pages to your Web's structure.

Web sites and Web pages

As we have advised in earlier chapters, we strongly recommend that you open and edit pages in FrontPage after first creating a FrontPage *Web*. Even if your Web site consists of a single Web page, you should still start by creating a FrontPage Web site, as you learned to do in Chapter 1. That way, you can include more-sophisticated features of FrontPage.

Even when working on a single page, you can benefit from allowing a FrontPage Web to organize your files. For example, as long as you open your pages from within a FrontPage Web, you can rely on FrontPage to organize all your graphics and other embedded files, including keeping track of them as you move them from folder to folder, or rename them.

Having made our case for starting with a FrontPage Web, we acknowledge that you can ignore our advice. If you know how to manage Web site files, you can skip the step of creating a Web site and go straight to Page view to design a page. If you elect to do that, we've warned you of the risks and assume that you'll take responsibility for overriding FrontPage's built-in features for keeping track of all the files associated with your Web page.

Exploring Page view

You can open an existing Web page in Page view by double-clicking it in any other view, including Navigation view. When you do so, you'll see your page open in Page view, as shown in Figure 5-1.

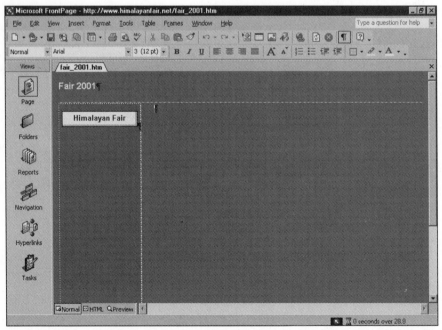

Figure 5-1: Even before you begin to edit page content, FrontPage may have assigned shared borders, navigation bars, and a color scheme.

The Standard and Formatting toolbars at the top of the Page view window will look somewhat familiar to you if you've used other Windows applications. Many tools (New Page, Copy, Cut, Paste, and others) do the same things in FrontPage that they do in other Windows applications, and they are very much like tools that you may be familiar with in other Office applications.

These toolbars are detachable, and can be moved off the top of the window by clicking and dragging on the toolbar (but not on a button). Detached toolbars can be re-anchored at the top of the window by dragging them back to the top of the screen. The Standard toolbar is shown in Figure 5-2.

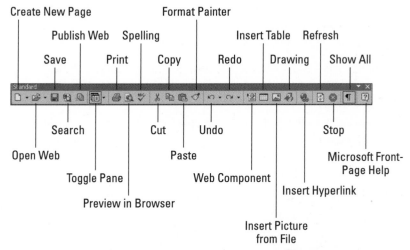

Figure 5-2: Page view's Standard toolbar handles basic editing tasks.

Although the Standard toolbar includes some buttons that you already know from other Office applications, many other buttons are unique to FrontPage. The following list explains what each tool does, and many of them are described in detail later in this chapter:

✦ **Create New:** Toggles between creating a new (blank) page, Web, task, folder, document library, list, or survey.

✦ **Open:** Toggles between opening a new file (Web page) or Web (site).

✦ **Save:** Saves the open, selected Web page file and all embedded image files within that page.

✦ **Search:** Searches your computer (not your Web site) for files, which is handy when you can't remember where you stashed the company mission statement text file that you wanted to copy into your Web page.

✦ **Publish Web:** Uploads Web files to a server.

✦ **Toggle Pane:** Switches back and forth between displaying navigational structure (Navigation pane) or file folder structure (Folder) to the left of the open Web page.

✦ **Print:** Prints the open page (and only the Web page) without allowing you to make selections in the Print dialog box. This is good when you're in an incredible hurry to rush page printouts to a client.

✦ **Preview in Browser:** Memorize this button! It displays the page *in your default browser*—which is the only way to really know how the page will look in a Web site.

✦ **Spelling:** Checks the current page.

✦ **Cut:** Also known as Ctrl+X.

✦ **Paste:** Better to exercise your fingers and choose Paste Special when copying in text—FrontPage provides more options for preserving (or not preserving) formatting.

✦ **Copy:** Grabs anything on the page, such as text, graphics, and video.

✦ **Format Painter:** First select text whose formatting you want to copy. Clicking on this tool temporarily transforms the cursor into a brush to "paint" the loaded formatting onto existing text.

✦ **Undo:** Saves lives! As in "Help! I deleted a page of text by accident!"

✦ **Redo:** Undoes undo.

✦ **Web Component:** Opens a dialog box full of FrontPage components such as Hover buttons and tables of contents (see Chapter 14 for a complete exploration of these features).

✦ **Insert Table:** Generates tables for displaying data or page layout (see Chapter 6 for the "how to").

✦ **Insert Picture from File:** Embeds an image file.

✦ **Drawing:** Opens the Drawing toolbar, which among other features allows you to use simple drawing tools right in FrontPage to generate vector markup language (VML) images. For proposed vml, see the article at the World Wide Web Consortium by all the big names in Web vector graphics at `http://www.w3.org/TR/NOTE-VML#h2:introduction`. You'll look at generated vml graphics in detail in Chapter 12.

✦ **Insert Hyperlink:** Assigns a hyperlink to the selected text or image.

✦ **Refresh:** Restores the last saved version of a page file.

✦ **Stop:** Stops uploading to the server.

✦ **Show All:** Displays invisible formatting elements such as paragraph marks, forced line breaks, and image anchors.

✦ **Microsoft FrontPage Help:** Opens a window to the right of the FrontPage window, with many options for online help.

✦ **Add or Remove Buttons:** Enables you to customize the Formatting toolbar.

Most of your Web page text formatting is controlled from the Formatting toolbar in Page view, shown in Figure 5-3.

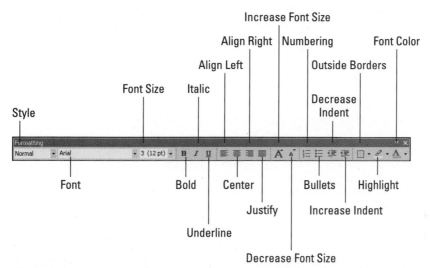

Figure 5-3: Many FrontPage formatting tools work differently than those in desktop applications.

The Formatting toolbar includes some tool buttons, listed next, that don't act like their twins in other Office applications:

✦ **Style:** The styles in the list are HTML styles, which are not customizable in the same way that styles are defined in word processors or desktop publishing applications. You can elect to assign formatting without worrying about what HTML style is assigned to text.

✦ **Font:** This drop-down list assigns fonts to selected text. How fonts display in a browser is dependent on whether or not the fonts are installed on a visitor's computer.

✦ **Font Size:** This drop-down list assigns font size to selected text. The limited selection of sizes reflects the limitations of HTML.

✦ **Bold:** Assigns boldface to selected text.

✦ **Italic:** Assigns italics to selected text.

✦ **Underline:** You can use this tool to *deselect* underlining for links, for that trendy, clean, no-underlined-links look.

✦ **Align Left:** Left-aligns selected paragraph(s).

✦ **Center:** Centers selected paragraph(s).

✦ **Align Right:** Right-aligns selected paragraph(s).

✦ **Justify:** Justification is supported by Netscape 4.5+ and Internet Explorer 4.0+, so you are constrained only by the odd spacing you might get between letters and words.

✦ **Numbering:** Assigns sequential numbering to selected paragraphs.

✦ **Bullets:** Assigns indenting and bullets to selected paragraphs.

✦ **Increase Indent:** Indents entire selected paragraph(s).

✦ **Decrease Indent:** Moves selected paragraphs to the left (undoes indenting).

✦ **Highlight Color:** Adds a background highlight to selected text.

✦ **Font Color:** Assigns colors to selected text.

✦ **Add or Remove Buttons:** Enables you to customize the Formatting toolbar.

Welcome to the World of HTML Formatting

If you are an experienced HTML coder, you may be pleasantly surprised by how much control you have over text formatting in Page view. If you haven't formatted Web page text before, you may be unpleasantly surprised by the reality that not as many formatting options are available in HTML (Web pages) as are available for printing.

The joys and limitations of FrontPage formatting and HTML

FrontPage frees you from needing to learn HTML to design a Web page. While you work in a WYSIWYG environment, FrontPage works behind the scenes to translate your formatting into HTML code. However, you are not freed from HTML in two ways:

✦ You can still achieve greater control over the appearance of your page by tweaking and editing the HTML code generated by FrontPage. In later chapters, especially Chapter 8, you'll learn how you can edit that HTML code in FrontPage.

✦ You are still constrained by HTML insofar as your page formatting options are limited to whatever formatting the Web browsers can interpret, relying on the HTML code they read when they connect with your page.

The ability to create HTML as if you are formatting a printed document is impressive. However, if you are transitioning from doing page layout and design for printed output, you may find the following aspects of text formatting somewhat disconcerting.

HTML is more limited as a page description language than are most word processing languages. If you have spent any time doing even basic desktop publishing with a word processor, you'll immediately realize that FrontPage's capabilities are limited in comparison with those types of applications. The reason for this is mainly that HTML was not originally designed as a page description language — although it is evolving in that direction, pushed by demands for more control over document layout and formatting.

FrontPage offers a mixture of standard HTML formatting and word processor-like formatting, resulting in some redundancy of function. Although FrontPage may seem limited in its formatting power, you will still find multiple ways to accomplish the same formatting task. This, too, is a product of HTML's evolution. For example, select a string of text and apply a Heading 1 style to it. Then, select a second text string, increase the font size, and assign boldface to that text. The results are about the same.

When you are designing your Web pages in FrontPage, you'll find that you can use the spacebar and the Tab key to insert spacing, and that you can control spacing with FrontPage's paragraph format features. The control that you have in FrontPage over white space, however, is restricted by the following:

✦ Many of the horizontal and vertical spacing controls in FrontPage, even things as basic as using the Tab key to separate words, are not widely recognized by other browsers.

✦ Because most monitor resolutions are as low as a grainy 72 dots-per-inch (dpi), you can't get too fancy in your space formatting. Small fonts are harder to read on Web pages than they are on paper.

Okay, that's enough warnings! The good news — and this is really the main news — is that you can easily apply all kinds of text and background formatting in FrontPage. Many formatting techniques are easier to apply to a FrontPage Web page than to a printed page, such as background colors, background images, and default colored fonts.

Formatting selected text

You can assign basic font attribute(s) to selected text by using the Formatting toolbar. First, select the text, and then click a toolbar button. For example, you can assign fonts from the Font drop-down menu, assign font size from the Font Size drop-down menu, and assign boldface by clicking the Bold button . . . you get the picture.

FrontPage Formatting and Cascading Style Sheets

FrontPage themes organize and incorporate many page and text style attributes by creating external Cascading Style Sheets (.css) files. (We'll explore the relationship between Themes and Style Sheets in more detail in Chapters 10 and 11.)

In this chapter, we assign formatting to selected paragraphs and text. FrontPage manages this formatting by generating embedded styles that apply to an entire page, and by generating HTML code for inline styles. At the end of this chapter, we'll take a brief look at defining styles for page-wide formatting. If you're not familiar with style sheets, no problem — FrontPage manages all this invisibly for you.

The wrinkle for those of you who are used to applying external style sheets is that when you apply a FrontPage *theme*, you effectively disable your ability to embed page styles and page formatting. If that poses an annoying obstacle to your page design plans, consider generating your own external style sheet files. For a full exploration of the themes vis-a-vis CSS dynamic, see Chapter 11.

You assign colors to selected text by clicking the down arrow next to the Font Color button. This opens the (detachable) Font Color palette, shown in Figure 5-4.

After you assign a color to the Font Color button, you can assign that color to selected fonts simply by clicking the button. You can also assign default font colors for a page. You'll learn to do that in "Defining page properties," later in this chapter.

Figure 5-4: The detachable Font Color palette assigns color to text. FrontPage keeps track of colors you have already assigned to your page in the Document's Colors area, which is handy for sticking to a consistent color scheme.

The formatting button that requires the most explanation is the Styles drop-down list. Styles can be defined either through FrontPage themes (see Chapter 10), or by defining your own Cascading Style Sheets (see Chapter 11).

More text style options

You can define additional attributes for selected text from the Format menu by selecting Paragraph, Bullets and Numbering, or Borders and Shading. These menu options control the basic look of text.

Additional text attributes can be assigned by choosing Position or DHTML from the Format menu. Formatting position on a page defines an exact location for selected text (or other objects) and is discussed in Chapter 6. Formatting DHTML (Dynamic HTML) is covered in Chapter 13.

Not all options in the Format menu work with all browsers. Therefore, let's explore that issue a bit before you go hog wild applying all kinds of shading and paragraph spacing to text.

Testing browser compatibility

As browsers gain more capability to accurately display text formatting, you can assign a wide variety of formatting to text in FrontPage, and expect visitors to see that formatting in much the same way you defined it. That said, if you come from a desktop publishing background, or you are thinking in terms of the kind of control you get when you send a Word file to your laser printer, you will have to adjust your perspective. How faithfully text formatting is displayed in a browser depends on what fonts a user has installed on his or her system. In addition, pre-version 3.0 browsers do not reliably interpret text-formatting effects such as background shading and borders.

If you want to restrict yourself to text formatting that will be interpreted by older browsers, choose Tools ➪ Page Options, and in the Compatibility tab, select 3.0 browsers and later from the Browser versions drop-down list, as shown in Figure 5-5. After you do that, some text formatting options will be grayed out in menus — preventing you from assigning formatting that older browsers don't recognize.

You'll note several compatibility options in the Compatibility tab of the Page Options dialog box. The most powerful of these additional options is the Enabled with Microsoft FrontPage Server Extensions checkbox. If you are publishing your Web to a server with FrontPage extension files, you can take advantage of additional features, including data management. Most FrontPage components require server extensions as well. We'll return to this dialog box throughout the book as we explore various page elements. If you find that features you want to apply to a page are grayed out, begin your troubleshooting by checking what browsers (or other constraints) are defined here.

Browser compatibility is, however, a moving target. It's one of the things that keep Web designers on the edge, and sometimes pushes them off the deep end. New versions of Netscape Navigator and Internet Explorer add new formatting-interpretation features. Ultimately, the only real test of browser compatibility for your Web pages is to view them with the latest versions of Navigator and IE, as well as older versions of both browsers. That way, you'll really know what visitors to your Web site see.

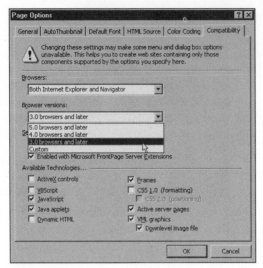

Figure 5-5: You can tell FrontPage to display only the formatting that can be read by both Netscape Navigator and Internet Explorer.

Defining paragraph spacing, bullets, and numbering

If your site audience is armed with version 5.0 or later browsers, you can apply an impressive array of paragraph-based styles to your text, giving your pages a decidedly non-HTML look.

To apply paragraph formatting to selected text, choose Format ⇨ Paragraph. In addition to alignment options (more easily accessed from the Formatting toolbar), you can assign indentation before text (on the left), after text (on the right), or to the first line only.

You can also assign vertical spacing by entering values in the Before or After spin boxes, and define word spacing by entering values in the Word spin box. You can choose between single spacing, 1.5 spacing, or double-spacing in the Line Spacing drop-down menu.

Units of Measurement for Spacing

The default unit of measurement in spacing is points. However, you can assign paragraph spacing in FrontPage in many units of measurement, including pixels (px), inches (in), centimeters (cm), ems (a unit of measurement the size of a letter m, often referred to as a *pica*), and percent (using the % symbol, such as 15%). The advantage of using percent as a spacing measurement is that it is adjusted depending on the size of the browser window viewing your Web page.

You can preview your spacing in the Preview area, as shown in Figure 5-6.

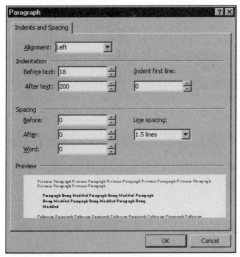

Figure 5-6: This paragraph has been assigned left alignment, six-pixel indenting on the left, and 200-pixel indenting from the right side of the page. Vertical line spacing is set to 1.5, and all effects are displayed in the Preview area.

Normal bullets and numbering can be quickly assigned from the Formatting toolbar. Detailed control over bullets and numbering is available for selected text by choosing Format ➪ Bullets and Numbering. The Picture Bullets tab enables you to choose an image for your bullets by clicking the Browse button and navigating to an image file. Of course, you will first need to design, or get and save, a small image to use as a bullet.

The Plain Bullets and Numbering tabs provide bullet and numbering options similar to those in Word — you can assign automatic numbering as roman numerals or letters, and define a starting number for a list.

The Enable Collapsible Outlines checkbox in each tab generates Dynamic HTML (DHTML) code that enables visitors in supported browsers to expand or collapse multilevel outlines. This feature is not supported in Netscape 4+ browsers.

If you select the Enable Collapsible Outlines option, you can indent lower-level bullets or numbering by selecting paragraphs in a bulleted (or numbered) list and clicking the Increase Indent button in the Formatting toolbar twice. This assigns lower-level status to a bulleted (or numbered) list item. When viewed in Internet Explorer, these items can be hidden or displayed by clicking the parent bulleted item.

Figure 5-7 shows two browser views of the same page — one with an outline expanded, the other with the outline collapsed.

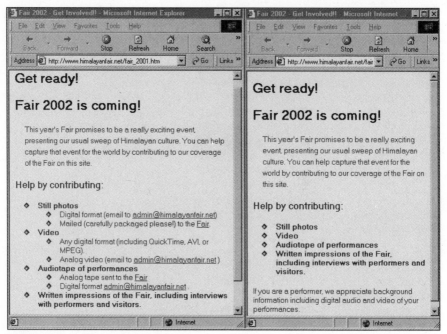

Figure 5-7: In the browser window on the left, the collapsible outline is expanded. In the window on the right, the outline is collapsed. Visitors can expand collapsed bulleted levels by clicking a bullet.

Tutorial 5-1: Assigning text and paragraph formatting

In this tutorial, you will experiment with assigning formatting to text fonts and paragraph attributes.

1. Open an existing Web site, and open a Web page with a paragraph of text.

2. Select the paragraph of text, right-click, and choose Paragraph Properties from the context menu.

3. In the Paragraph dialog box, assign 5% to all three of the indentation drop-down lists (Before Text, After Text, and Indent First Line).

Note   You can define indentation in percent by typing "5%" in any of the indentation spin boxes.

4. In the Before and After drop-down lists, select 5% spacing.

5. In the Line Spacing drop-down list, select Double.

6. From the Alignment drop-down list, choose Justify. Then, click OK in the dialog box and see how your paragraph looks in Page view.

7. Preview your page in your browser. Did all the paragraph attributes work?

Formatting borders and shading

Both borders and shading can be applied to selected paragraphs by choosing Format ⇨ Borders and Shading.

The Borders tab in the Borders and Shading dialog box enables you to assign a variety of borders around paragraphs, just as you can in Word or desktop publishing programs. You can select line style, color, and width, and then apply these attributes by clicking one of the four border buttons in the Preview area of the dialog box. The four Padding area spin boxes enable you to define space between the border and the text.

The Shading tab enables you to define a background color for a paragraph. The Foreground Color drop-down list defines the color of text.

Figure 5-8 illustrates a paragraph of text with a 2-pixel right black border, a 3-pixel black bottom border, a shaded background, and a brown foreground (text) color.

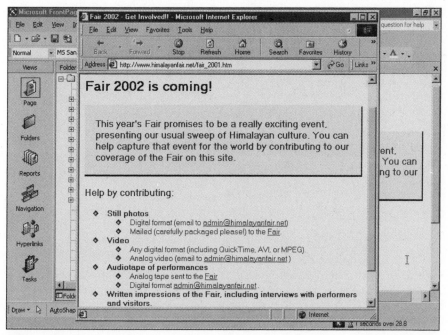

Figure 5-8: This shaded and bordered paragraph has a padding of 2 pixels on all four sides to create buffer space between the text and the border.

How do these border and shading effects play in Netscape? FrontPage assigns style code that is not standard HTML, and neither Netscape Navigator 4.7 nor 6.0 interprets it completely.

Should you, therefore, use shading and borders for effect? The trade-off is that these features make your Web page text stand out, but you have limited control over exactly how viewers will see your effects. In Figure 5-9, you can see the results of displaying shaded text with a border in each version of Netscape.

Defining page properties

Now that we've gone to the edge of what can be achieved with formatting applied to text and paragraphs, let's mix in formatting applied to an entire page. Web page properties define the look of your page, including background colors or images, default font colors, margins, page titles, and other features that apply to an entire Web page. These attributes are available in the Page Properties dialog box.

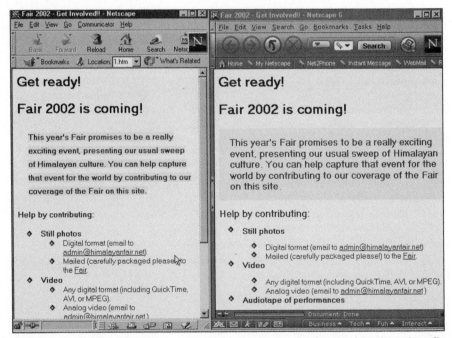

Figure 5-9: On the left, Netscape Navigator 4.7 interprets the combination of 1.5 line spacing and shading by displaying something that looks like highlighted text. On the right, version 6.0 handles the shading fine but doesn't display the border assigned in FrontPage.

Themes versus page properties

Because themes define so many properties automatically, they rob you of the free-dom to do your own page design. If you want total control over the look of your Web pages, you'll want to assign page formatting by hand.

To delete a theme from an open Web page, follow these steps:

1. Choose Format ➪ Theme.

2. Choose Selected Page(s) to apply your choice to only the open page.

3. Select No Theme from the list of themes on the left side of the Themes dialog box, as shown in Figure 5-10.

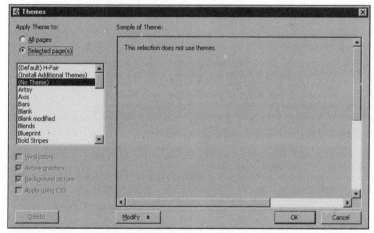

Figure 5-10: Select No Theme in the Themes dialog box to remove a theme from your Web page.

4. Click the OK button.

After you remove your theme, you can apply all the properties in the Page Properties dialog box. To access these features, choose Format ➪ Background.

The Page Properties dialog box is divided into six tabs, but the page properties associated with page appearance are in the General, Background, and Margins tabs. These tabs are described in detail here, followed by a brief look at the other tabs, which offer more esoteric page-property options.

Briefly, the nonpage formatting tabs are:

✦ **Custom:** Enables you to define HTML code, including meta-tags that define how your page is displayed in browsers. See Chapter 8 for a full explanation of meta-tags.

✦ **Language:** Defines the language character set required to view your page.

✦ **Workgroups:** Allows you to organize assignments. See Chapter 4 for a discussion of this feature.

If you find that page properties described in the following sections are not available, first make sure that no theme is assigned to the page, disrupting your normally available page properties.

Assigning page titles

Defining page titles is one of the more essential elements of creating a Web page. The page title displays in the title bar of a visitor's Web browser. Your Web page may be called `index.htm` or `default.htm` (these filenames designate home pages that open first when a visitor comes to your Web site). Alternatively, your page's filename may be `newpage4.htm`. Regardless, you can create a title such as "Himalayan Fair 2002," and that page title will display when visitors come to your Web page.

To enter a title for your page, right-click on the page and choose Page Properties. Enter a page title in the Title area of the General tab. Titles can break rules that apply to page *filenames*. Therefore, you can assign the same title to more than one page (technically possible, though likely to be confusing), and you can include any combination of uppercase and lowercase, numbers, symbols, and spaces in a page title.

Note   By default, FrontPage assigns a page title based on the filename you assign to a page. For example, a page named `fair_projects.htm` will be assigned a page title of Fair Projects.

Tip   You can also assign page titles by clicking on a page in Navigation view and pressing the F2 function key to enter a new page title.

Adding background sounds

You can also associate a sound file with your FrontPage Web page. The sound will play when your page is opened in a browser. Sounds can be overdone, however; think twice before adding a sound to your page. The downside of background sounds includes the following:

✦ Visitors get no warning that a sound is coming, which can be disruptive in some work environments.

✦ Sounds slow down page download time considerably, with longer sound files being the worst offenders.

✦ Browsers don't come with the capability to turn off a background sound easily, leaving unhappy listeners quite annoyed.

✦ Background sounds are not interpreted by Netscape Navigator.

Nonetheless, background sounds are appropriate in some situations. For example, you might have a link to a page that alerts visitors that they will hear music, voice, or other sound files at that page. FrontPage 2002 enables the inclusion of sound files in many audio file formats: .wav, .mid, .ram, .ra, .aif, .au, and .snd. These formats enable you to assign sound files created in all popular Windows and Macintosh audio software. Both page titles and background sounds are defined in the General tab of the Page Properties dialog box, shown in Figure 5-11.

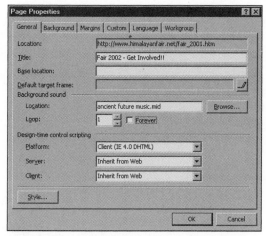

Figure 5-11: Add a page title and background sounds in the General tab of the Page Properties dialog box. The file is in MIDI (.mid) format, and will play just once.

The Loop spin box in the General tab of the Page Properties dialog box defines how many times the sound will play. The Forever checkbox plays a background sound repeatedly, as long as the page is open.

When you save a Web page, FrontPage will prompt you to save all embedded files — which includes a background sound file if you have assigned one.

Design-Time Control Scripting

What about the other options in the General tab of the Page Properties dialog box, the ones in the Design-Time Control Scripting area? These are very advanced features that you can ignore if you are relying on FrontPage to handle your HTML and scripting. If you're a coding daredevil and want to experiment with these features, here's our best advice to start you on your way.

A design-time control (DTC) is an ActiveX control that adds functionality to a development tool (in this case, FrontPage, but the model really comes from Visual InterDev), basically giving you a simplified way to configure certain elements of a Web page. In some ways, a DTC works like a FrontPage component: It writes scripting code onto the HTML page. This code is interpreted at run time (when the page is loaded).

The Page Properties section for DTC scripting enables you to define what scripting language FrontPage uses for DTC. The Platform option looks like it enables you to determine where the script is interpreted — either on the server side (as ASP) or on the client (browser) side (as DHTML). The other two options are analogous to the Default Scripting Languages properties in the Advanced tab of the Web Settings dialog box (choose Tools, Web Settings, and click on the Advanced tab) . In fact, the default — Inherit from Web — means that the DTC scripting language will use the values set in this dialog box. Alternatively, you can specify a scripting language on a per-page basis if you like.

Defining page background

Use the Background tab of the Page Properties dialog box to control your page's entire color scheme.

The Background tab lets you define both the page background and default text colors. Defining both simultaneously is handy. For example, if you create a dark-blue page background, you'll probably want to change your default text color to white, yellow, or another bright, light color that can be read against a dark background.

The features in the Background tab are as follows:

✦ **Background Picture check box:** Enables you to define a graphic image to tile in the background of your Web page. Tiled images repeat horizontally and vertically, as necessary, to fill all the space behind your Web page.

✦ **Browse button:** You can locate a background image on your local computer or Web site by navigating to the image file.

✦ **Watermark check box:** Freezes a background image on the browser screen; as visitors scroll up and down your Web page, the background image stays in the same place.

✦ **Enable Hyperlink Rollover Effects check box:** Enables you to assign special font changes when a visitor moves his or her mouse over your hyperlinks. If you enable rollover effects, you can click the Rollover Style button to open the Font dialog box, in which you can assign special font attributes to be displayed when a mouse is moved over a hyperlink. Alternatively, you can assign rollover effects with more control over triggering events by using DHTML (see Chapter 13).

✦ **Background drop-down list:** Enables you to select a color from a color palette to assign to your Web page background. Background images override background colors, so if you want the selected background color to work, deselect the Background Image checkbox.

✦ **Text drop-down menu:** Opens a color palette from which you can assign a default text color for your page.

✦ **Get Background and Colors from Page checkbox:** Enables you to link the current page to another page's background and colors. For example, you can use the Browse button to select the home page for your Web site as a source of background and color for your page. Then, when you make changes to colors and the background at your home page, the current page will change as well.

✦ **Hyperlink drop-down palettes:** Enables you to define colors for links on your page.

Page background approaches

The Background tab controls important page design options. You can assign default colors for page text, and the three states of page links here, as well as define a page background color or image.

With the advent of widespread broadband Internet connections, large background images become an option. Figure 5-12 shows a page with a large image used as a watermarked background. Text stands out because of contrasting colors, and by being set off in shaded and bordered text areas. The result is a distinctive look that enables text to be layered over an image.

Defining margins

Margins define spacing in a browser on the top and left edge of the page content. Margins do *not* affect background colors or images — they extend to the edge of the browser window. Oddly enough, the default margin for both Netscape Navigator and Internet Explorer is not zero. Instead, both browsers create some space on the top and left edge of pages by default. You can increase the default margins or you can redefine the margins to zero to create a clean, "marginless" look on your page.

The Margins tab in the Page Properties dialog box has two checkboxes and two spin boxes. The Specify Top Margin checkbox enables you to define an area at the top of the page that will be clear (except for any page background).

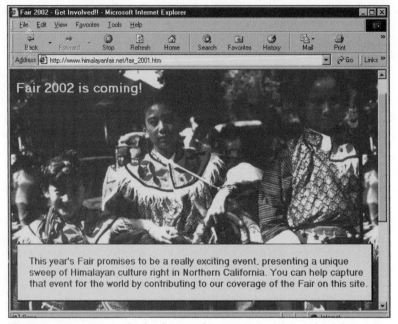

Figure 5-12: Because the background image is a watermark, visitors can scroll to see the entire image. Note, however, that if a browser window is too wide, the image will tile horizontally. And, watermarked backgrounds are not supported in all browsers.

The Specify Left Margin checkbox enables you to define a left margin. Both spin boxes are used to set the margin size in pixels. There are 72 pixels to an inch, so if you want to define a 1.5-inch margin on the right side of your page, for example, you would define a 108-pixel left margin.

The margins you define in FrontPage, unfortunately, do not work in Netscape Navigator. Netscape uses a different HTML tag to define margins. We've concentrated our discussion of HTML coding in Chapter 8, but if you want to add margins that work in Navigator, you need to jump to the HTML tab of Page view and enter the following code:

```
marginwidth=x, marginheight=y
```

x and y can be any value, and represent pixels. marginwidth defines the left margin in Netscape Navigator, and marginheight defines the top margin.

Figure 5-13 shows coding generated by FrontPage, along with additional coding to display margins in Navigator.

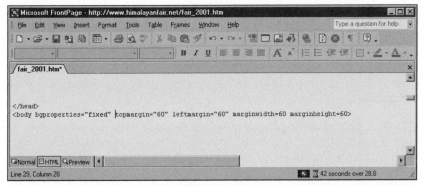

Figure 5-13: By adding marginwidth and marginheight HTML tags in HTML view, you can make your defined margins apply in Netscape Navigator.

Other page properties

The Custom tab enables programmers to alter coding in the Web site. The Workgroup tab helps teams work together to design Web pages, or helps a Web designer organize pages into categories. When you assign categories by using the checkboxes available in the Workgroup tab, you can then use those categories to generate reports in Reports view.

The Language tab enables you to set page defaults for dozens of languages, from Albanian to Zulu.

Editing and Checking Text

The beginning of this chapter introduced you to text formatting. If you've gotten this far, you've probably already figured out how to assign basic formatting to text and how to use the editing tools in the Standard toolbar. The Cut and Paste buttons work just as you'd expect, and click-and-drag editing is available in Page view.

Click the Spell Check button to check your spelling. FrontPage comes with a full-fledged spell checker. Not impressed? Okay, but did you expect a thesaurus in FrontPage? You've got one. Select a word and press Shift+F7, or select Tools ➪ Thesaurus when you're stuck for a missing synonym.

Another thing that you may not have expected is how easily you can import text, graphics, and even tables from other applications.

Getting text without typing

You can copy text from Word (or Excel, Access, and PowerPoint, for that matter) right into FrontPage's Page view. Select the text in another Office application, and click the Copy button in that application's toolbar to copy the text to the Clipboard. Then, open or switch to FrontPage's Page view and paste the text at the cursor's insertion point.

Much — but not necessarily all — of your formatting will be preserved when you paste text. In your other applications, you may be using formatting that's not available in HTML pages. FrontPage will do its best to keep your font type, size, color, and attributes when you paste text from other applications.

Editing text

The editing tools that are at your disposal in Page view include the following:

✦ Edit Find and Edit Replace enable you to find and/or replace text in Page view. You can also Find and Replace text globally, for an entire Web site — just select the Entire Web radio button in the Replace dialog box.

✦ The Spelling tool in the Standard toolbar enables you to check spelling for the open page in Page view. You can also spell check an entire Web site. To do that, click the Spelling tool while in any view except Page view, and you get the option to select the Entire Web radio button. The Add a Task For Each Page With Misspellings checkbox creates a link in Tasks view to each page that needs correcting.

Pushing the limits of HTML formatting

As alluded to at the beginning of this chapter, FrontPage is a bit schizophrenic when it comes to text and paragraph formatting. On the one hand, the Style drop-down list in the Formatting menu displays a list of traditional, standard HTML styles. Old versions of Web browsers relied on these styles as the main way of identifying font and paragraph attributes. On the other hand, if you want to assign paragraph and font attributes to selected text, you'll find more freedom and control by using the Formatting toolbar buttons, and the Paragraph and Font Properties dialog boxes.

Navigational aid with bookmarks

In Chapter 1, you learned the quick and easy way to create hyperlinks in a Web page. Simply typing a URL (Web site address) such as www.ppinet.com and pressing the spacebar or Enter creates a link to that site in your page. You can create links to e-mail addresses the same way, by typing an e-mail address on your page.

In Chapter 1, you also learned to assign hyperlinks to selected text or graphics by clicking the Hyperlink button on the Standard toolbar and then selecting a Web page in your site, or elsewhere on the Web.

An additional tool for assisting visitors to your site is to provide bookmarks on your pages, with links to them. Bookmarks are target locations on Web pages to which a link can be directed.

To create a bookmark, follow these steps:

1. Click a location in your Web page that you want to function as a bookmark, and select Insert Bookmark.

2. If you have text selected, that text will become the default bookmark's name. If you don't have text selected, you can enter a bookmark name, as shown in Figure 5-14.

Figure 5-14: Defining a bookmark

3. Click OK in the Bookmark dialog box. The new bookmark is displayed as a small, blue flag; or, if the bookmark is assigned to selected text, that text will be underlined with a dotted line.

With bookmarks defined, you can create links to them from other locations on your page. One useful technique is to create a bookmark at the top of your page, and provide links to it from other places on the page.

To create a link to a bookmark on your Web page, follow these steps:

1. Select text or a picture that will serve as the hyperlink to the bookmark.

2. Click the Hyperlink button. In the Create Hyperlink dialog box, click the Bookmark button. Select your bookmark from the Bookmark list, as shown in Figure 5-15.

Working with Bookmarks: Do's, Don'ts, and Considerations

You must save a page before you can assign bookmarks in the Hyperlinks dialog box. If you know hyperlinks on Web pages outside your site, you can add them to links by typing the pound sign (#) and the name of the bookmark. Bookmarks are also called *anchors*.

Bookmarks are particularly useful in long documents presented as Web pages. They enable users to easily navigate within a page. They can be disorienting for short pages, or when visitors think they have jumped to a new page, only to find themselves at the bottom of the same page at which they started. For image- and media-heavy pages, it's usually best to break text content into separate pages, and rely on links *between pages* to facilitate navigation through site content.

Figure 5-15: Making a bookmark a link target

3. You can test your hyperlinks to bookmarks by previewing your page in your Web browser, or in the Preview tab of FrontPage's Page view.

A Quick Look at Page Styles

Throughout this chapter, we've mainly examined formatting as applied to specific text on a page. This type of formatting — applied to selected text — is actually only one level of using styles to apply formatting.

Styles can also be applied to an entire page, or — as external style sheet files — to an entire Web site. The process of creating external style sheets is explored in detail in Chapter 11. Here, we'll look at creating styles that can be applied to a single page.

What's the advantage to defining page-wide styles? First, if you are formatting a page with a lot of text, page-wide styles enable you to quickly apply and revise formatting to assigned styles throughout a page — much as you do in Word or in desktop publishing programs. Second, if you later decide to take your page style "site-wide," you can copy the styles defined for one page into an external style sheet. We'll walk you through that in detail in Chapter 11.

Redefining a standard HTML style

If you click on the Style drop-down list in the FrontPage Formatting toolbar, you'll see six heading styles (Heading 1 through Heading 6), a normal text style, and styles for lists, as well as some other obscure styles that are holdovers from when all text formatting was restricted to a set of pre-defined HTML style formats.

Each of these styles can be redefined, and applied to an entire page. Style definitions can include font, size, font attributes, colors, background, borders, and paragraph attributes.

Once you define a style for a page, you apply that style by selecting a paragraph and choosing the defined style from the Style drop-down list.

In the hierarchy of styles, page-wide styles are *overridden* by formatting applied to selected text. This is true whether you defined the page-wide styles before or after you assigned specific formatting to selected text. If you want to get rid of *all* specific formatting applied to text, select that text and choose Format ➪ Remove Formatting from the menu.

Redefining headings and paragraph text

Normal (also referred to as Paragraph, or P) style is applied to text on a page that doesn't have any other style applied. By redefining the Normal style for a page, you reformat all text that does not have a style assigned to it.

To change Normal style attributes, deselect any selected text and choose Format ➪ Style. In the Style dialog box, choose HTML tags from the List drop-down menu at the bottom left corner of the dialog box. As you do, a list of all HTML tags appears, as shown in Figure 5-16.

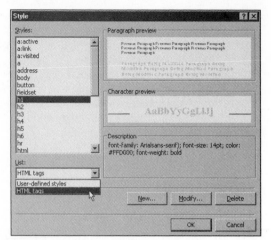

Figure 5-16: Standard HTML styles can be redefined, and then applied throughout a Web page.

The HTML tag for Normal text is "p" (as in Paragraph), so to redefine your page's Normal style, choose "p" in the list of HTML tags. Then click the Modify button. This opens the Modify Style dialog box. Here, you can use the Format button to assign Font, Paragraph, Border, and Numbering format to all normal text. (The Position selection assigns absolute location on a page, and is explored in Chapter 6.) As you define formatting attributes for your style, they are shown in the Preview area, and listed in the Description area of the Modify Style dialog box, as shown in Figure 5-17.

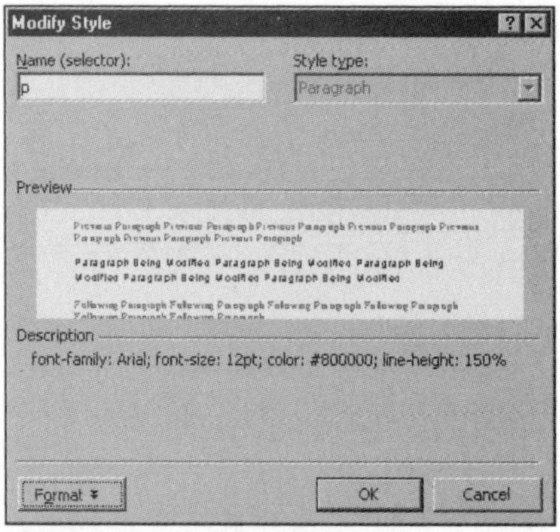

Figure 5-17: The Preview area and Description indicate that we've assigned a 12-point Arial font and 1.5 line spacing to the "P" style, which defines the look of normal text throughout our page.

Once you redefine your Normal (P) style, it will automatically be applied to all text on the page without other styles assigned to it.

You can use this same technique to redefine the heading styles, or any style. Define the style, select a paragraph on your page, and then apply the modified style by selecting it from the Style drop-down list.

Redefining link formatting

You can redefine how links are displayed throughout a page by modifying their styles. Choose Format ➪ Style to open the Style dialog box. Select HTML tags from the List drop-down menu.

The three styles that begin with "a:" define different states of links. The "a:link" style defines how a link looks before it has been used. The "a:active" style defines how a link looks while it is being followed by a browser. The "a:visited" link style defines how a used link is displayed. The "a" link defines how bookmarks appear in a browser.

Link styles do not need to be assigned. Like the Normal (P) style, they are applied automatically — in this case to links (or in the case of the "a" style, to bookmarks).

While you are defining link formatting, you can elect to get rid of the underlining that is assigned to links by default. The trend in page design evolution is toward eliminating underlining links. Because modern browsers indicate links with specialized cursors, and because you can denote a link with other formatting techniques, a good case can be made for pages free of underlining.

To remove underlining from link styles, select the No Text Decoration checkbox in the Font dialog box, as shown in Figure 5-18.

Creating a new custom style

In addition to reformatting standard HTML styles, you can create your own custom styles. For example, if you wanted to apply italics, indenting, and a background to chunks of text throughout a long page, you might define a style with those attributes, and apply it as needed.

To define a custom style, choose Format ➪ Style. In the List drop-down menu, choose User-defined Styles. Click New to define a new style (or Modify to revise a user-defined style if you already have one created).

Enter a style name in the Name box. FrontPage will add a period to the front of the name after you define the style (to conform to HTML rules), but you don't need to worry about that — just don't be disturbed when you see it.

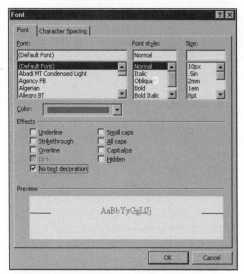

Figure 5-18: Removing underlining from link styles in the Font dialog box.

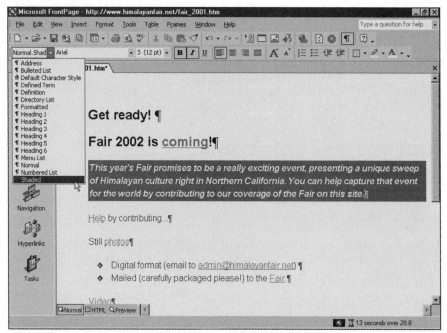

Figure 5-19: When you select a user-defined style, the HTML style name (such as Normal) appears in the Format menu.

Define formatting attributes for your user-defined style. After you OK the dialog boxes, you can apply your style by choosing it from the Style list in the Formatting toolbar, as shown in Figure 5-19.

Looking at style

Now that you have learned to define page-wide styles, you're on your way to creating external style sheets that can be applied to an entire site. It might be interesting, however, to see the HTML code that FrontPage generated as you created page-wide styles.

You can do that by choosing the HTML tab on the bottom of the Page view and scrolling up your page to the area bounded by the `<style>` and `</style>` tags. The generated HTML style definitions can be copied to other pages, or into an external style sheet. We'll walk you through that process in Chapter 11. You can see an example of style tags in Figure 5-20.

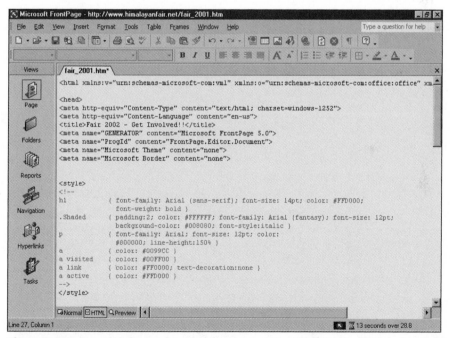

Figure 5-20: As you define styles, FrontPage generates HTML code. That code can be copied to other pages, or into an external CSS file that will control formatting for an entire Web site.

Summary

Text editing and formatting options in FrontPage come pretty close to what you can do in Word. You can copy and paste text, and rely on automatic spell-checking (those wavy red lines under misspelled words). You can apply formatting like text fonts, sizes, and attributes (like boldface or italic).

You can also format paragraphs, defining indentation and vertical spacing. Paragraph formatting is not interpreted by older browsers.

Page properties include page background color (or picture), background sounds, page titles, and margins.

If you use a Theme for your Web site, FrontPage will automatically format your pages and your text.

✦   ✦   ✦

Working with Layout: Tables and Layers

By now, you have learned to use FrontPage to create and edit your Web pages and to enhance them with themes, Office objects, formatted text, and graphic images.

FrontPage provides a variety of tools you can use to place text, graphics, and other objects on Web pages. The most basic technique for laying out pages is to create *tables*. Although tables can be used to display data in rows and columns, in FrontPage (and in Web page design in general), tables are more often used to lay out pages. For even more control over page layout, you can use absolute positioning. FrontPage facilitates placing text boxes or images at an exact point on a page. Because absolutely positioned objects can overlap (be on top of or behind one another), designing with absolute positioning is sometimes referred to as working with *layers*.

This chapter explores tables, absolute positioning, and other ways of designing pages including the new photo gallery component in FrontPage 2002.

Tables have two basic uses in Web design:

✦ To display text and images in columns and rows: If you have used spreadsheet applications such as Microsoft Excel, or created tables in Microsoft Word or Access, creating tables in FrontPage will be intuitive.

✦ To design pages: Although Microsoft and its rivals continue to add new interpretive powers to HTML, including the capability to recognize exact locations for objects, tables are still the easiest and most effective way to lay out information at an exact location on your page, or in columns or rows.

Creating a Table

Whether you are creating a table to display shipping prices in neat rows and columns, or 3-D animated graphics at different locations on your Web page, the process of defining a table is the same. To use tables as design tools or to display data, first define the location of your table, and then define how many rows and columns you need. These attributes are easy to edit.

Three ways exist to create a table in FrontPage. The simplest way is to use the Insert Table tool in the Standard toolbar. For the numerically oriented, the Insert Table dialog box enables you to define a table precisely. Finally, you can graphically draw a table and define columns and rows by using the Table toolbar. All three options are explored in the following sections.

After you create a table and place text or other objects in table cells, you can define table and cell properties. Fine-tuning the appearance of your table cells and rows is discussed in the sections "Editing Table Properties" and "Editing Cell Properties," later in this chapter.

Creating tables the quick and easy way

In many cases, you can use the Insert Table tool in the Standard toolbar to create a quick sketch of your table. Because you graphically create your table all in one step, the Insert Table tool is probably the most efficient way to add a table to your Web page.

With a Web page open in Page view, you can insert a table by following these steps:

1. Click to place your insertion point at the spot where you want the table to appear in your Web page.

2. Click the Insert Table button in the Standard toolbar.

3. Click and drag to the right in the Grid palette to add columns; click and drag down to add rows. Figure 6-1 defines a table that is nine rows long and three columns wide. Because it's easy to add or delete cells, don't spend much time agonizing over table size when you first generate a table.

Inserting and defining a table

Inserting a table by using the Insert Table dialog box (shown in Figure 6-2) provides greater initial control over the appearance of your table. Although not every table option is available in this dialog box, enough options are there to make setting up your table easier. These options, as well as others, are explained in detail later in this chapter in the section entitled "Editing Table Properties."

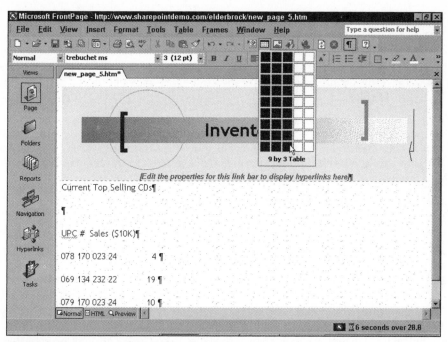

Figure 6-1: You can define tables graphically using the Insert Table tool in the Standard toolbar.

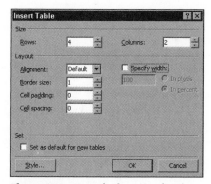

Figure 6-2: Even before you begin to edit table content, you can define basic table formatting.

The main options of initial concern are located in the Size and Specify Width sections of the dialog box. These options enable you to specify how many rows and columns your table has, and its overall width.

To insert a table, follow these steps:

1. Select Table ⇨ Insert Table to open the Insert Table dialog box.

2. Set the size, layout, and width options. If you deselect the Specify Width checkbox, FrontPage will generate a table just wide enough to display the content of cells.

3. If you want to assign inline styles, click the Style button and use the Format button in the Modify Style dialog box to define local font, paragraph, border, or number styles for your table. For more discussion of styles, see Chapter 5 for text and paragraph formatting, and Chapter 11 for a full exploration of styles.

4. Click OK to insert the table.

After the table is inserted, it can be manipulated in any of the ways detailed in the rest of this chapter.

Drawing a table

The Insert Table dialog box enables you to define many table properties digitally, by entering numbers in fields. The Table toolbar enables you to format your table in a graphical form, using the tools shown in Figure 6-3. (The function of each of these tools is explained in the section "Adjusting Table Structure," except for the Background Color tool, which is explained in the section "Editing Table Properties.")

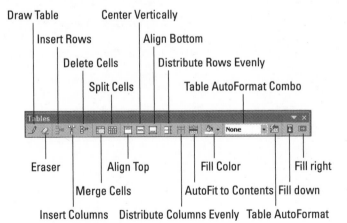

Figure 6-3: The Table toolbar

The Table toolbar provides much of the table formatting power you find in Word or Excel, such as cell background shading and alignment control. You get a nice selection of table auto-formatting features as well. Other table features are a bit odd or disappointing compared with formatting available in Word or Excel. Fill Down and

Fill Right speed up data entry, though not in the intuitive way you would expect. They simply *copy* the content of the top (or left) cell into cell(s) below or to the right of the selected cell(s). Therefore, applying Fill Down or Fill Right to a cell with Jan and a blank cell will not change Jan into Feb in the target cell; it simply copies cell contents. Moreover, if you were hoping, as we were, that Microsoft would introduce basic calculation and sorting features in version 2002, you'll have to keep waiting. In the meantime, tables with significant data will probably be best created in Excel or Word, and copied into FrontPage. Simply using Edit ➪ Copy and Edit ➪ Paste will move table content into FrontPage with most of the formatting preserved.

For the purposes of defining a new table, the important tool is the Draw Table tool. Appropriately named, this tool enables you to create a table simply by drawing its structure in your page. Use the following steps to create a table by using the Draw Table tool:

1. Select the Draw Table tool from the Table toolbar; if the Table toolbar isn't visible, select Table ➪ Draw table. The cursor changes to a pencil, and the Table toolbar opens.

2. Click and drag the cursor to define the overall rectangular shape of the table that you want to create. When the table is the size that you want, release the mouse button.

3. Add rows and columns to your table simply by drawing them (see the pencil-shaped cursor near the bottom of Figure 6-4).

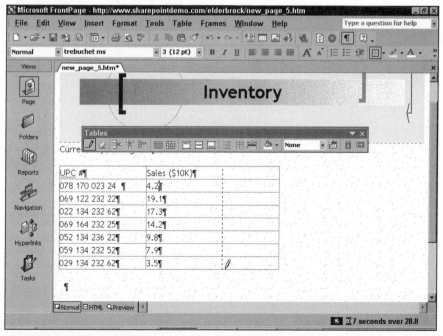

Figure 6-4: Adding cells by using the Draw Table tool

4. After you finish creating your table, click the Draw Table tool in the toolbar again to deselect it. The cursor returns to normal.

Placing text and other objects in a table

Adding content (text, graphics, form fields, videos, and so on) is the same as adding it anywhere else on a page. Click to place the insertion point where you want to add content, and then type or insert the content.

Resizing tables and rows

Table cells adjust in height and width as you place text and other objects in them. Inserting a large image in a cell enlarges that cell to accommodate the image. Typing unbreakable text strings (for example, long words) widens a column, as necessary. Typing additional text may lengthen your cell.

As you move your cursor over a row or column divider, a double-headed cursor appears, as shown over the vertical dotted line in Figure 6-5. Click and drag to the right or left to change column width, and up or down to change row height.

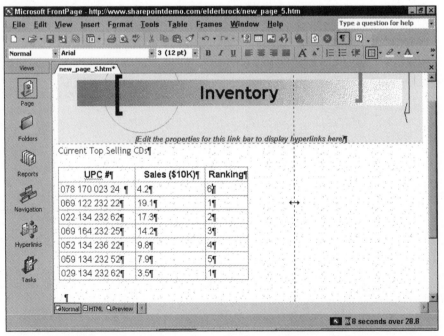

Figure 6-5: Click and drag row or column borders to change cell size.

Importing a table

As noted earlier in this chapter, you can format tables nicely in FrontPage, but your ability to create them is limited by disappointing datafill features and a lack of calculation or sorting power. Therefore, you're likely to create larger tables in Word or Excel, and then copy and paste them into FrontPage. The good news is that this works seamlessly, and most of your formatting is imported into FrontPage intact.

To copy spreadsheet cells into FrontPage:

1. Start Microsoft Excel, or another program with a table (such as Microsoft Access or Word), and open the file with your table.

2. Highlight the cells that you want to include in your page and copy the selection either by selecting Edit ➪ Copy or by using the command-key shortcut Ctrl+C.

3. Place the cursor where you want the table to be placed and either select Edit ➪ Paste or press Ctrl+V to paste the table into FrontPage.

If a cell is empty and the table has a border (which an imported table has automatically), no border appears around those cells.

Note When you copy a table into FrontPage that includes a calculation cell, the calculation cell is replaced by its value before completing the copy. If you need to retain the calculation, you need to rewrite the calculation by using one of the client-side scripting languages discussed in Chapter 18.

Another option for placing a formatted table in a Web page is to insert an entire spreadsheet file in your Web page. This is appropriate for small files in which you want to import an entire spreadsheet, not just a selected range of cells.

To insert a spreadsheet file into FrontPage:

1. Click to place your insertion point where you want to insert the spreadsheet.

2. Select Insert ➪ File.

3. In the Select File dialog box, select the file format for your spreadsheet from the Files of Type drop-down menu, and navigate to the folder with your spreadsheet files. Then, double-click the spreadsheet file to insert it in your Web page.

In Tutorial 6-1, you will import an existing spreadsheet into FrontPage.

Table Captions

A caption is a short phrase associated with a table. When you select Table ➪ Insert ➪ Caption (with a table already selected), FrontPage places the caption above the table. If you prefer the caption under the table, select the table caption and choose Table ➪ Table Properties ➪ Caption to display the Caption Properties dialog box. This dialog box enables you to designate the location for the caption, either at the top or the bottom of the table.

The advantage to using caption text is that you can keep that text with your table, no matter what changes are made to the rest of the page content. However, when you are using tables as design tools, you'll have more control over the location and appearance of text if you simply put it in a cell, rather than defining it as a caption.

Tutorial 6-1: Importing a table

In this tutorial, we'll import a table into a FrontPage Web page. In order to complete this tutorial, you will need a (preferably small) spreadsheet file saved on your computer. If you want your table to match this exercise, create a small spreadsheet file that tracks income over a few years.

1. Start with a new blank page: Select File ➪ New ➪ Page and select the Normal Page template.

2. Save this page as Table1.htm, with the title Income.

3. Type the heading **Project Income** for the page.

4. Select Insert ➪ File from the menu and choose Microsoft Excel Worksheet (.xls, .xlw) from the Files of Type drop-down menu.

5. Navigate to a spreadsheet file and double-click on the filename.

6. You can format or edit the imported table contents.

Editing Table Properties

Some attributes of your table are defined in the Table Properties dialog box, whereas others are defined in the Cell Properties dialog box. It's not particularly intuitive which properties are defined where. However, the basic distinction is that table attributes assigned in the Table Properties dialog box apply to the *entire* table, whereas cell attributes apply only to the selected cell(s). Therefore, for example, a table either has borders around cells or does not. You can't assign border attributes to specific cells. On the other hand, you can define both a table background color and a cell background color (although older versions of Netscape Navigator won't recognize your cell background colors).

Definable table properties include the following:

✦ Wrapping text around your table

✦ Border size (if any)

✦ Cell padding and spacing (the options that define how much space surrounds a cell and its contents)

✦ Background color

✦ Minimum table size (in pixels or percent)

Border width is perhaps the most basic formatting option available. Beyond that, you have almost complete control over how text aligns within cells, what color the cells are, and how much space exists between the cells.

Table Properties dialog box

The Table Properties dialog box provides quick access to all the formatting options available to the table as a whole. To open this dialog box, place the cursor within the table and select Table ➪ Table Properties, or right-click within the table and select Table Properties from the pop-up menu (see Figure 6-6).

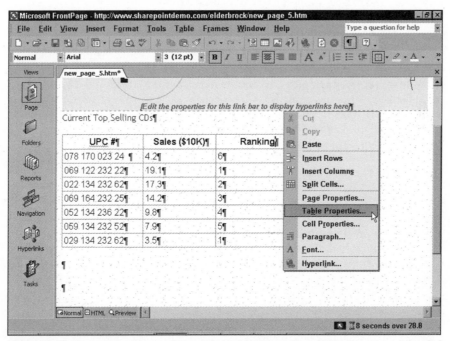

Figure 6-6: The easiest way to access the Table Properties dialog box is to right-click in any table and choose Table Properties from the context menu.

Layout

The Layout section of the Table Properties dialog box provides settings for specifying how other text interacts with the table and how individual cells are spaced within the table. The options in this area are as follows:

✦ **Alignment:** Determines where the table is located. Left places the table against the left margin, right against the right margin, and center aligns the table between the left and right margins. The default option typically places the table against the left margin, but this placement is determined by the browser.

✦ **Float:** Enables you to wrap text around the table, just as you can with an image.

✦ **Border Size:** Specifies the width of the outline placed around the table. A setting of 0 means that no border is displayed in a browser, though you can still see the dashed border when editing the page. Note that the thickness only applies to the outside border — when the border is active, only a thin line is placed between cells.

✦ **Cell Padding:** Specifies the space, in pixels, between the contents of a cell and the border around it. This option may be set regardless of whether the border is visible, and regardless of whether its size is greater than 0.

✦ **Cell Spacing:** Determines the spacing between individual cells.

Setting table width

The Specify Width checkbox activates the area of the Table Properties dialog box in which you can specify the overall height and width of a table. Height and width can be set in either pixels or as a percentage of the screen width. If the Width checkbox isn't checked, the table typically is 100 percent of the browser window width. If the Height checkbox is not checked, the table will be whatever minimum height is required to display everything in your cells.

Note   If table width is not specified, the table fills up as much space of the page as is needed to display the content, up to 100 percent.

If you set a table to be 50 percent of the height of the browser window, but the window is resized so that 50 percent of the height doesn't allow the entire contents to be displayed, the table will be larger than this setting.

Custom table background

Custom Background gives you the option of adding a background color or image to your entire table, much as you can add a background to an entire page. By default, the table is transparent, so that whatever background you have on your page shows through. Background images tile the same way that they do for entire pages.

Pixels Versus Percent

Should you define table minimum size in pixels or percent? Percent provides more flexibility for your table to be viewed with different monitor resolutions and different browser window sizes. If you define your table as 50 percent of the width of the browser window, your table will always take up half of a visitor's browser window.

The downside to defining the minimum width as a percent of the browser window is that if a visitor's browser window is very small, your cells become very narrow. The alternative is defining width in pixels, which gives you more exact control over table size. Your table will always be the same number of pixels wide, but your visitors may need to use their horizontal scroll bar to see all the columns in the table.

Defining table width in pixels is a very widely used technique for controlling the width of a Web page, regardless of browser size. For example, you can restrict your Web pages to 600 pixels in width by placing all content in a 600-pixel-wide, one-cell table.

To assign a custom background, click the Use Background Image checkbox. Choose a color from the Background Color drop-down menu, or use the Browse button to locate an image to tile as the background for the table. Custom-defined colors used in your Web page are available as background colors for your table.

To access the background table image and/or color options, you must tell FrontPage you are designing for an Internet Explorer site only (choose Tools ➪ Page Options, and in the Compatibility tab of the Page Options dialog box, choose Microsoft Internet Explorer Only from the Browsers drop-down list).

Border colors

In addition to setting the color of the table as a whole, you can set the color for the table's border in the Border Colors section of the Table Properties dialog box, which has three settings: border, light border, and dark border. The Border setting enables you to set a single color for the entire border.

The Light Border setting enables you to specify colors for the top and left edges of the border, and the Dark Border setting enables you to specify colors for the bottom and right edges of the border. This helps you give your table a 3-D look. Setting either of these options overrides the Border setting for that area.

Note   If you set Light Border to a dark color and Dark Border to a light color, your table will look as though it's indented into your page, rather than sticking out from it.

Note that if you leave all of these settings at their default, most browsers will display your table as though Light Border is set to silver and Dark Border is set to gray.

Assigning styles to a table

The Style button in the Table Properties dialog box opens the Modify Style dialog box. Use the Format button in the Modify Style dialog box to assign default font, paragraph, border, or numbering styles to your table.

Converting tables to text and vice versa

Before we end the discussion of what you can do with a table, you should know that you can easily convert a table into text. When you do, you don't lose any of the objects (text, graphics, and so forth) in the table; those objects become normal page objects, laid out in paragraphs. To convert a table to text, click anywhere in the table and select Table ➪ Convert ➪ Table to Text. Conversely, if you have text that you want to convert automatically into a table, select the text and then choose Table ➪ Convert ➪ Text to Table. You'll be prompted to insert cells as paragraphs, tabs, commas, or a symbol of your choice (for example, a dash).

Editing Cell Properties

Cell properties can be assigned to individual cells, columns, rows of cells, or selected blocks of contiguous cells. You can select the cells that you want to format from the Table menu. The options include Select Cell, Select Row, Select Column, and Select Table. Alternatively, you can click and drag to select cells.

Definable cell properties include the following:

✦ Horizontal and vertical alignment

✦ Text wrapping options

✦ Minimum cell size

✦ Background colors

If you move your cursor just to the left of a row, or just above a column, an arrow appears pointing to the row or column. By clicking, you can select an entire row or column, as shown in Figure 6-7.

The Cell Properties dialog box, shown in Figure 6-8, provides quick access to all the formatting options available to individual cells within the table. To open this dialog box, select the cells to which you will apply attributes, right-click, and then select Cell Properties from the pop-up menu. The following sections detail each portion of this dialog box.

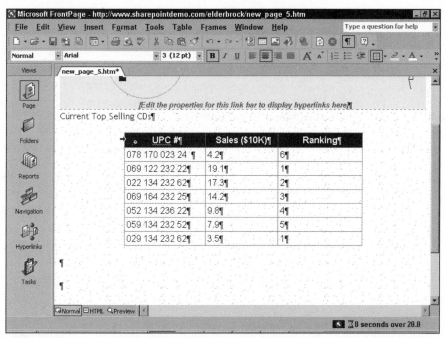

Figure 6-7: Entire rows or columns can be selected by moving your cursor to the top of a column or to the left edge of a row. Other rectangular groups of contiguous (touching) cells can be selected by clicking and dragging within a table. Noncontiguous cells can be selected using Ctrl+Click.

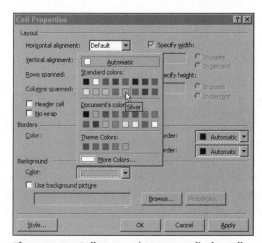

Figure 6-8: Cell properties are applied to all selected cells. Here, a silver background is being applied to alternate rows in a table to make the data easier to read.

Note Sometimes, either the Specify Width or Specify Height areas are grayed out in the Cell Properties dialog box. You can activate these areas by selecting the corresponding checkboxes.

Layout

The Layout section of the Cell Properties dialog box controls how text and graphics are placed within the cell. The settings in this area are as follows:

✦ **Horizontal Alignment:** Determines where the text or graphic is placed horizontally within the cell. The options are default, left, right, and center. Typically, browsers display the default setting as left. You can also perform this alignment by using the Align Left, Center, and Align Right icons on the toolbar.

✦ **Vertical Alignment:** Determines where the text or graphic is placed vertically within the cell. The options are default, top, middle, baseline, and bottom. Baseline makes the bottom of all letters in the row line up, no matter what the size. Oddly enough, the default vertical alignment setting is middle, instead of top. Therefore, you will usually want to change this so that text in cells aligns at the top of a row. You can also define these alignments (with the exception of default) by using the Align Top, Center Vertically, and Align Bottom icons on the Table toolbar.

✦ **Header Cell:** Makes the text within the cell bold (typically), although how it is actually displayed depends on the browser being used. This feature is a remnant of an earlier era when browsers were not able to interpret the same format commands that they recognize today. You probably won't find this feature too useful, because you can apply your own custom formatting to any cell in a table.

✦ **Rows Spanned and Columns Spanned:** You can use these spin boxes to merge cells by defining a cell as spanning more than one column or row.

✦ **No Wrap:** Forces text to remain on one line. This setting overrides the minimum size settings for other columns. Minimum size is discussed in the next section.

Defining cell height and width

The Specify Width and Specify Height checkboxes in the Cell Properties dialog box activate the fields that enable you to enter width and height for the selected cell(s). Note that the width setting applies to all cells in a particular column, and height applies to all cells in a row.

 Note Some browsers can't display tables if the height and width settings don't make mathematical sense, or the table layout gets distorted. For instance, if the overall width of the table is 500 pixels and the width of the individual columns (plus the cell padding and cell spacing for each column) is 510 pixels, the browser may display the table erratically, or may even crash. A good rule of thumb is as follows: If you specify your table width or height in pixels, set the columns and rows in pixels as well. As mentioned earlier, using percent instead of pixels is a safer way to define minimum table or cell size.

If you are editing a table, it is generally easier to set row and column sizing by clicking and dragging on the dividers between rows or columns in Page view, rather than defining sizes in the Cell Properties dialog box. An exception would be if you wanted to size a cell exactly — to match an image, for example.

To quickly make a number of columns the same width, highlight cells in two or more columns and then either select Table ⇨ Distribute Columns Evenly or click the Distribute Columns Evenly icon in the Table toolbar. To quickly make a number of rows the same height, highlight two or more rows and then either select Table ⇨ Distribute Rows Evenly or click the Distribute Rows Evenly icon in the Table toolbar.

Merging and splitting cells

Spanning cells are cells that take the space of two or more cells. Merging cells generally is easier and more intuitive by using the Table toolbar or the Table ⇨ Merge Cells menu option.

Merging cells can be a valuable creative technique when using tables as a design tool. For example, the table in Figure 6-9 combines a cell that spans two columns with other cells broken into different columns. The merged cell uses an aligned image to combine a picture with extra text.

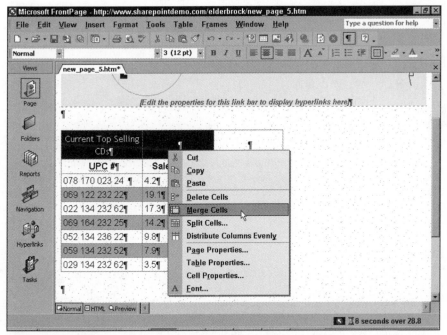

Figure 6-9: Merging cells that span two or more rows or columns are an effective design technique for displaying table data.

Custom backgrounds

As with the table and page, individual cells can have background colors. In addition, cells can have background images. If you select more than one cell and apply a tiling background image, the image will tile seamlessly between the cells.

Background images can be a particularly interesting layout tool, if used sparingly. They are a form of layering one object over another — usually text (in a table cell) on top of an image (as the cell background). In Figure 6-10, a picture of a graph has been used as the background image for the top cell in the table.

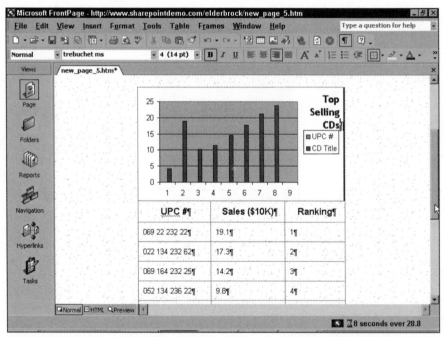

Figure 6-10: In this cell, the image is actually the cell background. The image has been "cropped" by sizing the cell height and width. The text "on top" of the image is the cell contents. The text in this instance has been forced to the right side of the image simply by embedding forced line breaks (Shift+Enter).

Border colors

The three options in the Border Colors section enable you to set the colors for the border of an individual cell, rather than the entire table. Light Border refers to the bottom and right edges of the cell, and Dark Border refers to the top and left edges of the cell — this is the opposite of their positions for the table's outline. If the table border is set to 0 width, these settings have no effect.

Should You Use Background Images in Cells?

One drawback to using background images in cells is that browsers of version 3 generation (or earlier) cannot interpret cell background images or colors.

FrontPage grays out the capability to assign cell and table background images unless you choose Internet Explorer Only as your target browser. (To do that, select Tools ➪ Page Settings.) Click the Compatibility tab and choose Microsoft Internet Explorer Only from the Browsers drop-down list.

There are subtle differences in how Netscape (various versions) and IE handle background images. You should test your page in each browser, but you can certainly experiment with using background images in cells or tables using either browser.

Adjusting Table Structure

You can easily add or delete rows, columns, and cells with the Table toolbar. The Table toolbar also enables you to merge cells easily to create irregular tables for design purposes. You can apply Table tools by selecting a table and then displaying the toolbar (Table ➪ Draw Table).

Inserting rows, columns, and cells

To insert a row by using the Table toolbar, highlight the row below where you want to add the new row and then click the Insert Rows icon. A new row appears. Each cell of the new row has settings identical to the one below it (the one that you highlighted).

To insert a column by using the Table toolbar, highlight the column to the right of where you want to add the new column and then click the Insert Column icon. A new column appears. Each cell of the new column has settings identical to the one to its right.

To insert a row or column by using the menu options, select Table ➪ Insert Rows or Columns. The Insert Rows or Columns dialog box opens, which enables you to add additional rows and/or columns to the table. New rows or columns can be inserted above or below the selected row, and to the left or right of a selected column. You can insert one or more rows or columns at a time.

To insert a cell, highlight the cell to the right of where you want the new cell located and select Table ➪ Insert Cell. A new cell with the original cell's properties appears.

An alternative way to create new cells is to split a single cell in two. To split a cell, simply place the cursor inside the cell (or highlight several cells) and then either select Table ⇨ Split Cells or click the Split Cells icon on the Table toolbar. This opens the Split Cells dialog box. Select the options that you want from this dialog box and click OK to split all the highlighted cells.

As discussed earlier in this chapter, you can also split cells by using the Draw Table tool, available on the Table toolbar. Select the tool and draw a vertical or horizontal line in the cell, or cells, that you want to split.

Reducing the number of cells, rows, and columns

Some options remove a table's cells, but not the text or graphics inside of them. To delete a row or a column, select the row or column to be deleted and select Table ⇨ Delete Cells. All the highlighted cells are removed.

Merging cells is a nondestructive alternative to deleting cells. When this option is used, all the text or graphics from the merged cells is placed within the new cell. To merge cells, highlight the cells that you want merged and then either select Table ⇨ Merge Cells or click the Merge Cells icon on the Table toolbar.

Note   You can also use the table eraser in the Table toolbar to merge cells.

Designing Layout with Tables

Using tables enables you to implement design features that are difficult or impossible to create with normal HTML formatting controls. The most widely used of these features is the capability to create column layouts on your Web pages. Many hard-copy layout designers suggest column layout for text to make it easier to read. With an imaginative use of columns, you can create a magazine-like appearance for your Web page.

Page Templates

Now that you know how to work with tables, you can explore some of FrontPage's page templates that use tables for page layout. To choose from these templates, choose File ⇨ New ⇨ Page or Web. Click the Page Templates link, and explore table-based templates by checking out the Preview section of the Page Templates dialog box as you click on templates, as shown in Figure 6-11.

You can also use columns to introduce two or more articles at the top of a Web page. Tables can also be used to manipulate a combination of images and text, as shown in Figure 6-12, which has a three-column layout that includes sidebar text, descriptive text, and matching images.

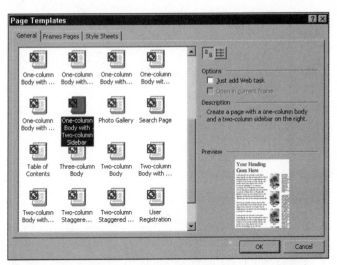

Figure 6-11: As long as you understand how to work with tables, you can start from one of FrontPage's table-based page layout templates, and add your own text and images.

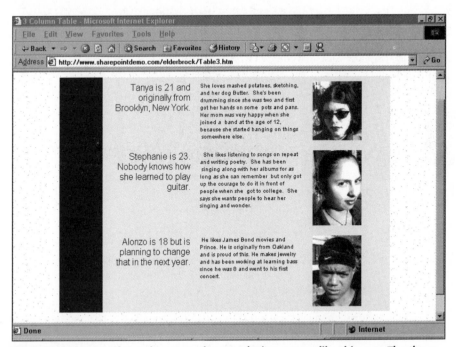

Figure 6-12: Tutorial 6-2 shows you how to design a page like this one. The three columns are defined by table cells. The column on the left was created by merging all cells in the first column.

Tutorial 6-2: Designing a three-column layout

In the following tutorial, you will create a Web page that combines text, graphics, and a third column that functions as a sidebar to what visitors see as a table.

For this tutorial, you can improvise your own text.

1. Start with a new blank page: Select File ➪ New ➪ Page and select the Normal Page template.

2. Save this page as `Table3.htm` with the title 3-Column Table.

3. Type a heading for the page.

4. Use the Insert Table tool to create a three-column, four-row table.

5. Select all the cells in the first column and then select Table ➪ Merge Cells.

6. Enter text in the cells, and add pictures.

7. Select all the cells and assign top-vertical alignment to them (use the Cell Properties dialog box).

8. Assign a yellow background to the table and a dark-colored background to the cell on the left side of the table. Format the text with a light-colored font.

9. Use the Table Properties dialog box to assign a border size of 0 (no border), and then assign 6 pixels for cell padding and 0 pixels for cell spacing.

10. Add font attributes (color, font type, and size). Save your table and then preview it in a browser.

Designing with Photo Gallery

FrontPage 2002 introduces a set of page templates that package together table layout, thumbnail generation, and descriptive text. In addition, the slideshow option enables you to set up a slideshow in which viewers can choose a thumbnail and see a full-sized picture on the same page.

Generating a table-based photo gallery

You can place a photo gallery anywhere on a page, but consider creating a new page for each gallery — to keep download time to a minimum and to keep your pages from appearing too cluttered.

With your cursor where you want to place the photo gallery, choose Insert ➪ Web Component, and click Photo Gallery in the list of components.

Choose one of the photo gallery options (except the slideshow) that is displayed on the right side of the Insert Web Component dialog box. Slideshows work a bit differently than other photo galleries, and we'll look at them in the next section. Once you choose a layout, click Finish. Don't worry, you're not truly finished — you will be prompted to add photos, captions, and descriptions. As soon as you click Finish, the Photo Gallery Properties dialog box opens.

The Layout tab of the Photo Gallery Properties dialog box enables you to change your mind about which layout to use. Select the Pictures tab to choose the images you want to display. The caption you enter for each image will be displayed under the picture (and also when a visitor's cursor hovers over it). If you chose a layout that allows descriptions, you can enter them here as well.

To add an image from a file to your photo gallery, click the Add button in the Photo Gallery Properties dialog box, choose Pictures from Files, and navigate to a picture file. Then choose Open in the Open File dialog box. If you are placing images directly from a scanner or digital camera, click the Add button and choose Pictures from Scanner or Camera.

After (or as) you add pictures, you can assign captions and descriptions. You can also assign fonts, font sizes, and font colors to captions and descriptions here. Some browsers display these captions, others don't — as shown in Figure 6-13.

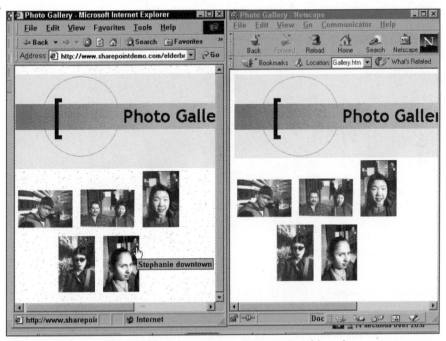

Figure 6-13: Captions are displayed when a visitor moves his or her cursor over a Photo Gallery thumbnail. Not all browsers support hovered captions.

When you finish adding pictures, captions, and definitions, click OK. When you do, FrontPage generates thumbnail (small) versions of your images for the photo gallery, and creates links from your thumbnails to full-size images.

If you need to change your photo gallery layout, just double-click the gallery in FrontPage Page view.

Creating a slideshow

Slideshows are similar to other photo galleries, except that selected images display in the same page as the gallery, as shown in Figure 6-14.

Figure 6-14: The slideshow photo gallery works best when full-size images fit in a browser window.

To create a slideshow, follow these steps:

1. Choose Insert ➪ Web Component ➪ Photo Gallery.

2. Click on Slideshow Layout in the Choose a Photo Gallery Option area of the Insert Web Component dialog box.

3. Click Finish to open the Photo Gallery Properties dialog box.

4. Click the Add button, and choose Pictures from Files (or Pictures from Scanner or Camera).

Note If you insert pictures from a scanner or camera, your options will depend on your installed hardware.

5. Double-click on a picture in the File Open dialog box to add it to the slideshow.

6. Enter text in the Caption and Description areas of the Photo Gallery Properties dialog box to add captions and descriptions to the photos.

7. Use the Add button to add more photos to your slideshow, and define captions and descriptions for each photo.

8. After you add photos, use the Edit button to change a selected photo, the Remove button to delete a photo from the slideshow, and the Move Up or Move Down button to change the order of the slideshow.

9. Click OK to generate the slideshow. You can test it in the Preview tab or in a browser.

Behind the scenes

When you generate a photo gallery, FrontPage creates a new folder in your Web site named _photogallery, and a subfolder for each specific gallery. You can see these folders if you view hidden folders (select Tools ➭ Web Settings, click the Advanced tab, and click the Show Hidden Files and Folders checkbox).

Each photo gallery folder contains picture files, HTML files, and JavaScript files. Picture files represent the images in the Photo Gallery, as well as the smaller-sized thumbnail images used in the gallery. The HTML pages in the folder are used to display the photos. If you used the slideshow photo gallery, your _photogallery folder also includes JavaScript files that control the slideshow page.

You can open (and edit) the generated HTML pages in photo gallery folders. You'll see that they rely on tables to control page layout.

Organizing Text in Blocks

Somewhere in between formatting pages and formatting tables lies the useful formatting technique of formatting text blocks. As a side effect of applying a border or shading to a block of text, FrontPage assigns *dimensions in pixels* to that block. The technical side of this relates to the <DIV> HTML code that FrontPage uses to control borders and shading. All we need to know, however, is that once you apply borders and shading to a section of text, you can shape that block of text.

Note   Chapter 5 explores using borders and shading. Here, we are "tricking" FrontPage into thinking we're applying borders and shading so that we can easily define dimensions for blocks of text and images.

To manage text width through an applied border, first select the paragraphs to which you will be defining dimensions. Then, with the paragraphs selected, choose Format ⇨ Borders and Shading. Choose *any* border or shading attribute — such as a light background. You can later change the background back to the page background so that visitors will not see any background or border effects applied to this text.

After you assign a border or shading, you'll note a dotted line around the block of text to which you applied border or shading effects. Clicking inside that block activates sizing handles on the corners and sides of the block. You can click and drag on side or corner handles to resize blocks of text, as shown in Figure 6-15.

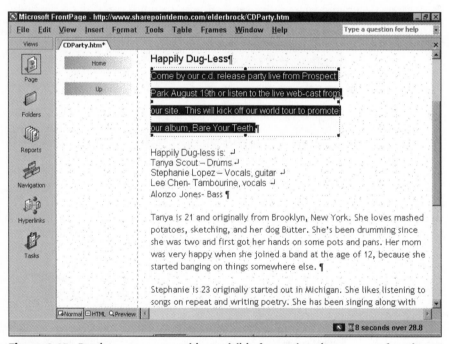

Figure 6-15: Borders, even ones with no visible formatting changes, can function as sizable page blocks.

Using Absolute Positioning As a Design Tool

With the advent of versions 4.0 of IE and Netscape Navigator, browsers began to support absolute positioning of objects on Web pages. Page designers eagerly anticipated the kind of object-location control that they enjoyed in desktop publishing and print design programs.

The biggest drawback to absolute positioning is that it is not interpreted by version 3 browsers and earlier. Beyond that limitation, Web page designers need to keep in mind that the biggest variable determining how viewers see your page is the size of their monitor. An absolutely positioned image that is located in the middle of a 640-pixel-wide screen will be on the left quarter of a 1,600-pixel-wide screen.

Absolute positioning is most effective when you are designing for a controlled audience, and you know the browser and monitor specifications of your viewers. With that kind of a managed environment, you can confidently locate images and text at exact locations on a page. Without such a closed environment, you need to carefully test the effect of your positioned objects on differently sized monitors and in differently sized browser windows.

Positioning images

To position a selected image, click the Position Absolutely button on the Pictures toolbar. As you do, a four-arrow cursor will appear when your mouse hovers over the image. Click and drag the image to any location on the page, as shown in Figure 6-16.

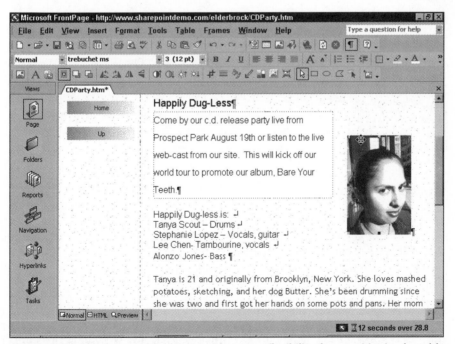

Figure 6-16: Absolute positioning provides more flexibility than positioning by tables, and is interpreted by browsers of generation 4.0 and later.

You have additional control over image position with the Positioning toolbar (select View ➪ Toolbars ➪ Positioning). Use the Positioning toolbar to control how overlapping images pile on top of one another. The Move To Front and Move To Back buttons in the Positioning toolbar enable you to control which of the overlapping images is on top, as shown in Figure 6-17.

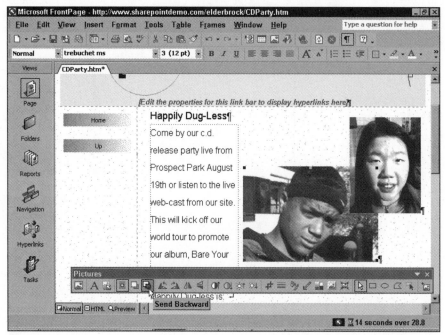

Figure 6-17: Absolutely positioned images can be moved in front of or behind each other.

Positioning text

To position text, first select the text, and then click the Position Absolutely button in the Positioning toolbar. The selected *paragraph* (not just the selected text, but the entire paragraph) becomes a movable text block. You can resize the movable text block by clicking and dragging on the bottom or right side handles that appear when the block is selected.

As with images, you can use the Bring Foward and Send Backward buttons in the Absolute Positioning toolbar to move text in front of other absolutely positioned objects. For example, in Figure 6-18, text has been positioned on top of a picture.

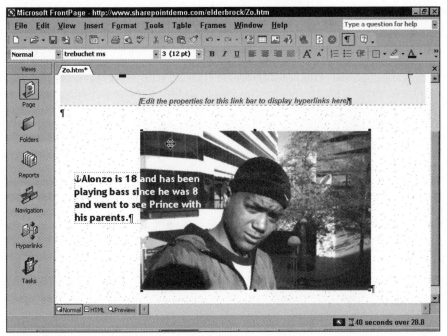

Figure 6-18: Here, the text is visible on top of the image in Netscape Navigator 6.0. Netscape 4.7 users, however, will not see the text, as that browser doesn't support the "front and back" features of absolute positioning as defined by FrontPage.

How absolute positioning works

In this chapter, we've looked at absolute positioning as a layout tool, and not delved much into what makes it work (or not work!). You'll learn how absolute positioning is achieved in Chapter 11, and examine different options for controlling and positioning objects.

In the following sections, you'll explore some important issues to consider in using absolute positioning.

Absolute positioning is defined by styles

Absolute positioning is an attribute of style sheets. Positioning is actually part of a style definition attached to HTML tags. We cut that process short in this chapter by using the Positioning toolbar. But while we were having fun moving objects around the page, FrontPage was actually generating styles that embedded the location information required to display images or text in defined positions.

Note   For a full exploration of how Cascading Style Sheets uses tags to define text positioning, see Chapter 11.

Absolute positioning compatibility issues

Because absolute positioning relies on Cascading Style Sheets 2.0 (CSS 2.0), only browsers that interpret CSS 2.0 are capable of interpreting absolute positioning.

In exploring browser compatibility issues related to styles in Chapter 5, we took a relatively tolerant and worry-free approach to browser compatibility. If a visitor comes to your site with a browser that does not faithfully interpret a border around text, he or she is still likely to be able to read text on that page. (An exception would be if you placed light text on top of dark paragraph shading, and used a light-colored page background. In this case, a browser that didn't interpret the border would render the text invisible.)

However, the likelihood of browser incompatibility problems with absolute positioning is much greater. If the absolute positioning is not interpreted by a browser, the page can be rendered dysfunctional, with text and images placed in random locations on the page.

 Note   On our request list for the next version of FrontPage would be a feature our Dreamweaver friends have had for some time – the ability to automatically convert page layouts from layers (absolute positioning) into tables.

If you are confident that all your visitors will be using Netscape 4+, or Internet Explorer 4+ browsers, you can utilize absolute positioning. However, even Navigator 4.7 does not fully support the front and back features of absolute positioning—as defined in FrontPage. If your site must be more fully browser-friendly, see Chapter 11 for a discussion of problems and solutions to browser compatibility issues for absolutely positioned objects.

If you want to design for older browsers (pre–version 3.0 for IE, and pre–version 4 for Netscape Navigator), you can disable absolute positioning. To do that, choose Tools ➪ Page Options, and click the Compatibility tab in the Page Options dialog box. You can either manually deselect the CSS 2.0 (Positioning) checkbox, or you can choose 3.0 or later in the Browser Versions drop-down list. In either case, you'll turn off FrontPage's absolute positioning features. These features will be grayed out in menus, and the Positioning toolbar will be grayed out as well.

Summary

One of the most effective ways to control page design is to use tables. The rows and columns of a table create cells that can hold text and pictures. Visitors to your site will see positioned text and pictures without seeing any evidence that a table is providing the layout structure for your page.

Tables are also used to present data in columns and rows. Tables can be easily copied or imported from Excel, Word, or Access.

FrontPage 2002 introduces another tool for page layout — the Photo Gallery. Four different options allow you to present pictures interactively on a page by automatically generating thumbnail image files, and tables to display your photos.

A more advance technique for placing objects on a page is absolute positioning. With absolute positioning, objects can overlap each other. The big drawback is that absolute positioning is not interpreted reliably by browsers.

✦　　✦　　✦

Designing Pages with Shared Borders and Frames

Both shared borders and frames enable you to design Web pages that combine fixed and changing elements. With shared borders and frames, you can "frame" Web pages with what are basically other Web pages. In this way, you can provide a consistent look to sections of your Web site, and anchor your visitors with elements that provide navigational links.

You were introduced to shared borders in Chapter 1, when you created your first Web site. You saw how these borders are shared between different pages in your Web site. Frames allow two or more discrete, scrollable Web pages to be viewed simultaneously in a visitor's browser window. Frames are more complex than shared borders and allow for more design options.

Although both shared borders and frames involve complex HTML coding, FrontPage 2002 makes it easy to create these elements graphically. In this chapter, you'll learn how to place, design, and fine-tune shared borders, and then learn how to create and link frame pages.

Working with Shared Borders

Normally, shared borders are used together with link bars. Embedded shared borders work well as a uniform element on multiple pages in your site. By including link bars in shared borders, you create dynamic navigational areas common to every page in your site.

However, you can add much more than navigation links to your shared borders. In fact, a shared border can include all the objects of a regular Web page, such as formatted text, graphic images, or even interactive elements (for example, a hit counter or table of contents). Figure 7-1 shows a Web page with a link bars in the top shared border, and text and a graphic in the left shared border.

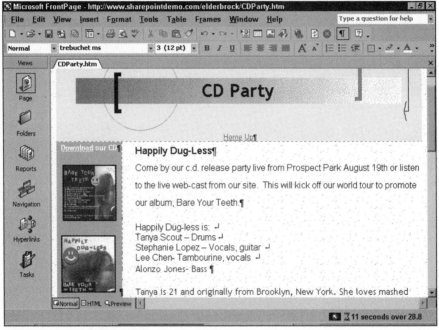

Figure 7-1: A Web page with shared borders

Note   In our seminars, we invariably find students who have unconsciously placed objects in shared borders, and then wonder why those objects appear on every page of their site. Remember that when you place any object in a shared border, that object appears wherever that border is embedded.

The page shown in Figure 7-1 has two shared borders — on the top and left sides of the page. The shared borders have their own page properties (namely, background color). In fact, they are separate pages, embedded within other pages. The border on top has a generated link bar, along with a generated title (based on the page title). The border on the left has a navigation link, as well as a couple of images that will appear on every page.

Adding shared borders

In Chapter 1, you learned to add shared borders to a Web page by selecting Format ➪ Shared Borders. By default, the Shared Borders dialog box adds shared borders to the right and top of your Web page. This chapter describes in detail how you can define the location of shared borders on your Web pages and throughout a Web site.

The Shared Borders dialog box opens when you select Format ➪ Shared Borders — in Page, Folders, Navigation, Hyperlinks, or Tasks view. However, this dialog box functions a bit differently in Page view, where you have the option of defining shared borders either for the page that you are editing or for the entire Web. When you open the Shared Borders dialog box in the other views, you have the option of defining shared borders either for selected pages or for the entire Web. In Folders view, you can choose which selected pages you want to control by holding down the Control key and clicking the page(s) in the Folder list. The Shared Borders dialog box that appears in Folders, Navigation, Hyperlinks, or Tasks view is shown in Figure 7-2.

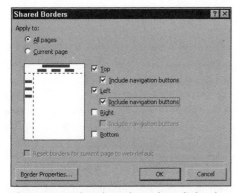

Figure 7-2: The Shared Borders dialog box is being used here to define top and left borders for the entire Web site.

The Shared Borders dialog box looks a little different when you select Format ➪ Shared Borders in Page view. In Page view, you can use the Format Shared Borders dialog box to turn off shared borders *only* for the open page. This is handy when you want to include in your site one-of-a-kind page layouts that don't have the same shared borders assigned generally throughout the site.

To assign shared borders, click the Top, Left, Right, or Bottom checkboxes to assign shared borders to the top, left, right, or bottom of the page(s), respectively.

Tip

Usually, designers avoid shared borders on the right side of a Web page. From a functional perspective, the right side of a page may be beyond the browser window, requiring a visitor to scroll horizontally to see it. From an aesthetic standpoint, most visitors are used to looking to the top or left side of a page for anchoring elements. Bottom shared borders can be useful for shared navigational links or other objects that function as a page "footer."

When you click the OK button in the Shared Borders dialog box, you are actually creating or editing *new HTML Web pages*. These special shared border pages are embedded in the left, right, top, or bottom of each page in your Web site. You can define up to four of these shared borders for the entire Web site. In other words, you can have only one top shared border, one left shared border, and so on.

Controlling link bars

The left and top shared borders that are generated with Web sites can include link bars — just check the Include Navigation Buttons checkboxes in the top and/or left shared borders. If you want to insert link bars manually into a shared border (or just in a regular Web page), follow these steps:

1. With your cursor where you want to insert a link bars (and that's usually inside a shared border), choose Insert ➪ Navigation. This opens the Insert Web Component dialog box, with Navigation already selected in the Component Type list.

2. In the Choose a Bar Type list, click Bar Based on Navigational Structure.

3. Click Finish to jump to the Link Bar Properties dialog box. For a discussion of the various approaches to link bar structures, refer to Chapter 2.

The links generated in link bars are based on the structure of your Web site. If you plan to include navigation links in your shared borders, *you must define a Web structure in FrontPage's Navigation view*. You can define a Web structure in Navigation view by dragging pages from the Folder list on the left into the Navigation view area on the right. Figure 7-3 shows a page being dragged from the Folder list into the Navigation view, where it is being defined as a child of an existing page in the navigation structure.

"But I want *different* links on each page...."

"Wait!," you protest, "What if want to manually define different navigation links on each page?" Then don't use link bars. You have to decide whether you want the convenience of having FrontPage generate your links, or you want to create them yourself. Of course, you can *supplement* the generated links in a link bars with additional links that you insert manually — either in a page or in a shared border. However, if you place link bars on a page, they will simply reflect the navigational structure you defined for your site in Navigation view.

Consider a couple of scenarios: If you are generating a 78,000-page intranet Web site that organizes personnel policies for your company, a handcrafted, artsy look and feel to your site isn't as important as a reliable, easily maintainable navigational structure that updates as your site changes. At the other extreme, a 12-page Web site for an art gallery devoted to iconoclastic abstract artists of the first century doesn't need generated site-wide link bars. For a site like that, you could just place links on each page manually, as needed. Sometimes you just have to try both approaches.

Caution   Our technical editor, who maintains a FrontPage help site, tells us he receives e-mails "almost daily" on this subject. Many people don't realize that you *must* create a navigation structure for link bars to work. Remember: *First* build a navigation flowchart in Navigation view, *then* add link bars.

FrontPage includes a handy feature that helps you to locate a Web page in Navigation view. To locate a file in your navigation flowchart, right-click the file in the Folder list and choose Find in Navigation from the context menu.

You can edit the structure of the navigation links in Navigation view by clicking and dragging Web pages in the flowchart. After you define navigation links in Navigation view, you can generate link bars for your Web site.

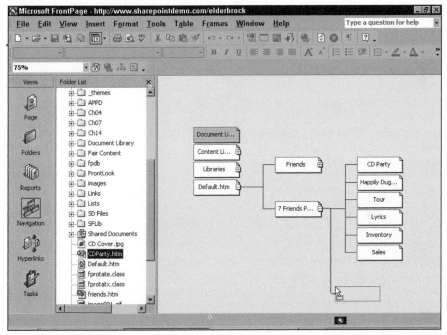

Figure 7-3: Dragging a page into the navigation structure controls how that page will appear in link bars.

The advantage of link bars is that you can instantly create a coherent and consistent series of navigational links in every page, or many pages, of your Web site. The disadvantage is that they are applied in a uniform way to every page in your Web and cannot be manually tweaked or customized for each page.

Figure 7-4 contrasts a Web site with extensive link bars, with a site that has only minimal, and manually created links.

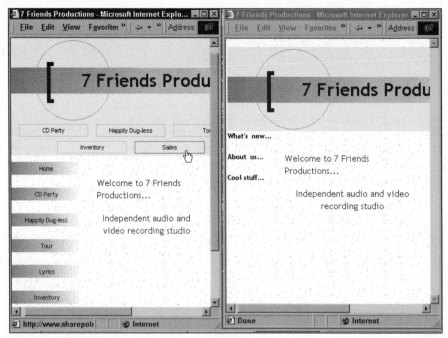

Figure 7-4: The page on the left uses "traditional" FrontPage-style link bars. The site on the right does not have link bars — instead it has a few links in a shared border that were entered by hand.

Changing shared border formatting

Compared to earlier versions, FrontPage 2002 makes it easy to modify the background color or image of shared borders. To assign a new color to a shared border, just right-click in any shared border on a page, and choose Border Properties from the context menu. In the Border Properties dialog box, use the Border drop-down menu to pick which border you want to format (if there is more than one border on the page).

Once you select a border, you can use the Color checkbox and drop-down menu to choose a background color, or the Picture checkbox and the Browse button to place an image behind a shared border, as shown in Figure 7-5.

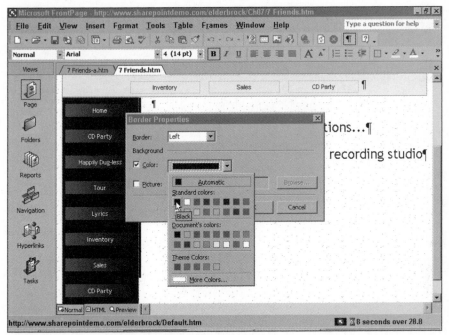

Figure 7-5: Here, we're assigning a black background to the left shared border.

Modifying shared border page properties

The new capability to edit shared border properties in FrontPage 2002 is nice, but if *we* ruled the world, we would have had the folks at Microsoft include the capability to define other page properties, such as default text colors, link colors, and other style options. You can still do that kind of formatting on shared border pages. You just need to find them.

Note   Keep in mind that embedded shared borders are actually *Web pages*.

To view shared borders pages, you must first tell FrontPage to show you hidden folders. To do that, choose Tools ➪ Web Settings, and click the Advanced tab in the Web Settings dialog box. Click the Show Hidden Files and Folders checkbox so the _borders folder in your Web becomes visible. This is where the HTML files that make up your embedded shared borders are found. You can open them from Folder view by double-clicking them. Figure 7-6 shows the contents of a _borders folder.

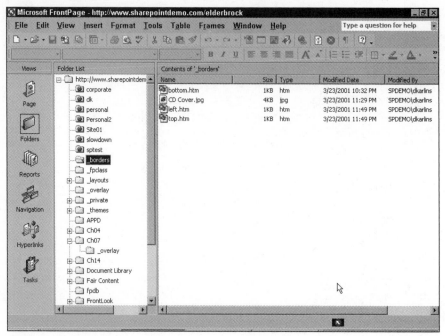

Figure 7-6: This shared borders (_borders) folder includes three HTML files for the top, bottom, and left borders used in the site. Note that an image file included in a shared border is also saved here. Any of these files can be opened and edited.

Changing shared border content

Shared borders can include much more than link bars. You can edit them in basically the same way that you edit any Web page. Following are two ways to edit shared borders:

✦ Edit the shared borders in a Web page.

✦ Open a page incorporating shared borders in Page view and edit the shared border option(s) as you normally would edit any other page. When you save the page, you are prompted to save the changes made to the shared borders.

The second option works well if you don't plan to edit the borders very much. By editing in place, you can see exactly how the border will appear.

Editing shared borders

You can change the content (and page properties) of border pages by opening them and editing them as you would any other page.

One downside to editing shared border pages in Page view, however, is that you have no direct control over the size of your borders, so it is difficult to gauge whether your edits will look good in your Web pages.

If you edit border content while looking at an open page (in which the border page is embedded), it's easier to determine how wide (or high) the border will be. Border page width is determined automatically by FrontPage. If you want to force a border to be wider, you can include an image of the width you want (a thin bar works well). Alternately, you can place a one-cell table in a shared border, and set the border width by defining the table width in pixels, as shown in Figure 7-7.

Figure 7-7: Although you cannot define the width (or height) of shared borders manually, our favorite work-around is to insert a one-cell table into a shared border, and use it to define border size.

Creating a Frame Set

Now that you understand how shared borders can be combined with Web pages, you can begin to explore the possibilities of combining more than one page within a browser window. Remember that the shared borders are actually separate Web pages. Therefore, when a visitor sees what appears to be a single Web page with shared borders, he or she is actually seeing more than one Web page in the browser window.

Frames allow more control than shared borders over the process of combining Web pages in a browser window. Pages designed with frames are called *frame sets,* because they are actually a set of HTML pages. Every frame page, or frame set, consists of at least three HTML files: the file that controls the frame structure, and at least two different HTML files that are displayed at one time.

Using frames as navigational aids

One of the advantages of working with frame sets is that each page that displays within a frame set can be navigated independently. Each frame page that appears in the browser window can have its own scroll bar, and hyperlinks from one frame can jump a visitor to another Web page, while other parts of the frame set remain in place. One of the most useful implementations of frames is using a navigation frame to display other pages, while the navigation link remains in the browser window — as illustrated in Figure 7-8. Here, the left frame has links that display pages in the right frame.

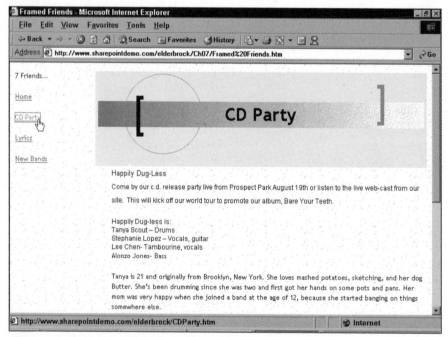

Figure 7-8: Navigation links in the left side of this framed page display pages on the right side of the framed page. The "framed" look on the left is mitigated slightly by the absence of a scrollbar.

Figure 7-9 is a peek behind the scenes at this Web page. You can see that two different Web pages are actually displayed in Page view.

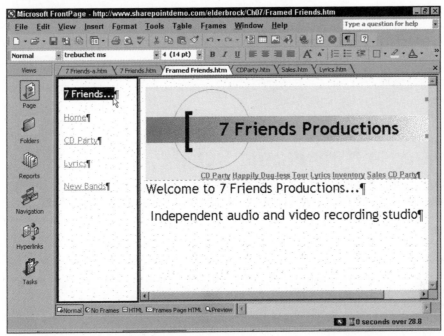

Figure 7-9: You can edit individual frames within a frame set in FrontPage.

Tip   Normally, you shouldn't use both shared borders and frames in a single page, because they play a similar role in page and site design, and they both take up some of your available page space.

Designing with frames can be somewhat complex. One of FrontPage's best features, however, is its ability to put together frame sets in a graphical manner. FrontPage simplifies the technical side of creating frames. The biggest challenge for you as a FrontPage Web designer is to put together an effective combination of pages.

Keeping frame hassles under control

Frames present a few unique challenges. One is aesthetic. A Web site crowded with complex frame sets can be distracting and annoying to visitors. Remember that most visitors are viewing your Web site with limited monitor space, and breaking that space into four or more frames divides that screen into unwieldy chunks.

Furthermore, not all browsers interpret frames. FrontPage makes this problem easy to solve by building in alternative Web pages for visitors who don't have frame-friendly browsers.

A third potential pitfall is that if links are not correctly designed, your visitors can find themselves wandering like Alice in Wonderland through a room full of increasingly smaller frames within frames within frames. "Creating Hyperlinks in Frame Sets," later in this chapter, describes how to avoid this particular snag.

Each of these challenges can be met if you decide that frames will enhance your Web site.

Creating a New Frame Set

The process of generating frames might seem a bit unwieldy in FrontPage. Not so when you understand what's going on behind the scenes. Remember that each frame set involves at least three Web pages: the *frame set* itself, and at least two pages that are displayed within the frame set.

The frame set, therefore, is a special kind of Web page. You don't put any content in it; it simply serves as a placeholder for the pages that will be displayed within it.

You can use a frame set to display existing Web pages or you can create pages for your frame set as you go. Either way, here's how to start creating a frame set in FrontPage:

1. In Page view, Select File ⇨ New ⇨ Page or Web.

2. Click Page Templates in the Task Pane. When the Page Templates dialog box opens, click the Frames tab to display the available pre-designed frame sets. These templates *are just a starting point*; you can make changes to any of the frame sets after you create the new page.

3. Select one of the frame sets from the list at the left, noting the layout shown in the right Preview window. To help make your decision, read the description of the frame set in the Description area. The default manner in which links work within the frame set is noted in this description. If you are unfamiliar with the way links work in a frame set, see the section "Creating Hyperlinks in Frame Sets," later in this chapter.

4. After you OK the Page Templates dialog box, your frame set will open. If you want to insert an existing page into a frame, click the Set Initial Page button in a frame, and navigate to and open an existing page. Alternately, you can click the New Page button, and begin to create and edit a new page from within the frame set.

5. As you edit the content of your frame set, notice the No Frames and Frames Page HTML tabs. These tabs enable you to view attributes that are available only in frames pages. These tabs are explained in the section "The two extra view tabs."

Editing or changing pages in a frame set

The current frame is the one indicated by the dark-blue border around it. You can change the current frame by clicking in another frame to select it.

To create a new page to display in a frame, click the New Page button. A clean, blank page appears. If you'd rather include a frame set within a frame (called a *nested frame*), select the frame and create a new frame set, making sure to check the Open in Current Frame checkbox.

FrontPage doesn't accurately display nested frames in Page view but instead shows a new View Frames Page button. Clicking this button changes Page view to display the frame set in the current frame. If you are editing a nested frame set, change the size of the Page view window to more accurately reflect the size of the frame in which the set is displayed in the main frame set. This will help you to picture how the frames will look in a browser. In addition, Preview mode does display nested frames properly.

To change the page in a frame, right-click in the frame and choose Frame Properties from the context menu. Use the Browser button to locate and insert a different page in the frame set.

After you create or add pages to your frame set, you can edit them as you would any normal page. Notice that when you select a different frame to edit, the dark-blue border shifts to that frame, and its filename appears in the FrontPage title bar.

Editing frame set properties

You can click and drag the border between frames to change frame sizes, as shown in Figure 7-10. Other frame properties can be changed in the Frame Properties dialog box.

The Frame Properties dialog box (accessed by selecting Frames ➪ Frame Properties or by right-clicking within the frame and selecting Frame Properties from the context menu) also contains other options relating to the frame.

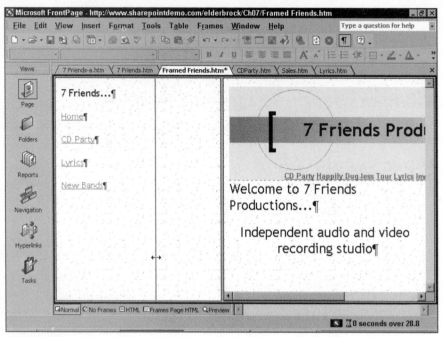

Figure 7-10: Resizing frames is easy — click and drag.

The following options are available in the Frame Properties dialog box:

✦ **Name:** The name given to the HTML file that defines the frame itself. The name is important because it is used to indicate the "target" for any hyperlink that may be intended for this frame.

✦ **Initial Page:** The page that appears automatically when the frame set is opened. Earlier, you learned to make this link by using the Set Initial Page button in a frame, and navigating to and opening an existing page. This is an alternative way to assign a page to a frame.

✦ **Frame Size Width and Height:** These two options determine the size of the frame. Changing the width or height of a frame affects other frames in the same row or column. Select units from the right list box and set the size in the left text box. Three units are available for frame sizing:

  • **Relative:** Sets the frame's size relative to the setting for other frames in the row or column, as long as they are using one of the other options. When using this option, set the amount in the left text box to 1.

  • **Percent:** Sets the frame's size as a percentage of the browser screen's height or width.

  • **Pixels:** Sets the frame's size as a specific number of pixels.

Note By default, the leftmost frame in a row and the topmost frame in a column are set in pixels; other frames are set to relative.

✦ **Margins:** The Width and Height spin boxes enable you to define margins for your frame set in pixels.

✦ **Resizable in Browser:** Used to enable users to resize the frame windows by dragging the divider bars. By default, all frames are resizable. Unless you have a good reason to constrict your Web site guests from resizing frame windows, this option generally makes your site more visitor-friendly.

✦ **Show Scrollbars:** The options in this drop-down list box are Always, which forces a scroll bar to always be present; Never, which forces no scrolling bar; and If Needed, which includes a scroll bar, if necessary, but doesn't show one if it's unnecessary. If Needed is the default option and is usually the most useful way for visitors to navigate your frame windows.

The bottom of the Frame Properties dialog box has the following additional two buttons, which reveal additional options:

✦ **Frames Page:** Opens the Frames tab in the Page Properties dialog box, which has two options:

• **Frame Spacing spin box:** Use to change spacing between frames in the frame set.

• **Show Borders check box:** Use to display (or hide) borders between frames.

✦ **Style:** Opens the Modify Style dialog box, in which you can click the Format button to assign inline style specifications for font type, paragraph alignment, and other default formatting.

Adding and deleting frames

If you need to add an additional frame to a frame set, you "split" an existing frame into two new frames. One of these two frames will contain the contents of the original frame, while the other will display the Set Initial Page, New Page, and Help buttons that are shown when the frame set is originally created. The following are the two ways to split a frame:

✦ Select the frame that you want to split and select Frames ⇨ Split Frame to open the Split Frame dialog box. Select either the Split into Columns or Split into Rows radio button and then click the OK button.

✦ Select the frame that you want to split and place the cursor over any border (including the four borders around the Page view window), so that the cursor changes to a two-headed arrow, and then use Ctrl+Drag to create the new frame.

The two extra view tabs

As mentioned earlier in the chapter, the bottom of the Page view screen has two additional view tabs that provide additional control over your frame set: No Frames and Frames Page HTML.

The No Frames tab displays the page content that is shown on browsers that don't support frames. By default, this page contains only the rather perfunctory message "This page uses frames, but your browser doesn't support them." Feel free to edit and embellish this page, as shown in Figure 7-11.

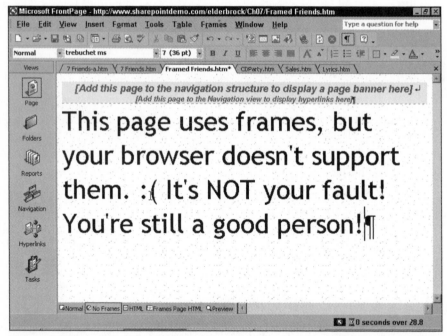

Figure 7-11: You can edit the No Frames page, just as you would any other page. Use this page to create access to your content for visitors with older browsers.

You can edit the No Frames page exactly like any other page. Remember, though, that browsers that can't display frames generally can't handle other "high tech" Web items, such as tables, JavaScript, and ActiveX controls, so you will want to avoid or limit their use. A useful way to fill the No Frames page is to copy the basic contents of your main frame (text and graphics) and paste them into the No Frames page.

The Frames Page HTML tab displays the HTML codes that define your frame set. The No Frames page codes are also contained here, between the tags `<noframes>` and `</noframes>`. In this case, the No Frames page only has the default message.

Creating Hyperlinks in Frame Sets

Creating hyperlinks within a frame set poses some new challenges. You need to indicate both the page to link to and the frame in which the page should appear.

When visitors click on a link in the navigation frame of a site, you generally do not want the target of that link to appear in the same frame. For example, in Figure 7-12, links in the top frame should open the target frame in the bottom frame. Otherwise, the top frame would be filled with content that didn't fit, and would not function as a navigation frame.

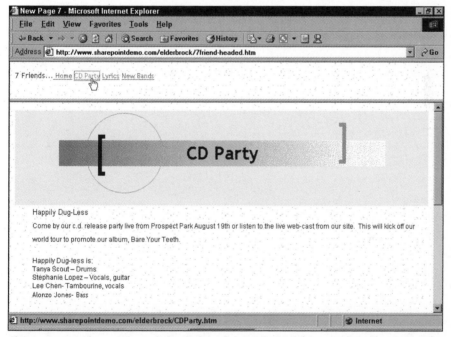

Figure 7-12: When visitors click a link in the top frame, they expect the target of the link to appear in the *bottom* frame — not the frame in which they clicked the link!

How does the frame set know to behave this way? HTML code located in each particular frames page within a frame set defines the default target for links on that page. If you want to explore the HTML, look at the Frames Page HTML tab in Page view and note that the tags defining the banner and contents frames (`<frame name="banner"` ... and `<frame name="contents"` ..., respectively) each contain the code `target="..."`. The name inside the quotation marks indicates the frame that should be opened when users click a link. The target information is also placed in each page's HTML code — click the HTML tab and notice the tag that reads `<base target="...">` near the top of the banner and contents frames.

FrontPage automatically adds the base target tag to your pages, whether you cre-ated them from scratch when you made the frame set or set them as initial pages later on. In the default links in the contents frame set template, for example, links from the left (contents) frame open pages in the right, main window. However, that's not always desirable. For example, if you have links from the contents frame to a Web page outside of your site, you may not want to display that page in your frame set. In that case, you have the option to change the target of a link.

Changing the link target

Changing the link target is done in the Target Frame dialog box. To change the default target for a page, follow these steps:

1. Open the frame set in Page view.

2. Select any link in the frame whose default target you want to change.

3. Select Insert ➪ Hyperlink, or click the Insert Hyperlink button on the toolbar, to open the Create (or Edit) Hyperlink dialog box.

4. Click the Target Frame button.

5. To open a link in one of the frames in your frame set, select the new target frame by clicking one of the frames in the Current Frames Page area, as shown in Figure 7-13.

Figure 7-13: Because the Set As Page Default checkbox is checked, the bottom frame is now defined as the default target for links in the top frame for this frame set.

Note To link to the default page for the frame set, choose the Page Default (main) option from the Common Targets list. The Same Frame option opens a link in the same frame as the link. The Whole Page option opens the linked page as a whole page. The New Window option opens the linked page in a new browser window. The Parent Frame option opens the link in the parent frame of a nested frame set.

6. To assign this target to other links in the page, select the checkbox labeled Set As Page Default.

7. Click OK in both the Target Frame and in the Insert Hyperlink (or Edit Hyperlink) dialog boxes to return to Page view.

8. Save your frame set. Notice that some extra time is taken to save — this is because FrontPage automatically changes the HTML code in the frames page.

Tip Different frame-link options are used for different navigation and design strategies. If you want to "lock in" visitors, display links from a contents frame in a main frame, leaving the visitor operating within your frame set. Alternately, you can open links in a new browser window. This option enables visitors to roam the Web from your site, while your site remains open in a separate browser window.

Keeping frame set files straight

As you work with and edit a frame set, recall that you are actually editing at least three different HTML pages. FrontPage will make sure you don't close a frame set without saving all the open pages. You might find yourself a bit confused about what page you are saving where, however.

Basically, FrontPage keeps track of which files in your frame set need to be saved. In some cases, you might need to save the HTML page that defines the frame, as well as several pages embedded in the frame set. In that case, the Save As dialog box will open, and the simple display on the left side of the dialog box will make it clear which element of the frame set you are saving, as shown in Figure 7-14.

As you save frame set pages, you can use the Change Title button to assign a page title to frame set pages.

Tip It's always good form to name page titles, but when a frame set displays in a browser, the only title visitors will see is the title assigned to the frame page itself — not the titles of the pages displayed within the frame set. Therefore, it's especially *important to assign a title to the frame set page*, rather than leave it at `newpage1` or something similarly uninviting.

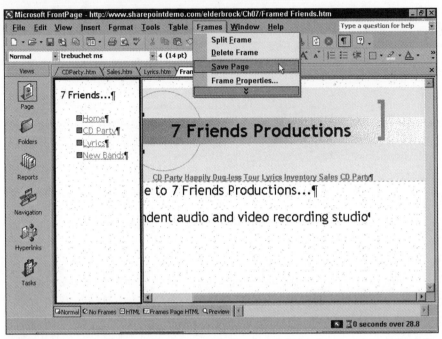

Figure 7-14: Here we are saving the HTML file that defines the contents of the left side of the frame set.

Using Inline Frames

Inline frames appear as independent browser windows *anywhere* within a page. Is that good? So far, we're unconvinced of the benefits of cluttering up pages with mini-browser windows inside of Web pages. Adding to the minus column for using inline frames is the fact that Netscape Navigator 4.7 does not interpret them.

However, it can be done if you are so inclined. If you know your visitors will not be using Netscape Navigator 4.7, and a busy interface is not a problem for your site... fire away with inline frames.

To insert an inline frame, select Insert ➪ Inline Frame. You'll see a grayed area on your page, with buttons that enable you to either set an initial page (embed an existing page) or create a new page.

If you click Set Initial Page, navigate to and open a page to place in the inline frame. If you click New Page, a new page will be created, and you can edit the page contents now in Page view.

When you click outside of and then back in an inline frame, you activate side and corner handles. These handles can be used to resize the inline frame. You can move an inline frame by clicking and dragging in the middle of the frame.

You can even assign absolute positioning to a frame, using the Absolute Positioning toolbar, as shown in Figure 7-15.

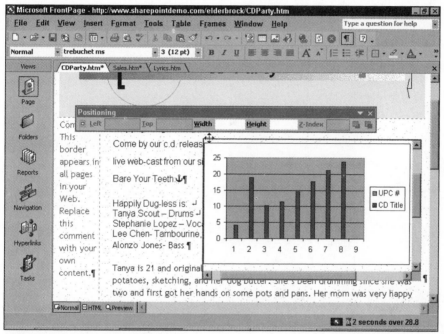

Figure 7-15: When this inline frame is viewed in a browser, visitors will be able to scroll in the embedded frame.

When you save a page with an embedded inline frame, you are prompted to save both the host page and the inline frame.

Figure 7-16 displays an inline frame in IE 5.5, and Netscape Navigator 4.7. Netscape Navigator does not support the inline frame. In Internet Explorer 5.5 (for Windows), the inline frame displays, but does not handle an embedded chart well. The result is that the inline frame is displaying text on top of a graphic.

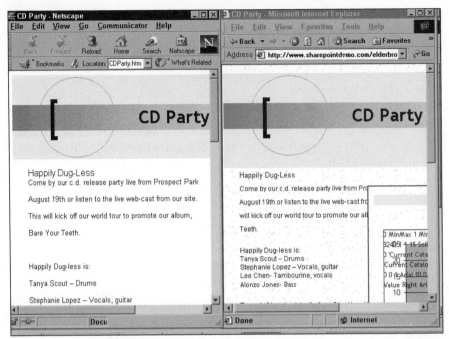

Figure 7-16: Netscape Navigator doesn't support inline frames. The results don't look good in Internet Explorer either — two good reasons to avoid using this feature.

Avoiding Frames Hate Mail

Frames can make a visitor's experience at your Web site more useful by providing helpful navigational tools and onscreen references. However, they can also be distracting or annoying. Visits to your Web site will not be pleasant or productive if visitors are using a browser that doesn't interpret the frames, if the frames are not implemented properly, or if the use of frames makes navigating your Web more difficult than it would have been without the frames. Even if you create a perfect implementation of frames, some people just don't like to use them. Following are some of the ways that you can reduce complaints:

✦ Always have a no-frames alternative built into each page — something more useful than the default "Your page doesn't display frames" page! Having a useful, full-featured alternative page should satisfy people whose browsers do not handle frames.

✦ Some people have frames-capable browsers, but they would rather not use frames. Consider giving users the option — at least from the home page, and potentially from other appropriate locations — to choose between a frames version and a no-frames version.

✦ Limit the number of frames. The more you break up the main window into little frames, the more cluttered your interface becomes. Remember the old saying "two's company, three's a crowd." Reserve as much space as possible for the main content window of your frame set.

✦ Be sure you have a better reason for using frames than the desire to show that you know how to use them! You should be able to explain why you chose to use frames, rather than a simpler approach.

✦ Avoid multiple frame sets in a single Web. The whole point of using a frame set is to create a consistent interface. If you are using multiple frame sets, you are defeating the purpose.

✦ Be sure that all hyperlinks target the correct frame windows. Avoid any circumstances that might result in a frame set document being opened in a frame window.

✦ Test your frame layout in browser windows of different sizes, including small browser windows used in mobile displays.

Summary

Shared borders and frames provide two similar ways of embedding Web pages *within* Web pages. Shared borders attach to the top, bottom, left, and/or right of Web pages. Since they are *shared* pages, they display the *same* content in every page to which they are attached.

Shared borders are often used to hold link bars. By combining link bars with shared borders, you can automatically provide navigation links in Web pages that reflect (in most cases) the navigation structure you define in Navigation view.

Frames provide more flexibility than shared borders. They are easier to resize. And you can define attributes like scrollbars, and allow visitors to resize framed pages. Frames are also more complex than shared borders, and require links that are targeted to an appropriate frame. Luckily for us, FrontPage 2002 manages much of the technical side of frame design by providing a nice selection of frame page templates. These templates have link targets already defined.

Frames can be a helpful design and navigation tool in Web design, particularly since most browsers now support them.

✦   ✦   ✦

HTML Editing

This chapter describes FrontPage's support for manual editing of HTML. As you have seen in the previous chapters, FrontPage enables you to create professional-looking Webs without having to learn or even pay much attention to HTML. However, you have also seen that there are some limitations to using FrontPage this way. Some effects can be achieved only by adding them directly to the HTML code, and under any circumstances, your Web pages will benefit by your ability to understand how they work. This chapter examines the ways in which FrontPage enables you to edit and extend HTML directly. For those who are already familiar with HTML and would like to be able to use FrontPage in conjunction with other HTML editing tools, this chapter provides basic information about how FrontPage deals with HTML.

Note This chapter does not instruct you in the use of HTML. If you would like to learn more about HTML, several good books on this topic are available for a wide range of audiences. If you are looking for an introductory-level book, one excellent choice is *Creating Cool HTML 4 Web Pages* by David Taylor, published by Hungry Minds (formerly IDG Books Worldwide), 2000.

How FrontPage Handles HTML

FrontPage 2002 makes it easy to create Web pages without any knowledge of what HTML is or how it works. Previous versions of FrontPage, however, didn't always make it easy for those who want to work directly with HTML. In fact, in its early versions, FrontPage developed a bad reputation (justly deserved, one might add) for rewriting HTML to its own specification, which sometimes wrought havoc with perfectly valid code that FrontPage just didn't happen to recognize or like.

Happily, one of the biggest improvements in FrontPage, beginning with FrontPage 2000, is that, for the most part, it leaves your HTML alone (it is not always so agreeable about server-side programming languages other than ASP, however). Not only does FrontPage let you control your own HTML destiny, it even enables you to tell it how you like to write HTML, and it will automatically format your HTML to suit your preferences! FrontPage has also improved the features of its built-in HTML editor, making it easier to write and edit code directly.

If you bought FrontPage precisely because you don't want to have to know anything about this technical stuff, you may happily skip this chapter. Quite possibly, you will never need to edit or even look at the HTML that FrontPage produces. However, some of the following reasons might prompt you to reconsider your blissful ignorance:

✦ Your curiosity about how HTML works gets the better of you and you want to use FrontPage to help you learn what is going on behind the scenes.

✦ Try as you might, FrontPage doesn't quite get right the effect that you want to produce, and you are forced to take matters into your own hands.

✦ You happen upon a way-cool Web page with a feature that you want to reproduce on your own site, but FrontPage doesn't have direct support for it, so you roll up your sleeves and dig in.

✦ You read one of the later chapters in this book describing advanced techniques that involve editing code directly, and you decide to take the plunge.

If none of these scenarios sounds mildly enticing, you are probably best served by skipping this chapter for the time being. If you are game, forge ahead. This chapter looks at the many ways that FrontPage gives you to work with HTML. The main questions addressed in this chapter include the following:

✦ Can I edit HTML directly, to take advantage of HTML elements or features not directly supported in FrontPage?

✦ Can I use FrontPage with my favorite HTML/Web programming technique?

✦ Can I use FrontPage in conjunction with the other development applications that I already use?

✦ Can FrontPage help with compatibility and validation of HTML?

Using the HTML Tab

Viewing the HTML source code of your Web page in FrontPage is as easy as opening a page in Page view and clicking the HTML tab at the bottom of the window (see Figure 8-1). The HTML tab functions just like a glorified text editor. You can use it to insert or edit HTML tags and text directly or to make adjustments to the HTML that can't be made in Normal view. All the standard text-editing features apply. You can insert and delete text, or cut, copy, and paste text selections. All of your favorite cut-and-paste shortcut commands work in HTML view. In FrontPage 2002, you can even drag and drop selected text.

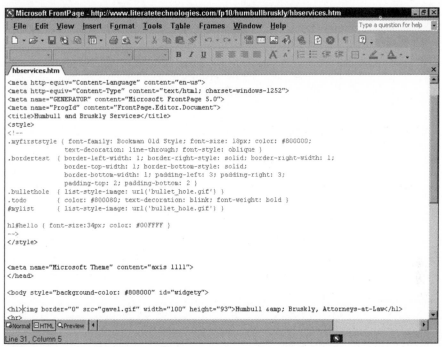

Figure 8-1: An HTML file in HTML view

Tip

If you insert the cursor at a given location or select text in Normal view and then switch to HTML view, the cursor remains at the same location or the text remains selected. This is a handy way to keep your place. Note that the same is not true when you switch from HTML view back to Normal view—the cursor or selected text remains where you left it.

Inserting tags

The ability to switch back and forth easily between Normal view and HTML view is very useful in its own right. You can make a change in Normal mode and then view the results in HTML mode, or vice versa. One of the recent improvements to FrontPage is the capability of inserting HTML tags by using the menu commands even when you are in HTML view. This means that you can insert HTML without knowing the correct syntax, and see the results instantly!

Caution

You may notice subtle differences between the behavior of menu commands issued in HTML view and the same commands in Normal view. For example, if you switch to HTML view and select Insert ➪ Form ➪ Form, FrontPage adds the following HTML:

```
<form></form>
```

In contrast, if you issue the same commands in Normal view, you get

```
<form method="POST" action="--WEBBOT-SELF--">
  <!--webbot bot="SaveResults" U-
File="file:///C:/WINNT/Profiles/Administrator.000/Person
al/My Webs/_private/form_results.csv" S-
Format="TEXT/CSV" S-Label-Fields="TRUE" -->
<p>
<input type="submit" value="Submit" name="B1">
<input type="reset" value="Reset" name="B2">
</p>
</form>
```

Another example: In Normal mode, you can toggle between Bold and UnBold text by repeatedly clicking the Bold button in the toolbar. Try this in HTML view, and you will find that it adds a new set of bold tags around your text each time you click the button.

To try this out for an image, switch to HTML view, place the cursor where you want to insert the image, and select Insert ➪ Picture. Select a picture file, just as you would in Normal view, and click OK. FrontPage inserts the appropriate <IMG> tag into the HTML page. If you find it disconcerting to insert a picture and see only a string of text, you can return to Normal view, where you will find the picture displayed as you would expect.

You can insert tags for the majority of the commands under the Insert menu, but there are some exceptions. You will not be able to insert inline frames, symbols, Web components, database results, files, bookmarks, and hyperlink tags. You can insert all table elements.

Caution FrontPage enables you to insert tags anywhere in HTML view. This means that you can insert an HTML tag accidentally into the middle of another HTML tag.

Editing tag properties

You may have noticed that when you are in HTML Tab view, you can't use the formatting menu commands. Perhaps this is to prevent people from inadvertently thinking that they can format the text in HTML view. At any rate, another way exists to access the formatting properties in HTML view: use the Tag Properties command in the HTML tab Options menu.

Note For what it's worth, even though most of the toolbar buttons are disabled in HTML view, the Bold, Italics, and Underline buttons remain enabled. You can also use keyboard shortcuts to insert these HTML formatting tags. First, select the text to format, and then either click the toolbar button or press the equivalent keyboard shortcut.

To demonstrate how the Tag Properties command works, create a standard paragraph of text in Normal view. Switch to HTML view. Your paragraph should have beginning paragraph (`<p>`) and ending paragraph (`</p>`) tags around it, something like the paragraph illustrated in Figure 8-2 (if not, you can always add them in HTML view!).

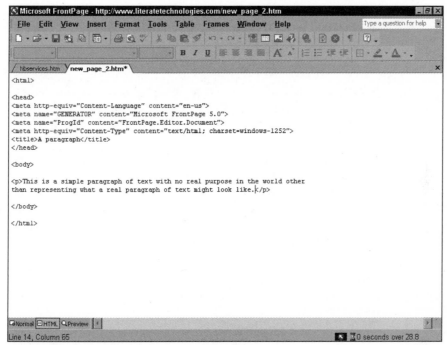

Figure 8-2: A standard paragraph in HTML view

Now, right-click the beginning paragraph (`<p>`) tag (alternatively, you can select the tag and then right-click anywhere on the page). Select Tag Properties in the Option menu. FrontPage displays the normal Paragraph Properties dialog box, enabling you to format the paragraph as you wish. For example, you might change the alignment from its default status to right alignment. Click OK to close the dialog box, and FrontPage updates the paragraph tag to (`<p align=right>`).

Try the same technique with other HTML tags. In each case, FrontPage displays the appropriate properties dialog box, enabling you to specify tag properties from within HTML view.

Finding and replacing text

In addition to the other regular editing features, the Find and Replace features are active in HTML view, to help you quickly find or replace HTML code in your pages. These features work just as they do in Normal view (except that you will notice that the Find in HTML checkbox is checked and unchangeable):

✦ To use the Find dialog box, select Edit ➪ Find or press Ctrl+F, enter the text that you're looking for in the Find What text box, and then click the Find Next button. The text (if it exists on your page) is now highlighted.

✦ To use the Replace dialog box, select Edit ➪ Replace or press Ctrl+H, enter the text that you want to replace in the Find What text box, and then enter the text that you want it to be replaced with in the Replace With text box. To review each change before it's made, click the Find Next button to highlight the text that you're looking for, and then, if you want to change it, click the Replace button. Replace changes the text and then highlights the next instance of the text. To replace all instances of the text at one time, click the Replace All button.

✦ Both Find and Replace support matching whole words and case via the Match Whole Word Only and Match Case checkboxes, respectively.

✦ If you enter "alt," for example, and check Match Whole Word Only, "alternative" will not be found. Note that the whole word option doesn't include punctuation or functions, such as the equals sign — in other words, entering "Bob" will return instances of "Bob's," and "alt" will return instances of "alt=." This is both a blessing and a curse, and means that you must be very careful when using Replace All.

Controlling color coding

By default, HTML view color-codes various HTML elements to help you distinguish them at a glance. The default color-coding is shown in Table 8-1.

Table 8-1 HTML Default Color-Coding	
HTML Element	**Color Code**
Normal text	Black
Tags	Blue
Tag attribute names	Blue
Tag attribute values	Black
Comments	Gray
Scripts	Dark red

If you prefer, you can turn off the color-coding feature. In HTML view, right-click anywhere on the page and then select the Show Color Coding option to uncheck it and render all text in standard black.

You can also adjust the colors to your own liking. Select Tools ⇨ Page Options and click the Color Coding tab, shown in Figure 8-3. Use the color-picker to adjust the display colors for any of the elements previously indicated. You can also use this tab to check or uncheck the Show Color Coding option. Note that you don't have to be in HTML view to adjust the colors, but it is useful for seeing the effects of your changes.

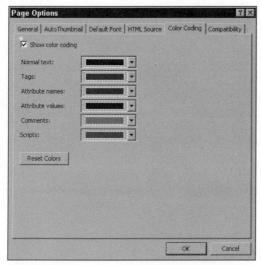

Figure 8-3: You can adjust color-coding in the Color Coding tab of the Page Options dialog box.

Finding a line number

One other useful feature in HTML view is the option of jumping to a particular line number. You access this feature by right-clicking the page in HTML view and selecting Go To from the options menu, which displays the Go To Line dialog box. Alternatively, you can use the keyboard shortcut, Ctrl+G. Type the number of the line in the dialog box, as shown in Figure 8-4, and then click OK. This feature is especially useful when you are trying to locate a scripting error from an error message identifying the line that contains the error.

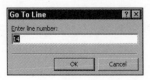

Figure 8-4: The Go To Line dialog box enables you to jump to a particular line number.

 Tip You can use the Go To feature as a quick way to determine the line number of a specific line in your page. Simply click to locate the cursor on the line in question, and then select Go To Line. The default line indicated is the line where your cursor is currently located.

Inserting HTML text

Try a little experiment. Create a simple Web page. Open it in Notepad or the text editor of your choice. Select the HTML and copy the page onto the Clipboard. Now, return to FrontPage and try pasting the Clipboard back into your page in Normal view.

All of your HTML is translated into formatted text (see Figure 8-5). This is just fine, if that's what you want to do — for instance, if you are writing an HTML page to explain how to create HTML. Sometimes, however, you may want the text that you copy to retain its HTML identity.

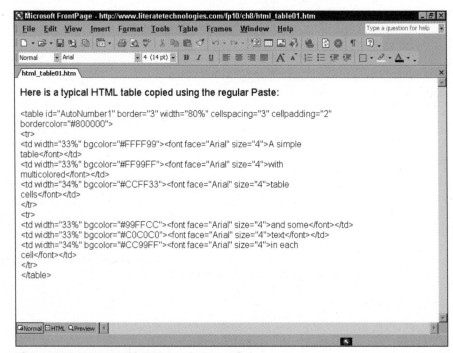

Figure 8-5: Formatted HTML text in Normal view

One relatively simple solution to this problem is to switch to HTML view and then paste in the text. When you return to Normal view, everything is as it should be: a simple Web page.

Suppose, however, that you would prefer to be able to accomplish this without ever seeing the HTML. FrontPage has a solution for you, too. Instead of doing a normal paste operation, use the Paste Special command:

1. Select Edit ➪ Paste Special to show the Convert Text dialog box (see Figure 8-6).

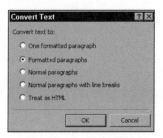

Figure 8-6: Use the Paste Special command to copy HTML text.

2. Select the Treat as HTML option.

3. Click OK to paste the Clipboard contents into FrontPage as HTML. Compare the results in Figure 8-7 with the normal paste operation results previously shown in Figure 8-5.

The Treat as HTML option of the Paste Special command copies only HTML from the body of an HTML document. Notice that in the example, it did not copy the title, which is in the head section of the HTML document. When you are copying complete HTML pages, you should do so in HTML view.

Tip If you anticipate that you will frequently use the Paste Special command and are concerned about saving time, consider customizing the FrontPage environment by writing a macro to save a few precious steps (see Chapter 22 for details).

Inserting custom HTML

In keeping with its spirit of leaving your code alone, FrontPage enables you to enter HTML-like code that it does not recognize. This is very handy if you are editing Web pages that contain elements from other programming environments — for example, XML, JSP, or PHP. FrontPage assumes that you know what you are doing. Of course, this means that if you inadvertently add invalid HTML to a page, FrontPage will not correct your error for you.

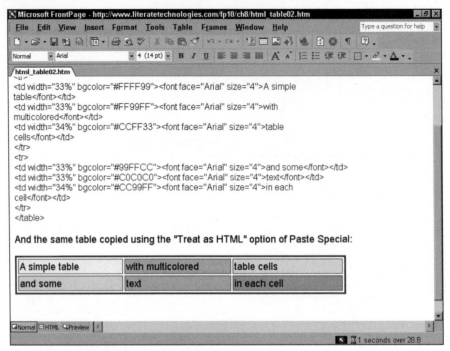

Figure 8-7: Pasting HTML as HTML in FrontPage

Another way to add custom HTML to your page is to use the HTML Web component designed for that purpose. This component, called HTML Markup component, enables you to add HTML to your page without FrontPage checking it for correctness.

Note   Because FrontPage doesn't currently check any unrecognized HTML for correctness, it is unclear why the HTML Markup component continues to exist. Backward compatibility, maybe? Perhaps someone else can think of a use for it.

To add an HTML Markup component to your page, select Insert ➪ Web Component, select Advanced Controls from the Component type list, and double-click the HTML item in the Choose a control list. This opens the HTML Markup dialog box, as shown in Figure 8-8. You can type whatever you want into this dialog box — text, HTML, pseudo-HTML — and FrontPage will not disturb it. Nor does it display it, at least not in Normal view. If you want to see some sign of its existence, you can do one of the following:

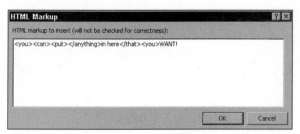

Figure 8-8: The HTML Markup Web component enables you to add HTML that FrontPage will not modify or check for correctness.

✦ **Turn on Reveal Tags:** When Reveal Tags (covered in the next section) are enabled, FrontPage displays a Question Mark icon to represent the presence of the HTML Markup component.

✦ **Select the Show All Icon:** This also turns on the Question Mark icon.

✦ **Switch to Preview Mode:** In Preview mode, FrontPage displays whatever portion of the inserted markup it recognizes (usually this means ignoring HTML tags and showing any text you added).

Figure 8-9 shows an example of an HTML page in Normal view with both Reveal Tags and Show All enabled. Note that if you simply enter unrecognized HTML in HTML view without using the HTML Markup component, FrontPage will attempt to display your text in Normal view; and with Reveal Tags on, it will attempt to translate anything that resembles HTML into tags.

To edit an HTML Markup component, you can double-click the Markup icon to open the HTML Markup dialog box and display the current markup text.

Do not confuse the Advanced ➪ HTML Markup command with the Comment command. Selecting Insert ➪ Comment places a FrontPage Comment component in the page. HTML Markup inserts HTML. Comments are represented by an Exclamation Point icon; HTML components are represented by a question mark. Both icons are illustrated in Figure 8-9.

Note

FrontPage tolerates unrecognized HTML tags in part to support the increasing use of XML in Web applications. XML, which stands for eXtensible Markup Language, is similar to HTML but much more powerful because it enables developers to define and use custom tags. FrontPage has limited support for XML, but you can at least open your XML files in FrontPage without worrying that FrontPage will alter them.

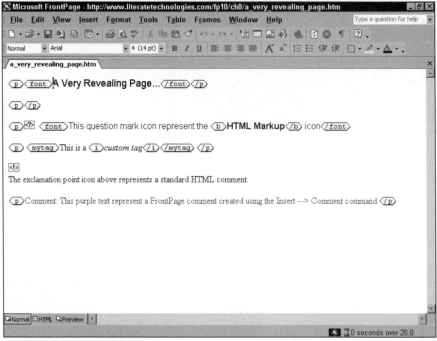

Figure 8-9: Signs of custom HTML in your Web page

Working with Reveal Tags

In addition to HTML Tab view, FrontPage enables you to see the HTML tags that it is inserting as you work in Normal view. This feature is called *Reveal Tags,* which is roughly equivalent to the Show All icon that reveals other "hidden" symbols, such as line and paragraph breaks. However, with Reveal Tags, FrontPage turns on icons that represent the beginning and ending tags in your HTML document (see Figure 8-9).

To show Reveal Tags, select View ➪ Reveal Tags. To hide the codes, select View ➪ Reveal Tags again. (Yes, we know, this is counterintuitive, but what can we say?)

Note   Do not confuse Reveal Tags, which shows you where your HTML tags are, with the Show All command, which shows you where "invisible" formatting elements, such as line breaks and paragraphs, are located. To enable the Show All command, click the icon containing the Paragraph symbol (a backward P) in the Formatting toolbar.

For the most part, Reveal Tags is just a convenience. If you are used to working with HTML and prefer seeing the tags as you work in Normal view, then Reveal Tags is for you. From a practical standpoint, Reveal Tags does have some limited value in that it provides a shortcut to the tag properties dialog boxes. If you double-click a

Reveal Codes tag, for example, you bring up the properties dialog box that corresponds to that tag set, just as selecting Tag Properties (described earlier in the chapter) in the HTML tab does.

Opening a Web Page in an Alternative Editor

If you are accustomed to using a particular text editor to edit HTML, you may find it useful to integrate that application with FrontPage so that you can use FrontPage to do what FrontPage does best, and use your favorite text editor to do what it does best. Unfortunately, no straightforward way exists to integrate these two applications and have them share control of your HTML files. You could simply open the page twice and cut and paste HTML back and forth between your application and FrontPage, but this would be rather tedious if you were doing a lot of HTML work.

A better alternative is to use the Open With facility in FrontPage to open Web pages in your editor. In either Hyperlink or Folder view, select a file by clicking the filename. Then, select Edit ➪ Open With or right-click and select Open With from the pop-up menu; either action presents a list of editors that FrontPage recognizes.

The trick to making this useful is to add your editor to this list. To do this, select Tools ➪ Options and then click the Configure Editors tab. Here, you see the list of editors that FrontPage recognizes, each of which is associated with a particular file type. You might think that you could substitute your editor in place of FrontPage for files of extension type .htm/.html, but this effectively disables your ability to open pages in FrontPage Page view.

In fact, it doesn't really matter which extension you associate with your editor, because you just want to add your editor to the list of options that FrontPage displays. One way to do this would be to make up an extension (.xyz, for instance) and associate your editor with that. Alternatively, you could substitute your editor for Windows Notepad (unless, of course, your favorite editor happens to be Notepad), which, by default, is associated with several extensions, including the special "." extension, which represents any otherwise specified file ending. Now, when you use the Open With function, your editor is one of the options, and you can open the file in this application simply by selecting it from the list.

This can get a little tricky if you open the file in an editor and in FrontPage simultaneously. FrontPage gives your text editor a temporary copy of the file, and FrontPage does not automatically update the original when you save a change to the temporary copy. You can work around this by saving changes in your text editor and then updating FrontPage using the View ➪ Refresh command. Alternatively, don't open the file in FrontPage until you have finished editing it in your text editor.

Note   You can use this technique with other file types as well — for example, style sheets or external JavaScript files.

Setting HTML Preferences

If you are accustomed to writing HTML by using a text editor, you probably have a set of conventions that you use to make your HTML more readable. Perhaps you use capital letters for all tags and attributes, to distinguish them from the content. You probably divide the lines of HTML and perhaps indent them, too, to make them easy to read. You may add comments internally to help you identify major sections of more complex pages.

Note   If you *are* accustomed to capitalizing HTML tags and attributes for readability, be prepared to amend this practice. With the increasing push toward making HTML XML-compliant, the preferred syntax is now the XML way, which means lowercase tags and attribute names.

One of the biggest improvements made in recent versions of FrontPage is the fact that it not only leaves your HTML alone, but it can also actually help you format HTML the way you like it. You can now fine-tune FrontPage to write HTML to suit your preferences.

You set your HTML formatting preferences by using the HTML Source tab. To access this tab, select Tools ➪ Page Options and click the HTML Source tab in the Page Options dialog box, shown in Figure 8-10.

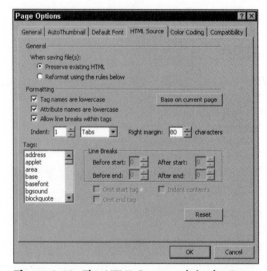

Figure 8-10: The HTML Source tab in the Page Options dialog box

HTML Source tab

The HTML Source tab contains two main sections: General and Formatting. In the General section, decide whether you want FrontPage to reformat your HTML to rules that you define, or to simply preserve the existing HTML. The options are as follows:

✦ **Preserve Existing HTML:** Select this if you want FrontPage to make no changes to the HTML as it shows up in the HTML view.

✦ **Reformat Using the Rules Below:** Select this if you want FrontPage to revise the formatting of the current page and all subsequent pages. Basically, the way this option works is that you designate formatting options and then specify for each and every tag how that tag should appear. (These options are reviewed in the next two sections.)

Caution If you change any of the Formatting checkboxes on this dialog box, FrontPage implements these changes to your HTML even if you have checked the Preserve Existing HTML option.

The following options are available in the Formatting area of the HTML Source tab:

✦ **Tag Names Are Lowercase:** Uncheck this option if you want HTML tags written in uppercase.

✦ **Attribute Names Are Lowercase:** Uncheck this option if you want HTML attributes within tags to be uppercase.

✦ **Allow Line Breaks Within Tags:** Uncheck this option to prevent tags from wrapping around to a second line (splitting a tag into multiple lines is perfectly valid in HTML).

✦ **Indent:** Select a quantity and a unit (spaces or tabs) to indicate how much to indent tags (in the Tags list at the bottom of the HTML Source tab) that have the Indent Contents checkbox selected.

✦ **Right Margin:** Select the number of characters to allow on a single line before wrapping occurs.

The remaining formatting options pertain to individual tags. To set these options for a specific tag, first select the tag by clicking it in the scrolling Tags list. Then, configure the following formatting options for that tag:

✦ **Line Breaks:** The options in this area determine whether a particular set of beginning and ending tags are placed on a separate line by themselves or are written on the same line with the content that they encompass. For example, by default, a `<blockquote>` tag is isolated on a line by itself, both before and after the text of the block quote itself. The following represents settings of 1 line break before and after both start and end:

```
Here is a paragraph of text
<blockquote>
Here is a block quote.
</blockquote>
Here is another paragraph.
```

If you change the preferences to 1 line break before the start and after the start, you get the following:

```
Here is a paragraph of text.
<blockquote>Here is a block quote. </blockquote>
Here is another paragraph.
```

And, reversing the settings so that you have 1 line break after the start and before the start results in the following:

```
Here is a paragraph of text. <blockquote>
Here is a block quote.
</blockquote>Here is another paragraph.
```

✦ **Indent Contents:** Check this to indent the contents between the start and end tags.

✦ **Omit Start/End Tag:** In some cases, you can omit the start/end tags without creating an error. A good example is with table cells. Because the beginning of a new cell tag, by definition, coincides with the end of the previous cell tag, writing the end tag is unnecessary. If you prefer to write your table code this way, this is where you stipulate your preferences.

One other important option in the HTML Source tab is the Base on Current Page button. When you select this option, FrontPage analyzes the current page to determine how you like your HTML to appear. You can use this to "train" FrontPage to do things your way. Of course, FrontPage assumes that your HTML stylistic practices on the model page are consistent.

Tip

If you plan to configure your HTML preferences only once and you are specifying only a few changes, using the Page Options dialog box is the easiest method. If you use multiple configurations or specify options for several tags, consider making a *template* that includes a sample of each tag you want to configure. Then, use the Base on Current Page feature of the HTML Source tab to set all the preferences simultaneously. This way, you can make multiple templates and adjust them quickly and easily.

Handling Browser Compatibility Issues

One of the original intentions behind HTML and the World Wide Web was to create a markup format that could be displayed consistently by any browser on any platform. Although this goal is partially realized in current browser practice, industry competition and changes over time to the HTML standards have resulted in a proliferation of small, but sometimes debilitating, differences in browser behavior. This is compounded by the pace at which new versions of browsers are released.

The upshot of all of this is that creating even a mildly sophisticated HTML page can introduce a host of compatibility problems. FrontPage tries to do its part to assist you in this regard by enabling you to dictate your compatibility preferences, using the Page Options dialog box's Compatibility tab.

To access the HTML Compatibility tab (see Figure 8-11), select Tools ➪ Page Options and switch to the Compatibility tab.

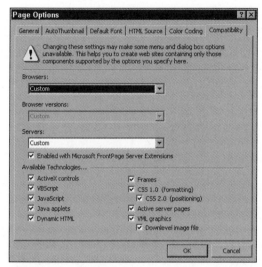

Figure 8-11: The HTML Compatibility tab in the Page Options dialog box

Specifying browser and server versions

Use the Compatibility tab to select the browsers you want to support. The Compatibility tab offers the following options:

✦ **Browsers:** You can specify the browsers you want to support. If you select one of the available options, you must also select a Browser version option before FrontPage makes any adjustments.

✦ **Browser versions:** Options include 3.0 and later browsers, 4.0 and later browsers, and 5.0 and later browsers (of course, only Internet Explorer has a 5.0 version, but who's counting?). If you select a browser version level, you must also select browser options before FrontPage makes any adjustments.

✦ **Servers:** Options include IE versions 3.0 and later (the current version is 5.0), and Apache. If you select Apache, FrontPage disables ASP support.

You also have the option of indicating whether your server supports the FrontPage Server Extensions discussed in Chapter 23. Unchecking this option causes FrontPage to disable any features that require the server extensions.

Setting available technologies

When you specify the particular browser or server versions that you need to support, you may notice that FrontPage automatically checks and unchecks the available technologies for your configuration. This results in FrontPage disabling particular menu items, to prevent you from creating compatibility problems.

If you leave the Compatibility tab browser and server options set to their default, custom, you can select the particular technologies you want to support, regardless of which browsers may happen to support those features. Your options include the following:

✦ **ActiveX controls:** Microsoft-based components that can be embedded in Web pages. See Chapter 15 for more details. Unchecking this option disables the ActiveX Advanced Control in the Web Components dialog box.

✦ **VBScript:** VBScript is a compact version of Visual Basic designed for use as a client-side scripting language. It is supported by Internet Explorer only. Unchecking this option disables VBScript support.

✦ **JavaScript:** JavaScript is a client-side scripting language used to provide user interaction. Unchecking this option disables all FrontPage features that require JavaScript. The use of JavaScript in your Web pages is discussed in Chapter 18.

✦ **Java applets:** Java applets, discussed in Chapter 15, are small Java-based applications designed to run inside a Web page. Unchecking this option disables the Java applet Advanced Control.

✦ **Dynamic HTML:** Dynamic HTML (DHTML) enables you to create dynamic effects in your HTML pages. Unchecking this option disables the Dynamic HTML Effects command, as well as several of the Web components. For more information on using DHTML, see Chapter 18.

✦ **Frames:** Frames enable you to create "embedded" HTML pages. Unchecking this option removes the Frames templates from the Page Templates dialog box and disables the Frames menu command and the Inline Frame command.

✦ **CSS 1.0 (formatting):** CSS stands for "Cascading Style Sheets," and it is the standard that FrontPage uses when you create styles. Unchecking this option disables the Styles menu command and removes the Style Sheet templates from the New Page Templates dialog box.

✦ **CSS 2.0 (positioning):** If you enable CSS 1.0 support, you can optionally select CSS 2.0 support, or at least the positioning aspects of CSS 2.0 that FrontPage supports. See Chapter 11 for more details on both CSS 1.0 and CSS 2.0.

✦ **Active server pages:** Active Server Pages (ASP) is a Microsoft server-side programming environment that uses VBScript. Unchecking this option disables FrontPage support for ASP scripting elements. Because this is a server-side programming environment, it is server-dependent, not browser-dependent as most of the other options are.

✦ **VML graphics:** VML, or Vector Markup Language, is an XML application that defines vector graphics using XML. It is currently the way in which all Microsoft Office applications define graphical elements, and FrontPage uses it to create Drawings, AutoShapes, and Word Art. Only the most recent versions of Internet Explorer support this feature. Unchecking this option disables these graphical features in FrontPage.

✦ **Downlevel image file:** If you enable VML graphics support, you can optionally select to support downlevel image files as well. This enables FrontPage to substitute an image file for the VML for browsers that do not support VML.

Alternatives to the Compatibility tab

The Compatibility tab provides basic protection against major compatibility problems. It assumes, however, that when faced with a potential compatibility issue, you want to avoid it altogether. Depending on the complexity of your site, however, you may have to make some tough compromises if you take this approach. The question that you have to ask is whether eliminating features creates more difficulties for your users than would the possibility of dealing with an incompatibility.

One alternative is to implement some method of checking your users' browser versions and then designing your Web pages to behave appropriately for various browser scenarios. The low-tech method of doing this is to create an initial page and ask users to select the link that corresponds to their browser. The more high-tech approach is to use scripting to perform *browser-sniffing,* detecting the user's browser version. (This is possible because all browsers identify themselves to the Web server when they request a Web page.) Using either of these methods, you can avoid the problem of potentially disappointing your users. However, this also means a fair amount of extra work for you, both in planning your site and in building it. Of course, some features, such as frames and scripting, have built-in ways to handle browsers that don't support that particular feature, but maintaining these options still requires extra work. You may have to develop multiple versions of key pages, or at least multiple options within pages; and each time you make a change, you have to make sure that the change is reflected in every version.

Ultimately, if you have anything more than a small Web site and are serious about handling browser compatibility issues elegantly, you may want to consider using scripting or programming to manage this task. Check out Chapter 18 for advice on this topic. In addition, you can use the resources mentioned in the next section to help you maintain compatible Web pages.

Validating HTML

HTML *validation* refers to the process of checking the accuracy of your HTML to ensure that you haven't made any typographical errors or used tags and their attributes incorrectly. The strictest validation methods parse your HTML against the actual Document Type Definition (DTD) that defines what elements are legal in various types of HTML.

Although you can use FrontPage to verify internal and external hyperlinks, it does not include any validation reporting capabilities for your HTML. On the one hand, the lack of a validation feature isn't a huge problem, because FrontPage is writing most of the HTML itself. On the other hand, the fact that you can still add your own HTML is reason enough to check your HTML for accuracy. Moreover, if you want to ensure that the HTML you are writing is standards-compliant, you should consider validating your HTML pages. Following are some resources to get you started:

✦ **W3C's HTML Validator (**validator.w3.org**):** Maintained by the W3C, the organization responsible for overseeing Web standards.

✦ **Bobby (**www.cast.org/bobby**):** Bobby is an online validator maintained by CAST (Center for Applied Special Technology) that is especially designed to identify problems with your Web pages that might pose accessibility problems for individuals with disabilities.

✦ **Dr. Watson (**watson.addy.com**):** A free service to analyze your Web pages.

✦ **Net Mechanic (**www.netmechanic.com**):** NetMechanic is a software vendor that specializes in both free and commercial HTML tools.

✦ **Web Site Garage (**websitegarage.netscape.com**):** Similar to NetMechanic; sponsored by Netscape.

✦ **AnyBrowser (**www.anybrowser.com**):** Shows you what your pages look like to viewers with designated browsers. A sobering experience, not to be missed.

✦ **Web Page Backward Compatibility Viewer (**www.delorie.com/web/wpbcv.html**):** Another free tool for checking page compatibility.

Handling Special Cases

This section concludes the chapter by describing some of the finer points of FrontPage's HTML usage. The topics covered here are by no means exhaustive, but they are representative and should give you a sense of the issues to watch out for if you plan to use FrontPage extensively.

Comments

FrontPage has a Comment feature that enables you to insert a comment into your Web page and view the comment in Normal view. The comment remains in the HTML, but it isn't displayed to users when the page is viewed in a Web browser.

To insert a FrontPage comment, first locate the cursor on the page where you want the comment to appear. Select Insert ⇨ Comment and type the text of your comment in the Comment dialog box, shown in Figure 8-12. Click OK to return to the page and view the results.

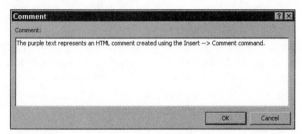

Figure 8-12: Entering HTML comments the FrontPage way

FrontPage's Comment feature is really a Web component with the quaint name `PurpleText`, alluding to the display style of the comment. Because this comment is embedded in a FrontPage component, you can double-click the comment text to bring up the Comment dialog box for further editing.

In addition to FrontPage's custom Comment feature, you can also insert standard HTML comments. An HTML comment is indicated by using the following syntax:

```
<!-- This is a standard HTML comment -->
```

You can insert a comment manually in HTML view, or you can use the HTML Markup feature, described earlier in this chapter. Either way, FrontPage represents this comment in Normal view with a highlighted yellow exclamation point. If you create your comment manually and then double-click the icon to edit the comment, FrontPage opens the HTML Comment dialog box, as shown in Figure 8-13. However, if you create the comment using the HTML Markup dialog box, double-clicking the comment icon reopens the HTML Markup dialog box. Go figure.

Figure 8-13: An HTML comment can be edited in the HTML Comment dialog box.

Meta tags

When you add or edit a Web page in FrontPage, you are working primarily with the *body* section of the page. Web pages also contain a *head* section, which stores information about the page that typically does not display. The Web page title that appears in the browser window's title bar is the most commonly used element that appears in the head element.

Meta tags are another of the HTML elements that are located in the non-displaying, head portion of an HTML Web page. Meta tags contain useful information about the HTML page, its creation date, the application that created it, the author, and so forth.

By default, FrontPage 2002 adds the following meta tags to the header of every HTML document:

```
<meta HTTP-EQUIV="Content-Language" CONTENT="en-us">

<meta HTTP-EQUIV="Content-Type" CONTENT="text/html;
charset=windows-1252">

<meta NAME="GENERATOR" CONTENT="Microsoft FrontPage 5.0">

<meta NAME="ProgId" CONTENT="FrontPage.Editor.Document">
```

You can add your own meta tag information using the Custom tab of the Page Properties dialog box. One common use of the meta tag is to create a list of keywords that text engines can use to index your Web pages. You'll see an example of how to create a keyword list in a moment. You can also include a short description of your site, which some search engines display with your URL when a search query matches your Web site.

To add a meta tag to the current Web page, right-click on the page and select Page Properties, or select File ➪ Page Properties from the menu bar. Click the Custom tab in the Page Properties dialog box, shown in Figure 8-14, which has options to add, modify, or remove two kinds of meta tags: system variables and user variables. System meta tags are standard, pre-defined HTTP headers. User meta tags can be user-defined, although some of these, such as the keywords meta tag, are considered fairly standard usage.

By way of an example, let's add keywords and description meta tags to the User Variables section of the Custom tab in the Page Properties dialog box.

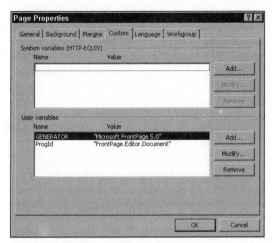

Figure 8-14: The Custom tab of the Page Properties dialog box. Use this tab to enter meta tags.

To add a meta tag, click the Add button next to the User Variables area. In the dialog box that appears, enter keywords in the Name field, and enter a comma-separated list of keywords or phrases in the Value field (see Figure 8-15 for an example). Click OK to add the keywords attribute. Repeat the process, using a description and a short paragraph that describes your site. Click OK in the Page Properties dialog box to accept your changes. Save the page.

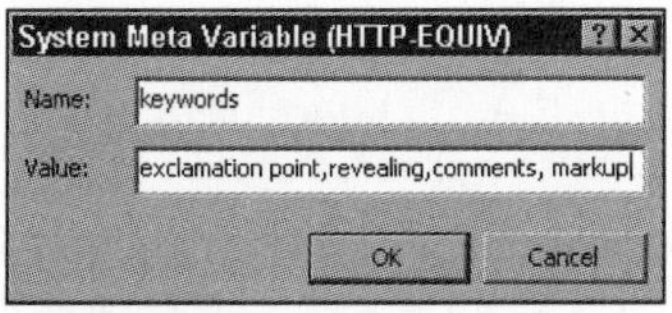

Figure 8-15: Adding keywords to an HTML page

To check the results, select the HTML tab. You should see the new meta tags added to the header of the HTML file, as shown in Figure 8-16.

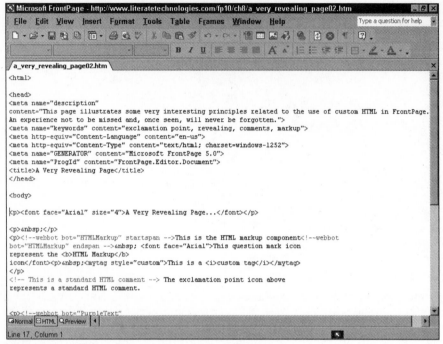

Figure 8-16: The results of adding user variables (meta tags).

Symbol entity references

HTML entity references are used to insert nonstandard ASCII characters into an HTML page. FrontPage correctly translates most typed character symbols, such as greater than (>) and less than (<) signs, or quotation marks ("), into their named entity references. You can also enter symbols by using the Symbol dialog box as shown in Figure 8-17, which is accessed by selecting Insert ➪ Symbol. This dialog box includes all the accented characters used in the romance languages, as well as symbols such as the copyright and trademark signs. FrontPage translates most of these symbols into a number entity reference or just leaves them as a symbol. In practice, this means that browsers on Windows platforms may see the character that you intended, but results are unpredictable on other platforms. To ensure that your pages are portable, use only the named entity references for non-alphanumeric characters. For a complete list of available entity references, check out this page from the W3C's HTML 4 specification: www.w3.org/TR/ REC-html40/sgml/entities.html. (For a slightly less technical list, try www. w3schools.com/html/html_entitiesref.asp.)

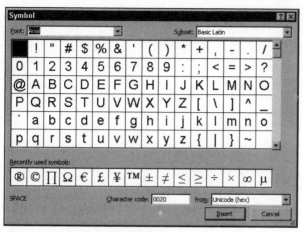

Figure 8-17: The Symbol dialog box

Nonbreaking spaces

You can indicate a nonbreaking space character in HTML by using the entity reference . Inserting this character forces browsers to display space characters where they normally ignore them. However, not all browsers recognize this entity reference, so using it isn't always advisable. FrontPage uses it liberally in a variety of circumstances.

FrontPage writes this symbol into blank paragraphs if, for example, you create two paragraph breaks in a row. It also often inserts this symbol into blank table cells. In addition, if you enter multiple spaces in Normal view, or attempt to insert a tab, FrontPage uses nonbreaking spaces to simulate this effect in HTML.

You can't prevent FrontPage from entering nonbreaking spaces. You *can* use the Replace feature in HTML view to eliminate these characters if you choose.

Summary

This chapter delved into FrontPage's support for controlling and editing HTML. You learned how to use the HTML view for editing HTML in your Web pages as well as some techniques for getting HTML into your pages. This chapter also identified the ways in which FrontPage enables you to control the HTML that it outputs, provided advice about how to use those features, and pointed out a few of their limitations. In Part III, we describe how to use FrontPage to design and organize a coherent Web site. The next chapter introduces FrontPage navigational elements, a feature that lets you control the ways in which your Web site is structured and accessed.

✦　　✦　　✦

Organizing FrontPage Webs

Building Navigational Elements

The ability to "click and jump" intuitively around a Web site is one of the things that makes browsing a Web page so useful. If you are designing only a single Web page, then you can custom craft links associated with text and pictures. But if you are managing a large Web site, then making sure each page has easy-to-find and intuitive links is a major job.

FrontPage does much of this work for you — by generating automated link bars that can be used to place useful sets of links on every page of your Web site automatically. Before we dive into creating automated link bars, we'll explore some cool options that can be applied to links, like screen tips (pop-up text associated with text links), and target windows. Then we'll explore link bars in detail.

Defining Link Properties

In Chapter 1, you learned to assign link properties to images and text. Here, we'll zoom in for a closer look at how you can control links.

One option to consider when defining links is whether you want the link to open in the current browser window or in a new browser window. You can also define the screen tip text for text links. Before looking into more complex ways to generate links, the following section will explore these link options.

Adding screen tips to link text and images

Screen tips are defined for images by the content of the Text field in the General tab of the Picture Properties box. However, you can also define tool tip text for text that is used as a link. A text screen tip is illustrated in Figure 9-1.

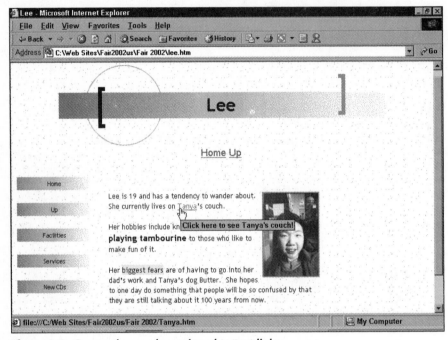

Figure 9-1: Screen tips can be assigned to text links.

To assign a screen tip to a text link, follow these steps:

1. Select the text to which you are applying the link.

2. Click on the Insert Hyperlink tool in the Standard Toolbar. The Insert Hyperlink dialog box opens.

3. Browse to a link in your site, or enter an external URL in the Address area of the Insert Hyperlink dialog box.

4. Click on the ScreenTip button in the Create Hyperlink dialog box. Enter text that will display as a screen tip when the link is *hovered* over (when someone moves their mouse cursor over the text without clicking).

5. Click OK twice to close the Insert Hyperlink dialog box.

You can test your hover text by clicking on the Preview tab in FrontPage, or by previewing the page in a browser (click on the Preview in Browser button in the Standard toolbar).

Opening a link in a new window

There is a particular advantage to opening *external* links (that lead out of your site) in a *new* browser window. If a visitor opens a link in a new browser window, he or she still remains rooted in your site. And when the link target browser window is closed, the visitor returns to your site.

To instruct a link to open in a *new* browser window, follow theses steps:

1. Select the text or image to which you are applying the link.

2. Click on the Insert Hyperlink tool in the Standard toolbar. The Insert Hyperlink dialog box opens.

3. Browse to a link in your site, or enter an external URL in the Address area of the Insert Hyperlink dialog box.

4. Click on the Target Frame button and choose New Window in the Target Frame dialog box, as shown in Figure 9-2. FrontPage attaches an HTML code _blank in the Target Setting area indicating that a new (blank) browser window will open when this link is activated.

Figure 9-2: Defining a link that will open in a new browser window

5. Click OK twice to close the Target Frame dialog box and the Insert Hyperlink dialog boxes.

Inserting Link Bars

You can insert link bars in a shared border or anywhere in a Web page. If you insert a navigation bar in a shared border, it will appear on every page (to which that shared border is assigned) in the Web site. If you place a navigation bar in a Web page (outside a shared border), it will appear only on that page.

The combination of placing link bars in, or out of, shared borders gives you more flexibility in creating convenient navigational links for your Web site visitors.

The tricky part of link bars is that the displayed links *are based on the site flow you define in Navigation view.* So, before you try to generate navigation links, it's important to make conscious decisions on how to structure your site flow.

Note You *can't* generate link bars without first defining a navigation flow in Navigation view. FrontPage won't know which links to create without being able to refer to the page relationships defined in Navigation view.

Defining site navigation flow

The link bars that you generate will apply the same link structure to each page. The links themselves will be different on each page, but the structure will be the same. This means that you have to choose which kinds of links to generate, and live with that choice throughout your site.

What if you want to apply a unique and specific navigational logic to just one Web page? You can do this by assigning link bars to specific pages, and placing them *outside* of a shared border. Similarly, you can use different navigation logic for different link bars in a Web site. For example, use Child Level links for a top shared border, and Parent Level links for a bottom shared border.

Site navigation logic

Before defining site navigation, it is helpful to think about the basic way you want visitors to navigate through your site. There are two fundamental options:

- ✦ Linear
- ✦ Hierarchical

A *linear* navigational approach is similar to a slideshow. Visitors go to page 1, then to page 2, and so on. They can have the option of going to the next or previous page, but really they are following a path you defined for them.

Linear navigational layouts are useful when information is to be presented in a very structured way, and when there is no basis, or need, to provide much freedom for a visitor to control his or her own "pathway" through the site.

Figure 9-3 shows a site with a linear structure.

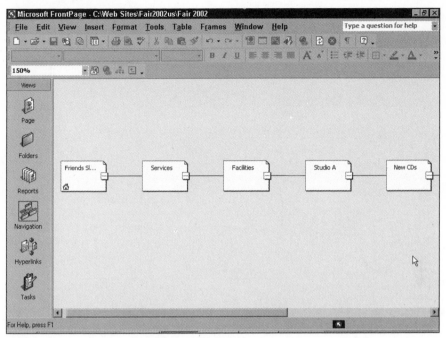

Figure 9-3: Linear site design leads visitors through site content page by page.

More typical is a hierarchical navigational approach, where site content is broken down into different areas, each of which has a *hierarchy* of pages. For example, a visitor might be given the choice of five divisions of the company. Each of those divisions could have its own home page, which would be the top page in that section of the site. Under each division's home page, there could be pages for different departments, and so on.

FrontPage uses a family metaphor to describe the relationship between pages in a hierarchical navigation structure. Pages on the top of the chart function as *parent* pages, while pages below them are *child* pages. These terms are relative, in that a child page can in turn be a parent page to pages beneath it.

Figure 9-4 shows a site with a hierarchical navigational structure.

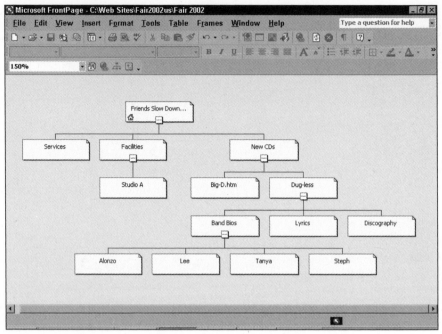

Figure 9-4: This site structure offers visitors a variety of options.

Defining link structure in Navigation view

To define a link structure for your site in Navigation view, click and drag to move pages from the Folder List into the Navigation View window.

Note   If the Folder View is not displayed, choose View ➪ Folder List.

Pages can be dragged to new locations within the navigational structure. And, you can drag pages from *any* folder on your Web into navigation view.

Defining link bars

To insert a link bar, click where you want to place the insertion point — either in a shared border or on a page.

Note   Remember, if you place a link bar in a shared border, it will appear on *every* page in your Web (where the shared border is displayed).

With your link bar location selected, choose Insert ➪ Navigation to open the Insert Web Component dialog box (with Link Bars selected). Double-click on "Bar based on navigation structure" in the Choose a Bar Type list, as shown in Figure 9-5.

Maxing Out in Navigation View

Navigation view is a handy place to take care of many file management issues. You can easily change a page title (the information that shows in a browser title bar when the page is open) by clicking twice (not double-clicking) and editing the page title.

You can find pages in Navigation view by right-clicking on a page filename in the Folder List, and choosing Find in Navigation from the Context menu. This is handy because pages often don't have the same file name and page title (for instance, index.htm can have a page title of "Welcome to the Fair").

You can change the orientation of the Navigation layout by right-clicking anywhere in the Navigation view area, and toggling between Portrait and Landscape using the Portrait/Landscape option in the Context menu. The Zoom features in the Context menu allow you to cram more pages onto your Navigation view screen.

And, of course, an easy way to edit any Web page (whether open or not) is to double-click on it in Navigation view.

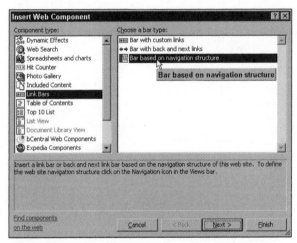

Figure 9-5: Selecting a link bar to embed in a page

You can skip the wizard and jump right to the Link Bar Properties box (where you define links more efficiently) by simply clicking on the Finish button in the wizard. That opens the Link Bar Properties dialog box with the General tab displayed, as shown in Figure 9-6.

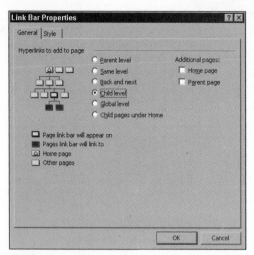

Figure 9-6: Link bar properties define how link bars will be generated.

The following options are available in the Link Bar Properties dialog box:

✦ **Parent level links:** Displays only a link to the page in the Navigation view flowchart that appears just above the page being viewed.

✦ **Same level:** Displays other Web pages on the same level of the Navigation view site flowchart.

✦ **Back and next:** Displays Parent and Child level links from the current page.

✦ **Child level:** Generates links only to pages directly below the current page in the Navigation view flowchart.

✦ **Global level:** Creates links to pages in Navigation view that are not connected to other pages.

✦ **Child pages under home:** Creates links to all pages that are direct child pages of the home page.

✦ **Home page:** Adds a link to the site home page to every page in the site.

✦ **Parent Page:** Adds a link to the parent page to each page.

As you define link options, they are illustrated in the chart on the left side of the Link Bar Properties dialog box, as shown in Figure 9-6.

The Style tab in the Link Bar Properties dialog box defines how links will look. From here, you can use a variety of graphic buttons or text, and you can arrange links in a horizontal or vertical list.

To generate link bars based on the theme assigned to your Web site, choose the default "Use page's theme" option in the Choose a Style list. Or, you can scroll down the list and find a better graphical theme to apply to your link bar. If you choose a new theme, you can use the "Use vivid colors" checkbox to substitute bolder colors, or the "Use active graphics" checkbox to generate interactive buttons with over, active, and down states.

The two radio buttons in the Orientation and Appearance area of the Navigation Bar Properties dialog box enable you to choose whether to line up your links horizontally or vertically, and whether to use Buttons or Text. Your selections are previewed in the small preview page in the lower-left corner of the dialog box.

Tutorial 9-1: Create a custom link bar in a shared border

For this tutorial, open or create a new Web site using a theme. Theme-based sites automatically generate shared borders with link bars. If your site doesn't have shared borders with embedded link bars, choose Format ⇨ Shared Borders. In the Shared Borders dialog box, select Top and Left, and select the Include Navigation Buttons checkboxes.

1. Double-click an existing link bar in the top shared border in any Web page in your Web site to open the Link Bar Properties dialog box.

2. Select the Child Level radio button, and both the Home Page and Parent Page checkboxes in the dialog box.

3. In the Style tab, select the Horizontal radio button in the Orientation and Appearance area, and then click OK.

4. Click and drag to select the text links that you just generated, and apply 14-point, Arial font.

5. Save your page, and select View ⇨ Refresh. Your top shared border should look something like the one in Figure 9-7.

6. Choose Format ⇨ Shared Border, and click in the Bottom checkbox. Click OK to return to the page, and scroll down to the bottom shared border and click inside of it.

7. Press Enter (if necessary) to create a new line, select Insert ⇨ Navigation, and click on "Bar based on navigation structure." Click Finish to open the Link Bar Properties dialog box.

8. In the Link Bar Properties dialog box, select the "Back and next" radio button, and both the Home Page and Parent Page checkboxes. In the Style tab, choose Horizontal, and scroll down the options in the Choose a Style area to select a style that displays text, like the one in Figure 9-8.

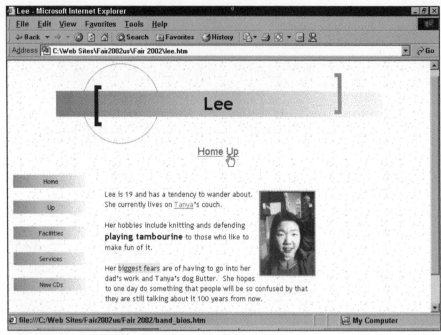

Figure 9-7: You can format the text of a link bar.

Figure 9-8: Generating text links in a links bar

9. Click OK in the dialog box. Not every link will be active. For example, if you selected a link to the home page, and you're at the home page, no link will appear.

10. Save your page, and preview your site in your Web browser. Test all the links in the top and bottom shared borders. Your links should look something like those in Figure 9-9.

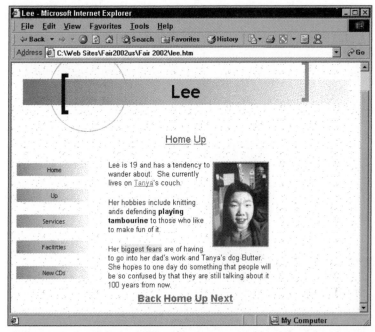

Figure 9-9: The links in this bar were generated based on the site structure in Navigation view and the link logic defined in the Link Properties dialog box.

Special Link Bars

In addition to *generated* link bars, that are based on your navigation structure, FrontPage 2002 allows you to create special link bars with customizable sets of links. For example, you might want to place all the departments in one area of a company or organization into a link group, and then drop a link bar into any page that includes links to all pages in that group. Or, you might want to create a link bar that has hyperlinks to your favorite five or six external Web sites, and place that link quickly in any page. You can do this using Custom Link bars.

Link bars with custom links

Link bars with custom links allow you to create a link bar that you can place on any page, with a custom set of links.

To create a *new* custom link bar, follow these steps:

1. With your cursor at the point where you want to insert a custom link bar, choose Insert ➪ Navigation, and choose Bar with Custom Links from the Choose a Bar Type list.

2. Click Finish in the dialog box. The Link Bar Properties dialog box appears. Click the Create New button to define a new custom link bar.

3. The Create New Link Bar dialog box opens. Type a name for your link bar and click OK.

4. Click the Add Link button in the Link Bar Properties dialog box, and navigate to a page to include in the link bar in the Add to Link Bar dialog box. Then click OK. (You can also include external links (to outside Web pages) in your link bar by entering a URL in the Address area of the Add to Link Bar dialog box.)

5. Use the Add Link button to add additional links. Your links will display in the Link Bar Properties dialog box, as shown in Figure 9-10.

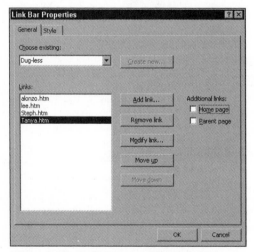

Figure 9-10: Defining a custom link bar

6. After you define your link bar, you can use the checkboxes to include a link to your site home page or parent page. The Add Link, Remove Link, Modify Link,

Move Up, and Move Down buttons allow you to edit your custom link bar. When you've finished the link bar, click OK. The custom link bar will appear in your page.

After you define a custom link bar, you can use it anywhere in any page in your Web site.

Link bars with Back and Next links

Link bars with Back and Next links are similar to custom link bars, except that instead of displaying page titles, they display Back and Next buttons only. The target of these Back and Next buttons depends on the links you define.

In effect, you are providing *blind links* for your visitors, asking them to follow the next link, trusting that this is the next thing they want to see. Back and next links appear in a browser as shown in Figure 9-11.

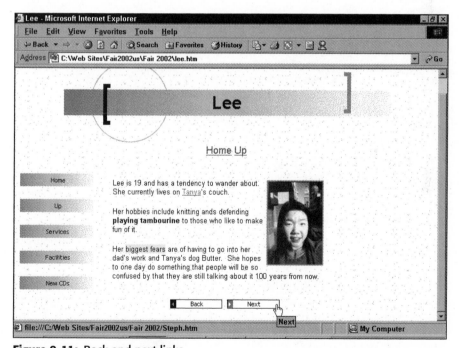

Figure 9-11: Back and next links

Note Both Custom link bars and link bars with Back and Next links appear in Page view with a clickable "add link" note. This text is not visible in browsers, but provides an easy way for you to quickly access the Add to Link Bar dialog box, enabling you to add links to your custom bars.

InterDev navigational links

An alternate way to embed button or text links is to use the somewhat inexplicably included InterDev Navigational Links option in FrontPage 2002. The InterDev option does pretty much the same thing as the Links dialog box, but in a different format. Because it's included in FrontPage, we'll take a quick look at it.

To insert a links bar using the InterDev Navigational Links box, click in a page and choose Insert ➪ Web Component. Scroll down the Component Type list, and choose Additional Components.

In the Choose a Component list, choose Visual InterDev Navigation Bar, as shown in Figure 9-12.

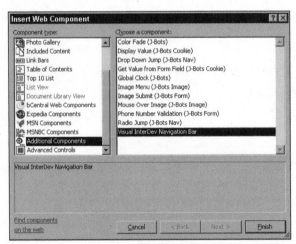

Figure 9-12: Selecting the well-hidden Visual InterDev Navigation Bar component

Click Finish to open the FrontPage Visual InterDev Navigation Bar Component Properties dialog box (Figure 9-13).

The Visual InterDev Navigation Bar Component Properties box is actually an easy way to generate text link bars without scrolling through the whole set of graphical options in the List Properties dialog box. To define text links, click on Rendering in the Settings list, and choose the Text option from the drop-down menu in the choice area, as shown in Figure 9-14.

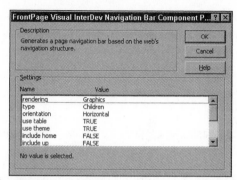

Figure 9-13: Defining a link bar (a.k.a. Navigation bar) using the FrontPage Visual InterDev Navigation Bar Component Properties dialog box

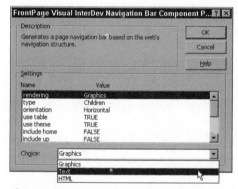

Figure 9-14: Generating a text links bar

The Graphics and HTML options for Rendering produce graphical buttons, but they are easier to define in the Links Bar properties dialog box.

After you define the InterDev property bar (same as a FrontPage links bar), click OK. You can edit the bar by double-clicking on it.

Note

There is actually no real functional contribution made by the Visual InterDev Navigation Bar Component. It simply duplicates the features created by a FrontPage link bar. And, further, it requires FrontPage 2002 server extensions (at least as far as our testers were able to determine at press time). So why is it in FrontPage and why did we explain it? The Visual InterDev Navigation Bar Component seems to be included in FrontPage 2002 as an *example* of an *Additional Component*. This category is really reserved for components produced by *third party vendors* (see Appendix D for a survey of FrontPage add-ins, including vendors who market additional components). If and when you install a third party add-in that provides additional components, you'll see many components listed in the Additional Component dialog box. Microsoft basically threw the Visual InterDev Navigation Bar Component in with FrontPage as a "freebie" example of a non-FrontPage component. And, it *does* work fine as a substitute for a link bar.

Link Bar Troubleshooting

Following are some of the most frequently asked questions about link bars at our FrontPage Forum at http://www.ppinet.com:

Q: How do I substitute my own graphics for the buttons supplied by my theme?

A: See the coverage of custom themes in Chapter 10. The horizontal, vertical, and other navigation buttons generated in link bars are determined by your customizable theme.

Q: Instead of getting a link bar, I get a message "Add this page to Navigation view to display hyperlinks here." Why???

A: A page must be included in the navigation structure (flowchart) defined in Navigation view, or it won't be part of the site's generated link bars. Go to Navigation view, and drag your page into the navigational structure.

Q: I don't have a navigational structure in Navigation view!

A: You can create one by dragging your home page (often default.htm or index.htm) into Navigation view from the Folder List.

Q: We have Link Bar components included in the top and left shared border. They look nice when the page opens up in the browser. But when the browser size is reduced, the global navigation buttons wrap to the next line within the top shared border. Is there any place to specify "No Wrap"?

A: Not easily. You can choose a smaller font size for your navigation bar text by simply selecting the text and assigning a font. Or, you can design your own, smaller, custom buttons. But you can't prevent link bars from wrapping if they don't fit in a browser window. You can place your link bars in a table, and define the table width in pixels — that will protect your text from wrapping, but visitors might need to scroll horizontally to see the entire button. Another solution: Change your navigation structure in Navigation view so that there are only three or four (or at the most five) child pages for any one parent page.

Q: The text in my link bar buttons doesn't fit on the button. For example, my page titled "Yummy Delicious Dinners" only displays "Yummy Del."

A: You can either shorten your page titles (retitle them in Navigation view) or make your text smaller. Or, design larger (custom) navigation buttons.

Q: I have to take my site home from work and work with it on my own computer. How to I keep the navigational structure intact?

A: Assuming you can't simply open your site from a remote server at home, try this: If your site fits on a Zip drive, choose File ➪ Publish, and publish your site to a Zip drive. Take it home and open it from the Zip drive. You won't have full FrontPage functionality, but your navigation structure will survive.

Q: Can you include external links in navigation structure?

A: Yes. Right-click on a page in navigation view, and choose Add Existing Page. The insert hyperlink window will appear. You can either add an existing page in your Web or *type in an external URL.*

Other Navigation Strategies

Link bars, especially when embedded in a shared border, are a powerful tool for generating intuitive, sitewide navigation. But they're not for everyone, and they're not for every site.

If, for example, your site has five pages, then link bars are probably overkill. Just add navigation links individually, on each page, as needed.

Or, if you are happy with your link bars, but want to add a separate link to a single page, don't try to beat that link out of a link bar. Just create a text link in your page.

Note

A generated table of contents can be a helpful navigation tool. It basically replicates the look and structure of your site's navigation view. For a full exploration of generating a table of contents, see Chapter 14.

Embedding Commercial Content

We have to confess that when we saw that Microsoft included the ability to embed links to MSN and MSNBC, our first question was, "And how much are we getting paid to place these links on our sites?"

That said, you may want to include links from your own site to news headlines, sports scores, and even localized weather forecasts.

Want to add a *Webwide* search box to your site (as opposed to the FrontPage search box that works for your own Web site)? You can do that with FrontPage 2002. FrontPage 2002 also comes with links to Microsoft's bCentral Web Banner Exchange Service, and Hit Counter.

Adding MSN search boxes and stock quotes

To include a search box for the Web on your page, choose Insert ➪ Web Component. Scroll down the Component Type list, and click on MSN Components.

Note   Don't confuse the Web Search component with the MSN search box. The Web Search component is used to search *your* site.

MSN offers two different options. You can let visitors search the Web, or look up stock quotes. Click on Stock Quote in the Choose an MSN Component list in the Insert Web Component dialog box. Then click on Finish in the dialog box. You'll get a stock lookup box on your page that looks like the one in Figure 9-15.

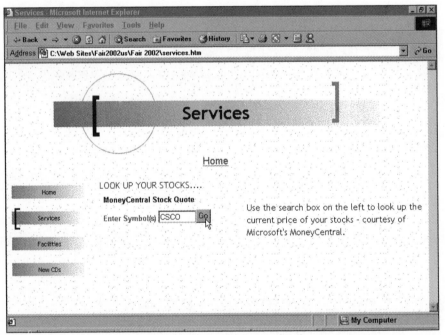

Figure 9-15: If folks check their stocks at your site, will they stick around?

To place a Web search box on your page, choose Insert ➪ Web Component. Scroll down the Component Type list and click on MSN Components. Choose Search the Web with MSN from the Choose an MSN Component list, and click Finish in the Insert Web Component dialog box to embed the search box. The embedded search box looks like the one in Figure 9-16 when viewed in a browser.

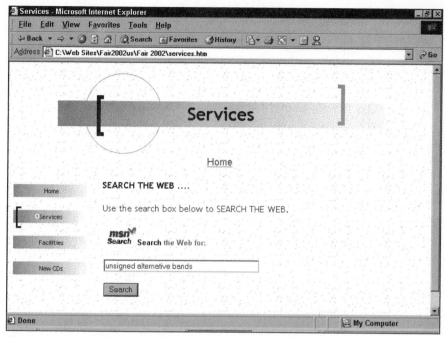

Figure 9-16: Including Web search resources at your site

Visitors who enter search criteria in your form will be sent to MSN's search engine and will be provided with a list of matching Web sites.

Can You Tamper with the Input Forms?

The MS Quick Quote and MSN search forms are based on input forms and form fields.

The Quick Quote input box is an input form that collects data and submits it to a database at Microsoft's www.moneycentral.msn.com site. That database then provides a current quote for the matching stock.

The search box sends results to http://search.msn.com/results.asp.

You can look at the form properties (but don't change them) by right-clicking on either form, and choosing Form Properties from the Context menu.

While you can't mess with the form properties, you can experiment with the form *field* properties. Refer to the discussion of form field properties in Chapter 16 to add default entries or validation scripts to the input forms.

Inserting News components

FrontPage 2002 offers six categories of news from MSNBC to display on your site. They are

✦ Business Headlines from MSNBC

✦ Living and Travel from MSNBC

✦ News Headlines from MSNBC

✦ Sports Headlines from MSNBC

✦ Technology Headlines from MSNBC

✦ Weather forecast from MSNBC

To embed any of these news features in your page, choose Insert ⇨ Web Component, and scroll down the list of components to select MSNBC Components. The list of available components appears on the right, as shown in Figure 9-17.

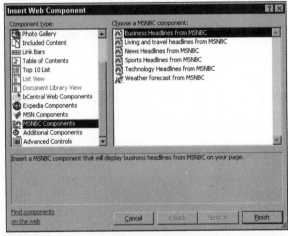

Figure 9-17: Free news from Microsoft and NBC. Who needs TV?

Click on any of the components, and click on Finish in the Insert Web Component dialog box to embed a link to the selected news feature.

If you choose the Weather Forecast component, you'll be prompted to enter a zip code in the United States, or a city (anywhere). This determines the location for the weather forecast that will be displayed at your site, as shown in Figure 9-18.

Figure 9-19 shows a site with five MSNBC components.

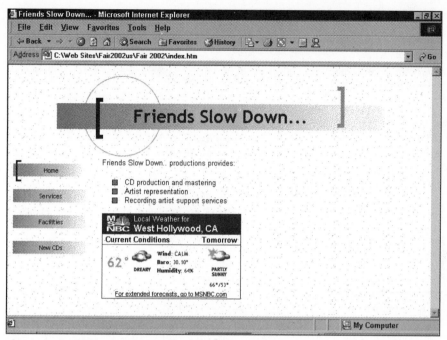

Figure 9-18: Will a weather link improve your site?

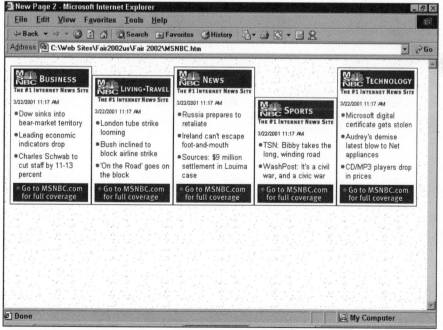

Figure 9-19: Loading up your site with free news sources

Can You Tamper with the MSNBC Links?

The MSNBC components are links to MSNBC. One option available to you is to change the MSNBC links so that the targets open in a new browser window. That way, you'll keep visitors locked into your site even if they stray off to MSNBC.

To change the link target, click on one of the embedded components, and click on the Insert Hyperlink button in the Standard toolbar. Click the Target Frame button, and choose New Window in the Common Targets list of the Target Frame dialog box. Click OK twice to close the dialog boxes, and save your page. The MSNBC link will now open in a new browser window.

Exchanging banner ads and signing up for bCentral's hit counter

With FrontPage 2002, Microsoft offers the option of signing up for Microsoft's own banner ad exchange deal. You can find banner ad deals all over the Web, where you post a banner, and someone posts yours. It's a way of generating hits to your site for free. Microsoft's bCentral deal is that you put two of their banner ads on your site, and they put one of yours' on someone else's site. (Unfortunately, you can't request http://www.microsoft.com as your exchange site!)

Microsoft's bCentral also offers a hit counter linked to a report that is sent to your e-mail address. It provides updates for you on who is visiting your site, and some statistical analysis of your visitors.

To sign up for either of these deals, choose Insert ➪ Web Components, and click on bCentral Web Components in the Component Type list. In the Choose a bCentral Component area of the Insert Web Component dialog box, choose either of the bCentral components and then click on Finish. You'll be sent to an online signup form that will collect quite a bit of required information, including your phone number (required). If that's cool with you, sign up and enjoy either of these services.

Summary

Once upon a time, Web developers had to add links to each page by hand. FrontPage allows you to automate this process in a couple ways. You can add link bars based on navigation structure, or you can create custom link bars based on groups of pages (or external links) that you define.

Placing link bars in shared borders further automates the process, because shared borders can be embedded in every page in your site. Simply by defining a link bar in a shared border, you can instantly create useful links throughout your site, no matter how large.

Finally, FrontPage 2002 includes a batch of new link options, including links to six different MSNBC news sources, MSN for stock quotes and Web search engines, and banner ad exchanges through Microsoft's bCentral.

✦　　✦　　✦

Using FrontPage Themes

In Chapters 1 and 2, you learned to apply FrontPage's (rather limited) set of pre-defined themes to a Web site. Themes are an extremely efficient way to apply a coordinated color scheme, standardized navigational icons, and global fonts and text formatting to a Web site. On the down side, there are only so many FrontPage themes, which limits your ability to create a distinctive Web site. In that sense, themes stand in the way of creating truly distinctive Web pages. The solution we focus on in this chapter is creating *customized* themes that define a unique look and feel for your site.

Themes — Behind the Scenes

You assign themes to an open Web by choosing Format ⇨ Theme, and choosing a theme from the list on the left side of the Themes dialog box. The All Pages options button applies the selected theme to an entire Web site, whereas the Selected Page option button applies the theme only to the open page (this option is available only in Page view).

In Chapter 1, we walked through the process of selecting a theme and applying it to your Web site. Theme elements are drawn from three categories:

- ✦ **Colors:** Includes the color assigned to text and the colors assigned to graphic and page elements, such as buttons and page backgrounds.

- ✦ **Graphics:** Includes the images used for buttons, page background, horizontal rules, and bullets.

- ✦ **Text:** Includes creating customized font styles in the Themes dialog box, which act in much the same way as styles in a word processing or desktop publishing program, with defined attributes such as font type, size, and color.

Each theme is a combination of assigned colors, embedded graphics, and text styles. Figure 10-1 shows a Web page with theme elements identified.

Figure 10-1: Theme elements are global, appearing on every page in a Web site.

If all you want to do is apply FrontPage's themes and customize them, skip ahead to the section "Customizing FrontPage Themes." If you aren't interested in economizing on Web design by applying site-wide formatting, skip this whole chapter! If you're curious — or more than curious — about exactly how themes work and how they interact with other approaches to Web design, read on.

Different Approaches to Using Themes

The ability to automatically assign dozens of text and page attributes, and to integrate dozens of graphic icons into a Web site instantly, tends to provoke different reactions in different kinds of Web designers.

The harried office assistant who has been assigned to have a prototype of the department's 700-page intranet, or the organization's 50-page Web site, online in a week may well breathe a sigh of relief and wonder, "How do I spiff these themes up a bit and slap them up on my site!?"

The HTML-trained Web developer will furrow his or her brow and wonder, "Exactly what kind of files am I dumping onto my Web site, and how will they interact with my external style sheets?"

And the full-time illustrator, who looks forward to carefully crafting the design of half a dozen Web pages to present the opening of an exhibit of stained glassware, may well have no use for themes at all.

What are themes made of?

As you apply themes to your site, FrontPage generates a folder called _themes on your Web site. This folder holds the files necessary to define the pictures, formatting, and other components of your theme. This _themes folder is a "hidden" file folder. To reveal it, choose Tools ➪ Web Settings, and choose the Advanced tab in the Web Settings dialog box. Click the Show Hidden Files and Folders checkbox, and then click Apply. You will be prompted to refresh your view; choose Yes. Figure 10-2 shows a typical themes folder and subfolder.

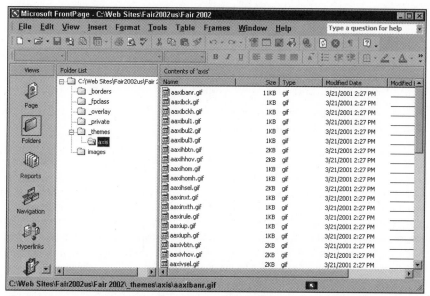

Figure 10-2: A typical _themes folder and subfolder

The _themes folder includes separate subfolders for each theme you apply to a site. FrontPage 2000 used to keep files from unused themes in your Web — which tended to add many unwanted files to your site. Our experiments with FrontPage 2002 indicate that it handles theme files better — when you change themes, old theme files are removed from your Web. You can find out if you do have unused theme files taking up Web space by switching to reports view. There is a report that shows how many unused themes are in that Web. If you click on the link in reports view that says Unused Themes, FrontPage will prompt you if you want to remove unused theme files.

Note   Microsoft stashes many important Web files in hidden folders, possibly to contribute to the illusion that there is no price to pay in terms of server space for various elements of FrontPage Webs (such as themes!). There is, however, no good reason to hide these folders. We suggest revealing all hidden folders as soon as you begin work on a Web.

With hidden files revealed, you can inspect the contents of any theme files you have generated. They will be composed of the image files (.gif and .jpeg images) used in your theme, and the Cascading Style Sheets (CSS) files that hold definitions for text and paragraph formatting. In addition, each theme folder will have a text file (.ut8) with basic information about the theme.

How CSS files define colors, fonts, and graphics

When you apply a theme, FrontPage generates files with .css extensions. These files, stored in the appropriate subfolder in the _Themes folder, define the graphics, colors, and fonts used in your theme.

+ Theme files that begin with the text "color" define colors for the theme.

+ Files that begin with "graph" define graphics for the theme — with or without active graphics. Themes with active graphics selected include additional graphic elements and color definitions for hovered-over navigation buttons.

+ The custom.css file defines fonts for generated navigation text that is placed on navigation buttons and banners.

+ CSS files that begin with the name of the theme (such as axis.css) are generated external style sheet files.

If you rely on FrontPage to generate your theme, there is no need to edit the content of these files by hand. If you want to do HTML coding to tweak your CSS files yourself (or if you just want to take a look at the files), you can open these files in Notepad by right-clicking on them in Folders view and choosing Open With from the context menu. Double-click on Notepad to open the files in Notepad. Alternatively, double-click on FrontPage to open the files in FrontPage.

For a full discussion of creating and editing CSS files, see Chapter 11.

Themes and style sheets

On one level, FrontPage themes conflict with external style sheets. If you're going to use Themes, it's difficult to later switch to standard Cascading Style Sheets. On the other hand, you can use FrontPage themes to quickly generate files that you can convert to traditional (non-FrontPage) style sheets.

As you apply a FrontPage theme, several Cascading Style Sheets (CSS) files that apply to the site are generated in your _Themes folder. If you are planning to apply an existing external style sheet, avoid assigning FrontPage themes.

On the other hand, if you are comfortable coding CSS files in HTML, you might still want to use FrontPage to generate your CSS files. You can always modify them.

Note Some of the functionality of FrontPage themes requires that you publish your Web to a server with FrontPage extensions. In Chapter 11, we'll show you how to use the "Apply Using CSS" checkbox to generate files that can be used to apply themes to sites without FrontPage server extensions.

Themes versus local formatting

What happens when colors, fonts, and graphic elements collide with objects or formatting assigned on a page? The local (page-assigned) formatting takes precedence.

For example, if you use the Formatting toolbar to assign black, Arial, 12-point font to text on a Web page, those attributes will not be affected by the colors and fonts you define for a theme.

Caution To take a problematic example, if you have assigned white text and a black page background to a page, and later assign a theme to that page with a white page background, the white text will stay white, but the page background will change — making your text invisible. This is why each time you apply a style, you get a warning telling you that fonts, colors, and other elements will be *changed* when the style is applied. Keep in mind, however, that some formatting will change, and some won't. Locally applied text formatting will not change when styles are assigned.

Customizing FrontPage Themes

There are essentially three ways you can customize themes:

✦ You can use the checkboxes in the Themes dialog box to select or deselect Vivid Colors, Active Graphics, and/or a Background picture. Figure 10-3 shows all three options selected.

✦ You can modify the color scheme for a theme by choosing from dozens of preset color scheme options.

✦ You can create a completely unique theme with your own graphic images, your own specified fonts for each theme element, and your own specified fonts (and substitute fonts) for any (or every!) font style used in your site.

In short, you have a rather impressive set of options for customizing themes, ranging from quick and simple to extremely detailed.

You can change themes by choosing Format ➪ Theme, and choosing a different theme. Alternatively, you can explore additional themes by clicking the Install Additional Themes option in the list of themes, and copying more themes from the FrontPage (or Office) CD.

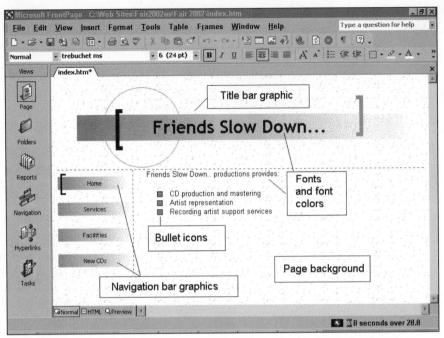

Figure 10-3: You can make significant changes to a theme simply by choosing different combinations of vivid colors, active graphics, and background options.

When you select a theme from the list in the Themes dialog box, you see a preview of the theme in the Sample of Theme window on the right. You can refine a selected theme by making selections in the Vivid Colors, Active Graphics, and Background Picture checkboxes, located in the lower-left corner of the Themes dialog box. As you select, or deselect, these checkboxes, the Sample of Theme window reflects changes to the page attributes:

✦ The Vivid Colors checkbox available for each theme substitutes a different (more "vivid") color scheme.

✦ The Active Graphics checkbox substitutes more colorful graphics for elements like bullets and banners. But the "active" part of this option generates interactive navigation buttons that display differently in their normal state, when hovered over, and when selected.

✦ The Background Picture checkbox toggles between a tiled graphic image background and a solid color.

Below the three checkboxes just described is the Apply Using CSS checkbox, which enables you to attach an HTML-coded Cascading Style Sheets (CSS) file. For a full discussion of Cascading Style Sheets, see Chapter 11.

Creating and Applying New Themes

To create a new theme, begin with an existing theme that has some elements you want to include in your new theme. From there, you will modify the theme, and save it with a new name.

Note   Can you just start from scratch to create a new theme? Nope. FrontPage requires that you create a new theme by starting with an existing one. If you plan to create a completely new theme, the process involves replacing all the inherited theme elements from the original theme. The Blank theme makes a nice starting point for creating completely new themes. Once you have created a new theme, you can use *that* theme as a starting point for additional new themes.

After you select an existing theme to work from, click the Modify button in the Themes dialog box, and then click the Save As button in the Modify area of the dialog box. The Save Theme dialog box appears, as shown in Figure 10-4. This dialog box enables you to save your theme with a new name. As you make additional changes to your own, new theme, a Save button will appear in the Modify area of the Themes dialog box.

Figure 10-4: You can't create a new theme from scratch, but you can resave an edited theme as a new theme.

Themes that are applied to Webs are saved on the Web server. Saved themes, whether they are applied to a Web or not, are saved on the local system. The default location for Windows ME is `C:\Windows\Application Data\Microsoft\Themes`. In Windows 2000, the default location is `C:\Documents and Settings\user name\Application Data\Microsoft\Themes`. If you need to move a saved theme (that is not yet applied to a Web), you can copy the files associated with that theme to a new computer.

Caution   If you need to move a saved theme, it is important that you not only save the files inside that folder but the folder itself too. For example, if you move the Axis theme, then all files for the Axis theme must be in a folder called Axis.

The Modify button opens, or hides, the area of the Themes dialog box that enables you to change theme elements. *If you're going to create a custom theme, you want the Modify buttons visible,* as shown in Figure 10-5.

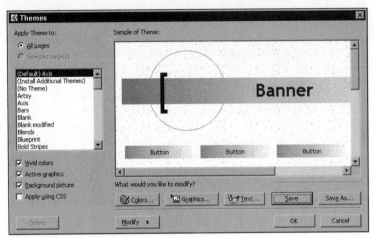

Figure 10-5: The real power of themes is hidden until you click the Modify button!

Defining theme colors

There are two basic ways to define theme colors. You can choose a color scheme, or you can assign colors to different elements of your pages individually. Preset color schemes are faster. For a carefully designed site, assigning specific colors to page elements provides much more control over how pages look.

Using color schemes

You can replace a theme color with one of many pre-defined color schemes by clicking the Colors button (visible only when Modify is selected). The Color Schemes tab of the Modify Theme dialog box (shown in Figure 10-6) illustrates each theme — although it doesn't tell you exactly how the color scheme will be applied.

If you see a scheme you like, click on it. Choose either the Normal Colors or Vivid Colors option button — as you do, the Sample of Theme area of the dialog box will illustrate how the theme will look. This is where you can find out exactly how colors will be applied to text and page background.

Click OK to apply your new color scheme to your theme. Then, click Save (or Save As, if you haven't yet saved your theme) to save the new color scheme as part of your theme.

For even more color scheme options, click the Color Wheel tab in the Modify Theme dialog box. The Color Wheel tab enables you to generate an aesthetically matched five-color color scheme to apply to your theme. (It's kind of like having an interior decorator for your home or office, and telling him or her that you want a color scheme built around the color blue, for example.) To generate a color scheme, click the Color Wheel tab in the Modify Themes dialog box. You'll see the Color Wheel, as shown in Figure 10-7.

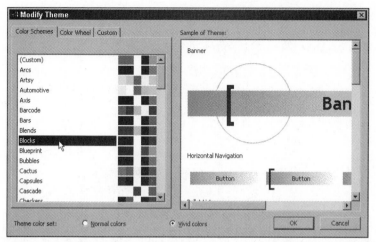

Figure 10-6: Microsoft drafted their fashion coordinators to design attractive color schemes. Any truth to the rumor that these are the folks who fashioned Bill Gates' wardrobe?

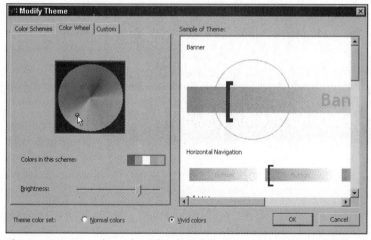

Figure 10-7: Use the color wheel to define your own color scheme.

To adjust the colors in your customized color scheme, change the setting of the Brightness slider. As you experiment with color schemes and brightness levels, you'll see the results previewed in the Sample of Theme area of the dialog box. You can also toggle between intense colors and muted colors by using the Normal Colors or Vivid Colors radio buttons, located at the bottom of the dialog box. Both options will be available after you complete your customized theme.

Assigning colors manually

For the most complete control over your theme color scheme, you can use the Custom tab in the Modify Theme dialog box (see Figure 10-8).

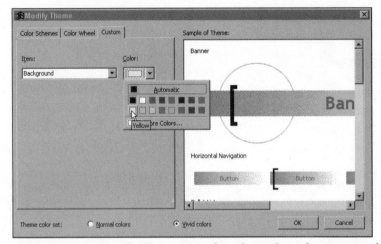

Figure 10-8: You can fine-tune your color scheme from the Custom tab of the Modify Theme dialog box.

With the Custom tab selected, pull down the Item drop-down list and select the page element (Background, for example) or the type of text to which you want to assign a color. Then, click the Color drop-down list and select a color to assign to that text element.

Here, too, you can define two sets of colors for your theme by using either the Normal Colors or Vivid Colors option button.

Not all of the colors you assign in the Custom tab will preview in the Sample of Theme area (for example, table colors won't appear, as there is no table in the Sample of Theme area). However, you can see enough of the assigned colors to get a good sense of how pages will look.

About custom colors

When you open the Color palette in the Custom tab of the Modify Themes dialog box, in addition to the 16 preset colors, you'll see a More Colors option. Click the More Colors option to open the More Colors dialog box, shown in Figure 10-9.

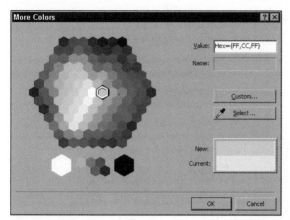

Figure 10-9: Colors in the hexagonal color palette will be accurately interpreted by both major browsers.

The hexagonally shaped color template (symbolic of the Web's six-digit color numbering system) displays colors that can be accurately interpreted by both major Web browsers.

Assign a color by clicking a color in the palette. If you are an experienced, professional Web designer working from your own palette of hexadecimal color values, you can select a color by entering a hexadecimal (six-character) color code in the Value field, in the format Hex={xx,xx,xx} (for example, Hex={FF,00,00} for bright red).

To create a custom color, click the Custom button, and use either the color grid or the two alternate color definition options (Hue, Saturation, Value; or Red, Green, Blue) to define a color.

Finally, you can use the Select button to turn your cursor into an eyedropper. With the eyedropper cursor, point and click anywhere on your screen to load a color into the palette.

Caution Although the colors in the palette of the Colors tab are browser-safe, custom colors are not. If you create your own colors by using the palette that appears when you click the Custom button, browsers will do their best to reproduce these colors by mixing, or dithering, pixels of the 216 available colors to simulate your color, with varying degrees of success. In short, there's no guarantee that the custom colors that you mix will be accurately displayed by browsers.

After you assign colors to your theme elements, click OK in the dialog box. You'll return to the main Themes dialog box, and you can now define custom font styles and graphics for your theme.

After you modify the color scheme of your customized theme, click the OK button in the Modify Theme dialog box.

Assigning fonts to styles

Click the Text button in the Modify area of the Themes dialog box to define text fonts for any HTML style.

You can define a font for a standard HTML style by first selecting that style (Heading 1, for example) from the Item drop-down menu in the Modify Theme dialog box. Then, click one of the fonts in the Font list. You can use the vertical scroll bar to see more fonts, if necessary.

You cannot define font *size* (or color), or other text and paragraph attributes for a theme this way. You can only choose a font. In order to define additional attributes, FrontPage makes us jump through a hoop or two.

To define additional text attributes for a style, click the More Text Styles button. Then, select your style from the list in the Style dialog box, as shown in Figure 10-10.

Figure 10-10: Font compatibility depends on whether the selected font is installed on a viewer's system.

With the style selected, click the Modify button. Then, use the Format button in the Modify Style dialog box to define a new style and assign font type, size, color, and even paragraph formatting. Choose from four categories of formatting: Font, Paragraph, Border, or Numbering. Use the dialog boxes that open to define different attributes for your style. These formatting attributes will be displayed in the Preview window of the dialog box.

After you define your additional style attributes, click the OK button in the Modify Style dialog box. Your new, custom-defined style will be available in the list of styles to edit in the Style dialog box. After you assign custom fonts to different styles, click the OK button to close this dialog box and return to the Themes dialog box.

> **Note** The Text section of the Themes dialog box controls only how text that *you* create will be displayed. It does not affect how *generated* text that is overlaid on graphics for navigation buttons and page banners will be displayed. Use the Graphics button in the Themes dialog box to define how overlaid text is formatted. See the section "Modifying theme graphics" later in this chapter for a complete explanation of how to control fonts in generated navigational theme elements.

Font substitution

The fonts assigned by FrontPage themes work only if the viewer's system supports those fonts. What happens, then, if the Trebuchet MS font that is part of your theme is not installed on a viewer's system?

This problem is addressed in the `themes.inf` file generated in the `root _themes` folder. The `themes.inf` file is a text file that can be opened in Notepad (right-click on it and choose Open With, and then choose Notepad). The `themes.inf` file lists all fonts that can be applied in a theme. Near the end of the file, however, it also has a substitution list that defines how unrecognized fonts will be handled by a browser. Therefore, for example, that unsupported Trebuchet MS font would be replaced with the default system variable font, and if one is not defined, with Swiss font.

> **Note** *Variable* font is a system's default proportionally-spaced font, whereas *fixed* is a system's default nonproportionally-spaced font. Characters in variable fonts are of different widths (for example, a w is much wider than an i); characters in fixed fonts (such as Courier New, for example) all take the same space.

Unique fonts definitely lend character to a Web page. But if your fonts are not interpreted by a visitor's system, you'll lose much of the style you are trying to express when a visitor's system substitutes other fonts. The site shown in Figure 10-11 contrasts the assigned font and a substituted font.

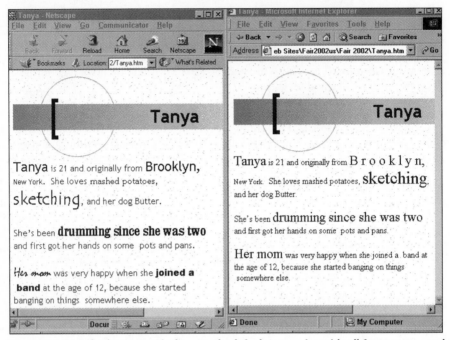

Figure 10-11: The browser window on the left shows a site with all fonts supported. The browser window on the right shows the same site viewed on a system that does not support the assigned fonts.

Substituted fonts have a fairly dramatic impact on the look of a Web page. Text blocks get longer or shorter, text flow around images is changed, and the overall lightness/darkness dynamic of a page is changed.

Nonsupported fonts are a much more common disruption in a presentation than browsers that don't support Web site features. Remember that font support is dependent on the computer system, not the browser of your visitor.

Modifying theme graphics

Theme graphics include the following:

- ✦ Background image
- ✦ Banner
- ✦ Bulleted list graphic icons (3)
- ✦ Global navigation buttons (1)
- ✦ Horizontal navigation buttons (3)
- ✦ Horizontal rule

- ✦ Quick Home button
- ✦ Quick Next button
- ✦ Quick Previous button
- ✦ Quick Up button
- ✦ Vertical navigation buttons (3)

The numbers after the elements in the preceding list identify the maximum number of each element used in a theme. Navigation buttons have a maximum of three different images — for the up, hovered over, and selected states of each button. There are three bullet images for three sizes of buttons.

When you apply an existing theme, a full set of graphic files is added to the _Theme folder in your Web site. These files provide images that are the background for navigational buttons and banners, as well as bullets (of different sizes), horizontal rules, and page background tiles.

If you want to create a unique theme, you need to (and can) create a full set of theme graphics. The numbers in the preceding list will help you as you create a full set of images to plug into your custom theme. Figure 10-12 shows a sample set of theme graphic filenames.

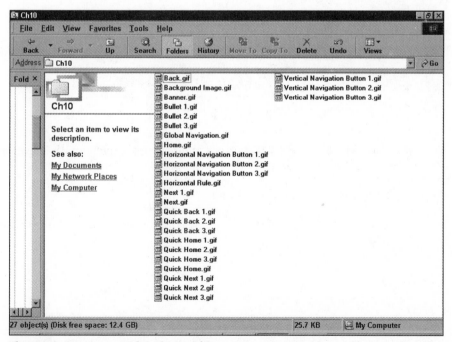

Figure 10-12: Use your favorite graphic program to create a set of icons to import into FrontPage, and use them as unique elements in a custom theme.

The text that is placed over these graphics (banners at the top of pages, and horizontal and vertical navigation buttons) is generated in either your Web pages or your navigation bars. You can assign custom images for each of these elements in your theme. You can also change the font of the text that is added to these images.

Therefore, when you create your own custom graphics for a FrontPage theme, do *not* include text in these images. Simply create the background buttons (and banner) and let FrontPage overlay text on them.

To customize theme graphics, click the Graphics button in the Themes dialog box. A Modify Theme dialog box opens, as shown in Figure 10-13.

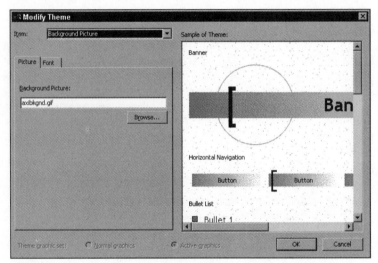

Figure 10-13: Choosing a background picture for a theme

Many graphic elements (navigation buttons and banners) include both images and text. Navigational buttons, for instance, consist of a graphical button and button text. Some graphic elements, such as the background page color, don't have text, so you don't need to define text fonts for them.

To define text for a graphic element, select the Font tab of the dialog box as shown in Figure 10-14.

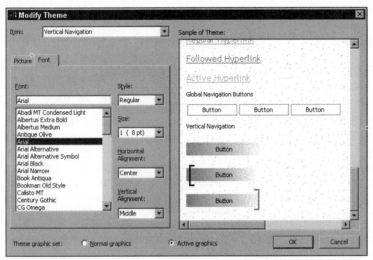

Figure 10-14: You can define a customized text font for each graphic theme element (such as navigation buttons and page title bars).

Font sizes and types for navigation buttons are controlled in the Graphics Modify Theme dialog box, but font colors are assigned in the Colors tab.

For an example of creating and applying custom graphics to a theme, try the tutorial in the next section.

Tutorial 10-1: Designing and applying a custom theme

In the following tutorial, you will design your own custom theme, including a custom background color, custom color scheme, and navigational buttons.

1. Open an existing FrontPage Web, or create a new one by using the Personal Web template.

2. Select Format ➪ Theme to open the Theme dialog box.

3. Click the Blank theme in the list of themes, and click the Modify button in the dialog box to display the three modification buttons.

4. Click the Colors button, and click the Custom tab in the Modify Theme dialog box.

5. Click the Active Colors radio button.

6. Choose Heading 1 from the Item drop-down list, and select Maroon from the Color palette.

7. In the same manner as in Step 6, assign blue to hyperlinks and yellow to background.

8. Click the OK button in the dialog box.

9. Click the Graphics button. Select Global Navigational Buttons from the Item drop-down list, and click the Font tab in the dialog box. Select a font from the Font list, and 10-point from the Size list. Click OK.

10. Assign pictures to each of the graphic elements used in the theme. Start with Background Picture, and use the Browse button to find a File.

You can create your own graphics from PhotoShop or another Web graphics program, or you can download a set of theme graphics from the book's Web site.

11. Click the Text button, and select Heading 1 from the Item drop-down menu. Click More Text Styles, and choose h1 from the Styles list. Click the Modify button in the Style dialog box, and then click the Format button. Choose Font from the pop-up menu. In the Font dialog box, select a font size of 14, and select Bold for the Font Style. Click OK. Change the Font sizes for the h2 style to 12-point Bold, and the h3 style to 10-point Bold in the same way. Finally, change the font for the Body style to 10-point (but not Bold).

12. Click the Save As button in the Themes dialog box, and enter a new name for the theme (make up your own name). Click OK.

13. Test your new theme: Click OK in the Themes dialog box to apply your new custom theme. Note the appearance of headings in your Web pages, the color of hyperlinks, and the page background.

If you don't want to save this custom theme, select your new theme in the Themes dialog box, click the Delete button, and then click Yes in the next dialog box.

Summary

FrontPage Themes are an effective way to apply many page formatting elements to an entire Web site. Theme elements include page background color, text fonts, sizes, colors, navigation icons, horizontal line images, and link colors.

The drawback to out-of-the-box Themes is that there are only about three dozen of them. Not only are your design options limited, but savvy Web surfers will recognize that you took your formatting from a FrontPage theme.

By defining your own, custom theme, you can combine the expediency of themes with the uniqueness of your own colors, graphics, and font formatting.

✦   ✦   ✦

Working with Styles and Style Sheets

Chapter 5 showed you how to apply basic formatting styles to the text of your HTML pages. In this chapter, you learn how to use style sheets to gain better control over text formatting within a particular page or across an entire Web. This chapter explains how to create a style sheet and apply it to your Web pages. It also demonstrates some advanced features of Cascading Style Sheets (CSS), with a special emphasis on using CSS to position elements on the page.

New Feature FrontPage 2002 adds some minor enhancements to the style capabilities introduced in FrontPage 2000. One important improvement is FrontPage's ability to handle both paragraph and character styles automatically.

Discovering Styles

When the HTML standard was originally conceived, it was envisioned as a method of defining the structural elements of a document rather than the formatting. It was left largely to the browser to decide how to display any particular element, and early Web browsers typically gave users control over the display of discrete HTML elements.

As the Web has increasingly become a media for publishing, however, developers have not been content to let viewers mangle their carefully designed Web pages. One symptom of this was the creation of new formatting HTML tags, like the insidious `<font>` tag, that give Web designers more desktop-publishing style control over the appearance of their pages. Even this has not provided a sufficient level of control over page elements, however. As the size and complexity of Web publishing enterprises have increased dramatically, people have sorely needed a mechanism to help control the consistency of pages within a site. Now that we are seeing the proliferation of "internet appliances," there is also a need for an easy way to define appliance-specific formatting. The answer: the Cascading Style Sheet (CSS) standard.

What are styles?

A *style* is a labeled set of formatting instructions, called *style declarations*, that can be applied to elements of a Web page. Once created, style declarations can be embedded directly in a particular page in order to control elements of that page, or they can be collected into a *style sheet* and linked to as many pages as needed to share a consistent look and feel. A style sheet is a collection of style definitions that can be applied to elements of an HTML page. These style sheets are plain text files that contain formatting codes using the CSS syntax (see Figure 11-1).

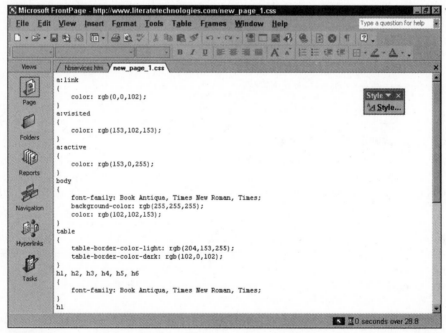

Figure 11-1: A sample style sheet illustrating style declarations for formatting Web page elements

Style sheet formatting is far more versatile than standard HTML, and you can use this versatility to make pages that you couldn't make without styles. By using styles sheets, you can add background images to individual paragraphs, make text an exact size (rather than be restricted to the seven logical sizes available to HTML), add borders around text, and even adjust the spacing between lines of text. In fact, the chief danger of learning to use styles is the temptation to abuse this power. There are two problems with relying too heavily on elaborate use of styles in your Web pages: (1) Web site visitors typically display a remarkable lack of patience with overly designed pages (can you blame them?); and (2) browser support for styles is neither complete nor consistent (and let's not forget about those browsers still in use that predate the advent of CSS). In the next section, we take a look at the current state of the CSS standards. Later in the chapter, we discuss some approaches to dealing with browser differences. You're on your own, though, to deal with the temptation to overuse styles.

The evolution of CSS

Cascading Style Sheets (CSS) is the standard that dictates how styles are defined. It is one of many standards that have been written by the World Wide Web Consortium, familiarly known as the W3C. Although the CSS Level 1 standard (CSS1) has been a recommended standard since December 1996, browsers have been slow to support the complete standard. Microsoft's Internet Explorer 3.0 was the first browser to incorporate any support (and it wasn't very well implemented). The version 4.x browsers, both Microsoft's and Netscape's, support the standard to varying degrees. The most recent versions, as of this writing, Internet Explorer 5.5 and Netscape 6, both have reasonably complete support for CSS1. CSS1 deals with the formatting properties of Web page elements. Most of this chapter focuses on creating and using the CSS1 elements that FrontPage supports.

CSS2 extends the original standard by providing support for media-specific style sheets, which can be used to adjust formatting to nontraditional Web page displays. It also provides support for downloadable fonts, table layout, and internationalization features. By far the most well-known portion of the standard, however, relates to the positioning of content on a page. This is an exciting prospect for anyone who has spent hours trying to lay out a complex page by using HTML tables and invisible spacer graphics. None of the browsers completely implement the CSS2 standard, but all of the 4.x and higher versions have some support for positioning. FrontPage 2002 includes support for the positioning properties and we discuss these later in the chapter. If you are interested in more details about the CSS standards, including the recent work on a CSS3 standard, check out the sidebar, "The CSS Standards."

Should I use styles?

Using FrontPage, creating style sheets is so easy—and using them will save you so many headaches down the road as you develop your Webs—that, in a sense, you would be foolish not to use a style sheet under any circumstance. Whether you are developing a new site or revamping an existing one, adding styles is a fairly straightforward process. If any of the following circumstances apply to you, you will be wise to consider implementing style sheets:

The CSS Standards

The Cascading Style Sheet standard is defined by the World Wide Web Consortium (W3C). Level 1 of the standard was approved in December 1996. It sets forth the basic concepts for style sheet notation and specifies the syntax for formatting elements of a Web page. Included in the specification are provisions for fonts, colors, text properties, alignment, margins, borders, and lists. You can read the complete W3C CSS1 Recommendation at http://www.w3.org/TR/REC-CSS1 961217.html.

In May 1998, the CSS Level 2 recommendations became an official W3C proposal. In plain English, this means that the Level 2 additions have been thoroughly discussed, resulting in enough agreement to present a formal proposal to the W3C. The proposal is not considered a standard until it is officially recommended by the W3C. In the interim, of course, the major browsers have already announced and begun to implement various aspects of the proposal (as well as some of their own variations). However, don't count on consistent behavior from the browsers until the proposal is accepted.

The most highly touted feature of CSS2 is its support for absolute and relative positioning of Web page elements. After the specification has solidified, designers will be able to lay out page elements precisely. Gone will be the days of kludging page layouts with tables and frames. Also, when combined with a scripting language, positioning styles can be used to create Dynamic HTML (DHTML) animations and sophisticated page effects.

Less noticed, but equally valuable, are provisions in the Level 2 proposal for specifying how page elements should be represented by different media types, such as printed output, a Braille device, speech synthesizers, handheld devices, and so forth. These provisions will enable devices other than standard computers to access and present Web pages easier. For more information, and to peruse the latest version of the W3C CSS2 proposed recommendations, visit http://www.w3.org/TR/REC-CSS2/.

Although the Level 2 standard has been around for some time, it has not been completely implemented by any browser. So, much of it remains theoretical and we will not cover it here because, not surprisingly, FrontPage doesn't support these features either. Not to be daunted, however, the W3C is already hard at work on the CSS3 recommendation. Initially, the CSS3 work is focused on "modularizing" the CSS specification into a number of distinct components so that it can be more readily updated. If you are interested in the latest developments, visit the W3C's CSS current work pages at http://www.w3.org/Style/CSS/current-work.

✦ Your site has more than 20 pages with a similar look and feel.

✦ Your site's content is developed or maintained by multiple authors and you want to enforce consistency.

✦ You would like to have more control over the look and feel of your pages (keeping in mind that "more" is a relative term).

Working with styles does require some thoughtful planning, however, given the vagaries in browser support. You will need to familiarize yourself with which style elements are cross-browser "safe" (keeping in mind that FrontPage will happily implement any CSS features supported by Internet Explorer) and implement some strategies to ensure that your pages "degrade gracefully" for those browsers that do not have CSS support. These issues are tackled at the end of this chapter.

Styles versus themes

But what if you are already using FrontPage themes on your site to control the formatting of your page? Do you need to switch? No, in fact, CSS and FrontPage themes can coexist together peaceably, or if you like, you can even have FrontPage generate your themes as CSS style sheets. Later in the chapter we will show you how you can even use FrontPage themes on a non-FrontPage Web server by converting them to styles.

Styles versus fonts

And what if you are happily using the `<font>` tag to format all of your font faces, sizes, colors, and styles? Why change that, especially if not all browsers support styles? There are several reasons. First, philosophically, using styles enables you to separate the structure of your content from its formatting, which is more consistent with the way the Web was supposed to be. Second, pragmatically, it is a lot easier to maintain styles than font tags. Finally, from a quality standpoint, using styles makes much cleaner, simpler HTML (especially in FrontPage which seems to want to write a new font tag set for every paragraph, whether the fonts have changed or not). For browser compatibility, see the last section of this chapter for advice on how to combine font and style usage judiciously to provide the best possible support for all users.

Defining Styles

This section walks through the process of creating a style definition in FrontPage. Once we have covered the basics, we will take a look at the various ways in which you can apply styles, and then examine some of the more detailed aspects of creating and applying styles.

Creating a new style

Implementing a style takes two steps: First, you need to define the style — and name it if you are defining a style for an existing HTML element — then, associate the style information with one or more page elements. This section explains these two steps in detail using a page from our Humbull and Bruskly intranet example. To create a new style, follow these steps:

1. Create a new Web page to contain your embedded style.

2. Select Format ➪ Style to open the Style dialog box.

The Style dialog box (shown in Figure 11-2) enables you to create user-defined style classes or to alter the default appearance of any standard HTML tag.

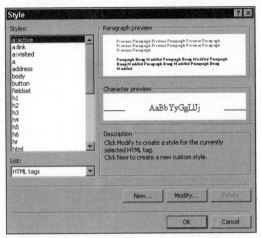

Figure 11-2: The Style dialog box enables you to create and edit embedded styles.

In the Style dialog box, you see a list of existing style elements (which should be simply existing HTML tag identifiers), preview boxes for Paragraph styles and Character styles, a brief description of what to do next, and a List selector with options for HTML tags (the default until you have created a style) and user-defined styles. To create a new, user-defined style from the Style dialog box, follow these steps:

1. Select "User-defined styles" from the List drop-down list. The Styles list above it should become empty.

2. Click the New button to bring up the New Style dialog box.

3. In the Name (selector) field, type a name for your style (for example, **myfirst-style**), as illustrated in Figure 11-3.

4. Select a Style Type from the drop-down menu — your choices are Paragraph, which applies the style at the paragraph level (e.g., to an entire paragraph of text), or Character, which applies a style to any entity you might select. (In a few moments, we will look at how this translates into CSS for those who are curious about such things.)

5. Click the Format button and define your style using one or more of the Formatting Properties dialog boxes for Font, Paragraph, Border, Numbering, or Position. Details on these are coming up in the next section.

Figure 11-3: The New Style dialog box showing the beginnings of your new style

6. Click OK once to return to the New Style dialog box. Note that the Preview window now contains a sample of your style as shown in Figure 11-4 (your results may vary, depending on how you defined your style). Also, the Description field shows you the CSS style definition that you have just created.

Figure 11-4: Previewing your newly created style in the New Style dialog box

7. Click OK twice more to return to your HTML page.

Caution

Make sure that you restrict style names to single words (no spaces). FrontPage *will* allow you to name a style "my new style," but you will not be able to use it. You can use the underscore character to separate multiple words, e.g. "my_first_style."

You now have a custom-defined style that appears in the drop-down list of available styles in the Styles list of the Formatting toolbar. Note that FrontPage puts a period in front of the name of the style that you defined. So, for instance, "myfirststyle" appears as `.myfirststyle`. The dot indicates that the style is really a style class that can be applied to any HTML element. (See the sidebar "Specifying Selector Types" for more information.)

When you create a style in this fashion, FrontPage embeds the style definition in the HTML page. You can see this code by switching to HTML view as shown in Figure 11-5.

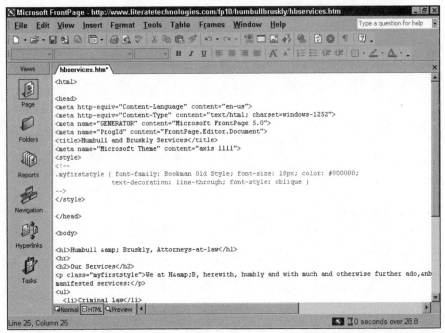

Figure 11-5: A glimpse of the CSS styles you can create using FrontPage's Style dialog box

A style sheet created in this manner, known as an embedded style, is written at the top of your HTML and can be applied to any element on the page. As you can see, it is enclosed in `<style>` and `</style>` tags with internal HTML comment tags to hide the style declarations from browsers that don't recognize CSS. The `<style>` tag is placed before the end `</head>` tag in the HTML page. The basic syntax for a style declaration is as follows:

```
selector {property_1: value_1;...property_n: value_n}
```

where `selector` is the name of the style, and each of the `property:value` pairs delimited by semicolons represents a formatting option you have applied.

Specifying Selector Types

Any valid HTML element can be used as a CSS selector (although, in practice, some elements lend themselves more readily to style sheet use than others). In addition, CSS permits the use of class and ID designators to give you more flexibility in how you assign styles.

In the style sheet syntax, a class is indicated by an initial period in front of the selector name. An ID is designated with an initial hash mark (#). You can also combine class names and/or IDs with selector names. The following code illustrates all the valid possibilities:

h1

.myClass

#myID

h1.myClass

h1#myID

h1.myClass#myID

.myClass#myID

To associate a particular HTML element with a class or ID identifier, simply add the class or ID identifier as an attribute of the tag. So, for example, to associate an HTML element with the selector `h1.myClass#myID` use the following:

<h1 class="myclass" id="myid">Some stylish text</h1>

In practice, you may never need to add these by hand to your Web pages. In most cases, FrontPage takes care of the dirty work. FrontPage does use, and assumes that you understand, the CSS terminology of selector, class, and ID.

What is the difference between a class identifier and an ID? Basically, a class is reusable. So, for example, you might create a style class called `.bigred`. You can then associate that class with as many different HTML elements as you want. An ID is guaranteed to be unique. It can only be associated with a single instance of an element.

And why does FrontPage support the use of ID selector names, but not provide any means for you to create one (other than by hand)? Maybe in the next version?

Modifying existing styles

Thus far we have concentrated on creating styles from scratch. You may have noticed that, by default, these styles are applied as classes to whatever element you are attempting to style. The power of this technique lies in the flexibility of the style. Another approach, though, is to modify the default style information for an existing HTML tag, say, for example, a Header level 1 (h1) or Bold (b). To modify an existing tag element, follow these steps:

1. Select Format ➪ Style.

2. From the List drop-down menu in the Style dialog box, select HTML Tags, to modify a standard HTML tag.

3. Select the tag, (for example, ul) from the Styles list.

4. Click the Modify button.

5. Click the Format button.

6. Make your Style selections, as desired.

7. Click OK on all dialog boxes until you return to Page view.

By using this method, all bulleted lists that you create on this page will inherit the style that you have defined for bulleted lists without your having to apply the style manually. Usually, you will create general-purpose style definitions for standard HTML elements and use class designations for more-specialized styles. To learn more about how to use the cascade principles in applying styles, see the section later in the chapter, "The Cascade."

Applying styles

There are two basic methods for applying a style to a page element. Which one you use depends in part on what kind of style it is and also on what element you are applying it to.

Styles created as classes are listed in the Styles drop-down list on the Formatting toolbar. (They are labeled with a paragraph sign.) To add a paragraph style from this list, click anywhere in the paragraph of text you wish to apply the style to, and select the style from the drop-down menu.

If the style you created was a character style, you will notice a character icon (a) next to the style name. To apply a character style, first select the text you wish to apply the style to, and select the character style. If you try to apply a paragraph style to selected text, FrontPage applies the style to the entire paragraph of text.

Note   You may be wondering how FrontPage distinguishes between paragraph and character styles (especially because there is no such distinction in CSS). The answer is simple: Paragraph styles are written as generic class-style selectors. When you apply a paragraph style, it adds the appropriate class name to the tags surrounding the paragraph of text. Character styles are written as class selectors for span elements. When you select text and then apply a character style, it adds a span tag around the selected text and adds the appropriate class attribute.

If you would like to apply a style to an element type other than regular text, you can define the style by using the Style button on the Properties dialog box of the given element. The following elements have Style buttons:

✦ line breaks

✦ horizontal rules

✦ images

✦ hyperlinks

✦ bullets and numbering

✦ page

✦ table

To add a style, select the Properties dialog box of the element and click the Style button. This opens the Style dialog box that you used to create a style. The one notable difference, as illustrated in Figure 11-6, is that the Selector name and Style type lists are unavailable, and under them have been added Class and ID lists. To add a style to this element, select the appropriate Class or ID name from the drop-down lists and click OK.

Note   As you may have realized, you can also use the Style dialog box here to create a new style and apply it immediately to the element in question. When you do this, you create an inline style, that is, a style that is applied *inline* to the element in question. This style cannot be shared among other elements on the page. We will discuss inline styles a bit later in the chapter.

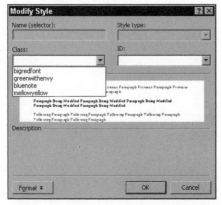

Figure 11-6: FrontPage's Style dialog box, showing Class and ID selector lists

As an example, let's create a list style that defines a new bullet image, and then apply the style to a list.

1. First, we create a list by creating the bullet point text elements, selecting them, and clicking the Bullets icon on the Formatting toolbar. Alternatively, we might have taken the longer way around by selecting Format ➪ Bullets and Numbering from the menu bar and then selecting the particular bullet style we wanted.

2. Next, to create a new style, we begin by selecting Format ⇨ Style to open the Style dialog box and click the New button.

3. In the New Style dialog box, name the style **bullethole** by typing the name in the Selector field. Select Paragraph from the Style type list.

4. Select Numbering from the Format drop-down menu to open the Bullets and Numbering dialog box.

5. We want to add a picture icon, so in the Picture Bullets tab, click the Browse button to locate the file you want. We will use a picture file called `bullet-hole.gif`. Once you have selected the file, click OK once to return to the New Style dialog box, where you should see the new style information in the Description window. Click OK again to return to your HTML page.

Note   You will find all of the example files referenced in this book, including `bullet-hole.gif`, on the book's Web site. For complete details on accessing this book's Web content, see the Preface.

6. To apply the new style, you have a choice. You can select an entire bulleted list, and select the `bullethole` style from the Style drop-down menu in the Format toolbar. Alternatively, right click on the list and select List Properties. Click the Style button and select `bullethole` from the class drop-down list. Click OK to return to your page. Sample results are shown in Figure 11-7.

Figure 11-7: Adding a bullethole style to your bulleted lists

Caution When you create a new style using the Style button for an element, you can, if you want, enter a class (or ID) name for that element. This will associate the class with the element and the style with the element. However, it will not associate the class with the style, as you might reasonably have intended. Nor will it even give you a named style that you can apply elsewhere. To accomplish either of these last two objectives, you must use the Format ⇨ Style menu item.

Style Properties

FrontPage provides you with property dialog boxes for several aspects of style formatting, namely:

✦ **Fonts:** for character formatting

✦ **Paragraphs:** for line and paragraph formatting

✦ **Borders:** for borders, boxes, and shading

✦ **Numbering:** for ordered and unordered lists

✦ **Position:** for positioning page elements

Note You may notice that all of these formatting commands are available directly through the Format menu list as well. In fact, several of the items create inline styles regardless of whether you thought you were using styles or not!

Of course, not all formatting options apply to every element. Note that FrontPage permits you to define and apply styles to elements even when it doesn't really make sense to do so. You will still need to exercise some judgment over the matter.

The following sections describe the various style formatting options in more detail.

Font

Use the Font property to select a font family, and then designate a color, size, style (bold, italics, or bold italics), and any special effects for the font family. You can also control a font's character spacing, both vertically (the position of the character relative to a line of characters) and horizontally (the space between characters).

CSS supports multiple font family references for a given style. A browser uses the first font in the list that it can find (this is the same behavior exhibited by the ⟨font⟩ tag). For example, you could create a style such as the following:

```
h1 {font-family: my_favorite_wacky_font, Arial, Helvetica,
sans-serif;}
```

The catch is that the Font dialog box does not directly support the use of multiple fonts. You have to type in the list by hand.

The Font dialog box used for style formatting (see Figure 11-8) is almost identical to the dialog box you get when you select Format ⇨ Font from the menu toolbar. There are, however, two subtle differences. The first is simply that this dialog box omits a number of checkboxes that the regular Font menu lets you apply. These are mostly little-used HTML tags that pertain to the format of text. (These include Strong, Emphasis, Sample, Definition, Citation, Variable, Keyboard, and Code.) These have no correlation in CSS, so isn't it nice that they aren't there to confuse you?

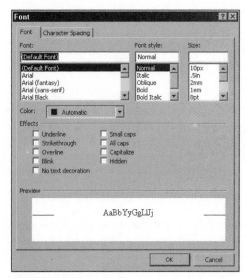

Figure 11-8: The Font formatting dialog box, as seen when formatting styles

The second difference is somewhat more interesting. You may have seen Web sites that have managed to get rid of the less-than-aesthetically-pleasing underline that has come to be identified with hyperlinks (to the point that you should avoid the underline tag for underlining on any Web page, because people will assume it is clickable). The trick to removing the hyperlink underline is a CSS property called "text decoration." (Isn't that just the cutest name for an underline? And you thought techies had no sense of poetry.) Simply check No Text Decoration on your font style, apply it to a hyperlink, and it will remove the underline from your hyperlinks. By the way, to learn a simple method for getting the underline to reappear when the user puts the mouse over the cursor, check out the Advanced Techniques section near the end of this chapter.

Paragraph

The Paragraph dialog box, shown in Figure 11-9, enables you to control a block of text's alignment, indentation, and spacing. This dialog box is the same as the one used to control line formatting in the Format menu. (See Chapter 5 for details on paragraph formatting.) In fact, here's a little secret: All of the formatting commands in the Paragraph dialog box, as well as in the Border and Shading dialog box and the Bullets and Numbering dialog box, create inline styles when you access them via the Format menu item. So you have been using styles all this time and didn't even know it!

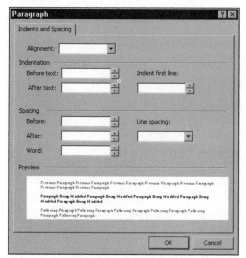

Figure 11-9: Set paragraph style options in the Paragraph dialog box.

Caution　If you produce a page that you intend to print, don't set the text size in pixels. If you set text size in pixels, then the text will probably print amazingly small! (For example, on a 300-dpi printer, text that is 10-pixels high prints at a height of about 1/32 inch.)

Border

The border formatting option uses the Borders and Shading dialog box to define border colors, width, and padding as well as shading properties such as foreground and background colors, or background images. To create a border, first select a setting: None, Box, or Custom. If you select Custom, you can create a border along any or all of the four sides of the block's rectangle. Select from a variety of line styles for the border, as well as border color and width, as illustrated in Figure 11-10. You can also dictate the padding between the border and the contents of the bordered element.

The Shading tab has options for background and foreground colors. In place of a background color, you can instead designate a background image and properties that control how it is displayed.

Caution　Be careful using border and shading style options — many of them are not cross-platform compatible in version 4.0 browsers.

All Units Are Not Created Equal

Many of the options available for styles involve distances (margins, line height, font size, and so on). While you may be used to having the units in a Web page forced on you (for example, table borders are always set in pixels), you have many options when you're using style sheets. You can choose from the following:

✦ **##px:** Specifies the distance in pixels.

✦ **##ex:** Specifies a height based on the height of the current font's uppercase X.

✦ **##em:** Specifies a height based on the height of the current font's lowercase letter m.

✦ **##in, ##cm,** and **##mm:** Specifies a distance in inches, centimeters, or millimeters, respectively. Note that the dots-per-inch (dpi) setting on most monitors is different, so the physical distances are different, too. A 15-inch monitor and a 17-inch monitor set to the same resolution have different dpi, which may not correspond to the dpi setting.

✦ **##pt** and **##pc:** Specifies a distance in points or picas, respectively. Both of these are typesetting measurements (you are probably familiar with setting font sizes in points). The same dpi considerations that apply for inches, centimeters, and millimeters come into play with point and pica measures.

Although it may not seem intuitive at first, we suggest that you always set font sizes in pixels rather than points. In addition, unless absolutely necessary, you should avoid all the absolute measurements (##in, ##cm, ##mm, ##pt, and ##pc) and stick with ##px, ##em, and ##ex. Because you have no control over the dpi settings for your visitors' monitors, text can display in sizes that are wildly different than what you intended. By using pixel measurements, you tell the browser exactly what size you want the text to be. And because the ex and em sizes are based on the font size, your display will be an accurate representation of what your visitors see.

Border and shading styles can be applied to any paragraph element. They can also be applied to tables, rows, and cells. You can also apply borders and shading to `<span>` and `<div>` tags, which, if positioned using the techniques described in the "Position" section, can be adjusted in size with more precision than a regular paragraph. Some examples of borders and shading are shown in Figure 11-11.

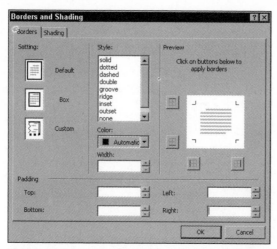

Figure 11-10: Select border-formatting options in the Borders and Shading dialog box.

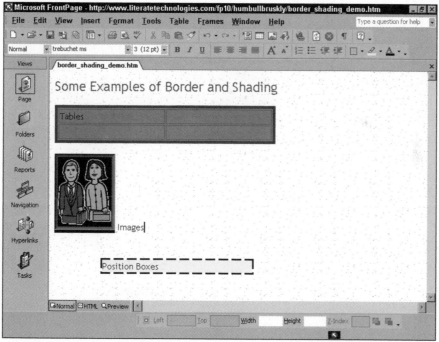

Figure 11-11: Some things you can do with border and shading styles

Numbering

The Numbering format option opens the Bullets and Numbering dialog box, shown in Figure 11-12. This dialog box enables you to set style properties for ordered and unordered lists. These formatting options are applicable only to lists, so it is good practice to create subsets of the <ul> or <ol> tags. Use this set of properties to designate a bullet style, choosing from a variety of numbering styles, HTML bullets, or custom-image bullets. The dialog box pictured here is similar to the dialog box accessed via the Format ➪ Bullets and Numbering menu item, although somewhat more restricted in its usage.

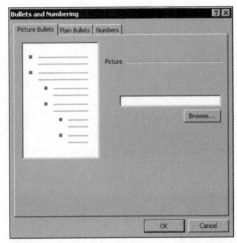

Figure 11-12: The style options for bulleted and numbered lists are found in the Bullets and Numbering dialog box.

Position

Selecting the Position item opens the Position dialog box, the same dialog box that is accessed via the Position menu item or the Positioning toolbar (see Figure 11-13). Specifying position information for a style enables you to apply consistent positioning to multiple elements. If you have ever tried to create a Web page that involved even a small amount of page layout, you know how limited HTML is when it comes to positioning elements on a Web page. (For a thorough discussion of using tables for complex page layout, refer to Chapter 6.) FrontPage makes it easy (well, relatively easy) to position text, graphics, form field inputs, or anything else exactly where you want it, by using the Position property, as defined in the CSS2 specification. This section describes the process of positioning page elements in detail.

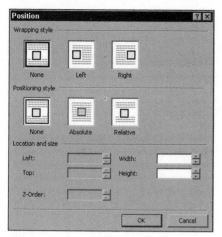

Figure 11-13: Positioning options available in the Position dialog box.

Wrapping style

Whether or not you want to apply positioning to an element, you can define its alignment, or "float," using what FrontPage calls the element's "wrapping style." Options here are None, Left, or Right. Keep in mind that if you combine the wrapping style with positioning, only elements positioned relatively are really affected.

Positioning options

When you use the Position dialog box to apply positioning to an element or style, you have the option of two types of positioning:

✦ **Relative positioning:** This option positions the selected element relative to the page elements that come before and after it in the normal page flow. Another way to say this would be that the relative positioning applied to an element moves that element relative to its original location. So, if you create a relatively positioned item and give it values of top=10 pixels and left=50 pixels, it will display 10 pixels lower and 50 pixels farther into the page than it did before you applied the positioning.

Caution

Relative positioned elements do not display in their actual location in FrontPage Normal view. Switch to Preview to view the element displayed correctly.

✦ **Absolute positioning:** This option locates an element in a defined location on the page. In this scenario, if you create an absolute positioned item and give it values of top=10 pixels and left=50 pixels, it will display 10 pixels from the top of the page and 50 pixels from the left edge of the page.

The difference between relative and absolute positioning is illustrated in Figure 11-14.

Note The CSS defines other position types as well: for example, "fixed," which stays in the same location relative to the screen even if the page moves (kiss those nasty frames good-bye!) — but browsers do not support these yet.

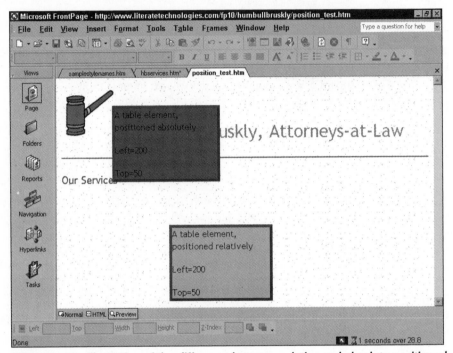

Figure 11-14: Illustration of the difference between relative and absolute positioned elements

Location and size

The final options concern the location and size of the position box around your element. Options include

✦ **Left:** This is the number of pixels from the left margin that marks the beginning of the left edge of the positioned element.

✦ **Top:** This is the number of pixels from the top of the page (in the case of absolute positioning) or from the previous element (in the case of relative positioning) before the top edge of the positioned element.

✦ **Width:** This is the width of the positioning box. This can affect text wrapping in the case of a positioned paragraph, or table size in the case of a positioned table. It does not affect image size.

✦ **Height:** This is the height of the positioning box.

✦ **Z-Order:** The Z-Order of an element represents the relative *layering* of items in a Web page. It is designated by setting its z-index property. When absolutely positioned items overlap, items with lower z-index numbers appear in front of, that is "on top of," elements with lower z-indexes. For example, if you super-impose two absolute positioned images, one with z-index=1 and the other with z-index=2, the image with z-index=1 will be visible, while the second image will be hidden behind it. Z-index numbers do not have to be unique or sequential. Two superimposed elements with the same z-index are displayed "bottom-to-top," in other words, the element defined last in the HTML page appears on top.

Caution The CSS2 standard permits negative z-index values. Internet Explorer supports the use of negative z-index values. Netscape, as of this writing, does not.

In the next section we describe the techniques you can use to create a position box around an element in FrontPage 2002 and discuss the pros and cons of each approach.

Formatting with the Position command

When you apply positioning formatting to an element, you create a *positioning box* around the element. Once created, you can control the properties of this box, including its pixel coordinates on the page. Moving the positioning box moves the elements in the box as well.

To create a positioning box using the position command, first add to the page the elements that you want to position. In our examples, we use an image, a paragraph of text, and a small table. These elements are shown in Figure 11-15 before being positioned.

Note In FrontPage, you must create an element and then position it. You cannot create an empty position box and then put an element in it. If you try to select Format ⇨ Position without selecting an element first, you will notice that the option is unavailable. Once you have created a position box, however, you can add and remove elements to it as you please.

After you create the elements, follow these steps:

1. Select the element that you want to position.

2. Select Format ⇨ Position to open the Position dialog box.

3. Select the desired positioning properties: Choose a wrapping style or posi-tioning style, and set any desired location and size values.

4. Click OK to return to Page view.

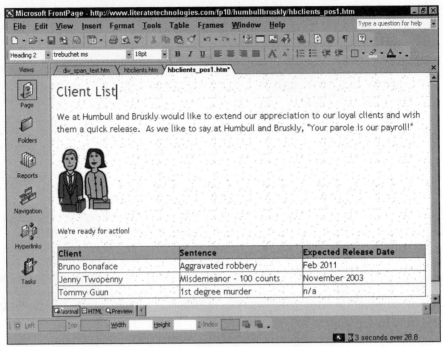

Figure 11-15: HTML page elements vying for their positions

After creating an absolutely positioned element using this method, you can click on the object and move it around to a new location on the page, automatically updating the top and z-level property values. You can resize the positioning box, updating the width and height values as necessary. You cannot, however, change the z-level value without first opening the Position dialog box (by selecting the item and then selecting Format ⇨ Positioning) or by opening the Positioning toolbar.

In the case of a relatively positioned element, you must reopen the Position dialog box to edit its position properties.

Tip   There is at least one additional method to get back to the Positioning properties for this element: Switch to HTML view, select the `<div>` tag that contains the positioning information, right click and select Tag Properties, and then select the Position option from the Format button on the Styles dialog box. Or, you could just open the Positioning toolbar. The choice is yours.

Using the Positioning toolbar

An alternate method of creating a position box is to use the Positioning toolbar. With this method, as with the Position dialog box, you should first create the element that you want to position. Then, select the element to position, and select View ⇨ Toolbars ⇨ Positioning to show the toolbar (see Figure 11-16).

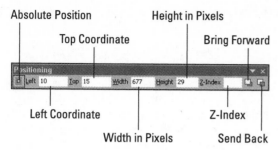

Figure 11-16: The positioning toolbar

To create an absolute position box around the selected element, click the Absolute Position icon at the left end of the toolbar. Use the other toolbar fields to specify the location and size values that you want to use, just as you did in the Position dialog box.

Inserting a position style

To create a position style, follow these steps:

1. Select Format ➪ Style.

2. Click the New button to create a new style.

3. Name the style, click the Format button, and then select the Position option.

4. Use the Position dialog box, as in the other examples, to define the Position attributes of your style.

5. Click OK three times to return to Page view.

6. Apply the Position style, as described earlier in the chapter, to an appropriate page element.

Advanced positioning properties

At this point, you know how to create and edit basic position properties for relative and absolute positioned elements. This section concludes by examining some of the finer points of working with CSS positioning.

Z-Order

One of the side effects of being able to position page elements precisely is that they can overlap. If you overlap several elements, how do you know which one is on top? The answer is the z-index property, which defines an element's relative z-order on the page. The smaller the z-index value, the closer to the top of the heap the element will be (in other words, an element with a z-index of 1 appears in front of an element with a z-index of 2). The z-index is a relative number: You can start with 1 or 100, it doesn't matter.

You can set the z-index by using either the Position dialog box or the Positioning toolbar.

> **Tip**
>
> It can be exasperating at times working with absolutely positioned elements if, for example, you end up with an element that completely surrounds another element. This renders the interior element unselectable. What do you do? (1) Move the bigger element out of the way, position the interior element, and put the bigger one back. (2) Switch to HTML view and edit properties directly in the HTML. (3) In some cases it makes sense to extend the position box way beyond the element it contains in order to give yourself a "handle" on the object. This works well when you are in the preliminary stages of developing a page and are doing a lot of repositioning. Once you have the element set, remember to shrink the box back to a more appropriate size—not doing so can sometimes produce unexpected results that can take a long time to identify.

Visibility

Another property that is useful with positioned elements is visibility. This property has three acceptable values: visible, hidden, and inherit. This property is of limited usefulness in a style sheet (why hide an element unless you want it to become visible under certain circumstances?), but it is very commonly used when scripting style properties, which we discuss in more detail in Chapters 16 and 18.

Span vs. div

When you create a position box, FrontPage places the positioned element inside either `<div>` or `<span>` tags. `<div>`, short for "divider," is a logical tag that identifies a self-contained unit, separated from any elements that come before or after it. Typically, browsers render `<div>` content by placing paragraph returns around it. In many cases, this is the appropriate behavior, but occasionally, you may want the element to fit seamlessly between other elements. In this case, you will want to use the `<span>` element in place of the `<div>` element. The difference is illustrated in Figure 11-17. FrontPage 2002 makes a reasonable guess as to which element makes the most sense in the context of what you are doing. Of course, you can always change it to suit yourself.

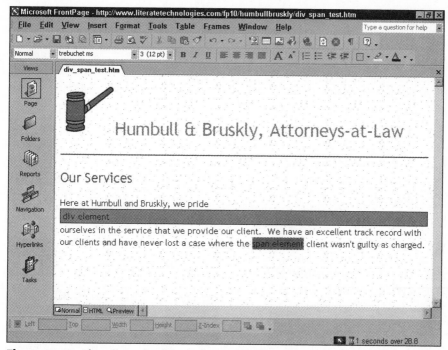

Figure 11-17: The effect of <div> and <span> elements on a block of text

Containment methods

As you have probably begun to surmise, there are a number of ways to add a style to a page element. In this section we take a closer look at the various options and then discuss how you decide the appropriate choice for your circumstances.

In CSS, there are effectively four ways you can insert style information:

- ✦ **inline:** Placed inside a particular element tag
- ✦ **embedded:** Placed at the top of the page that contains the elements you wish to associate with the style
- ✦ **linked:** Via a style sheet, which is the topic of the next section
- ✦ **imported:** Via a style sheet, which is automatically included in the Web page

These four style containment methods, illustrated in HTML format in Figure 11-18, are discussed in the following sections.

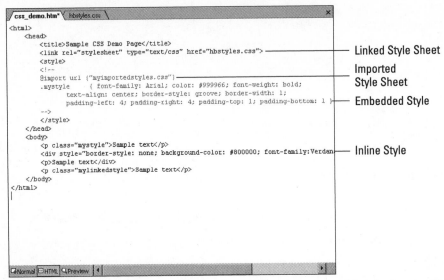

Figure 11-18: HTML view demonstrating four different ways to add styles to your Web pages

Inline styles

Inline styles are contained within a particular HTML tag and the style information pertains only to that element. Here is an example of an inline style contained within a Header 1 <h1> tag:

```
<h1 class="myheader" style="color: #6699AA; font-size: 12px">
```

Inline styles are useful for adding specific style elements on a one-time-only basis. If you find you are repeating the same style information on multiple occasions, then you want to stay away from this option.

Embedded styles

Embedded styles include a selector name as well as properties name:value pairs. They are typically written in the <head> portion of an HTML page. Because they include a label, or selector name, these styles can be associated with any appropriate element on the page, simply by referencing that selector name. FrontPage creates embedded styles each time you use the Style option in the Format menu.

Linked style sheets

The third method of including a style is to store your styles in a separate file, called a style sheet, and then link that style sheet to your page. This is the best way to create *global* style information that can be accessed by any file in your Web site. The next section describes the process of creating style sheets in detail.

Imported style sheets

The fourth way to add style information to your page is by using an import statement. An import statement is added to an embedded style block (that is, between `<style>` `</style>` tags), and it looks like this:

```
@import url("mystyle.css")
```

This method is similar to linking style sheets. Some older browsers that support styles do not support this usage. As a result, you can use an import statement to include style sheet definitions that you don't want the older browsers to see. (More on this in the browser compatibility section at the end of this chapter.)

The Cascade

With so many options, how do you know which to choose? What happens when styles overlap or contradict one another? The "cascade" in Cascading Style Sheets defines the hierarchy that specifies which styles receive higher priority in cases where several methods create conflicting style information.

The first rule of the cascade defines which styles take precedence. All things being equal, an author's style sheets override any styles that a reader has created, and the reader's styles override the default behavior of the browser. (This is complicated by the fact that it is possible to designate a style property as "important," in which case it will override normal styles that might otherwise have taken precedence over it.)

As for the order of precedence among the various ways of providing style information, the actual algorithm used to define the cascade order is unduly complex for our purpose. But, the general rule is that the closer the style definition is to the element it defines, the greater its priority. So, an inline style takes precedence over an embedded style, which takes precedence over a linked or imported style reference. In the case of multiple linked style sheets, references that occur later on the page supersede earlier references.

Styles also pass along information from the levels above them. So, for example, let's say that you have a page with a style sheet that defines all `<h1>` tags as having the font size of 14pt. You could also define the color of your header 1 tags in the style sheet as well, but you know that on some of your pages you want the header text to be red and on other pages you want it to be blue. To do this you must create embedded styles, one for red headers and one for blue headers. Now all of your headers will still have the same size, but the color will depend on which embedded style you include on a given page. Now suppose further that in one particular instance you want the font style of the header to be italic. Here you add a style attribute to that header and define the font style. The header will still inherit style information from the other header styles. The moral of the story? Take advantage of the cascade to make your styles more modular. Use style sheets to define general-purpose styles that you want to apply to all or most instances of an element, and use the more specific style types to override or augment those styles.

Using Style Sheets

As you have seen, with an embedded style sheet, applying a custom style to any element on your page is easy. This is a definite improvement over the inline style method, but it still doesn't serve the ultimate goal — consistent styles across all the pages of your Web. To accomplish this, you need to create an external style sheet and link it to any pages that you want governed by the style sheet.

Implementing and applying styles using a style sheet in FrontPage is a four-step process:

1. Create a style sheet.

2. Define the styles in the style sheet.

3. Link the style sheet to HTML pages.

4. Apply styles to the appropriate elements on the HTML page.

Creating a new style sheet

To create a style sheet in FrontPage, open the New Page drop-down menu in the Formatting toolbar, select Page, and click the Style Sheets tab in the Page Templates dialog box, shown in Figure 11-19, to select a style sheet template. (Alternatively, use the Page Templates link in the FrontPage 2002 sidebar.) FrontPage comes with a representative selection of predefined style sheets. You can also create a blank style sheet by selecting the Normal Style Sheet option.

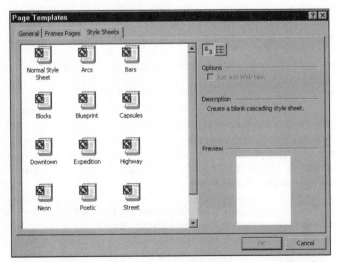

Figure 11-19: You can select from a number of predefined style sheets, or create your own.

Combining Styles and Themes

In contrast to CSS styles, FrontPage themes use a proprietary technique for attaching style information to your pages. They only work with Web servers using the FrontPage Server Extensions. If you are using a theme in your Web site, you can still make use of the CSS styles as well. In fact, you can think of your themes as the equivalent of a linked style sheet. If you add embedded and inline styles, they will override your themes just as they would override any linked styles.

You can also convert your theme to an actual CSS style sheet format. To do this, open the theme by selecting Format ➪ Theme and check the "Apply using CSS" option in the Themes dialog box.

The ability to convert themes to CSS style sheets means that even those people who are maintaining their sites on non-FrontPage Web servers can make use of themes. However, doing this is not as straightforward as you may think, because FrontPage does not actually embed the style sheet link information in the page until "run time," that is, until the page is requested. To work around this, you will need to replace FrontPage's embedded information with a standard style sheet link. Here is an example:

First create a page using your favorite style and check the Apply Using CSS box. Switch to HTML view and, near the top of the page, you will see that FrontPage has added a `<meta>` tag something like this:

```
<meta name="Microsoft Theme" content="axis 1011">
```

This is the information FrontPage uses at run time to link to the style sheet. The link reference will look like this:

```
<link rel="stylesheet" type="text/css"
href="_themes/axis/axis1011.css">
```

So, all you need to do is save FrontPage the trouble, and remove the `<meta>` tag and replace it with the appropriate link reference.

The last piece of information you need to know is that when FrontPage applies its themes as CSS, it creates a hidden folder named `_themes` to hold all of the necessary elements. You can show this folder by selecting Tools ➪ Web Settings and checking the "Show hidden files and folders" box in the Advanced tab of this dialog box. (You can also remove the underscore from its name and it will no longer be hidden. Just remember to update the link reference or your style sheet will no longer work!) Whatever you do with this folder, you need to make sure that you copy it and its contents to your Web server along with your Web pages.

Tip

Here's a big secret: A blank style sheet is nothing more than an empty text file with a `.css` extension (which lets FrontPage know it should treat it like a style sheet). When you open a CSS file in FrontPage, notice that many of the standard page editing tools disappear. For example, no tabs appear for HTML or Preview, and all the toolbar drop-down menus and menu items are disabled. The only menu item that you really need to use to create your style sheet is the Styles item in the Format menu (which you can also access via the Styles toolbar).

Defining style sheet styles

After you open a style sheet in FrontPage Page view, you can add and modify style definitions by using the same process that you used for embedded styles, as described earlier in the chapter. To review, the procedure is as follows:

1. Select Format ⇨ Style. (Alternatively, click the Style button on the Style menu that opens automatically when you edit a style sheet.)

2. Click New to create a new style definition, or, to modify an existing style, select either All HTML Tags or User-Defined Styles from the List drop-down menu.

3. Click the Format button and choose the formatting properties that you want to apply to this style.

4. Click OK on all open dialog boxes until you return to Page view, or continue to create additional styles.

When you return to Page view, FrontPage adds the appropriate CSS code to your style sheet. Save your style sheet to your Web, and you are ready to proceed to the final step of linking the style sheet to a Web page.

Linking to a style sheet

After you define and save your style sheet, you must associate it with any Web pages for which you want the styles to be in effect. Several ways exist to link style sheets to a Web page. You just point and click. FrontPage takes care of the details. The basic steps are as follows:

1. Select the page or pages to which you want to link the style sheet.

2. Select Format ⇨ Style Sheet Links to open the Link Style Sheet dialog box (see Figure 11-20).

3. Select either the All Pages, to have the style sheet linked to every page in your Web, or the Selected Page(s) option.

4. Click Add to locate the style sheet file in your Web (or elsewhere).

5. After you locate it, click OK to return to the Link Style Sheet dialog box.

6. Click OK again to accept your changes and return to your page.

After you perform these steps, peek at the HTML source for your Web page. Near the top of the page, somewhere between the `<head>` and `</head>` tags, you should see a line that resembles this:

```
<link rel="stylesheet" type="text/css" href="mystyles.css">
```

This tag tells the Web browser that the HTML page in question is governed by the style sheet `mystyles.css`.

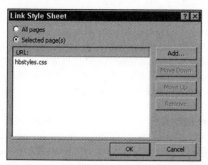

Figure 11-20: The Link Style Sheet dialog box enables you to link style sheets to your Web pages.

Tip The CSS standard also includes a mechanism for importing style sheets into an embedded style sheet. The syntax for this is @import mystyles.css. If you want to import rather than link your style sheets, you have to do it manually.

You can select a page for the linking operation in either of two ways:

✦ Open the page in Page view.

✦ Select one or more pages in Folder view.

Using Folder view is the only way to perform the linking operation on multiple Web pages simultaneously. To select more than one page in Folder view, hold down the Shift key and select the beginning and end of a range of files, or hold down the Ctrl key and click each file that you want to select. Then select Format ➪ Link Style Sheets and proceed as above.

Linking to all pages

To link a style sheet to all pages in your Web simultaneously, switch to Folder view and select the main Web folder. Now, when you select Format ➪ Link Style Sheets, only the All Pages option is enabled. Proceed as just described to link one or more style sheets to all HTML pages in the selected Web.

Using multiple style sheets

Occasionally, you may find that linking a Web page to more than one style sheet is useful. For example, you may create a generic style sheet that contains basic styles that apply to every page in your site, and then develop specialized style sheets for particular pages or sets of pages.

To link multiple style sheets to a page, use the same procedure previously described, but pay attention to the order of your style sheets. If the linked style sheets have overlapping style references (for example, if each has a style for h1 header levels), the style that is listed last dictates the style for that element.

Note It may seem counterintuitive that a style sheet listed lower on the list would have precedence over ones higher in the list. But, if you consider how the browser encounters the style information, this order makes sense. The browser reads the HTML page from top to bottom. When it encounters a <link> reference, it fetches the designated style sheet and reads it one line at a time, from beginning to end. When it encounters a style reference for, say, h1, it records that as the current style for that element. It then goes on to the next <link>reference and repeats the process. When it encounters another reference to an h1 style, it discards the earlier one and replaces it with the current one. So, the last style always wins.

To adjust the order of linked style sheets in the Link Style Sheets dialog box, select the style sheet that you want to reorder, and then click the Move Up or Move Down button until the style is positioned where you want it.

Tutorial 11-1: Creating a newsletter using style sheets

This tutorial reviews many of the techniques we have discussed and applies them to a real world example. Our objective is to create the front page for a newsletter that includes all of the basic elements of a newsletter as well as a stylish banner.

Step 1: Create the basic newsletter layout

To create a layout, you use the two-column page layout template that FrontPage supplies.

1. Open the Page Templates dialog box, either by clicking on this item in the sidebar or by opening the New Page drop-down menu from the Formatting toolbar and selecting the Page tab.

2. Switch to the General tab and select the Two Column Body with Contents and Sidebar template.

3. Click OK to open the template. Save the file as newsletter.htm.

Step 2: Link a default style sheet to the newsletter page

1. To import an existing style sheet, return to the Page Templates dialog box, switch to the Style Sheets tab, and select the style sheet that best expresses your creative spirit (we have selected blocks.css). Although specifics vary, most of the FrontPage style sheet templates define styles for some basic page elements: body, hyperlinks, tables, and headers.

2. Save the file as newsletter.css.

3. Link the style sheet to the newsletter page. Open or switch to the newsletter.htm page. Select Format ➪ Style Sheet Links, check the Selected Page(s) option, click Add, and select newsletter.css. Click OK to return to the Link

Style Sheet dialog box. Click OK again to apply the style sheet and return to the HTML page. You should notice that your page acquires a background color and a new text color. Save your changes.

Step 3: Define the required styles

The HTML template we are using has several elements that lend themselves nicely to style sheets: a masthead banner, feature text, navigation section titles and content items, and callout text. At the moment, all the formatting details that define these elements are contained in <font> tags. In a moment, we will create styles for each of these elements, but first we want to add a few of our own. Figure 11-21 shows what our page looks like after a few minor adjustments. We have added table cells to contain the newsletter volume and date, and added headlines and hyperlinks to the two columns of featured content on the front page of our newsletter.

We want to define the following general-purpose styles:

✦ table.newsletter: General purpose formatting for the newsletter table

✦ td.head: General purpose formatting for the headline section of the page

✦ td.toc: General purpose formatting for the contents of the left marginal column

✦ td.main: General purpose formatting for the main contents section of the page

✦ td.sidebar: General purpose formatting for the contents of the right marginal column

And these, more specialized styles:

✦ masthead: The banner text at the top of the page

✦ datelinetext: The volume and date information under the masthead text

✦ leadinhead: The headline for each article lead-in

✦ leadintext: The text of each article lead-in

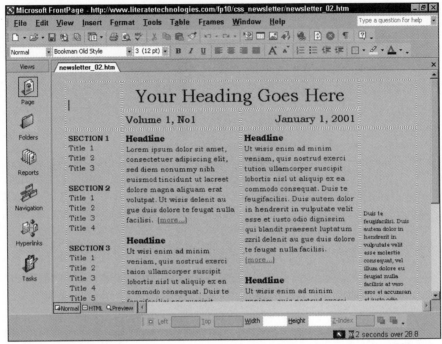

Figure 11-21: Our newsletter after some initial modifications to the page elements

- ✦ leadinlink: The link to more content at the end of each lead-in
- ✦ tocsection: Table of contents section titles
- ✦ tocitems: Table of contents items contained under each section title
- ✦ pullquote: A short quotation featured in the right margin of this layout

Step 4: Add the identified styles to the style sheet

For each style listed above, select the Style button on the Style toolbar (or select Format ➪ Style), click the New button to create a new style, give it an appropriate selector name, and select the Formatting properties of your choice. Note that the general-purpose styles should all be Paragraph style types. The more specific styles all need to be Character styles, because they are not all defined by paragraph breaks. (The one exception is the pullquote style, so you can do as you like with that one.) Figure 11-22 shows our style definitions in the style sheet.

Caution   FrontPage is not very sophisticated about how it adds style definitions to a style sheet. When you open a style sheet and add a new style, FrontPage simply adds it after the currently selected item in the existing Styles list. If you want to create a style sheet with the styles in a particularly order, you may find that the best approach is to define the style names without any definitions in your style sheet first, and then use FrontPage to modify them.

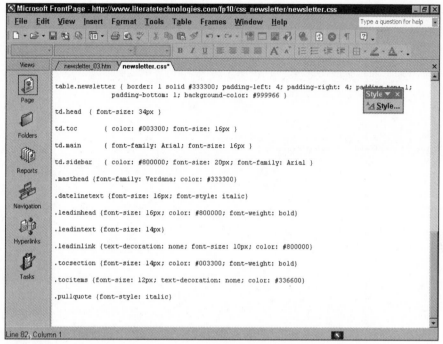

Figure 11-22: Detailed view of our newsletter style sheet (newsletter.css)

Step 5: Remove existing formatting

1. Once you have identified and created the styles that you want, you can remove all the existing formatting to avoid any conflicts between the style sheet and the existing formatting. (You could have done this to begin with, of course, but defining the style elements was somewhat easier with the default formatting intact.)

2. Select the entire page either by choosing Edit ➪ Select All or by using the Ctrl+A keyboard shortcut. Select Format ➪ Remove Formatting (you can also use the keyboard shortcut Ctrl+Shift+Z, if you think that is easier). By the way, you can use this technique for removing formatting if you plan to convert an existing Web to use style sheets. The page, stripped of its original formatting, should resemble Figure 11-23.

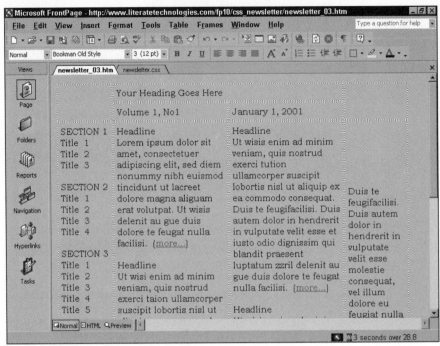

Figure 11-23: The newsletter page minus its original formatting

Step 6: Associate page elements with the appropriate styles

First add the general-purpose table and table cell class selectors. For each, select the appropriate Property dialog box, click the Style button, and type the name of the appropriate selector name from the class list.

Next, for each of the specific text items, select the text you want to apply the style to, and then select the style from the Style drop-down menu on the Formatting toolbar. The results of your labors are shown in Figure 11-24.

Step 7: Create a masthead banner using positioned elements

In this last step, you create a precisely positioned masthead for your newsletter page. Your headline banner will consist of three parts: small introductory text (actually the word "The"), which you want to offset from the main title; the main newsletter masthead title, including an attractive border; and a tagline positioned underneath the main masthead.

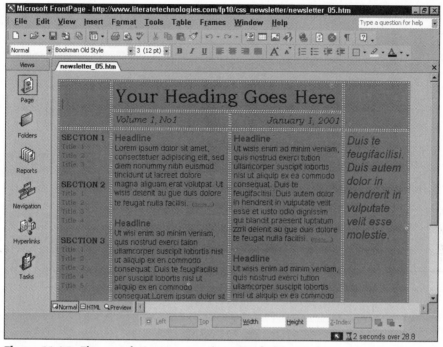

Figure 11-24: The newsletter page nearing completion

1. Add the text.

   You could just replace the existing Headline text, but this causes problems with the alignment of the table when you position the headline. Better to add the text at the top of the page, outside of the newsletter table, and then format the masthead after you have created the elements. Place the cursor at the top of the page and hit Enter to create a new line above the newsletter table. Type the three sections of the masthead, starting a new paragraph for each section, so that the Position command will work correctly.

2. Create three new character styles and add them to your stylesheet. The three styles you need are:

   * `premast`: Formatting for the "The" that precedes the main masthead title

   * `mastheadtitle`: Formatting for the main text of the masthead

   * `tagline`: Formatting for the tagline

Here you have the first hard decision to make, because the styles you want to create for these elements will contain positioning information as well as formatting. However, if you put the positioning in a style and apply that style to your text, you will not be able to re-position the elements by dragging and dropping them in Normal view. Your workaround for this is to create the styles, add positioning inline for each element, and position them where you want them. (If you wanted to, you could then take the next step and move the positioning information from the inline style to your style definition. But that's up to you.)

3. Apply the styles to each element, using the same method you used for the earlier character elements.

4. Add positioning information to each element.

The procedure is the same for all three elements, so you will step through it once. Place the cursor in the line of text you want to format, select Format ➪ Position, and click the Absolute Position style option.

Note that each time you format one of the elements to be absolutely positioned, it will "jump" out of its place in the normal order of the page, causing the next element on the page to push up behind it. This can make the page a little disconcerting to work with, so be prepared. You may want to move the newly created elements out of the way temporarily until you are ready for the next step.

5. Position the masthead elements in the newsletter.

Now you come to another challenge. When you remove the placeholder headline text from the newsletter table layout, it collapses the table cell where we want to put our headline. In effect, our new headline will "float" above the table, but we need some way to reserve space for our headline. One of the conventional methods for fixing the height and width of table cells used for layout is to use a transparent one pixel "spacer" image that can be resized as needed to force the table cells to remain the right size even if they are empty. (For details on using this and other table layout techniques, see Chapter 6.) In this case, we have elected to add a real image as well for some visual appeal. Our final results are shown in Figure 11-25.

Note   This tutorial is designed primarily to illustrate some of the principles we discussed in this chapter. Generally, we do not recommend trying to combine table layouts with absolutely positioned elements.

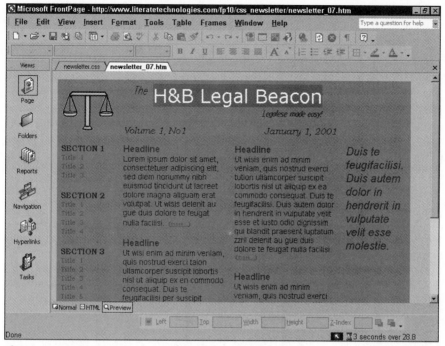

Figure 11-25: The finished newsletter with "stylish" text and an absolutely positioned masthead banner

Advanced CSS Techniques

At this point in the chapter, you know enough about style sheets to create and use them effectively in FrontPage. The remaining sections of this chapter briefly discuss some of the subtler aspects of style sheets, culminating in an explanation of how to use FrontPage to position elements on the page.

Hyperlinks

FrontPage 2002 doesn't provide any direct way to control the style of hyperlinks. However, you can designate styles for hyperlinks by modifying the default style for the hyperlink <a> tag. See "Modifying existing styles" earlier in this chapter for details on how to modify existing styles. In addition, you can create specific style information on each of the following hyperlink states:

✦ A:link: Any hyperlink that has not been visited

✦ A:active: The state of the hyperlink as it is being clicked

✦ A:visited: The state of a hyperlink after the user has clicked the link (after the user has *visited* the link)

For more information on these elements, see "Pseudo-classes and pseudo-elements," later in the chapter.

You may be pleased (or appalled) to learn that you can use a style sheet reference to remove the underlining that is part of the default appearance of hyperlinks. Use the following style reference to accomplish this feat: a {text-decoration:none;}.

Grouping styles

Frequently, you may want to apply the same style properties to several elements. For example, suppose that you want to use a special font called my_cool_font for all of your header levels. You could create a separate style for each element that repeats the same font designation, or you could create a grouping of elements. The grouping is just a comma-separated list of elements. For example:

```
h1, h2, h3, h4, h5, h6 {font-family: my_cool_font }
```

You can use the Style dialog box to create a group element. Simply select Format ⇨ Style and click the New button. In the Name field, type the comma-separated group and designate any formatting, as you normally would.

Using inheritance

Inheritance in the CSS world refers to the fact that HTML elements that contain additional elements pass on their styles to the contained element, unless that element has its own defined styles. In other words, the contained elements inherit the characteristics of the element that contains them.

Say, for example, that you have a line of text to which you apply the Header 1 style. One of the words in this line of text is italicized. By default, the italicized word inherits the characteristics of the Header 1 text: the same font size, font family, color, and so forth (the only difference is it is italicized). If you don't want the italicized text to inherit the characteristics of the Header 1 style, you need to create a specific style reference for italics, by modifying the <i> style. In this case, the italics style will override the Header 1 style.

Tip One useful way to use inheritance is to create a generic <body> style that designates a standard font type, size, color, and so on. Because all other tags are contained within the <body> tag, they inherit its style, unless you dictate otherwise.

Contextual selectors

Okay, you think that you've mastered the concept of inheritance and overriding inherited style characteristics. Now, consider again the example used earlier: You have a line of text designated as a Header 1 style that contains an italicized word. You saw in the last section how you can give the italicized word a different style from the Header 1. But, what if you want italicized text in the context of a Header 1 line to have a different style from italicized text that appears elsewhere? You could create a separate class selector to handle this, but fortunately, an easier way is available.

You can use the contextual selector syntax to indicate a style that applies only in certain contexts. For example:

```
h1 i {font-color: #6699FF}
```

This style reference says that any italics tags that are contained by a Header 1 style should use the style indicated. Italics anywhere else remain unaffected by this style.

You can create this style reference in FrontPage using the standard Style dialog box. Simply create a new style and name it by using the contextual selector syntax. Then, select the style properties by proceeding as you normally would.

The concept of contextual selectors may strike you as somewhat esoteric. One context in which it may come in handy is bulleted lists. Embedding one numbered or bulleted list in the context of another list isn't uncommon. You can use the contextual selector syntax to treat a standard list differently from one that appears embedded within another list (which, by the way, is exactly how FrontPage manages the three levels of bullets in its themes).

Pseudo-classes and pseudo-elements

CSS introduces the concept of pseudo-classes and pseudo-elements as a way to gain stylistic control over some elements of an HTML page that don't directly correspond to strict tag elements. This section briefly identifies the most commonly supported pseudo-classes and elements. Pseudo-classes and pseudo-elements can be used in CSS selectors, but do not exist in the HTML source. Rather, they are "inserted" by the UA under certain conditions to be used for addressing in style sheets. They are referred to as "classes" and "elements" because this is a convenient way of describing their behavior. More specifically, their behavior is defined by a *fictional tag sequence*.

Pseudo-elements are used to address sub-parts of elements, while pseudo-classes allow style sheets to differentiate between different element types.

Hyperlink pseudo-classes

Currently, the most commonly supported pseudo-classes are those associated with hyperlinks as described in the hyperlinks section above.

The pseudo-classes work just like any other selector. They just apply to special user-event-based circumstances.

Tip   Microsoft also supports another hyperlink pseudo-class, `a:hover`, which defines the style for a hover button.

"First" pseudo-elements

The most commonly supported pseudo-elements are the "first line" element and the "first letter" element. The first line element (designated as `p:first-line`) is used to apply a special style to the first line of a paragraph of text. Similarly the first letter element (`p:first-letter`) enables you to create drop-caps and other fancy typographical flourishes.

Style sheet comments

You can (and should) include comments in your style sheets, to help describe the purpose and effect of various style references. The syntax for CSS comments follows the C programming language conventions. The comment starts with `/*` and ends with `*/`, such as the following:

```
/* This is a sample CSS comment! */
```

Browser Compatibility Issues

Throughout this chapter, the fact that browser support for CSS is less than perfect has been reiterated. The most recent versions of Netscape Navigator (version 6) and Microsoft's Internet Explorer (version 5.5) as of this writing have implemented the majority of the CSS1 standard and some portions of CSS2 (see the earlier sidebar, "The CSS Standards," for details on the two levels of the CSS specification). What this means, in practice, is that some CSS techniques don't work as advertised anywhere, others work only on one or the other of the top two browsers, and some work on both browsers, but with slightly different results. Things only get worse when you try to incorporate CSS into a DHTML effect. If you want to know specifically which browsers support which features, check out *Webreview's* "Style Sheets Compatibility Chart" at `http://style.webreview.com/mastergrid.html`.

The problem is critical enough to have spawned the creation of yet another acronym: XBDHTML, or Cross-Browser Dynamic HTML. XBDHTML refers to the subset of DHTML features, including CSS, which is supported by both browsers. Netscape has posted numerous technical documents on the subject and even some tools to make your pages cross-browser-compatible. Look for these items at `http://developer.netscape.com/ docs/technote/dynhtml/xbdhtml/xbd-html.html`.

When working with styles, there are two issues you need to think about: (1) what to do about those users with browsers that do not support the CSS standard at all, and (2) what to do about those users with browsers that partially support the standard.

Working with older browsers: "Degrading gracefully"

Technically speaking, older browsers don't really pose a problem, because they will simply ignore the style information altogether. As long as you don't mind these users seeing "plain vanilla" pages, you don't have to do anything at all. (Of course, you do need to stay away from positioning elements, because the non-CSS support-ing browsers will simply show the contents of these elements as if they were stan-dard HTML.)

As an alternative to the plain vanilla approach, you could use regular HTML tags to reproduce as much of the style information as possible, and then use styles to over-ride this HTML for those browsers that support it. The problem with this approach is that it is labor intensive and hard to maintain, which, of course, eliminates one of the selling points for using CSS in the first place.

Some measure of compromise is probably the best approach. For example, you might establish a base font style for the page, including link color and visited link color in the <body> tag, and then leave the rest of the elements alone. In this way, users with older browsers are not subjected to bland pages and you are not sub-jected to hours of extra work.

Note For more detailed advice on this issue—as well as on the cross-browser compati-bility issue, check out the informative CSS "Masterclass" offered at `www.richinstyle.com`. Also, C/net has a nice article, although not as detailed, on the degrading issue at `http://builder.cnet.com/Authoring/CSSToday/`.

Dealing with incomplete CSS support

The next issue is how to deal with the browsers that only partially support the CSS standard, which is definitely the case for the 4.0 browsers still very much in circula-tion. If you happen to be lucky enough to know that your users have only the latest browsers: Internet Explorer 5.5 or Netscape 6, then you probably don't have to worry—as these browsers have pretty complete coverage of the CSS1 properties (no browsers yet implement the full CSS2 standard).

If you don't have this luxury, then you have some hard decisions to make. The safest, but not necessarily the most satisfying, route is to limit yourself to proper-ties that you know will work in all browsers that support CSS. There are a number of sites you can check to find out what these properties are (or aren't). Among these are:

✦ *Webreview* **Style Sheet Reference Guide:**
`http://www.webreview.com/style/index.shtml`

✦ **Western Civilisation's** *House of Style:*
`http://www.westciv.com/style_master/house/`

✦ *Rich in Style:* `http://richinstyle.com/`

✦ **CSS Pointers Group:** `http://css.nu/pointers/bugs.html`

✦ **Ian Graham's CSS Bugs and Implementation Problems, with Workarounds:**
`http://www.utoronto.ca/ian/style/cssbugs/toc.html`

Another alternative is to create alternate style sheets for different browsers and then incorporate a browser-checking script to determine which style sheet to use. Although the details of this scripting are beyond the scope of this chapter, if you are an experienced scripter, the basic method involves detecting the specific user agent type and then writing a style sheet link with an appropriate filename for that user agent (such as a browser).

Tip

Another CSS trick is to use the `@import` statement to include styles that you don't want earlier CSS supporting browsers to see, because this statement is not recognized by these browsers.

In general, we suggest you keep it as simple as possible — and check out any of the mentioned references for help in a pinch. They are all excellent sources of detailed information on CSS.

Summary

This chapter brings to a close the page layout and formatting techniques introduced throughout Part III. Using styles, you can create Web pages that are freed from the formatting limitations of plain HTML. We have shown you how FrontPage 2002 provides a WYSIWYG environment for creating and managing styles and style sheets. In addition, we have introduced the essential elements of Cascading Style Sheets, including multiple ways to add styles to your Web pages.

In Part IV, we delve into some of the many ways you can add interactive components to your Webs in FrontPage. Chapter 12 offers a complete look at working with pictures in FrontPage. Subsequent chapters discuss animation techniques, FrontPage Web Components, and the use of advanced components, such as plug-ins, ActiveX controls, and Java applets.

✦   ✦   ✦

Working with Pictures, Animation, and Multimedia

Using Pictures

First the bad news: You really can't *create* Web graphics in FrontPage. But there's much more good news. Once you find a picture file, or create an image yourself using another program, FrontPage not only makes it easy to insert and align that picture in a Web page. FrontPage even includes a decent set of picture editing tools that allow you to change brightness, contrast, and coloring in your pictures right in FrontPage.

A Quick Look at Web Graphics in FrontPage

FrontPage can insert any graphic in your Web page, regardless of the (original) format of the graphic file. FrontPage can handle the process of converting any image to a Web-compatible GIF or JPEG file, and will save the image file so that it will be seamlessly embedded in your Web page.

The following are the two easiest ways to place an image in your Web page:

 ✦ Insert an existing graphic image file in your Web page.
 ✦ Copy a graphic from another application into a Web page.

Inserting an image file

You can insert a graphic image file by placing your insertion point and choosing Insert ➪ Picture ➪ From File from the menu bar. The Picture dialog box appears, as shown in Figure 12-1. In Figure 12-1, the image is displayed in the Picture dialog box because Preview was chosen from the Views drop-down list in the Picture dialog box.

◆ ◆ ◆ ◆

In This Chapter

Adding pictures to your FrontPage Web pages

Controlling picture size and location

Managing picture attributes such as file type and transparency

Using FrontPage's rudimentary drawing tools

Assigning image map hotspot links to sections of a picture

◆ ◆ ◆ ◆

Figure 12-1: Choosing a picture file to embed in a Web page

Use the Look In box in the Picture dialog box to navigate to the folder or Web site with your image. Use the Files of Type drop-down list to select a desired picture file format (like GIF or JPEG), or just leave the setting at the default All Image Files to show all picture files in a selected folder. When you have selected an image in the dialog box, click on the Insert button to place the image in your Web page.

Adding clip art

To insert clip art, choose Insert ➪ Picture ➪ Clip Art from the menu bar. The Insert Clip Art window opens, as shown in Figure 12-2. To quickly find clip art, type a subject into the Search Text box in the Search For area of the Insert Clip Art window.

About Office XP Clip Art

Office XP includes Microsoft Clip Organizer, a program that organizes not just clip "art" but other media as well (including sound and video). These clips are available in any Office program, including FrontPage 2002.

The first time you search for clip art in an Office XP application, you'll be prompted to let Clip Organizer search and catalog any clip collections on your system. Clip Organizer will prompt you with options for sorting and organizing these clips. You can simply accept defaults to let Clip Organizer catalog your media files.

Clip Organizer can also be used to search for media files on the Internet by connecting to a site maintained by Microsoft that contains a wider selection of media clips than is available on the Office XP CD.

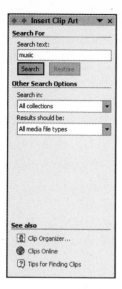

Figure 12-2: The Insert Clip Art window will search your installed clip art collections.

The Search In drop-down list allows you to choose from installed Office clip art sets. The Results Should Be list, shown in Figure 12-3, allows you to select the type of image file you wish to embed — clip art, photos, movies, or sounds.

Note   The basic routine for inserting clip art sound and video is the same as inserting a regular graphic. For a specific discussion of embedded video and sound, see Chapter 13.

When you have defined your search criteria, click on the Search button to open a gallery of images that match your search criteria. Then, click on the down arrow next to the image and choose Insert from the menu, as shown in Figure 12-4.

The Insert Clip Art window also has links to the Microsoft Media Gallery and the Media Gallery Online. The Microsoft Media Gallery, shown in Figure 12-5, displays your collections of installed clip art.

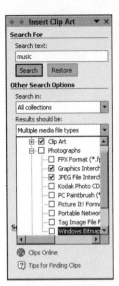

Figure 12-3: You can choose between clip art, photos, or media when you define search criteria.

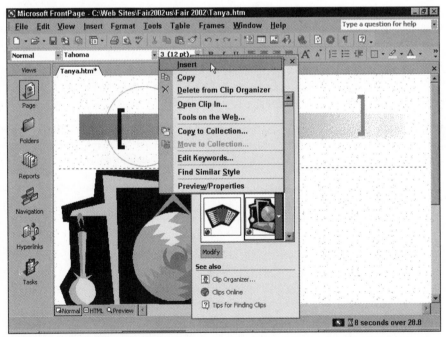

Figure 12-4: You can insert clip art, or preview it from the Insert Clip Art pane.

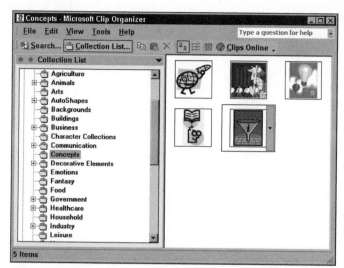

Figure 12-5: The Clip Organizer allows you to look at sets of images in folders, and to insert them into Web pages.

You can use the Clip Art Gallery to browse through whatever sets of Microsoft Office clip art are installed on your computer, and to insert images by copying them into the Windows clipboard (click on the down arrow next to the image, and choose Copy from the drop-down menu).

Caution

Many clip art images are saved in print formats with much higher pixel density than Web graphics. When you copy them into a Web page, they are often *way* too large for your page. Don't panic—just click on the (overly large) imported image to select it, and scroll to find a sizing handle in one corner. Click on a corner sizing handle, and drag towards the center of the image to resize it.

Simply resizing the picture in this manner will not decrease the file size. If you have an extremely large file with a large file size and you follow the warning above, you should also select the image and choose the resample button from the picture toolbar to reduce the file size for the image.

Note

You can copy a graphic image by creating or opening it (or a file that contains it) in any application. Copy the graphic to the Clipboard, and then paste it into a Web page that is open in Page view.

When you save your Web page, FrontPage converts all the graphics on your page to Web-compatible formats and prompts you to save these embedded files. The Save Embedded Files dialog box appears, as shown in Figure 12-6.

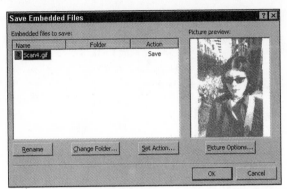

Figure 12-6: Embedded images are automatically saved as Web-compatible graphic files as you save your Web page.

Editing Pictures in FrontPage

When you select an image in Page view, the Picture toolbar at the bottom of the window becomes active. The tools in the Picture toolbar let you adjust the appearance of your graphic image right in FrontPage.

> **Note**   FrontPage gives you quite a bit of editing and tweaking power for a page editing program, but if you want to design new images yourself, you need an image editor like Adobe PhotoShop.

The picture tools enable you to add images and text, and change the appearance of a picture. You can increase brightness (something you frequently want to do with scanned images), increase contrast, change a picture to black and white (from color), and even crop an image.

The tool buttons on the Picture toolbar include the following:

✦ **Insert Picture:** Opens the Image dialog box, so that you can insert a new image.

✦ **Text:** Creates a text box in which you can enter caption text for the selected image.

✦ **Auto Thumbnail:** Generates a small version of your image. Thumbnails are often used as links to larger pictures, and their small size saves file space and speeds up page downloading.

✦ **Absolutely Positioned:** Locks the position of your image to any spot on your page.

✦ **Bring Forward:** Moves selected images in front of other objects on the page.

✦ **Send Backwards:** Moves selected images behind other objects on the page.

✦ **Rotate Left, Rotate Right, Flip Horizontal,** and **Flip Vertical:** Rotates your selected image.

✦ **More Contrast, Less Contrast, More Brightness,** and **Less Brightness:** Adjusts the brightness and contrast of your image.

✦ **Crop:** Creates a cut using a movable corner and side handles. Click and drag these handles to define crop marks for your picture, and then click the Crop button again to finalize your cut.

✦ **Line Style:** Sets line thickness in various point sizes, create colored lines, and choose various line styles, such as dashed lines or arrows.

✦ **Format Picture:** Set brightness and contrast, recolor your image, and specify cropping in inches from Left, Right, Top, or Bottom.

✦ **Set Transparent Color:** Displays an eraser tool. Point at and click any one color in your image to make that color disappear, allowing the page background to show through.

✦ **Black and White:** Converts images from color to black and white.

✦ **Washout:** Applies a watercolor-like effect to images.

✦ **Bevel:** Adds a 3-D frame around an image, suitable for navigation buttons.

✦ **Resample:** Saves your image as a smaller file if you've reduced the size of your image. The advantage is that the file size is decreased, which enables your Web page to open faster in a browser. The downside is that resampled images cannot be resized without losing quality.

✦ **Select:** Deselects other tools.

✦ **Rectangular Hotspot, Circular Hotspot,** and **Polygonal Hotspot:** Creates clickable links called image maps, which are discussed in detail later in this chapter.

✦ **Highlight Hotspots:** Helps identify hotspots.

✦ **Restore:** Undoes editing changes to your picture, as long as you haven't saved the changes.

Importing Images into a Web

When you save an embedded image, FrontPage automatically adds the graphic file to your Web. This means that the process of adding a graphic always involves two steps:

✦ An image is added to a Web page.

✦ The graphic is saved as part of the current Web site.

The order in which you perform these steps is entirely up to you. Probably the easiest and most intuitive way to add images is to first place them in a Web page, and then save the page, automatically saving the image as part of your Web site.

However, sometimes it will be faster and easier to import graphic files into your Web first, and then insert them in Web pages. For example, if you have dozens of photos that you want to use in your Web site, you can first import them, and then assign them to pages directly from the current Web site. You may have noticed when you created your Web that FrontPage created an empty folder called images, which is a convenient place to store your images.

To import images directly into your Web site before placing them on a Web page, follow these steps:

1. Select File ➪ Import to open the Import dialog box (see Figure 12-7).

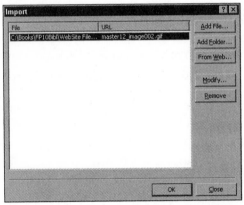

Figure 12-7: Selecting images to import into a Web

2. Click the Add File button to add a file from your local computer or network, or click the From Web button to add a file from a location on the Web or an intranet.

3. Navigate to and select the image file that you want to add to your Web site.

4. Add more files if you want by clicking the Add File or From Web buttons.

5. After you add all the files that you want to the list, click all of those that you want to import (use Shift+click to select more than one). Then, click the OK button in the dialog box, and wait while the image files are imported into your Web site.

After you import images, they appear in the list of image files in your Web site when you click the Insert Picture button in the Standard toolbar.

Note FrontPage automatically puts imported files in your site's root folder. If you want to import files into a specific folder, switch to folders view first, and have a specific folder selected.

Working with Image Objects

After you insert an image into your Web page, it exists as a separate object on the page, allowing you to alter it in a number of different ways, which are detailed in this section.

Resizing images

Select the image by clicking it. Notice how little black rectangles appear around it. These are its handles. You can resize the graphic any way you like by dragging these handles. If you drag from one of the corners, you can resize the graphic in two directions simultaneously, maintaining the height-to-width ratio of the graphic (see Figure 12-8).

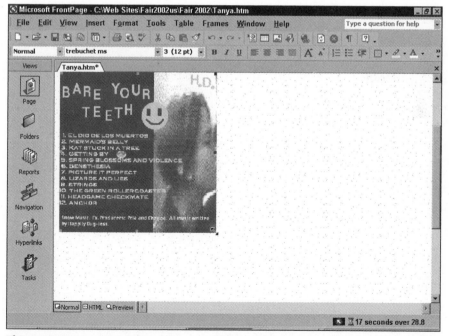

Figure 12-8: You can resize pictures by clicking and dragging on a sizing handle — use corner handles to maintain height-to-width ratio.

Resizing by clicking and dragging is quick and easy, and graphical. But keep in mind that you can easily distort the dimensions of an image if you drag on a *side* (as opposed to a corner) resizing handle.

Positioning images

You have two basic choices in positioning your image:

✦ **Align it in relation to a paragraph:** This option enables you to flow text around an image, and to have the image move with the associated text. This is explored later in the chapter in the section "Alignment options."

✦ **Position it at an exact spot on your Web page:** Absolute positioning enables you to drag your image to the exact point on the page where you want it to display. If you display an image on top of text or other page elements, you have the option of moving the image behind or on top of the other elements.

To assign an absolute position to an image, select it and click the Position Absolutely button in the Picture toolbar. Then, click the image and move it to a location, as shown in Figure 12-9.

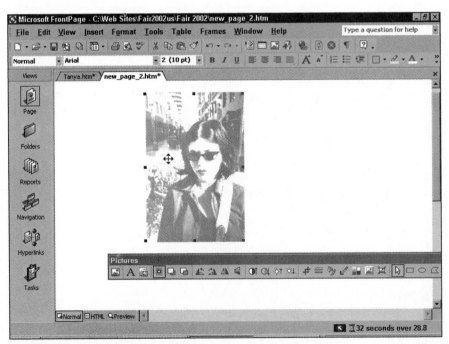

Figure 12-9: Images can be positioned at any location in a page.

Which Web graphics format is best?

Now that you've learned to control the basic appearance and location of images, you are ready to explore more-complex options for managing your graphics. One of those options is deciding what image format is best for your picture.

By default, FrontPage saves embedded images as GIF files. If you are adding an occasional icon to your Web page, that may be all you need to know. But FrontPage also makes it easy to save an image as any of the three widely recognized Web graphics formats (GIF, JPEG, or PNG). Which is best? Each of these formats has its advantages and disadvantages.

Graphics can be saved in a variety of formats; each has a slightly different method of storing the information necessary for a computer to render a bunch of 0s and 1s as a full-color image on your monitor. Until recently, almost all Web graphics were stored either as GIFs (GIF is variously pronounced "jiff," as in "I'll be there in a jiff," or "giff," as in "gift," but without the t) or as JPEGs (JPEG is always pronounced "jay-peg"). Recently, PNG (sometimes pronounced "ping") formats have come into wide acceptance, and are interpreted by recent versions of Microsoft Internet Explorer and Netscape Navigator.

These three formats are different, and each has its virtues in certain circumstances, but they share three characteristics that make them all well suited to the Web:

✦ They are not proprietary formats.

✦ They are not specific to any computer platform.

✦ They use compression to create reasonably small file sizes (although this is no guarantee that Web images will download quickly).

GIF: The all-purpose graphic format

GIF (short for Graphic Interchange Format) is a cross-platform graphics format invented by CompuServe to enable people to transfer graphic files easily over dial-up connections. This was the first graphics format used on the Web, and it continues to be the most prevalent even though the more recent Web browsers support both GIF and JPEG formats. Because of its compression techniques, the GIF format is particularly well suited to graphics that have horizontal bands of color or large areas of similar colors. Thus, GIF works well for most banners, buttons, and basic illustrations.

GIF images also have two interesting characteristics:

✦ Any single color in a GIF image may be *transparent*, allowing the background of your Web page to show through. These images are called *transparent GIFs*.

✦ A single GIF image can actually be composed of several individual pictures that are shown in sequence, giving the appearance of motion. These images are called *animated GIFs*.

Unfortunately, because of GIF's limit of 256 individual colors and its compression technique, GIF images are not particularly well suited to photographic images, which is where JPEGs come in.

JPEG: The format for photos

JPEG stands for Joint Photographic Experts Group, the name of the organization that created the format. The JPEG standard was devised as a method of compressing digitized photographs. Like the GIF format, it is a cross-platform standard. Although JPEG is used less frequently than GIF on the Web, you will see it used for complex images and for larger background images. One interesting aspect of JPEG images is that they can be created with varying amounts of compression, whereas a GIF is just a GIF. This is because JPEGs, quite simply, are compressed by throwing out some of the information in the image. In theory, enough information is removed to make the file smaller but not enough that anyone will notice without a magnifying glass. The more information that you throw out, the smaller the file becomes, and the more degradation to the image quality that results. For the technical-minded, this is called *lossy compression* (because the image loses quality when compressed).

PNG: The other image format

The PNG file format is a close (and younger) relative of the GIF file format. PNG (short for Portable Network Graphic) images share the GIF format's attributes of supporting transparency and incremental downloading (*interlacing*). The main drawback of using the PNG file format — and it is an imposing one — is that older browsers will not interpret these images at all. For the time being, that disadvantage probably argues for avoiding PNG files in your Web site.

Defining image properties

You've now taken a basic course in image file formats. Now you are ready to control the properties of the images in your Web pages, which you can do in the Image Properties dialog box. You can open this dialog box for a selected image in any one of three ways:

✦ Right-click the image and choose Image Properties from the context menu.

✦ Select the image and choose Format ⇨ Properties.

✦ Select the image and then press Alt+Enter.

Tip   You can open the Picture Properties dialog box by double-clicking an image.

The Image Properties dialog box gives you direct access to all the image properties in HTML. The dialog box is divided into three tabs: General, Video, and Appearance.

The Video tab, which contains properties specific to video images, is discussed in Chapter 13. The options on the General and Appearance tabs are examined in detail now.

Defining General properties

The General tab of the Image Properties dialog box enables you to edit some basic characteristics of the image, including the name of the image file, its format type, alternative representations that can be presented to users, and any hyperlink associated with the image.

Image Source field

The Image Source field displays the filename of the currently selected image. You can use this field to replace the current image with another. Click Browse, locate a new image file, and click OK. When you close the Image Properties dialog box, the new image appears in place of the former one.

Image Type

The Type option indicates the image format of the selected image. Click GIF, PNG, or JPEG to change the image format.

If the image is GIF format, two additional attributes of the image are indicated:

✦ **Transparent:** This enables you to designate one color in the graphic, typically the background color, that can be rendered transparently, allowing any background on the Web page to show through. Controlling transparency on a GIF image is explained in the next chapter. You cannot edit this property from the Image Properties dialog box. If the image contains a transparent color, the Transparent checkbox is checked. Otherwise, it is grayed out.

✦ **Interlaced:** This refers to an alternative way of storing the information about a GIF image. Some browsers are capable of displaying interlaced GIFs differently from noninterlaced images. By default, most Web browsers display images as they are downloaded. If the images are small, they appear to pop into the page. If they are larger, they draw in from top to bottom, which can be somewhat irksome if you happen to be the impatient type. Interlaced images can be displayed so that the entire image appears as the image is still downloading. The image at first appears blurry, and becomes increasingly focused as more of its information is downloaded. The effect is of an image materializing out of a haze of color. Interlacing was first introduced as a way of displaying the entirety of an image map quickly, so that the user could click some dimly recognized area in the image map without having to wait for the entire image to load. You can decide whether this really is a useful feature for your Web page. In practice, interlacing produces a pleasing effect for certain kinds of images, including photographs and illustrations. It can also be annoying, so use your judgment.

If the image type is JPEG, then two text boxes open, allowing you to specify more information:

✦ **Quality:** Adjust the quality of the image as a percentage from 0 to 100. The higher the number, the higher the quality of the image and the larger the file size. See the earlier discussion of the JPEG format for more information on how JPEGs work.

✦ **Progressive Passes:** This is essentially the same as interlace for GIF images. You do, however, have one advantage: You can specify the number of steps required to go from the extremely fuzzy version of your image to the full version. The number of steps can vary from 0 to 100.

Note   These above four options are not available when looking at the picture properties General tab. These options are only viewed when saving the files to a Web.

Alternative representations

Several reasons exist for why HTML includes provisions for designating alternative representations of images. One reason is that not all Web browsers are actually capable of displaying inline images. In addition, all Web browsers include an option to turn off the automatic display of images. This feature enables users with slower Internet connections, or users who may find the images distracting rather than useful, to browse the Web without waiting for images to download.

A more widely applicable use for alternative text is to function as an online caption for an image. Most modern browsers display alternative text when a visitor points his or her mouse cursor at a picture. Figure 12-10 shows alternative text displayed with an image in Microsoft Internet Explorer. To enter alternative text, just type the text in the Text field.

You can also define a low-resolution version of a graphic. This option is not universally supported, but it can be used for an interesting effect. It enables you to designate a temporary lower-resolution version of an image that is displayed first while the real image is still downloading. When the real image has completely downloaded, it replaces the temporary image. To make use of this feature, simply designate the image file to be used as the Low-Res version. Click the Browse button next to the Low-Res field in the Alternative Representations section to select an image for this purpose. (The Low-Res image and the main image must have the same dimensions.)

Alternative Low-Res images can be used to create the equivalent of a two-frame animation. One popular technique is to use a black-and-white version of an image as the low-resolution version. When the color version appears, it looks as if color is being painted into the image.

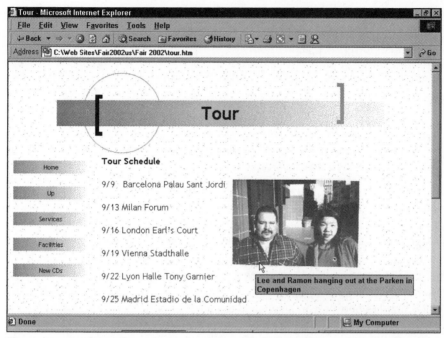

Figure 12-10: Alternative text appears next to an image when a visitor points his or her cursor over the image.

The default hyperlink

You can associate an image with a hyperlink in the same way that you associate a string of text with a hyperlink. For details on creating hyperlinks, refer to Chapter 2. When users click the image, they jump to the hyperlinked location.

If you associate your image with a hyperlink, that information appears in the Image Properties dialog box as well. Alternatively, you can use the Image Properties dialog box to create and/or edit an image's hyperlink. To add a hyperlink to an image, click the Browse button next to the Location field in the Default Hyperlink section. Locate the file and click OK.

Controlling image appearance

The Appearance tab contains image properties that directly affect the way the selected image is displayed. The options in the Layout section of the Appearance tab are described next.

Alignment options

The alignment options affect how an image is aligned in relation to the text around it. The most powerful alignment options are left and right alignment. Left or right alignment allows you to wrap text around a picture. Figure 12-11 shows text wrapped around a right-aligned image. The small arrow to the left of the paragraph indicates where the pictured is anchored, and the picture can be moved by clicking and dragging that anchor arrow.

Images can also be centered. But that's normally an odd way to lay out images, because text will break rather inelegantly on either side of the image. The other alignment options control how images are positioned in relation to a line of text. These options are somewhat esoteric, and are used for fine-tuning the exact alignment of tiny graphics inserted into text. These alignment features are used when an inserted image is smaller (shorter in height) than the line of text within which it is inserted. For example, if you were using a tiny graphic image as a trademark or degree symbol, you could align those images with the top of a line of text.

Horizontal and vertical spacing

Use the Vertical Spacing and Horizontal Spacing options to affect how much white space appears between an image and the surrounding text. These options are particularly useful when used in conjunction with the left- and right-alignment options to control how text wraps around an image.

Border thickness

If you associate an image with a hyperlink, by default, the hyperlink displays with a thin border that is the color of the other hyperlinks on the page around it. You can use the Border option to hide this border or control its width. In addition, you can use the Border option to add a border to non-hyperlinked images. To add a border to an image, simply designate its thickness, measured in screen pixels. The border displays in the color of the default text on the Web page.

Size options

The Size section of the Appearance tab indicates the width and height of the current image, designated in screen pixels. By default, these values are grayed out. You can alter them directly by first checking the Specify Size checkbox. This is the equivalent of resizing the image. Values for the size property can be given either in pixels or in percentages. If you select percentages, the size of an image changes in relation to the size of the Web browser window.

To maintain the same proportions between height and width as you resize, click the Keep Aspect Ratio checkbox. Then, when you change either the height or width, the other dimension will be reset automatically to keep the same aspect ratio.

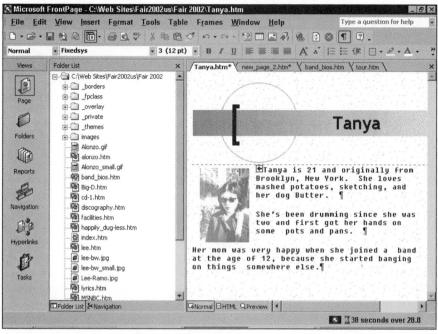

Figure 12-11: Wrapping text around an image

Tip

You can speed up downloading by using the following trick: Use the Size area of the Appearance tab to assign exact image size. To maintain the same proportions in your resized image, check the Specify Size checkbox, but leave the default values in the Width and Height text boxes (the original size of the image). This tells your visitors' browsers the size of the image before it's downloaded, so that your page doesn't redraw to accommodate the image's actual size each time an image is downloaded. This isn't a big thing, but it can make your pages easier to view.

Finding Images for Your Web Pages

You know how to work with an image once it is in FrontPage, but perhaps you are wondering how to fill your Web pages with beautiful artwork and interface elements like the ones you see on all the best professional Web sites.

There are many sources for Web site art, ranging from sites that allow you to download free art, to professional stock houses that provide images at prices that vary sharply but generally are well below the price of custom-designed graphics. This section briefly outlines some of the places you can look for images.

Online graphic resources

In addition to the clip art included with FrontPage, Microsoft maintains online resources that include sample media files and pointers to additional media resources. Two locations to check out are the following sites:

✦ **FrontPage Clip Art Resources:** At this writing, Microsoft has FrontPage clip art accessible at `http://dgl.microsoft.com/mgolen/eulaform.asp`

✦ **Cool Graphics:** `www.coolgraphics.com/`

Of course, you need not rely on Microsoft for everything. The Web has a store of freely available art that is expanding all the time. To get a sense of the possibilities, enter **free Web graphics** into the search box of your favorite search engine, and explore the hundreds of sites offering free icons, pictures, logos, and designs.

Saving images from the Web

Some people think it is one of the Web's greatest virtues, others think it is downright criminal, but the fact remains that copying images from Web sites is astoundingly easy. (In fact, merely in the process of requesting a Web page, your Web browser automatically copies the images to a temporary location on your computer.) If you have ever saved images from your Web browser, though, you know that you can save only one image at a time. What if you want to save all the images from a page? FrontPage makes this easy.

Caution

Legal warning! Under no circumstances should you make use of images that you find on the Web for your own profit, either directly or indirectly, unless those images come with explicit permission to do so. Using images in this manner is illegal, and it threatens to undermine the whole spirit of the Internet.

To save images from a Web page:

1. Select File ➪ Open from the Editor menu.

2. In the Open File dialog box, choose the Other Location tab and check the From Location radio button.

3. Type into the From Location field the URL of the Web page you want to open. Note that this can be any publicly accessible URL.

4. Click OK. The Web page opens in Editor (don't worry, you can't make changes to the original).

5. Select File ➪ Save. FrontPage prompts you to save the page to the current Web site, including the HTML file and any inline graphics.

Stock houses

You may notice that free images on the Web are of varying quality. In general, you can find many nice background textures (and some garish ones), and trinket art such as ruled lines and bullets. You are harder pressed to find decent illustrative art. Even nice buttons and icons are rare commodities. If you have some money to spare and want to add professional-quality illustrations to your Web pages, you may want to investigate some of the many stock photography and digital art companies. Here are two, large, representative examples of stock houses:

✦ **PhotoDisc** (`www.photodisc.com`): This service specializes in photographic images, and lots of them. These images are royalty-free, meaning that you pay for them once and then use them for their designated purpose as long as you like.

✦ **ImageClub** (`www.eyewire.com`): Affiliated with Eyewire, this is a source for your clip art needs. They have line art, icons, and fonts, as well as photography.

FrontPage's Rudimentary Drawing Tools

FrontPage 2002 includes a set of drawing tools, accessible from the Drawing toolbar. This tool set has been adapted from other Office applications, and is similar to the drawing tools available in Word, PowerPoint, or Publisher.

The fatal flaw with these drawing tools is that they are only supported by Microsoft applications. So if you're creating pages destined for the Web, or for a browser other than Internet Explorer, our advice, as we'll explain below, is to avoid these tools. After you read the following cautionary note, should you decide these drawing tools would be helpful in your development projects, we'll explain how to use them.

A word of warning

The drawing tools included for the first time in FrontPage 2002 have severe limitations for Web design. Okay, let's be more blunt: It's not a good idea to use these drawing tools for pages that you plan to post on the Internet.

Why is that? FrontPage's new drawing tools are based on VML technology. This technology has not been adopted as a standard for Web design. For example, objects created with FrontPage's drawing tools are not supported in Netscape 4.7, which is still, at this writing, a browser used quite broadly.

We need to further emphasize that with the discontinuation of bundling Microsoft Image Composer with FrontPage, it is now necessary to use a separate Web graphic program to design graphic objects for FrontPage, and no such package is included

How Compatible is VML Format?

In order to provide a Web-standards insider's view of VML compatibility with Web browsers, we're sharing this excerpt of an interview with Web strategist Elliotte Rusty Harold.

Q: Microsoft has promoted VML as a recognized tool for graphic development. They got representatives of other developers like Macromedia to sign on to the article they submitted to the World Wide Web Consortium (W3C) that governs Web standards proposing the adoption of VML standards. Is this a valid, recognized format for Web components?

A: As far as the W3C is concerned, VML is dead, dead, dead, DEAD. Did I mention that it was dead?

Q: Microsoft has incorporated VML tools into FrontPage 2002, and is promising support for them.

A: Microsoft has a horrible record of spreading huge amounts of misinformation about all sorts of XML technologies. Part of the problem is a severe internal communications failure there that has resulted in the salespeople, trainers, and documentation folks not having the foggiest clue what the programmers are doing. The trainers, for instance, are still pushing technologies the XML team at Microsoft replaced over a year ago.

Q: Well, VML is still useful for people who are designing for intranets, where everyone who accesses the Web site has Office XP, and therefore support for VML, right?

A: I doubt it. Bottom line: VML is a proprietary Microsoft technology supported by some (not all) Microsoft tools, and even then not all the time. There are only very limited circumstances in which one would consider using VML. Really only if you need to deal with graphics created in Office using the Office graphics tools. It doesn't do anything for graphics imported into Office from other programs, which is how most people work.

in FrontPage. There are, of course, many graphic design tools available, including Adobe PhotoShop, PaintShop Prop, CorelDRAW, and PhotoPaint, among others. The following resources provide a good overview of available Web graphic design tools:

✦ *Creating Great Web Graphics* by Laurie McCanna

✦ *<coloring web graphics>* by Linda Weinman and Bruce Heavin

✦ *<designing web graphics>* by Lynda Weinmann

All that said, you can use the drawing tools included in FrontPage for components of pages that will be viewed by folks using Internet Explorer and who have Office XP installed on their systems. Even here, we have reservations as to how much your VML drawings will be interpreted by a viewer's browser.

Drawing with FrontPage's drawing tools

Having warned you about the limitations of FrontPage's drawing tools, we'll now take a quick look at what they are and how they work. Figure 12-12 identifies the tools in the Drawing toolbar. To open the Drawing toolbar, choose View ➪ Toolbars ➪ Drawing (if it is not already opened).

The drawing tools that generate graphic objects are AutoShapes, Line, Arrow, Rectangle, Oval, Text Box, and Insert WordArt.

The Insert ClipArt and Insert Picture From File buttons duplicate features on the Picture toolbar, discussed in the section "A Quick Look at Web Graphics in FrontPage" at the beginning of this chapter.

The Fill Color, Line Color, Font Color, Line Style, Dash Style, Arrow Style, Shadow Style, and 3-D style tools apply effects to existing text or graphic objects.

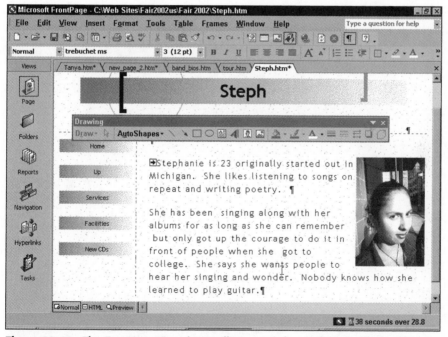

Figure 12-12: The FrontPage Drawing toolbar, not to be confused with the *Picture* toolbar, is used to insert and edit images.

AutoShapes

The AutoShapes tools include palettes of pre-set shapes. They are:

✦ **Lines:** Use this tool for freehand drawing. Double-click to complete a shape.

✦ **Basic Shapes:** Use this tool to draw a happy face, heart, trapezoid, and other shapes. Click and drag to define the size of the shape.

✦ **Block Arrows:** This tool provides a selection of different arrows.

✦ **Flowchart:** This is a palette of shapes used in drawing flowcharts.

✦ **Stars and Banners:** Every elementary school teacher needs these for his or her class Web site.

✦ **Callouts:** Cartoonists may want to check these out.

✦ **More AutoShapes:** Offers additional shapes.

Figure 12-13 shows the Block Arrows tool being used to insert an arrow.

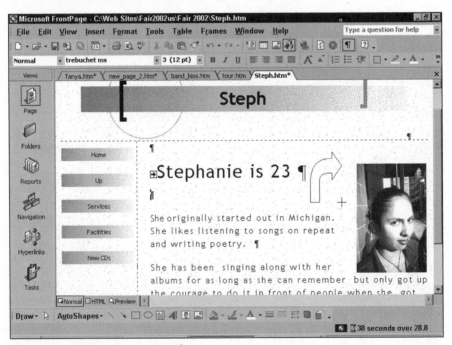

Figure 12-13: Inserting an AutoShape

Drawing lines and shapes

Draw a line by clicking on the Line tool, and then clicking and dragging on your page to create the line, as shown in Figure 12-14. In the case of both lines and arrows, you can force the angle of the line to 15 degree angular increments (for example 15 degrees, 30 degrees, 45 degrees, and so on) by holding down the Shift key as you draw.

Draw an arrow by selecting the Arrow tool, then clicking and dragging on the page. The direction you click and drag determines the direction to which the arrow is pointing.

Select either the Oval tool, or the Rectangle tool, and then click and drag on the page to create a shape.

Applying shape and line effects

You can apply shading, color, and other attributes to selected shapes. First, use the Select Objects tool (the white arrow in the Drawing toolbar) to select the object to which you are applying effects. Click on a shape with the Select Objects tool, and then use the Line Style, Dash Style (works only with lines), Arrow Style (works only with lines), Shadow Style, or 3-D Style tool to choose various effects from the pop-up palettes.

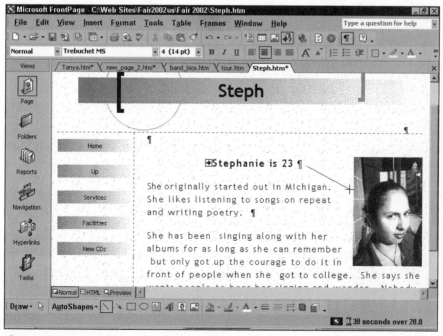

Figure 12-14: Drawing a line with the Line tool

To apply a fill or line color, or attribute, to a selected object, click on the Fill Color, Line Color, Line Style, Dash Style, Arrow Style, Shadow Style, or 3-D Style tool, and choose a color or style from the palette associated with that tool.

Figure 12-15 shows a color being applied to a selected shape.

Text boxes and WordArt

Text Boxes are similar to the shapes created with FrontPage drawing tools except that they cannot be rotated (we'll explore rotating other shapes and lines in the next section in this chapter).

To create a Text Box, choose the Text Box tool, and click and drag on the page to generate the box. A text cursor appears inside the box when it is selected, and you can insert and edit text within the box. You can format Text Box text by using the tools in the Formatting toolbar.

Caution   The Text Box drawing tool might be handier if it created text boxes that allowed text to wrap around them. However, text boxes sit *on top* of any existing page text, and so aren't suitable for that effect.

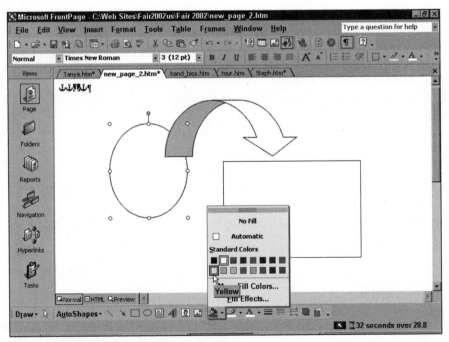

Figure 12-15: Applying effects to a shape

Ported from Microsoft Word, WordArt is a feature that allows you to apply an entertaining set of effects to text. To generate WordArt, click the Insert WordArt tool, and choose a style from the WordArt Gallery, as shown in Figure 12-16.

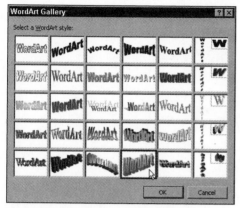

Figure 12-16: Picking a WordArt style

After you click on a style, and click OK, the Edit WordArt Text dialog box appears, as shown in Figure 12-17. Type your text in the Text area, and choose a font, font size, and bold or italic if desired. Then click OK to generate the WordArt.

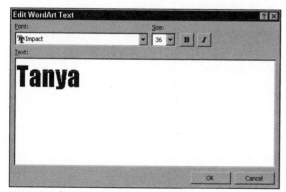

Figure 12-17: Generating WordArt

When you click on a WordArt object, a special toolbar appears, as shown in Figure 12-18. This toolbar allows you to edit, reformat, reshape, align, or space out the text.

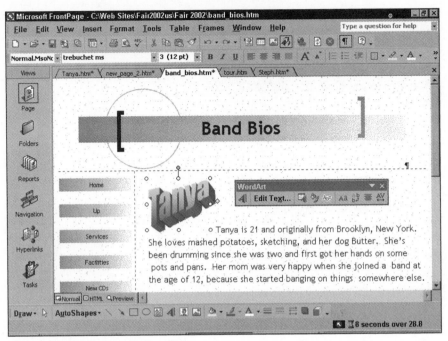

Figure 12-18: The WordArt toolbar

Moving, rotating, and grouping shapes and lines

You can resize, move, or rotate a selected line shape. Text boxes can be moved and resized, but not rotated.

Use the Select Objects tool to select the shape first. A selected shape displays with six handles (a selected line or arrow displays with two handles). Move selected objects by clicking and dragging on them.

Shapes, text boxes, and lines can be resized by clicking and dragging on either side or on the corner handles. (Lines have only two handles — one on each end.) Clicking and dragging on corner handles maintains the original height-to-width ratio, while clicking and dragging on a side handle can stretch or compress a shape, as shown in Figure 12-19.

You can *group* (temporarily combine) objects by holding down the Shift key while using the Select Objects tool to select more than one object, and then choosing Group from the Draw tool menu in the Drawing toolbar, as shown in Figure 12-20.

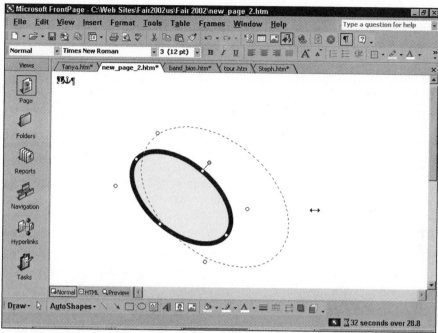

Figure 12-19: Reshaping an oval

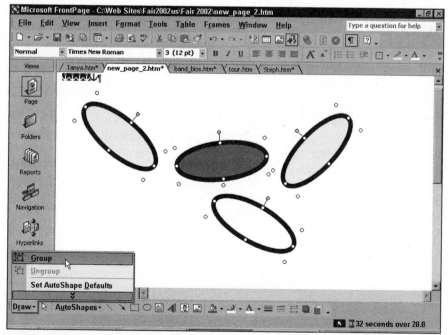

Figure 12-20: Grouping selected objects

Grouped objects can be moved, resized, or rotated together. You can also apply fill and line properties to a group of selected objects all at once. To ungroup a selected group, click on the Draw tool and choose Ungroup.

Defining shape layout

The Draw tool has features to align, locate, and flip selected objects. Align selected objects by clicking on the Draw tool in the Drawing toolbar, and choosing Align and Distribute. The options allow you to distribute (evenly space) or align objects.

The Snap option in the Draw tool menu allows you to set objects to snap to either another object, or a grid. In FrontPage 2002, there is no provision for defining a grid, so this option is inoperative. However, by choosing Snap to Object, you can easily align shapes next to each other. The Nudge option allows you to move any selected object(s) in small increments; and the Rotate option in the Draw tool menu allows you to flip objects horizontally or vertically.

Many shape and line features available in the Drawing toolbar are also accessed from the Format AutoShape dialog box which can be accessed by double-clicking on a Draw object, or by choosing Format ➪ AutoShape from the FrontPage menu bar.

Creating Graphic Links and Image Maps

Any image can serve as a hyperlink. Hyperlinks are assigned to images in the same way that they are assigned to text — first you select the object and then you assign a link. Image maps are graphics with more than one link. With an image map, a visitor clicks one part of the image to go to one link, and another part of the image to go somewhere else. Well-designed image maps can provide an attractive and intuitive way for visitors to jump to a desired destination.

Assigning hyperlinks to an image

The easiest way to assign a link to an image is to click the image and then click the Hyperlinks button in the Standard toolbar. The Create Hyperlink dialog box opens, and you can assign a link to a page in your Web site from the list at the top of the dialog box. Or, you can enter a URL. After you define your target, click OK in the Create Hyperlink dialog box. When you test your link in a browser, the target displays in the status bar of the browser, not in the alternative text caption that appears when you point to the linked graphic, as shown in Figure 12-21. Keep that in mind when you decide what alternative text to assign to a graphic.

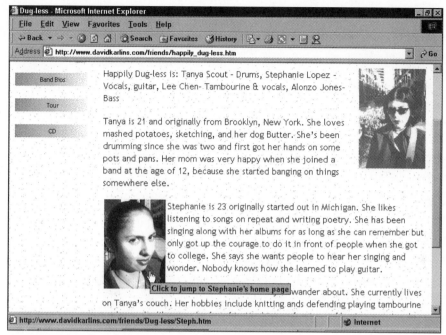

Figure 12-21: Your target displays in the browser status bar, not in the link alternative text.

Defining an image map

Defining an image map is as easy as drawing a rectangle, an oval, or a shape. First, click the image to which you are assigning links. Then, choose either the Rectangular Hotspot, Circular Hotspot, or Polygonal Hotspot tool from the Picture toolbar and (using the pencil cursor) draw an area on the picture that you want to associate with a link, as shown in Figure 12-22.

If you are drawing a polygonal hotspot, click points to create the outline, and then double-click to complete the shape.

After you complete your hotspot, the Create Hyperlink dialog box will open, in which you can define the target for the hotspot link.

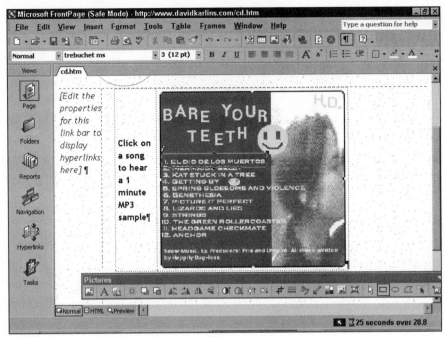

Figure 12-22: Defining a rectangular image map hotspot

Tutorial 12-1: Creating an image map

In this tutorial, you will create an image map with three clickable hotspots. Each of these hotspots will serve as a link to a different page in your Web site.

1. Open an existing Web page, or create a new one.

2. Select Insert ➪ Picture ➪ Clip Art, and type **map** in the Search Text box in the Insert Clip Art pane.

3. Click the Search button.

4. From the list of maps in your system's clip art collections, clip on a map clip art icon, and select Insert from the popup menu.

5. Click on the inserted clip art to select it. Use sizing handles to resize the clip art if necessary for the picture to fit on your page.

6. With the picture selected, click on the Text tool in the Picture toolbar (if the toolbar is not visible, choose View, Toolbars, and select Pictures).

7. Click OK if you are prompted to convert your image to GIF file format.

8. In the text box, type **We're on Tour**. You can use the formatting toolbar to format this text.

9. Click and drag on the text box to locate it.

10. Click the Rectangular Hotspot tool, and draw a rectangle around your text. As you release your mouse button, the Insert Hyperlink dialog box appears. Define a link target (any link target) here for this hotspot in your picture, and click OK to close the Insert Hyperlink dialog box.

11. Click the Polygonal Hotspot tool in the Picture toolbar. Draw line segments by clicking and dragging to outline part of your picture. When you have completed the outline, double-click to open the Insert Hyperlink dialog box. Define a link target for this hotspot, and click OK.

12. Define additional polygonal hotspots on your map, as shown in Figure 12-23.

13. Save your page, and test your image map in a browser.

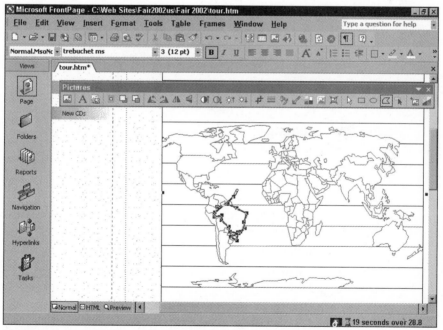

Figure 12-23: Drawing a polygonal hotspot in an image map

Summary

FrontPage provides a variety of tools to help you work with pictures. When you save a page, FrontPage allows you to save a picture as a GIF or JPEG file, regardless of the original file format.

You can use FrontPage to define image file properties — including how you want a picture to download into a browser, and what alternate text you want to associate with a picture. You can edit pictures for size, crop them, and resample them to reduce file size. You can use Picture toolbar tools to change contrast and brightness in a picture.

In addition to assigning links to a picture, you can define clickable hotspots (called image maps). Image maps allow you to connect several link targets to a single picture.

✦　　✦　　✦

Using Animation Effects

This chapter explores several ways of adding *dynamic* content to your FrontPage Web site. Dynamic content is the opposite of *static* content — images and text that just stay in one place and don't change.

Dynamic content changes, sometimes in response to a visitor action (like moving his or her mouse cursor over a spot on the page) and sometimes independently of visitor actions.

Dynamic Content: Animation and Multimedia

In this chapter, we'll explore a couple of different approaches to activating your site: using Dynamic HTML (DHTML) and using media (sound and video). DHTML can be used to animate elements of your site, such as fly-in elements, or text that changes color when scrolled over. Audio and video can be embedded in a page, or accessed via plug-in programs that work with browsers to enable different audio and video formats, like Windows Media, MP3 audio, or Flash movies.

As a side effect, this chapter also serves as a primer in Web-based multimedia formats, from relatively simple GIF animations to more sophisticated animation, audio, and video techniques.

What is DHTML?

DHTML, short for Dynamic HTML (HyperText Markup Language), is a method of adding animation and interactive effects to a Web page. DHTML works when combined with browsers that conform to a Document Object Model (DOM) that supports DHTML, including extensive support for Cascading Style Sheets (CSS). DHTML-friendly DOMs allow scripts (like JavaScript) to interact with page, image, and text formatting to create dynamic effects.

FrontPage allows you to assign DHTML formatting to pages and page content without any technical knowledge of what goes into DHTML. If you are interested in creating your own DHTML effects, check out Chapter 18 on client-side (browser-based) scripting languages. A deeper investigation of DHTML, including the problem of browser incompatibility, is found in the section "DHTML Effects: Behind the Scenes" later in this chapter. Before employing DHTML, you should read that section.

FrontPage DHTML Effects

DHTML combines many tools to create animation, interactivity, and media; and FrontPage powerfully automates the process of generating these elements for you. All you need to do is select effects and apply them to your page, and to the objects on your page.

FrontPage DHTML effects consist of numerous customizable animation effects that you can add to your Web page, or to your page objects, without worrying about the technical details. All that you really need to understand is how to add an effect to your page. DHTML animation for *page transitions* is explored later in this chapter in the section "Page Transitions." Here, we'll explore the process of assigning DHTML formatting to specific objects on a page.

The basic process of defining DHTML formatting involves three simple steps:

1. Create one or more elements that you want to animate. These elements may be text, graphics, or a combination of the two.

2. Select the element(s).

3. Use the DHTML Effects toolbar to select and configure the effect that you want to apply to the element(s) in the Position Box.

These steps are demonstrated in the upcoming DHTML Effects tutorial. First, take a look at the DHTML Effects toolbar and what it offers.

Using the DHTML Effects toolbar

To see the DHTML Effects toolbar, select View ➪ Toolbars ➪ DHTML Effects. The DHTML toolbar is illustrated in Figure 13-1.

Figure 13-1: The DHTML toolbar

The basic procedure for creating a DHTML effect is as follows:

1. **Choose an Event from the Choose an Event drop-down menu:** This is a technical way of saying you need to define what action will trigger the effect to do its thing. The event might be either something the user does, such as clicking the object with the mouse, or something the browser does, such as loading the page. Select an option from the drop-down menu to activate the Apply options.

2. **Choose an Effect from the Apply drop-down menu:** The effect is what happens when the event occurs. For example, the object might change its appearance or move around. Different events have different effects that can be associated with them, so depending on what you select in the first step, you see a different set of options for this step. Select an effect from the drop-down menu to activate the settings options.

3. **Choose Settings:** The settings are the particular properties of the effect. Each effect has its own set of settings.

In addition to the three main option menus, the toolbar has two other features:

✦ **Remove Effect:** This option is activated after you create an effect. It is always nice to have a way out!

✦ **Highlight DHTML Effects:** This option, represented by a page icon on the far right of the toolbar, adds a highlight to your effect in FrontPage. This is just a visual reminder to you that a DHTML effect is on the page (see Figure 13-2). The highlight doesn't show up on the Web page in a browser. This option is selected by default. Click the page icon to turn off highlighting.

The next several sections provide a brief description of the primary options available in the Events, Effects, and Settings option menus on the DHTML toolbar. If you are eager to try out DHTML, you can skip to the tutorial.

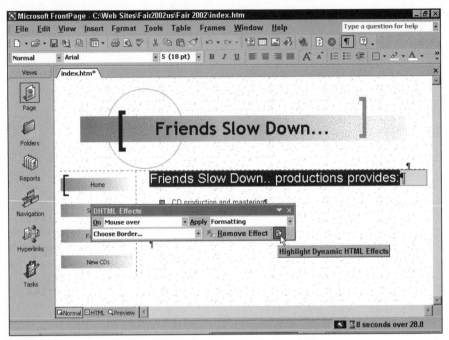

Figure 13-2: Highlighting DHTML effects in (Normal) page view

DHTML events

To create a DHTML effect, you first select one of the DHTML event options. The *event* is the action that initiates the effect. Most events are triggered by something that the user does, such as loading a particular page or clicking a particular page element. The following are the four events to choose from:

✦ **Click:** Triggered if the user clicks with any mouse button on the element contained within the Position Box. If the event involves a format change, clicking a second time undoes the effect (returns the element to its original state). Click events can trigger changes in the appearance (format) of the element or initiate a *fly out* that causes the element to move off the page.

✦ **Double-click:** Triggered if the user double-clicks the element in the Position Box.

✦ **Mouseover:** Triggered any time the user moves the mouse over the element within the Position Box.

✦ **Page load:** Triggered automatically when the page first loads. It is best suited for run-once animations, such as elements that move into place on the page.

DHTML effects and settings

Each of the four DHTML events has associated with it certain effects. After you select an event, you next choose one of the available effects for that event. The following list describes each of the available effects and, where appropriate, indicates which events have the effect as an option:

Note Not all effects are available for every event. The selection of available effects (like Formatting or Fly Out) will vary depending on the event you select.

✦ **Formatting:** Enables you to change the appearance of an element when an event occurs. This effect is available for Click, Double-Click, and Mouseover events. With Formatting selected, you can apply font and border formatting to activated text.

- **Choose Font:** Enables you to select a font change (typically a color change) to occur.

- **Choose Border:** Enables you to select a border change to occur.

The formatting choices can be used in conjunction with one another (it is not an either/or choice, as is the case with the animation settings).

✦ **Swap Images:** Appears only on the Mouseover event when the element is an image. It replaces the original image with an alternate, providing the equivalent of a "two-state" image. The only setting is Choose Image.

✦ **Fly Out:** Causes the affected element to disappear off the page in the direction designated by the setting option. Your choices are the following:

- To left

- To top

- To bottom left

- To bottom right

- To top right

- To top left

- To top right by word

- To bottom right by word

Note Formatting and Fly Out effects lend themselves nicely to effects initiated by the user after the page has loaded. Enabling these effects when the page loads doesn't make sense, because you will never see the formatting change, nor the elements that fly off the page before it loads.

The remaining effects are limited to the On Page Load event. They are all methods of moving elements onto the page with pizzazz.

✦ **Drop in by Word:** Displays a string of text one word at a time.

✦ **Elastic:** Text flies in and bounces up and down before coming to a stop. You can elect to bounce text up from the bottom of the page or in from the right.

✦ **Fly In:** The opposite of Fly Out. Settings are similar to those for the Fly Out effect (except that they are prefaced with From rather than To), with the addition of Along Corner, which causes the text to rise from the bottom and take an abrupt left turn to its final resting place.

✦ **Hop:** Causes a string of text to appear one word at a time, each word hopping in over the previous word.

✦ **Spiral:** Element appears in a sweeping arc from the upper-right corner of the page.

✦ **Wave:** Similar to Hop, except that each word does a loopy-de-loop (that's its technical name) when it appears.

✦ **Wipe:** Text reveals itself a line at a time. Settings are left to right, top to bottom, and from the middle.

✦ **Zoom:** Causes the element to grow or shrink to its final size. Settings are "in," in which case the element starts small and grows to its final size, and "out," which causes the element to start large and shrink down to its final size. Note that any size formatting you apply to this element is ignored.

Tutorial 13-1: Applying DHTML to text

In this tutorial, you create a simple but bold statement, punctuated with the dramatic effects of Dynamic HTML.

1. Create a new Web page.

2. Type your message, **Friends Slow Down...**

3. Now you bring this message to life. Select View ➪ Toolbars ➪ DHTML Effects and select the text message.

4. In the DHTML toolbar, select Page Load in the On drop-down list and select Hop in the Apply drop-down list, as shown in Figure 13-3. Now, the text will really "abound!"

Figure 13-3: Dynamic text

Now, preview the effects in the Preview tab, as shown in Figure 13-4. Notice that the effects always fire in order from top to bottom down the page. One of the limits of using DHTML effects in this way is that you cannot really create "synchronized" effects.

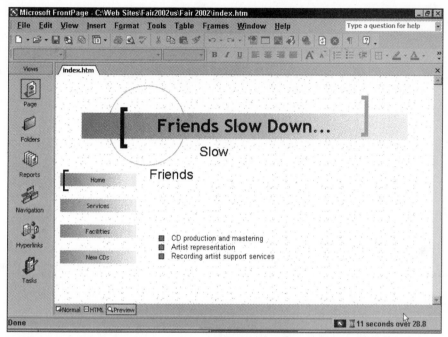

Figure 13-4: The Preview tab in Normal view will display DHTML effects.

Page Transitions

You can apply transition effects to specific text and graphic elements of your Web pages by using DHTML. But you can also apply dynamic effects to an entire page by assigning page transitions.

Note   Page transitions work only with Internet Explorer. On the other hand, it's not as if viewers who see your site in a Netscape browser will lose page content – they'll only miss out on your fun page transition effects.

Transitions assigned to a page can be activated when the page is first opened or exited. Alternatively, the transition effect can be set to activate only if the page is accessed when your site is first opened, or exited, in a browser.

To apply a transition to a page or a Web site, follow these steps:

1. Open the Web and view the page to which you are assigning a transition in Page view. Even if you are assigning a transition effect for when your site is opened or exited in a browser, you still need to have a Web page open in Page view.

2. Select Format ⇨ Page Transitions to open the Page Transitions dialog box.

3. Define the event you want to trigger the transition effect by selecting Page Enter, Page Exit, Site Enter, or Site Exit from the Event drop-down list.

4. Set a duration for the effect in seconds by entering a value in the Durations box, as shown in Figure 13-5.

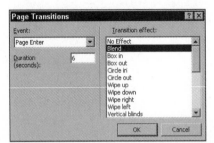

Figure 13-5: You can define the duration for a page transition, but the actual time will depend on a viewer's Web connection speed.

5. Choose one of the effects from the Transition Effect list. You can select a new event, and define another transition effect if you want. Then, click OK.

Note Contrary to what you might expect, if you define both a page and site transition effect on a page, the page transition effect takes precedence over the site effect.

Expandable and Collapsible Outlines

Collapsible and expandable outlines add dynamism to your page because they change based on actions (mouse clicks) performed by visitors to your page. You can present a collapsed outline on your page, and allow visitors to expand all, or parts, of the outline. In that sense, the page is interactive, and allows visitors to define their own viewing experience.

Figure 13-6 shows an outline with one section expanded, and the rest collapsed.

Expandable and collapsible outlines only function in Internet Explorer 4.0 or higher and not in any version of Netscape Navigator as of this writing. But they are a handy and helpful way to compress information on a page.

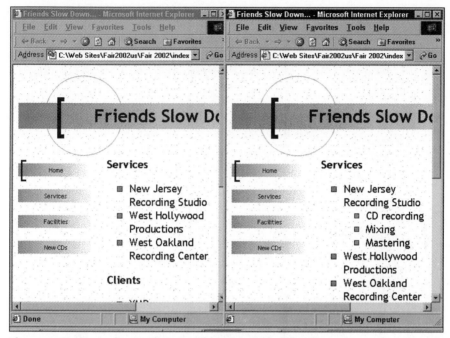

Figure 13-6: Expanding outlines can be expanded and collapsed.

To create collapsible outlines, follow these steps:

1. Type a list of items to which you will assign outlining using bullets or numbers.

2. Select the entire list, and assign either bullets or numbering to the list, using either the Numbering or Bullets icons in the Formatting toolbar.

Note

For more numbering or bullet list options, you can choose Format ⇨ Bullets and Numbering, and define the format of your list in the List Properties dialog box.

3. Select elements of the outline to demote, and click on the Increase Indent icon in the Formatting toolbar twice, to create an indented outline level.

4. Repeat Step 3 to indent (demote) other list items. You can create a new level of indentation by indenting selected list items two more times using the Increase Indentation icon. Figure 13-7 shows an outline with three levels of indentation.

5. After you have finished with your list, select the *entire outline*, and choose Format ⇨ Bullets and Numbering. The Bullets and Numbering dialog box opens.

6. Select the Enable Collapsible Outlines checkbox, as shown in Figure 13-8. You can also choose the Initially Collapsed checkbox to display the outline collapsed when a visitor first sees the page.

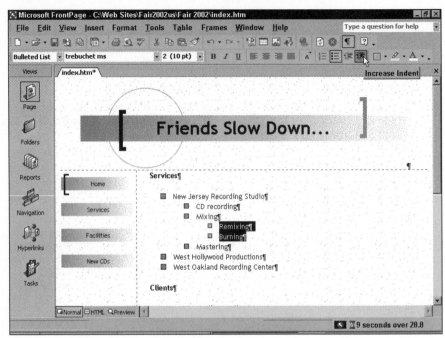

Figure 13-7: This outline can be expanded to three levels.

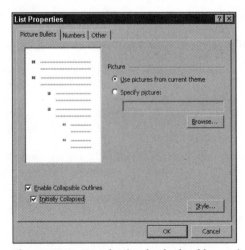

Figure 13-8: By selecting both checkboxes in the Bullets and Numbering dialog box, your outline will appear collapsed, but it is expandable.

Note   Visitors using Netscape browsers will see the outline expanded regardless of what options you select in the Bullets and Numbering dialog box. And they will not be able to collapse outlines.

Collapsible outlines, as displayed in Internet Explorer 5.5, are not particularly intuitive. For one thing, the cursor display does not change into an arrow, or change period, when a visitor hovers over an expandable or collapsible outline element. For that reason, it is generally a good idea to include some text on your page indicating to visitors that an outline is collapsible (or expandable). Visitors can be informed that they should click on an outline item to expand it.

Note   One effective technique is to combine collapsible outlines with linked text. This provides an interactive navigation tool, as shown in Figure 13-9.

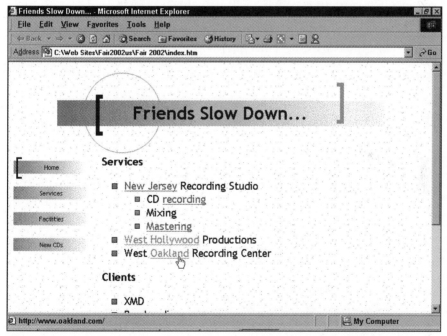

Figure 13-9: This collapsible outline functions as an interactive navigation bar.

DHTML Effects: Behind the Scenes

DHTML effects work (or *don't* work!) because (and *only when*) they are supported by a browser. Only Microsoft's Internet Explorer supports the full range of DHTML effects included with FrontPage 2002.

Why? Standards set for browsers by the World Wide Web Consortium (W3C) include specifications for what are referred to as a Document Object Model (DOM). Much of the thinking behind the DOM is to allow scripts (like JavaScripts) to be applied to any element in a Web site—ranging from the entire site, to a page, to a selected block of text or an image. Cascading Style Sheet (CSS) specifications fall within the realm of what is defined by DOM standards. CSSs contribute to DHTML by enabling embedded (inline) styles for selected text or images to interact with scripts.

Incompatibility problems with DHTML arise from the fact that Netscape Navigator, including version 6, has not adopted the W3C's DOM definitions as completely or aggressively as has Internet Explorer (IE). Thus, Netscape browsers do not fully support all of the CSS features included in IE, and do not allow CSSs to mesh with JavaScripts in a way that enables interactive changes in how text and images display.

DHTML and JavaScript

Much of the vitality of DHTML comes when JavaScript is combined with CSS styles. In effect, JavaScript enables CSS styles to *interact dynamically* with actions a visitor performs in his or her browser (like, for example, moving his or her cursor over an object on the page, or loading the page).

When you assign most DHTML effects, FrontPage generates a JavaScript file on your Web and embeds a reference to that file in the page in which the DHTML effect is employed. You can see these references to generated JavaScript files by looking at the HTML view for a page with DHTML elements.

For example, the HTML code `src="animate.js"` refers to a JavaScript file called `animate.js`. (This script is used for hover-over effects.) The file `outline.js` is used for expanding and collapsing outlines.

By default, these JavaScript files are saved to a JavaScript folder on your Web. You can open them in NotePad and edit them by double-clicking on a file with a `.js` extension.

Tip   Can't find your `.js` files? First, refresh your Web connection (choose View ⇨ Refresh) to make sure your Folder view reflects all the files on your FrontPage Web. You can search for files by choosing View ⇨ Reports ⇨ Files ⇨ All Files, and clicking on the top of the Type column to sort files by type.

While the entire ensemble of tools that make up DHTML are not fully supported by Netscape browsers, those browsers *do* support JavaScript. One option for developers is to take the generated FrontPage JavaScript files, and edit them. That option is explored in Chapter 18, which focuses on client-side scripting.

DHTML and browser compatibility

DHTML effects are very slick and remarkably easy to produce using FrontPage. Before you start adding effects to all of your pages, however, you may want to reflect on some of the limitations of DHTML. (By the way, this topic is discussed in gory detail in the scripting chapter, Chapter 18.) DHTML effects have three basic drawbacks:

✦ Not all browsers are capable of supporting DHTML. If you can count on (or insist on) your user having a Netscape or Microsoft browser, version 4 or greater, you are fine (and among the lucky few). If not, you have to remember that not everyone will see your cool effects.

✦ Even browsers that do support DHTML don't have exactly the same support for it. This means that any good DHTML implementation must check for the browser type and deal with it appropriately.

✦ FrontPage's method of handling the preceding drawback is to enable the effects only for IE (this drawback is specific to the DHTML effects).

In short, Netscape Navigator 4.7 and 6.0 do not support many FrontPage-generated DHTML effects because Netscape continues to use different CSS and DOM specifications than those adopted by Microsoft.

Managing DHTML (in)compatibility

Often, you will want to design pages that display differently in different browsers. That can work. Visitors with DHTML-less browsers see one thing, while DHTML-enabled browsers will display additional effects. Keep in mind, though, that viewing DHTML with an incompatible browser can produce two possible results:

✦ Your page won't look as cool and flashy when viewed with browsers that don't support DHTML.

✦ Your page will look awful when viewed with browsers that don't support DHTML.

For example, if you assign expandable and collapsible outlining to a list, the list will display fully expanded in Netscape Navigator 4.7 or 6.0. In many cases, that won't ruin your page design. Figure 13-10 shows the same page viewed with outlines collapsed in IE 5.5, and expanded in Navigator 6.0. The pages look different, but the Netscape page is a satisfactory presentation of the information.

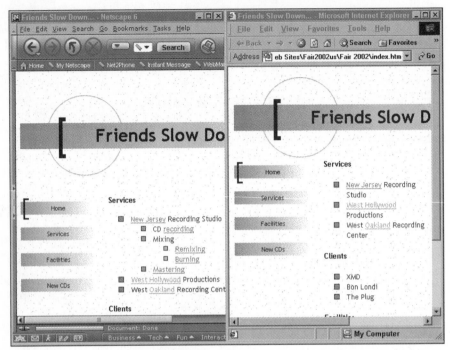

Figure 13-10: Expandable/Collapsible outlines in Netscape Navigator 6.0 and Internet Explorer 5.5

On the other hand, if you are *relying* on a DHTML effect to enable page content, as illustrated in Figure 13-11, then Netscape viewers will see *different* page content.

Disabling DHTML

You can disable some or all DHTML features in FrontPage. That way, you and your fellow developers will not be tempted to add features that will produce unpleasant results.

To control the availability of DHTML effects for an open page, choose Tools ⇨ Page Options, and click on the Compatibility tab. The Compatibility tab of the Page Options dialog box is shown in Figure 13-12.

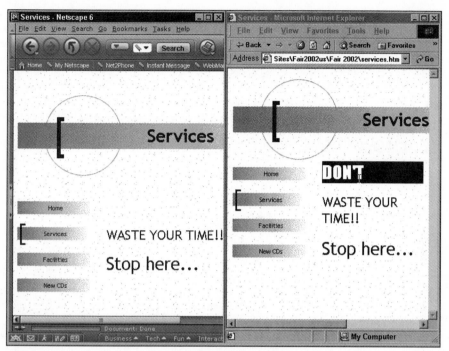

Figure 13-11: In this example, DHTML effects have been assigned to turn the text "DON'T" into a visible color only when hovered over. Because this effect is inoperative in Netscape Navigator 6, visitors get a very different message.

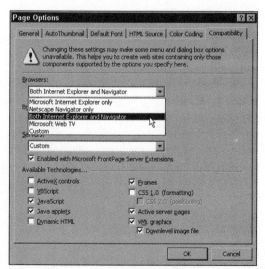

Figure 13-12: You can disable FrontPage's DHTML effects if you are designing for Netscape browsers.

There are two ways to disable DHTML effects that are not supported by Netscape Navigator or versions of Internet Explorer earlier than 3. You can choose browsers and versions from the Browsers and Browser Versions drop-down menus at the top of the Compatibility Page Options dialog box. Or, you can custom define supported DHTML features using the checkboxes in the bottom part of the dialog box.

Caution The built-in disabling that FrontPage assigns when you choose Both Internet Explorer and Navigator from the Browsers drop-down menu, and 4.0 Browsers and Later from the Browser Versions drop-down menu *do not* disable Dynamic HTML as shown in Figure 13-13. However, in reality, Navigator 4.7 (as well as version 6.0) does *not* reliably support much DHTML. If you want to disable DHTML, do it by deselecting the Dynamic HTML checkbox yourself.

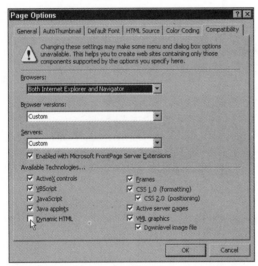

Figure 13-13: Here, we've told FrontPage that we're designing for browsers including Netscape Navigator 4.7. FrontPage still allows DHTML as an option, although these features are not supported by Navigator 4.7.

Designing for Web TV or Other Browser Devices?

Even as the two main browsers — Navigator and IE — move close to each other in terms of supported features, a plethora of new devices are emerging that support no, or almost no, DHTML. FrontPage does have an option in the Browsers drop-down menu of the Compatibility tab of the Page Options dialog box (Tools ➪ Page Options) that disables features not support by Web TV. Ultimately, there is no substitute for actually testing your pages in the browsers in which you anticipate viewers will see them.

DTHML vs. embedded media

DHTML is one option for providing animation and interactivity on your site, but it is very browser dependent. Less browser-dependent forms for providing animation, media, and interactivity rely on media files like sound, video, or animation objects.

What if you want to add bona fide multimedia to your Web? Well, you're in luck, because FrontPage provides support for this as well. The next sections in this chapter explore several multimedia technologies that FrontPage can assist you in adding to your site.

Adding Audio in Page Backgrounds

As Web pages continue to evolve in the direction of multimedia titles and interactive television programming, the ability to add background audio has become an increasingly prevalent element of multimedia Web pages. FrontPage includes support for a Microsoft-specific HTML extension that enables developers to embed an audio file in a Web page. When the page is requested, this audio file loads and plays automatically.

A Primer on Digital Audio Formats

FrontPage supports several digital audio formats. Without attempting to go into detail, here are the formats:

✦ **Wave Sound (WAV):** The Windows standard audio format.

✦ **Midi Sequencer (MIDI):** The format generated by synthesizers.

✦ **RealAudio files (RA):** This file format is supported by the downloadable RealPlayer application.

✦ **AIFF Sound (AIF, AIFC, AIFF):** The Macintosh equivalent of WAV files.

✦ **AU Sound (AU, SND):** A Sun audio format that is used on the Web and that has gained limited cross-platform acceptance.

✦ **MP3:** Popularized originally by Napster, MP3 files produce relatively good quality sound from files that are compressed to download quickly. Many media players including the QuickTime player and Windows Media Player handle MP3 format sound files.

Wave, AIFF, and AU sound files are sampled audio, also known as waveform audio. Waveform audio formats record, or "sample," sounds, much as a tape recorder does. MIDI, unlike a sampled sound format, records a set of instructions about how to re-create, or "synthesize," a particular sound. As a result, MIDI has a more limited repertoire than waveform audio, which can copy any sound that you feed into a microphone. MIDI is, however, far more economical in the size of its files than is waveform audio. Many online musical compositions are distributed in MIDI format.

In addition, you can embed audio files in many formats as playable files within a Web page. When these files are activated, an associated player (like RealPlayer or Windows Media Player) opens to play the sound file.

Getting audio files

To add background audio to your Web page, you first need an audio file. You have two options: Either create a digital audio file yourself or obtain a file from an existing source. Several sites on the Internet maintain sample sounds and music clips (see the "Audio resources" section later in this chapter). Always be aware of any possible copyright issues before you download and use audio files from the Internet, however.

For purposes of experimenting with sound, or for adding short sound clips to pages, Windows provides a selection of WAV and MIDI files. In Windows ME, those files are installed by default in the Windows\Media folder. If you don't find that folder on your system, or you don't find sound files there, you can search your system for sound files (select Start ⇨ Search from the Windows taskbar, and select For Files and Folders. Specify WAV files (or another sound format) to locate sound files on your system.

Figure 13-14 shows a listing of some of the available sound files that come with Windows ME. You can test them by double-clicking on a filename to open the sound file in the Windows Media player (or other sound player depending on your installed media software and system defaults).

Caution   Turn down your stereo speaker before you check out sound samples. Or make sure everyone in your office is prepared for some audio stimulation!

A Quick Look at Ripping Sound Files

Assuming you have permission to do so, you can extract (*rip*) audio files from CDs, and then use them in FrontPage Web sites.

There are many freeware, shareware, and downloadable commercial packages that allow you to do this with Windows, including Poikosoft (download at http://www.poikosoft. com/cdda/). Most of these programs convert your CD files into WAV format sound files.

You can also download software (like CoolEdit, http://www.cooledit.com) that converts WAV files into MP3 and other audio file formats.

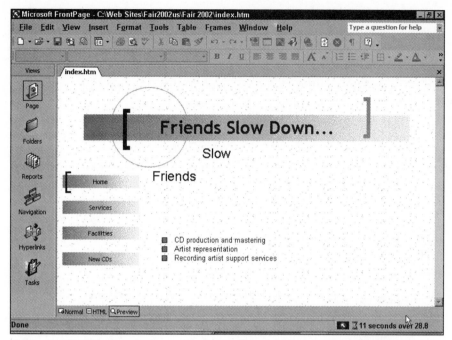

Figure 13-14: Windows comes with sound files you can experiment with.

Adding background sounds to your Web pages

After you locate a file on your local drive (or save one there from the Internet), you can assign that sound as a background for any open Web page. To insert a background audio into a Web page:

1. Open the Web page in FrontPage.

2. Select File ⇨ Properties. The Page Properties dialog box shown in Figure 13-15 appears.

3. In the Location field of the Background Sound area, click the Browse button and browse to the folder with your audio files. Select the audio file to play when the page is loaded.

Note

The Windows Media folder has both MIDI and WAV files. Because MIDI files are much more efficient, you can add a much longer background sound that takes less time to download by finding a MIDI file to use as a page background sound.

4. Click Open.

5. To loop the sound indefinitely, select the Forever checkbox. To play the sound a set number of times, deselect the Forever checkbox, and enter a number in the Loop spin box.

6. Save the Web page. You are prompted to add the sound file to your Web, if it is not already there.

7. Preview the sound in your Web browser and dance along with the background sound file.

Note   This feature is easy to implement, although it does not offer much in the way of user control. Remember that it is also Microsoft-specific, and not supported by all browsers.

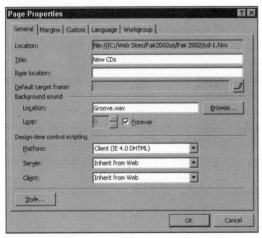

Figure 13-15: You can assign a background sound to a page in the Page Properties dialog box.

Setting audio properties

After you create a background sound, you can control a few properties. For instance, as with GIF animations, you can set the sound file to loop a designated number of times. To do this, select File ⇨ Page Properties, and in the General tab, indicate the number of times to loop the sound file. You can also use the Page Properties dialog box to change the name of the background sound.

Embedding Audio Files in Web Pages

In addition to including audio files as part of a page background, you can also embed audio files anywhere in a Web page. These files can be of any format supported by the visitor's system media player. Windows folks will likely have Windows Media player, which supports WAV, SND, AU, AIF, AIFC, WMA, and MP3 audio files. AIF files are supported by Macintosh systems. The next most accessible sound player is the RealPlayer, which supports it's own RA sound files, most of the same files supported by Windows Media Player, and SMIL (or SMI) format audio files.

The easiest way to embed these audio files is to import them into your Web (File ⇨ Import, then navigate to the file and import it). You can now simply create links directly from a page to a sound file, as shown in Figure 13-16.

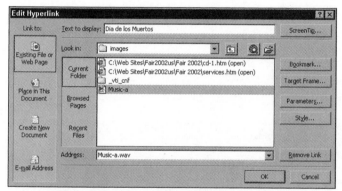

Figure 13-16: Visitors who click on this link will launch their system's media player, which will play the sound file.

One thing that is a bit odd about playing embedded audio files is that they automatically launch an associated player program. That makes sense for linked video files, because viewers will want to watch the video in the associated player. However, because there is no audio associated with video files, visitors end up looking at an empty player window. In order to keep all their senses entertained, Microsoft's Windows Media Player allows visitors to display various transforming shapes while "watching" an audio file, as shown in Figure 13-17.

Audio resources

If you are looking for sound bytes to add to your Web, or if you want to learn more about sound formats, the following are several Web resources that you may want to investigate:

✦ **WWW Virtual Library:** Maintains lists of Internet resources on a variety of topics. Each topic is maintained by a volunteer. The library's list of audio resources is located at `http://www.comlab.ox.ac.uk/archive/audio.html`. It contains links to sound archives, software, newsgroups, and online radio.

✦ **Harmony Central:** An excellent site for MIDI resources and information. Everything from MIDI forums to software and links to MIDI archives. `http://www.harmony-central.com/MIDI/`

✦ **The MIDI Farm:** Another full-service MIDI site with a well-organized potpourri of MIDI-related content. `http://www.midifarm.com/`

✦ **Webplaces Internet Search Guide:** This bare-bones site has links to all sorts of searches. The Audio Browser section has links to numerous sound file archives. `http://www.webplaces.com/html/sounds.htm`.

✦ **Internet Underground Music Archive (IUMA):** If you are looking for music on the Web, this should be your first stop. Lots of audio, and an ultra-cool, award-winning interface. `http://www.iuma.com`.

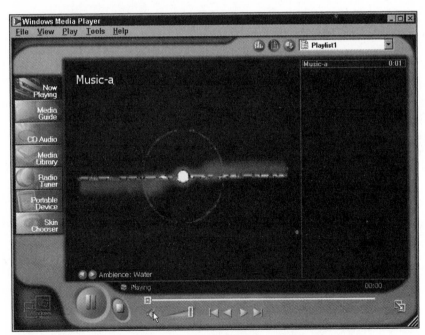

Figure 13-17: "Watching" an audio file in Windows Media Player

Audio players

Two media player programs will handle just about any audio file you want to test. They are the Windows Media Player that comes with Microsoft Windows, and RealPlayer.

If, for some reason, you don't have Windows Media player, you can download it for free at `http://www.microsoft.com/windows/windowsmedia/en/download/default.asp`.

RealPlayer supports RealAudio (RA) files. RA is the original streaming audio format, and still the most popular. Unlike the standard audio formats, which require users to download an entire file and then listen to it, streaming audio plays as it downloads. It can even be used to broadcast audio in real time. You can download either the free or a commercial version of RealPlayer at `http://www.realnetworks.com/`.

In addition to these two industry-standard (as of this writing) audio and video players, other media players include:

✦ **QuickTime Audio:** Apple Computer's video format can also be used to prepare audio files. QuickTime files can be saved for "fast-start," enabling the QuickTime video files to begin playing as they download. For more information, see the QuickTime WebMaster's Page, `http://www.apple.com/quicktime/download/`.

✦ **Crescendo:** A MIDI plug-in from LiveUpdate, is available in Netscape and Microsoft versions. You can download either the free version, or the Plus version, at `http://www.liveupdate.com`.

✦ **Liquid MusicPlayer:** This audio player from Liquid Audio is designed to allow users to download and play CD-quality audio, as well as to view art, lyrics, and credits: `http://www.liquidaudio.com`.

Including Video in Your FrontPage Web Site

In the following sections of this chapter, we'll explore various options for including video in your FrontPage Web site.

The simplest, if not the crudest, way to include video is to use animated GIFs. These files look and act like regular GIF images, but have animation embedded within them. They look like static graphics in Normal Page view, but do their animated thing in Preview or when viewed in a browser.

The next step in video sophistication is to embed either a Windows Media (AVI) file or a RealMedia (RA) file in your FrontPage Web. FrontPage makes this easy to do, and gives you some control over how the video is displayed in the page. The biggest advantage of embedded video is that it appears right in your Web page.

Finally, you can include video in your Web site that launches plug-in media players. These players (like Windows Media Player, RealPlayer, or QuickTime) provide viewers with sophisticated video controls so they can play, pause, stop, or rewind videos, as well as controlling display and sound volume.

Where do movies come from?

FrontPage 2002 provides a number of ways to present movies in your Web site, but it does not include tools for creating video. An exploration of options for creating digital video is well beyond the scope of this book, but we can note a few of the sources for video.

✦ **Find them on the Web:** You can search for free, downloadable video in various formats, and find a wide array of video on the Web.

✦ **Create video in an animation program:** Programs like Flash, Shockwave, Adobe Premier, and QuickTime are used to design and generate digital video.

✦ **Windows ME built-in video tools:** While a bit behind Macintosh in built-in video tools, Windows ME does include Windows Movie Maker — not a full-featured movie editor, but acceptable for editing digital video.

✦ **Capture video with a digital camera.**

A good starting point for investigating digital video is the book *Digital Video For Dummies* by Martin Doucette (IDG Books Worldwide, 1999).

Easy animation with animated GIFs

One of the most primitive, but still effective, formats for animation is animated GIF files. Animated GIFs are simply a series of GIF images sequenced and saved as a single GIF file. Animated GIF files do not have the features of more sophisticated animation formats, such as sound and custom controls, and the quality is generally more choppy than animation displayed in online video. However, GIF animation has three big advantages:

✦ Animated GIFs are supported by the widest array of browsers of any form of animation.

✦ Animated GIFs are usually smaller than the other formats.

✦ Amimated GIFs are easy to make yourself, and FrontPage's clip art includes a selection of Animated GIFs.

Note

FrontPage 2002 ships without Microsoft Image Composer. Darn!

Image Composer is a powerful Web graphics package that came free with FrontPage 97, FrontPage 98, and FrontPage 2000. Image Composer included a cool little program called GIF Animator that generated animated GIFs.

Dumping Image Composer (and GIF Animator) appears to conform to Microsoft's strategy of meshing FrontPage more firmly into the Microsoft Office family, as opposed to developing FrontPage into an increasingly robust Web design tool — a disturbing trend that FrontPage users can only continue to protest.

Even though we lost GIF Animator, there are many free programs available for creating animated GIFs. You can find MediaBuilder's GIFWorks at `http://www.gifworks.com`. Desktoppublishing.com provides links to several downloadable GIF animation packages at `http://desktoppublishing.com/graphutilgifanim.html`. You can download a trial version of Ulead's professional-quality GIF Animator at `http://www.ulead.com/ga/trial.htm`. (For more exploration of Ulead's GIF Animator, see Appendix D.)

To insert animated GIF clip art, choose Insert ➪ Picture ➪ Clip Art. In the Results Should Be drop-down menu, in the Insert Clip Art window, check only Movies, and click on Search. Hover over images that appear to identify the file type, as shown in Figure 13-18.

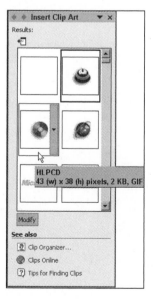

Figure 13-18: This GIF at the end of the tool tip indicates this clip art movie file is in (animated) GIF format.

When you find an animated GIF, choose Insert from the drop-down menu next to the image.

Tip

As an alternative to inserting a selected clip art image using the drop-down menu, you can also click and drag the icon onto your page.

After you insert an animated GIF in your page, save your page. As you do, you will be prompted to save the animated GIF as well. You can change the filename (or destination folder) of your saved file just as you would a static Web graphic. Animated GIFs can be resized, and normal picture formatting can be applied by right-clicking on the picture and choosing Picture Formatting from the Context menu.

Note

Picture formatting options in the Appearance and General tabs of the Picture Properties dialog box can be applied to animated GIFs, but not the options in the Video tab.

Embedding AVI and RealVideo clips in your Web pages

FrontPage allows you to embed Windows Video (AVI) files and RealAudio (RA) files in your pages. To embed a Windows Video or RealAudio file in your page, follow these steps:

1. Select Insert ➪ Picture ➪ Video.

2. In the Video dialog box, use the Look In list to scroll to the local folder or Web folder with your video files.

3. Select an AVI or RealAudio file that you want to include, and click OK. A preview of the video appears in the Web page, showing the initial frame of the video clip.

You now have video in your Web page. When you save the page, you are prompted to save the video in the current Web. To preview it, select the Preview tab.

Setting video properties

The properties for video clips are located on the Video tab in the Picture Properties dialog box. Select the video to format, and then select Edit ➪ Picture Properties, or right-click the image and select Picture Properties from the pop-up menu. The Video tab of the Picture Properties dialog box is shown in Figure 13-19.

You can edit the following elements of a video display in the Video tab of the Picture Properties dialog box:

✦ **Video Source:** As with other inserted objects, you can alter the source name, effectively substituting another video for the current one.

✦ **Repeat:** Just as with animation and sound, you can elect to loop the video clip as many times as you want to subject the poor user to the sequence.

✦ **Start:** By default, the video begins to play when the file loads. Alternatively, you can have it begin when the user passes the mouse over the video. If you use this option, you may want to prompt the user to do so, unless you just want them to guess for themselves.

Note In addition to the video formatting options in the Video tab of the Picture Properties dialog box, some of the options in the General and Appearance tabs also affect video. You can define wrapping style, alignment, border thickness, horizontal and vertical spacing, and size in the Appearance tab. In the General tab, you can define alternate text, and a link for your video.

Figure 13-19: You can edit looping (how often a video repeats) and other play options in the Picture Properties dialog box.

Including Video Plug-Ins

AVI videos are easy to embed with FrontPage, but they have important limitations. Although players are available for the AVI video format on all major computer platforms, AVI is not considered a cross-platform standard. Nor does it have the best compression methods available. Even relatively short video clips are likely to be 300K and larger, more than the average user is going to want to confront unannounced on a Web page. For more sophisticated video, it is necessary to embed more advanced video file formats.

The RealAudio format *is* a more sophisticated video file format capable of compressing sound and quality video into bandwidth-friendly file size. And RealAudio files *can* be embedded in FrontPage Web pages. However, when you embed RealAudio (RA) files in FrontPage, they play without displaying the RealPlayer viewer. That's good if your visitors don't have, and don't want, the RealPlayer. The downside is that they don't get control over volume, image size, and other features that are available when videos are viewed with the RealPlayer.

Figure 13-20 shows a side-by-side comparison of watching a movie in the RealPlayer, and watching it embedded in a FrontPage Web site.

Note   As we put this book to bed, support for RealVideo files in FrontPage 2002 is still unreliable. The two competing media formats and media player producers appear to not be meshing their products particularly well at this moment.

In addition to embedded media, you can include video in your site that depends on *plug-ins*, or additional software on the viewer's system. For instance, you can embed a Flash movie in your FrontPage Web page, and viewers will need to have the Flash/ Shockwave Player installed. If they don't have that player associated with their Web browser, or installed on their system, you can prompt them to download the software necessary to view the movie.

Note   It's often helpful to include a link to a media software vendor when you embed a video in that vendor's format. For example, if you embed a RealPlayer file, you can include a link to www.real.com.

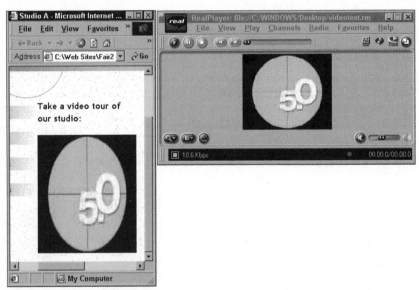

Figure 13-20: The embedded RealVideo does not provide viewers with the same control as a RealVideo that launches the RealPlayer.

Making video files available at your site

Plug-in video can work two ways: It can be embedded right in a FrontPage Web page, or it can be played in viewing software like Windows Media Player or Real-Player that are launched when the movie file is opened.

The easiest way to include movie files in your site is to open them as you would a picture. To do that, follow these steps:

1. With your Web page open, choose Insert ➪ Picture ➪ Video.

2. In the Video dialog box, navigate to your video file, and click Open. Your video will appear as a small icon on your page.

3. Double-click on the embedded video icon to open the Video tab of the Picture Properties dialog box. Here you can define looping and the Start method for the video.

That's pretty much it! When a visitor clicks on a link to a video file, that file will open in whatever media player he or she has associated with the video file format in his or her operating system.

One obvious shortcoming with this is your visitors may not have a video player that supports the file you are providing. For this reason, sites usually include a link to a download site, so that viewers can acquire the required software to watch your video.

Popular download sites for video formats are shown in Table 13-1.

Table 13-1
Popular Video Formats

Video Format	Download Site
Windows Media Player Plays WAV, MPEG, and AVI movies	`http://www.microsoft.com/windows/` `windowsmedia/en/download/default.asp`
RealPlayer Plays RealNetworks (RA) files	`http://www.realnetworks.com/`
QuickTime Player Plays QuickTime movies	`http://www.apple.com/quicktime/` `download/`
Macromedia Shockwave Player and Macromedia Flash Player The Shockwave player supports both Flash and Shockwave movies	`http://www.macromedia.com/downloads/`

By providing a link to a video file, and a helpful link to download the required viewer, you can easily add video to your site. Figure 13-21 shows a movie playing in the QuickTime player.

Some video format plug-ins can function within FrontPage to present video from *within* a Web page. In the following sections, we'll explore those options.

Embedding Macromedia's Shockwave and Flash movies

Macromedia's Shockwave (SWF) format is the export file type for Flash movies and for animations created by Macromedia Director. The SWF file format is supported by browsers equipped with the Shockwave/Flash Player.

Over the last couple of years, Flash has evolved into the standard for vector-based animation applications. You can download a trial version of Flash (version 5 at this writing) from Macromedia's Web site, http://www.macromedia.com.

Flash video can be embedded in a FrontPage Web page. However, visitors must still have the Flash (or Shockwave) viewer in order to see the video (so you may well want to include a link to the Macromedia site for viewers to download the player if necessary).

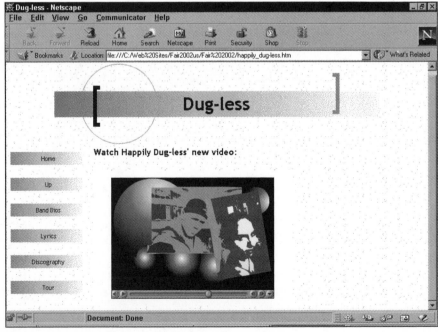

Figure 13-21: Watching a QuickTime movie

To embed a Flash SWF movie in an open Web page, follow these steps:

1. Select Insert ➪ Web Component ➪ Advanced Controls.

2. In the Choose a Control area of the Insert Web Component dialog box, select Plug In, as shown in Figure 13-22.

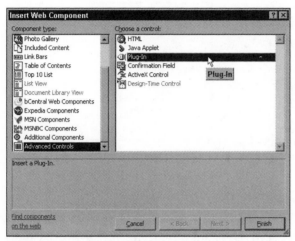

Figure 13-22: Inserting a plug-in for a movie

3. Click on Finish. The Plug-In Properties dialog box appears.

4. Use the Browse button to locate a Flash Player (SWF) file on your local system or on the Internet.

5. In the Message For Browsers Without Plug-In Support box, enter text that will be displayed if a visitor does not have an installed viewer for Flash movies (for instance, **You must download the Flash Player from Macromedia to see this movie.**).

6. You can use the Height and Width boxes to define the size of the plug-in display.

7. Use the Alignment drop-down menu to align the plug-in on the right or left side of a page, allowing text to flow around the plug-in.

8. You can use the Border Thickness box to define the thickness of a border (in pixels). Use the Vertical and Horizontal spacing boxes to define buffer space around the plug-in.

9. After you define the plug-in, click OK. The plug-in will display in Normal Page view only as a plug-in icon, as shown in Figure 13-23. You can test the video in Preview Page view or by previewing your page in a Web browser.

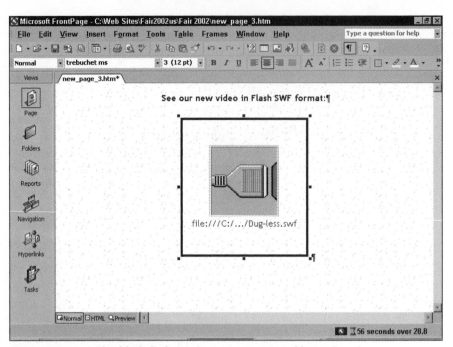

Figure 13-23: Embedded Flash movies are represented by an icon in Normal Page view.

If your plug-in file was not imported into your Web, you'll be prompted to save it when you save your Web page.

Flash plug-ins can be resized in FrontPage by simply clicking and dragging on the sizing handles.

Most of the parameters of how a Flash movie plays are built into the movie itself (for example, whether it loops, as well as the controls to play or stop the movie). However, visitors can play, stop, and rewind movies by right-clicking on them, so you may want to include that information on the Web page, as shown in Figure 13-24.

Embedding RealMovies

If visitors to your site have RealPlayer installed on their systems, they can see RealMovies (RM) embedded within FrontPage Web pages.

Note RealMovies are inserted in FrontPage by using the Plug-In advanced control. In the discussion that follows, we'll sometimes refer to RealMovies as "plug-ins."

As mentioned earlier, as we went to press, we were having inconsistent results embedding RealMedia video in FrontPage Web pages. Some RealMedia files were not recognized as video files by FrontPage, and some were.

Figure 13-24: Visitors have some control over how Flash movies play in their browsers.

To embed a RealMovie in an open Web page, follow these steps:

1. Select Insert ⇨ Web Component ⇨ Advanced Controls.

2. In the Choose a Control area of the Insert Web Component dialog box, select Plug In.

3. Click on Finish. The Plug-In Properties dialog box appears.

4. Use the Browse button to locate a RealMovie file on your local system or on the Internet, as shown in Figure 13-25.

5. In the Message For Browsers Without Plug-In Support box, enter text that will be displayed if a visitor does not have an installed viewer for RealMovies (for instance, **You must download the RealPlayer to see this movie.**).

6. You can use the Height and Width boxes to define the size of the plug-in display.

7. Use the Alignment drop-down menu to align the plug-in on the right or left side of a page, allowing text to flow around the plug-in.

8. You can use the Border Thickness box to define the thickness of a border (in pixels). Use the Vertical and Horizontal spacing boxes to define buffer space around the plug-in.

9. After you define the plug-in, click OK. The plug-in will display in Normal Page view only as a plug-in icon. You can test the video in Preview Page view or by previewing your page in a Web browser.

If your plug-in file was not imported into your Web, you'll be prompted to save it when you save your Web page.

Sizing a plug-in for a RealMovie requires a bit of experimenting,in order to provide a plug-in large enough to include the RealPlayer controls. If you don't create a large enough plug-in, the controls won't be visible.

Note   Viewers can access additional control over RealMovies by right-clicking and choosing options from the context menu.

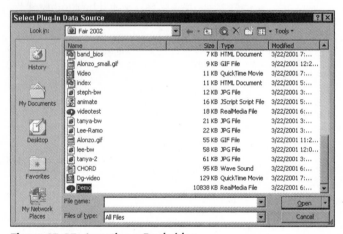

Figure 13-25: Inserting a Real video

Embedding MPEG movies (or WAV media files)

Like Real media files, MPEG and WAV media files are also inserted using the Plug In advanced control in FrontPage. To embed an MPEG movie (or WAV media file) in an open Web page, follow these steps:

1. Select Insert ➪ Web Component ➪ Advanced Controls.

2. In the Choose a Control area of the Insert Web Component dialog box, select Plug In.

3. Click on Finish. The Plug-In Properties dialog box appears.

4. Use the Browse button to locate an MPEG file on your local system or on the Internet.

5. In the Message For Browsers Without Plug-In Support box, enter text that will be displayed if a visitor does not have Microsoft's Windows Media Player installed.

6. You can use the Height and Width boxes to define the size of the plug-in display.

7. Use the Alignment drop-down menu to align the plug-in on the right or left side of a page, allowing text to flow around the plug-in. You can use the Border Thickness box to define the thickness of a border (in pixels). Use the Vertical and Horizontal spacing boxes to define buffer space around the plug-in.

8. After you define the plug-in, click OK. The plug-in will display in Normal Page view only as a plug-in icon. You can test the video in Preview Page view, or by previewing your page in a Web browser.

If your plug-in file was not imported into your Web, you'll be prompted to save it when you save your Web page.

Figure 13-26 shows an MPEG video file playing in a Web page.

Note If you make the plug-in too small, the Windows Media Player plug-in will not include all controls.

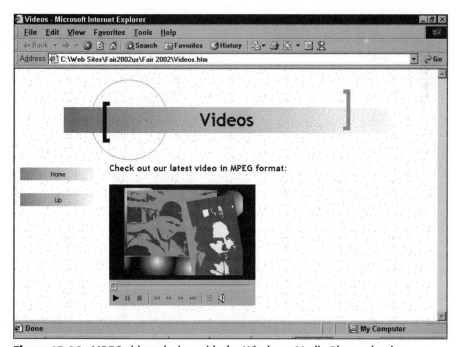

Figure 13-26: MPEG video playing with the Windows Media Player plug-in

Adding QuickTime movies to FrontPage pages

QuickTime movies can also be embedded in FrontPage Web pages as plug-ins. Visitors must have the required viewing software to see them.

To embed a QuickTime movie in an open Web page, follow these steps:

1. Select Insert ➪ Web Component ➪ Advanced Controls.

2. In the Choose a Control area of the Insert Web Component dialog box, select Plug In.

3. Click on Finish. The Plug-In Properties dialog box appears.

4. Use the Browse button to locate a QuickTime file on your local system or on the Internet, as shown in Figure 13-27.

Figure 13-27: Locating a QuickTime movie to embed in a Web page

5. In the Message For Browsers Without Plug-In Support box, enter text that will be displayed if a visitor does not have an installed viewer for QuickTime movies.

6. You can use the Height and Width boxes to define the size of the plug-in display. You will want to experiment later to ensure that you have created a large enough sized plug-in to accommodate the QuickTime control panel, as shown in Figure 13-28.

7. Use the Alignment drop-down menu to align the plug-in on the right or left side of a page, allowing text to flow around the plug-in.

8. You can use the Border Thickness box to define the thickness of a border (in pixels). Use the Vertical and Horizontal spacing boxes to define buffer space around the plug-in.

9. After you define the plug-in, click OK. The plug-in will display in Normal Page view only as a plug-in icon. You can test the video in Preview Page view or by previewing your page in a Web browser.

If your plug-in file was not imported into your Web, you'll be prompted to save it when you save your Web page.

Sizing a plug-in for a QuickTime movie requires a bit of experimenting in order to provide a plug-in large enough to include the QuickTime controls. If you don't create a large enough plug-in, the controls won't be visible. The controls allow visitors to play, rewind, and stop videos, as well as control sound volume.

When visitors play QuickTime movies in their browser, they can also configure plug-in settings to define their download speed, streaming options to minimize download wait time, and other rather advanced features for controlling how movies are downloaded and played.

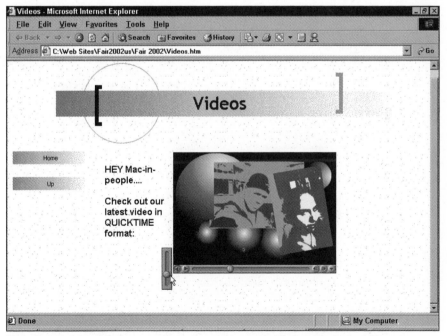

Figure 13-28: QuickTime movies come with embedded controls, including the sound (volume) control.

Summary

In this section, we explored the process for creating video plug-ins for four of the most popular movie formats: RealMedia (RM), QuickTime movies (MOV), Flash or Shockwave movies (SWF), and Windows Media (MPEG). Each type of plug-in appears somewhat differently in FrontPage Web pages, each displaying their own set of controls for managing movies in unique ways.

Nevertheless, the basic routine for embedding movie plug-ins is similar for any video format. Choose Insert ➪ Web Component ➪ Advanced Controls, and select Plug-In in the Insert Web Component dialog box. Click on Finish. Then browse in the Plug-In Properties dialog box to locate a video file. Use the Plug-In Properties dialog box to define how the video will be displayed, and experiment with video size to make sure plug-in controls are visible.

And, remember to provide handy links so that visitors can download the player necessary to view your video.

✦   ✦   ✦

Adding FrontPage Web Components

This chapter introduces FrontPage Web Components,
a.k.a. FrontPage components, a.k.a. Web components,
and a.k.a. just plain ol' components. These handy features
allow you to do everything from generating and automatically
updating a table of contents, to creating hover buttons that
change when a visitor scrolls across them with a cursor.

Adding FrontPage Web Components

Many of the Web components add *interactivity* to your site.
These interactive elements respond to the actions of visitors.
For example, a *hit counter* responds to a visit by changing the
number of visitors displayed, and *search boxes* respond to a
visitor's query with a list of matching pages.

> **Note** Prior to FrontPage 98, FrontPage components were called
> WebBots. Now we are in the new millennium, and
> Microsoft still uses WebBots in the HTML codes for
> FrontPage components. As you add components to your
> page, you can click on the HTML tab to see the WebBot ter-
> minology in place.

Defining and using components

FrontPage components actually are small programs that are
embedded in FrontPage. You don't need to know how Web
components work to use them, but you should be aware of
two particular attributes of components:

✦ Web components enable you to use preprogrammed elements that normally require a scripting language to create.

✦ Many (roughly half) of the Web components work *only after your Web is published to a Web server with FrontPage extensions.*

Note We'll explore the implications of having (or not having) access to a server with FrontPage extensions throughout this chapter, both in relation to using components in general, and in relation to specific components.

Web components are programs

Web components are pre-fabricated programming modules that you can customize and insert into your Web pages. When you add a Web component to your Web page, FrontPage inserts HTML tags that reference it, much as HTML is used to reference a graphic, a sound file, or a Java applet.

Customization of components is done through HTML attributes in the component tag. Figure 14-1 shows an example of the HTML used to point to a component; in this case, you can see WebBot tags for a Substitution component.

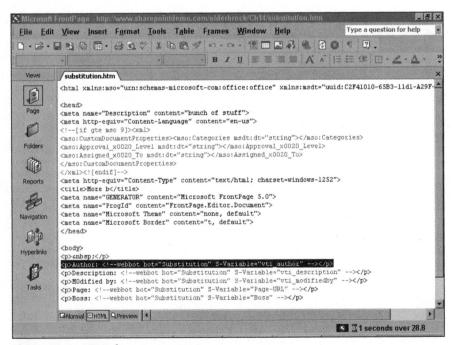

Figure 14-1: HTML for a component

If FrontPage components are little programs, where the heck are these programs stored? That depends. Components that require FrontPage server extensions are stashed on Web servers, and simply called by the code that FrontPage inserts into your page. No connection to a FrontPage Web server? In that case, these components won't work.

While about half of the FrontPage components rely on FrontPage Server Extensions to work, other components (like the Photo Gallery, new to FrontPage 2002) generate JavaScript code. All recent version browsers (going back to version 4) support JavaScript, and so the programming support for these components is essentially in a visitor's own Web browser. Still other components (like hover buttons or the Banner Ad Manager) generate Java programs, which are saved to your Web.

Many Web components require FrontPage extensions

The following FrontPage components *only work* when your site is published to a Web server with FrontPage extensions:

✦ Web Search

✦ Hit Counter

✦ Top 10 List

✦ List View

✦ Document Library View

If you aren't publishing your Web to a server armed with FrontPage extensions, you can disable the components that require extensions by selecting Tools ➪ Page Options, and clicking the Compatibility tab. Then, deselect the Enable with Microsoft FrontPage Server Extensions checkbox. After you do that, only those components that do not require FrontPage extensions will display. The rest are grayed out, and display the message shown in Figure 14-2.

If you are saving your Web to a disk folder (a disk-based Web), the FrontPage extension-requiring Web components will be grayed out automatically.

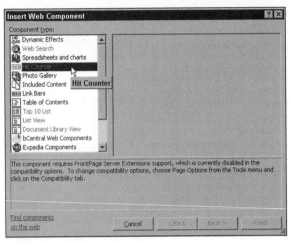

Figure 14-2: Hit counters are a component that require FrontPage extensions.

Because components require FrontPage-enabled servers, they are less portable than standard CGI applications or Java applets and are more akin to other Microsoft technologies, such as Active Server Pages (ASP), that are limited to servers supported by Microsoft. But, if you have access to a FrontPage-enabled Web server, the ease with which you can add components makes using them hard to resist.

Developing on a Disk but Developing for a Server?

Suppose that you are developing your Web site using a drive-based Web or a server that doesn't have FrontPage extensions, but you plan eventually to publish your Web to a server that *does* have FrontPage extensions. If you are using a server without FrontPage extensions, you can still *install* (non-working) components. In this scenario, do not disable components. You can still place them on Web pages — you just can't test them or use them in a Web site until you publish to a FrontPage-friendly Web server with FrontPage extensions.

On the other hand, if you are developing your site using a disk-based Web, but eventually plan to publish it to a server with FrontPage extensions, you have to *turn on* the features that require FrontPage server extensions. Do this by choosing Tools ➪ Page Options, and *selecting* the Enabled with FrontPage Server Extensions checkbox in the Compatibility tab of the Page Options dialog box. In this scenario, you are fooling FrontPage, telling it that your site is published to a FrontPage Web. Remember, some components *won't work* until you actually publish your site to a FrontPage server.

Still not satisfied? You don't have a server with FrontPage connections? Check out Chapter 23.

If you don't plan to publish your Web site to a FrontPage server, and you are inclined to do your own scripting and programming, you can jump ahead to Part V of this book, which introduces other programming components that you can use to create many of the same functions, with perhaps a bit more labor on your part.

Many components don't require FrontPage extensions

If you are creating a Web for a server without FrontPage extensions, you can use the components identified in Table 14-1. Some of these components simply generate HTML code. Others generate Java applets, and others create JavaScript.

Table 14-1	
Coding and Scripting for Various Web Components	
Component	*Type of Script or Coding*
Hover buttons	Java applets
Marquees	HTML
Banner Ad Manager	Java applets
Photo Gallery	JavaScript
Included Content	HTML
Link Bars	HTML
Table of Contents	HTML
Commercial components (bCentral, Expedia, MSN, etc.)	Remote sites linked through HTML
Advanced Controls	Various scripting languages

Some components require SharePoint servers

As if all this wasn't complicated enough, some Web components are only functional when you are publishing a Web to the SharePoint server that comes with Office XP. SharePoint servers are designed with built-in intranet tools, like bulletin boards, uploaded document libraries, and customizable interfaces. You can use the SharePoint server as-is, out of the box, on your intranet (or Internet). Or, you can customize a SharePoint server by editing pages in FrontPage, and adding lists and other features proprietary to the SharePoint server.

Spreadsheet Components

Spreadsheet Web components (Office Spreadsheet, Office Chart, and Office Pivot Table) are actually embedded pieces of Microsoft Excel.

The basic deal with these components is that they allow visitors to your Web site to see and interact with elements of a spreadsheet. In order to do this, visitors must have Excel installed, or they can download programs that function as a kind of limited Excel viewer.

As we go to press, Microsoft has not yet released a public domain downloadable Excel viewer for Excel 2002. However, downloadable viewers for older versions of Excel are available at `http://office.microsoft.com/Downloads/`.

Web site visitors who use a downloaded viewer will not have full functionality for spreadsheet components, but will be able to view spreadsheet data.

Both in their use, and their function, the three Spreadsheets and Charts components fall more into the category of Microsoft Office application integration, and so we explore them in detail in Chapter 4.

We examine customizing the SharePoint server in detail in Chapter 24. In this chapter, we'll take a quick look at the components that require SharePoint servers; but our focus is limited here to publishing your FrontPage Web on Office XP's SharePoint server, and to the lists and other special features available for this server.

Inserting Components

You have two ways to add a component to your Web page:

✦ Insert the component directly into your Web page (the primary method).

✦ Use one of the many Web page templates and wizards that come with preconfigured Web components (secondary method).

Page Templates that generate components include:

✦ **Confirmation Form:** Generates a confirmation form for an input form, using the Confirmation Field Component (found in the Advanced Components submenu).

✦ **Table of Contents:** Generates a page with a table of contents.

In addition, many page templates include comments. And most Web templates include many components.

To insert a component in an existing Web page, first position the cursor where you want the component to appear. Select Insert ⇨ Web Component, or click the Web Component icon in the toolbar. The Insert Web Component submenu is a dialog box, as shown in Figure 14-3.

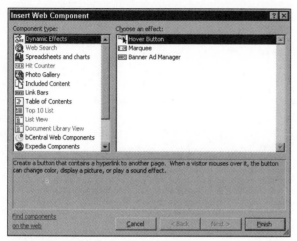

Figure 14-3: Choosing Web Component from the Insert menu brings up this dialog box.

After you select a component, additional options may appear, enabling you to customize the component's properties. After you add a component to your Web page, you can edit it by double-clicking it. Alternatively, you can right-click the component and select (Component's Name) Properties from the pop-up menu.

Components that Aren't "Components"

In addition to the components listed in the Insert Web Components submenu, the main Insert menu includes a few miscellaneous but highly useful objects that work like components, such as Date and Time (which works like a time stamp), and Comments. These features are explored in this chapter, even though they aren't listed in the Component submenu.

Using Date and Time and Comments

The Date and Time and the Comments elements could have been put in the Components submenu, but they weren't. Nevertheless, they work like components. When you insert a Date and Time code, you create a time stamp WebBot code in HTML. Comments also generate WebBot coding.

The Date and Time component displays the modification time and date of the Web page on which it resides. In other words, you can tell visitors exactly when the page was last changed, so that they can quickly decide whether the material at your Web site is current enough for their needs.

Including a last-modified date on your Web pages is a courtesy to visitors, because it helps them judge whether the information on your site is up to date. Of course, if currency isn't that important to your Web page, you certainly aren't required to have a time stamp on it.

Every time that you save your Web pages, the time stamp (Date and Time code) updates. So, the only "revising" reflected by your time stamp may simply be that you actively maintain the page. Manually updating the modification date by resaving a page is one way of indicating that you are maintaining the page, even if the content has not changed recently.

To add a Date and Time code, position the cursor at the location where you want the component to appear. Select Insert ⇨ Date and Time. The Date and Time Properties dialog box appears, as shown in Figure 14-4.

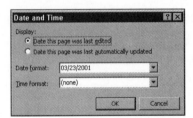

Figure 14-4: Adding a time stamp to a page

The Date this Page Was Last Edited radio button revises the displayed date when you update the page. The Date this Page Was Updated Automatically radio button changes the Date and Time code if the page was changed by the action of a Web component or other applet, or if an embedded page changed.

Note

Still don't get the difference between the Date This Page Was Last Edited button and the Date this Page was Last Automatically Updated button? Here it is in a nutshell: When you select the Date this Page was Last Edited button, merely opening the page in the Page view will update the time stamp. You don't even have to change the page—just open and close it.

When you select the Date This Page Was Last Automatically Updated button, the time stamp will also update every time you open the page. However, and in addition, if you include content (such as a table of contents or another HTML page), and you change the embedded content, the time stamp updates then as well.

Use the Date Format drop-down menu to select from a variety of date formats. Use the Time Format drop-down menu to select from a list of time formats.

After you make your selections, click OK to insert the Date and Time code in your page. The time stamp appears just as it will look in the Web page. You can also format the date text. When you edit in Page view, you can distinguish the date and time data from regular text because its code has an icon over it rather than an insertion cursor, as shown in Figure 14-5.

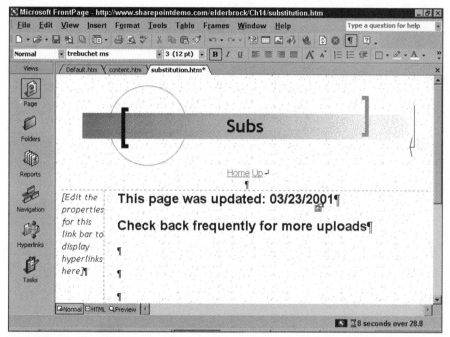

Figure 14-5: The Web Component icon is your clue that this date is not text, but a generated component.

Note The Date and Time component only displays a date. If you want text like "Date page was last updated," you have to add that yourself.

Adding comments

To add a comment, position the cursor where you want the comment to appear in the Web page, and then select Insert ➪ Comment. The dialog box allows you to enter the text of your comment.

Comments show up in FrontPage in the visited link color as shown in Figure 14-6, which is purple by default (in fact, the actual name of this component is PurpleText, as you can see if you look at the HTML). Comment text doesn't appear when the page is viewed by a Web browser, because the entire component is enclosed in a standard HTML comment tag.

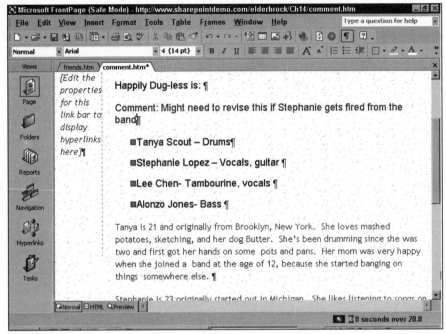

Figure 14-6: Comments don't show up in Web browsers.

Caution   The Comment may not appear on the Web page, but it is still there in the HTML, viewable by anyone who decides to view the HTML source code of the page. As a result, use of the Comment component to record your trade secrets or the combination of your safety deposit box is, as they say, discouraged!

The Comment component is used in almost every template, to instruct you about the purpose of the template or to teach you how to customize it.

Exploring Web Components

This section briefly examines the operation of all the components that come packaged with FrontPage 2002.

Dynamic effects

The Dynamic Effects option in the Insert Web Component dialog box offers three options for presenting *active* page elements: hover buttons, scrolling text marquees, and banner ads (that rotate images). These elements (text and/or images) are active, as opposed to *static* text and images that just sit there.

Other options for dynamic objects include Dynamic HTML formatting, which is explored in Chapter 13. Dynamic HTML (DHTML) effects rely on a browser's ability to accurately interpret the DHTML specifications that FrontPage uses to generate animation and interactivity. Some of these effects are not supported by Netscape Navigator 4.7.

As opposed to DHTML effects, the dynamic effects Web components rely on HTML and Java to generate small programs right in your Web site to produce interactivity. Therefore, *these* Web components are compatible with Netscape 4.7. And, they do *not* require FrontPage Server Extensions, or even a Web server to work. Cool, huh?

Hover buttons

Hover buttons display an effect when visitors to your page pass their cursor over the button. Hover buttons provide a way to make boring buttons more interesting. Effects range from a glow to color changes. You can even define images and sounds to display for the button, to provide a more interactive look and feel to your pages.

To add a hover button, select Insert ➪ Web Component ➪ Hover Button. The Hover Button Properties dialog box appears, as shown in Figure 14-7.

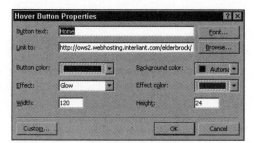

Figure 14-7: Defining a hover button

Hover button options

You can make the following selections in the Hover Button dialog box:

- ✦ **Button Text:** The text that is displayed on the button's face. You can change the font, color, style, and size by clicking the Font button.

- ✦ **Link To:** The page or file that is opened when the button is clicked by visitors. Enter the URL directly in the text box, or click the Browse button to select a page.

- ✦ **Button Color:** The button's "static" color when you don't use an image; the color that displays when a visitor does not move his or her cursor over the button.

✦ **Background Color:** The color for the button's background. This color shows through even if you use a transparent GIF as a button image.

✦ **Effect:** You can choose between these effects:

- **Color Fill:** The entire button changes color.

- **Color Average:** The entire button changes to a color halfway between the button color and the effect color.

- **Glow:** The center of the button changes to the effect color, with the color fading toward the edges.

- **Reverse Glow:** The center of the button remains the button color, but it fades to the effect color at the outside edges.

- **Light Glow:** A muted version of Glow.

- **Bevel Out:** The button takes on a 3-D appearance, as if it is protruding from the page. This effect works best with relatively light button colors.

- **Bevel In:** The reverse 3-D appearance of Bevel Out, so that the button looks like it is indented into the screen.

✦ **Effect Color:** The button's "hover" color that displays when you don't use an image. When a visitor's cursor passes over the button, this color shows, in combination with the effect that you apply.

✦ **Width:** The button's width in pixels. It does not automatically change if you select a large font size or a large image; you have to change the size manually.

✦ **Height:** The button's height in pixels. It does not automatically change if you select a large font size or a large image; you have to change the size manually.

Adding sound effects to hover buttons

To add sound effects to your hover buttons, click the Custom button in the Hover Button dialog box to open the Custom dialog box. This dialog box has two fields, for up to two different sounds. You can assign one sound to play when a visitor hovers over the button, and a different sound (or the same one) when a visitor clicks the button. The trick is that the sound files must be in the AU sound file format.

Note   AU format audio files were discussed briefly in Chapter 13. You might expect that, being a *FrontPage* Web component, hover buttons would support the WAV file format that is generally accepted in Microsoft Office applications. However, hover buttons generate Java code that requires sound files in the AU file format.

The following are the two sound options for a button:

✦ **On Click:** Plays a sound when a visitor clicks the hover button.

✦ **On Hover:** Plays a sound when a visitor passes the cursor over the hover button.

You can use the Browse buttons associated with each sound field to attach sounds to either of these two options. Just remember that you must attach a sound file in the AU file format.

Displaying custom images in hover buttons

The Custom dialog box also enables you to assign custom images that display when a visitor either moves his or her cursor over a hover button or clicks a hover button. The following two fields in the Custom dialog box represent your options for specifying custom images:

✦ **Button:** Displays the image when a visitor is not hovering over the button.

✦ **On Hover:** Displays the image when a visitor hovers over the button.

Again, you can use the Browse buttons associated with each image field to attach images to either of these two options.

Note   The hover button does not resize to fit an image, so you have to do that manually.

Hover buttons: Behind the scenes

When you define a Hover Button, FrontPage generates files with names that begin `fphover`, and end with a filename extension of `.class`. These files contain the Java code required to activate the button effects. You can view these files in Folder view, and look at the Java code by right-clicking on one of the `.class` files and choosing Open With from the context menu. Select Notepad, and you can take a quick look at the Java coding associated with your hover button.

And yes, you Java coders can feel free to touch-up the coding if you wish. The rest of us will just appreciate that FrontPage generated it for us.

Caution   Be judicious in your use of Hover buttons. Each hover button is a single java applet. For every hover button you insert on a page the browser must load a java applet. Ten hover buttons load ten separate java applets. This puts intense demands on computer processors, and can cause slower systems to crash. Use java applets sparingly, or pay the price of alienating and annoying many visitors.

Scrolling marquees

Scrolling marquees present text scrolling across your screen. A scrolling marquee is one Web component that doesn't require you to save your site to a Web server. You don't need to preview your Web page in a browser to see how your marquees will look. You can test them in the Preview tab of Page view.

To create a scrolling marquee, click in Page view to set the insertion point for the marquee. Then, select Insert ➪ Web Component ➪ Dynamic Effects, and double-click on Marquee. The Marquee Properties dialog box displays, as shown in Figure 14-8.

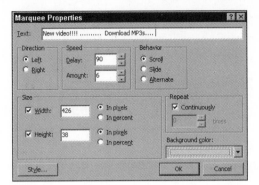

Figure 14-8: The Marquee Properties dialog box

Defining scrolling effects

You can adjust many scrolling text properties via the Marquee Properties dialog box. The Background Color drop-down menu lets you select a background for the scrolling text. Experimenting with the three radio buttons in the Behavior area is pretty safe. And you can use the Right or Left radio buttons to define the direction of your scroll. You can also fiddle with the Delay and Amount spin boxes in the Speed area of the dialog box.

After you enter text in the Text field, click OK. You can see how your scrolling text will look in a browser by using the Preview tab of Page view. To resize your scrolling text marquee, click and drag side or corner handles (back in the Normal tab of Page view).

Experimenting with marquee properties

For those of you determined to blaze the cutting edge of scrolling text displays, feel free to experiment away with the various options available. Remember that if you get in trouble, you can always delete a messed up marquee and start from scratch with the default settings. The following are the available options in the Marquee Properties dialog box:

✦ **Scroll:** The text starts at the left (unless you have Right set under Direction) and moves to the right until all the text has moved off the screen, and then it repeats.

✦ **Slide:** Similar to Scroll, except that when the first letter hits the right edge of the marquee, the text disappears and starts again at the left.

✦ **Alternate:** The text bounces back and forth between the left and right edges of the marquee, like a Ping-Pong ball.

You can edit many of the marquee properties in Page view using the Formatting toolbar. For example, you can click the marquee and select text size, color, and font, and apply attributes such as italics or boldface. You can also resize the marquee in Page view by clicking and dragging the sizing handles.

Banner ads

Banner ads rotate two or more images in a space, creating an animated presentation for visitors to your Web site. The first step in preparing a banner ad is to gather some images that you want to display. You don't need to insert pictures into your page to include them in your banner ad, but you do need to have the pictures available in file form. With your images picked out, select Insert ➪ Web Component ➪ Dynamic Effects, and double-click on Banner Ad Manager. The Banner Ad Manager Properties dialog box appears, as shown in Figure 14-9.

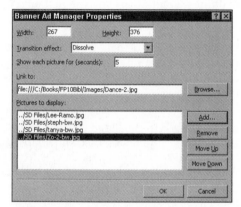

Figure 14-9: The Banner Ad Manager Properties dialog box allows you to create a list of images that will display one after another.

Adding links to banner ads

Banner ads may function as graphic hyperlinks (although they don't have to). To define a page to which you want your banner to link, use the Browse button or enter a URL in the Link To field of the Banner Ad Manager Properties dialog box. Or, use the Browse button to navigate to a link target.

Banner ad effects

You can define the transition effects between images using the Transition Effect drop-down list. The transition effects are:

✦ **None:** The images change, but with no effects.

✦ **Blinds Horizontal:** Pictures transition with an effect that looks like horizontal window blinds.

✦ **Blinds Vertical:** Pictures transition with an effect that looks like vertical window blinds.

✦ **Dissolve:** Pictures fade into each other like the faces Michael Jackson's video "Black and White."

✦ **Box In:** A rather weird transition effect where images change starting with the outer edges, and ending with the center changing.

✦ **Box Out:** Images change starting with the center, and ending with the outer edges.

You can set the timing for each image (in seconds) in the Show Each Image For (seconds) box.

You can either use the Height and Width boxes in the Banner Ad Manager Properties dialog box to define the size of the banner ad, or you can just click and drag on the banner ad in Page view to resize the display.

Note The trick in creating banner ads is to first collect and prepare a set of images that are *the same size*. While it is not necessary to have rotating images that are the same size, most banners look better if each picture fills the entire banner.

Adding images to a banner ad

Use the Add button in the dialog box to add images to the list of those that will display in your banner ad. The Add Picture for Banner Ad dialog box, shown in Figure 14-10, displays your image when you select it. You can either pick images from your Web site or use the Clip Art button to include clip art in your banner ad. You can also select the Use Your Web Browser button or the Select a File on Your Computer button in the lower-right corner of the dialog box to include files from the Web or your local computer.

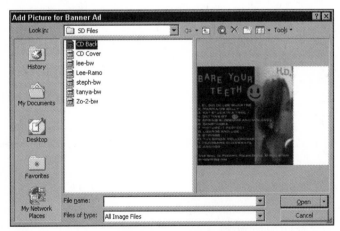

Figure 14-10: Adding images to a banner ad

You can edit your display list by using the Remove, Move Up, or Move Down buttons in the Banner Ad Manager Properties dialog box (refer to Figure 14-9). Define the size of your banner ad in the Width and Height fields. Choose a transition effect from the drop-down list. Then, select a number of seconds to display each image. After you define your banner ad, click OK in the dialog box.

Caution Like Hover buttons, Banner Ads are java applets. Inserting too many on a Web page can strain a slower processor, causing computers to crash. Also, avoid using more than a few images in a Banner Ad because every image must download before the applet can run.

Web search

The Web Search component creates a form that allows visitors to search all or part of your Web for pages containing one or more text strings. Results of a search are displayed by listing the titles of matching pages, with each title hyperlinked to the actual page. Details of the results page can also be controlled via the Search Form component. If you have a content-rich Web and are looking for a relatively simple way to enhance the usability of your Web site, the Search Form component could be just the thing.

Note Search forms only work if your Web is published to a server with FrontPage extensions.

To place a Web search form in your Web page, place your insertion point where the search box should appear, and select Insert ➪ Web Component ➪ Web Search, and double-click on Current Web in the Insert Web Component dialog box. The Search Form Properties dialog box appears, as shown in Figure 14-11.

Figure 14-11: Defining a search box

At this point, you can either click OK to insert a default search box, or you can adjust both the way the search box collects input and the results that it generates.

Search form properties

The redundantly named Search Form Properties tab of the Search Form Properties dialog box enables you to define how your search form will look. You can change these options:

✦ **Label for Input:** Displays a label for your search box input field. You can change it to "Tell us what topic you are interested in" or "What are you looking for?" or some other label. Often, the default "Search For:" works fine.

✦ **Width in Characters:** Controls only how wide the display is of the input field, not how much users can input. Visitors can still enter 40 characters in a 20-character field.

✦ **Label for "Start Search" Button:** Displays a name for the button that starts the search. Keep the default, or create your own.

✦ **Label for "Reset" Button**: You can change the default name for the button that clears whatever a visitor has typed into the search box field.

Caution

The width in characters displays differently in Internet Explorer and Netscape Navigator. Test your page in both browsers to ensure that your visitors are seeing what you intend them to see.

Displaying search results

The Search Results tab in the Search Form Properties dialog box controls which pages are included in search results, and how results are displayed.

The three radio buttons at the top of the Search Results tab, control which part of your Web is searched. They are:

✦ **Entire Website:** Searches all folders in your Web site including subwebs, except those that begin with an underscore, like `_private` or `_borders`.

✦ **This Web:** Searches only the selected Web, and *not* subwebs.

✦ **Directory:** Allows you to define a single folder or directory in your Web. This is especially useful for restricting searches to sets of documents in a folder. If you select this option, use the Browse button to locate a folder or directory for the search.

The seven checkboxes at the bottom of the Search Results tab define what information is displayed about the pages that are located:

✦ **Last Time File was Changed:** Tells visitors how recently a matching page was updated.

✦ **Size in Bytes:** Adds the file size to the results list.

✦ **Score (Closeness of Match):** Adds a numerical rating (*score*) to each page that matches the search criteria. Larger numbers indicate a closer match. The logic for this number is somewhat arbitrary, but visitors can elect to try pages

Search Result Options Vary

Not only is the Web Search component dependent on a server with FrontPage Server Extensions, but the options for displaying search results vary depending on which version of server extensions are installed, and even vary depending on *what kind of server* you are using.

Most Web component options that require FrontPage extensions work the same on any kind of server — UNIX, Linux, Microsoft Internet Information Services (IIS), etc. However, Search Form properties are a little different for IIS, and other servers. The description of search results options here may differ slightly from your options depending on what kind of server you use.

If your site is published to a server running IIS, the search form uses Microsoft's Indexing Service to search the text index. Since Indexing Service has more extensive support for searching Microsoft Office documents, you get more search options when your site is connected to an IIS server.

If you publish your site to a server using FrontPage extensions on a non-IIS server, FrontPage uses a different search engine — the Wide Area Information Server (WAIS) to search the text index.

Finally, depending on what server you publish to, sometimes index files have to be activated by server providers. If your search engine isn't working, contact your server provider and make sure the necessary index files have been created at the server.

As we go to press, Microsoft is providing information on these issues at:

`http://www.microsoft.com/TechNet/sharepoint/admindoc/owsi06.htm`

Is all this too much hassle? One option is to use one of the free, downloadable search boxes available from folks like FreeFind.com (`www.freefind.com`) These search boxes don't require FrontPage Server Extensions.

with a, score of 100 before trying a page with a score of 10. Even if you don't select this checkbox, results are still ordered by score.

✦ **Author of Document:** Displays the author of the page, as determined by the user's system information

✦ **Comments:** Displays comments (if there are comments on the page). Comments are defined by right-clicking on a page in Folders view, clicking Properties in the context menu, and defining a comment in the Summary tab of the page Properties dialog box.

✦ **Document Subject:** Displays the page title for Web pages.

✦ **Matches:** Displays the number of matching files.

Figure 14-12 shows a the Search Results tab of the Search Form Properties dialog box.

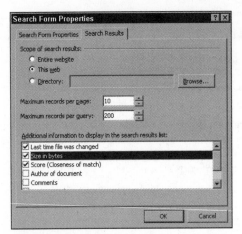

Figure 14-12: FrontPage allows tremendous control over how search results are displayed.

Hit counters

The hit counter component displays the number of times that a particular page has been accessed, or *hit*. To insert a hit counter, select Insert ➪ Web Component, and click on Hit Counter. Then, select one of the counter styles that appear on the right side of the Insert Web Component dialog box, and click Finish. The Hit Counter Properties dialog box appears.

Defining a hit counter

In the Hit Counter Properties dialog box, click a radio button to select a style for your hit counter. Use the Reset Counter To checkbox if you want to enter a starting number other than zero (which is the default). Use the Fixed Number of Digits checkbox to enter a set number of digits for your hit counter. After you define your hit counter, click the OK button in the dialog box. Your hit counter displays when you preview your Web page in your browser. You will see a code Hit Counter in Page view.

A small placeholder indicates where the counter will be displayed on your page, as shown in Figure 14-13.

Hit strategies

Hit counters record how many hits your Web site has received. Hits pretty much correspond to visits (if a visitor refreshes his or her browser window, that counts as an additional hit). The following are the two basic approaches to using a hit counter:

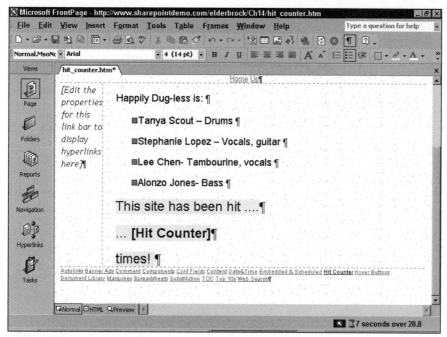

Figure 14-13: Hit Counters don't work in Page view.

✦ Use it to show off how many hits your site is getting. Of course, the credibility of a hit counter is somewhat suspect, because (as you'll soon see) you can set your own starting number. Still, sometimes a valid reason exists to display a count of how many folks have been to a site.

✦ Use it for your own purposes, just to keep track of how effective your site is. You can place a hit counter at the bottom of a page, where visitors are not likely to notice it.

Figure 14-14 shows a hit counter that is subtly stashed at the very bottom of a Web page, where it quietly keeps track of visitors.

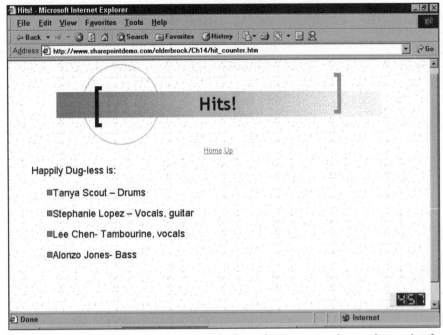

Figure 14-14: Hit counters can be placed where they are not a focus of attention for visitors. In this page, the counter is in the lower right corner of the page.

Photo gallery

The photo gallery Web component generates a JavaScript element that allows you to display photos in tables. With your cursor where you want to place the Photo Gallery, choose Insert ➪ Web Component, and click on Photo Gallery in the list of components. Choose one of the photo gallery options (except the slideshow) that display on the right side of the Insert Web Component dialog box. When you click Finish, the Photo Gallery Properties dialog box opens allowing you to define your photo display. The Photo Galleries options are covered in detail in Chapter 6.

Included content

The Included Content category of Web components has five helpful ways to embed content from your Web site in a Web page. The options vary from embedding the content of one page in a second page, to embedding a picture based on a schedule.

Free Hit Counters on the Web

Want a Hit Counter, but don't have FrontPage extensions? Many companies offer free, embeddable hit counters. In turn, they have you display ad banners for their service. You can find free hit counters at `http://www.cybercount.com/`, `http://www.beseen.com/hitcounter/`, and `http://www.easycounter.com/`.

And guess what? These hit counters provide a lot more information than the FrontPage version. Many provide detailed logs of where your visitors came from, what time they visited your site, the browser they used, and other valuable information if you are trying to closely monitor and evaluate the traffic on your Web site.

Third party providers let you embed their hit counters in your site by providing you with some lines of HTML that you insert in your site. Often they email this code to you, other times they provide it on their Web site. In either case, copy the HTML code into the clipboard. To paste it into FrontPage, click to place your insertion pointing Page view, and choose Edit, Paste Special. From the Paste Special dialog box, choose the Treat as HTML options button, and click OK. The HTML code will be pasted into your page, and the third-party hit counter will appear.

With a little work, you can set up one of these free Hit Counters with the accompanying banner ad stashed quietly out of everyone's way. (Hint: try making them smaller.)

All the Included Content Web components are tools for *automating* site content. For example, you can use the Page option to create an "updateable" page that is embedded in other pages. Every time you update the embedded page, the content changes on all pages in which this page is embedded.

Substitution

Suppose you are responsible for a 28,000-page Web site, and the slogan of your corporation is on each of those pages. When you show up for work on Monday morning, you learn that the company motto has changed, and must be substituted on every page where it appears.

Yes, one option is to search and replace, but that's tedious, and requires that the text being searched for is a perfect match. The other option is to create a *parameter* called `motto`, and then simply change the definition of that parameter when you need to update your Web site.

Figure 14-15 shows all the default substitution fields displayed in a browser.

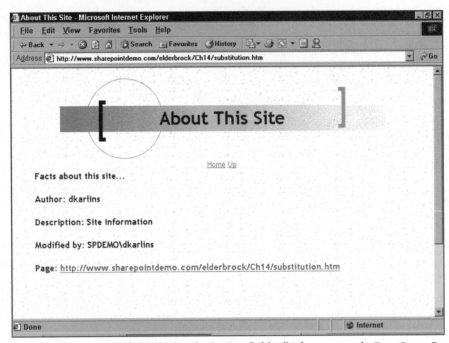

Figure 14-15: Not all the default substitution fields display content in FrontPage. Preview your page in a browser to see the displayed information.

To add parameters, select Tools ➪ Web Settings, and click the Parameters tab. This tab displays your existing parameters, as shown in Figure 14-16.

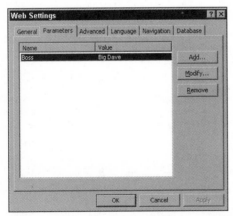

Figure 14-16: Substitution fields are used to instantly update the content of an entire site. They are defined in the Parameters tab of the Web Settings dialog box.

You can add a new parameter by clicking the Add button, entering a name and value for your parameter, and then clicking OK, as shown in Figure 14-17.

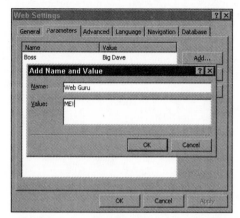

Figure 14-17: Creating your own substitution field in the Add Name and Value dialog box

Use the Modify button in the Parameter tab of the Web Settings dialog box to change a parameter value, or the Delete button to delete the parameter. After you define parameter names and values, click OK in the FrontPage Web Settings dialog box.

With your own parameters defined, you can insert them into any Web page. Just set your insertion point, and select Insert ⇨ Web Component ⇨ Substitution. Pull down the Substitute With list and select a field. When you modify the Substitution parameter value, your Web pages are updated with the new value. Each time visitors view your Web page or refresh their browser window, they see the latest value for a Substitution component.

Note   Sometimes substitution values aren't automatically changed. When that happens, you can force FrontPage to update substitution values by choosing Tools ⇨ Recalculate Hyperlinks.

Including pages

The Include Page component enables you to insert the contents of another file into your Web page.

If you want a page embedded in the top, bottom, right, or left of your page, use shared borders. Creating a bottom shared border usually is easier than creating a new page to function as a footer (see Chapter 7 for more information on working with shared borders).

The Include Page component is useful as a way to include elements that are common to many pages (see Figure 14-18), such as a chunk of page data that you want to embed in several different pages. By including these elements in a separate Web page, you can edit the included page, and the changes will be reflected on all pages.

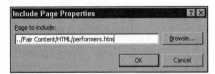

Figure 14-18: Including a page in a page

To edit the *content* of an included page, double-click on the included page area. This will open the included page in a new Page view.

Embedding a page based on schedule or a picture based on schedule

With the Page Based on Schedule and Picture Based on Schedule Web Components, you never again have to worry about your Web page advertising a fantastic offer that expires on June 1, 2002. Scheduled Pictures and Scheduled Include Pages can be defined so that they vanish on a set date, or are replaced by new content.

To add a page or picture based on a schedule, position the cursor on the Web page where you want the page or image to appear. Select Insert ➪ Web Component ➪ Included Content. From the Included Content choices, click on either Page Based on Schedule or Picture Based on Schedule. Then click Finish.

In the Scheduled Picture Properties or Scheduled Include Page dialog box, indicate the image or page to include, the starting and ending times to display the picture or page, and, optionally, a picture or page to display before and after the scheduled time frame.

In Figure 14-19, we're defining a picture that will display until March 24, 2001.

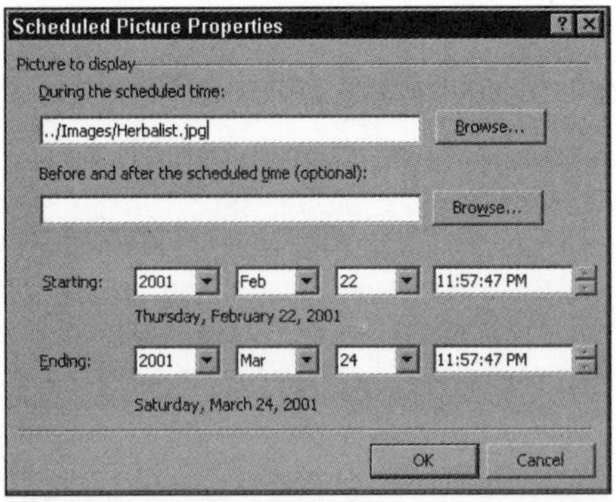

Figure 14-19: Defining a starting (and ending) date for an included picture

If the current time is within the range of the scheduled image time, the selected picture or page displays in Editor. If not, FrontPage displays an error dialog box notifying you that you've defined an invalid date range.

Including a page banner

Page banners display the page title either as text, or (if you have a theme assigned), as a graphic. To embed the page title, position the cursor on the Web page where you want the title to appear and select Insert ➪ Web Component ➪ Included Content. From the Included Content choices, click on Page Banner, and then click Finish. The Page Banner Properties dialog box appears, as shown in Figure 14-20.

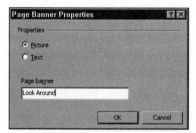

Figure 14-20: Page banners will only display as a picture if a theme is assigned to a page.

In the Page Banner dialog box, choose either Text or Picture and click OK. You can format the text of a banner using the regular text formatting tools in Page view. If you change a page title, the content of the banner will change.

Tip   If you place a Page Banner component in a shared border, the component will reflect the title of the page in which the border is embedded. This is a quick and easy way to add the page title to every page in your Web.

Link bars

Link Bar components provide a variety of generated links on a page. This component can be accessed two ways, either through the Insert ➪ Web Component menu, or through the Insert ➪ Navigation menu. Link bars can be based on a defined set of pages, or they can be generated by a site's navigational structure. We explore them in detail in the section "Inserting Link Bars," in Chapter 9.

Inserting a table of contents

FrontPage 2002 introduces improved options for generating tables of contents. You can create a table based on the entire Web site, or based only on a selected category of Web pages.

A table of contents can be an effective tool for embedding automatically updated site maps in a page. Figure 14-21 shows a site using a TOC as a navigation tool.

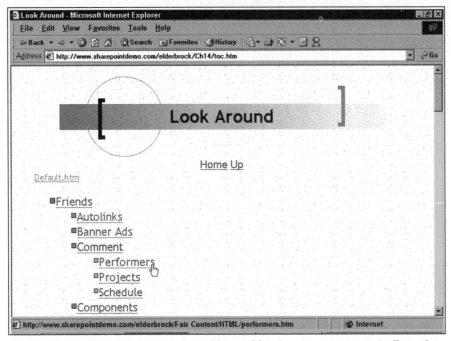

Figure 14-21: This site map, generated by a table of contents, automatically updates whenever the site is updated.

To add a table of contents, position the cursor on the Web page and select Insert ⇨ Web Component ⇨ Table of Contents. From the Included Content choices, click on either For This Web Site, or Based on Web Category. Click Finish.

Assigning categories

If you choose Based on Page Category, the Categories Properties dialog box appears. Categories can be assigned to a page by right-clicking, choosing Page Properties from the context menu, and selecting one or more categories in the Workgroups tab of the Page Properties dialog box as shown in Figure 14-22. These assigned categories then govern which pages are included in a table of contents that is restricted to only certain categories.

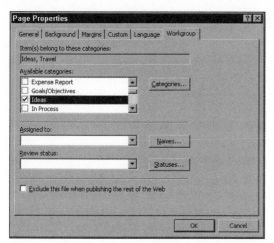

Figure 14-22: A table of contents can be restricted to only pages assigned to defined categories.

Table of contents options

Whichever method you use for selecting pages to include in a table of contents, you can define what information to display when the Table of Contents is generated. Depending on which type of Table of contents you are creating, different dialog boxes will allow you to define whether or not to include the date a file was last modified, and/or comments added to the file in the generated table of contents.

If you generate a TOC for an *entire* site, the Table of Contents Properties dialog box allows you to define a starting point for your TOC. The Page URL for Starting Point of Table box in the Table of Contents dialog box only defines the page that will serve as a title for your TOC. And the Heading Font Size drop-down list defines the size of the title, based on the defined heading styles for your site or page.

Using the Table of Contents template

The quickest way to get a Table of Contents is to use the provided page template to create a separate Table of Contents page. To use this template, select File ➪ New ➪ Page, and click on Page Templates in the Task Pane (that opens when you choose New Page from the menu).

Clicking on Page Templates in the Task Pane opens the Page Templates dialog box. In the General tab of the Page Templates dialog box, click on the Table of Contents template, as shown in Figure 14-23, and then click OK. This opens a new page.

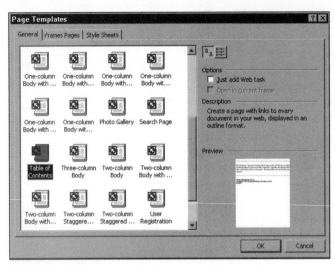

Figure 14-23: Need a quick TOC? Use the template.

Of course, you are free to change the introductory text provided by the template. If you want to modify the table of contents generated by the template, double-click on the TOC to open the Table of Contents Properties dialog box.

Top 10 lists

Top 10 lists work for pages saved to Webs on servers with FrontPage 2002 extensions. They generate lists based on data collected by the server when visitors come to your site.

Top 10 lists are a way of sharing with your visitors information similar to what you see *internally* when you view Usage Reports. To see a Usage Report, choose View ➪ Reports ➪ Usage, and select one of the Usage Reports listed. For example, the information shown in the Browsers Usage Report tells you how many people visited your site using what browser. That same information can be shared with visitors in a Top 10 browsers list. The available Top 10 lists are:

✦ Visited pages

✦ Referring domains

✦ Referring URLs

✦ Search strings

✦ Operating systems

✦ Browser

All lists are embedded in a page the same way:

1. Select Insert ⇨ Web Component, and click on Top 10 List.

2. Choose one of the available lists.

3. Click Finish to display the Top 10 List Properties dialog box.

   Top ten lists do not display in FrontPage Page view, but do display in a browser window, as shown in Figure 14-24.

4. You can edit the default list title by entering new text in the Title Text area of the dialog box.

5. Select the Include Date Usage Processing Was Last Run checkbox to let visitors know when the list was last updated.

6. Choose one of the four formats for displaying your list, and click OK.

Top 10 lists must be previewed *in a browser* (not in Preview tab) in order to see actual content.

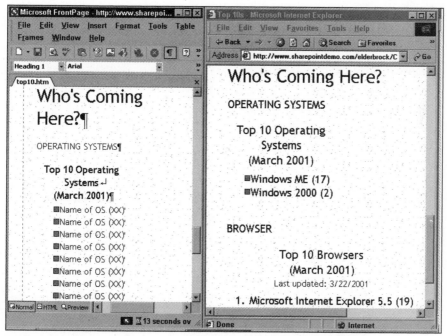

Figure 14-24: Top 10 lists can be displayed in a variety of list formats.

The latest version of FrontPage 2002 available at this writing, does not allow you to apply local (inline) formatting to the text generated by Top 10 lists. To format the fonts in these lists, you can instead use page or external style settings. These are covered in detail in Chapter 11.

Here's one way to change the formatting of a Top 10 list: right-click on a page and choose Page Properties to open the Page Properties dialog box. Click on the Style button and choose Format ⇨ Font. Define a font, and then click OK. This will define a new default font style for your page, which will be applied to your Top 10 list.

Top 10 lists require servers with the SharePoint Extensions.

List view and document library components

List views and document libraries are interactive ways for visitors to a site to upload documents, and contribute to online discussions. *These components require that a site is published to a server with SharePoint Extension files.*

List views and document libraries are a central part of the SharePoint Office Server shipped with the current release of Microsoft Office. This server, and its built-in features, are mainly designed to quickly generate an out-of-the-box intranet portal for an organization.

SharePoint Office Server, and its features, are explored in detail in Chapter 24.

Commercial and additional components

FrontPage offers a number of embedded commercial content options. These options are generally self-explanatory content that is provided by other companies (or Microsoft). When you embed this content in your page, the trade-off is that you advertise their product, provide a link to their site, and facilitate their sales. In return, you get their content. We discuss using these components in more detail in Chapter 9.

You can purchase additional Web components from third-party vendors, including J-Bots, which creates Java-based interactive components for Web sites, and FrontLook, the maker of additional themes and other FrontPage enhancements. If you do incorporate such third-party add-ons, they attach themselves to the Component submenu and appear when you select Insert ⇨ Web Component ⇨ Additional Components.

You can see a list of third-party add-ons for FrontPage at `http://www.ppinet.com/resource.htm`. In addition, the most widely used and useful add-ons are outlined in Appendix D.

Tutorial 14-1: Creating a page with Web components

In the following tutorial, you will create a Web page with a scrolling text marquee, hover buttons, a hit counter, and a Date and Time stamp.

1. Create a new FrontPage Web from the Personal Web template (select File ➪ New ➪ Page or Web. Click on Web Templates in the Task Pane, and then double-click Personal Web).

2. Open the file Index.htm in Page view.

3. Click at the end of the first line of text ("Welcome to My Web Site") and press Enter to create a new line.

4. Select Insert ➪ Web Component ➪ Dynamic Effects ➪ Marquee, and click Finish.

5. Type **Welcome to the ultimate Web site** in the Text field and click OK in the dialog box.

6. Place your cursor at the end of the second paragraph and press Enter to create another blank line. Select Insert ➪ Web Component ➪ Dynamic Effects ➪ Hover Button.

7. Type **Photos** in the Button Text field, and photo.htm in the Link To field (or use the Browse button to find the file photo.htm). Click OK. Create a few additional hover buttons linked to the Interests and Favorite pages.

8. Press Ctrl+End to move to the end of the page. Select Insert ➪ Web Component ➪ Hit Counter, and click Finish.

9. In the Hit Counter Properties dialog box, click the radio button next to a hit counter that has a style you like. Click OK.

10. Note that the Web template generates a Date and Time field on the home page (at the bottom of the page). You can identify the date as a Web Component because when you hover over it, an icon appears. Double-click the date to open the Date and Time Properties dialog box, and add a Time format from the drop-down menu. Click OK.

In Page view, your Web page should look something like the one in Figure 14-25.

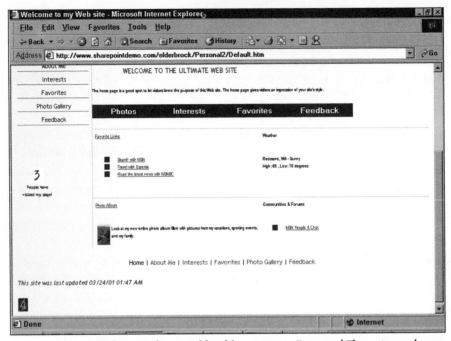

Figure 14-25: A Web page shown with a hit counter, a Date and Time stamp, hover buttons, and a scrolling marquee. The hit counter requires a server with FrontPage extensions to work.

Summary

Much of the value in using FrontPage comes from it's impressive set of Web components. Unfortunately, most of these components are rather inelegantly packed into a single menu option, and therefore can be hard to find. A good percentage of the best features in FrontPage are found by choosing Insert ➪ Web Component in the FrontPage menu.

Web components are mini-programs, and they utilize different scripting languages to do their jobs. Therefore, some components work in all development environments, while others are browser- or server-specific. FrontPage 2002 includes a few components, like Top 10 Lists, that require that your site be published to a site with SharePoint Server Extensions.

Web components can be used to make sites interactive. Search engines react to user input to help visitors find pages in your site. Hit counters react to each visit by counting visitors.

Other components are used to automate site content. The Table of Contents component generates a table of contents automatically. Included pages can be used to automatically update many pages.

Finally, some components provide site content, like those that link to MSNBC, MSN, or bCentral sites for news, sports, stock quotes, and Internet search engines.

✦   ✦   ✦

Embedding Components: Plug-ins, ActiveX, and Java Applets

In the previous chapter, you learned about the many types of Web components that are included with FrontPage 2002. In this chapter we examine how you can use FrontPage to add advanced programming components that add functionality to your Web pages. We will explore the following technologies in this chapter: plug-ins, ActiveX controls, and Java applets.

New Feature FrontPage 2002 has reorganized its menu items so that all advanced controls, including Java applets, plug-ins, and ActiveX controls are now found in the Web Components dialog box.

Introducing Advanced Web Components

First we need to get straight on some terminology. FrontPage 2002 uses the term *Web Component* to refer to any number of ways that you can insert programming functionality into your Web pages; and FrontPage can insert many of these Web components into your pages for you. These components, once called FrontPage components (and before that, WebBots), are discussed in Chapter 14. In addition to its built-in component support, FrontPage also enables you to add standard programming components, such as Netscape plug-ins, Microsoft ActiveX controls, and Java applets. FrontPage refers to all of these as *advanced controls*.

Note
The FrontPage Web Components Advanced Controls list includes an HTML component, a Confirmation field, and Design-Time controls, in addition to the components discussed in this chapter. The HTML component is discussed in Chapter 8, the Confirmation field is discussed in Chapter 17, and Design-Time controls are discussed in Chapter 22.

This chapter divides the discussion of these controls into two sections, according to the two main ways that the technologies discussed are utilized. The first section focuses on using the advanced controls to add *embedded content* to your Web pages. Embedded content consists of content files, in any of a variety of formats, that can be made to appear directly in your Web page — in the same way that GIF, JPEG (and in some cases PNG) images display directly in your Web page — even though the actual content files are stored separately.

The second section of the chapter explores the slightly more technical aspects of inserting Advanced Controls in your Web pages. These controls can be scripted to add interactive functionality to your site. In contrast to embedded content, these controls embed the actual functional component in your Web page, and not a separate content file.

Working with Embedded Content

When the HTML standard was first defined, it was limited in terms of the kinds of content that could be incorporated into a Web page. The main provision for embedded content was the inline GIF image. To allow for the inclusion of other kinds of content, browsers worked with helper applications — separate programs designed to display certain kinds of *rich media* content external to the browser.

The ability to view content in external applications is perhaps better than nothing (and in some cases is actually to be preferred), but it is not a particularly elegant approach to delivering content. With a helper application, every content file must be viewed separately, so any possibility of a seamlessly integrated, multimedia experience is lost. Not to mention the fact that you have to locate, download, install, and maintain a separate utility for every application. Embedded components have been implemented using a variety of technologies to attempt to solve this issue in a more satisfactory way. The first half of this chapter examines the primary forms of embedded content as they pertain to using FrontPage.

The next stage in the evolution of active content via the Web was Netscape's development of the plug-in, which was first unveiled in the Netscape Navigator 2.0 browser. One way to characterize a plug-in is to say that it is a "smarter" helper application that lives inside a Web page. When the user selects content to be displayed in a plug-in, the content downloads to the user, just as in the helper application scenario. With the plug-in, however, the content is handled by an application that works in conjunction with the Web browser. The browser opens the application, which displays itself inside the browser window, just as graphical images typically appear. (In a sense, a browser's method of displaying graphics in this fashion is a prototypical plug-in.)

> **Note** Like the `<embed>` tag typically used to add plug-ins to a Web page, plug-ins remain principally a Netscape phenomenon, although Internet Explorer has also had the ability to display plug-ins since version 3.0. In practice, IE developers typically use ActiveX controls instead, which have some advantages over plug-ins and provide the developer with more flexibility.

Not to be outdone, Microsoft quickly introduced its own means of embedding content into its Internet Explorer browser in the form of ActiveX controls Although it is capable of working with plug-ins as well, IE is typically configured to use ActiveX controls that provide the same functionality. For the plug-in developers, this has typically meant developing two versions of their product, one for Netscape users and one for users of Internet Explorer. For developers and Web page authors, it is important to devise your pages to accommodate both.

In this section of the chapter, we first examine how to add plug-ins and ActiveX controls in FrontPage, and then examine some popular examples of plug-ins.

Inserting plug-ins with FrontPage

Using FrontPage to add Embedded Content to your Web page is a three-step process:

1. First, you should have the plug-in installed. This is not essential to creating the page, but it is essential if you want to preview the page to make sure everything is working correctly. In most cases, you will already have the plug-in installed, so this step will not be a major burden.

2. Locate a file in the format you want to embed in your page. Many of the file formats that have existing plug-ins are proprietary in nature, which means that although the "viewer" may be free, the authoring application is not.

3. Once you have obtained a file, you can insert it into your Web page using FrontPage's Plug-in Control Properties dialog box.

> **Note** If you do not have the Flash plug-in, you can obtain it by downloading the free Flash player from the Macromedia Web site (`www.macromedia.com`).

Adding a reference to a plug-in is relatively straightforward. This next section describes a simple example of how to do this, using a sample Macromedia Flash animation.

Note You can find this sample file (`hbsplash.swf`) on the book's Web site. See the Preface for instructions on locating and downloading example files.

First, verify that you have the appropriate plug-in installed. You can check on the status of your plug-ins in Netscape by selecting Help ➪ About Plug-ins. This displays an internal HTML page listing all installed plug-ins. An example of the About Plug-ins page is shown in Figure 15-1.

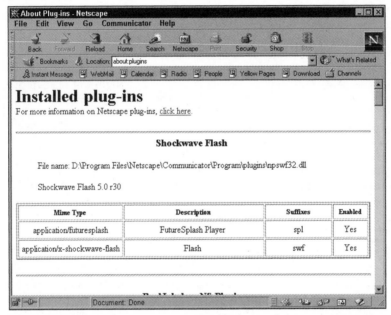

Figure 15-1: More than you ever wanted to know about your Netscape plug-ins can be found in the About Plug-ins page.

To use `hbsplash.swf`, you must first import it into your Web by selecting File ➪ Import. To embed the file in a Web page, select Insert ➪ Web Component to open the Insert Web Component dialog box. Select Advanced Controls from the Component Type list, and then select Plug-in from the Choose a Control list, as shown in Figure 15-2.

Select Finish. This opens the Plug-in Properties dialog box as illustrated in Figure 15-3.

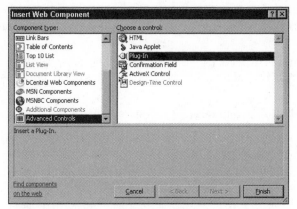

Figure 15-2: Add a Plug-in component from the Advanced Controls list in the Insert Web Component dialog box.

Figure 15-3: The Plug-in Properties dialog box

The Plug-in Properties dialog box features several fields, the most important of which is the Data Source. Click the Browse button to locate the file that you want to have displayed via a plug-in. In addition to the Data Source field, you can configure your plug-in using the following options:

✦ **Message for browsers without plug-in support:** Insert text and/or HTML to be displayed by browsers that do not recognize the plug-in tag. For example, you might insert a link enabling the user to download the file in question rather than display it in the browser.

✦ **Size (Height and Width):** Indicates the dimensions of the plug-in, in pixels. Once you have inserted the content and plug-in, you can also adjust the height and width of the plug-in by dragging and moving its icon. For our example, set the width to 480 and the height to 320.

✦ **Hide Plug-in:** Check this box to render the plug-in invisible. This normally is used with audio or other plug-ins for which a visible component to the plug-in isn't needed.

✦ **Layout:** Designates various aspects (Alignment, Border Thickness, Horizontal Spacing, and Vertical Spacing) of the visible characteristics of the plug-in on the page.

✦ **Style button:** Use this button to add relevant CSS style formatting to the plug-in.

When you are happy with your selections, click OK to return to the Editor window.

As shown in Figure 15-4, FrontPage puts a placeholder plug image in your page to represent the plug-in.

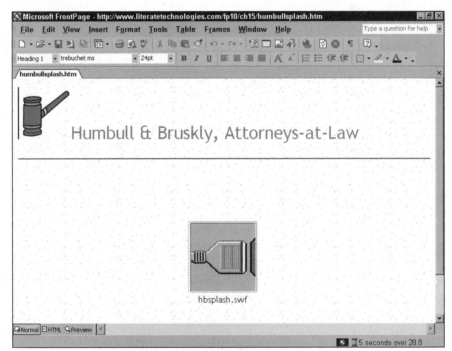

Figure 15-4: FrontPage marks your plug-in with a plug icon.

You can preview your plug-in either by using the Preview tab or by selecting File ➪ Preview in your browser. If you click the plug-in image to select it, you can then drag a corner to resize the plug-in window. Double-clicking the plug-in image brings up its Properties dialog box for additional editing.

The plug-in <embed> tag

When you issue the Insert Plug-in command, FrontPage creates an `<embed>` tag for the plug-in, as shown in the following code:

```
<embed width="480" height="320" src="hbsplash.swf">
```

FrontPage supports the following `<embed>` tag attributes via the Plug-in Properties dialog box:

✦ `Src`: Identifies the URL of the file to be displayed by the plug-in. Its type is identified by its filename extension.

✦ `Height`: The height of the plug-in window, in pixels.

✦ `Width`: The width of the plug-in window, in pixels.

✦ `Border`: Places a border around the plug-in window with the designated thickness, in pixels.

✦ `Align`: Alignment of the plug-in window.

✦ `Hspace`: Horizontal space, in pixels, between the plug-in window and the surrounding elements.

✦ `Vspace`: Vertical space, in pixels, between the plug-in window and the surrounding elements.

✦ `Hidden`: Hides the plug-in element from view. This is most useful for audio plug-ins, when you want the audio file to play without any visual elements.

Caution

Although commonly used, the `<embed>` tag is a pure Netscape invention and has never been part of any official HTML standard. The `<object>` tag discussed later is the preferred method of embedding content in HTML.

The <noembed> tag

In addition to the properties (or attributes) of the plug-in, you can use the Plug-in dialog box to create a simple text message that displays for users with browsers that don't support the `<embed>` tag for plug-ins. Any text placed in the "Message for browsers without plug-in support" textbox appears only if the user has an incompatible browser. This message is placed within a `<noembed></noembed>` tag set.

Adding plug-in attributes manually

FrontPage makes it easy to add a plug-in to your Web page. However, the Plug-in Properties dialog box does not provide a means for editing all possible attributes that might be associated with a given plug-in. For example, our Flash animation is set to loop infinitely by default, but you're not always going to want your animations to loop. If you prefer the animation to play once and stop, switch to HTML view and set the `<embed>` tag's `<loop>` attribute to false, thus:

```
<embed loop="false" width="480" height="320"
src="hbsplash.swf">
```

We can also add information that tells the browser where to locate the plug-in for this file, if the user's browser does not have the plug-in installed. For this, we add a `<pluginspage>` attribute, and give it the appropriate URL, obtained from Macromedia's Web site:

```
<embed
pluginspage=http://www.macromedia.com/shockwave/download/index.
cgi?P1_Prod_Version=ShockwaveFlash loop="false" width="480"
height="320" src="hbsplash.swf">
```

Note　For more information on using the `<embed>` tag with Flash, see the Flash Support section of Macromedia's Web site, at `http://www.macromedia.com/support/flash/`.

Embedding Content using ActiveX

About the time that Netscape was introducing plug-in technology, Microsoft was realizing that it needed to remake itself, and simultaneously re-make the nature of the Internet, to avoid being left in the virtual exhaust dust of the information super-highway. The introduction of the ActiveX technologies is the result of Microsoft's efforts to put itself back in the driver's seat.

ActiveX is Microsoft's answer to Netscape plug-ins. To a large degree, the ActiveX name is really just a repackaging of preexisting Microsoft technologies (most notably, the Object Linking and Embedding specifications, or OLE), and fine-tuned a bit for their new role on the global Internet. These technologies make possible the reuse of application components and enable applications to communicate with one another and even embed parts of themselves in other applications.

Now, let's insert the same content we used in the last section into a new page, this time using an ActiveX component. As we noted earlier, most of the vendors who have developed plug-ins for their content have developed both a plug-in version for Netscape users and an ActiveX version for Internet Explorer users.

Inserting an ActiveX control

Assuming that you have the Flash ActiveX control installed, you can insert the Flash file by selecting Insert ➪ Web Components ➪ Advanced Controls. Select ActiveX Control and then click the Next button. This opens the Insert Web Components dialog box where you can select an ActiveX control, as illustrated in Figure 15-5. Select the Shockwave Flash Object.

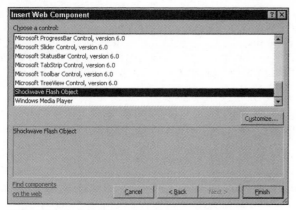

Figure 15-5: Selecting an ActiveX control

Note

If you do not have the Flash ActiveX control installed, you can obtain it by down-loading the free Flash player from the Macromedia Web site (www.macromedia. com).

If you do not see the control you need, click the Customize button to open the Customize ActiveX Control List dialog box, which features a list of all registered ActiveX controls on your computer. (You may be surprised at the number of controls in this list!) Scroll until you locate the Shockwave Flash Object (shown in Figure 15-6) and check its selection box to add it to the Components list. Click OK to proceed. (If you don't see the Shockwave Flash Object in the Customize list, then it is not installed on your computer.)

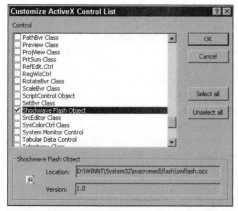

Figure 15-6: Locating an ActiveX control from the list of registered controls on your computer

Select Finish to insert the control into the page. To configure the control, open the Flash Component's Properties dialog box by double-clicking on the control in Normal view (note that it will be invisible — except for its selection handles — until you configure it). The first step in configuring the control is to add the URL of the Flash file in the Movie URL field of the Flash Properties tab as shown in Figure 15-7.

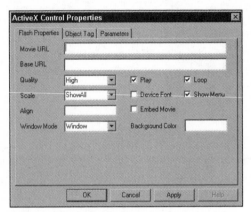

Figure 15-7: The Flash Properties tab of the Flash ActiveX Control dialog box

Notice that in contrast to the Plug-in Properties dialog box, the ActiveX Control Properties Dialog box contains specific property input fields for all of the control's properties. Still in the Flash Properties tab, uncheck the Loop checkbox. In the Object tab, set the width to 480 and the height to 320 (pixels) and give the component a name, as shown in Figure 15-8.

Click OK when you are finished. You may notice that FrontPage displays the actual embedded content even in Normal view. (In some circumstances, it displays the red and black ActiveX control icon instead).

Caution

When you use FrontPage's ActiveX Control Properties dialog box to configure your ActiveX controls, you may notice that FrontPage adds several parameters that you did not ask it to. You can see these in the Parameters tab, where you can remove the ones you aren't using. However, each time you open the ActiveX Control Properties dialog box, FrontPage insists on putting them back. Also, FrontPage insists on converting Boolean values (true or false) to integers (0 or 1), which can sometimes cause problems for the control.

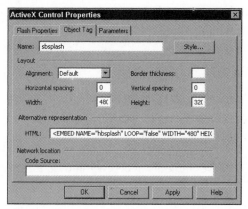

Figure 15-8: The Object tab of the Flash ActiveX Control dialog box

The <object> tag

Switch to HTML view and look at the code FrontPage generates for your ActiveX control (see Figure 15-9). It uses the `<object>` tag, a general purpose tag that enables the embedding of various kinds of content. It is similar to the `<embed>` tag, but encloses its property statements in `<param>` tags, each of which contains a name and a value.

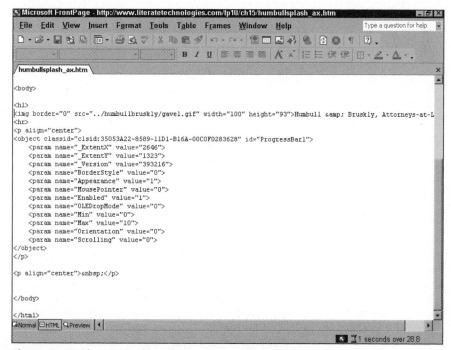

Figure 15-9: The HTML view of your ActiveX control

Notice, too, that the ActiveX control registers itself using a `classid` that consists of an impressively long string of letters and numbers. This `classid` is a unique identifier, and shows why it's a good reason to let FrontPage insert your ActiveX controls for you, as it adds this automatically.

Cross-browser embedded content

So now you have an Embedded Content page with a plug-in for Netscape and another page with an ActiveX Control for Internet Explorer. Does this mean you have to maintain two pages for every instance of Embedded Content on your site? Fortunately, this is not the case. There is a commonly accepted method for creating a single page to handle both instances.

This method takes advantage of the fact that the `<object>` tag can include HTML text to display for browsers that do not support this tag. The trick is to insert an `<embed>` tag as the alternate text, so that browsers that do not support the `<object>` tag but do support `<embed>` (namely Netscape) can still see the Embedded Content.

One way to do this in FrontPage is to create separate instances of the Embedded Content for the plug-in and for the ActiveX control, as we have done, and then cut and paste the `<embed>` tag information you have created into the ActiveX Control's Property dialog box. Here are the steps, assuming that you have already created the two components as we have previously described.

1. Switch to the HTML view of your Flash plug-in page. Select the `<embed>` tag with all of its attributes, then select Edit ➪ Cut — or use the shortcut Ctrl+X — to cut the HTML.

2. Open the page containing the ActiveX Flash control. Double-click the control to open the Properties dialog box.

3. Switch to the Object tab and paste the `<embed>` tag information into the Alternative Representation HTML field (you may not be able to see the entire tag in the field, but you can scroll the text to see that it is all there.) Refer back to Figure 15-9 to see this.

4. Test in both Netscape and IE to be certain that your content displays in both browsers.

Popular plug-ins and ActiveX controls

When Netscape first introduced the plug-in concept and made available the resources for developers to build their own plug-ins, dozens of companies who had proprietary file formats rushed to create plug-ins for their file types. This has resulted in over 150 plug-ins listed on Netscape's site (see the following section, "Where to find plug-ins"). In practice, however, only a few plug-ins have achieved any real acceptance. Most have disappeared, or are really just special purpose tools. Although plug-ins to handle Embedded Content have the advantage over helper applications of being able to run inside the Web browser, they are still a fair amount of hassle and there too many ways for things to go wrong. The same is true for ActiveX controls. That said, the following section profiles some of the major "players," so to speak, who have managed to stay the course.

Where to find plug-ins

If you are looking for a plug-in, the main source, not surprisingly, is the Netscape plug-in site, located at `http://home.netscape.com/plugins/index.html`. (A link to this location is provided in the About Plug-ins page contained in the Netscape browser.) Another good site for finding good plug-ins is Browser Watch, located at `http://browserwatch.internet.com/plug-in.html`. However, for most of the well-known plug-in vendors, you may find it easier just to point to the particular vendor's Web site.

Caution

One problem with both the Netscape and Browser Watch sites is that they do not weed out products or companies that have long since vanished from cyberdom. Be prepared for a number of dead-ends.

Where to find ActiveX controls

Microsoft maintains information on ActiveX at `http://ww.microsoft.com/com/tech/ActiveX.asp`, but does not maintain a list of ActiveX controls. Two other sites worthy of mention are

✦ C/Net's ActiveX site download site: `http://www.activex.com`

✦ Browserwatch ActiveX Arena: `http://www.browserwatch.com/activex.html`

Keep in mind when searching for ActiveX components that you are likely to find more listings of programmable components, or "controls," — as we discuss in the next section — rather than the kind intended for delivering Embedded Content.

Popular embedded content formats

This section provides a brief overview of the most important forms of Embedded Content on the Web today.

Animation

The hands-down leader in this category continues to be Macromedia (`http://www.macromedia.com`), who was one of the first companies to capitalize on the plug-in format. Macromedia developed a viewer for its Director file format — called *Shockwave* — and rechristened it for the Web community. Since this humble beginning, Macromedia has released versions of Shockwave to run Authorware applications and Freehand presentations. Its most recent entry is Flash, a vector-based animation program that produces compact animations geared toward bandwidth-limited media. Flash currently enjoys an immense popularity — see Chapter 13 for a detailed introduction to integrating Flash and FrontPage.

Document formats

No question here, Adobe's Acrobat Reader for its own Portable Document Format (PDF) is the run-away winner in this category. Recently Adobe (`http://www.adobe.com`) has also entered the e-book arena and is championing a new vector graphics format, Scalable Vector Graphics, or SVG, and XML application which enables the creation of dynamically adjustable images and diagrams

Streaming media

Currently there are really only three contenders left in this arena: Windows Media Player from Microsoft (`http://www.microsoft.com`), RealPlayer from RealNetworks (`http://www.real.com`); and Apple's QuickTime (`http://www.apple.com`). Each supports a wide array of audio, video, and animation formats, including SMIL (Synchronized Multimedia Integration Language), an XML application for producing synchronized multimedia presentations.

Web3D

VRML, short for Virtual Reality Markup Language, and often pronounced "vermel," is a programming language for creating 3-D objects and virtual worlds, through which you can navigate by using the mouse pointer. The issue of whether VRML is a cool technology that has come and gone or is still just a little ahead of its time remains unclear. It has never quite lived up to its promise.

Recently, a more general term, *Web3D*, has emerged to describe any of a handful of 3-D technologies designed for the Web. Who knows, XML may yet save the day for the VRML folks. Of the once crowded VRML plug-in field, Cortona, a VRML viewer from ParallelGraphics (`http://www.parallelgraphics.com`), the Cosmo browser, once owned by SGI and currently in the hands of Computer Associates (`http://www.cai.com/cosmo/`), and Blaxxun's Contact (`http://www.blaxxun.com`), remain as the most viable products.

Working with Advanced Controls

In the first half of this chapter we examined how you can use plug-ins and ActiveX components to embed a wide variety of content formats in your Web pages. Components can also be used to add programmable, interactive controls to your Web page. Any of the "big three" component technologies we listed at the beginning of this chapter (i.e., plug-ins, ActiveX, and Java applets) can be used to do this. In practice, because plug-ins are difficult to work with in this capacity, ActiveX controls and Java applets are more often used for this purpose. This is what we concentrate on in this portion of the chapter.

ActiveX Controls

Earlier in the chapter, we saw how ActiveX can be used as a substitute for Netscape plug-ins. Although ActiveX is often associated with the Internet, it is really just a set of general-purpose technologies that happen to work on the Internet. This is both its strength and its drawback. On the one hand, it virtually eliminates the boundary between the computer system and its local and remote resources on the Internet. On the other hand, all of the ActiveX technology is platform- and operating system-dependent.

An ActiveX control is simply a reusable, modular programming component. It can be inserted into another application or into a Web page, and it can be configured or scripted to perform a variety of tasks. It can range in size from something as simple as an option button to a sophisticated spreadsheet application. Because ActiveX controls tend to be easier to use than to explain, the next section provides a hands-on example of how to add an ActiveX control to your Web page.

A Short, Acronym-Cluttered History of ActiveX

First came Visual Basic Extensions (VBE), custom controls that can be accessed using the popular Visual Basic programming language. Then came Object Linking and Embedding (OLE) and OLE Controls (OCXs). OLE technology essentially enabled developers to put one document type inside another. You have experienced OLE if you have ever embedded, say, a spreadsheet in your word processing document.

When Microsoft first discovered the Internet, it quickly extended the OLE technology to operate via the Internet. Then it gave OLE a catchy marketing name. Voila! ActiveX was born.

For a time, Microsoft tried using ActiveX as the umbrella brand name for all of its Internet programming technologies, but the term soon fell out of vogue. Then for a while, Microsoft referred to the totality of its Web programming technologies and applications as DNA, which stands for Distributed interNet Application. Most recently, they unveiled their .NET (pronounced "dot Net") platform, and now everything is "dot Net." Now, ActiveX is only used in connection with ActiveX controls, as discussed in this chapter.

In somewhat more formal terms, ActiveX refers to any of several technologies that use the Microsoft Component Object Model (COM) specification—and more recently DCOM, COM+, etc.—to create programming entities that can be combined, reused, scripted, and delivered via a network such as the Internet. Thus, ActiveX encompasses an array of applications that use the core concepts of OLE and COM.

Inserting an ActiveX control

If you have followed along from the beginning of the chapter, you already know how to insert an ActiveX control. When we added a Flash component earlier, we only had to tell the component where its content file resided and it took care of the rest. The ActiveX controls we examine in the following sections will not be very useful until we supply them with some properties and, later in the chapter, add some scripting to control them..

To insert an ActiveX control, select Insert ➪ Web Components. Select Advanced Controls from the Components Type list, and then select ActiveX Control from the Choose a control list. Click Next to view the list of ActiveX controls that FrontPage knows about in the Web components dialog box.

The main purpose of this dialog box is to select the control that you want to insert into your Web page. You can also customize this dialog box so that it lists only the controls that you might actually want to use. To customize the list, click the Customize button and deselect any items that you don't want to appear on the list. (Don't worry, if you change your mind later, you can always return and recheck any items that you remove from the list.)

Note   When a control is registered on your computer, which typically happens when you install a piece of software, a reference is created in your System Registry file. It is quite likely that some of the controls listed by FrontPage no longer exist on your system. You can remove them from sight by using the Customize button. (Or, better yet, get a utility to remove the reference completely from your Registry.)

After you select a control from the list, click OK. For the purposes of demonstration, we will select a simple ActiveX control, the Microsoft Forms 2.0 Label control.. Figure 15-10 illustrates what the Label control looks like when it is first inserted with some initial text. Not very exciting at this point. The next section examines how to manipulate the control to serve a better purpose.

Editing control properties

Being able to use an ActiveX control like a plug-in is useful, but the real power of ActiveX begins to be more apparent when you configure a control to your liking. In many ways, ActiveX controls are much like any other HTML object in that they have properties you define that change how the controls look and/or behave. FrontPage gives you access to these properties. As we will see, however, FrontPage does not offer you as much flexibility as you might like in working with these controls. After we describe how to work with an ActiveX control in FrontPage, we will suggest some alternatives for those who need more functionality.

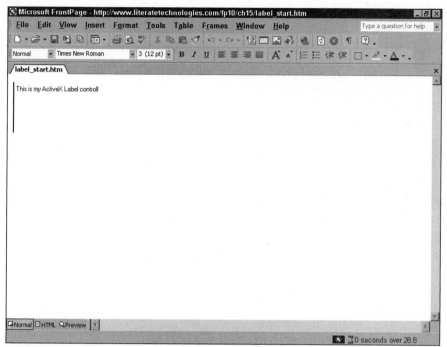

Figure 15-10: A basic ActiveX control icon inserted in Normal view

Using the ActiveX Control Properties dialog box

Let's first try out the ActiveX Control Properties dialog box. To access it, double-click the ActiveX control in Normal view of your Web page. If you are using the Label control (as described in the previous section), you should see a Properties dialog box that resembles Figure 15-11.

The Properties dialog box for the Label control has two tabs: Object Tag and Parameters. The number of available tabs and their names vary from control to control. The options available for the Label control are representative of many basic ActiveX controls.

Object tags

The Label control's Object Tag tab enables you to define the control's general placement and appearance on the page. With the Object Tag tab selected, you can give the control a name, define layout properties (alignment, horizontal spacing, width, height, Border thickness, Vertical spacing), you can define alternative HTML to present to users who do not have a browser capable of displaying ActiveX controls, and you can point to the codebase for the control to enable users who do not have it installed to obtain it. This tab does not affect how the control functions (which you define by using the control's Parameters tab, discussed in the next section). The following are the options available on the Object Tag tab:

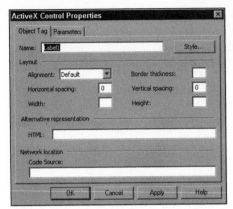

Figure 15-11: The ActiveX Control Properties
dialog box for the Microsoft Forms Label control

✦ **Name:** The control's name is used to reference it when using a client-side
scripting language, such as VBScript or JavaScript. The name cannot contain
spaces and must begin with either a letter or an underscore.

✦ **Layout section:** Enables you to adjust the following properties that affect how
the control appears on the page:

- **Alignment:** Like an image, an ActiveX control can be positioned in various
ways relative to the elements around it.

- **Border Thickness:** By default, the border attribute is 0. Set this to a posi-
tive number to indicate the thickness of the border, in pixels.

- **Horizontal Spacing:** The spacing, in pixels, between the control and any
elements to its left and right.

- **Vertical Spacing:** Spacing, in pixels, between the control and elements
above and below it.

- **Width:** The width of the control, in pixels. Typically, you adjust the
width and height by dragging and moving the ActiveX icon to an appropriate size. Use these fields for fine-tuning.

- **Height:** The height of the control, in pixels.

✦ **Alternative Representation:** Enter any text, including HTML, that you want
presented to users with browsers that don't support ActiveX.

✦ **Code Source:** Indicates the URL to which users should go to download the
ActiveX Control when the page is loaded, if the user does not already have the
control.

Parameters tab

If you click on the Parameters tab (see Figure 15-12), you will notice that this tab contains a lengthy list of user-configurable parameters that the control recognizes. The parameters of an object enable you to change the behavior and/or appearance of an ActiveX control. These parameters are stored in the HTML as part of the `<object>` tag. As we describe in the next section, you can add, modify, or remove parameters from this list.

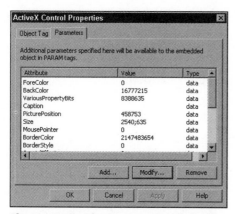

Figure 15-12: The Parameters tab for the ActiveX Label Control Properties dialog box

The following is the list of the principal parameters available for the Label control:

✦ **Caption:** The text that the control displays

✦ **Angle:** The angle of the text (0 is horizontal)

✦ **Alignment:** Options are as follows:

  • 0 = left top

  • 1 = centered top

  • 2 = right top

  • 3 = left centered

  • 4 = centered

  • 5 = right centered

  • 6 = left bottom

  • 7 = centered bottom

  • 8 = right bottom

✦ **Mode:** Options are as follows:

- 0 = simple no rotation
- 1 = simple rotation
- 2 = user-defined no rotation
- 3 = user-defined rotation

✦ **Fillstyle:** 0 = solid, 1 = outline

✦ **ForeColor:** An integer representing the foreground (the text) color

✦ **BackColor:** An integer representing the background color

✦ **FontName:** Any valid font

✦ **FontSize:** An integer representing the pixel size of the font

✦ **FontItalic:** True/false

✦ **FontBold:** True/false

✦ **FontUnderline:** True/false

✦ **FontStrikeout:** True/false

Adding or modifying parameters

From the Parameters tab, you can add, modify, or remove parameters from the parameter list. You can add a parameter to the list or remove an existing parameter. Keep in mind that you are only adding and removing parameters from the list included in the HTML. You cannot change the functionality of the control itself with this dialog box.

It is at this point, when we try to define values for these parameters, that we begin to run up against some limitations in FrontPage. As long as we only want to enter text parameters, we are fine. The trouble starts when we want to provide a value for parameters that get their values from a list of valid options. But we are getting ahead of ourselves...The first thing we would like to do is put some text in our Label control. This is easy enough to do by selecting the Caption attribute in the Parameters tab and clicking the Modify button to bring up the Edit Object Parameter dialog box as illustrated in Figure 15-13.

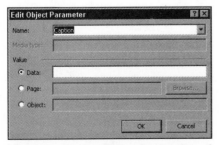

Figure 15-13: Modifying the Caption of a Label control in FrontPage

The Name field in this dialog box shows the parameter that you selected. You can select a different parameter from the drop-down menu. The Edit Object Parameter dialog box offers three options for how values are provided to the control:

✦ **Data:** The most common (and the default) option. Use this option whenever you want to enter the value directly to the parameter as an alphanumeric character string.

✦ **Page:** Enables you to enter a value that is a URL reference to another resource. This is typically used when the control incorporates external media, such as graphics, sounds, video, and so forth. Note that selecting this option also enables the Media Type field under the Name field.

✦ **Object:** Enables you to enter a value that references the id of an `<object>` declaration in the same page.

For our purposes here, type the text message you want for your label in the Data field and click OK to return to the Parameters tab.

Easy, right? OK, now let's change the color of the label text. Again, there is a parameter to do this — it is the ForeColor parameter. Select it from the Attributes list and click Modify. The Edit Object Parameter tab looks very much the same as it did when we edited the caption. The only problem is that the ForeColor parameter takes a numerical value. What number do we use for, say, green text? We are left to guess because ActiveX controls do not use standard Web color notation. They use something called *packed integer notation*.

So how do you ascertain what values to use? First, we should acknowledge that the Label control is not the most up-to-date ActiveX control available. One approach would be to find controls that use values that are easier to determine without a fancy interface. At the other end of the spectrum, if you suspect you will be doing a lot of work with ActiveX controls, we suggest you look into purchasing an application that is better suited to this purpose. A good option for Web-related development is Microsoft Visual InterDev (also part of the Visual Studio suite of development tools). If you were to open the Label control in Visual InterDev, you would be presented with a color picker from which to select colors. No need to brush up your RBG to packed integer notation skills in this case!

Caution   As we write this, Microsoft is working on the Visual Studio.NET product, which folds the InterDev product into its Integrated Development Environment (IDE). Before you purchase Visual InterDev, check out the current status of the Visual Studio.NET release.

The ActiveX Control Pad

For our simple purposes, Visual InterDev is overkill. We simply need a method of ascertaining the correct color values for our label control. Our solution, in this case, is to use an outdated, but still serviceable, utility from Microsoft called the *ActiveX Control Pad*.

Caution   You might think that the Microsoft Script Editor could help us here. Unfortunately, it is not better than FrontPage itself at providing a user-friendly interface to our Label control.

Tip   You can download ActiveX Control Pad (it's a freeware utility) from C/Net's Download.com `http://www.download.com`. Search for "ActiveX Control Pad." Ironically, users of older versions of FrontPage may recognize this tool as having once been a part of FrontPage itself.

Install this tool by double-clicking on the installation executable and following the instructions. Once you have installed the Control Pad, open it using the Start Menu shortcut it installs. It starts up with an empty HTML document as shown in Figure 15-14. All we want to use it for is its ability to help us set ActiveX control properties.

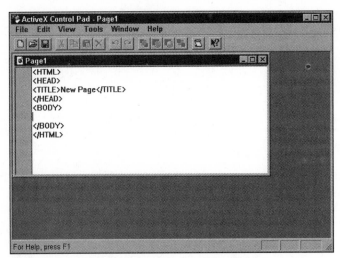

Figure 15-14: The ActiveX Control Pad interface

Select Edit ➪ Insert ActiveX Control to open a control selection list that by now should look familiar. Locate the Microsoft Label control and click OK. The Control Pad opens two new windows: the first, labeled Edit ActiveX Control, shows a visual representation of the control; the second, labeled Properties, contains a list of the control's properties. Now, if you select the ForeColor property, you can click the little button in the upper right corner of the Properties dialog box (the one marked with three dots) to open up a color picker tool to help you select a color (see Figure 15-15). Similarly, the other properties have appropriate selection options.

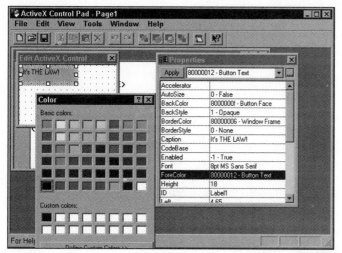

Figure 15-15: The ActiveX Control Pad provides access to control parameter options.

Once you have finished setting your Control parameter options, close the editing windows. Control Pad will create the <object> tag information you need. You can copy and paste the necessary object and parameter tags into your FrontPage Web page (or you can save the page in Control Pad and import it into FrontPage).

Note You can also use the Control Pad's Script Wizard to script your controls. However, the Control Pad is old technology and sometimes performs unpredictably, especially when confronted with newer controls. Use this workaround at your own risk.

Examining the object tag

You have now inserted and configured an ActiveX control, all without a stitch of programming. Just to show you what you have accomplished, look at the HTML that FrontPage generates for your control. When FrontPage inserts an ActiveX control into a Web page, it creates an instance of the <object> tag, an example of which is shown here:

```
<OBJECT CLASSID="clsid:99B42120-6EC7-11CF-A6C7-00AA00A47DD2"
  ID="MyLabelControl"
WIDTH="199" HEIGHT="140" BORDER="2">
  <PARAM NAME="_ExtentX" VALUE="5265">
  <PARAM NAME="_ExtentY" VALUE="3704">
  <PARAM NAME="Caption" VALUE="Welcome to ActiveX">
  <PARAM NAME="Angle" VALUE="45">
  <PARAM NAME="Alignment" VALUE="4">
  <PARAM NAME="FontBold" VALUE="1">
  <PARAM NAME="FillStyle" VALUE="0">
  <PARAM NAME="ForeColor" VALUE="#FF0000">
```

```
<PARAM NAME="BackColor" VALUE="#000000">
<PARAM NAME="FontName" VALUE="Arial">
<PARAM NAME="FontSize" VALUE="12">
<PARAM NAME="FontItalic" VALUE="0">
<PARAM NAME="FontBold" VALUE="0">
<PARAM NAME="FontUnderline" VALUE="0">
<PARAM NAME="FontStrikeout" VALUE="0">
<PARAM NAME="TopPoints" VALUE="0">
<PARAM NAME="BotPoints" VALUE="0">
<PARAM NAME="Mode" VALUE="1">
Sorry, your browser does not support ActiveX.
</OBJECT>
```

The <object> tag set contains several attributes. The most important of these is <classid> (CLSID). This is the unique key stored in the Registry that identifies the control. Entering this string by hand is both time-consuming and error-prone (and memorizing too many of these numbers is tough). So, in this case, FrontPage does you a favor by automatically inserting the correct ID number.

In addition, the <object> tag includes an <id> attribute, which is the name used to identify the object within the HTML page. The <height> and <width> attributes define the size of the object on the page. The <border> attribute indicates that this object has a 2-pixel border around it.

Within the beginning and ending <object> tags are two elements:

✦ A series of <param> tags that correspond to the parameters that you configured earlier using the FrontPage ActiveX Properties dialog box.

✦ Optional text displayed by browsers that don't support the <object> tag. How to deal with browser compatibility issues is the subject of the next section.

Scripting a control

In addition to controlling the properties of an ActiveX control at design time, you can access your control via client-side scripting. This enables you to create sophisticated Web pages and ActiveX controls with minimal effort.

This section illustrates the process of scripting the Label Object control used in the earlier example. This chapter assumes that you are familiar with basic client-side scripting techniques. If you are not, you may want to peek at Chapter 18 before tackling this section.

Scripting the Label Object control

In this example, you add some additional ActiveX controls to the Label Object control example that you constructed earlier in the chapter. These new controls enable you to change the appearance of the label interactively. To follow this example, you need to have the Microsoft Forms 2.0 ActiveX Controls registered on your computer. If you do not, you can substitute standard HTML form elements and obtain similar results.

Start with a new Web page and insert a Label Object control, as previously described. Using the ActiveX Control Properties dialog box, name the control MyLabelControl and make it 200 × 200 pixels square. Modify the Caption parameter to suit your tastes (and the size of the control).

Adding form controls

You are going to add a series of ActiveX form controls. These are similar to the standard HTML form elements, only much more versatile.

1. Create a table to hold the form controls. You are going to add a form control to modify the label caption, height, width, style, angle, and color. You can use Figure 15-16, which shows the form control labels already inserted, as a guide to create the table.

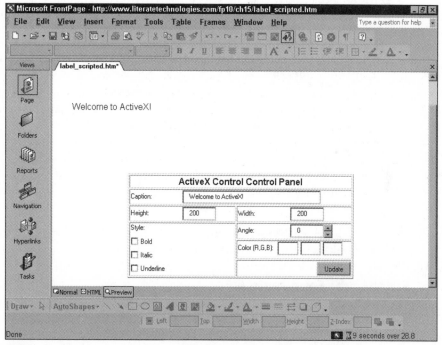

Figure 15-16: Our form for controlling the Label control's attributes

2. Add the necessary form label controls. Place the cursor in the first table cell and select Insert ➪ Web Components ➪ Advanced Controls and select ActiveX Control. Select the Microsoft Forms 2.0 Label control. Edit the form label properties by double-clicking the label. Name the first control lblCaption, change its height value to 20, and modify its caption parameter value to Caption:. Repeat this step for the other label controls.

3. Add the remaining form controls. You may have noticed that the Microsoft Forms 2.0 controls include a long list of form controls. You are going to use only three: the TextBox control, CheckBox control, and SpinButton control. Of these, only the SpinButton control has no standard HTML equivalent (and, if you are really clever, you can probably imagine a way to emulate this control by using standard HTML form buttons and some additional scripting).

4. To add a TextBox control, select Insert ⇨ Web Components ⇨ Advanced Controls and select ActiveX Control and select the Microsoft Forms 2.0 TextBox control from the list. If the TextBox control is not on the list of current controls, click the Customize button to locate it and add it to the list. Name this textbox control `tbCaption` and insert it next to the Caption Label control. Adjust the size, as needed. Repeat the same process to create TextBox controls for height, width, and angle. Create three boxes for the RGB color values.

5. To add a CheckBox control, select Insert ⇨ Web Components ⇨ Advanced Controls and select ActiveX Control and select the Microsoft Forms 2.0 CheckBox control. Name this control `cbFontBold`. Click the Parameters tab and modify the Caption parameter to Bold. Set the value of this checkbox to 0 (the default is 2). This makes the checkbox not selected by default. Repeat for italics and underline.

6. To add a SpinButton control, select Insert ⇨ Web Components ⇨ Advanced Controls and select ActiveX Control and select the Microsoft Forms 2.0 SpinButton control. Name it `sbAngle`. Place this control next to the Angle textbox control.

7. You also need a button control. Select Insert ⇨ Web Components ⇨ Advanced Controls and select ActiveX Control and select the Microsoft Forms 2.0 Command Button control. Name it `btnUpdate` and modify the Caption parameter to `Update`.

You now have a nifty Web page control panel for your Label control. In the next section, you hook up the control to the control panel.

Scripting the Form controls

The idea is simple. You want to be able to edit the values of any of the available Form controls and click the Update button to register the changes with the Label Object control. To do this, you must write a few simple scripts.

Creating Event subroutines

To write these simple scripts, we will use VBScript, mainly because VBScript has built-in support for ActiveX control events. To set the page to use VBScript rather than JavaScript as its scripting language, insert the following scripting block (note that all of the code defined below will go in this scripting block):

```
<SCRIPT LANGUAGE=VBScript>
<!--//
    Scripting to go here...
//-->
</SCRIPT>
```

The Command button includes a Click event method. To script that event, you create a subroutine called `btnUpdate_Click`:

```
Sub btnUpdate_Click
    Our code will go here
End Sub
```

You also need an event subroutine for the SpinButton control. Each time that the top spin button is clicked, you want the value of the Angle textbox to increase, and each time the bottom spin button is clicked, you want the value of the Angle textbox to decrease. The SpinButton control has two events, `SpinUp` and `SpinDown`, to handle these events. The code that you add here is relatively straightforward:

```
Sub sbAngle_SpinUp
    If (tbAngle="") Then
        tbAngle=0
    End If
    tbAngle=tbAngle+1
End Sub
Sub sbAngle_SpinDown
    If (tbAngle="") Then
        tbAngle=0
    End If
    tbAngle=tbAngle-1
End Sub
```

Completing the update event code

When the Update button is clicked, you need scripting that checks the status of each update element and then makes any necessary changes to the parameters of your Label Object control. This is a relatively straightforward matter of setting each of the parameters in the Label Object (`MyLabelControl`) to the value of the form control. Here is the code:

```
Sub btnUpdate_Click
    MyLabelControl.Caption=tbCaption
    MyLabelControl.Height=tbHeight
    MyLabelControl.Width=tbWidth
    MyLabelControl.Angle=tbAngle
    MyLabelControl.FontBold=cbFontBold
    MyLabelControl.FontItalic=cbFontItalic
    MyLabelControl.FontUnderline=cbFontUnderline
    MyLabelControl.ForeColor = setColor(tbR,tbG,tbB)
End Sub
```

Dealing with color values

One complication to the update routine in the previous section is the color designation. Although FrontPage allows you to designate Web page colors using hexadecimal notation (such as #FF0000), the scripting object doesn't accept this format. Instead, it requires a packed integer notation. The good news is that our script will include a conversion function, setColor(r,g,b), that accepts color values from 0 to 255 for red, green, and blue. It translates this into the requisite packed integer and sends it along to the Label Object control. The following is the code for this function:

```
Function setColor (r,g,b)
    'converts RGB values to packed integer
    Dim iColor
    If StrComp(r,"")=0 Then
        r=0
    Else
        If cInt(r)> 255 Then
            r=255
        End If
    End If
    If StrComp(g,"")=0 Then
        g=0
    Else
        If cInt(g)> 255 Then
            g=255
        End If
    End If
    If StrComp(b,"")=0 Then
        b=0
    Else
        If cInt(b)> 255 Then
            b=255
        End If
    End If
    iColor = (b * 65536) + (g * 256) + r
    setColor = iColor
End Function
```

At this point, you have everything in place to use the Label Object control panel. Try it out! Compare your results with those in Figure 15-17.

Setting the default values

In this section, you make one last refinement to your control panel. You need to add a routine to set the control panel fields to the default value of the Label Object control.

Note   Why add this routine? Well, the first time I tried out the update routine, I forgot to put in values for the height and width. When I clicked the Update button, poof! The control was gone. Or, rather, it was still there, but it was just 0-pixels wide by 0-pixels high. Therein lies the value of being able to reset the defaults.

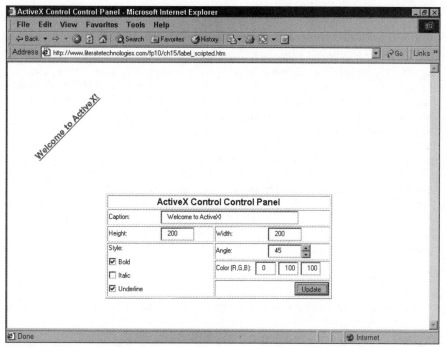

Figure 15-17: Updating the Label Object control with your ActiveX control panel

Create a subroutine called `onPageLoad`. Create a series of assignments that are the reverse of the ones in the update routine. The code is listed here:

```
Sub onPageLoad
    tbCaption=MyLabelControl.Caption
    tbHeight=MyLabelControl.Height
    tbWidth=MyLabelControl.Width
    tbAngle=MyLabelControl.Angle
    cbFontBold=MyLabelControl.FontBold
    cbFontItalic=MyLabelControl.FontItalic
    cbFontUnderline=MyLabelControl.FontUnderline
End Sub
```

You want to call this routine when the page first loads. To do this, update the `<body>` tag of the Web page to the following:

```
<BODY ONLOAD="onPageLoad">
```

Now, the initial values of all the form controls are set when you initialize the page.

ActiveX controls and security

When you allow a remote computer to send a program to you to be run on your local computer, as is the case with both ActiveX controls and Java, you open up the possibility of security problems. What is to stop someone from sending you a "malicious" program that wreaks havoc with your computer system? The question is always how to safeguard your computer to a reasonable degree of certainty from such attacks without completely foregoing the advantages that the ability to send programming across the Internet affords.

Microsoft has addressed security issues with its ActiveX technologies by creating a method of digitally signing their code. This digital signature technology is called *Authenticode*. When the user arrives at a Web page that contains active content requiring a control that isn't currently installed on the user's system, the Web page issues a request to download the software. It checks the sender's digital signature and, if the signature is correct, displays a certificate-like graphic and asks for permission to download the control.

Success of this method relies on two assumptions:

✦ The entity who signs the digital certificate is trustworthy and will not cause any harm.

✦ The digital signature has been generated by its actual owner; and the person receiving the programming can make a reasonable decision about whether or not the owner is deserving of trust.

After you determine that the entity is legitimate and safe, you grant the program license to do as it pleases.

Setting security in IE 4 and IE 5

In Internet Explorer 4.x, you can set a similar range of general security levels. Internet Explorer 5 adds a "Medium-Low" level of security. This is similar to Medium in the level of security, but does not prompt you. In addition, in both IE 4 and 5, you can customize security options by setting the level of numerous potential security risks. To do this, select View ➪ Internet Options, and click the Security tab, as shown in Figure 15-18.

Select one of four zones: Local Intranet Zone, Trusted Sites Zone, Internet Zone, or Restricted Sites Zone. The Internet zone is the default zone for any location not specified as being part of one of the other zones. To add a location to a zone, select that zone and click the Add Sites button.

Select a security level option: High, Medium, Medium-Low, Low, or Custom. This last option gives you very fine-grained control over your security choices, as shown in Figure 15-19.

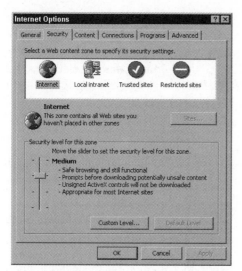

Figure 15-18: Setting security options in Internet Explorer 5.x

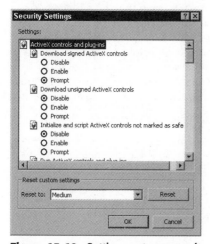

Figure 15-19: Setting custom security options in Internet Explorer 5.x

All of these options may help to make you feel safe, but if you happen to allow a bad piece of code through, no physical layer of security can protect the computer system. This is the main difference between security as it is implemented by Microsoft in its ActiveX technologies and Sun Microsystems's Java programming language, the topic of the next section.

Java Applets

This section explores what you need to know to use FrontPage to add Java applets to your Web pages. Java is another of the advanced programming elements that FrontPage supports and makes easy to incorporate into a Web page, even if you're not a programmer.

What is a Java applet?

First, you need to understand that Java isn't just a technology for building applets. Java is quite capable of creating full-scale applications (although arguments are ongoing as to how capable "quite capable" is). Java is a programming language. In that respect, it is no different than C, C++, Visual Basic, or FORTRAN. You can write regular applications in Java. However, Java has been designed from the beginning for a multiplatform, networked environment, such as the Internet.

A Java applet is only one specialized kind of Java application, designed to operate within a Web browser environment — that is, embedded in a Web page — rather than as a standalone application. Usually, an applet is smaller and simpler than a Web application, because it has to download to the user's browser. It is also limited somewhat in its operations by the security restrictions that Java places on remotely accessed applets. The main difference between an applet and a Java application, however, is that the applet has some special characteristics associated with starting and stopping the applet. This is because an applet does not run independently of a browser the way a standard application is run. An applet must be able to start when it is loaded with a Web page. Likewise, it must respond intelligently when a user stops the Web page from loading, clicks the Back button to return to the page it is on, and so on.

The next section illustrates the process of adding Java applets to your Web pages in FrontPage. The simple Java applets that are used in the examples are freely available on the Internet, so you will not have to script any of your own applets as we explore the following two examples:

✦ The first example focuses on inserting an applet into a FrontPage Web page and configuring the applet.

✦ The second example goes a step further, demonstrating ways that you can control how an applet operates from a scripting language, such as JavaScript.

Inserting a Java applet

This section starts by inserting a simple but eye-catching applet, called Fireworks, into a Web page. As you might guess, this applet produces an animated display of fireworks on your screen. It is easy to use and provides a good sense of some of the animation capabilities that Java offers for a Web page.

Note   The three Fireworks classes: `firework.class`, `Rocket.class`, and `Bullet.class` can be downloaded at `http://www.wistrand.com/fireworks/`.

Before you can insert the applet into a Web page, you must import into your Web the required classes for this applet. Select File ➪ Import, locate the classes, and add them all to the same directory on your Web site.

To add the Fireworks applet to your Web page, open the page and place the mouse cursor at the spot where you want the applet to appear. Select Insert ➪ Web Components ➪ Advanced Controls, and select Java Applet, which opens the Java Applet Properties dialog box, shown in Figure 15-20.

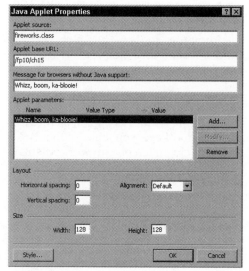

Figure 15-20: Inserting a Java applet with the Java Properties dialog box

This dialog box provides the following options:

✦ **Applet source:** The name of the applet class file (in this case, `firework.class`). (Note that the name is case-sensitive, so be sure to use lower case.)

✦ **Applet base URL:** The path name of the directory that contains the class files for this applet.

✦ **Message for browsers without Java support:** You can include an optional message that displays only when a user's browser isn't capable of displaying a Java applet. This message also displays if the user has turned off Java support in their browser. This message can include HTML tags.

✦ **Applet parameters:** An applet may have one or more parameters that you can configure. Use this dialog box to add, modify, and remove parameter names and values (this is examined in more detail in the next section, "Adding parameters to an applet").

✦ **Layout:** You can set the following attributes, which work for applets in the same way that they work for images:

- **Horizontal Spacing**: Dictates the amount of space between the applet and any page elements on either side of it.

- **Vertical Spacing**: Dictates the amount of space between the applet and any page elements above or below it.

- **Alignment**: Determines how the applet is oriented relative to other elements on the page.

✦ **Size:** Adjust the Width and Height attributes. It is easier to modify these visually by dragging the applet icon in Normal view.

✦ **Style:** Use this button to add style formatting to the java applet. This will be effectively limited to placing a border around the applet.

Adding parameters to an applet

If you set the applet source and base URL for the Fireworks applet, as previously indicated, and then attempt to preview it in FrontPage, you'll notice that the applet appears to load, but then not much happens. Not much of a fireworks display, is it? If you want a real display, you need to provide the Fireworks applet with some information about how to display the fireworks. You communicate this information to the applet via parameters.

How do you know which parameters the Java applet accepts? In contrast to what it knows about ActiveX controls, FrontPage has no idea what parameters are available for any specific Java applet. You must rely on documentation from the applet itself for this information.

The Fireworks applet accepts the following parameters:

✦ **Rockets:** The number of rockets (default = 3).

✦ **Points:** The number of points in each rocket (default = 3).

✦ **Pointsize:** The size in pixels of each point (default = 2).

✦ **Lifelength:** The duration of rockets in number of frames (default = 100).

✦ **Grav:** Affects how quickly the fireworks fall. The lower the number the less gravity (default = 10).

✦ **Delay:** Delay in milliseconds between frames (default = 50).

✦ **Trail:** The number of trailing points (default = 10).

✦ **Color:** The color of the applet background (RRGGBB).

To add parameters to the applet, double-click the big "J" Java applet icon in Normal view (see Figure 15-21) to open the Java Applet Properties dialog box.

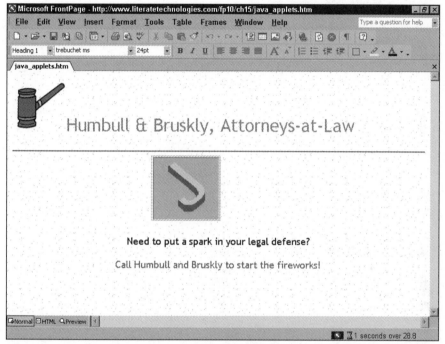

Figure 15-21: FrontPage Normal view represents your Java applet as a big "J" icon.

In the Applet Parameters section of the dialog box, click the Add button to open the Set Attribute Value dialog box, shown in Figure 15-22. Type the name of one of the fireworks parameters in the Name field, check the Specify Value checkbox, and add an appropriate value to the Data field. Click OK to return to the Java Applet Properties dialog box. You should see the parameter information added to the parameter list.

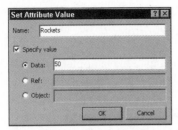

Figure 15-22: Set Attribute Value dialog box for adding parameters to your Java applet

To edit or remove a parameter from the list, first select the parameter from the list in the Java Applet Properties dialog box. To edit the parameter's name and/or value, click the Modify button. This opens the Set Attribute Value dialog box with the current parameter information. To remove a selected item from the list, click the Remove button. One example of a complete configuration is shown in Figure 15-23.

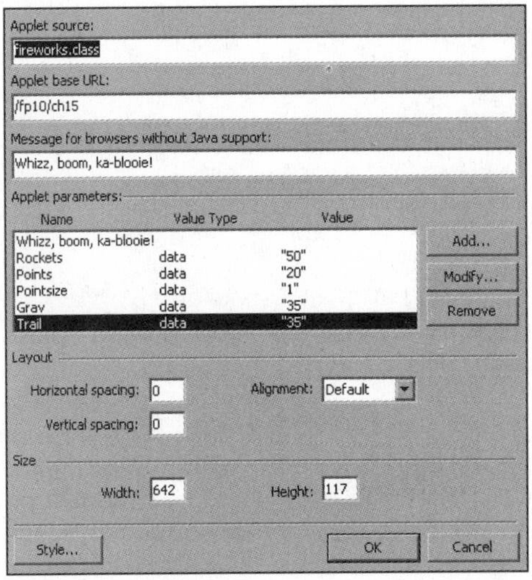

Figure 15-23: Sample configuration for the Fireworks applet

Java applets in HTML

You have learned the basics of adding a Java applet to your Web page. Now, look at what FrontPage has created for you behind the scenes. FrontPage adds a Java applet to an HTML page using the `<applet>` tag. The following is the HTML for the Fireworks applet:

```
<applet width="642" height="117" code="fireworks.class"
  codebase="/fp10/ch15">
    Whizz, boom, ka-blooie!
    <param name="Rockets" value="50">
    <param name="Points" value="20">
    <param name="Pointsize" value="1">
    <param name="Grav" value="35">
    <param name="Trail" value="35">
</applet>
```

Caution

Be advised that the official HTML 4.0 standard has deprecated the `<applet>` tag and recommends the use of the more general `<object>` tag instead. Interestingly, although FrontPage insists on using the `<applet>` tag for applets, you can manually change the `<applet>` tags to `<object>` tags and FrontPage will not object. It will, however, consider your object an ActiveX control and display the wrong icon in Normal view. However, you can still double-click on the object and edit its parameters in the ActiveX Properties dialog box!

The source filename for the applet is designated by using the `code` attribute. The directory path to the Java classes is contained in the `codebase` attribute. Each of the parameters that you used is contained in a separate `<param>` tag, with attributes for the name and value of the tag. The alternative text for non-Java-enabled browsers is indicated within the `<applet>` tag, as well.

Scripting a Java applet

The Fireworks applet is a splendid example of the visual effects that are possible in a Java applet (see Figure 15-24).

You might feel, however, that it is somewhat limited in its usefulness. The next example is more useful. It displays a scrolling message in the applet. It is a variation of a "ticker tape" applet, one of the most popular Java applets.

The name of this applet is TinyScroller. It is freely available from `http://www.javaboutique.com`.

Inserting the applet

The TinyScroller applet is designed to scroll a series of text messages vertically across the screen. It can scroll the message up (the default) or down. You can adjust the background color and foreground text color, as well as the font and spacing. This applet is only 4K in size, which means that it loads quickly.

Start by importing the `TinyScroller.class` file into your Web. Next, open the Web page where you want the applet to appear. Select Insert ➪ Web Components ➪ Advanced Controls, and select Java Applet to open the Java Applet Properties dialog box. Designate the Applet Source name as `TinyScroller.class` and the Applet Base URL as the path within your Web to the applet. You can add a text message to display for non-Java browsers. Adjust the size and alignment of your applet to suit your circumstances.

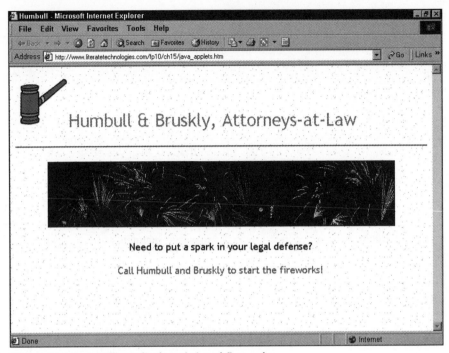

Figure 15-24: A brilliant display of virtual fireworks

The TinyScroller applet recognizes several parameters, but the only required parameters are the ones that indicate the lines of text to scroll. These are indicated with a series of LINE parameters, beginning with LINE1 up to as high as LINE100 You need to define only as many lines as you want, but you should use consecutive numbering, because the applet stops looking for lines after the first sequential number that is missing. For example, define the following lines:

```
LINE1 = "Welcome to our Web site!"
LINE2 = "We hope you like all the cool features"
LINE3 = "you will find here...."
LINE4 = ""
LINE5 = "Like this cool scrolling applet, for instance!"
```

Notice that in LINE2 and LINE3 the text is manually "wrapped," because the applet doesn't automatically wrap a long line of text. Alternatively, you can make the applet wider. Also note how LINE4 is used to include a blank line between lines of text.

Now, test your applet. The result, with formatting added, but minus the scrolling effect, is shown in Figure 15-25.

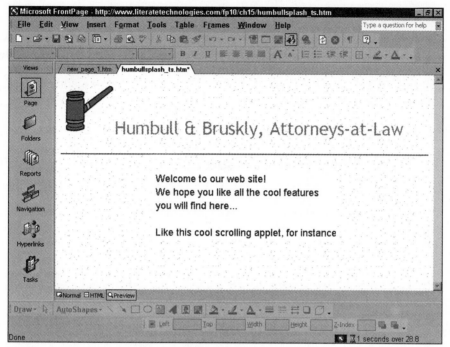

Figure 15-25: A shot of the TinyScroller applet in action

Additional parameters

In addition to the LINE parameter, the TinyScroller applet has numerous optional parameters, including:

✦ BGRED, BGGREEN, BGBLUE: Defines the background color (white is the default). Each parameter can have a value between 0 and 255.

✦ FGRED, FGGREEN, FGBLUE: Defines the foreground (text) color (black is the default). Each parameter can have a value between 0 and 255.

✦ FONTNAME, FONTSIZE: Defines the font typeface and size. If you use one of these, you must use both.

✦ SPACING: Defines the line spacing between lines (12 is the default).

✦ DELAY: Dictates the time delay between line movements (100 milliseconds is the default).

✦ XPOS: Controls the horizontal position of the lines in the applet (5 is the default).

✦ DIRECTION: To scroll up, choose 0 (the default); to scroll down, choose 1.

✦ BACKGROUND: Designate an image to display in the background, in either JPEG or GIF format.

Communicating with your applet

The ability to configure an applet by using `<param>` tags is very helpful, but what if you want the user to be able to interact with your applet? For example, a scrolling message window is very nice, but it would be nice to provide the user with a way to stop the applet if they have seen it enough times. Even better, wouldn't it be fun if the user could change the text displayed? This section examines how you can achieve these effects without becoming a Java programmer. All it takes is a recent version (4.0 or better) of either Netscape or Microsoft Internet Explorer.

Controlling your applet with scripting

Any browser that is capable of displaying a Java applet must have access to a Java Virtual Machine (JVM), the *run-time* engine that knows how to process Java on your user's computer. Browsers that are more recent have taken this one step further, enabling developers to control a Java applet from either JavaScript or VBScript. This requires only that the applet have methods or properties that are declared public (in other words, accessible from outside the applet itself).

Because all applets derive from a generic `applet` class that is defined by the Java base classes, you can guarantee that any applet will have a minimum set of methods that are public. The fine points of this are beyond the scope of this book, but what is important is that two of these public methods are the methods that start and stop an applet.

To add Start and Stop buttons to your TinyScroller applet, perform the following steps:

1. Open the TinyScroller example created in the previous section.

2. Add a name identifier to the `<applet>` tag. Because the Java Applet Properties dialog box does not include a Name field, you have two ways to add a name identifier:

   - Switch to the HTML tab and add a `name=YourAppletName` attribute to the `<applet>` tag by hand, substituting the actual name of your applet for `YourAppletName`.

   - Double-click the Java applet icon (J) in Normal view to open the Java Applet Properties dialog box. Click Style to open the Style dialog box for the Applet, and then type `YourAppletName` in the ID field.

3. Create the form buttons. Select Insert Form ⇨ Push Button to create a form element with a push button. (FrontPage also adds a Submit and Reset button by default. You should delete these.) Double-click the Push button to open its Properties dialog box. Change its name to `btnStart` and its value to Start. Be sure to keep the Normal option selected. Repeat the process for a second button, named `btnStop` with a value of Stop.

4. Script the Start and Stop buttons. To call any public method of the applet, you first identify the applet, using the object name that you created in Step 2, followed by the method name. For example, the call to the stop method of an applet, `YourAppletName`, would look like this:

```
document.YourAppletName.stop()
```

5. You can add this to the `onclick` event for each button. Switch to HTML view and add the following to the `<input>` tag for the Stop button (remember to substitute the actual name of your applet for `YourAppletName`):

```
onclick="document.YourAppletName.stop()"
```

6. Repeat for the Start button, using

```
onclick="document.YourAppletName.start()"
```

Your page should now resemble Figure 15-26 when displayed in the browser. Test the Stop and Start buttons.

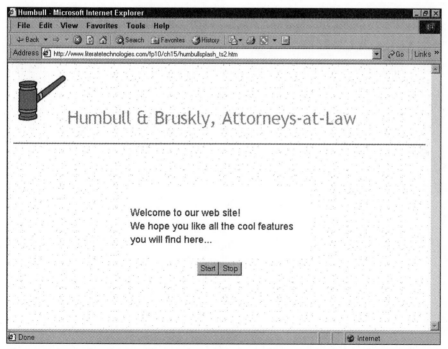

Figure 15-26: The TinyScroller applet with Start and Stop buttons added

Tip   If you use the applet tag's id in place of `YourAppletName` above, your code will work in Internet Explorer but not Netscape. Try giving the applet a `name` attribute that is the same as the `id`.

Java security

Java uses a different security method than Microsoft's ActiveX. Java is essentially paranoid. It assumes that any code is potentially vicious, and therefore limits the capabilities of certain kinds of activities. In Java lingo, the code is said to run in a *sandbox*, which is Java lingo for a self-contained field of operation. The applet code can "play" with all the "toys" in the sandbox but it cannot get out of the sandbox to get at your computer. This is a good idea since it doesn't rely on the user to make appropriate choices about which software to allow and which to deny (although you can still do this by using the facilities provided by your Web browser). However, the sandbox also limits (some would say unduly limits) an applet from doing things that can otherwise be productive. For example, a Java applet under normal circumstances cannot read files or write files.

As a result, Sun has made adjustments to the sandbox method to allow developers and systems administrators, working in a "trusted environment," to enable more functions within their Java code.

Summary

This chapter showed you how to work with plug-ins, ActiveX controls, and Java applets using FrontPage. We discussed the basic operations associated with each kind of control and provided examples to show how to insert this active content into your Web pages. You also learned how to control both ActiveX controls and Java applets with some basic scripting techniques. Reading this chapter, you should be able to make decisions about what kind of active content to include in your pages, how to get that content into the page correctly, and how to use controls effectively.

✦   ✦   ✦

Activating Web Pages

Designing Forms

I n this chapter, you learn to create forms in FrontPage and connect them to built-in FrontPage components that are available for processing and managing form input. After a brief overview of how HTML forms work, this chapter examines the built-in FrontPage form handlers, including the Database handler. You will learn how to customize confirmation pages, and how to use forms to collect information from visitors to your site. You will learn how to design forms, define input validation, collect form input, and display a result or confirmation page after the data is processed. This chapter also serves as the foundation for later chapters, which explain how to use programming elements that provide even more options for handling form input.

New Feature FrontPage 2002 includes several new form elements that are part of the HTML 4.0 specification: Labels, group boxes, advanced buttons, and picture elements. FrontPage 2002 also adds automated support for file uploads.

Discovering Interactive Forms

The Web pages that you learned how to build in earlier chapters have a limited ability to accept input from users. For example, including your e-mail address (and a link to it) in a Web page is a basic level of interactivity. A visitor can easily send you e-mail. However, e-mail links don't give you much control over the input that you receive.

Form elements open up a whole new level of interactive possibilities. Forms can be used as a way to collect information from users, request feedback, initiate a database query, or facilitate a discussion. All of this is possible without any programming by using built-in form handling components in FrontPage. You can build on these same form elements to create applications that enable users to access and share information, conduct business, play games, and perform a variety of complex tasks. All of these things are possible because forms provide various means for users to add their input via a Web page and get back information based on that input.

Creating HTML Forms

All Web page forms are composed of three parts:

✦ One or more form field elements that collect user input.

✦ A means of submitting the input for processing (typically a push button).

✦ A programming component for processing the results and responding to the input, typically by returning a confirmation Web page.

Standard HTML provides for a number of standard form field elements, which can be grouped together and submitted collectively to whatever programming component is processing the results. HTML also offers a variety of options for submitting results. FrontPage adds the ability to validate the information users provide before they submit it. Even more critically, FrontPage has several built-in methods of processing form results, including e-mailing the input to an e-mail address, storing the input in a text file or HTML page, or sending it to a database. FrontPage also makes it easy to create a custom response page. In the following sections, we examine how to use each of these options.

Note   In order to make use of FrontPage's form processing features, you will need to use a Web server that supports the FrontPage Server Extensions. See Chapter 23 for details.

A basic form

In general, the simplest form consists of an input field, a button to submit the results, and a results message. Let's start by looking at what it takes to create a simple form, from start to finish, in FrontPage. After you understand the basic process, everything else is just details.

Creating a form

To create a form in FrontPage, first create a new blank page by selecting Insert ⇨ Form, and then select a form element to add to your form. For our simple form, select a textbox, the most common form element. Notice that when you add a textbox form element to your blank page, FrontPage automatically adds a form element, represented by the dotted lines around the form field element and buttons. (Don't worry, those lines only show up in Normal view, not when you view the form in a browser.) The textbox form element is inserted, complete with Submit and Reset buttons.

Tip   If you would prefer that FrontPage stop second guessing you and only do what you tell it to do, select Tools ⇨ Page Options, and in the General tab uncheck the "Automatically enclose form fields within a form" option.

Let's add a second textbox just for good measure, and then add a regular HTML text label in front of each (not the Form element label, which we discuss later), so that our hypothetical user knows what to enter in each field. Label the first field **Name** and the second one **Email.** Thus far, your results should resemble Figure 16-1.

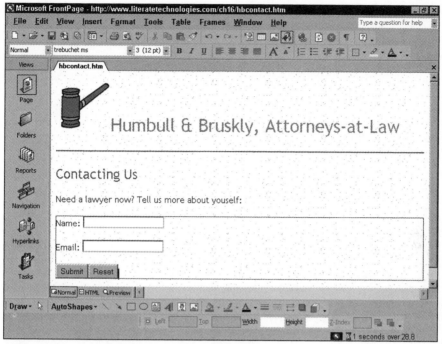

Figure 16-1: The beginning of a great HTML form

Next, let's do a little formatting of the textbox input fields. Notice that if you click on the field box to select it, you can drag the corners to make it longer or shorter but not taller. For that you will need the Text Area field, which is discussed in the later section, "The Standard Form Elements." If you double-click on the field box, it opens the Text Box Properties dialog box, as shown in Figure 16-2. Give each textbox a name that matches its caption.

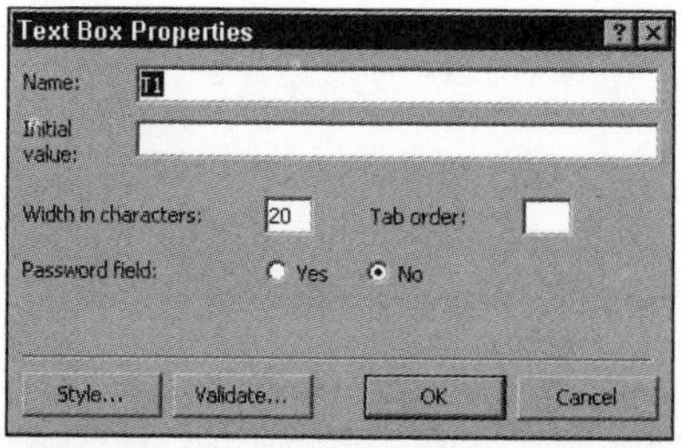

Figure 16-2: Double-clicking a text box element opens the Text Box Properties dialog box, where you can edit this element's properties.

Caution   Note that field names can only consist of a single word (no spaces). FrontPage 2002 will complain if you try to insert a space in the Name property of your form field.

Handling the submitted form

FrontPage has already taken care of adding a Submit button, so next you need to tell FrontPage what you want to happen when the form is submitted. To do this you must configure the form's properties. You can either right-click somewhere inside the dotted lines that define the form or, with the insertion point somewhere in the form, select Insert ➪ Form ➪ Form Properties. This opens the Form Properties dialog box, shown in Figure 16-3.

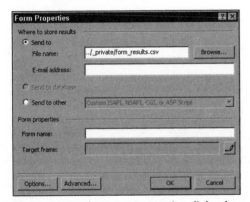

Figure 16-3: The Form Properties dialog box

Tip   By the way, keep your eye on the form's dotted lines. It is relatively easy to delete the form element inadvertently, and if you do, your form may not submit correctly.

The Form Properties dialog box is packed with features, which we will cover in detail in a moment. For now, simply note that our form is already set up to store information in a comma-separated text file (CSV).

Issuing a response

As it turns out, our form is also set up to return a default confirmation message. To see for yourself, click the Options button in the Form Properties dialog box, and then select the Confirmation Page tab from the Saving Results dialog box. This tab, shown in Figure 16-4, allows you to define your own custom confirmation page, but in the absence of one, it returns a default page. The default will serve just fine for now. Simply click OK to exit the Form Properties dialog box, and save your form.

Testing our form

That's all there is to it. Well, not quite. In order to see this form work, you need to publish it to a Web server running the FrontPage extensions. If you don't, you will get a stern warning message when you try to submit your form.

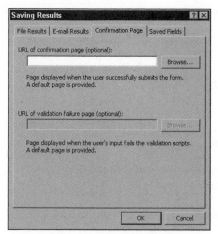

Figure 16-4: Use the Saving Results dialog box to configure form results and a confirmation page.

Once you have your form on a proper Web server, select File ➪ Preview in Browser, type a name and e-mail address into the appropriate forms, and hit the Submit button. You will see a plain-vanilla confirmation page, like the one in Figure 16.5. You can also locate the text file, which, if you accepted the default configuration, should be named `form_results.csv`, and should be located in the `_private` Web folder on your site.

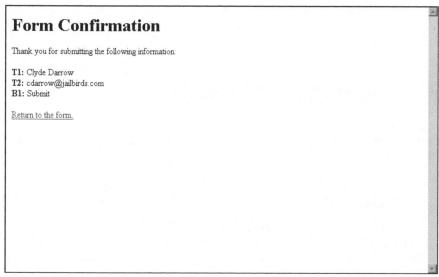

Figure 16-5: A reassuring confirmation that your input has been submitted successfully

You have just created your first form—not very exciting perhaps, but a definite start. In the next section, we explore some of the pre-built forms that come with FrontPage and which can make the task of creating a real form even easier.

Working with form templates

FrontPage includes several templates that contain pre-designed forms. If you are looking for a relatively standard form type, starting with one of these templates is likely to save you some time. A Form Wizard is also available, which is discussed in the section "Using the Form Page Wizard." The following are the form templates available in the Page Templates dialog box (unfortunately, they are somewhat randomly mixed in with various other kinds of templates):

✦ **Feedback form:** A simple form designed to solicit comments from users on a variety of company-related topics. It uses the Save Results component to send input to a text file.

✦ **Guest book:** A basic text-input form that enables site visitors to record a comment, much like the guest register of a small hotel or bed-and-breakfast inn. Although this form is a relatively simplistic way to encourage user involvement on your Web, a surprising number of people actually take the time to sign your guest book (especially if you let them read what they and others have written). The Guest Book form uses the Save Results component to send comments to an HTML page that can be viewed by visitors to your Web site.

✦ **Search page:** A simple one-field text-string search form used in conjunction with FrontPage's built-in text search engine.

✦ **User registration:** Enables users to enter a user name and password that allows them to access a designated access-controlled Web. This component is restricted to certain Web servers and must be saved in a root Web. Results are processed by the Web Registration component.

Working with Form Elements

In the next several sections we take a more detailed look at each of the form elements available on the Forms submenu (by selecting Insert ➪ Form) or on the Forms toolbar.

Tip

Form fields display differently on different browsers. To keep your form looking nice and neat, you should consider using a table to line up its parts. After you insert your first form field (and create the form container), insert a table within the dashed container box. You can now drag the form items into the appropriate cell in the table. (See Chapter 6 for more information about constructing tables.)

The options in the Form submenu can be detached and made to float on your FrontPage Page Editing window. To detach the Form menu (which then becomes a toolbar), select Insert ➪ Form and move your cursor to the gray stripe at the top of the submenu. The ScreenTip text, "Drag to make this menu float" appears, as shown in Figure 16-6.

Figure 16-6: You can detach the Forms menu and turn it into a toolbar.

Tip   Of course the ScreenTip appears as long as you have not disabled ScreenTips by unchecking the Show ScreenTips on toolbars checkbox located on the Options tab of the Customize dialog box (select Tools ➪ Customize and select the Options tab).

Click and drag this bar to move the menu onto your Page Editing window. The menu becomes a floating toolbar, whose tools are identified in Figure 16-7. Throughout the rest of this chapter, when you are asked to select a menu option from the Form submenu, you can alternatively click that tool in the floating Forms toolbar if you prefer.

When you are designing complex forms, you might find the floating toolbar a bit annoying. In that case, you can drag the toolbar's title bar and dock the toolbar on any side of the application window: at the top, on the left, the right, or on the bottom. What fun!

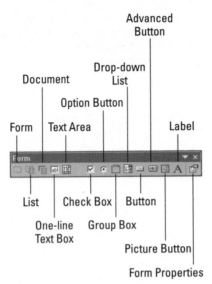

Figure 16-7: Options in the Form submenu are also available from the floating Forms toolbar.

The standard form elements

In this section, we examine the form elements and their properties that you will use most often. These are discussed in the order they appear on the Form submenu, except for the elements that are new to FrontPage 2002, which are discussed in their own section. We do this partly as a convenience for experienced FrontPage users and partly because these HTML 4.0 elements are specialized elements only supported by more recent browser versions.

Note

To keep things relatively simple, the following sections refer to the Form submenu commands. But, as you explore the different components of form fields, remember that you can insert form components from either the Form submenu or the Forms toolbar.

Textbox

The one-line textbox is the staple of most online forms. It is suitable for short input, such as is shown in the Contact form in Figure 16-8.

To create a one-line textbox, select Insert ➪ Form ➪ Textbox. To resize the input box, select it and drag either side handle of the box. A one-line textbox can't be resized vertically (in other words, it can be made wider or narrower, but not taller).

Textbox properties

To edit the textbox properties, double-click the input box, or right-click the box and select Form Field Properties. The Text Box Properties dialog box is displayed (refer to Figure 16-2).

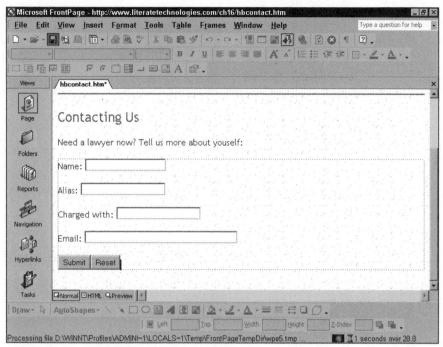

Figure 16-8: Collecting input through one-line text form fields

You can edit the following properties in the Text Box Properties dialog box:

✦ **Name:** The name of the form field. This name is used internally when the form is processed. By default, the name of a text field is "T" plus a number corresponding to the number of text fields that have been placed on the form. To keep track of your input, you should assign names to these fields that describe the field's data input. For example, a field that collects last names could be called "LName."

✦ **Initial value:** Default text that appears when the form is first opened or when it is reset. The initial value is empty, by default. Normally, text input fields should be blank.

✦ **Width in characters:** The horizontal length of the field. This value is adjusted automatically whenever you resize the form by using the mouse, as previously described. This number designates the physical size of the textbox. It does not limit the amount of text that can be entered in the box. For information on limiting text input, see the section "Validating Text Input," later in this chapter.

Caution

You may find that the text-input box size that you define in FrontPage does not exactly match the size of the box when viewed in a Web browser. The only way to see exactly how fields will look is to view your input form in a browser. It does not display exactly in FrontPage preview.

✦ **Tab order:** When filling out a form, your visitors can use the Tab key to switch between fields. By default, the order in which your users tab between fields is the order in which the fields appear on-screen. To change this order, enter a number in this textbox to indicate the elements order in the tab sequence (remember to give each field a different number, in sequential order).

✦ **Password field:** Generally, the text-input box echoes to the screen any characters that the user types into it. If the input box is created as a password field, by choosing the Yes option button for the password property, placeholder characters are echoed instead. This feature provides a modicum of security for user passwords. For example, if you are collecting input that a visitor would not want someone to read over their shoulder, password fields hide that input, as shown in Figure 16-9. Recognize, however, that this property only governs the screen display. It does not provide any encryption of the input when it is sent back to the server.

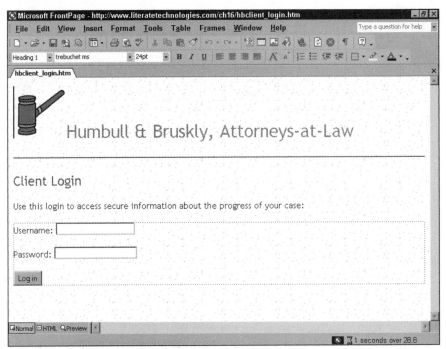

Figure 16-9: A password field conceals the content of input on the screen.

Formatting textbox input

You can define font attributes, paragraph formatting, and borders for text fields. These formatting features are available through the Style button in the Form Field Properties dialog boxes. Font attributes can be applied to any input form field that displays text.

Note   Formatting that is applied to input form fields is referred to as a style, and is a basic form of applying Cascading Style Sheets. For more discussion of higher levels of Cascading Style Sheets, see Chapter 11.

To add style attributes to a textbox, click the Style button in the Text Box Properties dialog box and then click the Modify Style button. In the Modify Style dialog box that appears, click the Format button, and select one of the options discussed next to format your input field.

Text area

A multiline, scrolling textbox, called a *text area* in HTML, is used for data input that is longer than a few words. Typically, a scrolling textbox is used when a paragraph of text is called for, such as comments or messages.

To create a scrolling textbox, select Insert ⇨ Form ⇨ Text Area, or click the corresponding icon on the Forms toolbar. You can resize a text area element both horizontally (make it wider or narrower) and vertically (make it taller or shorter) by dragging any of the eight corner or side handles that appear when the box is selected. Figure 16-10 shows a scrolling text area being enlarged in both height and width.

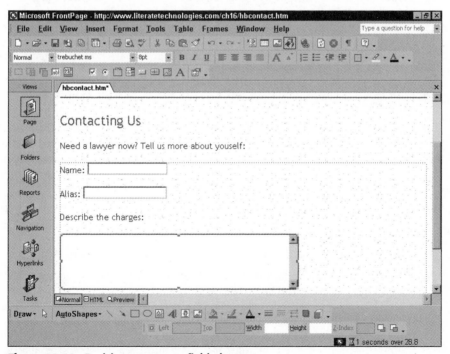

Figure 16-10: Resizing a text area field element

Text area properties

To edit the text area properties, either double-click the input box or right-click the box and select Form Field Properties to open the TextArea Box Properties dialog box, shown in Figure 16-11.

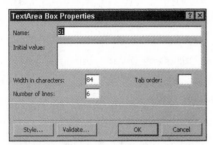

Figure 16-11: The TextArea Box Properties dialog box

You can edit the following properties in the TextArea Box Properties dialog box:

✦ **Name:** The name of the textarea is used internally when the form is processed. By default, the field name is "S" plus a number corresponding to the number of scrolling text fields that have been placed on the form. You probably want to change this name to a field name that helps you to keep track of the data that you are collecting. For example, if you are collecting feedback on a product, you might call the field "Feedback."

✦ **Initial value:** The default text that appears when the form is first opened or when it is reset. The Initial Value field is empty by default.

✦ **Width in characters:** The horizontal width of the field is adjusted automatically whenever you resize the form, as previously described. Note that this number designates the physical size of the textbox. It does not limit the amount of text that can be entered in the box. For information on limiting text input, see the "Validating Form Input" section later in this chapter.

✦ **Number of lines:** Designates the vertical height of the textbox. This value is adjusted automatically whenever you resize the form by using the mouse, as previously described. Note that this number designates the physical size of the textbox. It does not limit the amount of text that can be entered in the box.

✦ **Tab order:** Enter the position number that you want this field to have when your visitors use the Tab key to move through the form's fields.

Tip

Wrapping text refers to the ability of text to start a new line automatically any time that the text approaches the end of the textbox. In Internet Explorer, scrolling textboxes wrap by default. In Netscape Navigator, they do not. To enable text wrapping in all versions of Netscape, open the form page in Editor and select View ➪ HTML. Locate the `<text area>` tag that corresponds to the scrolling textbox. Add the attribute `<wrap>` inside the tag (`<text area wrap>`). See Chapter 8 for help on using the HTML view.

Checkbox

Checkboxes enable users to indicate a selection by clicking a small, typically square, box. Selecting a checkbox typically marks it with an "x" or a check mark. Checkboxes are used for simple yes/no input. Although checkboxes are often used for a group of options, they are nonexclusive, which means that checking one box does not restrict the user from checking another box in the same grouping. This is the chief difference between checkboxes and option buttons. Option buttons are exclusive, which means a user can select only one option button in a group.

To create a checkbox, select Insert ➪ Form ➪ Checkbox. To add some text next to the checkbox to describe what a visitor is selecting, simply type the text next to the checkbox. If you want to turn the text into a label element associated with the checkbox, select both the text and the checkbox, and then select Insert ➪ Form ➪ Label.

Checkbox properties

To edit the checkbox properties, either double-click the checkbox or right-click the box and select Form Field Properties. The Check Box Properties dialog box, shown in Figure 16-12, is displayed. You can edit the following properties:

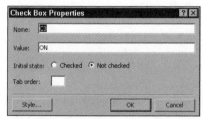

Figure 16-12: The Check Box Properties dialog box

✦ **Name:** The name of the checkbox, which is used internally when the form is processed. By default, the name is "C" plus a number corresponding to the number of checkboxes that have been placed on the form.

✦ **Value:** The value that is sent by the checkbox if it is checked. By default, the Value is ON. Typically, you'll want to create a more meaningful value, perhaps a value related to the label text, to aid you in interpreting the form's output.

✦ **Initial state:** Selecting the Checked option causes the checkbox to be checked already, by default, when the form is first accessed or when it is reset.

✦ **Tab order:** Enter the position number that you want this field to have when your visitors use the Tab key to move through the form's fields.

Often, when you are creating checkboxes, you are creating a list of items that your visitors can select from. For example, you might have a series of checkboxes that are each labeled with a different type of animal, asking your visitors what types of pets they have. To help keep your form reply more manageable, you will find that it is easier to provide all the checkboxes in this type of series with the same name, but with different values. In other words, name all the checkboxes "pet," and then assign each checkbox a different value, such as cat, dog, orangutan, and so on.

Attaching labels to checkboxes

Attached labels enable a visitor to select a checkbox (or option button) by clicking text associated with that checkbox. Checkboxes are small, and label text makes it easier to select a checkbox. You can assign label text to a checkbox by typing **text** next to the checkbox. Then, click and drag to select the text and the checkbox, and select Insert ➪ Form ➪ Label. Figure 16-13 shows a label being assigned to a checkbox.

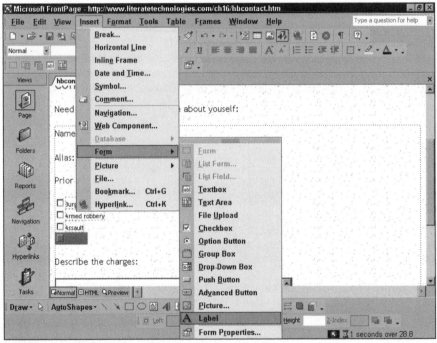

Figure 16-13: Assigning a label to a checkbox field

Labels are supported by versions of Internet Explorer 4.0 and above. However, visitors viewing your forms with browsers that don't support labels are still able to make selections by clicking directly on the associated checkbox or option button.

Option button

An option button, also known as a radio button (presumably because it functions like old car radio buttons — you push one in and the others pop out), refers to a hollow, round circle that contains a smaller, solid-black circle when selected. Option buttons are always used in an exclusive grouping, meaning that only one option in the group can be selected at a time. Selecting a new option automatically deselects any previous selection.

To create an option button, select Insert ➪ Form ➪ Option Button.

Although creating a single option button is possible, in practice, option buttons are usually grouped. Groups of option buttons are analogous to a multiple-choice question on a test. A visitor selects one, and only one, button in a group. By default, additional option buttons that you create are grouped with any button(s) that precedes them. To change groupings, use the Option Button Properties dialog box, as described in the next section.

Option button properties

To edit the option button properties, either double-click the option button or right-click the button and select Form Field Properties. The Option Button Properties dialog box, shown in Figure 16-14, is displayed. You can edit the following properties:

Figure 16-14: The Option Button Properties dialog box

✦ **Group name:** This name is shared by all option buttons in the same group. Users can select only one option from the group. By default, the group name is "R" plus a number corresponding to the number of option button groups that have been placed on the form. Every option button in a group must have the same group name. The common group name ensures that only one of the option buttons (within the group) can be selected.

> **Tip**
>
> Maintaining the exact same group name for each option button in a group is important. The easiest way to make sure that all option buttons have the same group name is to create a button, assign a group name, and then copy that button. Later, you can change the value for each button within the group. To create more than one group of option buttons, create the first option button of the second group, change its name to differentiate it from the first group, highlight it, press Ctrl+C, and then Ctrl+V to paste copies of it.

✦ **Value:** This is the value that is sent by the option button when it is checked. A option button value needs to be unique within its group, to distinguish responses. By default, the value is "V" plus a number corresponding to one more than the value of the preceding option button. FrontPage increments this number automatically each time you add a new option button.

✦ **Initial state:** Choosing the Selected option causes the option button to be selected by default when the form is first accessed or when it is reset. Note that only one option button in a group can be selected, by default. Choosing Selected for a given button automatically causes any previously selected button to lose its default selection.

✦ **Tab order:** Enter the position number that you want this field to have when your visitors use the Tab key to move through the form's fields. Option buttons tab as a group, so it is only necessary to set this once per group. When you tab into an group of option buttons, the tab stops on the currently selected button in the group. Within a group, you can use the arrow keys to move the selection.

Drop-down box

Drop-down boxes, also referred to as select lists, are similar to checkboxes or groups of option buttons in that they enable a visitor to make selections from a group of options. The difference is mainly in the appearance of the form field. Most often, drop-down menus enable a visitor to choose one option from a list. Figure 16-15 shows a drop-down menu with several options.

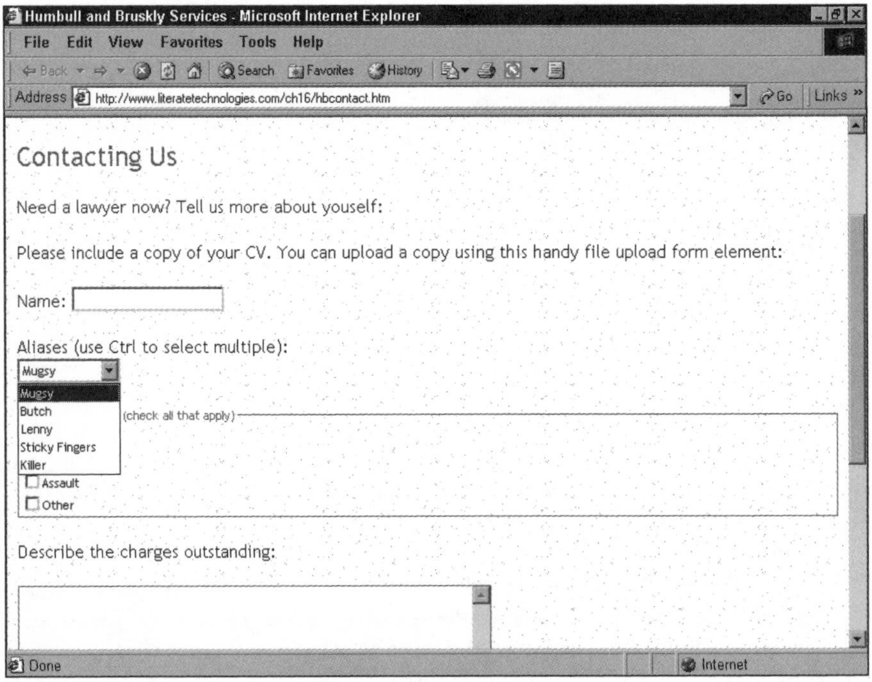

Figure 16-15: A sample drop-down menu

Drop-down menus can also be defined so that a visitor can select more than one option from the list. When you allow for more than one selection from a list, displaying multiple lines in a list is helpful, as shown in Figure 16-16.

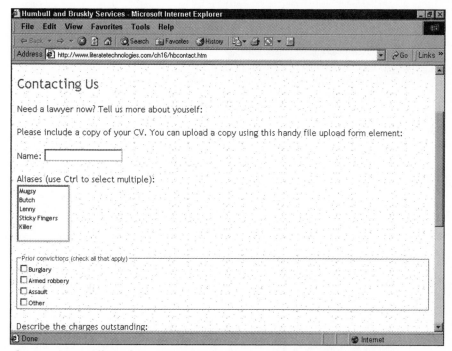

Figure 16-16: A drop-down menu configured to accept multiple selections

To create a drop-down menu list, select Insert ➪ Form ➪ Drop-Down Menu. This creates an empty drop-down menu, which is not very useful. To add items to the menu list, edit the drop-down menu properties, as described in the following section.

Drop-down box properties

To edit the drop-down box properties, either double-click the drop-down box or right-click and select Form Field Properties. The Drop-Down Box Properties dialog box, shown in Figure 16-17, is displayed. You can edit the following properties:

✦ **Name:** The name of the drop-down menu field, used internally when the form is processed. By default, the name of a drop-down menu is "D" plus a number corresponding to the number of drop-down menus that have been placed on the form.

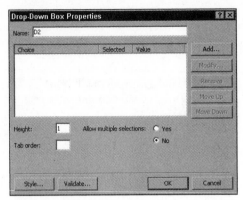

Figure 16-17: The Drop-Down Box Properties
dialog box

✦ **Choice:** The location in which you create the list of items that appears in the
drop-down menu. To add an item, select Add. This opens the Add Choice dialog box, as shown in Figure 16-18. Type the list item into the Choice input
field. Optionally, check the Specify Value field and type a value to be sent
when the form is submitted. If you do not specify a value, the form uses the
Choice text, so you only need to specify a value if you need the information
sent to be different from the Choice text. Select the Selected option button to
have this item selected by default.

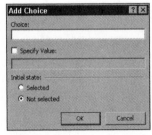

Figure 16-18: Use the Add
Choice dialog box to add
items to a drop-down menu.

After you add at least one choice item, use the Modify button to edit an item,
the Remove button to delete an item, or the Move Up and Move Down buttons
to change the order of items.

✦ **Height:** By default, the height of the drop-down menu is 1. You can edit this number to display more items in the list simultaneously. Using any number greater than 1 causes the menu list to change from a drop-down menu to a menu list. If the number of items in the list is greater than the height, the menu list will include a vertical scroll bar. If the number of items is less than or equal to the height, the menu list simply displays all items. In Normal view, Editor usually displays menu lists of more than one line with an extra line that isn't visible in a browser.

✦ **Allow multiple selections:** If this option is checked, users can select more than one choice by using a method appropriate to their browser and operating system. (On a Windows system, hold down the Shift key to select a range of items; hold down the Control key to select noncontiguous items.)

Specialized form elements

This section discusses some of the more specialized elements in the Forms menu (and one that isn't there, but should be).

File upload

Using a form to upload a file from the user to your Web server is often handy. It is also not a simple undertaking to create by hand but FrontPage has made it easy by combining the ability to add a specialized file upload form element with built-in processing that can deal with the file that is uploaded. In this section, we describe what it takes to add the file upload form element to your page. Processing uploaded files is discussed in Chapter 17.

Caution   If you are using tab orders in your form, note that the file upload component actually uses two tabs — one for the text input and one for the button, even though the File Upload Properties dialog box only allows you to specify one tab order.

Select Insert ➪ Form ➪ File Upload to add the file upload element to your page. The file upload element consists of a text field box and a Browse button (Figure 16-19). The user can type a filename directly into the text field, or click the Browse button to locate the file on their local computer.

Note   For those interested in such things, adding a file upload element to your form also causes FrontPage to change the form's encoding type from the default to "multipart/form-data" which is required in order to process an uploaded file. Of course, like the other form elements, you must configure your form to handle this upload before it actually does any useful work. See chapter 17 for details on the FrontPage form handling capabilities.

Microsoft FrontPage - http://www.literatetechnologies.com/ch16/hbcontact.htm

File Edit View Insert Format Tools Table Frames Window Help   Type a question for help

Normal ▾ | trebuchet ms ▾ | 8pt ▾ | B *I* U | ≡ ≡ ≡ ≡ | A ⁒ | ≔ ≔ ≔ ≔ | □ ▾ ✎ ▾ **A** ▾ ▾

hbcontact.htm

Contacting Us

Need a lawyer now? Tell us more about youself:

Please include a copy of your CV. You can upload a copy using this handy file upload form element:

Curriculum vitae: [   ]   Browse...

Name: [   ]

Aliases (use Ctrl to select multiple):
[Mugsy   ▾]

┌─ Prior convictions (check all that apply) ──────────────────
│ ☐ Burglary
│ ☐ Armed robbery
│ ☐ Assault
│ ☐ Other

Describe the charges outstanding:

Normal ⊟HTML ⌕Preview | ◦

Done   ⊠ ⌛2 seconds over 28.8

Figure 16-19: The file upload form element

Group box

The group box element, which corresponds to the HTML 4.0 `<fieldset>` tag, is a visual border you can use to organize form elements into labeled boxes. It has no functionality of its own. A group box is especially handy if you have a long form that would benefit from breaking the input elements into sections of related items.

To add a group box, select Insert ➪ Form ➪ Group Box from the menu to open the Group Box Properties dialog box (Figure 16-20). Click on the caption title to change it in Normal view. Alternately, if you have good aim, you can double-click on the border of the group box to bring up the Group Box Properties dialog box (you can also right-click anywhere in the element and select Group Box Properties from the option menu). From here, you can change both the label and the alignment of the group box, as well as its style formatting.

Group Box Properties   ? X

Label: [Prior convictions (check all that apply)]
Align: [Default   ▾]

[Style...]   [OK   ]   [Cancel]

Figure 16-20: The Group Box
Properties dialog box

Label

Typically, when you create an HTML form, you label fields using standard HTML text. The label element enables you link a label specifically to another form element. As we mentioned when describing option buttons, the label element may bring with it some additional functionality for your page. At the moment, though, it is only mildly useful, and is likely incompatible with all but the most recent browsers.

Because it is tied to another field element, the label element is created differently from other elements. To add a label element, first create another form field element. Then type the label you want to use. Select both the label and the form element and from the menu select Insert ⇨ Form ⇨ Label. You will notice that FrontPage puts gray dashed lines around the label, which you can see by referring back to Figure 16-19.

Hidden form fields

One additional form element is worth mentioning here, even though FrontPage has chosen not to treat it along with the other elements. This is the hidden field. A hidden field is a field element that gets submitted along with the rest of the form, but does not appear on the Web page that the user sees and cannot be changed (at least not directly) by the user. Hidden fields are used primarily as a way of passing parameters to the processing element.

To add a hidden field, right click your form and select Form Properties (or use the Insert ⇨ Form ⇨ Form Properties menu route if you prefer). Click the Advanced button (maybe Microsoft thought that hidden fields meant they had to hide their Properties as well?) to open the Advanced Form Properties dialog (a.k.a. Hidden fields) as shown in Figure 16-21.

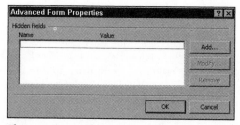

Figure 16-21: The Advanced Form Properties dialog

Note   In defense of FrontPage's handling of hidden fields, it is frequently useful to see the entire list of hidden fields at once. But why couldn't they just add hidden field form elements to the menu and toolbar that bring up this dialog box?

Use the Advanced Form Properties dialog box to add, modify, or remove hidden fields. To add a hidden field, click Add, and designate a name and value for the field in the Name/Value Pair dialog box (Figure 16-22). To modify an existing hidden field, click Modify and change the name and/or value. To remove a hidden field, click Remove. Pretty advanced, wouldn't you say?

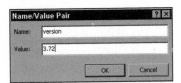

Figure 16-22: Creating a new hidden field

Push buttons

Using the form elements described above you can create just about any form you might need. But without some means of allowing the user to submit their information, all your form designing will be for naught. This section describes the various mechanisms at your command to provide the user that means.

Submit and reset buttons

The submit button is the mainstay of any form. It is a special purpose button, which automatically instructs the Web browser to send back the form input. All you have to do is add it to the page. If you created a form element by selecting Insert ➪ Form ➪ Form, you may already have both a submit and a reset button, since FrontPage adds them automatically.

You can change the name and the label of the submit button by double-clicking the button in Normal view, or by right-clicking on it and selecting Form Field Properties from the Option menu. This opens the Push Button Properties dialog box (Figure 16-23). You can give your button a new name (usually of little importance to a submit button — although it is possible to use multiple submit buttons and then script them to perform different actions depending on which one is clicked). More importantly, you can change the button's Value/label, which is the text that displays on the button itself. You can also change the Button Type in this dialog box. Your choices: Submit, Normal, and Reset. What difference that makes will become clearer after we discuss Reset and Normal buttons.

The reset button is another single-purpose button that performs its job without any need for direction from you. The reset button returns a form to the state it was in when the page first loaded. Note that this is not the same as clearing the form, which removes any information from the form. It is often the case that a form loads with default data in its fields. Resetting the form restores this default state.

Figure 16-23: The Push Button Properties dialog box

If you want to create a reset button, you can either rely on the default button that FrontPage provides when you create a new form, or select Insert ➪ Form ➪ Push Button to create a Normal button and then edit the button's "type" to change it to Reset. Note that you use the same procedure to create a submit button, and that neither of these button types is directly available from the menu list or toolbar.

Normal button

A normal button is a general purpose button without any predetermined function. You can change its name and the value associated with it, but unless you program it to do something, it will just sit on your Web page looking, well, normal. (See Chapter 18 for ideas on ways to use client-side scripting to give life to your normal buttons.)

Advanced button

From a nontechnical standpoint, an *advanced* button (Microsoft likes this word, don't they?) is just a normal button that you can resize and type the name directly into rather than having to pop up a properties box for the privilege. Some people might consider this more "basic" than "advanced" functionality, but those people have not been around the Web development world for very long. See Figure 16-24 for an example of the different buttons available.

To create a new Advanced Button, select Insert ➪ Form ➪ Advanced Button. Click on the button's label to change the button text . Drag the corners of the button to change its width or height. Or, if you prefer, double-click the button and edit these elements directly in the Advanced Button Properties dialog box (Figure 16-25). You can also change the button type here. As with the normal button, you must program the advanced button if you want it to do anything beside look advanced.

Note   For the technically inclined, the advanced button uses the HTML 4.0 designation, which places the button label between a `<button>` open and `</button>` close tag.

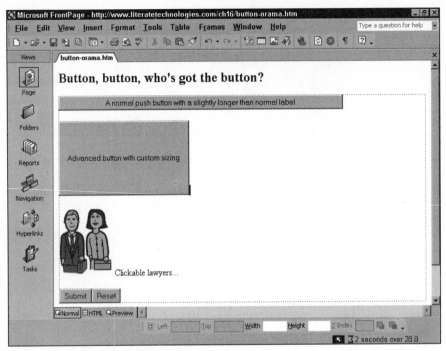

Figure 16-24: Buttons, buttons everywhere

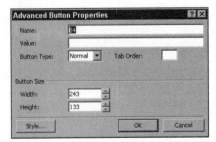

Figure 16-25: The Advanced Button Properties dialog box

Picture button

If you want total control over the look and feel of your button, you can create it using a picture (a.k.a. image) button. However, keep in mind that you will lose the automatic push button feel of the standard buttons. If you want to have the button change its appearance when users click on it, you will have to add programming to your picture button.

You can use any standard picture as buttons, although users are more likely to click on pictures that resemble buttons (unless you provide some instructions). To create a picture button, select Insert ⇨ Form ⇨ Picture, and select the image you want using the regular Picture dialog box. Recognize that although it appears that you are simply adding a picture to your page, you are in fact adding a button. Clicking on this picture causes the page to submit, much as it would if you had used a submit button.

One difference between the submit button and a picture button is that the picture button sends along the pixel coordinates of the spot on the picture where the user clicked. These are returned as `button_name.x` and `button_name.y` where `button_name` is the actual name of your button. Unfortunately, unless you are creating custom forms, this extra information may be of little use to you, although you can use this facility to create a variation on an "image map." Image maps are discussed in Chapter 12.

To edit the picture's properties, use the normal means of opening its Properties dialog box. In addition to the standard picture properties, you can also edit the input field name of this picture button.

Designing Forms

Well-designed input forms collect valuable information. The following approaches can be integrated into designing forms:

✦ **Ask for specific information.** If you want to find out what product a visitor has purchased, providing a list of option buttons or a drop-down menu might yield more accurate information than a one-line textbox.

✦ **Explain to visitors why providing form information is in their interest.** For example, explain to visitors who fill out a survey how their input will be used. Or, explain to visitors filling out an order form why it is important to collect all the information in the form.

✦ **Keep forms as short as possible, but collect all the information that you need.**

✦ **Testing your own form is a good idea.** After you create it, save your Web page and view it in a browser. Better yet, view it in several different browsers. Put yourself in the place of a visitor. Are your questions clear? Is your form design easy to follow? Is the tab order correct? Does it have repetitious questions that can be avoided? In general, test, test, and test again to create a form that invites a visitor to fill it out.

If you are perplexed by the fact that form elements look different in different browsers and on different computer platforms, you may be pleased to learn that you can use styles to dictate the appearance of form elements. However, before you get too excited by this prospect, keep in mind that styles are not consistently supported even by the most recent browsers. If you are determined to apply styles to form elements, we advise that you test the results on as many browsers, versions, and computers as possible.

Caution   Be especially wary of trying to position form elements using the Position style option. Even browsers that support positioning have trouble dealing with form elements in layers.

The other difficulty with form elements and styles is that FrontPage will happily let you apply style attributes that have absolutely no effect on that element. For example, you can apply font styles to a checkbox, or paragraph styles to a drop-down box, without producing any change in the appearance of these elements. In general, common sense — combined with a healthy dose of testing — should be your guide in selecting styles. The following list indicates which formatting options are appropriate for each element. (Note that this list does not guarantee that the style changes will actually display the way you intend. For more details on creating and applying styles, see Chapter 11.)

- ✦ **Fonts:** This option can be used in most of the elements that display text, including text fields and buttons.

- ✦ **Paragraphs:** Not particularly useful for most form elements. You can use it to align elements in your form, but not within the elements themselves.

- ✦ **Borders and shading:** This option can be used to create "boxes" around most form elements. For input boxes and buttons, this typically replaces the standard beveled box look with your style. You can also use this option with drop-down menus to create more pleasing styles than the standard, industrial-age form element look.

- ✦ **Bullets and numbering:** Like paragraphs, this option is not particularly useful when applied to form elements, but can be used to help organize elements in your form.

- ✦ **Positioning:** Use this option with extreme caution, since many browsers have trouble rendering form elements properly in a positioned layer.

Validating Form Input

So, now that you have created a beautiful form, complete with an appropriate method to enable the user to submit the information back to your Web server. Let's pause and think about what you are about to do here. The ability to collect input from your user and store the results is a very powerful tool. For better or worse, though, the quality of the information you collect is only as good as the user makes it. How do you ensure that the user does not inadvertently (or maliciously) enter invalid, even potentially harmful, input into your form elements? And how do you ensure that the user has the best possible experience? (We all know how much we love filling out forms, Web-based or otherwise.)

One way to improve your form is to add validation to the form elements to catch any blatantly erroneous input. This section describes you how you can easily add sophisticated form input validation to your FrontPage forms.

Validation: Client-side versus server-side

Validating form input means inspecting the input to see that it meets certain criteria. If it passes the inspection, we collect the data. If not, we tell the user that they need to make some changes before the information is acceptable.

There are two general ways you can perform validation. The first is to inspect the data once it has been received by the server. In this case, if there is a problem, the server has to return a message to the user telling them to try again. The downside to this approach, as you probably can tell, is that it is time consuming to send the information to the server and back, not to mention the fact that because the user has already submitted the form, they now have to "go back" to it and try again if there is a problem. Sometimes this is unavoidable, for instance when data has to be validated against some preexisting data, as in the case of a username and password stored in a database. But for most general purposes, the preference is to validate data on the client-side before the user submits their form (or, to be more precise, before the browser sends the data back to the server).

In client-side form validation, you insert a checking mechanism between the time that the user clicks the submit button (or whatever kind of button you have designed) and the time that the browser sends the data back to the server. If you can catch errors here, then you can prompt the user about the problem before the page is gone. Client-side form validation is normally done using JavaScript. FrontPage has taken the pain (or at least the programming) out of this process by generating the validation programming automatically based on the validation options you set. We'll now look at those options and just how much you can do.

Text field validation

The discussion of validation is divided into two sections. The first, and more involved, looks at ways you can validate text input. The second describes how you can validate selection input (option buttons and select menus).

To access any form element's validation dialog box, first use one of the many methods to open the element's Properties dialog box. Then click the Validate button on the Properties dialog box.

Tip   Any time that you specify validation options, and especially if the restrictions are not obvious ones, be sure to alert your user to the presence of those options on the form itself. A good example is any fields that you designate as "required." Failing to alert users is likely to reduce the number of people who complete the form, and probably will result in some curt messages from users who do not appreciate surprises.

The Text Box Validation dialog box is shown in Figure 16-26. This dialog box is the same for both textbox input and text area input. It includes several options for specifying what input is accepted by the form. By default, the form field's accepted Data Type option is set to No Constraints, meaning that any input is accepted, including no input. The data type constraints that you can place on fields in a form are explained next.

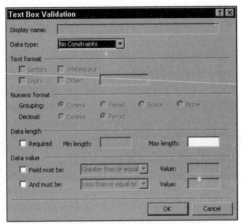

Figure 16-26: Text input validation options

The Text Box Validation dialog box is actually not as complex as it looks. Basically, for any text input, you can restrict the input to a particular kind of data (text, numerical values, or just integers, i.e., whole number values). Based on which kind of data you pick, you may also have some additional formatting options. No matter what data type you select, you can specify values for the maximum and minimum length of the text input as well as the actual input values. Here is a rundown of the available options in the Text Box Validation dialog box:

Display name

If you select one of the available constraints Constraint in the Data Type pull-down menu, you can also designate a display name for the field, in the Display Name textbox at the top of the Text Box Validation dialog box. This name is used to identify the field to users, in the event that they haven't entered valid data in the form field. By default, any error message uses the name of the field that is specified in the form field properties. Use the Display Name field if you are using shorthand field names (such as T1) and want to include a more recognizable name in any error messages. For example, if you have a field named "Code" in which you are collecting area codes, you can identify the nature of the input, so that visitors are told that they need to enter an area code to complete the form. Note that this field remains unavailable until you have selected some validation constraints.

Data type constraints

Selecting a data type constraint activates additional validation options. The following are the options available for each of the data types :

✦ **Text:** If you choose to limit data input to text, the additional validation options in the Text Format area of the dialog box are activated. You can restrict the text that a field accepts to Letters, Digits, Whitespace (space, tab, carriage return, and line feed), and/or Other. To include one or more of these formats, check the box next to its name. If you select Other, you must also type the other characters that you want to permit, such as a comma, hyphen, dollar sign, or an at-sign (@).

✦ **Integer:** If you choose to limit input to integers (in other words, whole numbers) the data types that are accepted by a form field, the Grouping option buttons are activated in the Numeric Format area of the dialog box. You can designate how the digits of the number should be grouped. The options are Comma (1,234,567), Decimal (1.234.567), or None (1234567).

✦ **Number:** If you choose to limit input to numbers the data types that are accepted by a form field, the Decimal option buttons are activated in the Numeric Format area of the dialog box. You can designate the decimal character by selecting either the Comma or Period option button. Note that the Grouping character and the Decimal character cannot be set to the same character.

✦ **Data length:** Selecting Required means that the minimum length must be at least 1. This is why the Minimum option remains unavailable until you check the Required checkbox. You can also set a Maximum number of characters. This is good protection for your form, and if you do nothing else, you would be wise to use this validation option.

✦ **Data value:** Now we get to the fun part! Here you can set up to two rules to define acceptable values in your form element. First, select a condition: Less than, Greater than, Less than or equal to, Greater than or equal to, Equal to, Not Equal to. Then indicate the value to compare against.

Data length

Even if you don't want to limit the data type, you can still restrict the data length and values. In the Data Length area of the Text Box Validation dialog box, you can stipulate that input in the field is required. Required means that the minimum length must be at least 1. This is why the Minimum option remains unavailable until you check the Required checkbox. You can also set a Maximum number of characters.

Tip   You should always designate a maximum length in any text field. This prevents potential misuse of the form, either inadvertent or intentional. Give users a reasonable length limit, but no more than is necessary.

Data value

The Data Value section of the Text Box Validation dialog box enables you to restrict input to a range of acceptable values. Here you can set up to two rules to define acceptable values in your form element. First, select a condition: Less than, Greater than, Less than or equal to, Greater than or equal to, Equal to, Not Equal to. Then indicate the value to compare against. Keep in mind that the conditions mean different things depending on the format of the data you specify:

✦ If you restrict the data type to integers or numbers, FrontPage checks results numerically (e.g. 45<145 and 12=12).

✦ If you limit the data type to text or don't set any constraints, input is compared by using text character order ("a" < "b" and "145" < "45").

Selection field validation

Although the text input elements have by far the most validation options, it is also possible to validate input for the other elements, as we describe in this section.

Option buttons

You can use option button validation to require that users select one of the options from a option button grouping. To access an option button's validation dialog box, use the Validate button on the Properties dialog box.

Tip   Option buttons are frequently designed so that a selection is required. After a button has been selected, it is difficult to deselect all buttons. If one of the options for a set of option buttons is None, you should include this as an explicit choice and make it the default.

The Option Button Validation dialog box is shown in Figure 16-27. Select the Data Required checkbox to require that users select one of the option buttons in a grouping. Note that checking this option for one of the buttons in a group activates the validation for all buttons in the group. In addition, you can designate a display name to be used if it is necessary to prompt the user to select an option.

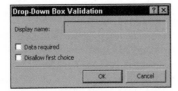

Figure 16-27: Option Button validation options

Drop-down menus

You access a drop-down menu's Validation dialog box via the Validate button on the Properties dialog box.

The drop-down menu has two different validation menus, depending on whether the menu has been configured to accept one or multiple selections. The validation option for menus that allow only single selections is shown in Figure 16-28.

Figure 16-28: Validation options for drop-down menus when only one choice is allowed

Check the Data Required checkbox to require users to select an option from the menu. Select Disallow First Item if you want to place a direction, such as Select an Item, as the first item in the list and don't want this to be included as a valid selection. If you have made the menu required, you can optionally designate a name to be used to identify the menu field to the user if they fail to make a valid selection.

The Validation dialog box for menus that allow multiple selections has an additional option, as shown in Figure 16-29. In this case, you can stipulate a minimum and maximum number of allowable choices, using the Minimum Items and Maximum Items fields.

Figure 16-29: Validation options for drop-down menus when multiple selections are allowed

Why no checkbox validation?

No mechanism exists for validating a checkbox. Why not? Well, mainly because a checkbox doesn't have much to validate. Users either select the checkbox or they don't. Of course, there are some occasions where you want to insist that the user check a certain box (think about all those Terms of Use agreements out there with their Agree/Don't Agree boxes).

How Does FrontPage Validation Work?

FrontPage uses your validation configuration options to generate a series of JavaScript functions that are created when the user requests the page on a Web server enabled with FrontPage Server Extensions. When the user submits the form, these JavaScript routines validate the input based on the options you selected. If it encounters a problem, it prompts the user. (In the case of more than one problem, it only prompts the user regarding the first issue encountered.)

And what happens if the user has their JavaScript turned off? In this case, FrontPage will fall back to checking validation on the server side, assuming that you are working on a server with the FrontPage Server Extensions installed.

By the way, with a little bit of work, you can get your JavaScript validation functions to work, even if you are not using a FrontPage enabled server. How, you ask? Preview the page in question locally, so that FrontPage generates the script. View the source of the generated Web page, and copy the JavaScript back into your page. You will also have to replace the FrontPage component calls with standard JavaScript. If that last sentence makes sense to you, then you are probably qualified to try this. Otherwise, I suggest you not try this at home. Of course, you will no longer be able to edit the validation options.

If you want to ensure that users check a particular box on a form before they proceed, then you need to add some simple scripting to the checkbox. (Scripting languages are discussed in Chapter 18.) Alternatively, you can use option buttons for this purpose and validate them as described above.

Using the Form Page Wizard

In addition to the form templates described earlier in this chapter, FrontPage also includes a Form Page Wizard that can help you to construct a sophisticated form quickly. (Although to be honest, we think it is faster just to build the form using the Forms Toolbar.)

To create a form by using the Form Page Wizard, select File ➪ New and choose the Form Page Wizard from the Page Template dialog box. You are greeted with the first screen of the Wizard, as shown in Figure 16-30. Click Next to continue.

The form questions

In the next dialog box, you select the questions you plan to include in your form. Click Add to add a new question. Select the type of input to include from the drop-down list, shown in Figure 16-31, and customize the prompt question to your liking.

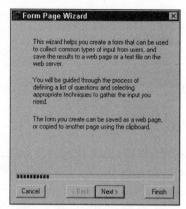

Figure 16-30: The opening screen of the Form Page Wizard, which you can use to generate a custom form quickly

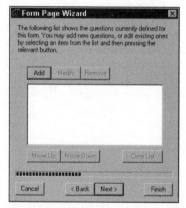

Figure 16-31: Using the Form Wizard, you can create a form with a variety of question types.

The following are the many questions to choose from:

✦ **Contact information:** Builds form fields to capture name, affiliation, address, and phone number.

✦ **Account information:** Prompts for username and password.

✦ **Product information:** Asks for a product name, model, version, and serial number.

✦ **Ordering information:** Produces a form to take a sales order, including a list of products to order, billing details, and shipping information.

✦ **Personal information:** A form that collects information such as username, age, and other personal characteristics.

✦ **One of several options:** A form item that requires users to pick exactly one option.

✦ **Any of several options:** A form item that enables users to pick zero or more options.

✦ **Boolean:** Prompts to input a yes/no or true/false question.

✦ **Date:** Prompts to input a date format.

✦ **Time:** Prompts to input a time format.

✦ **Range:** Creates a rating scale from 1 to 5.

✦ **Number:** Creates an input box for a number.

✦ **String:** Creates a one-line textbox.

✦ **Paragraph:** Creates a scrolling textbox.

Input options

After you select question input type for your form, click the Next button in the dialog box. You are prompted for details about the specific form data that you want to include in this form. For example, if you ask for contact information, you can use the checkboxes in the dialog box shown in Figure 16-32 to define exactly what contact information you want to collect.

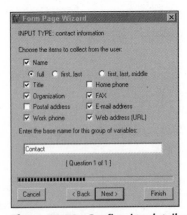

Figure 16-32: Configuring detailed options for each question input type in your form

After you define one question for your form, click the Next button to return to the dialog box that lists the questions that you've created. Use the Add button to place additional questions in your form.

After you create a list of questions to ask in your form, you can click any of those questions and use the Move Up or Move Down buttons to move a selected question up or down on the page. You can Modify a question, Remove it, or Clear out the whole lot and start again. After you complete your list of questions, click the Next button to move to the Presentation Options dialog box in the Wizard.

Presentation options

The Presentation Options dialog box, shown in Figure 16-33, enables you to define the look of your form page.

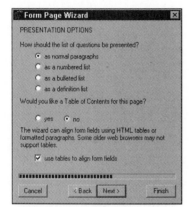

Figure 16-33: Defining page layout in the Form Page Wizard

The group of four option buttons at the top of the Presentation Options dialog box enables you to lay out your questions as normal paragraphs, as a numbered list, as a bulleted list, or as a definition list. (Numbered lists, bulleted lists, and definitions lists are discussed in Chapter 5.) Select one of these options for organizing your form questions.

The yes and no option buttons under "Would you like a Table of Contents for this page" enable you to place a table of contents on your form page. The table of contents generates links within the page to each question, so that a visitor can jump directly to a selected question. For a simple form, a table of contents usually isn't necessary. For input forms with lots of questions, a table of contents can be helpful. Click the "Use Tables to Align Form Fields" checkbox to let FrontPage organize your questions in table cells, for a more orderly layout. (Using tables for page design is covered in Chapter 6.)

After you define your presentation options, click the Next button to select output options for your form.

Output options

In the Output Options dialog box (Figure 16-34), you determine what happens to the data submitted in a form. Select the "Save results to Web page" option button to send the input to a page that can be viewed in your browser. Or, select the "Save results to a text file" option button to send the results to a file that can be opened with a word processor. CGI scripts require customer programming, a topic we tackle in Chapter 19.

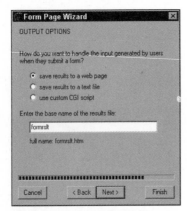

Figure 16-34: Configuring your form's output options in the Form Wizard

After you select an output option, click the Finish button to generate a Web page with your form.

Tutorial 16-1: Designing a form

In the following tutorial, you will create a feedback form that uses the five basic types of form fields.

1. Click the New Page tool (top-left button in the Standard toolbar) to create a new Web page.

2. Click the Save button, type feedback.htm in the filename field, and then click OK in the dialog box.

3. At the top of the page, type a title for the page: **Your comments on this Web site are appreciated!** Press Enter to create a new line.

4. Select Insert ⇨ Form ⇨ Form to create a form. Press Enter to create a line above the Submit and Reset buttons, as shown in Figure 16-35.

Figure 16-35: Start your feedback form with Submit and Reset buttons.

5. In the new blank line in your form, type **Please rate this site**, and press Enter to create a new line. Insert an option button by select Insert ➪ Form ➪ Options button.

6. Double-click the option button to open the Option Button dialog box, and enter **Rating** in the Group Name field. Enter **1** in the Value field, and make sure the Selected option is checked. You can leave the Tab Order field blank to use the default tab order, for visitors who use the Tab key to move between fields. The Option Button Properties dialog box is shown in Figure 16-36. Click OK to return to your form.

Figure 16-36: Configuring an option button

7. Back in the form, type a space after the option button and then type the label **Excellent**. To make this text a form element label and connect it to your option button, first select both the button and the text and then select Insert ➪ Form ➪ Label from the menu item. FrontPage draws a light gray box around the text to indicate that it is now a label.

8. After you define the first option button, you can use the Copy and Paste tools in the toolbar to paste copies of the option button and label to subsequent rows. Change the label text to something appropriate. Then open each button's Properties dialog box and check the group name (FrontPage should keep this the same) and rating number (FrontPage tries to increment this automatically). Compare your results with Figure 16-37.

Figure 16-37: A complete set of option buttons

You will notice when you start copying the option button, that FrontPage makes the most recent button in the group the selected option. If you want the first button selected, wait until you are done and then reset it in its Properties dialog. Note that FrontPage updates other option buttons in the group when you do this.

9. To create a group box for these option buttons, locate your cursor just above or below the existing group of buttons and select Insert ⇨ Form ⇨ Group Box. Insert the question, "How would you rate this site?" as the caption for the group box. Cut and paste (or drag and drop) the option buttons into the Group box.

10. To create a question with a Drop Down Box list, place your insertion point after the set of option buttons, press Enter to start a new question, and then type **How often do you visit this site?** (Alternately, use another group box to do this.) Select Insert ⇨ Form ⇨ Drop-Down Menu from the menu bar, and double-click the empty drop-down menu.

11. Type **Visits** in the Name field of the Drop-Down Menu Properties dialog box, and click the Add button. Enter an appropriate value in the Choice field, check the selected option, and press Enter. Add additional options as needed. Leave the other properties at their default settings. Your dialog box should look similar to the one in Figure 16-38. Click the OK button.

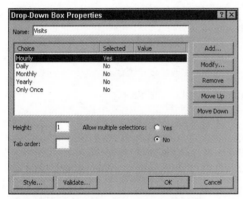

Figure 16-38: Adding options to your drop-down list

12. Click to place your insertion point at the end of the drop-down menu and then press Enter to start a new question. Type **Any Advice?** and add a line break. Select Insert ⇨ Form ⇨ Text area. Double-click the textbox, change the Name to **Advice**, and press Enter. Click the right-top corner handle to stretch the box to the width of your page, so that the text area looks similar to the one in Figure 16-39.

13. Place your insertion point at the end of the scrolling textbox and press Enter to start a new question. Select Insert ⇨ Form ⇨ Check Box. Press the spacebar and type **Please contact me**. Double-click the checkbox and change the Name to **Contact** and the Value to **Yes**. Select the checked option button and then click OK in the dialog box.

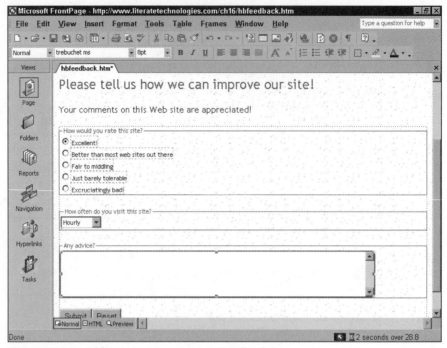

Figure 16-39: Adding a text area to your feedback form

14. Click and drag to select both the checkbox and the checkbox text, and then select Insert ➪ Form ➪ Label. Click after the label and press Enter.

15. Type **My Email Address** and select Insert ➪ Form ➪ Textbox. Double-click the One-line textbox and change the Name to **Email**. Click the Validate button and click the Required checkbox. In the Min Length field, enter **6**, because any legitimate e-mail address will be at least that long (a@b.xy). Set the Max length to 100, which should be ample. Click the OK button in the Text Box Validation dialog box, and then again in the Text Box Properties dialog box.

16. Save your page, and Preview in your browser by selecting File ➪ Preview in browser or by using the Preview button in the toolbar.

Your input form should resemble the form shown in Figure 16-40. Of course, if you customized the form or experimented with other options, that's fine! Try applying some text formatting or other embellishments. Have fun designing your form! In the next chapter, we'll explore how to publish forms, so that you can collect and store the data your users send you.

17. You can experiment with entering data into your form in your browser, and using the Reset button to clear the form. In the next chapter, you'll learn to implement forms, so that you can actually collect form input.

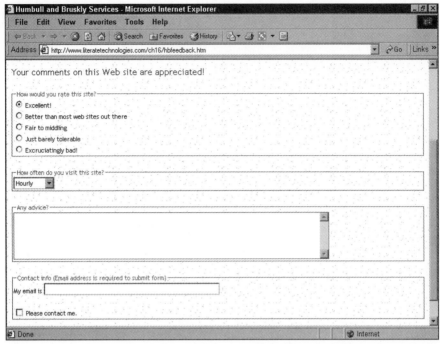

Figure 16-40: Our finished feedback form (or at least the most important parts)

Summary

In this chapter, you learned how to design interactive HTML forms that enable you to collect input and data from users. We have described all of the major form elements. You have learned out to use FrontPage to add custom input validation to your form elements, and you have seen how you can use the FrontPage form Wizard to speed the creation of a new form. Now it is time to learn how to use FrontPage to configure form submission.

In the next chapter, you'll learn a variety of ways that you can collect and store the data that is submitted via your HTML forms. FrontPage makes it easy to send form data to a Web page, a text file, to e-mail, and even to a database, all without programming. However, in case, you want to do some programming, Chapter 17 also introduces some custom scripting techniques you can use for managing input data.

✦   ✦   ✦

Activating Forms

I n Chapter 16, you learned to create and design forms in FrontPage. In this chapter, you learn how to connect your form to built-in FrontPage components that are available for processing and managing form input. This chapter examines the built-in FrontPage form handlers that enable you to save form results to a text file or send them to a designated e-mail recipient, and use the results to create an HTML page or store the results in a database. You will also examine the newly added file upload support as well as the capability to create a customized confirmation page for your users.

Working with Form Properties

You previously learned how to create and configure the input fields in your form. You also learned various ways to enable users to submit their input results. Now the question is, what do you do with this input and how to you do it? FrontPage makes it very easy to answer these questions without requiring a degree in computer science. This chapter explores in detail the built-in FrontPage options for dealing with form results.

Note   If you are interested in learning various ways to create custom form handlers, see Chapter 18 on client-side scripting, Chapter 19 on server-side programming, and Chapters 20 and 21 on working with databases.

You configure your form to handle input results by using the Form Properties dialog box. To access this dialog box, you first need a form. The Feedback Form template that comes with FrontPage is used in this section to illustrate how the Form Properties dialog box works. This form is a good example of a basic HTML form, partly because it includes an example of almost every possible HTML form element. The Feedback Form template shown in Figure 17-1 is used as-is, except for the addition of a theme and background to improve its visual appeal.

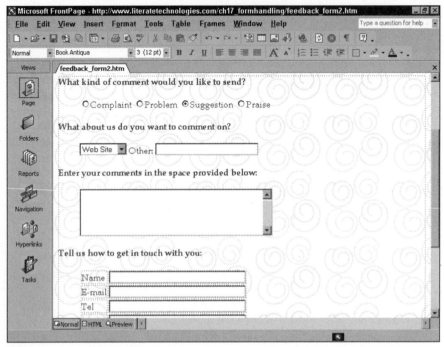

Figure 17-1: A basic feedback form awaiting configuration to handle user input

Note

For those interested in technical details, the Form Properties dialog box works by setting the action attribute of the <form> tag element. If you select the Send to Other option, FrontPage assumes that you are providing the programming to handle the form submission. In this case, FrontPage does not add any FrontPage-specific information. All other predefined handlers are controlled by a FrontPage Web component.

To configure your form's properties, open the form in FrontPage, right-click anywhere inside the form (as indicated in Normal view by the dashed lines around form field elements) and select the Form Properties item from the options menu, which displays the Form Properties dialog box (see Figure 17-2). Alternatively, you can select Insert ➪ Form ➪ Form Properties. Note that this option is only available when the insertion point is inside a form.

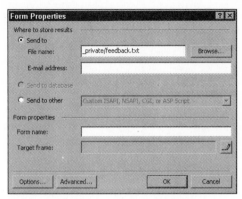

Figure 17-2: The default settings for the feedback form's Form Properties dialog box

The Form Properties dialog box consists of two principal parts: a section to designate where to send the form results and a section to designate basic form properties. The Where to Store Results area of the dialog box includes the following:

✦ **Send To:** Click this button to send form results to either (or both) of the following:

- **File Name**: Store results in any of several file formats. (The feedback form is preconfigured to send results to a text file, feedback.txt, that is created and stored in the _private folder of the current Web).

- **E-mail Address**: Formats and sends results to a designated e-mail address.

✦ **Send to Database:** You can choose to send results to a database. Selecting this option requires an understanding of how to set up a database in FrontPage. This chapter describes the basic process of configuring a form to store data in a database. For detailed instructions on working with databases in FrontPage, see Chapters 20 and 21.

✦ **Send to Other**: You can designate your own custom form handler. Selecting a form handler is as simple as clicking one of the three options and setting some basic option parameters. See Chapter 18 for examples of custom form handling in both Perl and ASP.

These options require more detailed attention, and we discuss each of them in the next several sections. For now, let's look at the remainder of the Form Properties options. The Form Properties section of the Form Properties dialog box (kind of redundant, isn't it?) includes options for the following:

✦ **Form Name:** Giving all of your form elements descriptive names is always a good practice. In many cases, you many never have need to use this name, but if you do any scripting of your Web pages, having the name references is helpful.

✦ **Target Frame:** You can specify a target frame for the page returned (either confirmation page or error page) when the form is submitted. If you are using a frame set, use the target frame to specify the name of the frame in which you want the confirmation page to appear. If you are not using frames, leave this alone.

Note   To learn more about frames and setting target names, refer to Chapter 7.

The following sections describe each of the options available to you for handling form results automatically. Custom form handlers are discussed in the later section, "Additional Form Handling Options."

Sending results to a text file

By default, all FrontPage forms are configured to send results to a comma-delimited text file (sometimes called a CSV). This file records your form's field names in the first row. Subsequent rows contain the data submitted, with each item separated by a comma. Using the Form Properties Options button, you can control the type of file to which the data is output, and the quantity of information that is output. You can even save the results to two separate files, each with a different format.

The steps described in the following sections explain how to configure your results page using the Form Properties dialog box.

Designating the results file

First identify the results file in the File Name field of the Form Properties dialog box. If the file already exists in the current Web, click the Browse button to locate the file. Otherwise, type the full path name to the file. If the file doesn't exist, FrontPage creates it the next time that you save your Web page.

Tip   Although FrontPage limits you to browsing for a results file within the current Web, the file doesn't have to reside within the Web. In fact, unless you want to make this file available for anyone to view, you are better off storing the file outside of your Web. Standard FrontPage practice calls for using the _private directory for this purpose. You can just as easily use any directory to which the Web server can write.

Next, click the Options button to display the Saving Results dialog box (see Figure 17-3). This dialog box shows the name of the results file that you indicated in the previous step. (You can also go directly to this dialog box and configure the filename here if you prefer.)

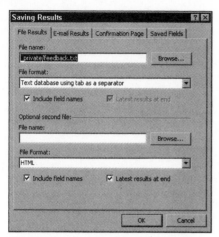

Figure 17-3: Use the Saving Results dialog box when saving form results as text.

Now you are ready to configure various options for your results file.

Selecting a file format

FrontPage enables you to save form results in one of several file formats: as a basic text file that is suitable for logging purposes, as an HTML file that can be made available to your Web site visitors, or as a delimited text file that can be imported into another application, such as a spreadsheet or database. Within these types, FrontPage enables various formatting style options. The following list describes the details of each of the available file formats:

✦ **HTML:** Displays the form input in an HTML page. If Include Field Names is checked, it creates a list of the input formatted, as follows:

```
Field_name: Field_value
```

Note

Input from text area fields is listed separately at the end of the results list. The field name is formatted as a level-three header (<H3>), and the results are listed as a separate paragraph.

Tip

FrontPage provides very little control over where or how the HTML input is recorded on the page. By default, FrontPage adds new responses to the bottom of the HTML page, making it difficult to create a page footer. However, a workaround to this exists. First, create your page without the footer. Then, test the page and submit some results. The first time that results are submitted, FrontPage adds a FormInsertHere Web component to the HTML page. Open the updated HTML page in FrontPage and add your footer after this component. (Don't forget to remove your bogus input!)

✦ **HTML definition list:** Same as HTML just described, but formats results by using an HTML definition list. If Include Field Names is checked, results are listed as follows (note that some browsers may display definition lists differently):

```
Field_name
  Field_value
```

✦ **HTML bulleted list:** Same as HTML, but formats results by using an HTML bulleted list. If Include Field Names is checked, results are listed as follows:

```
Field_name: Field_value
```

✦ **Formatted text within HTML:** In FrontPage terminology, formatted text refers to what HTML calls preformatted text, text contained within a <PRE> tag. This tag was initially designed to represent text as-is, maintaining spacing, tabs, and so forth. It is typically displayed using Courier type, such as the following (note the wider tab):

```
Field_name:          Field value
```

You can use a style sheet to control the formatting of your HTML results page. For more information about using style sheets, refer to Chapter 11.

✦ **Formatted text:** Generates a text page that resembles the formatting of the HTML pages previously described. For each set of results submitted, FrontPage creates a "ruled line" composed of asterisks, and then lists elements, as with the formatted text within HTML:

```
*****************************************
Field_name:          Field_value
```

Note that if you inadvertently use this option within an HTML page, the elements are displayed in one long line, because HTML ignores standard text line returns.

The Latest Results at End checkbox is disabled for all text file formats.

✦ **Text Database using comma as a separator:** Records the results in a data file format that later can be imported into a spreadsheet or database application, as illustrated in Figure 17-4. Each result set is written in a single line, with individual fields separated by commas. All field values are marked by quotation marks (mainly so that a comma sent as part of the results is not confused for a comma separator). If the Include Field Names option is checked, the first record in the file indicates the field values. (Note that this line is written the first time that results are submitted from the form.)

✦ **Text Database using tab as a separator:** Similar to the previous option, except that it uses tabs as field separators instead of commas.

✦ **Text Database using space as a separator:** Similar to the previous two options, except that it uses spaces as field separators instead of commas or tabs.

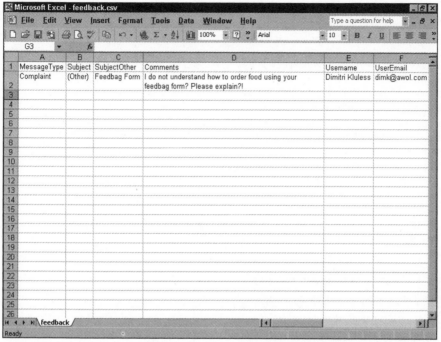

Figure 17-4: Sample form results saved to a comma-delimited (CSV) file opened in Excel

Selecting additional file format options

Check Include Field Names to include both field names and values in your file. Uncheck this option to include only the values submitted.

If the Latest Results at End option is available, check it to append new records to the bottom of the page. Uncheck this option to have the most recent submissions appear at the top of the page. The latter format is appropriate for content that will be viewed by users, which is perhaps why this option is enabled only for the HTML formats.

Optional second file

You might want to save the results in two different file formats. For example, you might want to log the results both to a tab-separated file that you can examine in Excel and as an HTML bulleted list that you (and, optionally, anyone else) can look at from the Web. Alternatively, perhaps you just want to record the same information in the same format in two different files, just to be safe. You can use the Optional Second File option to do this.

Note   FrontPage happily lets you configure your form to submit results to the same file twice, which is great if that is what you want to do.

Sending form results to an e-mail address

In many instances, it is helpful to be alerted whenever anyone submits a form from your Web site. The classic example is a customer-support form, for which the expectation of a rapid response time is fairly high (thanks to that old, outmoded device called a telephone). If FrontPage Server Extensions have been configured for your mail, sending results to an e-mail address is quite simple:

1. Right-click the form element and select Form Properties.

2. Type the e-mail address of the recipient in the E-mail Address field.

3. To specify e-mail options, click the Options button and select the E-mail Results tab, as illustrated in Figure 17-5.

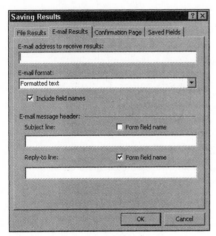

Figure 17-5: E-mail Results tab configuration options

E-mail options

As with the results file, you can specify the format of the e-mail message that is sent. All the file formats previously listed for the results file apply here as well. The chief difference is that an e-mail message always contains data for one record. In addition, remember that your e-mail reader must support HTML formatting if you want to receive the file in one of the HTML formats:

✦ **Include Field Names:** Check to send field names as well as the input values.

✦ **Subject Line:** You have two ways to designate a subject line for the e-mail
  results:

  • In the field provided, you can type what you want to appear in the sub-
    ject line. For example, typing "Customer Service Web Form" causes this
    line to appear in the subject heading of every e-mail message sent from
    this form.

  • You can designate a form field whose contents you want to appear in the
    subject line. To do this, first check the Form Field check box just above
    the subject line and then type the field name in the subject line. When
    the e-mail is sent, it will contain the value of the field indicated.

✦ **Reply-to Line:** Similar to the Subject Line option, except that the default is to
  put a field name in the Reply-to Line field (assuming that you are most likely
  to reply to the e-mail address of the person who submitted the e-mail results).
  If this is what you want, leave the Form Field Name checkbox checked, and
  indicate the field name in the Reply-to Line input box. If you want to insert a
  static value into the Reply-to Line field, such as the e-mail address of the person to whom certain e-mail results are escalated, uncheck the Form Field
  Name checkbox and type the Reply-to Line value in the designated field.

When you are finished, click OK to return to Page view. If your server has not been
configured to send e-mail, FrontPage warns you, as shown in Figure 17-6.

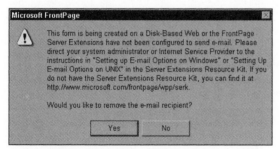

Figure 17-6: This warning appears if your server
is not already configured to send e-mail.

Designating saved fields

By default, FrontPage sends the value of every form element to the file and/or
e-mail address you designate. This may not always be what you want. As a prime
example, you probably have a button that submits the form results. You most likely
don't need to record the name and label value of this button each time the form is
submitted. You can use the Saved Fields tab of the Form Properties dialog box,
shown in Figure 17-7, to specify which field values to record.

Configuring Your Server Extensions to Send E-Mail

E-mail is configured in the FrontPage Server Extensions, so unless you are managing your own server, you shouldn't need to worry about this. If you do manage your own server, the steps required are as follows:

1. Open the Microsoft Management Console (MMC) by clicking Start ⇨ Programs ⇨ Configure Publishing Extensions.

2. Right-click the server you want to configure, and then select Properties from the options menu.

3. In the Options section of the Publishing tab, click the Settings button next to Specify How Mail Should Be Sent.

4. Specify the mail server address. Optionally, indicate a Web server's mail address, which appears as the From line of any e-mail sent. The Contact address is listed in case any problems occur submitting a form via e-mail.

For more information on the MMC and how to use it, see Chapter 23 on administering server extensions.

By the way, versions of FrontPage Server Extensions before FrontPage 2000 rely on a configuration file called `frontpg.ini` that, by default, resides in the Windows folder. Open this file in your favorite text editor. Entries in this configuration file are divided by port numbers.

To configure the server extensions to send e-mail, you need to specify a mail server for the particular port (or virtual server) that you are using. The line looks like the following (substitute the name of your mail server in the appropriate place):

```
SMTPHost=<name_of_your_mail_server>
```

Save the configuration file and restart your Web server. For details about other configuration options in this file, consult the Server Extension Resource Kit (SERK). Details on obtaining the current version of the SERK can be found in Chapter 23.

By default, all fields are listed in the Form Fields to Save list. To remove an item from the list, simply select and delete it (this may look like a select list, but it isn't — it is just a list of items separated by line breaks in a textbox). You can add items by typing them on a separate line. Note that this configuration is in effect for all versions of the information you save: one or both files, any e-mail you send, and the confirmation message. Unfortunately, you cannot save one set of information to an HTML file for general viewing and another to a comma-delimited file for your records.

Figure 17-7: Designating which fields
to save in your results file

You can also use the Saved Fields tab to add additional information to your saved
results:

✦ **Date:** The date of the submission, in various formats.

✦ **Time:** The time of the submission, in various formats.

✦ **Remote computer name:** The full host name if available, or an IP address.

✦ **Browser type:** Type and version, as reported by the browser.

✦ **Username:** Only records if you require users to authenticate using standard
HTTP authentication (as opposed to user names stored in a database)

Creating a confirmation page

Recording users' input is all fine and well, but you can also reassure users that you
have received their information by returning a confirmation message to them.
FrontPage calls such a message a *confirmation page.*

To provide your visitors with feedback, you don't have to designate a confirmation
page. FrontPage does this by default. As Figure 17-8 shows, the default confirmation
page is adequate, although somewhat less than inspirational. Fortunately, you can
easily create your own custom confirmation page that includes only the input field
information that you select.

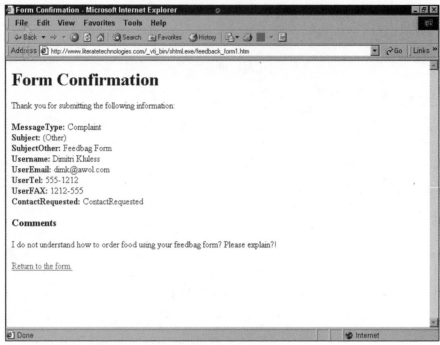

Figure 17-8: FrontPage's default confirmation page

Creating a confirmation page is a simple three-step process:

1. Create the basic confirmation page, just as you would any HTML page. If you like, you can use the Confirmation Form template that FrontPage provides for this purpose by selecting File ➪ New and choosing the Confirmation Form from the Page Templates dialog box. Save space for any results information that you plan to include on this page.

2. Insert placeholders for any results fields that you want to include in the confirmation page. To insert a result field placeholder, place the cursor where you want the field results to appear, select Insert ➪ Web Component ➪ Advanced Controls, and select Confirmation Field from the list of options. Type the name of the field whose value you want to appear on the page. Be careful to enter the name correctly, because FrontPage doesn't have any way to check for you When you save this information, FrontPage places the name of the field in brackets as a placeholder on the confirmation page, as illustrated in Figure 17-9. To edit this component, double-click the bracketed text.

Tip You can check field names by right-clicking the field in question and selecting Form Field Properties, or by using the Save Fields tab described earlier and checking the name in the list of saved fields.

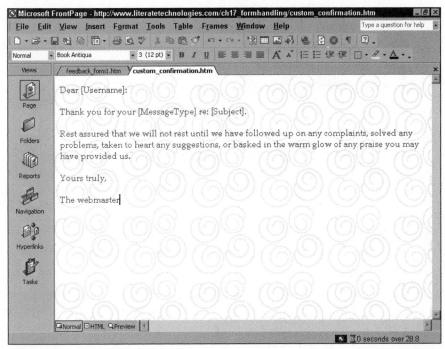

Figure 17-9: A sample confirmation page, showing Confirmation Field components in brackets on the page

3. Attach your custom page to your form page. To do this, open the form page, select Form Properties, select the Confirmation Page tab, and type or select the name of your confirmation file. You can designate a filename before you create the file, but in this case, FrontPage doesn't create a file. It simply creates the link to the file and complains that the file doesn't exist.

Tip The Confirmation Page dialog box indicates that you should provide the file URL. However, you can also store the file outside of your Web site document directory and link to it by using the full path name of the file.

Creating a validation failure page

In the previous chapter, you learned how to configure validation properties on HTML form fields. Here's a quick review. To set validation options for a given field, right-click the field and select Form Field Validation (you can also select Form Field Properties and click the Validate button in the properties dialog box). Select the validation options that you want, and click OK to return to Page view.

When you designate validation requirements, FrontPage adds a Validation component to the page. When a visitor to your site requests the page, FrontPage replaces the component with script functions that correspond to the requirements you designated (what kind of script depends on how you have configured your default scripting languages in the Advanced tab of Web Settings). If the visitor fails to complete a field validly, by default, the page displays a dialog box indicating the error.

What if the user doesn't have a script-enabled browser, or does but has disabled the use of client-side scripting? This is where the Validation Error page comes into play. By default, FrontPage returns a page that indicates the nature of the validation failure (see Figure 17-10).

Figure 17-10: The default validation error page

Using the Confirmation tab, you can designate your own Validation Error page. You can use this option to include a somewhat more sophisticated Validation Error page.

Tip   You can include a special confirmation field to return the same bulleted list of validation errors that you see in the default Validation Error page. Select Insert ➪ Component ➪ Confirmation Field, and type `Validation-Error` as the name. This still works in FrontPage 2002; however, Microsoft seems to have forgotten about it, because the Confirmation Field Web component now refuses to let you create a confirmation field name with a hyphen. You can work around this problem by giving the Confirmation Field a name FrontPage will accept and then switch to HTML view, and change the name as indicated above. Note that the field name is case-sensitive, so be sure to retain the capitalization as shown.

Creating a Multi-Step Form

Nobody likes to fill out a long form. In cases where there is no alternative but to provide a long form, some developers prefer a long, scrolling form, divided into clear sections to guide the user through the input process. Others prefer to divide the form into multiple pages, something like the way wizards function in the Microsoft Windows world. If you fall into the latter category, read on.

Because of a known bug in FrontPage's form handling, trying to set up a multiform submission process can be a little tricky. (Frankly, if you are savvy enough to understand the workaround to this problem, you can probably write your own custom form handler.)

Here's the problem: When the user submits the first form page, the next page that you want to show is the confirmation page, containing the second form. Unfortunately, when you try to set this up, FrontPage submits the form on the second page (which, of course, isn't completed) and returns instead the confirmation page of the second form. (If this also happens to have a form element, the process simply repeats.)

Microsoft's official workaround to this condition is to set up the confirmation page to do an automatic redirect to the second page of the form. Before the second page loads, the user first sees the real confirmation page, which might contain a cheerful message like "One moment, please, while we process your information." (which is *not* what you are doing, but is probably a more palatable explanation than the truth: "One moment, please, while I work around a known bug in FrontPage to make you fill out yet another form page.").

This approach has two problems. First, this requires a modicum of scripting to pull off, which you might regard as counter to the reason why you are using the built-in form handler in the first place. Second, passing information from one page to the next using the Confirmation Field component is somewhat tricky. It can be done, but we suggest a custom mechanism if this is what you are trying to achieve. For an alternative approach to creating a multi-page form, see Chapter 19.

Note that you must turn off scripting in your own browser in order to test your validation page.

Working with File Uploads

FrontPage 2002 includes a new file upload component that makes it painless to create forms that enable users to select a local file to send to the server. The capability to do this is part of the HTML standard. However, the standard does not include the programming required to deal with the file once it is sent. This is where FrontPage 2002 can help.

Creating a file upload form

The first step is to create a form that includes a file upload form element.

1. Create a new HTML page.

2. Add a form element and whatever fields you like using the Insert ⇨ Form menu items.

3. Add a file upload form element by selecting Insert ⇨ Form ⇨ File Upload. A simple file upload form is shown in Figure 17-11.

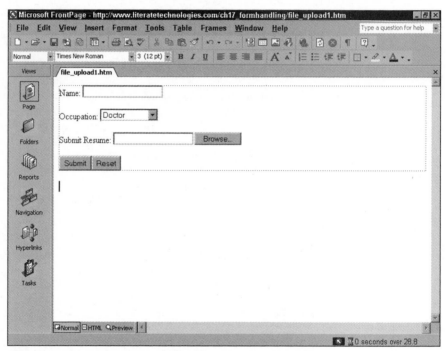

Figure 17-11: A simple form with a file upload form element

The file upload form element differs from most of the others in that it consists of a text field and button combination; and the button is already hardwired to permit users to browse their local file system and select a file. You cannot change either the button's behavior or its name. This is a small price to pay in exchange for the functionality that the upload element offers you, though, so don't sweat it.

Configuring file upload options

Once you have a form with a file upload form element, it is time to configure the form to deal with the upload.

1. Select Insert ⇨ Form ⇨ Form Properties (or right-click the Form element and select Form Properties from the option menu). After getting to the Form Properties dialog box click on Options.

2. Select the File Upload tab (you will notice that this tab only appears when you have a file upload form element in your form), as shown in Figure 17-12.

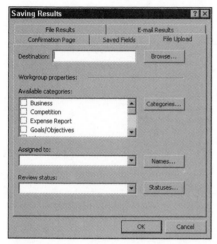

Figure 17-12: The File Upload options tab

3. Select a destination for the uploaded file, either by clicking the Browse button and locating a folder on the Web server or by typing a location directly into the form element.

4. If you like, you can also automatically assign uploaded files to workflow categories, assign them to a reviewer, and/or mark their status.

That's all there is to it! Now users can submit files via your form.

Caution   FrontPage does not currently provide a method of limiting the size or type of files that will be accepted. For this reason you should limit use of this option to circumstances where you are reasonably confident that your user's will not attempt to misuse this capability.

Adding Results to a Database

The most recent addition to FrontPage's automatic form handling bag of tricks is the ability to send the results directly to a database file. This is a very useful handler if you want to store and manipulate form results in a database, such as Access. (If you are interested in more information on connecting your Web site to a database, see Chapters 20 and 21.)

To activate this database file option, right-click your form and select Form Properties. Select the Send to Database option and then click Options to configure the database connection using the dialog box shown in Figure 17-13.

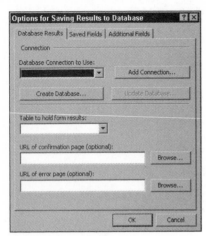

Figure 17-13: The Options for Saving Results to Database tab

> **Note** To use the database handler, you must have the current version of FrontPage Server Extensions installed on your Web server. You also must have Active Server Pages extensions installed. If the database handler option is grayed out on your dialog box, you probably don't have one or the other of these installed. (See Chapter 23 for more information on FrontPage Server Extensions.)

Creating a database

If you don't have an existing database that you are working with, FrontPage will generate a simple database that corresponds to your form elements.

Click the Create Database button. FrontPage creates a new Access database, with an .mdb extension. By default, FrontPage names the database file after the page name and stores the database in an fpbd folder in the root directory of your Web. FrontPage then creates a Results table in the database, connecting fields with names that match the form fields you have created. Figure 17-14 shows a sample confirmation message that FrontPage displays after it has created your database. Figure 17-15 shows the database fields generated in Access for our original feedback form.

> **Caution** If you have an HTML form that you attach to a database, you need to change the file extension from .htm (or .html) to .asp. FrontPage will prompt you to do this when you create the database.

Figure 17-14: When you create a database to save form results, FrontPage displays a confirmation message.

Field Name	Data Type	Description
ID	AutoNumber	
MessageType	Text	
Subject	Text	
SubjectOther	Text	
Comments	Memo	
Username	Text	
UserEmail	Text	
UserTel	Text	
UserFAX	Text	
ContactRequested	Text	
Remote_computer_name	Text	
User_name	Text	
Browser_type	Text	
Timestamp	Date/Time	

Figure 17-15: The database fields generated in Access for our feedback form

Updating a database

What happens if you make a change to your form after you create your database? You can use the Update Database button to modify your database to reflect any fields that you have added, modified, or deleted.

Using an existing database

In most cases, after you design your form, letting FrontPage create your database is the simplest option. However, this isn't always possible (you may, for example, be creating a form expressly for an existing database). Therefore, FrontPage also lets you manually map your form fields to a database. This is a three-step process:

1. Create a connection to this database within FrontPage.

2. Connect this database to the form.

3. Select a table from the database to contain the data and designate a mapping between each form field that you want to capture and the field names in the database. To create the mapping, select the Saved Fields tab of the Options for Saving Results to Database dialog box, shown in Figure 17-16. To modify a default mapping, click the Modify button, and select a database field name from the option menu. Use the Additional Fields tab to map non-form information — such as the user's browser type, the date, and so on — to database fields.

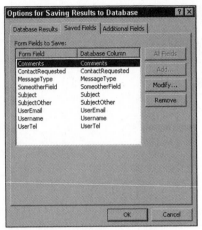

Figure 17-16: Map form fields to database fields in the Options for Saving Results to Database dialog box.

Note   FrontPage only supports saving data to a single table. If the fields that you need to save span multiple tables, you may be able to create a new table to store the data temporarily, and then use database functions to copy the data to its appropriate places. Typically, however, such applications require more sophisticated measures than FrontPage can easily provide to ensure that proper linkage between tables is maintained. Sometimes the better solution is to break your form up into multiple pages that pass along any required linkage information. See Chapters 20 and 21 for more information about working with databases in FrontPage.

Adding database connections

If you need to add a new database connection, use the Add Connection button. This button opens the Web Settings Database tab, which enables you to configure database connection information for your Web. You can connect your form to a database using any of four methods:

✦ **A database file in the current Web:** This is the easiest method, especially if you use a remote hosting service. FrontPage automatically adds a connection for any database file you import into your Web.

✦ **A system data source on the Web server:** With this method, you can set up an ODBC data source for your database file.

✦ **A network database:** If you are connecting to a network database, such as Oracle or MS SQL Server, use this option.

✦ **A custom database connection:** If you need to define connection parameters other than those supported by the methods above, use this option.

Refer to Chapter 20 for more details about these database connection options.

Defining additional database options

In addition to defining basic database-connection information, the Database tab enables you to define the following options:

✦ **Confirmation page:** This is the page users see after submitting your form. FrontPage creates a default confirmation page. Use this option to create a custom page as described above.

✦ **Error page:** You can also create a custom error page for your form submission.

Tutorial 17-1: Creating a guest book

The following tutorial reviews what you have learned thus far. In this tutorial, you create a standard guest book application by using the Guest Book template as your starting point. The Guest Book template is set up to record input to a separate file that is then included on the guest book page. Each time the page is reloaded, any newly submitted results are added to the page.

1. Open FrontPage, select New ➪ Page, and select the Guest Book template (see Figure 17-17).

2. Add a theme to your guest book page to give it a bit of life.

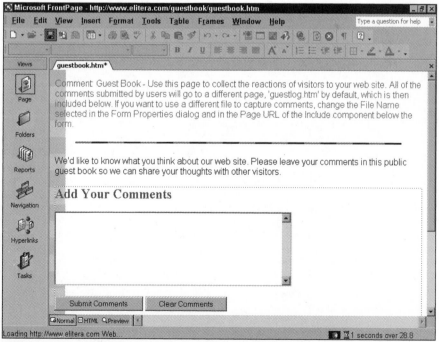

Figure 17-17: Creating a guest book using the FrontPage Guest Book template

3. The template provides only a single input field for comments. You want to capture a bit more information from the user, so add a Name and an E-mail field.

4. To make sure that guests actually complete all fields, configure the form validation properties for each of the form fields. Set each of the text box fields to no constraints between 1 and 100 characters. Set the Comment field to no constraints and a required length between 1 and 500 characters. Give each validation element a display name, which is the name that appears in the error message when the form is not correctly completed.

5. Configure the results display. You want to display the field values without the field names. Right-click the form and select the Form Properties dialog box. Note that the template has already designated a filename, `guestlog.htm`, as the results page. Leave this as it is. Click Options, and in the File Results tab, select HTML as the file format, and uncheck both the Include Field Name and Latest Results at End options.

6. Click the Saved Fields tab. First, verify that all three fields — `GuestName`, `GuestEmail`, and `Comments` — are included in the list of fields to be recorded, as shown in Figure 17-18. Select a format to display the time and date that the guest comment was sent. Uncheck all other options.

7. Test your guest book.

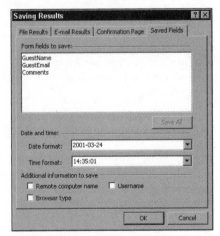

Figure 17-18: The Saved Fields tab of the Saving Results dialog box

Additional Form Handling Options

The Form Properties dialog box also enables you to select alternative form handlers for your results. To select an alternative form handler, check the Send To Other option button in the Form Properties dialog box and pick the appropriate handler from the list. Three options are available: a custom script option, a registration component option, and a discussion component option. These are explained next.

Custom ISAPI, NSAPI, CGI or ASP Script

This option enables you to attach your form to a custom form handling program. Personally, I think calling this option "Custom Form Handler" would have been amply descriptive without all the acronyms. At any rate, to configure your form to use a custom script, select this option and then select the Options button. This opens the Options for Custom Form Handler dialog box, illustrated in Figure 17-19. This dialog box provides four options you can configure (which correspond to the <form> tag attributes):

Figure 17-19: Custom Form Handler options

✦ **Action:** The form's action attribute points to the URL of the file that provides the form handling. This attribute is required for your form to work properly.

✦ **Method:** The method used by the server to send form results to your custom form handler. Options are POST, which sends input "invisibly" via standard input, or GET, which sends form results through a URL query string. This attribute is also required.

✦ **Encoding Type:** This attribute defines the encoding format of the form input. The default is application/x-www-form-urlencoded, which you only need to include if you want to show off. The only time you really need to worry about encoding type is if you are uploading files in your form. In this case, the encoding type needs to be multipart/form-data.

✦ **Style:** You can use the Style button to set the style for a form element. This includes fonts, borders, and shading. Note that if you set font styles for the form, they will apply to all normal text within the form but not to text entered into form elements.

Note In the current release of FrontPage 2002, you can only add a style to your form from the Custom Form Handling dialog box. Why Microsoft did not put the Style button on the main Form Properties dialog box is a mystery.

The Registration component

The Registration component serves the specialized purpose of allowing users to register with a user name and a password, to enable them to access password-protected Webs. Forms that use the Registration component must be saved to the root Web of a FrontPage Web server.

The Discussion component

The FrontPage Discussion component is also a specialized form handler, designed to store messages that are input from a discussion form. The Discussion component stores each message as an HTML page, and adds the page to a discussion table of contents, arranged according to messages and their responses.

Summary

In this chapter and the previous one, you learned to design, create, and enable HTML forms. You have examined the capabilities of the built-in FrontPage form handlers, and you have caught a glimpse of the larger world of custom form handlers available with some amount of programming. You now have the ability to save submitted form data in a variety of ways: in an e-mail message, in a text file, in HTML, or directly to a database table. You have also learned how to configure a file upload form to save files to the Web server. At this point you have explored all of the ways you can create sophisticated, interactive Web content without the need for programming. In the next two chapters, we examine how FrontPage can assist and support you if you choose to add your own custom client-side scripting and/or server-side programming.

✦   ✦   ✦

Client-side Scripting: JavaScript and DHTML

This chapter introduces you to client-side scripting using the Microsoft Script Editor (MSE). Client-side scripting enables you to handle some processing directly on the user's browser, so you don't need to send a call to the server. FrontPage doesn't have much support for scripting, however, the Microsoft Script Editor comes with FrontPage and this chapter shows you how to use it. A primary goal of this chapter is to provide you with some working scripts, so that even if you don't plan to become a scripting guru, you can use these in your Web pages.

Understanding Client-side Scripting

Scripting refers to programming code that is stored in text format and interpreted by another program. There are two principal methods of adding scripts to your Web page: client-side scripting and server-side scripting. In networking terminology, a *client* program is one that makes requests of a server application — in the case of your Web site, the client is the user's browser. Client-side scripts are programs that are embedded in the Web page and processed by the browser once it receives the page. Server-side scripts are programs that are processed on the Web server before the Web page is delivered to the browser. They are the subject of Chapter 19.

Client-side scripts are typically short and easy to create, so you can add interactive effects to your page without being an advanced developer. Because they run in the browser, client-side scripts are effective at handling events like responding to the user's mouse movements, or manipulating and validating form input. Of course, being browser-based also means that client-side scripts are entirely dependent on the ability of the user's browser to handle those scripts. Server-side scripts, conversely, are entirely browser-independent.

The good news is that there is a standard for client-side scripting languages. The current standard for client-side scripting is known as *ECMAScript* (ECMA is short for European Computer Manufacturers Association). Even better news is that both Microsoft Internet Explorer (through its JScript) and Netscape Communicator (through JavaScript) have relatively consistent support for the standard.

By using a client-side scripting language, you can increase the interactive character of your Web page without forcing the Web browser to send a request to the server and reload the page with a response. With scripting, for example, you can do the following:

✦ Have images on the page change when the user positions the mouse over them.

✦ Perform calculations and automatically update form field information.

✦ Pop up a message if the user enters invalid information into a form field.

✦ Design your Web page to display different information to the user depending on the type of browser he or she is using.

Best of all, client-side scripting languages are easy to learn and use. Of course, having some experience with other programming languages helps, but even if you don't, you should be able to follow the example scripts provided in this chapter and adapt them to your own use. Scripting languages are not suited for large-scale applications, but they provide a quick way to increase the flexibility and interactivity of your Web pages.

The problem (you didn't think I was going to stop with the good news, did you?) arises when the scripting language is extended to be able to access all of the HTML elements on the Web page itself. The ability to control all page elements has given rise to a special set of scripting called *Dynamic HTML* or DHTML. DHTML is not a programming language; it is just a name for using a scripting language like JavaScript to manipulate Web page elements. To do this, you need a standard convention for referring to all the elements in a Web page. This standard is known as the *Document Object Model,* or DOM. Unfortunately, IE and Netscape have historically had very different DOM support, so creating DHTML that is cross-browser compatible can be a challenge.

In this chapter, we'll first examine what you can achieve with standard JavaScript, and then look at some DHTML examples. Because FrontPage itself has no real features to help you with scripting (except that it will leave it alone), we also use this chapter to introduce the Microsoft Script Editor, the Office tool in search of a raison d'etre. MSE provides some useful support for your scripting needs.

Genealogy of Scripting Languages

The first scripting language to hit the Web development world was Netscape's JavaScript. Contrary to what many people assume, Netscape's JavaScript, although it has some similarities in syntax to Sun Microsystems' Java, is not directly related to the popular programming language. JavaScript (in version 1.2 as of this writing) is also the basis of the recently defined standards-based scripting language, ECMA-262, also known as *ECMAScript*. ECMAScript is the work of ECMA (European Computer Manufacturers Association), an international standards body. Both Microsoft and Netscape have announced their support for this standard, although both continue to support functionality that isn't contained in the standard. One way to ensure compatibility is to use only the standard definition when developing, although this currently is somewhat difficult, due to a lack of ECMAScript-aware development tools. The ECMAScript specification is now in its third edition (`www.ecma.ch/ecma1/STAND/ECMA-262.HTM`).

Originally, JavaScript was known as LiveScript. The name was changed partly to signify that JavaScript syntax bore some similarity to Java, but mainly (one suspects) to capitalize on the rising popularity of the hot new programming language. Microsoft, in its Internet Explorer browser, has developed support for a JavaScript-like language, which Microsoft refers to as JScript, for obvious reasons avoiding any clear associations with the Java name. Because of its support for JScript, Internet Explorer works correctly with the majority of JavaScript scripts. You need to test any scripts that you develop in both Netscape and Microsoft browsers to ensure that they work correctly in both environments.

In addition to its support for JScript, Microsoft has developed a second scripting language, called *VBScript*. VBScript, the full name of which is Microsoft Visual Basic Scripting Edition, is a subset of Microsoft's popular programming languages, Visual Basic and Visual Basic for Applications (VBA). If you already know how to program in Visual Basic, learning VBScript is a snap. Also, if you are planning to develop a Microsoft-based Web solution using ActiveX technologies, you may find some advantages to using VBScript. (See Chapter 15 for a discussion of ActiveX.) Remember, however, that only Internet Explorer contains support for VBScript. You need to know that your users have this browser; or you must be prepared to deal with those who do not. For this reason, VBScript can be an appropriate choice for intranet developers, when a company uses only Internet Explorer. It also works fine for server-side scripting languages, such as ASP (discussed in Chapter 19), for which browser support does not matter. In this chapter, we will restrict our discussion to JavaScript.

Both scripting languages have server-side versions, so you can use the same programming environment to write scripts for both server- and client-side uses.

To script or not to script

Any time that you want to add simple interactivity to your Web pages, you may want to consider using a scripting language. Remember that if you create script-based functionality that is essential to the operation of the page, you need to find a way to accommodate users who are using browsers that are not compatible with scripting languages. The following are some of the tasks that scripting languages are well suited to do:

✦ Simple animation

✦ Pop-up messages

✦ Calculations

✦ Form field updating

✦ Form field validation

✦ Window and frame control

✦ Dynamic control of page elements

✦ Browser detection

Scripting languages are useful, fun, and easy to use, but they are not suited to every task. The following are occasions when using client-side scripting may not be appropriate:

✦ If you need to access or process data or files that reside on the server

✦ If you need to record user input to a storage device

✦ If you have a large, complex programming task

✦ If you need to protect your proprietary code

✦ If you need to support a lowest-common-denominator browser

Discovering Scripting

This discussion will start with a simple example that will illustrate how JavaScript works and will also demonstrate a situation when it can be a better solution than server-side programming. Suppose that you have created a form that asks users to supply their name and e-mail address. You realize that a fair number of people are likely to input their e-mail address incorrectly. (At least you would realize this if you have ever had occasion to try to collect e-mail addresses from users.) You would like to have a simple way to catch those who unintentionally mistype their e-mail address. (Verifying the legitimacy of e-mail addresses is a much thornier issue, and won't be discussed here.)

You could write a program to perform this task using Common Gateway Interface, commonly called CGI, which is the lingua franca of Web applications. The user would need to submit the form to the server. The CGI application would read the e-mail address input by the user, and compose a reply message prompting the user to confirm his or her e-mail address. The user would then either successfully confirm his or her address, in which case the form would be resubmitted; or the user could edit his or her e-mail address, in which case the original form would have to be reloaded with the existing data and the whole process repeated until the user got the e-mail address right.

This CGI solution has two obvious drawbacks:

✦ A fair amount of programming overhead is involved in building any CGI application, more overhead than you want for such a simple function.

✦ Your users are likely to find this function mildly distracting, if not annoying, particularly if they need to correct their e-mail address.

To implement this enhanced behavior more simply, you need some way to create a "smart" Web page, one that can perform this function without intervention from the server. That way involves using client-side scripting.

Now, imagine that instead of using a CGI program, you could pop up a message box with the same confirmation request when the form was about to be submitted. In this case, if the user makes a mistake, he or she is prompted to try again. No information is ever submitted until it is correct. This method is easy on the Web server and easy on the user. Plus, because no connections are made across the Internet, the confirmation process is blazingly fast, even on the slowest dial-up connection.

Note   The completed version of this script — and all the other scripting examples found in this chapter — are available for downloading from the HMI Web site. Details for accessing the site and obtaining examples files can be found in the Preface.

Creation of this script requires three simple steps:

1. Create the form. (See Chapter 16 for details on building forms in FrontPage.) Your example form is shown in Figure 18-1. Set the form element's name to ex1. Configure the form to send the results of the form wherever you like. (See Chapter 17 for details on activating your forms.)

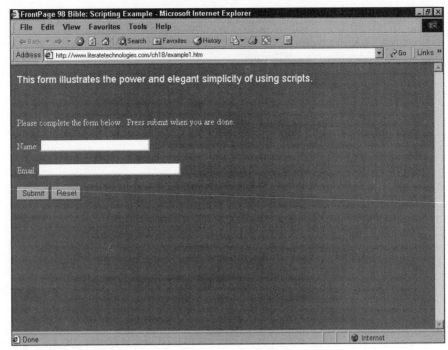

Figure 18-1: The beginning of your e-mail confirmation script

2. Switch to the HTML tab, and insert the custom script function necessary to perform the confirmation. Later in the chapter, you learn how to use Microsoft Script Editor to add a script. For now, just follow along. The script in question has a single function, called `confirmEmail`, which looks like this:

```
<script LANGUAGE="JavaScript">
<!--
function confirmEmail(name,email)
{
var confirmedEmail = window.prompt(name + ", \
Please retype your email to confirm:","");
  if (confirmedEmail != null && confirmedEmail !="") {
    if (email==confirmedEmail) {
      document.ex1.submit();
      return true;
    }
    else {
      window.alert("First address (" + email + ") \
does not match confirmation (" + confirmedEmail + "). Please
try again.");
      document.ex1.Email.value="";
      return false;
    }
```

```
    }
    else {
      return false;
    }
}
//-->
</script>
```

Insert this script as shown in Figure 18-2 just before the end of the head section of the page; that is, just before the `</head>` tag.

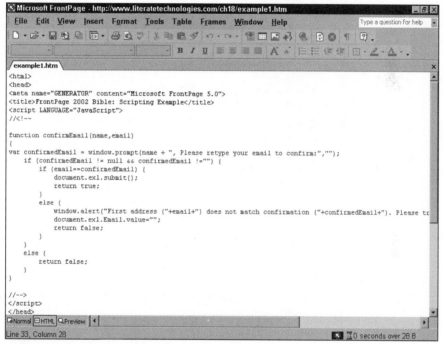

```
<html>
<head>
<meta name="GENERATOR" content="Microsoft FrontPage 5.0">
<title>FrontPage 2002 Bible: Scripting Example</title>
<script LANGUAGE="JavaScript">
//<!--

function confirmEmail(name,email)
{
var confirmedEmail = window.prompt(name + ", Please retype your email to confirm:","");
    if (confirmedEmail != null && confirmedEmail !="") {
        if (email==confirmedEmail) {
            document.exl.submit();
            return true;
        }
        else {
            window.alert("First address ("+email+") does not match confirmation ("+confirmedEmail+"). Please tr
            document.exl.Email.value="";
            return false;
        }
    }
    else {
        return false;
    }
}

//-->
</script>
</head>
```

Figure 18-2: Placing a script

3. After you insert your script, while still in HTML view, update your form's button tag to bind the `confirmEmail()` function to the button's `onClick` event handler. This added code causes the button to execute the `confirmEmail` function when it is pressed by the user. The button tag should resemble this:

```
<input type="button" value="Submit"
onclick="confirmEmail(this.form.Name.value,
this.form.Email.value)" name="btnConfirm">
```

Now save and test the page. When you click the submit button, it executes the script, causing the `confirmEmail` function to spring into action, as shown in Figure 18-3.

Figure 18-3: The e-mail verification script in action

JavaScript Basics

Unfortunately, we do not have the space here to provide a complete introductory course in JavaScript. If you are interested in learning more, a great way to learn is using Danny Goodman's *JavaScript Bible*.

Our assumption here is that you may find yourself working with scripts in FrontPage, whether you write them yourself or acquire them elsewhere. It helps to have a basic understanding of what scripts look like, what it takes to get them into your Web pages, and what they can do for you once you get them there.

Elements of a script

As we saw in our initial example, even a simple script consists of several components working together. In this section, we identify some of the key elements that make up scripts and that make them work. These include

+ **The script tag:** This is an HTML tag that tells the browser to regard anything inside it as programming rather than as HTML.

+ **Event handlers:** These are special functions that are associated with some action, frequently user initiated, such as a button click or moving the mouse.

+ **Variables and functions:** These are the code statements that execute commands.

+ **Provision for nonscripting browsers:** HTML also enables you to deal with browsers that don't support scripting.

The script tag

All scripts are defined by a `<script>` start tag and a `</script>` end tag. You can have multiple script blocks on any given Web page, and script tags can be embedded practically anywhere on the page. The script tag can define scripts that are contained within the script block, or it can provide a URL reference to a page containing external scripts, roughly the equivalent of "including" a scripting library in the page. Typically, scripts are written in a single block contained within the `<head>` section of the page, before the beginning of the `<body>` section. All code in a scripting block is executed immediately when it is loaded into the browser, unless it is contained in a separate function. Functions are executed when they are called, either somewhere in the scripting itself or by an event handler, as described in the "Event handling" section.

Note The choice of location of scripts is partly convenience and partly because browsers typically process Web pages from top to bottom, and it is helpful to have the scripting processed prior to the page elements.

The script tag also has some important attributes:

✦ LANGUAGE: Use this attribute to identify the scripting language in which the current script is written (such as "JavaScript", "JScript", or "VBScript"). This attribute is currently in common use, but as of the HTML 4.0 specification the TYPE attribute is preferred for this purpose. Note that FrontPage 2002 uses this notation.

✦ TYPE: This attribute specifies the scripting language (using MIME notation) of the element's contents and overrides the default scripting language set by the LANGUAGE attribute. The scripting language is specified as a content type (for example, "text/javascript"). You must use this method if you want your Web pages to conform to the HTML 4.0 specification.

✦ SRC: This attribute specifies the location of an external script in URL format (for example src="../js/myscripts.js").

Event handling

Having scripts that execute when your Web page is loaded in the browser is nice, but somewhat limited. In most cases you will find yourself wanting something to happen in response to the user doing something on the page: moving the mouse, clicking a button or a link, or typing input into a form field. The technical name for something happening on your Web page is an *event*. Scripting allows you define handlers for specified events by attaching scripting to the specified event handler. The primary event handlers as defined by HTML 4.0 include the following:

✦ onload: Occurs when the browser finishes loading a window or all frames within a FRAMESET. This attribute may be used with BODY and FRAMESET elements.

✦ onunload: Occurs when the user agent removes a document from a window or frame. This attribute may be used with BODY and FRAMESET elements.

✦ onclick: Occurs when the pointing device button is clicked over an element. This attribute may be used with most elements.

✦ ondblclick: Occurs when the pointing device button is double-clicked over an element. This attribute may be used with most elements.

✦ onmousedown: Occurs when the pointing device button is pressed over an element. This attribute may be used with most elements.

✦ **onmouseup:** Occurs when the pointing device button is released over an element. This attribute may be used with most elements.

✦ **onmouseover:** Occurs when the pointing device is moved onto an element. This attribute may be used with most elements.

✦ **onmousemove:** Occurs when the pointing device is moved while it is over an element. This attribute may be used with most elements.

✦ **onmouseout:** Occurs when the pointing device is moved away from an element. This attribute may be used with most elements.

✦ **onfocus:** Occurs when an element receives focus, for example, when it is clicked or selected, either by the pointing device or by tabbing navigation. This attribute may be used with the following elements: A, AREA, LABEL, INPUT, SELECT, TEXTAREA, and BUTTON.

✦ **onblur:** Occurs when an element loses focus either by the pointing device or by tabbing navigation. It may be used with the same elements as onfocus.

✦ **onkeypress:** Occurs when a key is pressed and released over an element. This attribute may be used with most elements.

✦ **onkeydown:** Occurs when a key is pressed down over an element. This attribute may be used with most elements.

✦ **onkeyup:** Occurs when a key is released over an element. This attribute may be used with most elements.

✦ **onsubmit:** Occurs when a form is submitted. It only applies to the FORM element.

✦ **onreset:** Occurs when a form is reset. It only applies to the FORM element.

✦ **onselect:** Occurs when a user selects some text in a text field. This attribute may be used with the INPUT and TEXTAREA elements.

✦ **onchange:** Occurs when a control loses the input focus and its value has been modified since gaining focus. This attribute applies to the following elements: INPUT, SELECT, and TEXTAREA.

JavaScript vs. VBScript

Scripting is agnostic about what scripting language you use in your scripts. You can use FrontPage to designate either JavaScript or VBScript as your default scripting language. If you are a VB guru and you know you will be working in a Microsoft-only environment, then you are probably better off going with VBScript. For all other uses, JavaScript (either the Netscape or Microsoft variety, officially JScript) is the better choice for client-side scripting. Save your VBScripting for server-side scripting, where the language you select does not matter to your users — it only matters to your Web server. To designate a default scripting language, select Tools ⇨ Web Settings and select a default scripting language on the Advanced tab.

To define an event handler, you add the handler to the HTML tag of the page element whose event you want to handle, and set the value of the handler to the scripting code you want to execute when the event occurs. To take a simple example, say you have a normal push button on your page and that you want to pop up an alert message when the user clicks the button. Before defining the event handler, the HTML for your button looks like this:

```
<input type="button" name="btnMyButton" value="Click here!">
```

To activate the button, add the `onclick` event handler and appropriate scripting like this:

```
<input type="button" name="btnMyButton" value="Click here!"
onclick="window.alert('Thanks, I needed that!')">
```

Caution
Be careful to enclose the event handler code in quotation marks and to use single quotation marks (apostrophes) for any string quoting you need to do within the scripting itself, as in the button example here.

Defining custom functions

In the button example in the previous section, the event handler you defined was pretty simple: click a button, pop up a message. For tasks like that, you can place the scripting code right in the tag, as you saw. But what if you have more grandiose plans, such as the e-mail confirmation script presented at the beginning of the chapter? It would be cumbersome at best to try to place all of that code in the button tag. The solution is to write a *function* and then *call* the function in your event handler. A custom function is a named block of scripting that performs a particular programming task. It may take parameters and return a value at the end of the function, but this up to you. Let's create a slightly more elaborate version of our button clicking script. This time we make our button toggle between two different values after you click on it the first time. Here's how:

1. First, create a function called `toggleMe` that takes a simple string value parameter. The function looks like this:

```
function toggleMe(s)
{
    if (s=="Thank you!")
    {
        return true;
    }
return false;
}
```

The function definition consists of the keyword `function` followed by the name of the function, with any parameters in parentheses. If your function has no parameters, you still need to include the empty parentheses. The script itself is contained within a {} block. Code statements are terminated with a semicolon (;), although JavaScript is relatively forgiving about this in cases where it can reasonably assume the end of a statement. In this case, the function looks to see if the value of the parameter equals "Thank you!" and if it does, the function returns a value of `true`. If not, the function returns `false`. Note that functions can return other values besides `true` or `false` — for example, a string of text or a number.

2. Next, you need to add the event handler to the button. You will use the same button as in the previous example. This time, the event handler is a bit trickier:

```
<input onclick="return toggleMe(this.value)?this.value='You
are welcome!':this.value='Thank you!';" type="button"
value="Click here!" name="btnMyButton">
```

You will notice, first of all, that the event handler calls the function in this script, and passes it the expression `this.value`. The `this` is shorthand for the object referred to in the current tag, in this case, the button. And `this.value` refers to the value attribute of the button. So, in essence, you are passing to the function the current value of the button. The rest of our script uses another special scripting command that is shorthand for "if the expression being evaluated is true, do the first thing in this list; if it is false, do the second thing." The shorthand syntax looks like this:

```
expression?<do if true>:<do if false>
```

Applied to this example, the `toggleMe` function returns either `true` or `false`. If true, then the statement `this.value='You are welcome!'` is executed. If false, the statement `this.value='Thank you!'` is executed. The net result is that the first time you click on the new button, it responds by changing its label to say "Thank you." Click on it again, and it says "You are welcome." After that, it toggles back and forth between the two statements as long as you care to continue the experiment.

The no-script alternative

Believe it or not, not everyone uses the latest version of either Netscape's or Microsoft's browser (a pill that is very difficult for most developers to swallow). And even if they are using one of these browser versions, some users turn off their browser's support for active elements, such as Java, ActiveX, and scripting, primarily for security reasons.

For such users, you can prevent their browsers from displaying the script as if it were normal text. You also can define an alternative to the scripting functions that you include in your page.

Hiding scripts from old browsers

You can hide your scripts from older browsers by enclosing the script itself in a slightly modified comment tag. Comment tags begin with an exclamation point, followed by two hyphens `<!--`. The comment tag is closed with two hyphens, `-->`.

If you look back at the HTML created by Script Editor in the first two example scripts, you see that Script Editor automatically wraps your script in comment tags, as shown in Figure 18-2. In the JavaScript version, the end tag is preceded with a double slash, //, which is the JavaScript comment indicator. If your user's browser does not support scripting or if scripting is turned off, the browser interprets the script as a comment and ignores it. You should use a similar syntax any time that you insert a script manually. Note that the comment tag is placed inside the script tag—otherwise, even script-enabled browsers would ignore the scripts.

Alternatives for nonscripting browsers

Wrapping your scripts in comment tags ensures that incompatible browsers will not dump your code into your Web page, but this still leaves these users with a blank spot where useful information is meant to appear.

In most cases, you cannot provide these users with the same information (if you could, you wouldn't need a script). You can, however, inform these users that they are missing out on something. To include a message for nonscripting browsers, place the message in a <NOSCRIPT> tag.

Unfortunately, although both Netscape Navigator and Microsoft Internet Explorer support the NOSCRIPT syntax, FrontPage does not. Consequently, you have to insert this tag manually.

Return to the first JavaScript example at the beginning of this chapter. Select the HTML tab to view the document source. Insert the following immediately after the end of the <SCRIPT> tag:

```
<NOSCRIPT>
<H6>This page requires a JavaScript compatible browser with
JavaScript currently enabled.</H6>
</NOSCRIPT>
```

Select the Normal tab to return to the WYSIWYG mode. Notice that FrontPage displays the comment tag icon around the inserted text, indicating that it does not recognize this NOSCRIPT tag. Not to worry. Select the Preview tab, and you should see the appropriate display for a JavaScript-enabled browser.

To see the NOSCRIPT text displayed, select File ➪ Preview in Browser and select your favorite browser. If you have a JavaScript-compatible browser, you should see the current time displayed correctly.

To view the NOSCRIPT text in Internet Explorer 4.x and 5.x, select Tools ➪ Internet Options. In the Options property window, select the Security tab and uncheck the Run ActiveX Scripts checkbox. Return to the Web page and reload it, either by clicking the Refresh button or by selecting View ➪ Refresh. The current time should no longer be displayed. In its place is the alternative message.

To view the NOSCRIPT text in Netscape Navigator 4.*x*, select Edit ➪ Preferences. Select the Advanced item and uncheck the Enable JavaScript checkbox. Return to the Web page and reload the page, either by clicking the Reload button or by selecting View ➪ Reload. In Netscape 3.*x*, select Options ➪ Network Preferences, select the Languages tab, and then uncheck the Enable JavaScript checkbox. Return to the page and reload it as described for Netscape 4.*x*.

Using the Microsoft Script Editor

The Microsoft Script Editor (MSE) is a shared Office tool. According to the official Microsoft literature, MSE is intended to be used to edit HTML in Office documents. This is reasonable until you ask why FrontPage, an Office tool designed for editing HTML documents, would need to have a tool designed for editing HTML documents? This is a conundrum, which one can only hope the smart folks at MS will put their heads to solving. In the meantime, we can sidestep the dilemma by billing MSE as a specialized environment for adding scripts to the Web pages you create in FrontPage. As it turns out, FrontPage is not a particularly good environment for creating scripts. Besides this fact, there are two reasonably compelling arguments for creating and editing scripts in MSE:

✦ **Autocompletion:** MSE knows scripting and pops up a list of available scripting objects as you type your script, which helps jog your memory and speeds development by cutting down on the time spent looking up arcane syntax references.

✦ **Debugging:** MSE comes with a Web debugging tool that helps you track down errors in your scripts.

In this section, we take a spin through the MSE tool with attention to its scripting features.

Starting Microsoft Script Editor

Microsoft Script Editor is designed for editing and debugging HTML, JavaScript (and JScript), VBScript, DHTML, and Active Server Pages (server-side script).

Note   If you have never used MSE and you didn't explicitly install it when you installed FrontPage 2002, when you first try to open MSE, you may receive a warning message "Microsoft FrontPage can't use Web Scripting. The feature is not currently installed. Would you like to install it now?" Select Yes, and have your installation CD-ROM handy.

To start MSE, open a Web page in FrontPage (MSE is not accessible without an open page) and select Tools ➪ Macro ➪ Microsoft Script Editor. The selected HTML page is opened in the Source tab of MSE's HTML editor.

Working in the MSE environment

By default, MSE opens with the following windows, shown in Figure 18-4:

✦ A main HTML Editor window in the center

✦ A window on the left side containing tabs for Document Outline view, Script Outline view, and HTML toolbox

✦ Two half-size windows on the right side, with the Project Explorer window on top and the Properties window on the bottom

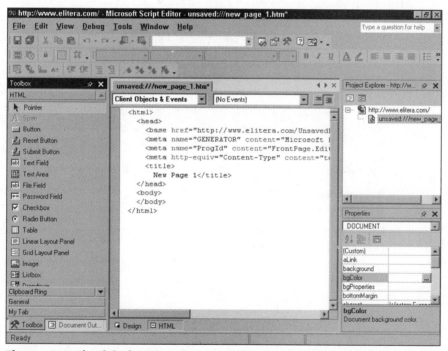

Figure 18-4: The default MSE environment, showing the HTML editor, HTML toolbox, and the Project Explorer and Properties windows.

In addition to the windows visible in the default layout, several other windows exist that you can work with in MSE. The next sections briefly describe each of the principal windows in the MSE environment and list some of the methods that you can use to customize the MSE environment to suit your needs.

MSE windows

MSE contains a multitude of windows. Besides the HTML editor window, in which you do most of your work, the other windows typically provide various views of the contents of the page that you are editing, lists of available objects to add to the page, or debugging information. The following are the main MSE windows, with a brief description of their functions:

✦ **HTML outline:** Displays a tree view of the HTML elements currently in the HTML document that you are editing. Double-click an item in the list to locate and select the item in the HTML editor window.

✦ **HTML toolbox:** Contains a list of elements that you can add to the current HTML page. You can customize this toolbox by adding new elements to the list.

✦ **Script outline:** Provides a tree-based view of scripting objects and events that you can add to your pages.

✦ **HTML editor:** Enables you to edit the FrontPage HTML page. The HTML editor window consists of three views:

   • **Design view:** Available only for pages that are created directly in MSE. Any pages created using FrontPage 2002 have this view disabled. (In essence, FrontPage controls the Design view for its own pages.) When available, Design view functions as a WYSIWYG HTML editor, much like the Normal view in FrontPage.

   • **Source view:** The default view for the HTML editor, it displays the HTML source of the page for editing.

   • **Quick view:** Equivalent to FrontPage's Preview tab, this allows for quick previewing of the page you are editing.

✦ **Project explorer:** Displays a hierarchical list of all MSE projects and the items contained in each project. Use this window to navigate through your projects by selecting a project or item to make it active.

✦ **Properties:** Lists the properties of a selected object in the editor. Use this window to edit an object's properties.

✦ **Object browser:** Displays the various elements (classes, properties, methods, and events) available for use in your project. It is primarily a dictionary. Use it to find the syntax of objects and their elements.

✦ **Output:** Displays runtime messages when you run a script. It is typically used for debugging purposes.

✦ **Debug windows:** Series of windows that provide information that is helpful in debugging scripts. Debug windows include Immediates, Autos, Locals, Watch, Threads, Call Stack, and Running Documents. You can also access these windows from the Debug toolbar.

MSE toolbars

MSE provides the following toolbars for easy access to commonly used commands:

✦ **Standard:** Contains buttons for most of the basic file operations.

✦ **Debug:** Provides button access to the main debug features and windows.

✦ **Design:** Active only in Design view (which is unavailable from FrontPage, as previously indicated). It includes functions that affect how a page is displayed in Design view, and that enable you to add absolute-positioned elements to your HTML page.

✦ **HTML:** Contains HTML formatting elements to add to the page that you are editing. This toolbar is similar to the Formatting toolbar in FrontPage.

✦ **Window UI:** Provides shortcuts to manipulate the MSE windows and environment.

✦ **Fullscreen:** Single-item toolbar that toggles MSE between full and partial screen.

Customizing the environment

The MSE environment consists of a sophisticated set of windows and toolbars. After you are familiar with MSE's major features, you can customize the environment to suit your preferences. This section describes some of the general methods that you can use to alter the MSE environment to your liking:

✦ **Tab-linking windows:** Most of MSE can be superimposed in a single window with multiple tabs. To tab-link a window, click and drag the window on top of another existing window. MSE creates a single window with two tabs. You can tab-link additional windows to this window in the same way.

✦ **Dockable windows and toolbars:** Many of the windows and toolbars can be fastened (or docked) to the top, bottom, left, or right side of the MSE environment. To dock or undock an item, click and drag it to the desired location.

✦ **Customizable toolbars:** You can add items to existing toolbars by using the Customize Toolbar feature. FrontPage has a similar feature. For details, see Chapter 22.

✦ **Customizable toolbox:** You can also add elements to the various toolboxes. To customize a toolbox, right-click the toolbox and select Customize Toolbox. Select one or more items to add to the toolbox from the list of available elements.

✦ **Define Window Layout:** Use this command to define a custom layout that you want to be able to recreate. MSE has several default layouts (Debug, Design, DevStudio, Edit HTML, Full Screen, and Visual Basic). To add your own layout, first arrange the layout as you want to save it. Select View Í Define Window Layout and give the layout a name. Select Add to add this name to the list of available layouts.

Editing an HTML page

As a preliminary example of how you can work with MSE, the following process creates a simple JavaScript form that prompts users to enter the year in which they were born, and then returns a message informing them which animal is associated with their birth date in the Chinese calendar:

1. Create a new, blank Web page in FrontPage.

2. Select Tools ⇨ Macro ⇨ Microsoft Script Editor to open the blank Web page in this application. Unless you have already reconfigured the MSE environment, the page opens in the HTML tab of the Editing window, as previously illustrated in Figure 18-4.

   You need to create a form with one text-input box and a button. Of course, you could do this in FrontPage, but you need to practice your MSE skills. MSE includes a Design view, which is the equivalent of FrontPage Normal view, but it works only for pages that are first created in MSE. So, you work in Source view, the equivalent of FrontPage HTML view. Before continuing, make sure that you have the HTML toolbox, Document/Script outlines, and Properties windows all opened. You can arrange these windows in any way that you like; try grouping the toolbox and Outline view to the left of the main editing window, and then placing the Properties window to the right. If you need details on how to customize the MSE environment, refer to that information earlier in the chapter.

3. Select your new page in the editing window. You should see the DOCUMENT properties displayed in the Properties window; select the Title property and change the text to **Your Birth Year Animal**. Note that the text between the `<title>` and `</title>` tags is updated in the Source tab.

4. In the Source tab of the main editing window, place the cursor inside the `<body>` tag of your blank HTML page. Notice that the Properties window changes to reflect the properties list for the selected tag. To change the color of the page, select the `bgcolor` property and click the three-dot (...) button to its right in the value field. Select the Web Palette tab in the MSE Color Picker and select an attractive color for the background of your page (for example, #666699). Click OK to accept the color and update your page. Note that the color is registered in the `<body>` tag as well as in the Properties window (see Figure 18-5).

5. To preview your page color, you can switch back to FrontPage and see that your page has been updated in Normal view.

6. Create your form. Place the cursor between the `<body>` and `</body>` tags. Select the HTML menu and Form to add a `<form>` tag set to the page. Select the Form element by placing the cursor in the `<form>` tag element. Alternatively, select the Document Outline window. Two elements are listed: a `<body>` tag and a `<form>` element. Click the Form element to select it.

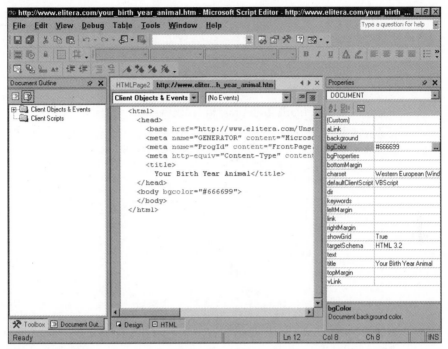

Figure 18-5: Your new page in MSE after adding a background color in the Properties sheet

7. In the Properties dialog box, change the form name from the default `form1` to `birthform`. (You also can change the `ID` attribute, although it isn't used in this example.) Because you are implementing a client-side script only, the Action attribute associated with this form isn't needed, so you can leave it blank.

8. Select the Toolbox window. Place the cursor between the `<form>` and `</form>` elements in the editing window and double-click the Textbox item to add a textbox to the form. Change the name of the Textbox from `text1` to `byear`, using the method described in the previous step.

9. Repeat the preceding steps to add a form Button after the Textbox. Change its value to **Get Animal!** Figure 18-6 shows the form as it is shaping up.

   It is time to add the scripting to your form, but first, this is a good time to save your work. Click the Save button on the MSE toolbar. Notice that MSE switches back to FrontPage momentarily to save the page, and then returns.

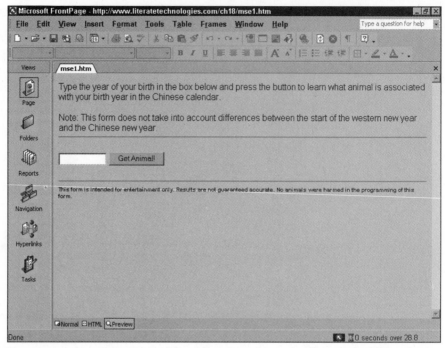

Figure 18-6: Your form page after adding some form elements and additional text

10. By default, MSE is configured to use VBScript as both the client and server scripting languages of choice. You want to use JavaScript (or JScript in this case), so you must first change the document properties to reflect this choice, which you can do in either of two ways:

   • Select the `defaultClientScript` property in the DOCUMENT properties window and change its value to JavaScript.

   • Select View ➪ Property Pages and change the Client Default Scripting Language to JavaScript.

Note   MSE defaults to VBScript as the default client scripting language regardless of how you have configured your Web Settings in FrontPage.

11. Select the Script Outline window and open the Client Objects and Events folder (if it isn't already open). In addition to the default Window object, you should see your form and, under it, the textbox and button objects: `button1`, `form1`, and `text1`, as illustrated in Figure 18-7.

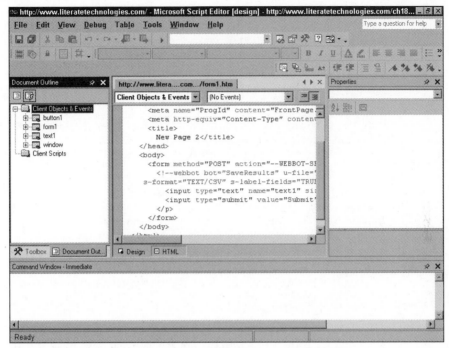

Figure 18-7: The objects in your new form page as seen by MSE

Note

You can hide or show the events available for each object by right-clicking any object in the Script Outline window and selecting Hide Events or Show Events.

Open the button object and show its events. Double-click the onClick event, which causes two things to happen to your Web page. First, MSE adds some stub JavaScript to the header section of your page:

```
<SCRIPT ID=clientEventHandlersJS LANGUAGE=javascript>
<!--

function button1_onclick() {

}

//-->
</SCRIPT>
```

This represents a script block with an empty function, called `button1_onclick()`, which is called when the button is clicked. To connect this code to the button, MSE also adds code to the button's `<input>` tag itself, so that the tag now looks like this:

```
<INPUT type="button" value="Get Animal!" id=button1
name=button1 LANGUAGE=javascript onclick="return
button1_onclick()">
```

Your task is to write the code that makes the page work to your specification. At this point, because you haven't yet learned how JavaScript works, concentrate more on how to use MSE to insert this code rather than on how the code works.

12. Your objective for this form is to take the year entered by the user, figure out which of the twelve animals of the Chinese calendar is associated with that year, and return a message informing the user which animal sign they were born under. When the form button is clicked, you need to take the value entered into the textbox and pass it to a function called `get_sign()`, the code for which follows:

```
function get_sign(yearoffset) {
   signs = new Array("Dragon","Snake","Horse","Sheep", \
"Monkey","Rooster","Dog","Pig","Rat","Ox","Tiger","Hare");
   return signs[(yearoffset % 12)];
   }
```

Manually enter this code into the Source view window. Basically, this function subtracts the input year from 1880, which is known to be a year of the dragon and long enough ago that it is unlikely someone born before this year will try to use the form. The `get_sign()` function then divides the offset year by 12 and uses the remainder to figure out which of the twelve animals to return.

13. Add code to fill out the `onclick` function that MSE created for you. The barebones version of this function looks like this:

```
function button1_onclick() {
   var baseline = 1880;
   var byear = parseInt(document.birth_form.byear.value);
   var offsetyear = byear-baseline;
   window.alert("You were born in the year of the " +
get_sign(offsetyear) + "!");
   }
```

A couple of notable things happen as you type in this code. When you type `parseInt`, MSE reminds you of the proper syntax for this JavaScript function (see Figure 18-8). It is even smart enough to recognize your own `get_sign()` function and show you its syntax when you start to type it. Also, when you type the `document` object keyword and then the period, MSE pops up the valid completion of this object, including the form name. You can continue to type this object identifier or select it from the pop-up list. MSE refers to this ability to prompt you to complete object specifications as *Intellisense*.

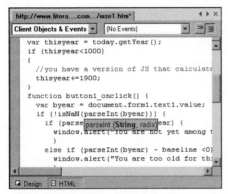

Figure 18-8: MSE remembers proper JavaScript syntax, so you don't continually have to hunt for that JavaScript reference book.

14. At this point, your JavaScript works fine (see Figure 18-9), as long as you type something reasonable into the form.

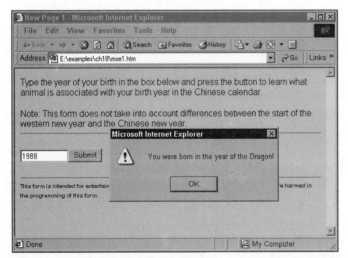

Figure 18-9: Signs of intelligent life from your JavaScript form!

If you make a mistake and type a year before the baseline year or after the present year, or if you type your name instead of a year, bad things can happen. To handle, or trap, some of the more obvious kinds of errors, add a more elaborate version of the `onclick()` method, as follows:

```
function button1_onclick() {
  var baseline = 1880;
  var byear = parseInt(document.birth_form.byear.value);
  var today = new Date();
  var thisyear = today.getYear();
  if (thisyear<1000)
  {
    //compensate for pre-Y2K browser dates
    thisyear+=1900;
  }
  if (!isNaN(byear)) {
    if (parseInt(byear)> thisyear) {
      window.alert("Sorry, you are not yet among the
living!");
    }
    else if (parseInt(byear) - baseline <0) {
      window.alert("You are too old to waste your time on
this!");
    }
    else {
      var offsetyear = byear-baseline;
      window.alert("You were born in the year of the " +
get_sign(offsetyear) + "!");
    }
  }
  else {
    window.alert(document.birth_form.byear.value + " is not a
valid year!");
  }
}
```

You can try out this code yourself, or use the version provided on the this book's Web site: www.hungryminds.com/extras/076453582x/.

Debugging scripts

One of the most difficult tasks associated with programming in a Web environment is debugging errors. Just trying to pinpoint the location of an error can sometimes be tricky, given that the files containing the scripts are passed around from Web server to browser. MSE contains tools for helping you track down those nasty bugs and squashing them with a minimum of grief. This section introduces you to some of the main debugging features offered in MSE.

There are two primary ways that MSE attempts to help you identify bugs: the first is by providing you with "insider" information about what is going on in your scripts; the second is by enabling you to start and stop your script at various points to examine what is happening along the way.

Enabling debugging

Perhaps it is cynicism on Microsoft's part, perhaps it is their personal experience — whatever the reason, it remains the case that MSE does not install with the debugging tools by default. To install the debugging tools, select Debug ➪ Install Web Debugging from the MSE menu and have your FrontPage CDs handy.

MSE includes a number of useful tools for helping you track down, decipher, and eradicate errors from your scripts. A full discussion of these tools and how to use them in developing your pages is beyond the scope of this book. Our brief tour through MSE debugging capabilities focuses on two key concepts: using tools to control your program's execution and then using watch windows to inspect your program and understand what it is doing as it runs.

Controlling program execution and setting breakpoints

Debugging a script or program is a bit like watching a video in freeze-frame mode. What you want to be able to do is advance the program a little bit at a time and examine what is going on — how have the values of various expressions changed? Which fork in the procedural road has the program taken, and why? Ideally, you also would like to be able to experiment with changing variables or calling functions with different values to see how they behave. MSE gives you an array of tools to do this. In the following, we briefly identify the principal ways that you can control the execution of your program:

✦ **Setting the execution point:** The execution point is just a marker that you can use to indicate where you would like to pause the execution of your program. In MSE it is represented by a yellow arrow in the margin of the script window. You can set and move this point. When you run your script (or continue it, if you have paused it), the script runs to this point and breaks.

Note   When you are debugging a program, your program will be in one of three modes: it may be running, in break mode, or stopped. *Break mode* is really just computer jargon for pausing while the program is still in memory.

✦ **Running to the cursor location:** Another way to break your program at a designated place is to set the cursor to the place in your program where you want to pause and then select Debug ➪ Run to Cursor.

✦ **Setting breakpoints:** The first two methods work well if you want to pause in one place. If you want to make a series of stops in predetermined locations, you can do so by setting breakpoints. *Breakpoints* are essentially smart pause markers. You can designate a breakpoint at a given function, a particular file location, or a specific memory address. In addition, you can set conditions on the breakpoints, causing your program to pause only if those conditions are met.

✦ **Stepping through your program:** Sometimes you don't know exactly where you want your program to break. You just want to advance it slowly and watch what happens at each step. This is called *stepping through* a program. If you select Debug ➪ Step By, you have the option of stepping through your program By Line or By Statement. You can also use Step Into, Step Over, and Step Out — all of which provide various ways of dealing with functions. Running Step Into causes your program to break once it starts into a function. Step Over, executes the function and then pauses. Step Out is used when you have paused the debugger inside a function and you want it to proceed to the end of the function and stop when it gets out.

Of course, being able to start, stop, and pause your program at will is a powerful capability. It is only useful, however, if you can glean some useful information about what your program is doing at each step of the way. That is where the various inspection windows in MSE come into play. These are the topic of the next section.

Gathering information about your script

Typically, when you encounter an error in your programming, you hear about it only at the end. In the best case scenario, you might receive an error message with a helpful message like "object xyz does not exist." You are certain you set this variable. There is no possible way it could not exist. What is going on?

In cases like this, what you would like is some way to peek in on your program and see exactly what it is doing along the way. MSE provides several facilities for doing these — all variations on the same theme: open a window that reports on the changing state of some portion of your programming as it runs. Typically, these are used in conjunction with some execution control, so that you have time to ponder the significance of what you are witnessing. The available debugging windows include:

✦ **Autos window:** This window displays variables used in the current or previous statement. Open the Autos window by selecting Debug ➪ Windows ➪ Autos Window.

✦ **Locals window:** This window displays variables that are local to the current context, typically the function where you have temporarily stopped execution.

✦ **Quick Watch dialog box:** The Quick Watch dialog box lets you quickly zero in on a particular expression whose value you would like to know at a given point in your program. Open the Quick Watch dialog box by selecting Debug ➪ Quick Watch, or right-click on a variable in your program and select Quick Watch from the options menu.

✦ **Watch window:** The Quick Watch dialog box is a good choice if you want information on a particular expression. The Watch window is the better choice if you want to keep track of a number of expression. Open the Watch window by selecting Debug ➪ Windows ➪ Watch. You can add expressions to the watch list by typing in their names or by dragging and dropping them into the list. The Watch window keeps track of these expressions until you delete them.

✦ **Call Stack window:** Although this window has a hard-core programmer kind of name, its function is straightforward enough. It displays a list of functions that are running or slated to run. The Call Stack window displays a variety of technical information about the functions: their programming language, line numbers, byte offsets, and other fascinating tidbits. One of the most useful features of this window is that you can double-click a function to run it and then examine the results in one of the other windows. Just another way to control execution of your program.

In addition to watching as your program changes these various entities, you can also change variables manually by typing them into the appropriate window. This way you can experiment with what happens to your function if you make a change to a variable.

In the remainder of this chapter, we offer a number of scripting examples, using both JavaScript and DHTML, to illustrate several scripting functions that you may find useful in your Web pages.

We'll start with some simple but useful JavaScript techniques that you can incorporate into your FrontPage Webs. Then, we apply what you have learned about JavaScript to a basic introduction to DHTML.

JavaScript Examples

You can enlist a scripting language like JavaScript to help you with some of the common tasks described in this section. This is by no means a thorough introduction to JavaScript, but these examples should give you some ideas about how to use it. The examples are roughly arranged from simple to more complex.

A status-bar message

The status bar is the thin band at the bottom of your browser window that displays various text messages in the course of your Web surfing. Left to its own devices, it typically displays status messages as a new page loads.

You can control the status bar messages with scripting as well. Typically, this is done in association with moving the mouse over a hyperlink as a way of providing users some contextual clues about where the link is leading. (Of course, this is only useful if the user happens to look at the status bar as they move their mouse over the link.)

Interface design issues aside, you accomplish this by adding a `window.status="msg"` statement to the `onmouseover` event handler for the hyperlink. The following steps explain how to do this:

1. Create a hyperlink that looks something like this in HTML:

```
<a href="mylink.html">Click here to see my link</a>
```

2. Add the mouseover event handler:

```
<a href="mylink.html" onmouseover="window.status='pay
attention to this space!'">Click here to see my link</a>
```

A suggestion: If you add a mouseover status message, also add a default message — or perhaps no message — that appears when the user moves the mouse off of the hyperlink.

```
<a href="mylink.html" onmouseover="window.status='pay
attention to this space!'"
onmouseout="window.status=''">Click here to see my link</a>
```

Caution   One problem with using hyperlinks to display status messages is the fact that browsers tend to display the link URL when you put the mouse over a link. This may take precedence over your status message.

Pop-up message boxes

You have already seen a couple examples of using standard scripting pop-up messages. JavaScript defines three basic pop-up message box types:

✦ **Alert:** Displays a simple text message with an OK button.

✦ **Confirm:** Displays a message with two buttons: Yes and No.

✦ **Prompt:** Displays a prompt message and a text entry field with an optional default value.

Because previous examples illustrated the use of the alert and confirm message boxes, the following is a prompt example. The prompt method takes two parameters: the message to display and a default value for the text input field. If the user presses the Cancel button, the method returns a null value. If the user presses OK, it returns whatever value is in the text input field. The following script function, illustrates how you can make use of this:

```
function promptme()
{
    var s = prompt("Your name?","here")
    if (s==null)
    {
        alert("You cancelled me!");
    }
    else
    {
        if (s=="David")
        {
            alert("Aren't you the\nlucky one!");
        }
        else
        {
```

```
        alert("Oh, I'm so sorry.");
      }
    }
  }
```

For the most part, this script should be straightforward. The one detail worth noting is the use of the \n in the alert message response. This represents a new line character and demonstrates that it is possible to dictate line breaks in your message box text — by default it will return one long string of text.

Pop-up window

Opening a new browser window is a simple technique. Frequently, sites will open any external links into a new browser window, presumably in an effort to keep you on their site. And, of course, there is always the annoying pop-up advertisement window.

Popping up a window is easy — far too easy, one might say. To do it, you call the open() method of the window object. This method has three parameters: the URL of the page to open in the new window, the window name, and a list of window features to enable. Here is an example:

```
onclick="window.open('newwindow.html','newwin',
'titlebar=yes,width=200,height=100')"
```

Notice that the feature list is represented by a single, comma-delimited string in which each feature is designated with a name=value pair. Most values take a yes, which means the feature is enabled, or no, which means it isn't. Others like height and width take a pixel value. Unfortunately, there is no definitive standard here, so acceptable values vary from browser to browser. (For example, Netscape uses ScreenX and ScreenY to define the location of the window, IE uses Left and Top.) Omitting any reference to a feature, causes it not to appear in the window you create. Some relatively safe feature options include:

Height	Status
Location	Titlebar
Menubar	Toolbar
Resizable	Width
Scrollbars	

Note　Some sites like to open new browser windows with abandon. If you are like us, you probably find this annoying, especially because if people want to open pages in separate windows they can use their browsers to do it themselves. You probably should only open a new window if you are creating what amounts to a dialog box, with input that will alter the state of the initial page, or if you are creating a standalone presentation or application that needs to run in its own space, typically stripping out browser buttons and other interface features.

Here is an advanced lesson in window opening (with a bit of a jump on the later section regarding form field manipulations). This example takes a simple one-field form in the main window and passes its current value to a field in a pop-up window. It then enables you to set the value of the field in the original window from the pop-up window — just like a dialog box would. It is a basic lesson in interwindow communication. Here are the steps:

1. Create a simple HTML page with a single textbox form and a normal push button. Call the page `mainform.htm`. Name the form element `f1`, and the textbox `tb1`. Set the value of `t1` to `This is a test`.

2. Create a second HTML page, which will be the pop-up dialog box. Call it `dialogbox.htm`. Create a select list with some values in it. (The example has a list of educational degrees.) Name the form element on this page `f2` and the select list `s1`. Add a textbox field, called `tb2` and a normal push button. The results should resemble the two windows shown in Figure 18-10.

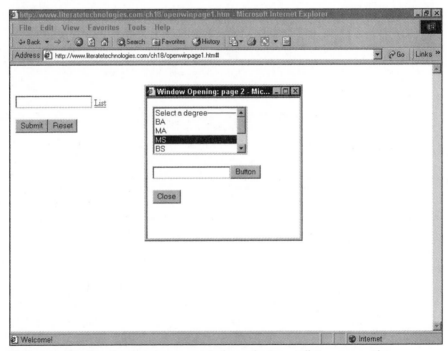

Figure 18-10: Creating two browser windows that can talk to one another

3. The next step is to create a function that will open the dialog box (`dialogbox.htm`) and populate its textbox (`tb2`) with the current (default) value of the original page's textbox (`tb1`). To do this, do the following:

   • Create a script block in `page1.htm` and define a variable `newwin`.

   • Add a function called `openDialog()` that takes no parameters.

- Add a single line of code to openDialog() as shown below:

```
<script>
<!-- //
var newwin;
function openDialog()
{
    newwin =
window.open('page2.htm','dialog','width=300,height=250');
}
//-->
</script>
```

So far, you have a function that, when called, opens a new window and returns a reference to that new window (in the newwin variable). Next you need a link that calls the function to open the dialog box. Create a simple text hyperlink and set its onclick handler to the openDialog() function:

```
onclick="openDialog();".
```

Now all you have to do is set the field value in the new window to whatever you want it to be. Except for one small problem: you need some way to know that the new window has actually finished opening before you make a call to its field objects. Otherwise, you will generate "Object not found" errors. Do to this, you have to get the dialogbox.htm to tell you when it is finished loading.

4. To this end, create a new function in mainform.htm, called callMe(). This function is responsible for setting the value of the field in page2.htm. It looks like this (don't worry about where the setMyField comes from yet):

```
function callMe()
    {
        var o = document.f1.t1; //this is the page1 field
newwin.setMyField(o);
    }
```

5. Now it is time to deal with dialogbox.htm. Open this file. In the body tag, add an onload event handler:

```
<body onload="doOnLoad();">
```

This script will call back to mainform after dialogbox is finished loading. The function itself (see the next listing) first calls back to mainform to let it know it can set the targetField object. Then it gets the value of that field and puts it into its own textbox. Notice the use of the opener property, which is a convenient (in fact, essential for this example) property of windows that contains a reference to the window responsible for opening them (mainform.html).

6. Now you need to create a function that enables page1.htm to pass along the field information to dialogbox.htm that will enable it to set field values back in the original page. This is where you create the setMyField function mentioned earlier. Add a script block to dialogbox.html that looks like this:

```
<script>
<!--//
var targetField;
```

```
function setMyField(o)
{
    targetField=o;
}
function doOnLoad()
{
    window.opener.callMe();
    document.f2.t2.value=targetField.value;
}
//-->
</script>
```

7. Last but not least, you create a function called doOnClose() to fire when a
user clicks the button on dialogbox.htm. This function performs two operations: First it sets the value of the textbox in mainform.htm to the selected
value from the list in page2.htm. Then it closes the pop-up window. Here it is:

```
function doOnClose()
{
    opener.document.f1.degree.value=document.f2.s1.options
[document.f2.s1.selectedIndex].text;
    window.close();
}
```

Whew! Now try it out. Open mainform.htm. You can change the default text in the
text field or leave it as it. Click on the link to open the dialog pop-up box. Its textbox
should contain the same value as the initial textbox. Now select a value from the
select list and click the dialog box's close button. It should update the
mainform.html textbox and then close.

Page redirects

A *page redirect* refers to the ability to have one page redirect the user to another
page. There are lots of uses for this. One of the most popular is to create a drop-
down navigational device that lists the pages on the site. Selecting a page automatically redirects you to that page. Here's one way to do that, using a basic page
redirect function:

1. First create a select list with the names of pages in the list. Set the value of
each option to the URL for the page. You should have a form that looks something like this when you are finished:

```
<form name="f1" method="POST">
  <p><select name="s1" size="1" name="D1">
  <option selected value="0">Select a page</option>
  <option value="zero.htm">home</option>
  <option value="two.htm">Page two</option>
  <option value="one.htm">Page One</option>
  </select></p>
```

2. Add an `onselect` event handler to redirect the browser based on the user's selection. The redirect is triggered by setting the `href` property of the page's `location` object to a valid URL (i.e., `location.href=someurl`):

```
onChange="this.selectedIndex>0?
location.href=this.options[this.selectedIndex].value:'';"
```

Caution

Make sure you have your page set so that it resets this menu list each time the user loads the page. Because the event only fires when the selection changes, if the user comes to the page and the Page one option is already selected (for example), they will go nowhere if they reselect Page one.

You may have begun to notice a certain pattern in the JavaScript examples provided above. In most instances, a user initiates some action that triggers your JavaScript to perform some designated task. In this way, you create a truly interactive experience for your users. Granted, these examples are basic, but for the most part, sophisticated JavaScript applications are just more of the same.

One thing that is missing from these examples, though, it the ability to interact directly with elements on the page. That, as we will see in the next section, is in large part the attraction of Dynamic HTML techniques.

Discovering DHTML

Dynamic HTML (DHTML) refers to Web page programming that manipulates page elements at the time that they are presented in the browser. DHTML makes the following features possible: page-level animation, expandable navigation menus, drag and drop, and a generally more sophisticated, dynamic Web page.

DHTML accomplishes all of this by combining a client-side scripting language, such as JavaScript or VBScript, with some means of accessing page elements. The programming interface that enables this interaction is called the Document Object Model (DOM) by both Navigator and Internet Explorer. Unfortunately, although the two major browsers have agreed on a name for this entity, they haven't agreed on an implementation. As a result, one of the chief difficulties of working with DHTML is dealing with browser compatibility issues.

A full account of the DOM and how it works is beyond the scope of this chapter. The goal here is to give you a general overview of the DOM, including some of the issues facing you if you take on a DHTML project. (You can find more information on adding DHTML animation effects to your pages in Chapter 13.)

The Document Object Model

The Document Object Model is the terminology that defines how you can refer to elements of the HTML document. The purpose of the DOM is to enable programmers to interact with and make changes dynamically to HTML pages.

The W3C has released a specification for DOM Level 1, which includes the core objects that make up the DOM. This is good news in the near future for developers, but the reality is that, at the moment, Netscape and Microsoft have evolved separate DOMs that bear a resemblance to each other but use different syntax and give access to different elements of the HTML document. Presently, this means that the biggest challenge in using DHTML in a real-world application is making certain that the programming works in both browser worlds. (Of course, if you happen to work in an environment such as an intranet, in which you need to worry about only a single browser type, you are among the lucky minority.)

Note   As if worrying about DOMs isn't enough of a problem, you also need to know how to reference and manipulate style sheet elements via programming. The terminology for doing this sometimes is referred to as the *Style Sheet Object Model*. For more information on style sheets, see Chapter 11.

The main purpose of the DOM is to give programmers access to the elements of an HTML page. Netscape Communicator 4.x does this by exposing elements of the page that it refers to as *layers*. This includes elements contained inside a <LAYER> tag, which is supported only by Netscape. It also includes elements that FrontPage calls Position boxes, namely DIV and SPAN elements. Because these are standard tags, you are should probably use these for any elements that you want to access via the DOM.

In addition, Netscape has developed in its version 4 browser a set of JavaScript elements to refer to style sheet elements that don't correspond to the CSS syntax. Things are significantly improved in version 6, but as long as older browsers remain in use, this babel of name differences will continue to cause confusion. The example in the next section does a reasonable job of pointing out the degree of the headaches involved, and (fortunately) illustrates one approach to dealing with the problem.

Internet Explorer, in contrast, exposes all the tags on a given page, using a collection object named all as well as a set of "children" collections that refers to HTML tags contained within a specific tag. IE also exposes all the elements defined in <STYLE> tags, by using the styles collection associated with a particular element. Most importantly, IE allows for real-time updating of any element on the page. Netscape currently does not.

Note   This example assumes that you are familiar with JavaScript programming as we have discussed in the first half of this chapter. It will also help to have read chapter 11 which covers Cascading Style Sheets (CSS).

Developing a DHTML script

This section steps through the process of creating a relatively simple (from a conceptual standpoint) DHTML program, and then shows how it is complicated by the need to make it cross-browser compatible. The program that you create is a simple pop-up message box, similar in concept to Windows ToolTips. Your program is called *Pop-ups*.

1. Create the pop-up message box. Open a new page in FrontPage and type something—anything to serve as temporary text for your pop-up box. Add a DIV element around the text. The simplest way to do this is by hand. (You can use the position box command in FrontPage to create this tag, but you will end up having to remove attributes manually. Alternatively, you can use MSE, which can insert <DIV> tags. Select HTML ⇨ Div and choose the Inline option.)

Switch to HTML view and type the following:

```
<div id="popupbox">Our Sample Pop-up Text</div>
```

2. Create a local style for your position box. Select Format ⇨ Style. Click the New button to create a new user-defined style. Name it #popupbox (the # designates a style ID) and click the Format button to set the following font, border, and position attributes:

```
#popupbox    {
    font-family: Arial;
    font-size: 10pt;
    color: #660033;
    background-color: #FFCC99;
position: absolute;
left: 50;
top: 40
    border: 1 solid #660033
}
```

The results are illustrated in Figure 18-11.

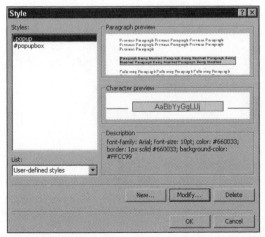

Figure 18-11: Defining the pop-up style using CSS

3. After you create this style, apply it to the DIV element that you made in Step 1. When you are satisfied with the way the box looks (disregard the fact that it's too long; you will fix that in a moment), add the following line to the STYLE:

```
visibility: hidden
```

4. Before you leave the HTML view, you need to add some text with a hyperlink. When you pass the mouse over this link, you want it to pop up your message. To do this, you need to trap mouseover and mouseout events, using the following code:

```
<a onmouseover="showPopUp()" onmouseout="hidePopUp()">Here is
some text</a>
```

5. Next, you will create JavaScript routines to hide and show this element. For now, these functions are simple wrappers for methods to change the visibility attribute of the position box. However, you will need to add to these functions when you create cross-browser versions of your program.

You use MSE for the scripting work (more for the practice than from necessity — your scripting needs are fairly simple and could just as easily be done in the HTML tab). Select Tools ➪ Macro ➪ Microsoft Script Editor to open the HTML page in MSE. Select View ➪ Property Pages and set the default client scripting language to JavaScript (ECMAScript).

Right-click in the HTML source window at a location between the end of the <title> tag and the end of the <head> tag. Select Insert Script Block ➪ Client to insert an empty scripting block in the header of your page. Add the following functions:

```
<script language=javascript>
<!--
function showPopUp() {

document.all.popupbox.style.setAttribute("visibility", \
  "visible");
  }
function hidePopUp() {

document.all.popupbox.style.setAttribute("visibility", \
  "hidden");
  }
//-->
</script>
```

6. If you followed the directions accurately, you should see the text message pop up when you run the mouse over the hyperlink. When you remove the mouse button, the message disappears.

7. All you really need to add to this procedure are the capabilities to change the text message dynamically and to position the dialog box on the page.

Modifying the text is easy (until you begin to make the script Netscape-compatible). Simply pass a `text` parameter to the `showPopUp()` function, and then add the custom text to the `onmouseover=` event.

To position the pop-up message correctly, you need to find the location where the pop-up box is invoked. To do that, pass an event object to your function. Then, use the event object's `clientX` and `clientY` properties to get the necessary mouse coordinates. You relocate the top and left properties of the `popupbox` style relative to these mouse coordinates. As shown here, the top left corner of the popup box appears fifteen pixels to the left, and ten pixels above the mouse position. When you are done, the `showPopUp()` function looks like this:

```
function showPopUp(e,text) {
    //replace the text inside the DIV tag
    popupbox.innerHTML=text;
    //x-offset
    document.all.popupbox.style.setAttribute("left", \
      e.clientX+15);
    //y-offset
    document.all.popupbox.style.setAttribute("top", \
      e.clientY+10);
    //show popupbox
    document.all.popupbox.style.setAttribute("visibility", \
      "visible");
    }
```

The `MouseOver` event of the hyperlink tag should resemble the following (note the use of single quotes around the text string, to avoid clashing with the double quotes around the function call):

```
onmouseover="showPopUp(event, 'This is a test...')"
```

That is it. You can even use this mechanism with an image map, to provide custom pop-up messages.

Adding non-DHTML support

If you were content with having your DHTML work only with IE 4 or greater, you would be done now. However, your page currently doesn't work in Netscape Navigator 4. To create cross-browser DHTML, you need to determine which browser you are dealing with, and then build your DHTML accordingly.

The first (and frankly easier) task is to provide alternative functionality for those users who have pre-version 4 browsers. To do this, you set up three true/false variables: `IsIE`, `IsNN`, and `DoesDHTML`. Then, initialize them after checking the browser name and version. This code, listed here, is added to the top of the script block that you created in the previous section:

```
var IsIE = false;
var IsNN = false;
var DoesDHTML = false;

if (navigator.appName == "Netscape") {
  IsNN = true;
  }
else if (navigator.appName == "Microsoft Internet Explorer") {
  IsIE = true;
  }

if (parseInt(navigator.appVersion) >= 4) {
  DoesDHTML = true;
  }
```

Now, make two small changes to your showPopUp() function:

1. Wrap your current functionality in checks, to make sure that you perform them only if you have a version 4 or later IE browser.

2. Add a generic function at the end of this function, to set the status bar with the text that you passed to your function.

In a version 3 browser (or any current non-IE browser), this is all that happens. Notice, as illustrated by the Netscape browser screen shot shown in Figure 18-12, that it doesn't yet know what to do with the supposedly "hidden" position box text that it displays at the top of the page. You also need to add code to the hidePopUp() function, to set the status bar back to its default value. Here is the revised function:

```
function showPopUp(e,text) {
  if (DoesDHTML) {
    if (IsIE) {
      popupbox.innerHTML=text;
document.all.popupbox.style.setAttribute("left",
  e.clientX+15);
document.all.popupbox.style.setAttribute("top",e.clientY+10);
document.all.popupbox.style.setAttribute("visibility",
  "visible");
      }
    }
  window.status = text;
  return true;
  }
```

Note   When you set the window.status property, you also add code to return a true value from your function. To accommodate this, you also update the onmouseover call as follows:

```
<A onmouseover= "return showPopUp(event, 'This is a
test')"
A similar change is made to onmouseout.
```

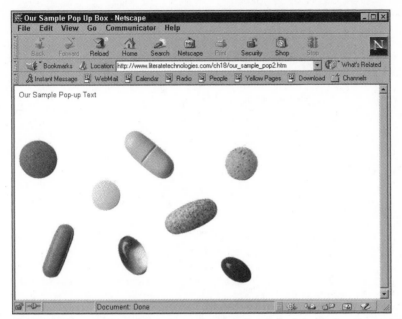

Figure 18-12: Netscape's browser, showing the default behavior of your DHTML script for non-IE browsers. (Notice that Netscape does update the status bar!)

Adding cross-browser compatibility

The language used in this section's title requires some clarification. You actually have already made your script "cross-browser-compatible," but only if that means (as the marketing departments of the major browser companies mean) that your script won't break in any browser. What you really want, though, is comparable behavior in both Navigator and IE. To get that, you have to work a bit harder.

The first question to address is why Netscape doesn't recognize the position box that you created. The answer is that Navigator chokes on the style information that FrontPage produces. Specifically, it does not like the way that FrontPage designates border information about the pop-up message (`border: 1 solid #660033;`). You can alleviate the problem by removing the offending line from the style designation and adding it into the `showPopUp` code for IE:

```
document.all.popup.style.setAttribute("border","1 solid
#660033");
```

Note It appears that more recent versions of Netscape (v. 4.7, and later for example) deal with FrontPage's style sheet designations correctly. If you are working with only current browser versions, some of what follows may be unnecessary.

Now, Netscape will hide the position box text, and you can add Netscape-specific code to render the text visible. Netscape's DOM has a very different way of referencing elements in the page. Here is the code to make Netscape show the position box at the appropriate location (added to the showPopUp routine):

```
else if (IsNN) {
    document.popupbox.visibility="visible";
    document.popupbox.top=e.pageY+10;
    document.popupbox.left=e.pageX+15;
    }
```

And here is the code added to hidePopUp:

```
else if (IsNN) {
    document.popupbox.visibility="hidden";
    }
```

You still have a couple differences to overcome. Although you have referenced the event object to find the mouse-cursor coordinates (note Netscape's use of pageX and pageY rather than clientX clientY), you haven't yet added code to update the text of your pop-up message with the text variable that you pass to your function.

The challenge is that Netscape, unlike IE, doesn't update page elements automatically. It doesn't even have a way to reference the text inside a tag, in the way that you used the innerHTML property in your IE code.

One way to update the text of a layer element (including DIV and SPAN elements, as well as the Netscape-specific LAYER element) is to call that layer's document.write() method. So, to change the text of the pop-up message in Netscape, use the following code (the second line is necessary to ensure that the next popupbox call does not simply append additional text to the existing text):

```
document.popupbox.document.write(text);
document.popupbox.document.close();
```

Now, you can update the text in your Netscape pop-up message. However, if you look closely at the results, you may notice that you have lost all the formatting of your position box, including font and border styles. Unfortunately, when Navigator calls the document.write() method, it overwrites everything that it knows about the popupbox element, including all of its styles. Are you starting to sense that this process takes you two steps forward and one step back? The next section offers a workaround to this new problem that actually solves several difficulties simultaneously.

One way to retain the style information when you rewrite the Netscape layer object (as just detailed) is to store that information in a separate class style and then write the class name back into the layer. This is easier to show than to describe. First create a new class style, called .popup, and give it the following styles (note that you need to create this style manually, because several of the style designations are Netscape-specific, and FrontPage cannot generate them using the Style dialog box):

```
.popup {
     font-family: Arial;
     ffont-size: 10pt;
     fcolor: #660033;
     fbackground-color: #FFCC99;
     fborder-color: #CC9966;
     fborder-width: 1px;
   }
```

Now, revise the original #popupbox style to include only the minimal style information needed:

```
#popupbox   {
    visibility: hidden;
    position: absolute;
        }
```

Finally, revise the Netscape document.write() line to read as follows:

```
document.popupbox.document.write("<span class=popup>" + text +
"</span>");
```

Admittedly, this last statement is a bit of a hack, because it requires writing a second layer element inside the original one. However, it works, and given the amount of fussing necessary just to get this far, we, personally, can live with this. Now, compare the final results in both Internet Explorer (Figure 18-13) and Netscape (Figure 18-14).

One other adjustment was required to get the Netscape pop-up box to fill in the background as shown in Figure 18-14. Prior to adding the extra line, Netscape insisted on creating a line of white between the border and the background color, which stubbornly resisted all efforts to go away. Adding the following line to the Netscape portion of showPopUp routine seemed do the trick, although we can't explain why and haven't seen this documented anywhere:

```
document.popupbox.bgColor="#FFCC99"
```

If you look closely, you'll notice that it still retains the extra padding around the text, but at least it is filled with color.

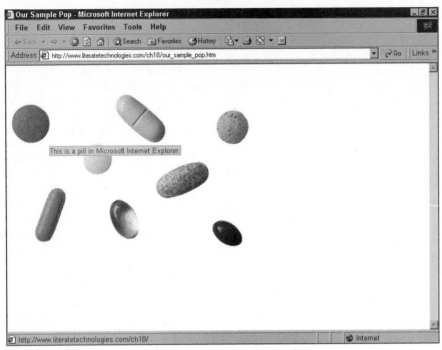

Figure 18-13: Your pop-up box in IE

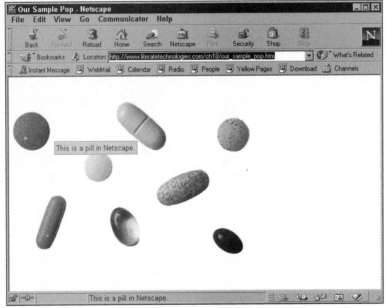

Figure 18-14: Your pop-up box in Netscape

Browser compatibility

This DHTML example has gone beyond simply demonstrating what is required to create a DHTML script in FrontPage; it has demonstrated what is required to create a real-world DHTML script using FrontPage. Most of the challenges involved have little to do with FrontPage and everything to do with the disparate state of the various DOMs still in the process of coalescing around a standard. However, you may also notice that FrontPage does not provide much assistance for creating cross-browser scripts. FrontPage is more helpful if you decide to develop to the lowest common denominator (in other words, to use only those capabilities that are common to both browser environments). You may suspect that in the current state of DHTML, that fact leaves precious little to work with.

Summary

This chapter has introduced you to the world of client-side scripting. As we discussed, having certain items update themselves on the user's browser enables you to validate information and produce interesting effects without making resource-intensive server calls. The chapter discussed JavaScript and walked you through several simple script examples. The Microsoft Script Editor was introduced, which provides a lot of your script language for you and makes it easy to coordinate your scripting tasks with FrontPage. Finally, we discussed DHTML, and how conflicting standards make it difficult for you to create DHTML scripts that work in both popular browsers. The next chapter moves from client-side scripting to server-side scripting.

✦   ✦   ✦

Server-side Programming: CGI and ASP

I n this chapter, we go a step beyond the programming support built into FrontPage and examine how you can extend your Web site's functionality with *server-side programming*. We examine two general approaches to server-side programming: classic CGI scripts and server-side processing languages. For each type, we walk through a full-length example — a CGI Perl script and an ASP page — in part to illustrate how you can work with these in FrontPage and in part to compare the virtues of each method. It is not our intent to try to teach you to become ace programmers in a single chapter. This chapter is designed to help you understand how these two types of server-side programming operate so that you can decide if either is appropriate for your Web development needs.

> **Note**
>
> If you are interested in online CGI tutorials, try www.cgi101.com (or get the complete version in book form, authored by Jacqueline D. Hamilton). For a list of technical resources, see www.w3.org/CGI. There are also a number of good online resources where you can find sample scripts, including the CGI resource, www.cgi-resources.com and the CGI Directory, www.cgidir.com.

Overview of Server-side Programming

There are two basic types of programs that can interact with a Web server. The first, *CGI programming*, involves a mechanism that enables the Web server to pass information to an external process and have it return data to the Web browser. CGI applications are thus stand-alone programs, which can be written in any of a number of standard programming languages. The examples we provide in this chapter were written in Perl.

The second type of server-side programming we discuss in this chapter is *server-side scripting*. In the case of server-side scripting, you embed programming blocks directly into your Web page and save your Web page with a special file ending. The Web server is then instructed to send these pages to a special *preprocessing application* that interprets and executes the scripts in the page and then returns the page to the browser. Our examples of this type of programming are limited to Active Server Pages (ASP), Microsoft's popular server-side processing language.

Introducing CGI

Common Gateway Interface (CGI) is the basis for communication between a Web server and an external process or application. CGI is not itself a programming language. It simply defines a standard for how information should be passed from a Web server to an external program, and how the external program should pass information back to the server. CGI's name is derived as follows:

- ✦ **Common:** CGI is common not because it is low-class, but because it is a defined standard that uses a basic data-passing mechanism, one to which all good Web servers adhere.

- ✦ **Gateway:** CGI defines a gateway because the program that you write serves as a gateway between the Web environment and any other application (a database, for instance) that you might want to send Web data to or return data from. In many cases, of course, the CGI application serves as an end unto itself.

- ✦ **Interface:** CGI is an interface because it defines how two separate entities — the Web server and your program — can communicate with one another.

A CGI program can be written using any programming language that can execute on the same system as your Web server. Some of the more common programming languages used to create CGI applications include the following:

- ✦ **Perl:** Perhaps the most commonly used CGI programming language, Perl is an acronym for Practical Extraction and Report Language. Perl was originally written for UNIX and ported to Windows and Macintosh, and is perhaps the most portable CGI language (besides C). Perl is an *interpreted language,* which means that the source code is read and interpreted when the Perl program is run (as opposed to being compiled beforehand, like a C program).

- ✦ **C/C++:** The C programming languages are reputedly harder to learn than languages such as Visual Basic and Perl, and so you see fewer freely available C-based CGI programs. Because it is a compiled language, C typically produces faster CGI code than most other languages.

✦ **Java:** Although Java is more commonly used to write applets that run inside a Web page (see Chapter 15 for more detail), as a cross-platform programming language, Java is perfectly suitable for CGI programming as well.

✦ **Visual Basic:** VB is the most popular Windows programming language, and its applications are fairly simple to implement.

CGI pros and cons

The choice of which programming language to use depends on several factors, including the scope and complexity of the task, time and budget constraints, and who you enlist to do the work and what their experience is. Ultimately, any one of the programming languages listed in the previous section produces serviceable CGI code.

The chief virtues of a CGI application are that it can be written in any of a variety of programming languages and that the CGI interface specification itself is very easy to understand and use. As a standard, CGI is supported by practically all commercial Web servers.

One disadvantage of a CGI application is that it is relatively slow and can be a drag on system resources, particularly if you have a CGI application that is frequently invoked by many people simultaneously. The server has to start a separate instance of the CGI application for each user, pass the data back and forth, and then close the application when it is finished.

Another limitation of CGI is that it can only be invoked via the server. This means that to process any information, the CGI application must have the information submitted via an HTML form. As soon as the CGI application processes the information that it receives and returns its response, it is done. This creates a challenge for any application involving multiple transactions by a user, because as far as the CGI is concerned, each time that the user calls the application, it is the first time. In other words, there is no straightforward way for data to carry over from one application call to the next.

POST versus GET

A few simple CGI examples are coming up, but before you delve into the details, you need to understand the basic principles of how a Web server sends form input to a CGI application.

Basically, two methods exist by which the server can send form input to an external, gateway application. These two methods are called GET and POST.

Note   GET and POST are part of the larger HTTP specification. If you are interested in the nitty-gritty details of this specification, check out http://www.ics.uci.edu/pub/ietf/http/rfc1945.html.

The POST method of submitting input is preferred. POST instructs the server to output the form data to *standard input* (STDIN), a well-known repository that the CGI program can monitor and, when data comes in, from which it can pick up data. In addition, the POST method sets a variable called CONTENT_LENGTH that tells the CGI program how long the string of text is that it wants to pick up. One of the chief virtues of the POST method is that the data is passed behind the scenes, without attaching the input to the URL. Only HTML forms are capable of invoking the POST method.

The GET method is more of a general-purpose method for handling data than is POST. GET is not as powerful or elegant as POST, perhaps, but it is serviceable in certain circumstances. GET can be used to send form data, or it can be invoked directly from a URL. For this reason, GET is limited to a maximum length of 255 characters.

With the GET method, form input data is attached to the URL itself before being sent to the server. The basic format for a GET URL is as follows:

```
http://www.myserver.com/cgi-bin/
myhandler.cgi?name=david&rank=101&serialno=345
```

Data is separated from the body of the URL by a question mark (?). Data elements are separated by ampersands (&), and each data element consists of a name/value pair, linked by an equals sign (=), for example, in this URL, the user's name is passed as david. The CGI application receives the data portion of this URL in a variable called QUERY_STRING.

Armed with the preceding information, you are ready to configure an HTML form to work with a custom form handler. But first you need a form handler, so you create one in the next section.

Custom Form Handling with CGI

We are going to walk through two examples. The first is very basic, just enough to give you a taste. Then we provide an example that is a bit more involved, but also more useful.

A simple Perl CGI

A typical CGI program performs several basic functions. These include

✦ Determining whether data is submitted via GET or POST

✦ Parsing the data input into name/value pair variables

✦ Processing and storing the data input in a useful format — and possibly calling on other external programs to assist in this

✦ Returning an appropriate Web page response to the user via the Web server

Note   If you are looking for more information on Perl, the the primay source is `www.perl.com`.

Your Perl script, `simplecgi.pl`, doesn't do anything fancy, but it does illustrate each of these steps. A complete discussion of Perl is beyond the scope of this chapter, but the next four sections point out some of the salient parts of the program.

Note   You can find a copy of this script on the Web site for this book, `www.hungryminds.com/extras/076453582x/`.
See the Preface for additional details on accessing this site.

Running Perl on Windows

You can use Perl on just about any version of Windows, including Windows 95, 98, Me, Windows NT and 2000. Before you can run a Perl script on your Windows Web server, however, you need to perform several preliminary steps (or have a system administrator perform them for you):

1. Obtain a copy of the Perl for Windows executable. The most commonly used version of Perl for Windows is available from ActiveState at its Web site, `www.activestate.com`. Note that if you are not running Windows 2000 or Me, you may need to upgrade the Windows Installer first.

2. Install Perl in an appropriate and secure location (see the section on scripting security in this chapter), not in a directory that is Web-accessible.

3. Configure your Web server to recognize Perl scripts and associate them with the Perl application.

Perl is a flexible and powerful programming language, and the one thing that you don't want to do is to put the executable someplace where any Web user could have access to it. Under no circumstances should you place the executable in the `cgi-bin` directory of your Web server or in any other directory that has been set up to execute CGI scripts. To do so would open a gaping security hole in your system.

Instead, you should place Perl executables in a location that isn't directly accessible from a Web browser, but is somewhere that the server can find the Perl when it needs to. You can use one of two approaches to do this.

Option 1 is to create a shell, or wrapper program, that sends the appropriate information to the Perl executable. This approach is safer because it filters out any of the nasty things that someone might do by accessing Perl directly. This wrapper program can be created as a batch file (a not-so-great idea) or as a Visual Basic or C program (a better idea).

Continued

Continued

Option 2: Associate Perl scripts with `perl.exe` in the Windows Registry. This approach is the official Microsoft explanation for setting up Perl with Internet Information Server (IIS). An equivalent explanation isn't provided for Microsoft's Personal Web Server (PWS), but it seems to work just fine. This method requires making a change to your system Registry information, so you should be comfortable with editing the Registry before trying this. These are the basic steps:

1. Open the Registry database by using RegEdit.

2. Navigate to:

`HKEY_LOCAL_MACHINE::System::CurrentControlSet::Services::W3 Svc::Parameters::ScriptMap`

3. Right-click in the right side and select New ➪ String value.

4. Enter .pl.

5. Right-click the string value that you just created and select Modify.

6. Enter the full path to the Perl executable; for example, `C:\perl\bin\perl.exe`.

7. Add a space and `%s` after the path name; for example, `C\perl\bin\perl.exe %s`.

8. Close the Registry.

Parsing the data

This section of the script, contained in a subroutine called `parseResults()`, is the most complicated. `parseResults()` first determines whether the results have come from a `GET` or a `POST` method, and then obtains the results string from the appropriate place:

```
$contentLength  = $ENV{'CONTENT_LENGTH'};
$requestMethod = $ENV{'REQUEST_METHOD'};
    if ($requestMethod eq 'GET') {
      $resultString = $ENV{'QUERY_STRING'};
    }
  elsif ($requestMethod eq 'POST') {
    read(STDIN, $resultString, $contentLength);
    }
```

After this, `parseResults()` massages the results string, placing the data in an associative array (`%results`) that makes the data relatively easy to work with.

Saving the data

After it has parsed the form input, `simplecgi.pl` proceeds to write the field values to a file. The path and name of this file are held in the variable `$logfile`, which you can configure to point to a valid file. The log writing is performed in the `&saveResults()` subroutine. This routine is not particularly flexible, although you can configure the field separator (a comma, by default) by changing the value of the `$FS` variable. Only field values are written to the file.

Returning the data

Finally, a simple confirmation page is returned. The HTML for this page is formulated by the Perl program. The data-results display is formatted in a separate subroutine, which makes changing the formatting relatively easy. Even if you are not familiar with Perl commands, you should recognize that this section of the `&returnResults()` subroutine is primarily standard HTML:

```
$resultsHTML = <<"returnHTML";
<HTML>
<HEAD>
<TITLE>$title</TITLE>
</HEAD>
<BODY BGCOLOR=#FFFFFF>
<H1>$title</H1>
$fResults
</BODY>
</HTML>
returnHTML
```

Configuring a custom CGI handler

With your simple CGI form handler ready to go, it is finally time to create and configure a form to send data to your custom handler. Note that to make this work, you need to make sure that Perl is installed and running on your server, and that you have a scripts directory (typically either `scripts` or `cgi-bin`) that is configured to permit the execution of programs such as `simplecgi.pl`. (Even if you can't run the script, however, you can still follow the steps necessary to configure the form.)

1. Create a form. Because `simplecgi.pl` is completely generic, you can create any number of form fields; see Figure 19-1 for an example.

2. Right-click the form element and select Form Properties from the options menu.

3. Select the Send To Other option, and select Custom ISAPI, NSAPI, CGI, or ASP script.

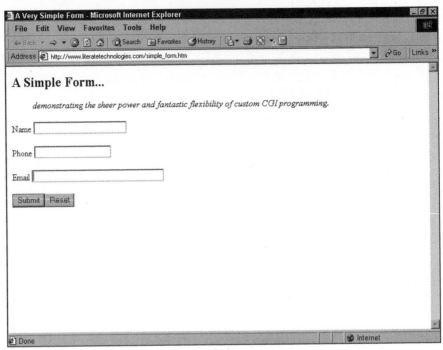

Figure 19-1: A simple form for your simple CGI script

4. Click the Options button to bring up the Options for Custom Form Handler dialog box.

5. Set the Action field to the URL for the script file; for example, `/scripts/simplecgi.pl`.

6. Set the Method field to `POST` (the default).

7. Leave the Encoding Type field blank (the default, `application/x-www-form-urlencoded`, is fine unless you are performing a file upload).

8. Click OK to return to the Form Properties dialog box. Click OK again to return to Page view.

9. Save the form and preview it. Don't forget that you may need to change the name of the log file in the Perl script. To do this, open the script in your favorite text editor and adjust the `$logfile` variable to suit. When you submit the form, you should see results that resemble Figure 19-2.

10. Check the log file to see whether the input values are recorded there as well.

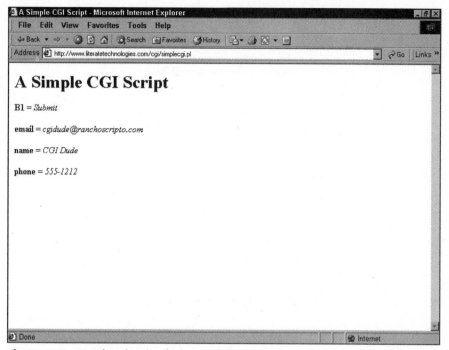

Figure 19-2: Results of a simple form, as processed by your custom Perl script.

Security precautions with CGI

If you plan to use any CGI programs on your Web site, you need to be aware of the potential security problems that running scripts can present. Any time that you introduce programming elements onto your site, you open up a potential entrance to your computer system. This is not intended to scare you away from using scripts, only to alert you to the need to take precautions. The following is general advice to help avoid problems. It applies as well to any type of custom form handlers.

✦ **Keep program executables out of public directories.** By definition, your scripts directory must allow general access to execute programming. For this reason, placing the `perl.exe` interpreter in the scripts directory, or any accessible directory, is incredibly dangerous. See the earlier sidebar, "Running Perl on Windows," for directions on how to avoid this.

✦ **Limit access to script directories.** For similar reasons, make sure that you or your system administrator has turned off Read access on your script directories. Visitors have no reason to browse this directory. It is enough that they can execute scripts.

✦ **Control the functionality of scripts.** Although the `simplecgi.pl` script that has been used to illustrate some basic CGI principles has nothing intrinsically dangerous about it, it isn't a particularly intelligent script, partly because it doesn't sufficiently trap for errors. Equally important, however, is that it doesn't sufficiently limit its own functionality. It has nothing to prevent someone with Web access to create a form with hundreds or thousands of fields, fill each field with volumes of text, and then pointing their form at your script. The result could easily bring down a Web server. A good CGI script should check the authenticity of the form that calls it.

NSAPI and ISAPI form handlers

CGI programs are relatively simple to create, and they function adequately under normal circumstances. Because CGI programs are separate programs from the server, however, they have several limitations. Each time that they are invoked, they have to be started. Likewise, when they finish their task, they have to be stopped. Also, because CGI programs run in their own memory space, if 100 people request a script simultaneously, the Web server has to start 100 copies of the program, which can quickly eat up system resources on heavily used sites. *NSAPI* and *ISAPI* form handlers are an attempt to overcome some of the limitations inherent in CGI.

NSAPI stands for Netscape Application Programming Interface. ISAPI, Microsoft's equivalent to NSAPI, stands for Internet Server Application Programming Interface. Although they differ in particulars, both of these entities define methods by which a programmer can construct a CGI-like application that is loaded within the memory space of the Web server. In this fashion, all the previously mentioned limitations of CGI programs are largely overcome.

Note FrontPage Server Extensions for Internet Information Server are an example of ISAPI applications.

So, why doesn't everybody just use these API-based handlers if they are so great? In the first place, they are much more difficult to write than a standard CGI application. In all but the most complex situations, the time and cost involved to create them isn't worth using them. Secondly, this type of handler is highly Web-server dependent, as witnessed by the fact that Netscape and Microsoft Web servers have separate APIs.

Using the CGI.pm module

If you do any amount of custom CGI scripting, you will find that you are repeating the same basic processes repeatedly just to handle the basic communication between your programming and the Web server. To simplify some of these tasks, there is a Perl module — an extension to the core Perl programming language — designed to handle basic CGI functions. This module, written by Lincoln Stein, is called `CGI.pm`.

Note

> `CGI.pm` and instructions on installing as well as a wealth of documentation and examples on its use can be found at `http://stein.cshl.org/WWW/software/CGI/cgi_docs.html`. All scripts described in this chapter can be downloaded from this book's Web site: `www.hungryminds.com/extras/076453582x/`.

To see if you have `CGI.pm` correctly installed on your system, you can use the `testcgipm.pl` script found in the Chapter 19 examples on the book's Web site. Place this script in your `cgi-bin` directory and point to it with your Web browser. If you see something resembling Figure 19-3, you know you have `CGI.pm` installed.

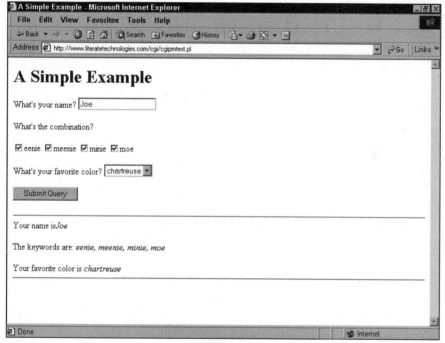

Figure 19-3: Results for the testcgipm.pl script

To understand more about how to work with the `CGI.pm` module, we recommend reading the documentation that comes with it. In the meantime, here is an example of how this module can save time and effort in your CGI programming. You may recall the `parseResults()` method in the `simplecgi.pl` script that assembled form input into an associative array. Using the `CGI.pm` module, this is all taken care of. You can access any form input using the following syntax:

```
param('form_element_name')
```

Single-item results are returned as strings; multi-item results (as in a multiple select list or checkboxes) are returned as arrays.

`CGI.pm` also contains methods for creating HTML forms (or any other basic HTML for that matter.) As with any other programming aid, it takes some time to learn the details of `CGI.pm`, but once you do, writing custom form handlers will be a breeze. Here is the code that produces the simple form in the `textcgipm.pl` program:

```
print start_form,
    "What's your name? ",textfield('name'),
    p,
    "What's the combination?",
    p,
    checkbox_group(-name=>'words',
        -values=>['eenie','meenie','minie','moe'],
        -defaults=>['eenie','minie']),
    p,
    "What's your favorite color? ",
    popup_menu(-name=>'color',
        -values=>['red','green','blue','chartreuse']),
    p,
    submit,
    end_form;
```

The Perl `print` statement is followed by a series of `CGI.pm` methods, all of which return HTML. The most interesting of these are: `textfield()`, `checkbox_group`, and `popup_menu()`, each of which defines an HTML form element. The `start_form` and `end_form` methods add in the form element tags, and the `submit` method adds the submit button. Having a basic understanding of how to build a form using `CGI.pm` will help you in the next section, when we outline an example that creates a multipage form.

A multipage form program

Our final Perl CGI example addresses a shortcoming we pointed out in the chapter on FrontPage's built-in form handling capability (see Chapter 17) namely, FrontPage's inability to handle multipage forms efficiently. This script allows you to configure a set of form pages, collect up all of the results, show them on a final review page, and then save the results to a file.

Note   This script is a slightly modified version of a sample script by Lincoln Stein, the author of the `CGI.pm`. More information about this Perl module can be found at this Web site: `http://stein.cshl.org/WWW/software/CGI/cgi_docs.html`.

The script, named `multipage.pl`, can be found in the Chapter 19 examples folder on the Web site for this book. To use the script, you must have Perl 5 and the `CGI.pm` module installed on your server. If you have not done so already, you can use the sample script discussed above to test whether `CGI.pm` is available and working on your site.

The first step is to define the form pages in your multipage application. For this example, we have created a three page "Travel Survey." The (extremely sophisticated) marketing questions on the three pages are as follows:

✦ **Page 1** (Contact Information): Name (textbox), e-mail (textbox), and nearest airport (select menu)

✦ **Page 2** (Favorites): Favorite foods (checkboxes), favorite forms of entertainment (checkboxes), and favorite vacation spots (checkboxes)

✦ **Page 3** (Ideal Get-Away): Describe your ideal getaway (text area), and how much would you be willing pay for this getaway? (option buttons)

Once you have defined your pages and the form elements you want to put on them, open the sample `multipage_template.pl` CGI program, save a new copy of the file, and make the following changes (you can review the sample provided to see these changes):

1. Change the `@PAGES` array to the list of page names in your multipage form.

2. Update the `%FIELDS` associative array with your page and field names.

3. Update the `$direction` and `$apptitle` variables to suit your needs.

4. In the `print_form` subroutine, add a call to a print subroutine for each form page in your form, following the model provided: `form_page_1()`, `form_page_2()`, and so on. These subroutines, which we explain in the next step, are used to create the HTML forms. After each subroutine call add a conditional statement to define which form page in the sequence is being generated. So, for a three-page form, this section looks like this:

```
print_form_1() if $current_page eq 0;
print_form_2() if $current_page eq 1;
print_form_3() if $current_page eq 2;
```

5. This step involves some real work. For each form page, you need to create the form in its appropriate subroutine as defined in the previous step. You can include any kind of HTML form you want. For help, check the `CGI.pm` documentation, or check out the finished example, `vacation.pl`, which has at least one example of each of the major form elements. Here is the form definition for the first page of the form:

```
sub print_form_1 {
#ADD THE FORM ELEMENTS HERE
print "Your full name? ",textfield(-name=>'Name',-size=>20),
```

```
p,
"Your email address? ",textfield(-name=>'Email',-size=>50),
p,
"The nearest airport? ",popup_menu(-name=>'Airport',-
values=>['New York','Atlanta','Chicago','Dallas','Los
Angeles']),
p;
}
```

6. If you want to customize the Confirmation page, make changes to the `print_confirmation()` subroutine.

Now, all you have to do to run the multipage survey is to put the script in an appropriate `cgi-bin` directory and point to it in your browser. The script will take care of the rest. Figures 19-4 through 19-7 show the results.

Note   You will notice that as written, this script does not save its results. But, hey, it's an exercise — we have to leave something for you to figure out. In the next section, we present an ASP script that will save results — and read them back in.

![Screenshot of Multipage Survey Title in Microsoft Internet Explorer showing a Contact Information form. Address: http://www.literatetechnologies.com/cgi/vacation.pl]

Contact Information

Please complete all questions.

Your full name? [   ]

Your email address? [   ]

The nearest airport? [New York ▾]

[Next]

[Restart]

Figure 19-4: A series of HTML forms beginning with contact information

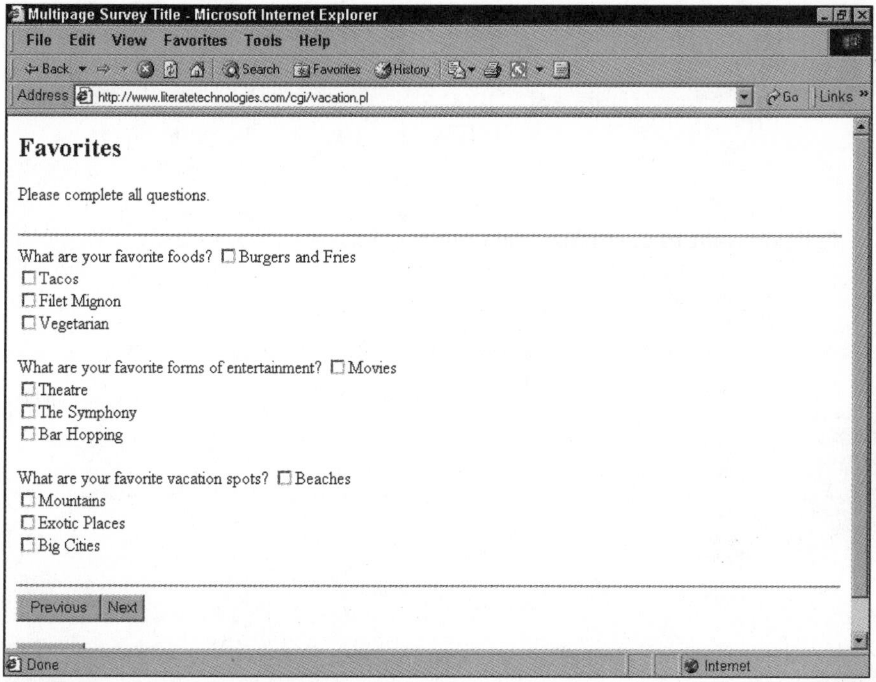

Figure 19-5: Survey of favorite foods

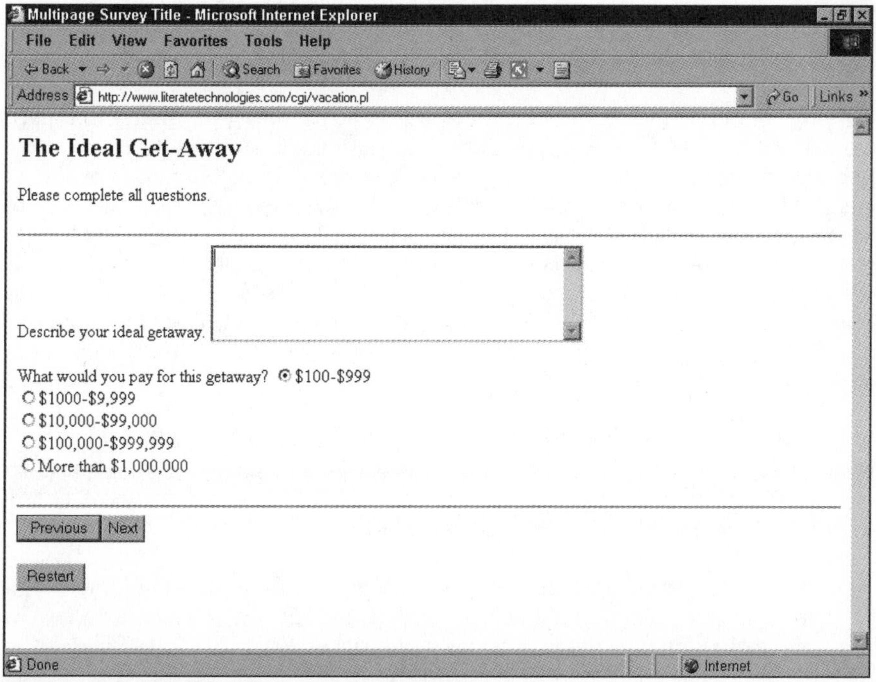

Figure 19-6: Form for "The Ideal Get Away"

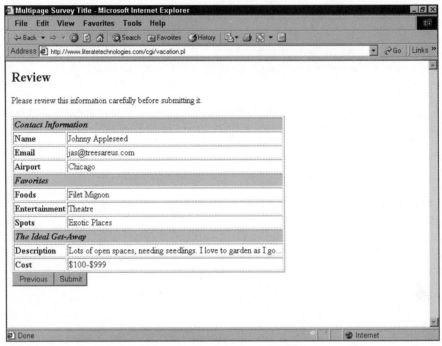

Figure 19-7: Review of multipart survey

Introducing Active Server Pages

CGI programming adds a whole level of sophistication to your ability to create dynamic Web sites. However, you may have noticed, even in the previous examples, that it is not always that easy to combine the programming elements of a CGI language with the ultimate goal — returning an HTML page to the user. This, combined with the fact that CGI doesn't really scale that well on large sites, has led to the creation of a number of server-side programming languages designed to be embedded directly into an HTML page. In this sense, they may seem more like a client-side programming language (as discussed in the previous chapter). The difference is that in a server-side programming language, the scripting blocks are processed before the page is returned to the user.

There are a number of server-side programming languages, but the one most at home in FrontPage is Microsoft's Active Server Pages. Active Server Pages (ASP) is really just a fancy name for VBScript designed to be run at the server. The remainder of this chapter provides an overview of ASP.

Note It is a little-known fact that ASP does not actually rely on VBScript for its programming language. You could just as easily write ASP using server-side JavaScript, although using VBScript is generally more convenient.

Again, we do not have the ability to provide an introductory course in ASP. We show you how to incorporate ASP into your FrontPage Web pages, and we try to give you enough of a sense of how ASP works to decide if it something you want to pursue further. As with the other scripting languages we have discussed, ASP is fairly easy to use for some basic functionality without needing a lot of programming expertise.

If you want to learn more about Active Server Pages, a good place to start is with Eric Smith's *Active Server Pages Bible* (IDG Books Worldwide, 2000). For online resources, check out Charles Carroll's extensive `http://www.learnasp.com//`.

ASP versus CGI

OK, you know you need to do some server-side programming. How do you decide whether to dive into a CGI programming language like Perl, or to embark on the Active Server Page route? There are a number of factors to consider:

✦ **Ease of Use:** CGI applications like Perl require you to have access to special server directories that can run external programs. ASP, on the other hand, is scripted right in your Web page. It still requires a server that supports it, but is typically regarded as easier on the novice developer.

✦ **Portability:** Active Server pages are largely limited to the Microsoft server environment. There are programs that enable the use of ASP in a Unix server environment, but you are more likely to encounter ASP as the default server-side programming language in an NT/Windows 2000 environment. Perl, on the other hand can run on Windows, Unix, or Macintosh. So, if portability is an issue, CGI scripts may be your best bet.

✦ **Performance:** The general wisdom here is that CGI scripts are not ideal in high-transaction environments. Unless you are talking about hundreds of simultaneous hits on your application, however, this is less likely to be a deciding factor for you. Under normal usage, CGI and ASP are going to perform similarly.

✦ **Power Tools:** If you are looking for rapid application development (RAD), you are more likely to go with ASP. The CGI world is still largely an advanced text editor development world. If you want to do rapid ASP, you will want to look into Microsoft's Interdev or the whole Visual Studio suite of tools. Again, for small-scale tasks, the difference is less prominent, and if you are looking for a low-cost rather than a rapid-development solution, you may find CGI (or a different server-side programming language, like PHP) more suited to your situation.

Server-side Scripting with Active Server Pages

In contrast to the other scripting techniques previously discussed, ASP is a server-side scripting language. ASP code is processed at the server before it is sent to the Web browser. The drawback to this technique is that only a server that understands and can interpret ASP code is capable of presenting ASP pages. The good news is that after you have an ASP-enabled server, your ASP code is entirely browser-independent. Also, you have less need to worry about proprietary code being stolen by users poking around in the HTML source code, because your ASP code is processed before it gets to the user.

The other good news about ASP is that, basically, it is simply standard scripting that is processed by the server rather than by the Web browser. Thus, if you are familiar with VBScript, you are already halfway over the ASP learning curve.

The main difference between client-side VBScript and server-side ASP is that ASP has access to additional resources (for example, objects) at the server side that are beyond the reach of your standard VBScript. These additional resources include the following:

✦ **Application and Session Objects:** These are objects that help you to manage user-state information by enabling your application to set and track application- and session-specific information about a user. These objects are managed by using a configuration script called `global.asa`.

✦ **Request Object:** This is a set of collections that provides access to information submitted by a user via a standard `POST` or `GET` command. It enables use of ASP as an alternative to CGI scripts.

✦ **Response Object:** This object deals with responses back to the browser from the server.

✦ **ServerVariables Collection:** This collection retrieves a set of headers (elsewhere known as CGI environment variables) passed from the browser to the server.

✦ **Cookies Collection:** Cookies enable you to store in the browser data that can then be retrieved later by your ASP application.

✦ **FileSystemObject Object:** This object provides access to file system information and server-side file objects.

✦ **Additional Server Components:** These components are built into the Internet Information Server (IIS) as well as third-party components.

✦ **Database Access Components:** These components provide connectivity between the Web server and databases.

✦ **Collaboration Data Object:** This object provides support for messaging, calendaring, workflow, and collaboration applications.

Note   ASP can also be augmented by writing Active Server components that extend the functionality of a particular server — somewhat analogous to the extended client-side functionality that an ActiveX component combined with VBScripting adds to the client side.

If you do not have a server that is capable of supporting ASP, you can disable ASP support in FrontPage. To do so, select Tools ⇨ Page Options, select the Compatibility tab, and uncheck the ASP support check box.

ASP by Example

In this section, we present two short samples of some fundamental ASP techniques as well as a fully developed tutorial example. This is not intended as a crash course in ASP coding. This section is intended to give you some sense of the kinds of things ASP can do, a feeling for how easy it is to learn ASP, and finally, something you may find useful, even if you never understand the programming involved.

ASP basics

As noted earlier, ASP is just VBScript that is processed at the server. You write ASP in blocks of code that are inserted directly into your Web page. The page is then saved with an .asp extension to tell the server that the page needs to be handed off to the ASP preprocessor before being sent back through the server to the user's browser.

An ASP code block is designated with <% and %> symbols. Anything inside these symbols is interpreted as code. You can place a code block anywhere on the page, with a few reservations: Some code is designed to write HTML text, and should be placed at the location where you want the HTML to appear; and some ASP is designed to be run before the HTML page begins to be displayed, and should come before any HTML in the page.

ASP and HTML can also intermingle. For example, you can create a conditional statement in ASP that normally displays some HTML, and under other conditions displays a different set of HTML. We demonstrate this in the first example, an ASP confirmation page.

Using ASP to create your confirmation page

In this example, we show you how you can create your own custom confirmation page that reads results from a form. In fact, you can embed the confirmation page right in the form page and add a detector to determine whether you need to show the form or the confirmation.

Using ASP in a confirmation page

As we discussed in the CGI section of this chapter, you know that form input comes to the server either via the GET method or the POST method. ASP has two constructions to access the data in each of these methods. Using one of these constructions, you can easily create a custom confirmation page that includes input from the submitted form, just as you did in Chapter 17 with the help of the FrontPage Confirmation field component.

Accessing GET method input

Data from a GET request is stored in the ASP Request.QueryString() collection. To identify a particular GET request field, insert the field name as a parameter in this object. For example, if you want to retrieve the value of the Name field in your form, you would write Request.QueryString("Name").

Accessing POST method input

Data from a POST request is stored in the ASP Request.Form() collection. As with the GET method request, you identify a particular form field value by inserting the field name as a parameter to this object. So, if you want to retrieve the value of the Name field in your form, you would write, Request.Form("Name").

Accessing general input

ASP also supports a general-purpose way to identify request input, using the Request() collection. If, for example, you want to retrieve input from a Name field, but you are not sure whether the input will come from a GET or POST request, you can use the use the Request("Name") syntax. This looks through both Request collections, in turn, until it finds a Name variable.

Creating a simple ASP confirmation page

Armed with the preceding information, you can easily create an ASP page that handles either type of input, much as you did in the simplecgi.pl Perl script described earlier. The final confirmation page, used in conjunction with the simple form page that you developed in the CGI section, looks like this:

```
<html>
<head>
<title>A Simple ASP Program</title>
</head>
<body bcolor="#FFFFFF">
<%
    If Not (request("Name")="") Then
        method = Request.ServerVariables("REQUEST_METHOD")
        name = Request ("Name")
        rank = Request ("Rank")
        serialno = Request ("SerialNo")
%>
<p>This is a <%= method %> request method.</p>
```

```
<p><b>Name</b> = <i><%= name %></i></p>
<p><b>Rank</b> = <i><%= rank  %></i></p>
<p><b>Serial Number</b> = <i><%= serialno  %></i></p>
<%
    Else
%>
<form name="f1" method="post" action="simpleasp.asp">
    <p>Name: <input type="text" name="Name" value=""
size="20"></p>
    <p>Rank: <input type="text" name="Rank" value=""
size="20"></p>
    <p>Serial Number: <input type="text" name="SerialNo"
value="" size="20"></p>
    <p><input type="submit" value="Submit" name="B1"></p>
</form>
<%
    End If
%>
</body>
</html>
```

Although this ASP file doesn't have exactly the same general functionality as the earlier Perl script, because it is "hardwired" to this particular form, you may be surprised by how much less code is required to accomplish effectively the same task. Even more, the ASP file contains both the form and the form results page. When the ASP page is processed, it first checks to see if a name input has been submitted. If so, it displays the submitted data. If not, it displays the form for inputting data.

Having the form and the results pages together and all of the programming embedded into the HTML page greatly simplifies page maintenance. For example, if you decided to add a new field, such as Age, you would simply have to make two changes to this file: adding the new input field to the form section and a new statement to display the data that the user has input.

Using ASP to read and write files

The capability to return to users the form data that they submitted is useful, but it isn't really sufficient to be considered form handling. To be complete, your ASP handler also needs to be able to write the data that it receives. The following ASP snippet makes use of the FileSystemObject, one of the built-in ASP objects, to generate code that opens, appends text to, and then closes a log file:

```
<%
Dim fs, a
Set fs = CreateObject("Scripting.FileSystemObject")
Set a = fs.OpenTextFile("c:\temp\logfile.txt", 8, True)
a.writeLine("This is a test")
a.Close
%>
```

Note   If you are curious about such things, the 8 that appears as the second parameter to the OpenTextFile method is the one responsible for defining the type of file handle obtained, in this case the ability to append to a file.

Tutorial 19-1: Form processing in ASP

You will create two ASP pages in this tutorial: a simple form that asks you to input some of your favorite things, and the form response page. The most interesting aspect of the two pages is that they remember what you have input, within the confines of a particular user session. Along the way, a few ASP basics are illustrated.

You will use the Microsoft Script Editor to create this file. If you have not read the discussion of MSE in the previous chapter (Chapter 18), you may want to take a look at that because we assume you have a basic familiarity with the tool and dive right in here.

Creating the form

1. Create a simple form, as pictured in Figure 19-8. The main consideration is that you need a form element with two input elements: a scrolling textbox for entering new "favorite things," and a scrolling list input, created by inserting a drop-down menu and setting its Height to 6 in the form field properties dialog box. Name the scrolling textbox **NewThings**. Name the drop-down menu **OldThings**.

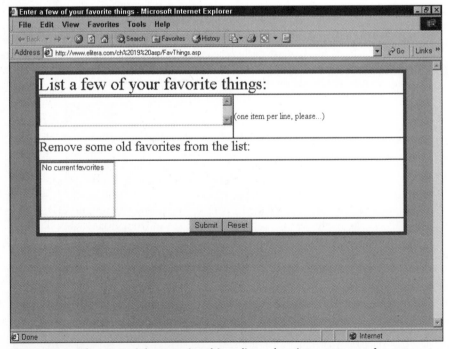

Figure 19-8: The start of the Favorite Things list — showing a text area for new favorites and a drop-down list for removed items

Note   For complete coverage of creating forms, refer to Chapter 16.

2. Right-click the form element and select Form Properties from the option menu. Choose the Send to Other option and click the Options button. Enter **FTResults.asp** as the Action. Click OK twice to return to the form.

3. Save the form as `FavThings.asp`. (Don't forget the `.asp` ending rather than `.htm`.)

4. Make sure that the folder that contains this ASP page is set to enable scripts to run. Although you haven't added any ASP script to your form yet, it is still designated an ASP page and needs scripting permission to run. To enable scripts to run, click the Folder icon in FrontPage Folder view and select Properties from the option menu. Check the box labeled Allow Scripts of Programs to Be Run. You will know that your folder does not have ASP enabled if it tries to save the page rather than display it when you select File ↪ Preview in Browser.

Creating the form response

Now create the results page, in which you get to add your ASP scripting:

1. Create a new page in FrontPage and design the form results. Include a placeholder for newly added favorite things, removed favorite things, and a counter (see Figure 19-9).

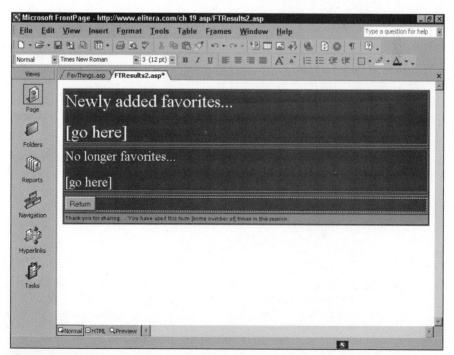

Figure 19-9: The start of your Favorite Things results page — awaiting some ASP

2. Save the results page as FTResults.asp. With the new file open, select Tools ➪ Macro ➪ Microsoft Script Editor.

3. Create a script block for your main ASP. Place the cursor somewhere in the header of the HTML page and right-click. Select Script Block ➪ Server from the option menu to insert an empty server-side script block into your page.

4. This script block contains the main script elements to be run when the page is loaded. It also contains functions that you will call from within the HTML results. When the results page is called, it needs to do the following:

   • Show the list of newly added favorite things.

   • Show the list of items removed in this session.

   • Update the list of current favorites.

   • Update a simple page counter.

   • Configure the return button to return to the page that called it.

5. You get the list of newly added favorites from the NewThings field in your FavThings.asp form. In ASP, form elements are passed in a Request.Form collection, in which the value of each form element is referenced as Request.Form("fieldname"). Create a simple function called getNewFavorites that returns the list of NewThings from the Request.Form. Your function takes one parameter, a string delimiter that enables you to change how the list is displayed in the results page. If no NewThings have been added, return a generic message. The function code should look like this:

```
Function getNewFavorites(delimiter)
'This is the list of newly added items from FavThings.asp
'
If Not StrComp(Request.Form("NewThings"),"")=0 Then
 getNewFavorites =
Replace(Request.Form("NewThings"),chr(13)&chr(10),delimiter)
Else
 getNewFavorites = "No new favorites."
End If
End Function
```

After you add the function, you simply reference it from the appropriate place in your HTML page. To do that, you can use a shorter syntax to designate an ASP script block to display text:

```
<%= getNewFavorites("<br>") %>
```

which is short for

```
<script language=vbscript runat=Server>
Response.Write(getNewFavorites("<br>") </script>
```

6. Add the counter next, simply because it provides a simple example of using Session variables, which you will also use to store the currentFavorites and oldFavorites lists. Your counter simply counts accesses to this page

from a specific user during a specific session. When you first access an ASP page within a particular application on your Web server, the server starts an ASP session for you, which it maintains by sending you a session ID cookie. You can create custom session variables that are retained during the lifetime of a session, simply by invoking a new item in the Session collection.

Take your counter as an example. You create a simple counter function called updateCounter(). This function takes no input parameters, and returns the current counter value, after first incrementing the value by one:

```
Function updateCounter()
    Session("Counter") = Session("Counter" )+ 1
    updateCounter = Session("Counter")
End Function
```

You call the function in the appropriate spot in your HTML with the following:

```
<% = updateCounter() %>
```

If you experiment with this, you will discover that the counter resets any time that you quit your browser and restart, or if you sit long enough that the session times out (by default, 20 minutes).

7. Create a session variable to hold all the current favorites and to add any new items to that list. This is the list that you eventually display in the initial FavThings.asp form.

First, create a subroutine called updateCurrentFavorites(). The job of this routine is to both add new items and delete any old ones. In this step, you deal with adding new items. The next step addresses deleting old items.

```
Sub updateCurrentFavorites ()
   'This adds new favorites to current list
   aList = split(Request.Form("NewThings"),chr(13)&chr(10))
   For Each strItem in aList
     If Not checkMatches(strItem, _
Session("CurrentFavorites")) Then
       AddCurrentFavorite(strItem)
     End If
   Next
End Sub
```

To perform the adding of new favorites, you create two utility routines:

- checkMatches(): This routine is designed to compare a string against a list of strings to see whether the particular string is in the list. It returns a true/false value.

- addCurrentFavorite(): This subroutine takes a new string to be added and adds it to the CurrentFavorites list. Note that you elect to store your Session variable as a delimited string rather than as an array or collection, which means that each time you make changes, you have to convert the list to an array and then back to a delimited string.

The two routines look like this:

```
Function checkMatches(tmpItem, tmpList)
  bMatch = false
  aList = split(tmpList,"$")
  For Each strItem in aList
    If StrComp(strItem,tmpItem) = 0 Then
      bMatch = true
    End If
  Next
  checkMatches= bMatch
End Function

Sub AddCurrentFavorite(tmpItem)
  If Not StrComp(Session("CurrentFavorites"),"") = 0 Then
    Session("CurrentFavorites") = Session("CurrentFavorites")
& "$"
  End If
  Session("CurrentFavorites") = Session("CurrentFavorites") &
tmpItem
End Sub
```

8. You also want to be able to list all the removed favorites during a given session, which requires adding any newly removed items to the list of accumulated removed items. Simultaneously, you want to remove any newly removed items from the list of current items. The process is analogous to Step 7. GetOldFavorites() first updates the list of removed items and then returns the updated list. UpdateOldFavorites() is responsible for the updating, and AddOldFavorite() adds a deleted item to the list of OldFavorites. Here are the new routines in their entirety:

```
Function getOldFavorites(delimiter)
  updateOldFavorites()
  getOldFavorites =
Replace(Session("OldFavorites"),"$",delimiter)
End Function

Sub updateOldFavorites()
'This is the list of newly removed items from FavThings.asp
aList = split(Request.Form("OldThings"),",")
For Each strOldItem in aList
    If Not checkMatches(strOldItem, Session("OldFavorites"))
Then
      AddOldFavorite(strOldItem)
    End If
Next
End Sub

Sub AddOldFavorite(tmpItem)
  If Not StrComp(Session("OldFavorites"),"") = 0 Then
```

```
    Session("OldFavorites") = Session("OldFavorites") & "$"
  End If
  Session("OldFavorites") = Session("OldFavorites") &
tmpItem
End Sub
```

Simultaneously, you want to remove any old items from the list of current favorites. To do this, you first create a RemoveCurrentFavorites() routine and then add a call to it in your updateCurrentFavorites() routine. The new routine looks like this:

```
Sub RemoveCurrentFavorite(tmpItem)
  aTmpList = split(Session("CurrentFavorites"),"$")
  For Each strItem in aTmpList
    'add back any non-matches
    If Not StrComp(strItem,tmpItem)=0 Then
      If Not StrComp(NewList,"")=0 Then
        NewList = NewList & "$"
      End If
      NewList = NewList & strItem
    End If
  Next
  Session("CurrentFavorites") = NewList
End Sub
```

The additional code in UpdateCurrentFavorites()—added to the end of the preceding routine—looks like this:

```
'This removes any old favorites
aList2 = split(Request.Form("OldThings"),",")
For Each strItem2 in aList2
  RemoveCurrentFavorite(strItem2)
Next
```

9. Add a Return button that returns to the page that called the results page. This is not a necessary part of the script, but it does show how ASP accesses system variables via the Request.ServerVariables collection.

One of the system variables, or CGI environment variables, that the server and the client typically pass is HTTP_REFERER. This designates the name of the page that referenced the current page. Armed with this piece of information, scripting the button is fairly simple. The code looks like this:

```
<%= Request.ServerVariables("HTTP_REFERER") %>
```

10. The final step is to return to the FavThings.asp form and update the code for the list box, so that it displays the current list of favorites, enabling the user to select ones to remove from the list. Because you created this form as an ASP page initially, you can simply add the requisite code to build the list of items in the appropriate place within the HTML page. Switch to HTML view and enter the following between the <select> and </select> tags for the list box:

```
<%
        If Not StrComp(Session("CurrentFavorites"),"")_
  = 0 Then
                aList = split(Session("CurrentFavorites"),"$")
                For Each strItem in aList
                    Response.Write("<OPTION VALUE=""" _
& strItem & """>" & strItem)
                Next
        Else
                Response.Write("<option value="""> _
No current favorites")
        End If
%>
```

Now you have a complete "Favorite Things Tracking System." Figure 19-10 shows the system in action. Within a session, you can add and delete favorite things, and ASP remembers both the total list of deleted items and the list of current items. Of course, if you really want to make this system functional, you need to connect it to a database. (For information on database programming using FrontPage, see Chapters 20 and 21.)

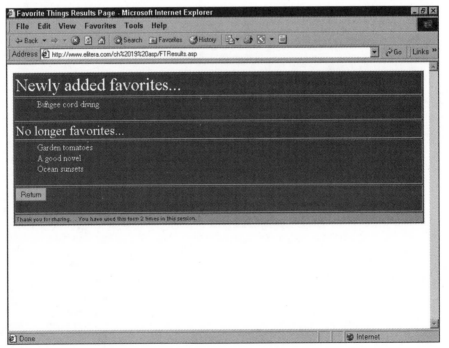

Figure 19-10: Keeping track of your favorite things is a snap with ASP.

Who knows, perhaps you will soon be adding ASP programming to your list of favorite things?

Using ASP to read server files

The final ASP example demonstrate ASP's ability to read files from the server, enabling you to interact with them via a Web page. You will build a simple log file viewer. This viewer first asks for two configuration items: the name of the log file and the file delimiter. Based on that, it then looks at the file and returns a list of the columns in the file. You can select one or more of the columns, and then the program returns the list of those columns in the file.

You can find this file, `simple_log_viewer.asp`, on the book's Web site. We do not have time to cover this example in detail, but here are the salient points:

1. To use this file, first open it and change the directory variable to point to the directory where your log files are located. It would be possible to write this application to open any file on the server, but this would create all kinds of security issues. Hard-wiring a directory name limits the scope of the application. As a further precaution, it would be a good idea to examine the filename entered and strip out any directories entered as part of the filename — a check that is not currently made.

2. When you request this page, it first checks to see if it has been sent a `logfile` parameter. If not, it sends you to the start page, where you can enter a `logfile` name and select one of the delimiter options as shown in Figure 19-11.

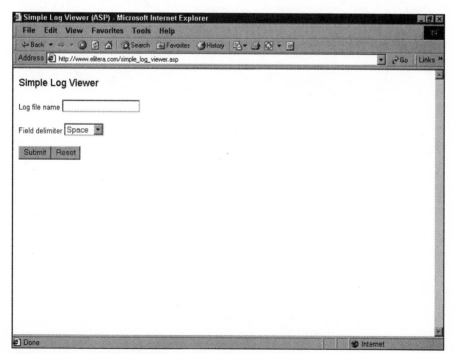

Figure 19-11: Start form for the log reading ASP program

3. If it does find a `logfile` name, it then checks to see if you have sent a list of columns. If so, it is ready to return the file contents. If not, it first opens the `logfile`, reads in the first line, which is presumed to contain a list of the column names (this is the way that the built-in FrontPage results are saved), builds a select list form element from the column names, and returns that to you to make your selections. An example of this is shown in Figure 19-12.

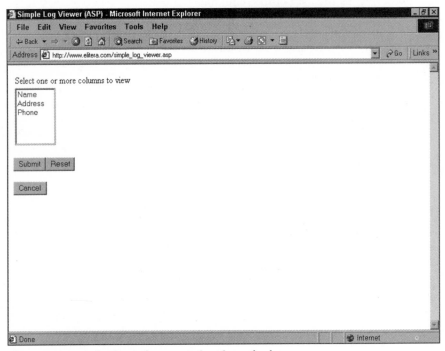

Figure 19-12: Selecting columns to view from the log

4. Finally, if the page detects both a log file and column names, it reads in the log file and displays the results as illustrated in Figure 19-13.

5. There is one other configuration item that you can change without recoding the application. The viewer defines a two-element color array, which it uses when it displays the contents of the file, alternating colors for each row. You can set these two elements to any valid color designations.

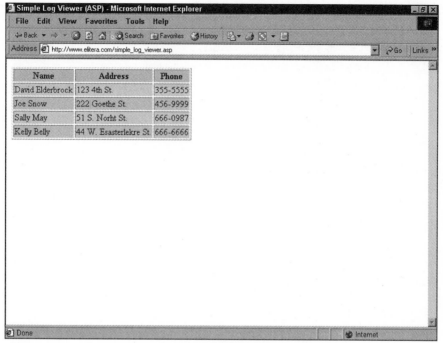

Figure 19-13: The results of the log-reading program

Summary

This chapter introduced you to the two prominent forms of server-side scripting: CGI programming and Active Server Pages and illustrated some of the differences between them. Server-side scripting can be a powerful addition to the usefulness of your pages, and can perform many functions, such as processing data input and reading and writing files that are cumbersome or impossible to do using client-side scripting. You have many choices of languages in creating your server-side scripts, but all require some familiarity with a general understanding of the server-side processing concepts we have discussed. One of the most common uses of scripting is to enable your pages to interact with a database, which is the subject of the next two chapters. In these chapters you will discover that FrontPage takes care of much of the database programming for you, and we will show you how you can extend those capabilities even further.

✦   ✦   ✦

Connecting Databases to the Web

Working with Databases in FrontPage

This chapter is the first of two chapters about working
with databases in FrontPage. This chapter introduces you
to some of the basic concepts you need to understand when
accessing databases via the Web. It describes all of the built-in
support that FrontPage offers for connecting to, querying, and
displaying the results of queries from databases. The next
chapter expands the topic of database access to show you
how to build a complete database application.

Understanding Web Database Access

In many respects, the capability of a Web site to access and
display data from a database source is at the heart of what
has made the Internet so revolutionary. This capability to
access databases has made e-commerce possible; it has been
the occasion of companies opening up to their customers, and
even the public, information that was previously difficult, if
not impossible to obtain (at the same time replacing customer
service with customer self-service); and it has equally
changed the way companies manage their own internal information and knowledge systems.

Access to database applications comes in two basic varieties.
The first type, the topic of this chapter, is limited to extracting
information out of databases. It involves "read only" access, if
you will. This covers areas such as reporting, searching and
filtering, data mining, and business intelligence analysis. The
second category of database access involves full-featured

database applications that allow various levels of access to data, but include the capability to add, update, and delete data (and possibly perform the same operations on database elements). In other words, this category of Web database application uses the Web browser as a complete database access client. Using FrontPage to build such an application is the topic of the next chapter.

Components of database access

Several components are needed to build a successful relationship between your Web site and a database. Fortunately, FrontPage is capable of assisting you with each of these items, greatly simplifying the task of Web-enabling your database:

✦ **Opening a connection:** This involves establishing a communication link between the server and the database, as well as handling the passing of messages between the two entities.

✦ **Issuing a query request:** Once you have a connection established with the database, you can issue a query, typically using some version of the Standard Query Language (SQL) that defines a common set of terms to describe a database request. The FrontPage Database Results Wizard is capable of building single-table queries automatically for you. If you want to build queries that involve joins, you have to create them by hand (or use Access Designer to assist you as demonstrated in the next chapter).

✦ **Handling and displaying results:** Any good query deserves a response, and dealing with the data set that is returned is the most challenging part of any database application. FrontPage has built-in support for generating basic table, list, and select drop-down menus from database elements.

Using the Database Results Wizard

FrontPage uses ASP and ADO to communicate with data sources. When you use the Database Results Wizard (DRW) to guide you through the process, it takes care of the messy programming and configuration issues for you. This section demonstrates the basic capabilities of the wizard. In subsequent sections, you'll examine each of its capabilities in more detail — with an eye to pushing FrontPage's database capabilities to the limit.

To use the Database Results Wizard (DRW), follow these steps:

1. Open an existing Web page or create a new Web page to contain the database results.

2. Select Insert ⇨ Database ⇨ Results to bring up the opening screen of the DRW.

The DRW consists of a series of five screens. The following sections walk you through the steps of the Wizard, with a simple example to get you started.

Note
This database Wizard has gone through a number of name changes. Initially it was called the Database Connection Wizard, emphasizing the fact that it helped create the connection between the Web page and a database. In FrontPage 98, it was renamed the Database Region Wizard, suggesting that it helped to define the region that displayed database results. Starting in FrontPage 2000, it was called the Database Results Wizard, highlighting the fact that it helps you formulate the query that gets data from a data source, and formats the results for the user.

Step 1: Connecting to a database

The first step in creating a Database Results page is to create a connection to a database or data source. As shown in Figure 20-1, the DRW presents you with three basic options:

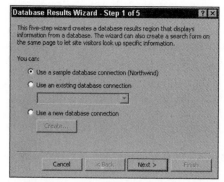

Figure 20-1: The first screen of the Database Results Wizard — selecting a database connection

✦ **Use a sample database connection (Northwind):** FrontPage's sample Northwind Traders database is good for practice and testing your setup.

✦ **Use an existing database connection:** If you haven't set up a database connection yet in this Web, no items are listed in this drop-down menu. Once you have used a database (including the Sample database), it is listed here.

✦ **Use a new database connection:** Use this option to create a new database connection to a pre-existing database.

Tip
You can also check the list of previously created database connections by selecting Tools ➪ Web Settings and clicking the Database tab.

Do You Have the Right Stuff?

In FrontPage 2002, you can create database access pages using the Database Results Wizard even if you do not have a local FrontPage-enabled database. This enables you to develop your pages offline. However, to test and/or display the results of any pages you create, you need to publish the pages to a Web server that has FrontPage 2000 or 2002 server extensions installed. That server also needs to have the ASP extensions installed. The best way to determine whether your system currently supports database access is to create a simple Database Results page as described in this chapter and if it works. If the test fails, try the following:

1. Check that you have opened the page from a Web server that is enabled for database connections. If you start FrontPage without opening a Web, or if you open a Web that isn't connected to a Web server, the database features will work in FrontPage, but your pages will not work correctly. Open an existing Web or create a new Web on the appropriate server and publish your pages to this server. If you need to install a Web server, see Chapter 23.

2. If you opened a Web on your Web server and the database features still aren't enabled, you are missing a current version of the FrontPage Server Extensions (either FrontPage 2000 or 2002) , or ASP, both of which are required. If your Web server is Internet Information Server (IIS) 4 or later or Microsoft Personal Web Server (PWS) 4 or later, chances are good that ASP is installed and that you need to upgrade FrontPage server extensions. (See Chapter 23 for details about upgrading FrontPage Server Extensions.)

3. If you are unsure whether your server has ASP capabilities, you can use one of several methods to check this. If you have administrative privileges and are familiar with the Windows Registry, you can use RegEdit (or an equivalent) to check for ASP functionality. If you have only user access to the server, the simplest test is to create a basic ASP page and see whether it works. See Chapter 21 for details about creating a simple ASP test page.

For the purpose of our examples in this chapter, we will use the sample Northwind database that comes with FrontPage. If you want to learn how to create a new connection, skip ahead to the section entitled, "Working with Database Connections." Otherwise, select the option button labeled Use a Sample Database Connection (Northwind) and then click Next.

 Note   When you select the sample database, FrontPage creates a new data source, named Sample, and uses it as the data source. In subsequent sessions with the sample database, you can use the existing connection instead of selecting the Use a Sample Database option.

Step 2: Select a data record source or custom query

In the next DRW screen (see Figure 20-2), you select a record source to use in the query. Typically, a record source is a table in the database, but it may also be a stored query (view only) in the database application. The DRW provides you with a list of available record source names. Select one from the list. If you want to retrieve results from multiple tables simultaneously, you need to create a custom query (see "Creating Database Queries," later in this chapter).

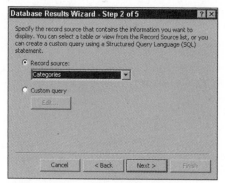

Figure 20-2: The Database Results Wizard — selecting a record source

For now, select Products from the drop-down list. Click Next to continue.

Step 3: Designate fields to display and advanced query options

Having selected a database and record source, you can now indicate which fields to include in the results. The third screen of the DRW (see Figure 20-3) lists the fields currently slated to be returned. By default, all fields are displayed.

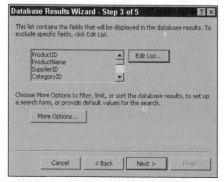

Figure 20-3: The Database Results Wizard — selecting fields to display

To edit the list of fields, click the Edit List button to display the Displayed Fields dialog box (see Figure 20-4). To add a new field to the list, select the field name from the Available Fields list and click the Add button. To remove a field, select a field from the Displayed Fields list and click the Remove button. To change the order in which the fields are displayed, select a field and click the Move Up or Move Down button to change its relative order in the display. Click OK to return to the main Wizard screen after you finish editing the Displayed Fields list.

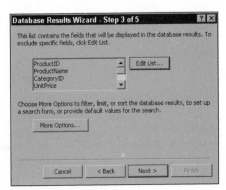

Figure 20-4: Editing the Displayed Fields list in database query results

In this example, you will display the `ProductID`, `ProductName`, `CategoryID`, `UnitPrice`, `UnitsInStock`, `UnitsOnOrder`, and `Discontinued` fields, so select the other fields from the Displayed Fields list and click the Remove button (to select multiple fields, hold down the Ctrl key and select each field) . The removed fields are transferred to the Available Fields list. Click OK to return to the main DRW screen.

Tip   The order of the fields determines the order in which they appear in the table created by the DRW (which, of course, you can change if you like).

You can also use this DRW screen to designate advanced query options by clicking the More Options button. These options are examined in detail in the section "Setting Advanced Query Options." For this example, you are ready to proceed to the next step. Click Next to continue.

Step 4: Select results formatting options

You have now completed the database query setup. In the final two steps of the DRW, you select options regarding how results from the query will be displayed.

New
Feature   The ability to create select lists from database records is new in FrontPage 2002.

In this DRW screen, you can choose to display the results in a table format, with or without the field names as column headers, as lists in a variety of formats, or as a drop-down list. We will describe each of the available formatting options at this point, although for the purposes of our example, we will use the "Table-One Record per Row" option.

When you choose "Table – one record per row" from the drop-down list, the following options are available (see Figure 20-5):

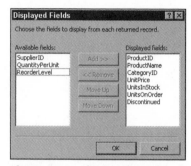

Figure 20-5: The Database Results Wizard options for displaying results in a table

✦ **Use table border:** Check this if you want the border to appear. If you uncheck this option, the table border is turned off. Once you have created the table, you can format it however you like.

✦ **Expand table to width of page:** Check this to create a table that resizes itself to the full width of the browser window. If this option is not checked, the table cells are sized to the width of the widest column value. Again, you can adjust this and all other aspects of the table once the Wizard has created it.

✦ **Include header row with column labels:** Check this to include the field names in a header field in the first row of the table. The Wizard uses the database field names as column headings, which you will typically replace with more descriptive, people-friendly labels.

When you choose "List – One field per list" from the drop-down list, the following options are available (see Figure 20-6):

✦ **Add labels for all field values:** Check this to include the field name before each value. This is similar to the include header row option for tables.

✦ **Place horizontal separator between records:** Check this to include a horizontal line between records.

✦ **List Options:** Select a format for the list of field values. The numerous list formats include paragraphs, line breaks, bulleted lists, numbered lists, definition lists, tables, formatted text fields, and scrolling text fields. The last two options enable you to put the data results into a form for submitting updates to the database.

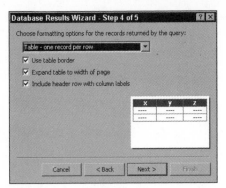

Figure 20-6: The Database Results Wizard options for displaying results in a list

When you choose "Drop-Down List – one record per item," the following options are available:

✦ **Display values from this field:** Select the table field to use as the text that is displayed in the drop-down list.

✦ **Submit values from this field:** This is the value that is actually submitted by the form (the value attribute of the select element's option element).

As previously mentioned, for now, select "Table – One Record Per Row" and check all three available options. Click Next to continue.

Step 5: Select grouping options

The final step of the DRW is in some ways its most valuable contribution, and the simplest to select. Use this dialog box (see Figure 20-7) to split records into groups of a designated number or to display all results together. If you elect to group the results, FrontPage automatically adds to the Web page a set of four buttons: First, Next, Previous, and Last, as illustrated in Figure 20-8. These buttons enable the user to page through the data one group at a time. FrontPage automatically adds the programming necessary to keep track of which group is currently being viewed, and reloads the data accordingly. We will keep the default option to split the records into groups of five records per group.

If you have included input parameters, this Wizard screen also offers you the option to generate a submission form, to collect inputs on the same page as the search results. In many cases, you collect that input on a prior page, but this feature can be useful for situations in which the user may need to reenter the input values. When it is available, the option is a simple checkbox labeled Add Search Form.

Click Finish to complete the DRW and return to the Web page.

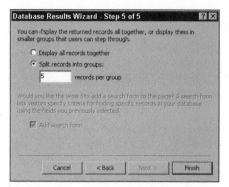

Figure 20-7: The Database Results Wizard —
you can show all records or group them
into separate pages.

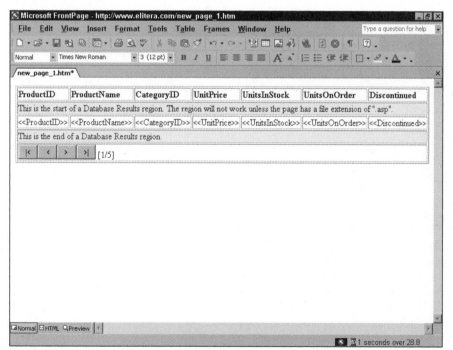

Figure 20-8: Product database created using the Database Results Wizard

Previewing the results

To preview the Database Results page, first save the page and then select File ➪
Preview in Browser. If you attempt to use the Preview tab, you are warned that it is
unable to display database results. Figure 20-9 shows our initial sample page, after
some revision, as it should look when viewed in a Web browser.

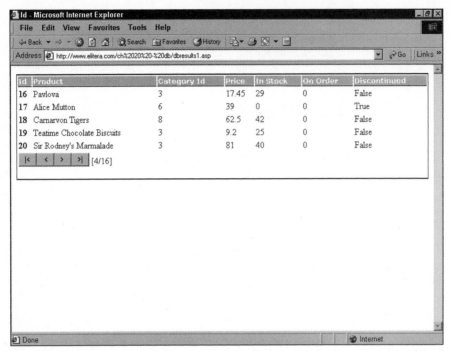

Figure 20-9: The sample database Web page displayed in the browser with a bit of formatting applied

This section has demonstrated the basic steps necessary to create a database connection. The next section shows you some ways to customize the process.

Editing an existing Database Results page

You can modify the query and results configuration of an existing Database Results page by double-clicking the start or end indicators of the database region (shown in neon yellow in Normal view). When you pass the mouse over the database region, the cursor changes to a hand holding a piece of paper. Alternatively, you can right-click in this region and select Database Results Properties from the option menu.

As noted earlier, once you have created your database region, you can adjust the formatting to your liking. You can make changes to the HTML within the Database Results region (indicated with the yellow table cells), but be careful not to disturb the Column value components — indicated with double angled brackets. In addition, if you make changes in HTML view, FrontPage will complain if you attempt to edit any of its Webbot information, including the ASP code it inserts into the page.

Modifying column values

In addition to modifying query results, you can alter the selected column value components displayed in the Database Results page. Column value components are indicated in Normal view by double tag brackets (e.g., <<ColumnValue>>). You can add additional column values, edit the names of existing values, and delete values from the Database Results page.

To add a new column value, place the cursor somewhere between the yellow database region's start and end indicators (refer to Figure 20-8) otherwise, the Column Value menu option is disabled. Select Insert ➪ Database ➪ Column Value to open the Database Column Value dialog box (see Figure 20-10), which consists of a single pop-up menu, showing all available column names. Select a column name from the available list. Click OK to return to the Database Results page.

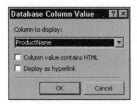

Figure 20-10: The Database Results Wizard options for displaying database column values

Note

If the column that you want to include is not listed in the Database Column Value dialog box, you may need to modify your query to include this column (although it appears that in FrontPage 2002, the Database Column Value dialog box lists all available fields, not just ones you have already selected).

To modify an existing column, double-click the Column Value region to open the Database Column Value dialog box. Alternatively, right-click the existing column value and select Database Column Values Properties from the options menu. Select the alternative column name that you want to use. Click OK to return to the Database Results page.

To delete an existing column, select the Column Value region and click the Delete button.

The Database Column Value dialog box contains two new checkbox options in FrontPage 2002:

✦ **Column value contains HTML:** Check this option if the data in this field contains HTML

✦ **Display as hyperlink:** Check this option if the data in this field contains a URL that you want to display as hyperlinked text.

Working with Database Connections

The initial example used the FrontPage 2002 sample Northwind database as the source for your Database Results page. This is a handy way to test that your database access is working correctly and to practice using the DRW, but you won't likely use this option very often except for testing. This section describes the standard methods of connecting your FrontPage Web to a real database.

ADO database connections

By default, FrontPage manages database connections through ActiveX Data Objects (ADO). When you add a database to your FrontPage Web, FrontPage creates a `global.asa` file that contains the connection information necessary to connect to the database. This makes it easy to create Web-to-database connections even if you do not have administrative access to the Web server.

Note   ADO is a language-neutral object model that exposes data through an OLE DB data provider. OLE DB is a set of Microsoft interfaces that defines common access methods for retrieving any kind of data. FrontPage uses the OLE DB provider for Open Database Connectivity (ODBC) to access local and remote data sources.

Adding a database to a FrontPage Web

Two ways exist to add a new ADO database connection to your FrontPage Web. You can use either of these methods:

✦ Use the DRW, as previously described, and select Use a New Database Connection in the first step of the Wizard (refer to Figure 20-1). This opens the Web Settings dialog box to its Database tab (see Figure 20-11).

✦ Select Tools ⇨ Web Settings, click the Database tab, and click the Add button to create a new database source directly.

Tip   You also use the Database tab of the Web Settings dialog box to modify, remove, and/or test database connections from the Web.

Once you open the Web Settings Database tab, you can click the Add button on the Database tab to open the New Database Connection dialog box (see Figure 20-12). Select one of four ways in which to designate a database connection. In each case, you select the appropriate option, indicate a name for the data source that you are creating, and then click the Browse button.

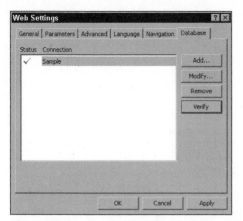

Figure 20-11: Use the Database tab to create database connections in your FrontPage Web.

Figure 20-12: Add a new database connection to your FrontPage Web using the New Database Connection dialog box.

✦ **File or folder in current Web:** Click the Browse button to locate the database file in the current Web. You can select from a wide variety of data file types, including Access, FoxPro, and dBase database files; Excel spreadsheets; and even comma-separated text files. (See the section, "Importing a database file into the current Web" for more details.)

✦ **System data source on Web server:** Click the Browse button to select from the list of available system data source names (DSN) defined on the Web server. (See "Configuring a data source," later in the chapter, for details.)

✦ **Network connection to database source:** This option creates a connection to a database server application. Click the Browse button to select the type of database server that you are using, designate the server's host name in the Server Name field, and designate the name of the database in the Database Name field.

✦ **Custom definition:** This option creates a connection to a file data source name (DSN) or Universal data link (UDL) file in the current Web. Use this to access database drivers that require parameters FrontPage does not support directly.

Advanced connection options

If necessary, you can use the Advanced button on the New Database Connection dialog box to configure additional driver information. As shown in Figure 20-13, the Advanced Connection Properties dialog box enables you to specify additional parameters for the connection:

Figure 20-13: Use the Advanced Connection Properties dialog box for selecting advanced options when creating a new database connection.

✦ **Authorization:** Specify the user name and password FrontPage should use when connecting to the database application.

✦ **Timeouts:** Specify values for the Connection and Command timeout values. Default values are 15 seconds and 30 seconds, respectively.

✦ **Other parameters:** You can create a custom connection string for your database driver if necessary.

Importing a database file into the current Web

If your database is an Access or Excel file, the simplest method of identifying the data source in FrontPage is to import the file into your Web. Use the following steps to import a database:

1. Open Folders view in FrontPage. Select the folder into which you want to import the database.

2. Select File ➪ Import and click the Add File button.

3. Locate the database file and click Open to return to the Import dialog box. Click OK to import the file.

4. When you import a database file, FrontPage prompts you to provide a name for the database. If you elect to name the database when you import it, FrontPage adds it to the list of available databases. You can then use the DRW to create a query to access this database.

5. If you elect not to provide a name for the database when you import it, you need to use the Database tab of the Web Settings dialog box to name the database and add it to the list of available databases before you use the DRW.

Working with data sources

If you are working with a database application such as Access, importing the database file into your Web is the most convenient method of configuring it to work with your site. In some situations, however, moving an existing database isn't feasible. In this case, you need an alternative way to identify it to FrontPage. One method is to set up the database as an ODBC system data source.

When you select the "System data source on Web server" option in the New Database Connection dialog box, you are given a list of existing system data sources from which to select. If your database is already configured, simply select it from the list. If you need to configure the data source, read on.

Configuring a data source

To identify to FrontPage a database outside the current Web, you need to register your database as an ODBC data source. ODBC is an industry standard for accessing database information. It is supported by most database systems, and it is the means — directly or indirectly (through OLE DB) — that ASP/ADO uses to communicate with a database.

To create your ODBC data source, use the ODBC Data Source Administrator (see Figure 20-14) found in the Windows Control Panel. To locate this utility, select Start ➪ Settings ➪ Control Panel. Double-click the icon named ODBC Data Sources icon (the exact name of which varies depending on the version of Windows you happen to be using).

Note   In Windows 2000, the ODBC Data Source Administrator is located in the Administrative Tools folder in the Control Panel folder.

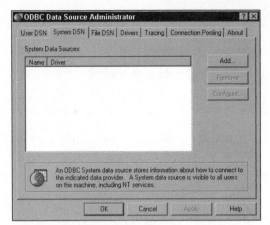

Figure 20-14: The ODBC Data Source Administrator is used to configure your database as an ODBC data source.

The utility contains several tabs, three of which are important to our purposes:

✦ **User DSN (Data Source Name):** A data source visible only to you, the current user.

✦ **System DSN:** A data source visible to local users of this computer. This includes services running on the computer (such as a Web server).

✦ **File DSN:** Used to access remote data sources.

To create a DSN for your application, select the System DSN tab, click the Add button, and choose the appropriate ODBC driver for your application (for example, Excel or Access). Figure 20-15 shows the Microsoft Access Driver being selected. Click Finish to continue setting up the data source.

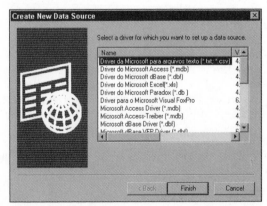

Figure 20-15: Select the appropriate ODBC driver in the ODBC Administrator.

Next, you need to configure your data source, using the dialog box shown in Figure 20-16 (this example shows the ODBC data source setup for a Microsoft Access database). Designate a data source name for your data source and provide a short description of the database. Next, configure the data source to use your newly created database. Click Select, locate your database file, and click OK three times to save your configuration and exit. FrontPage can now access this DSN using the "System data source on Web server" option.

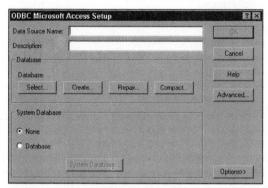

Figure 20-16: Naming and locating your ODBC data source

Working with a network database

Your Web also can access a database on another networked server, a fairly typical scenario if you happen to have a large Web site or are working on a corporate intranet application. The first requirement is that you have a database application that can be shared across a network; Microsoft SQL Server or Oracle, for example. In addition to knowing the type of database server being used, you need to know the identity of the server (typically a host name or IP address) and the database name. In most cases, you will also need to provide authentication parameters — a user name and password. To configure a network connection–to-database server, select this option from FrontPage's Network Database Connection dialog box and identify the type of database driver used, the server name, and the database name, as shown in Figure 20-17.

Figure 20-17: Creating a connection to a network database server

Using the Web Settings Database tab

In addition to providing a way to add new database connections to your Web, the Web Settings dialog box's Database tab (refer to Figure 20-11) enables you to make changes to and test those connections. From the Database tab, you can perform the following functions:

✦ **Modify a database connection:** Select an existing connection name, click the Modify button, and make any changes that you want to the database connection properties.

✦ **Remove a database connection:** Select an existing connection name, click the Remove button, and confirm that you really want to delete this connection. (You aren't deleting the database itself, just the currently defined connection to the database.)

✦ **Verify a database connection:** Select an existing connection name and click the Verify button. Database connections that have been verified are displayed with a green checkmark next to their name.

✦ **Configure advanced database connection options:** Select an existing connection, or click Add to create a new connection. In the Database Connection Properties dialog box, click the Advanced button to bring up the Advanced Properties dialog box. Use this to configure any required user name and password for the database, to set timeouts, and to add any additional parameters that are necessary for connecting to the database.

Caution

If you are working in an environment in which you are developing your Web site locally and publishing to a Web server, you need to ensure that you keep the Web server version of the database and your local copy of it in sync.

Creating Database Queries

In the previous example, you used the DRW to create a simple database query, without having to worry about how that query was formulated. This is fine for simple queries, but for most real-world applications, you need more control over how your data requests are formulated. This section describes the mechanisms that you can use to designate various kinds of data queries.

Setting advanced query options

One of the easiest ways to customize a query is to use the More Options button in Step 3 of the FrontPage DRW (refer to Figure 20-3). Clicking this button opens the More Options dialog box, shown in Figure 20-18, which has the following options:

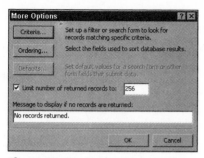

Figure 20-18: Setting more options in the Database Results Wizard

✦ **Criteria:** Click this to open the Criteria dialog box, in which you can specify for designated fields the conditions that you want to use to limit the records returned by the query. By default, all records are returned. You can add, modify, or remove items from the criteria list. Click Add to add a new criterion to the Add Criteria dialog box, shown in Figure 20-19, which offers the following options:

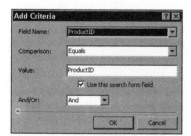

Figure 20-19: Use the Add Criteria dialog box to add new criteria to your database query

- **Field Name:** Select a name from the drop-down menu of available fields.

- **Comparison:** Select a comparison from the drop-down list of available options. The comparison options vary with the type of data contained in the field.

- **Value:** Indicate a static value for the comparison, or check the Use this search form field Get Value from This Query Parameter option and indicate the name of the field from which to obtain the comparison value.

- **And/Or:** Select And if all criteria must be true in order for the comparison to be true. Select Or if any one of the criteria will satisfy the comparison.

If you include input criteria from query parameters, the DRW gives you the option of including form elements on the Database Results page to collect these inputs.

Note If you create a custom query, as described later in this section, FrontPage disables the Criteria and Ordering buttons.

✦ **Ordering:** Click this to open the Ordering dialog box (see Figure 20-20), in which you can select fields to use to sort the records returned. You can select multiple sort order fields, and you can indicate what kind of sort to perform, either ascending or descending. The order of the fields makes a difference when, for example, you have a list of names that you want to sort based on Last Name and First Name fields. If you sort on first name and then last names, you group all the "Toms" together, for example, arranged alphabetically by their last names. If you sort on last name and then first names, all the "Smiths" are grouped together, arranged alphabetically by first names — probably more likely what you want. The buttons in the Ordering dialog box are used to do the following:

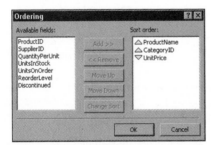

Figure 20-20: Set the order of results returned in the Database Results Wizard.

- **Add:** Click to add the selected field(s) to the list of Sort Order fields. Use the Ctrl and/or Shift keys to select multiple items. (You can only select multiple items from the Available Fields panel).

- **Remove:** Click to remove the selected field(s) from the list of Sort Order fields.

- **Move Up/Move Down:** Click these buttons to change the relative position of a selected item in the Sort Order list if you have included multiple sort order fields.

- **Change Sort:** By default, the sort order on a field is ascending, from lowest to highest for numbers, and from 0 to 9 and A to Z for mixed character strings . The sort order is indicated by a yellow triangle next to the field name in the Sort Order list. To change the sort order to descending, select the Sort Order field and then click the Change Sort button. Alternately, double-click the item in the Sort Order field.

- **Defaults:** Use this dialog box to set default values for any search form parameters or other input parameters you are using. If you create a search form that expects input parameters, it is vital that you set defaults for these items, as the database results bot returns an error if it does not receive an input parameter and no default value is set.

✦ **Limit number of returned records to:** Set a maximum number of records to be returned. You may want to limit the number of records that can be returned to protect your interest in proprietary data that you don't want to give away to every passing Web surfer, or to improve the performance of your Database Results page. If you have a large database, and users are accessing many fields, your Web server resources can be drained, particularly if you have numerous visitors.

✦ **Message to display if no records are returned:** Use this small text field to indicate the message to present to the user when no records are returned by the query. This message may contain embedded HTML.

Creating a custom query

Using the More Options dialog box in the DRW, you can create a variety of sophisticated queries without worrying about the database programming required to formulate the query. The DRW doesn't handle all circumstances, however, so if you need to create a query that it doesn't support, you can use one of several approaches:

✦ Use the DRW to create a custom query. This necessitates some knowledge of Standard Query Language (SQL), the general-purpose programming language that is used to query a database. The next section, "Joining results from multiple tables," examines a relatively simple example, combining results from two tables. If you don't know how to construct SQL statements but you have a tool with a database query designer, such as Access, you may be able to use this tool to help you develop queries (an example of this is provided in the next chapter). Otherwise, you may want to consider one of the other methods in this list.

✦ Use a prepared query stored in the database. This requires understanding of, and access to, the application used to create the database (such as Access or SQL Server). This approach is particularly effective if you are working in a team environment, with database experts maintaining the database and Web authors creating the Database Results pages. In this scenario, the database developers can write queries that can be accessed via the DRW for use by nonprogrammers. A detailed example of this approach is provided in "Accessing an Access query in FrontPage."

✦ Create in the database a new table that contains the joined records. This is the easiest method, assuming that you are able to add tables to your database. The chief advantage of this approach is that it keeps the query simple, which improves your application's performance. If your database changes with any frequency, however, maintaining this table so that it stays in sync with the original tables can become a database management challenge.

To insert a custom query in the DRW, select Insert ⇨ Database ⇨ Results, select a database source in the first screen, and click Next to go to the second Database Results Wizard dialog box (refer to Figure 20-2).

Select the Custom Query radio button to enable the Edit button. Click the Edit button to open the Custom Query dialog box, shown in Figure 20-21. You can type a valid SQL SELECT statement in the text field. Other query types (INSERT, UPDATE, DELETE, and so forth) are also supported, assuming that you have the capability to make changes to the database you are working with. In addition, you can click the following Custom Query dialog box buttons to select the actions described:

Figure 20-21: Use the Custom Query dialog box to create a custom database query.

✦ **Insert Parameter:** This is the same function performed automatically by the DRW when you define query criteria by using the More Options button, previously described. To insert a parameter field, create the criteria clause of your SQL statement. Place the cursor at the point where you want to insert the parameter value. Click the Insert button to open the Insert Form Field Parameter dialog box. Type the name of the form field that contains the value to insert (do not include the double colon delimiters (::) — that is the dialog box's job). Click OK. FrontPage inserts the field name, including the proper parameter identifiers into your SQL statement. (Of course, you can always just type this identifier yourself.)

✦ **Paste from Clipboard:** Use this option to cut and paste into the SQL Statement box an SQL query statement that you create with another application, such as Microsoft Access. (You can also use the paste shortcut, Ctrl+V, or right-click to bring up a menu list that includes cut, copy, and paste options)

✦ **Verify Query:** Use this to verify that the SQL statement you typed is valid. FrontPage tests the SQL statement and returns a success or error message. Oddly, the Wizard attempts to verify the SQL statement anyway when you click OK, and refuses to let you leave the dialog box until you correct your error. Therefore, one can only assume that the button is there to provide you with the illusion of control.

Be aware that the Verify Query option indicates that your query is OK even in some cases when it is not. For example, if you inadvertently create a SQL statement containing mismatched type information (which usually happens when you forget to put quotation marks around text field parameter values), the Wizard will claim that the query is valid. Unfortunately, your Web page will not be so forgiving.

Joining results from multiple tables

The DRW supports queries on a single record source. In most cases, this record source is a single table in the database. For relatively simple databases, this may be adequate. However, many databases store related information in multiple tables, mainly to eliminate the need to repeat information in multiple records.

For example, imagine that you have a customer database in which you want to store your customers' addresses. A given customer may have several addresses — for home, work, shipping, billing, and so forth. You could construct your database with a single Customer table, with separate fields for each of the various types of address, including street, city, state, and zip code fields for each type. Alternatively, you could create several records for each customer, each with a different address.

As a third alternative, you could create separate Customer and Address tables. In the Address table, you would have a field containing the customer ID, keyed to the customer record in the Customer table. You also would have a field that indicates what kind of address the particular record is. In this scenario, every customer has one record in the Customer table and one or more records in the Address table.

This method of structuring data is called *normalizing* the data. It produces a relatively efficient database, with little repetition of information. It does, however, require a little more work on your part to retrieve a particular customer's address. Suppose that you want to create a query form that prompts customers for their first and last name and returns a detailed list of their known addresses. (Of course, your task would be much simpler if you could prompt customers for their customer ID, but customers typically are better at remembering their name than an ID number!) The query that you want should find all the addresses for a specific customer name. To achieve this query, you need to join the Customer and Address tables. The query to do this looks something like the following:

```
SELECT * FROM Customer, Address
    WHERE Customer.customerid=Address.customerid
    AND Customer.FirstName = '::FirstName::'
    AND Customer.LastName = '::LastName::'
    ORDER BY Address.AddressType
```

This example uses the WHERE clause to specify the join information. Alternately, you can use a JOIN clause, as follows:

```
      SELECT * FROM Customer, Address
      INNER JOIN Customer ON
Address.customerid=Customer.customerid
      WHERE Customer.FirstName = '::FirstName::"
      AND Customer.LastName = '::LastName::'
```

The first WHERE clause in this SELECT statement links together the Customer and Address table records. The last two criteria provide a match on the database. Note that when you create a custom query, several of the DRW's More options, such as Criteria, Ordering, and Defaults, are disabled, whether or not you include criteria statements.

Caution You may well wonder what happens to your database query if you include multiple tables without joining them as described above. Basically, you will get one record returned for each matching record times the number of records in any other tables. As you might imagine, it does not take too large a database to produce a mammoth, run-away query. Therefore, it's best not to forget the join clauses.

Once you have created a query joining multiple tables, you can generate database results that combine information from multiple fields.

Using Access to create a custom query

The previous section assumes that you have some familiarity with SQL statements and are comfortable creating your own. Even if you aren't a SQL guru, you can create custom SQL statements by using a visual query-design tool, such as the one provided with Access, and then pasting the resulting SQL statement into the DRW. This section discusses two methods that you can use to create queries in Access: The Simple Query Wizard and the Query Design tool.

Simple Query Wizard

Before you start the Simple Query Wizard, you first must make sure that you have defined any necessary relationships between the tables that you plan to use in this query.

To define relationships between tables in Access, select Tools ⇨ Relationships to open the Relationships layout window. If prompted, add both the Customer and Address tables to the Relationships layout by using the Show Table dialog box, shown in Figure 20-22. If you are not prompted, right-click the Relationships layout window and select Show Table to open this dialog box.

After you add both tables to the Relationships layout, select CustomerID from the Customer table and drag it across to the Address table. The mouse cursor changes to a long, thin rectangle, representing the field; when you release the mouse button, the Relationships dialog box opens, with the link between the two fields defined. Click Create to create the relationship, indicated by a line connecting the `CustomerID` field in the `Customer` table to the `CustomerID` field in the `Address` table (see Figure 20-23).

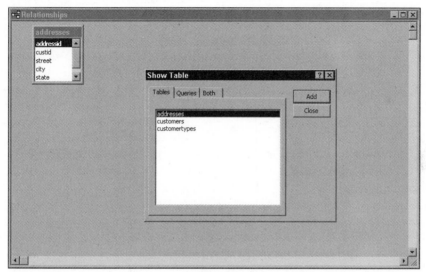

Figure 20-22: In Access, select the tables that are part of the relationship you want to define.

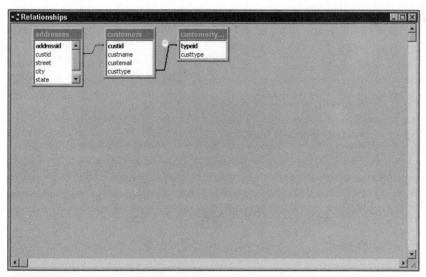

Figure 20-23: Define any data relationships before using the Access Simple Query Wizard.

After you define all necessary table relationships, you can begin the Simple Query Wizard (SQW). To use the Simple Query Wizard in Access, open your database, select Queries from the Objects list, and select the Create Query by using wizard item.

The first SQW screen, illustrated in Figure 20-24, prompts you to indicate which fields you plan to include in your query. You must include at least one field from each table that is part of the query. For this example, select all the fields from both the Customer and Address tables. Click Next to continue.

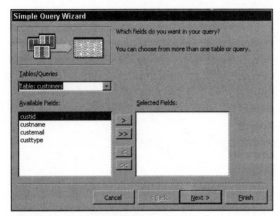

Figure 20-24: Select fields to include in your query using the Simple Query Wizard.

You are next prompted to select either a Detail query, which returns all the selected fields for every record in the database, or a Summary query, which enables you to create some simple groupings of data, based on the kind of data in your database. Select Detail and click Next.

In the final SQW screen, give the query a name. Note that the SQW can't insert query parameters or sort order information. You have to add this manually, using the Design view described in the next section. For simple joins, however, the SQW is an easy tool to use. Click Finish to complete the SQW.

To copy the query statement to the Clipboard, open the query in Design view and then switch to SQL view by selecting View ➪ SQL View. Select all and copy. Return to the DRW in FrontPage and paste the SQL statement into the custom query window.

Query Design tool

The Query Design tool in Access provides a more sophisticated way to define a query without manually constructing the SQL statement. To use the Query Design tool, open your database, select Queries from the Objects list, and select the Create Query in Design View option.

The Query Design view window appears, as shown in Figure 20-25, and immediately opens the Show Table dialog box to prompt you to add the tables that you want to include in the query. Using the earlier example, select and add the `Customer` and `Address` tables. Click Close to close the Show Table dialog box.

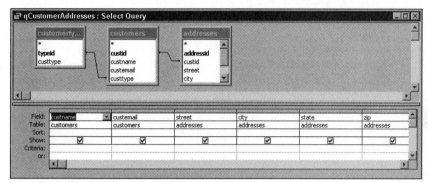

Figure 20-25: Access Query Design tool

The next step is to add the fields that you want to return in the columns of the Query Design tool. Select each field that you want to include, one at a time, and drag the field into the top row of an empty column in Query Design view. (Alternatively, you can double-click the field name to have it appear in the next available column.) As a shortcut, to include all fields, you can select the star (*) items at the top of each table.

At this point, you may be finished, or you can continue to refine the query in several ways. You may have noticed that when you added the tables initially, Access created a relationship between the two tables. You can edit this relationship by right-clicking the line that connects the two tables.

You can designate criteria for the query by using the Criteria row for each column. If your query includes multiple criteria, use the And row to indicate whether multiple criteria should be linked as And or Or clauses. Similarly, you can use the Sort row to indicate sort order instructions.

After you finish designing your query, test it in Access and save it with an appropriate name (use `qCustomerAddresses` for this example). Then, switch to SQL view by selecting View ➪ SQL View (see Figure 20-26). Select the entire text of the SQL statement (it is selected by default) and select Edit ➪ Copy. Switch back to FrontPage and use the Custom Query option of the DRW to paste in the SQL statement.

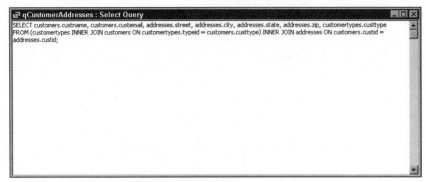

Figure 20-26: Creating a query in Access for use in FrontPage 2002

Accessing an Access query in FrontPage

In the previous section, you created in Access a database query called `qCustomerAddresses`, which you then pasted into your FrontPage Database Results page. Alternatively, you can access the query directly from the FrontPage DRW and save yourself the trouble of creating the custom query in two places. After you create a query in Access, it becomes available to the DRW as a record set, in the same way that all the database tables are presented.

To demonstrate this, create a query with either the Access SQW or the Design Query tool and save the query in Access. Then, return to FrontPage and launch the DRW. Select the appropriate database source and, in the second screen of the DRW, as shown in Figure 20-27, you will see the query name in the list of available record sources.

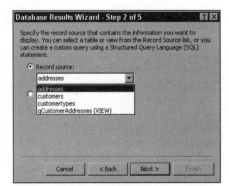

Figure 20-27: The Database Results Wizard lists your Access query as an available record source option.

Passing parameters to an Access query

Being able to create queries in Access and then use them in FrontPage is very helpful. But what do you do if you want to change the query based on input from the
user? This is what parameters are used for — and as we have seen already, adding a
parameter to a custom query in FrontPage is easy. What do you do if the query is
stored in Access?

You can create a parameterized query in Access and pass parameters to it from
FrontPageStart by creating a general-purpose query in Access, as described in the
previous section. Include any static criteria (criteria that always remains the same),
but omit any variable criteria. Next, return to FrontPage and start the DRW. Select the
Access query from the list of available record sets. Click Next to continue. Click the
Advanced Options button to access the Criteria dialog box. Add the variable criteria,
as described earlier in the chapter. Complete the rest of the DRW and save the page.

Customizing Query Result Sets

After you use the DRW to create a basic Database Results page, you can use
FrontPage's page editing features to adjust the appearance of the page. Of course,
you can create the basic design of the page first, before you run the DRW, but you
still need to make some formatting changes to the data results section itself.

The main thing to be careful about if you make formatting changes is not to disrupt
the database region component or the column value components. You can make
changes to a column value's font by selecting the column value component and then
applying formatting. If you are careful, you can even cut and paste these elements to
different locations on the page (as long as you don't move a column value component
outside the database region). Keep in mind that any page elements that you add
inside the database region will be repeated for each record returned by the query.

Caution   You should save any formatting of the database region itself until you are relatively
confident that you won't need to edit the query. If you rerun the DRW, it regenerates
the database region, occasionally undoing formatting changes that you have made.

Passing Parameters via Hyperlinks

One of the most common uses of database applications is to display a summarized
list of results and then to link each item in the list to detailed information about it.
Consider, for example, a catalog search form that enables users to search for keywords in the catalog descriptions. The results of the search might be displayed in
list form, arranged by product name. The product name is then linked to another
database function that returns the detailed product information regarding the designated item.

The key to making this application work is the ability to pass to the second database function a parameter that identifies the product. FrontPage includes a parameter feature in its Hyperlink dialog box that makes setting this up a breeze.

To illustrate, use the sample Northwind database that accompanies FrontPage 2002. First, you need to create the initial database search:

1. Create a new page and select Insert ➪ Database ➪ Results.

2. Referring back to Figure 20-1 use the DRW to create a connection to the Northwind sample database by selecting "Use a sample database connection (Northwind)" If the connection already exists, select the Sample database from "Use an existing database connection" instead. Click Next to continue.

3. Select Products from the Record Source drop-down list. Click Next to continue.

4. In the step three of the Wizard (refer to Figure 20-3), click the Edit List button. Remove all fields except `ProductName` and `UnitPrice`. Click OK to return to the main DRW screen. Click Next to continue.

5. Instep four of the Wizard (refer to Figure 20-5), select "Table – one record per row." Check "Include header row with column labels." Uncheck the other boxes. Click Next to continue.

6. In the last step, select "Display all records together." Click Finish.

   The results should resemble Figure 20-28.

   Now you create the second database function, which expects to be passed a `ProductID`, and returns detailed information about the product. (The Northwind database doesn't include product descriptions, but it does include a lot of additional information about the product.)

7. Create a new page. Select Insert ➪ Database ➪ Results to start the DRW.

8. Select the sample Northwind database, as described in Step 2. Click Next to continue.

9. Select Products from the Record Source drop-down list. Click Next to continue.

10. This time, you want to display every field in the `Product` table, so you can leave the Displayed Fields list as is. Click the More Options button.

11. In the More Options dialog box, select Criteria. Click Add. In the Add Criteria dialog box, select `ProductID` as the Field Name; select Equals as the Comparison; check "Use this search form field"; and then type `ProductID` in the Value textbox. Click OK to return to the Add Criteria dialog box. Click OK again to return to the More Options dialog box.

12. In the More Options dialog box, check "Limit number of returned records to" and type 1 in the input field. Click OK again to return to the main DRW screen. Click Next to continue.

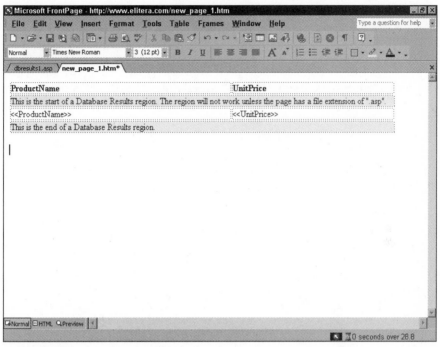

Figure 20-28: Creating a simple product list to link to a Detail view

13. In the results formatting screen, select "List – One field per item" and then select a Table list from the List Options drop-down list. Check "Add labels for all field values." Do not check "Place horizontal separator between records." Click Next to continue.

14. In the last DRW screen (refer to Figure 20-7), select "Display all records together." Uncheck "Add search form." Click Finish to view the completed page.

15. Save this page, shown in Figure 20-29, with an appropriate name (such as `ProductDetail.asp`).

    Now you can join the two database lookups by using a hyperlink that passes the appropriate parameter.

16. Return to the first database page (`productlist.asp`). Select the `<<ProductName>>` column value component. Either click the Hyperlinks icon in the toolbar and select Insert ➪ Hyperlink, or right-click the column value and select Hyperlink from the option menu.

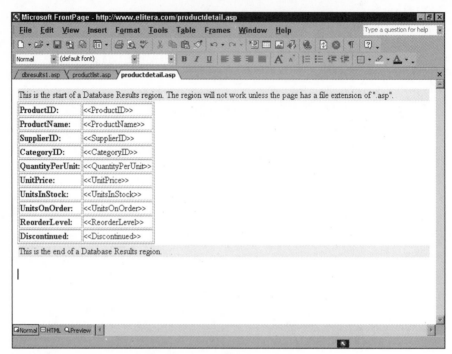

Figure 20-29: The Detail view for your product catalog

17. In the Hyperlink dialog box, select the `productdetail.asp` file as the URL. Click the Parameters button to open the Hyperlink Parameters dialog box (see Figure 20-30).

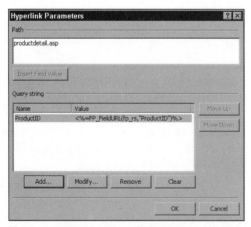

Figure 20-30: The Hyperlink Parameters dialog box

18. Click the Add button underneath the Query String input area. In the Add Parameter dialog box, select the parameter name, ProductID, and FrontPage inserts some ASP code in the value field, as shown in Figure 20-31. Click OK to return to the Hyperlink Parameters dialog box. Click OK again to return to the Insert Hyperlink dialog box, and click OK a third time to return to the Database Results page.

Figure 20-31: Creating a simple product list to link to a Detail view

19. At this point, the ProductName column value component should be hyperlinked.

20. Preview this page. Click one of the hyperlinked product names in the initial list. You should get a second page showing details (although, frankly, not very interesting details) for that record.

Tutorial 20-1: A Web database phone directory

This tutorial provides a real-world example to demonstrate some of FrontPage's database access capabilities. The next chapter expands this example by adding the capability to add, update, and delete records.

Note All files used in this example are available from the book's Web site. Information on downloading files from the Web site can be found in the Preface.

The scenario

Using a Microsoft Access database, you are going to create a company telephone directory. Users can search the directory for listings. By clicking an entry, they can view detailed information about the person listed. This portion of the directory application consists of three pages:

✦ **Search form:** This enables users to search on all or a portion of a name, and filter results by department. In the first portion of the tutorial, we create a simpler search form — and then refine it later.

✦ **Results listing:** This shows results either alphabetical by last name or organized by departments. In the first portion of the tutorial, we develop the more standard alphabetic results list, again refining it later.

✦ **Detailed listing:** This shows all the fields for a specified individual. This page will be linked to the results list via a hyperlink that passes an ID parameter to the detail page.

The database

This application uses a simple online phone directory database, opd.mdb. Start by importing the database into your Web and creating a data connection for it:

1. In FrontPage, select File ➪ Import, click the Add File button, and locate the opd.mdb database file.

2. When you import the file, FrontPage prompts you to give the database a name. Call it **OPD** and click Yes to finish adding the database to the Web.

Create the search form interface

The first step is to create a basic telephone directory search interface:

1. Create a new Web page, opd.asp.

2. Select Insert ➪ Database ➪ Results and select the OPD database. Click Next to continue.

3. Select the Employees table and click Next to continue.

4. You want to display an initial list of search results, so edit the list of fields returned to limit it to LastName, FirstName, and HomePhone. Click the Edit List button and remove all other fields. Click OK to return to the DRW screen.

5. Click More Options and then click the Criteria button to designate search criteria. Click Add and select LastName as the field name, select Begins With as the comparison, check the "Use this search form field" box, and select LastName as the form input name. Click OK twice to return to the More Options dialog box.

6. Click Ordering and select the LastName and FirstName fields for an ascending sort order. Click OK to return to the More Options dialog box.

7. In the text field provided at the bottom of the dialog box, indicate a message to display if no records are returned. Click OK to return to the DRW screen. Click Next to continue.

8. Select the Table display format and check "Include header row with column labels." Click Next.

9. Select "Display all records together" and check the option to create a search form on the Results page. Click Finish.

    Next, you tidy up the display a bit. Add some color, a more pleasing font, and so on. The results are displayed in Figure 20-32.

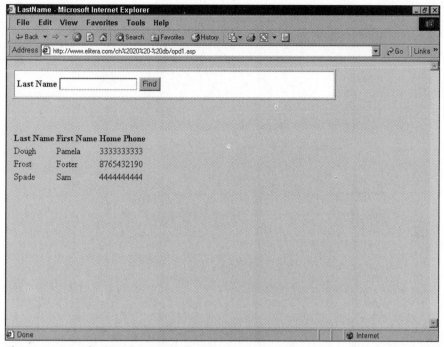

Figure 20-32: The initial Contacts list after some sprucing up

These results have a few problems. One is the format of the phone number. Another is the lack of any link to additional information. The formatting problem is easily fixed, but it requires some hands-on work with the database query generated by the DRW.

10. Double-click the Database Results region to open the DRW. Click the Custom Query button. The current query opens in an editing box. To format the telephone number, make the following change (indicated in bold italics) to the SQL statement:

```
SELECT *, Format(HomePhone, '(000) 000-0000') as fHomePhone
FROM Contacts WHERE (LastName LIKE '::LastName::%') ORDER BY
LastName ASC,FirstName ASC
```

Next, we add a visual interface, using letters of the alphabet, as shown in Figure 20-33.

11. Add the alphabet images, which can be obtained from the book's Web site, or alternatively, create your own set of images. (Of course, if you are really in a hurry, you can just use text links instead).

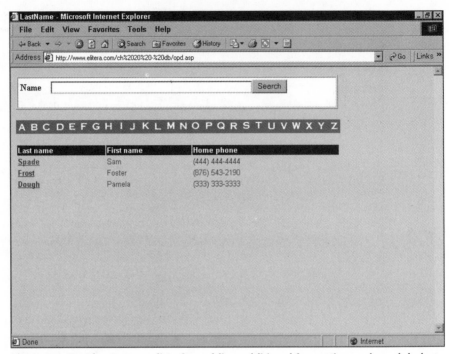

Figure 20-33: The Contacts list after adding additional formatting and an alphabet lookup interface

12. For each letter, select the image and click the Hyperlink toolbar icon to open the Hyperlink dialog box. Alternatively, right-click the image and select Hyperlink from the option menu.

13. In the Hyperlink dialog box, select the same page, opd.asp, as the URL.

14. Click the Parameters button at the bottom of the dialog box. Click Add, and in the Name field of the Add Parameter dialog box, type LastName. In the Value field, type the appropriate letter of the alphabet, (for example, **A**). Close all dialog boxes. Now, try clicking a letter of the alphabet. The query should return all database entries that begin with the corresponding letter.

Tip   Any time that you redo the DRW search results, you are prompted to re-create the output. This means that if you revise your query, as you are doing here, after you format the output, you have to reformat the page. For this reason, you usually should postpone formatting until you are sure you are done.

Create the Detail view

In this section, you create a Detail view and link it to the Database Results page via the telephone directory record ID:

1. Create a new Web page and save it as `opddetail.asp`.

2. Select Insert ➪ Database ➪ Results and select the OPD database. Click Next to continue.

3. Select the Contacts table as the record source. Click Next to continue.

4. Select More Options. Click Criteria, click Add, and select `ContactID` as the field name, Equals as the comparison, and a form field Value of `ContactID`. Click OK twice to return to the More Options dialog box. You want to include all available fields in this detailed view, so you don't need to edit the list of displayed fields. Check "Limit number of returned records to" and designate 1 as the maximum. An occasion to display more than one record shouldn't arise, but it never hurts to be sure.

5. Before you leave the More Options dialog box, you also need to set a default value for `ContactID`. Again, in theory, you will always pass a value via a hyperlink parameter. What if someone tries to access the page directly? The page shouldn't display a record, but if you don't define a default value, it will generate an ASP error.

   Click the Defaults button in the More Options dialog box. The Defaults dialog box shows the `ContactID` parameter. Click Edit and set the default value to **-1**. Click OK to leave this dialog box, and click OK again to return to the main DRW screen. Click Next to continue.

6. In the formatting options screen, select "List – one record per list," and choose the Table format from the List Options drop-down list. Check the "Add labels for all field values" checkbox (you will edit these labels to make them a bit more user-friendly, but you might as well let FrontPage do as much of the work as possible). Click Next.

7. Select the "Display all records together" option, and don't check the "Generate form to collect input parameter" option, because you will pass the ID as a query string parameter from a hyperlink. Click Finish.

   Figure 20-34 shows your Detail Results page after some cleanup work. Next, you link the List Results page to the Detail Results page.

8. Open the List Results page, `opd.asp`, and select the `<<LastName>>` column value component. Click the Hyperlink icon in the toolbar or use another method to open the Hyperlink dialog box. Locate `opddetail.asp` and identify it as the target URL. Click the Parameters button. Click Add and select `ContactID` from the drop-down Parameter Name list. FrontPage automatically writes the ASP code to include the appropriate field value as the parameter value. Click OK twice to return to the main page.

9. Save your work and preview. Click a last name in the search results to view the detail record for that record.

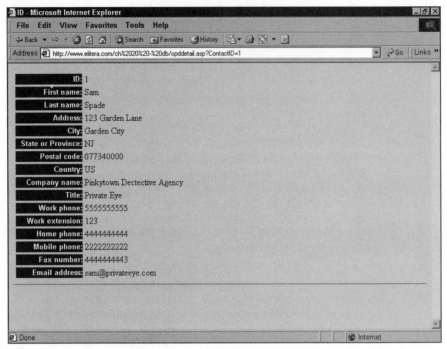

Figure 20-34: The Detail view of your telephone directory

Tutorial 20-2: Building an advanced search form

Earlier in the chapter, you learned how to use the Database Results Wizard to add a simple search form element to the database results. However, the Wizard is limited to creating basic text input search form elements. This is fine for basic text searching, but it isn't always the most practical solution when working with structured data in a database. In this section, you'll learn how you can push the envelope of FrontPage's capabilities to create a slightly more sophisticated search form. The point of this exercise is largely to illustrate that with some creativity and a small amount of programming, you can use FrontPage to create more real-world database examples than you might realize.

Using the sample database, we will create a search form with the following features:

✦ A text entry field to match product names

✦ Option buttons to select cases in which product name matches should be exact matches, start with the text entered, or just contain the text entered

In this example, we assume that you have been following along and don't need us to spell out everything in complete detail. If need be, refer back to the section "Using the Database Results Wizard" at the beginning of the chapter for details.

Step 1: Create the basic search results

To create the basic search results, do the following:

1. Create a new page to contain the search results. Save the page as `productsearch.asp`.

2. Open the Database Results Wizard by selecting Insert ➪ Database ➪ Results.

3. In Step 1 of the Wizard, select Sample from the "Use an existing database connection" drop-down menu. Click Next.

4. In Step 2, select "Products" as the record source. Click Next.

5. In Step 3, click the Edit List button to select the fields to include in the results: `ProductName`, `UnitPrice`, `UnitsInStock`, and `UnitsOnOrder` are our choices. Click OK to return to Step 3 of the Wizard.

6. Click the More Options button, and in the More Options dialog box, click the Criteria button. In the Criteria dialog box, click Add, select `ProductName` as the field name, select Like for comparison, and select `ProductName` in the Value drop-down menu. Make sure the "Use this search form field" option is checked. Click OK. (We will have more to say about this "Like" comparison in a moment.)

7. Back in the Criteria dialog box, add a second criterion, where `CategoryID` equals `CategoryID`, again making sure that the "Use this search form field" option is checked. We are going to alter this form element later, but adding the criterion now will save us from having to edit the query statement later. Click OK.

8. In the More Options dialog box, click the Ordering button, and add `ProductName` to the Sort Order list. Click OK to return to the More Options dialog box. Click OK again to return to Step 3 of the Wizard. Click Next.

9. Still in the More Options dialog box, click the Defaults button. You need to set default values for the two search form fields so that the page will work when the user first comes to it. You can take one of two approaches here. One option would be to show no results until the user selects something. In this case, you can put **"-1"** as the defaults for both parameters, and then edit the message returned if no records are found to something like "**Enter a product name and category ID and click Find.**" The alternative approach is to give users some results by default. In this case, you can enter any valid values for the two defaults.

Tip

OK, we know, what you would really like to do is return *all* results by default. Because you are using a LIKE criterion for `ProductName`, you can set the default to "%" to return any product name. The problem is `CategoryID`, which is a number field and will not accept a wildcard value. One way to accomplish this is to replace the `CategoryID=::CategoryID::` portion of the SQL with the following:

```
(CategoryID =  ::CategoryID:: OR -1=::CategoryID::)
```

Then set the default `CategoryID` to -1.

10. In Step 4, select whatever formatting options you prefer. Click Next.

11. In Step 5, select whatever record display format you prefer. Make sure the "Add search form" option is checked. Click Finish.

12. Edit the field labels by putting a space in "Product Name" and removing the "ID" from the Category label. Edit the button labels: Change the Submit Query button label to "Find" or "Search" or any name you prefer. Remove the Reset button if you like. Adjust formatting to suit yourself. Your results should resemble what is shown in Figure 20-35.

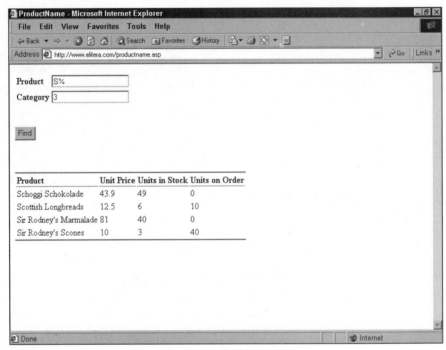

Figure 20-35: The initial version of your search form

Step 2: Add Option buttons

In Step 1, we set up the criterion for `ProductName` as a `LIKE` comparison. In SQL, a `LIKE` comparison differs from an equals (=) comparison in that it allows the insertion of wildcard characters using a percent sign (%) as the wildcard. For instance, you could create a criteria statement that says "...`WHERE ProductName LIKE 'Abc%`" to find any product names that begin with "abc" and have zero or more additional characters.

Without altering our form at all, you can take advantage of this if you type `%<sometext>%` into the form and then do a search. The database will return all products that contain the text you typed between the percent signs. If you use a percent sign only at the end, you could find all text that started with the input text. If you wanted to add a little note explaining this "hidden feature" of your search form, you could skip the whole business of adding option buttons to do this. For the purpose of this tutorial, however, we will make the cynical assumption that users would be perplexed by having to add weird percent sign characters to their search terms, so we are going to "automate" this capability using our option buttons.

1. Add a set of three option buttons after the Product Name form element. To do this, insert a new row into the form. Then merge the columns of this row and insert a three-column, one-row table into this row. (Remove the automatic styling that FrontPage 2002 "kindly" adds to tables.) Insert three option buttons, one into each cell of the table. Label the first one "Exact"; the second "Starts with"; and the third "Contains." (Note that you could do an "ends with" as well if you like, but this seems a bit esoteric.) Change the Group name of each option button to searchType and change the value to match its label. Mark the first option (Exact) as selected by default.

2. To enable our option buttons, we create a simple JavaScript function that fires when the user submits the form. This function determines which option the user has selected. If "Exact" is selected, it does exactly nothing; if "Starts with" is selected, it adds a percent sign to the end of the input; and if "Contains" is selected, it adds percent signs to both ends. Here is the function:

```
function setSearchType()
{
        selobj = document.f1.type;
        for (var i=0;i<selobj.length;i++)
        {
                if (selobj[i].checked)
                {
                        if (i==1)
                        {
                                document.f1.ProductName.value +="%";
                        }
                        else if (i==2)
                        {
                                document.f1.ProductName.value = "%" +
                                document.f1.ProductName.value + "%";
                        }
                }
        }
}
```

Place this function in a script block in the head section of the page's HTML (see Chapter 18 for details about how to do this).

3. Finally, add an onSubmit event handler to the form element that calls this function:

```
<form name="f1" onsubmit="setSearchType(); method="POST"
action="productsearch.asp">
```

4. Test your changes. You will notice one unfortunate side effect of your new functionality: When the page reloads, it adds the altered search term back to the Product Name search form. This is not debilitating, but a bit of a distraction to the user, who has no idea where this percent sign came from. Therefore, we will add one more JavaScript function to deal with this issue.

5. Create a new function called `init()`. Add the single line of code for this function as noted below. The trick here is to grab the altered version of the input and strip out any percent characters. (We limit our trimming to the beginning and end of the term in case the user has legitimately entered a percent sign in the middle of the text — unlikely, but you never know.). Note, too, that this code assumes that your form element has the name `f1`; make adjustments as needed.

```
function init()
{
document.f1.ProductName.value =
trimChar(document.f1.ProductName.value,"%");
}
```

The `trimChar()` function is listed below as well:

```
function trimChar(str,char)
{
        //trim first char if necessary
        if (str.substring(0,1)== char)
{
        str = substring(1);
}
if (str.substring(str.length-1)==char)
{
        str.substring(0,str.length-1);
}
return str;
}
```

6. Add an `onLoad` event handler to the body tag to run the `init()` function when the page loads. This will reset the input text to the state it was in before the user submitted the form.

7. Test the option buttons to make sure they are working correctly.

Note   The final version also includes code to set the option button to the previously selected value.

Step 3: Add a drop-down menu

Next, we would like to enable users to filter results by category. We could have used the Database Results Wizard to add a `CategoryID` text field element, but this would not have been very useful. A user would have no idea what category IDs are available or valid, let alone what category name they corresponded to. In this case, having a drop-down menu of available options is far more efficient. If you wanted, you could open the database, find out the available categories, and create a drop-down menu item to do this. This method is easy from a programming standpoint, but not very maintainable. Every time you change the database, you have to remember to redo your drop-down menu.

A much better approach is to create the list from the database itself. Fortunately, FrontPage 2002 enables you to save results as Select lists. To accomplish this, we are going to create a second Database Results region inside the search form:

1. Change the label of the `CategoryID` form element that FrontPage added to Category. Delete the text input element.

2. Place the insertion point in the second column of this new table row, where the now deleted text input field was, and open the Database Results Wizard as described earlier.

3. In Step 1, select the Sample database again. Click Next.

4. In Step 2, select Categories. Click Next.

5. In Step 3, click the Edit List button and remove the Description field, leaving `CategoryID` and `CategoryName`. Click OK to return to the Step 3 dialog box.

6. Click More Options, select Ordering, and add Category Name to the sort order list. Click OK twice to return to the Step 3 dialog box. Click Next.

7. In Step 4, select the "Drop-Down List – one record per item" option. Select `CategoryName` as the display field, and `CategoryID` as the values to submit. Click Next.

8. In Step 5, because you selected the drop-down menu option, you have no options here. Click Finish.

9. You now have a drop-down menu named `CategoryID`, which sends the `CategoryID` value corresponding to the Category name that the user selects. Guaranteed to be in the database—though not guaranteed to have any products associated with it.

Tip

If you want to create a drop-down menu that you know will return results, you can build the Category list using a join on the `Product` table. That way, only categories that have corresponding entries in the `Product` table will be displayed. Here is the SQL to do it:

```
SELECT DISTINCT c.CategoryID, c.CategoryName
from Categories c, Products p
WHERE c.CategoryID=p.CategoryID.
```

10. One little problem you may notice — when the form reloads, it returns to its default value, which is confusing if you can't remember what you selected that returned the results you are looking at. It would be better if you could have the form retain the last selected value. To do that, we add a little more JavaScript magic to our `init()` method:

```
var selval = "<%=Request("CategoryID") %>";
var selobj = document.f1.CategoryID;
for (var i=0;i<selobj.options.length;i++)
{
        if (selobj.options[i].value==selval)
{
            selobj.selectedIndex=i;
          }
      }
```

This code grabs the submitted value from the Categories drop-down menu and sets the drop-down menu to the item that matches this value. Now you have the completed search form. Compare your results with Figure 20-36.

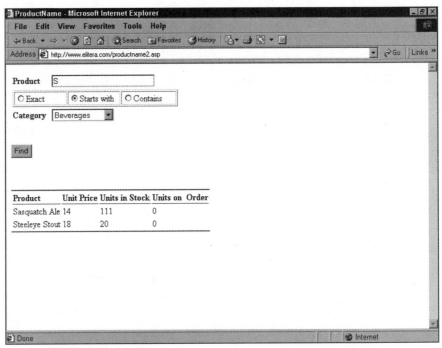

Figure 20-36: Our completed advanced search form, with option buttons and a drop-down Category select list

Step 4: Create a custom sort order form

Wouldn't it be nice if you could create your database results so that the user could sort them however they wanted? Well, here's one way to do it:

1. Create the database.

2. Open the Database Results Wizard and select the Sample database.

3. Select Custom Query. Create the query and add `ORDER BY ::sortField::`.

4. Add a Default value for `sortField` (for example, `ProductID`).

5. Save in table format.

6. Hyperlink the header title to `<pagename.asp>?sortField=<fieldname>`.

Tutorial 20-3: Creating a hierarchical results list

Note This tutorial introduces some relatively sophisticated SQL. It does not require any special programming knowledge, but you will want to be comfortable with creating custom queries in FrontPage before attempting this tutorial.

You have a search results list sorted alphabetically by last name. For small databases, this may be perfectly adequate. Imagine, however, that what you really want to do is organize the results hierarchically by department, placing the department name as a summary header over each grouping. How would you do it? The main problem is retrieving the data organized the way you want it.

Step 1: Create the Query

We create this query in the Access database using the Query Designer. To accomplish the results we want, we are going to create a somewhat unorthodox `UNION` query, which you can only create manually even using the Query Designer tool, but once created, this query will be easier to access from FrontPage.

1. Open the `Employee` database. Select Queries from the list of Database Objects. Double-click the "Create query in Design view" option.

2. Using the Show Table dialog box, add the `Departments` table to the query designer grid and close the Show Table dialog box.

3. Drag the `DeptID` and `DeptName` fields into the grid. This is as far as we go using the design interface. From here on, we will have to edit our SQL by hand.

4. Select View ➪ SQL View to open the SQL text editing window. Currently, the SQL should resemble the following:

```
SELECT Departments.DeptID, Departments.DeptName
FROM Departments;
```

Now a bit of explanation for what we are about to do. The goal is to return a set of records that displays the Department name alone in a record followed by a list of records that display the Employee Name alone for each employee in that department. To do that, we are going to use a UNION query. A UNION query enables you to take two separate queries and combine the results. The catch is that the fields in both queries have to match. We want to do a UNION on the Departments table and the Employees table, but they don't have all the same field information. To solve that problem, we use another SQL trick that enables us to define field names for our query in the query itself. In this case, the contents of the fields will be empty, but that is what we want anyway.

5. Revise the SQL in SQL View to the following:

```
SELECT DeptID, DeptName,'' AS EmployeeName, '' AS eeid
FROM Departments
UNION SELECT DeptID, '' AS DeptName, lnam e & ', ' & fname AS
EmployeeName, eeid
FROM Employees
ORDER BY DeptID, DeptName DESC, EmployeeName;
```

Note the following salient points about this query:

* It creates a UNION between Departments and Employees by "padding" each table with necessary empty fields. These will show up as empty table cells in the Results page, which will give us the hierarchical results we are after.

* The Employee SELECT statement includes a concatenated field that combines Last Name (lname) and First Name (fname)

* The ORDER BY clause sorts by DeptID (which we will not display) to get all the employees in the same department together with the department name record. It then sorts in reverse order on Department Name, which puts the Department record containing the actual name first and all of the employee records after it in alphabetical order.

6. Save the Query as qEmpByDept (or whatever you want to call it).

Step 2: Create the results page

1. Return to FrontPage, create a new Web page and save it as empByDept.asp.

2. Open the DRW and select your database. Click Next and select the query you just created from the Record source drop-down list. Click Next to go to Step 3.

3. Click the Edit List button and remove the DeptID and EmployeeID fields, leaving DeptName and EmployeeName. Click OK and Next.

4. In Step 4, select "Table – one record per row." You can format the table as you wish, but you will probably want to uncheck the "Include header row" option. Click Next.

5. Select "Display all records together" (trying to break this query up into pages would produce disjoined results). Click Finish to return to your Web page. Save the results.

6. Optionally, do some formatting of the results — at a minimum, you may want to change the font style of the `DeptName` column to highlight the department names. You can add a background color as well, but keep in mind that the color will be displayed in the empty `DeptName` columns as well.

7. Now take a look at the results — illustrated in Figure 20-37. Not bad for no programming!

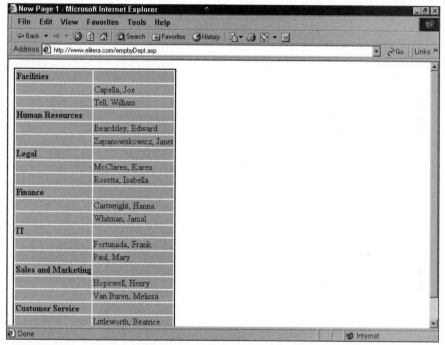

Figure 20-37: A list of employees, arranged hierarchically by department

Summary

In this chapter, you have learned how to use the Database Results Wizard to create dynamic, database-driven Web pages quickly and easily. You have practiced a number of methods for connecting your database in FrontPage. You have learned how to define database queries in FrontPage, including some advanced techniques that produce results you may have thought were not possible without custom programming. You have explored ways to coordinate Access with FrontPage, including using Access to design and store your database queries and passing parameter values from one application to the other. In addition, you have learned a number of important techniques for displaying data in your Web pages, including the ability to pass a database parameter via hyperlinks from one Web page to another. Not bad for one chapter, but we are not done yet with working with databases. So far, we have concentrated exclusively on techniques for viewing database data. The next chapter focuses on building a complete database application that enables you to add, edit and delete information from your database. Our focus will be on the new FrontPage 2002 Database Interface Wizard, which simplifies the job for us. As in this chapter, however, we will venture beyond the basics so see just how to accomplish some sophisticated tasks as well.

✦   ✦   ✦

Building a FrontPage Database Application

This is the second of two chapters on the topic of connecting your Web to a database. The previous chapter dealt with issues related to extracting data from a database and viewing it in your Web pages. This chapter shows you how you can use FrontPage to create a complete database application, including the ability to add, modify, or delete database records.

New Feature The early release versions of FrontPage 2000 limited the ability to create database update pages without resorting to custom ASP programming. In FrontPage 2002, this has been amended with the introduction of the Database Interface Wizard. In addition, MS has reinstated the ability to use the FrontPage Results Wizard for `INSERT`, `UPDATE`, and `DELETE` queries as well.

Understanding Web Database Applications

In this section we explain what we mean when we talk about a "Web database application" and briefly describe the components that typically make up a complete database application.

What are the components of a complete database application?

A complete database application includes all of the interfaces you need to maintain the data in your database — by adding, updating, and deleting records — in addition to the means that you use to access that data (via reports, etc.). You might want to include database update mechanisms in some of these ways:

✦ User self-service applications that allow end users to maintain personal database records

✦ User transaction services that record user functions and requests — such as making a purchase, booking an airline ticket, or performing a task

✦ Administrative access to maintaining database table records

✦ DBA access to managing database structure, queries, user information, etc.

At a minimum, a complete Web database application needs both a user "view only" component and an administrative data maintenance component to insert, update, and delete database records. These are the functions we focus on in this chapter.

Why maintain database records via the Web?

It's easy to understand why one might want to provide data-view access to a database over the Web, because it makes that data available to a much wider audience with nominal costs and maintenance requirements. Similar arguments apply to the case of Web-enabling database update functionality as well. A Web-based database application can be a cost-effective way to create easy-to-use, distributed access to key database functions. It also makes possible a model of *distributed maintenance*, otherwise known as *self-service* applications, which depend on granting limited maintenance access to users in order to have them keep records that matter to them up-to-date.

Extending that model to include traditional database administrative functions introduces some additional challenges as well, however. These include security (controlling access to database update functions) and data integrity (ensuring the quality of the data updates). For these reasons, it is necessary to consider all of the implications of extending database update functions to a wider audience via the Web and to create an appropriate model to define the level of access you plan to grant to various types of users.

Coordinating FrontPage and Access

Most users of FrontPage will find themselves creating applications that connect to a Microsoft Access database application. However, Access has very sophisticated support for building native client applications in Access. In addition, the recent versions of Access have a variety of means by which you can get your data from Access to the Web — without needing FrontPage at all.

In Access you can put database data on the Web in one of three ways:

✦ **Export data to a static HTML page**. You can create static HTML files from tables, queries, forms, and reports in Access. Access produces a different HTML formatted page, depending on the type of data view you are converting to HTML. This method is appropriate if you want to make available data that changes infrequently.

✦ **Create Server-Generated Database Report Forms**. Access is capable of generating ASP (as well as IDC/HTX — the predecessor to ASP) pages that can be added to your Web site to provide dynamic view-only database information. This method is appropriate if you want to make available data that changes frequently but does not require updating.

✦ **Use a database access page**. A data access page is a Web page that is connected directly to the data in your database. Use these pages to view, edit, update, delete, filter, group, and sort live data from either Access of Microsoft SQL Server. Data Access pages offer a flexible way to provide complete data update access to your database in Microsoft Internet Explorer 5 or later. It is appropriate for situations where you know your users have Internet Explorer 5 or later and you want to provide them with data update capabilities.

Given the capabilities of Access, you may wonder if there are any compelling reasons to use FrontPage to construct your database. In fact, if you are comfortable using Access and you are working in an environment where you can guarantee that all users of your application will have Microsoft Office support (such as you might find in an intranet environment), then using Access data access pages may prove a better solution than using FrontPage to generate a Web-based database application.

If, however, you need to ensure that your application supports general Web standards, use Access as the data repository — potentially even as the source of your database queries — and use FrontPage to build the application.

Using the Database Interface Wizard

On the assumption that you are ready to create a database application in FrontPage, let's look at the mechanism FrontPage 2002 provides to do that — namely, the Database Interface Wizard (DIW). The DIW is an extension of the Database Results Wizard (DRW), discussed in the previous chapter. The DIW uses the DRW to create an entire set of database access pages using the FrontPage Web Wizard capabilities. Using the DIW, you can create

✦ **Database results pages:** Similar to the pages you can create using the Results Wizard

✦ **Database submission forms:** That make use of the Send to Database capability, discussed in detail in the Activating Forms chapter

✦ **Database editing functions:** To add, edit, and delete data from a database table

✦ **Login functions:** To control access to database editing functions

Creating a new database interface

In this section, we walk through the steps to create a basic database interface using the Database Interface Wizard. By way of illustration, we use the Northwind sample database that comes with FrontPage. You would use similar steps to create an interface for any existing database. Once we have gone through the basic steps we will look at various options, including using the wizard to create a new database and working with multi-table databases.

To use the Database Interface Wizard, select Page ➪ New ➪ Webs to open the Web Site Templates dialog box. Select the Database Interface Wizard, shown in Figure 21-1, and decide whether to create your application as a separate Web or within the current Web. Name your Web, if necessary. Click OK to start the wizard.

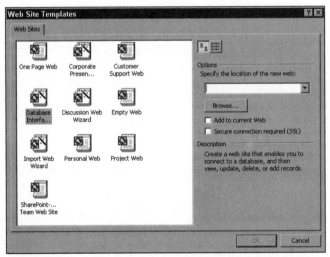

Figure 21-1: The FrontPage 2002 Web Site Templates dialog box, including the new Database Interface Wizard

Step 1: Selecting a database and source table

In the first step, shown in Figure 21-2, you are asked to identify the data source for your application.

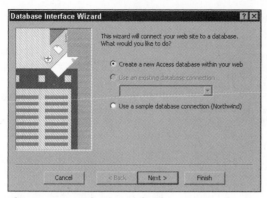

Figure 21-2: Selecting a database source for your database interface

You can use any of the following three sources to create your database application:

✦ **Create a new Access database within your Web:** This creates a single-table database within FrontPage. We provide an example of this process in the following section. Note that you will be limited to a single-table database if you take this route.

✦ **Use an existing database connection:** This allows you to select from an existing database the table you want to work with to create the database application. In order to create multiple table functions, you will have to run the DIW once for each table. This is illustrated in the section, "Editing Multiple Tables" below.

✦ **Use a sample database connection (Northwind):** Always a good way to practice and hone your DIW skills. We use this method in this initial example.

Select the "Use a sample database connection (Northwind)" option and click Next to continue.

Note You cannot set up a database connection to an existing database using this wizard. If you plan to connect to an existing database, first create a connection as described in the previous chapter, and then run the DIW.

Once you have selected the Sample database, you are next prompted to identify the table to use as the source of the database application. As illustrated in Figure 21-3, select Employees from the drop-down list and click Next to continue.

Step 2: Defining form field types

After you have selected the source table for your application, the wizard prompts you to define what form fields to associate with each field in your database table.

To modify a form field type, select the field in the list as shown in Figure 21-4, and click Modify (you will note that the other buttons are unavailable at this time).

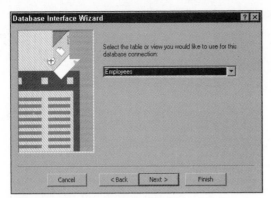

Figure 21-3: Selecting a table from the data source for your database interface

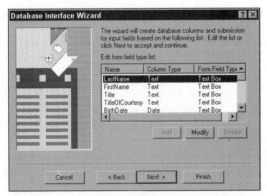

Figure 21-4: Selecting fields from the table in your data source for your database interface

You can define a form field type as one of the following (see Figure 21-5):

✦ **Drop Down Box:** A pull-down style menu of choices

✦ **Option Buttons:** An option button selection style of choices

✦ **Text Box:** A text entry field (the option shown in Figure 21-5)

If you elect either of the two select-style options, you can also designate how many options to include. FrontPage fills in the form field with dummy options, which you will need to edit by hand after completing the wizard.

Figure 21-5: Modifying form field types for the database fields in your database interface

The wizard is only capable of creating static option lists. It cannot create lists based on other database tables.

Once you have defined all of the form-field options to your satisfaction, click Next to go on to the next step.

Step 3: Selecting the pages to generate

Once you have selected, your database and a source table for your application, the next step is to identify the pages you would like the wizard to generate for you (see Figure 21-6).

Figure 21-6: Page options offered by the Database Interface Wizard

As illustrated in Figure 21-6, you have the following options:

✦ **Results Page:** A Web page to display contents from your database

✦ **Submission Form:** A form for inserting results into your database

✦ **Database Editor:** A collection of pages to review, add, delete, and update records in your database

Select all options by clicking on the checkbox for each option. The Results Page and Submission Form are selected by default. (This seems odd, because the primary reason to run the DIW in the first place would be to create the editing pages, but perhaps FrontPage just wants to make sure you are serious about this.) Click Next to continue.

Step 4: Defining authentication options for database editing

If you selected the Database Editor option, you are next prompted to enter a user name and password for database editing (see Figure 21-7). By selecting the "Don't protect my Database Editor with a username and password." checkbox, you can forgo the security of user name and password protection, which means that anyone can access and edit your database — not a highly recommended option for most Web-based applications.

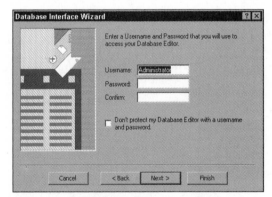

Figure 21-7: Configuring authentication options for your database interface

If you do opt for a username and password, the wizard will create a few extra pages to handle this, including a login form and login verification ASP code.

Caution   As discussed in more detail in "Extending the Login Model," later in this chapter, this authentication mechanism is very rudimentary and is inadequate for any but the most basic needs.

Click Next after you have entered your user name and password (twice).

The final page of the wizard lists the pages it will create and where those pages will be located. Click Finish to generate the interface Web for your database. The next section will examine these pages in more detail.

What the Database Interface Wizard creates

When the dust settles, you should find that the wizard has created the following pages (as shown in Figure 21-8).

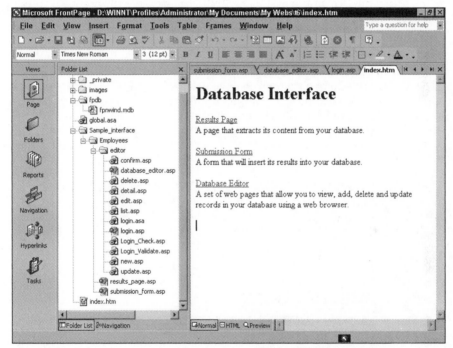

Figure 21-8: The FrontPage 2002 Database Interface Wizard's handiwork

The DIW creates the following files in the main folder it creates in your Web:

✦ Index.htm: A table of contents page that links to your other pages.

✦ Results_page.asp: If you selected a results page, FrontPage creates a bare bones database results table, using all of the default settings in the Database Results Wizard. The results page is a simple table format that shows five records per page. You can edit this page as described in the previous chapter.

✦ Submission_form.asp: If you added a submission form, FrontPage creates a basic form with an input field for each of the fields in your database. This form uses the Send to Database results component (discussed in Chapter 17) to insert a record into your database.

✦ `Database_editor.asp`: If you elected to add database editing files, FrontPage creates a set of files that allow you to add, edit, and delete records in the database table you designated.

✦ `Login.asp`: If you protected your database editing function with a user name and password, FrontPage adds a login form and validation pages to your database. FrontPage creates a `login.asa` file which contains (in plain text) your user name and password. Also generated is `Login_Check.asp`, an include file which is added to any page that needs to check for login, and `Login_Validate.asp`, the page the `Login.asp` submits to.

Note   The user name and password are stored in a plain text file, which is not exactly high security. On the plus side, you can easily edit the user name and password by opening `login.asa` in a text editor and changing the information.

The database editor is the most complex element that the wizard creates. Its main interface consists of a two-frame Web page (see Figure 21-9). The top frame shows a list of records in the database. Click the Add New Record button to add a record using the Submission form. Check one or more records in the list and then click the Delete Selected Records to delete items. Or you can click the hyperlinked item field to view detail results for the record and either edit or delete the record.

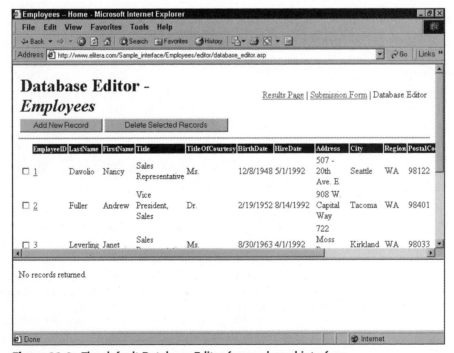

Figure 21-9: The default Database Editor frames-based interface

Now that we have seen how the DIW behaves using an existing database, let's see how it can help us create a new database from scratch.

Creating a new database

In addition to using the DIW to create your Web database interface, you can also use it to generate a new database. The DIW is best used when you want to create a simple form that stores information in a single database table. It is not suitable for more elaborate database applications.

To create a new database using the DIW:

1. Start the wizard by selecting File ➪ New ➪ Page or Web, selecting Web Site Templates (Figure 21-1), and selecting the Database Interface Wizard from the list of available Web templates.

2. In the first wizard screen (Figure 21-2), select "Create a new Access database within your Web."

3. Enter a name for your database connection. Click Next to continue.

Use the Edit column and form field type list to designate fields and form field elements to correspond. To add a field, click Add, name the column, select the column type (in other words, the data type) and a form field element to use in any Web page forms created. If you create a select-type form field — either a drop-down menu or option buttons, you must also indicate how many options FrontPage should include. You will need to edit the options after the wizard has completed. Use the Modify button to edit any existing columns, or delete to remove columns. Once you are finished and click Next, FrontPage generates the database and places it in the fpdb folder in your Web.

Note
In addition to any fields you designate, FrontPage also creates a Key field of type autonumber that is used as the index field for your database. This is not an option.

Using an existing connection

The final option available to you when using the DIW is to create an interface to an existing database. In order to use an existing database, of course, you must first have created a connection to a database. The procedure to do this is described in detail in Chapter 20. Once you have defined a connection to an existing database, you can use the DIW to generate the Web database interface, much as we did earlier using the sample Northwind database.

To create an interface for your existing database, select "Use an existing connection" in the first screen of the wizard. In the next screen, select a table or view to use. Then configure the fields as described in the preceding section. Note that you cannot add or delete fields from this list, and you can only modify the form-field element property of the existing fields. If you want to alter the submission form, you will have to do so after the wizard completes.

Editing multiple tables

If you have a very basic database application, you may be content to edit a single table. Most database applications, however, involve more than one table of information. The question is how to manage that using the DIW. The easiest (although not necessarily most elegant) solution is to add multiple versions of the application using the DIW — one for each table.

To build a complete set of database interfaces for a multitable database, use the following techniques:

1. Create a first database application as described in the previous sections. Note that when you create this application in your Web, FrontPage places it in a folder called `<mydatabase>_interface` and then creates a folder inside that with the name of the table or view. Inside that are the interface pages.

2. With the Web containing the database application still open, create a second Database Interface application. This time, when you are creating the new Web in the Web Site Templates dialog box (refer back to Figure 21-1), check the Add to Current Web option. Follow the same procedure you used for the first interface to create a new set of forms for a second table in your database. You will now have a second folder in your `<mydatabase_interface>` folder.

Tip If you want to be able to navigate easily from one editing application to another, be sure to use the same user name and password for authentication in each one.

3. Repeat this process for each of the tables in your database that you need to edit. When you are finished, you may want to create a single page with links to each of the interfaces you have created.

At this point, you have mastered the basics of creating a complete database application in FrontPage using the handy Database Interface Wizard. If you find that the DIW creates everything that you need for your database application, you need read no further in this chapter. However, you may find that although the DIW is a significant enhancement to FrontPage's ability to generate database functionality quickly and painlessly, it still is less than is needed for most real Web-database applications. To illustrate some of the issues raised by FrontPage's limitations, the remainder of this chapter is devoted to examining a simple but realistic example using a modified version of the Online Phone Directory we created in the previous chapter.

Note The database files used in this chapter can be found on the book's Web site. For complete instructions on downloading all the sample files for the book, see "About the Book's Web Site" in the Preface.

Designing a Self-service Database Application

You have employee information. Each employee has an ID number. You want to create a phone directory that will enable users to maintain their own information. In addition, you want to have an administrator who has the ability to update any employee's records and a system administrator who can make changes to all tables in the database.

Even before we start, you can probably see that the DIW is going to handle some but not all of our objectives. In general, the DIW relates to our needs as follows:

- ✦ **Areas where the DIW will be perfectly adequate:** Mostly in maintaining basic database records
- ✦ **Areas where the DIW will almost but not quite cut it:** These are mostly ease of update issues
- ✦ **Areas where the DIW is just inadequate:** Most evidently in the authentication

Whatever your particular database project, you will find the DIW more or less adequate to your task, but we are willing to bet that you will have the same range of issues. The goal, in working through this example, is to provide you with a model for addressing your own challenges. So, our plan for building the application will be first to use the DIW to create the entire application, then make adjustments as needed, and finally make wholesale replacements where we can't avoid them.

The Database

We have tried to keep this database relatively simple in order to focus on essentials, but also representative of a real-world phone directory. The database consists of six tables:

- ✦ `Departments:` A list of department names keyed by department id (`deptid`) to employees.
- ✦ `Employees:` A list of employees with names, addresses, and e-mail addresses. The `Employee` table is linked to the `Users` table by `userid`. You could simply add the user information to the `Employee` table, but sooner or later someone will want to give customers access to the directory as well, or if not customers, then family members, or some other non-employee entity, so having the user information in a separate table is just a hedge against the future.
- ✦ `Phones:` This table has `phonenumbers` and `typeids` linked to employees via the `Employee` table key (`eeid`). Again, you could simply add phone information to the `Employee` table, but that makes your database a bit more rigid. This way, if the CEO has 3 cell phones, you can add them all.

✦ `PhoneTypes`: A list of available phone types.

✦ `Roles`: A list of valid user roles.

✦ `Users`: User information, including `username`, `password`, and `roleid`.

For a complete picture of this database, its tables, and columns, see Figure 21-10.

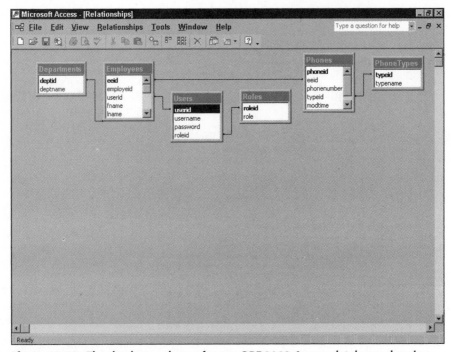

Figure 21-10: The database schema for our OPD2002 Access database, showing column names and table relationships

Step 1: Building the basic application

To begin building the Online Phone Directory database application, do the following:

1. Import the database into an existing Web. Select File ➪ Import, locate the database file, `opd2002.mdb`, and import it into the Web. FrontPage asks if you would like to create a new database connection for this file. Yes, thank you, you would. Name the connection `OPD2002`. Click Yes. FrontPage recommends that you put the database in the `fpdb` folder, and asks if we want to do this. Click Yes. The database is added.

2. Run the DIW by selecting File ➪ New ➪ Page or Web, selecting Web Site Templates from the Task Pane and then selecting the Database Interface Wizard. You are going to add your application to the existing Web, so check the Add to Current Web checkbox and click OK.

3. The DIW prompts you to choose a database connection option. Select "Use an existing database connection," and select `OPD2002` from the drop-down menu list. Click Next.

4. At the next DIW screen, you have to select a table to work with. You are going to create a separate application for each of the six tables, so you might as well start at the top, and select `Departments`. Click Next.

5. In the next dialog, edit the list of fields and form fields that correspond to those in your table. The default, which lists `deptname` as a Text type and Text Box as form field is fine for `Departments`. Click Next.

6. In the next dialog, you only need the Database Editor portion of the application for the `Departments` table. Uncheck Results Page and Submission Form and check Database Editor. Click Next.

7. Next, you have to select a user name and password. You may anticipate that you will have to change the login mechanism, but your goal at this point is to leverage as much of the DIW's hard work as possible. So go ahead and create a user name and password, because this will generate all of the login related files. Click Next to review the DIW's plan, and Finish to generate the files.

8. You should now have a folder named `OPD2002_interface` that contains a `Departments` folder that contains an `editor` folder that contains all of the database editor files we need to maintain the `Departments` table.

Step 2: Repeat for remaining database tables

Now you have to repeat this procedure for each of the other five tables in your database. Each time, the DIW will create a new folder for your files, which as you may guess will mean a fair amount of redundancy (let's hope that the next version of the Database Interface Wizard has support for multiple tables). In the meantime, the next sections describe the specifics for each of the remaining tables.

✦ **Employees:** You would like to display the `employeeid` without allowing it to be edited. Not an option in the DIW, so you will deal with it yourself. You want to remove `userid` and you want `Deptid` to be a drop-down menu. `Modtime`, which is just a time stamp indicating when the record is updated, you want to display but not edit, because it will update automatically when the record is updated. You want `Modby` to populate with the user's name, without their intervention. You will have to edit these manually, once you finish the wizard. For the pages to generate, you actually need to create two versions of this page — one which will allow a user to edit their own information, and one which will allow an administrator to edit anyone's information. Your solution will be to create a form for the administrators and a separate login for users. For now, select Database Editor and Results pages.

✦ **Phones:** This is the other table that will modified by users. Ultimately, you would like to combine user editing of employee information and phone information into a single form. This is complicated by the fact that a given employee will have multiple phone records.

✦ **PhoneTypes:** Similar in concept to the `Departments` table, this is a simple lookup table that lists phone type name by id. Database editing will be limited to adding, updating, and deleting items from this table.

✦ **Roles:** Another lookup style table, treated the same as `Departments` and `PhoneTypes`.

✦ **Users:** This is the database table you will use for your customized authentication purposes. For now you just need to be able to add, update, and delete users from the database. It would also be nice to give users the ability to update their passwords in this table.

Step 3: Organize the various functions

Having created the multiple database applications, one per table, you now go about the tasks of cleaning up and consolidating functionality. The main tasks to perform:

✦ Consolidate the interfaces with a single entry point for database administration functions, and a second entry point for users who will have access to their own records. If you only created database editor pages for each table, FrontPage does not bother to create a table of contents at all. You create a simple list that points to each of the database editing framesets — one for each table. In a moment, you will revise this page to require a login prior to accessing it, but for now, you will only be prompted to login when you click on one of the links.

✦ Speaking of logging in, by default each of the database editing applications you created currently has its own individual login facility. This is potentially useful, if for instance, you want a different person in charge of each table of your database — but it is more likely that you will want to consolidate these into a single login mechanism. Mainly this is just a matter of reorganizing some files and changing a few links. The steps are as follows:

1. Copy the four login files `login.asa`, `login.asp`, `Login_Check.asp`, and `Login_Validate.asp` from one of the database applications into the main interface folder.

2. Open each database editor file and repoint the included file directive to the new location of `Login_Check.asp`.

3. Check the form submission action in `login.asp`. It may need to be repointed to the new location of `Login_Validate.asp`.

4. Open `Login_Validate.asp` in HTML view. After validating the user and setting a session cookie, it redirects to a new page. The default redirect page is the `database_editor.asp` file in each database application. Change this to point to the new table of contents you created.

5. Open the table of contents file, and add an include file directive as follows (note that this assumes you have placed the table of contents in the same directory as the login files):

```
<!--#include File='Login_Check.asp'-->
```

Now if you open the table of contents page, it will redirect you to the login page. After you login, you will be sent back to the table of contents, where you can proceed to any of the database editor functions.

✦ The next clean-up step is to make changes to the individual database forms. You can edit form field labels with more descriptive names (the defaults are the actual database field names); you may want to remove some fields from editing — for example any key fields that link one database table to another.

Caution   If you do remove a field from an editing form, be advised that it will break the functionality of the update page. One way around this dilemma (since it is likely that you will have fields that you don't want users to edit) is to pass field data that you do not want to be edited through hidden fields.

✦ You might want to add a theme to the database editing pages, to give your application a consistent (and somewhat more eye-pleasing) look and feel.

✦ Finally, you'll want to make changes to individual form elements. This includes removing some fields from the input list — because you do not want them to be edited — and customizing the input fields for some others. Here you run up against your first snag. You would like to use select lists populated from the database in your forms (as you did in the search form example in the previous chapter), but unfortunately it is not possible to nest a Database Results Region (for your select list) inside another Database Results Region (used to generate the form). The next section pursues — in some detail — a workaround to this problem.

At this point, you have a serviceable database application for a multiple table database. However, several issues remain:

✦ The fact that login is restricted to a single user name, password combination

✦ The fact that it is not possible to add database-generated select lists to your input forms

✦ The fact that there is no way to edit linked database tables together

These are not the only issues, but they point out some typical features that the DIW does not support. By way of illustrating how far you can push the FrontPage database mechanism, we will examine each of three issues in the remainder of this chapter.

Extending the login model

The DIW creates a serviceable login for a personal database application that you, or someone like you, will maintain on your own — and that only requires a mild dose of security. It is not sufficient for a multi-user environment, nor for an application that defines multiple roles to users.

One way to amend that is to store user information in the database and let it manage logins. That is the approach we take in our phone directory application. This section briefly describes the steps needed to revise the DIW's login to accommodate the use of database tables to manage users and user roles.

Note   In the following sections, I assume a fair degree of comfort with Active Server Pages. If you are unfamiliar with ASP programming, you may want to glance at Chapter 19 before proceeding. Better yet, pick up a copy of Eric Smith's *Active Server Pages Bible* (IDG Books Worldwide, 2000), which covers ASP programming in far more detail than we can manage here.

Step 1: Using a database table for login

In this first step, we add a database query to the login page, so that we can maintain multiple usernames and passwords somewhat more securely than in a text file.

1. The first step is to use the Database Results Wizard to create a new login validation routine based on the `Users` table in your database. You are going to insert your new validation directly into the `login.asp` page, for reasons that we will explain in a moment. Place the cursor above the login form in `login.asp` and run the wizard. Select the phone directory database, and then create the following custom query:

   ```
   SELECT Count(*) As LoginCount FROM Users WHERE
   username='::login::' AND password='::password::'
   ```

   The `Count(*)` function returns the number of matching records: 1 means you have a valid user; 0 means you do not. (More than 1 means you have trouble in your database!)

2. Once the wizard has created its default database region, you need to delete all of the visible elements and add a small block of ASP that evaluates the count returned from the database and sends the user on to their desired destination if the count is 1, and lets them know that the login failed otherwise. Here is the code to do that, which needs to be inserted somewhere inside the database region in order to pick up the `LoginCount` value from the database.

   ```
   <%
   If (FP_FieldVal(fp_rs,"LoginCount")=1) Then
        Response.Redirect "database_editor.asp"
   End If
   %>
   ```

3. When you redirect the user to another page you introduce one other complication: the redirect command works with a standard element of the HTTP response mechanism in your Web server. To function properly, the redirect command has to be issued before the page starts to load. (If you try to run this command as is, you will get an error message indicating that it is too late to be redirecting folks.) To make this work, you need to use a capability within ASP that allows you to *buffer*, that is, to build but not to send, the page until you are ready. To do this, add the line `Response.buffer=true` in an ASP

block at the top of the page. Once you know whether you will be redirecting the user, you can issue another statement Response.flush to release the buffer and start loading the page.

4. Next, add an error message in the case of an invalid login. This is, in part, the reason for wanting to build the login validation right into the login page. You can define an error message in the ASP and then display it on the login page — later in the HTML — without having to redirect the user at all. To do that, you check to see if any login information was submitted. If it was, and you do not have a matching record from the database, you display an error message. To do this, create a flag, HasLoginData and set it initially to false. If login data is submitted to the page, update the value of the flag to true. Here is the code added to our original routine:

```
HasLoginInput=false
If StrComp(Request.Form("login"),"")>0 Then
     HasLoginInput=true
     If (FP_FieldVal(fp_rs,"LoginCount")=1) Then
          'Go to database start page
          Response.Redirect "database_editor.asp"
     End If
End If
End If
```

If HasLoginInput is true and the page does not redirect, you know that the user submitted login information that was invalid and you can display a custom error message. In the body of the page, just above the login form itself, add this block of code:

```
<% If HasLoginInput Then %>
     <p><font size="2" color="red">Error: Invalid username
or password. Please try again.</font><p>
<% End If %>
```

Of course, you can change the HTML error message to suit yourself. The key is to create the conditional check for HasLoginInput and only display the error message if its value is true.

5. Next, add back the cookie setting routine used by Login_Validate.asp so that the application does not have to recheck the database each time the user goes to a new page that requires authentication. You will use a simple variation on the original cookie code in Login_Validate.asp. Instead of setting the cookie data to the username and password, however, simply set the login cookie to some text string, as shown in the code below.

```
Response.Cookies ("ADMIN")("login") = "VALIDLOGIN"
```

6. Finally, we need to update all of the database editing pages to use our new login mechanism. This is not difficult, just a bit tedious. By default, each page checks the Login_Check.asp page in its directory for a valid login. One option is that you can update all of the existing Login_Check.asp pages (one per table in your application) so that they check for the existence of the new cookie you created and redirect the user to your new login page if it is not found. The other option is to create one central Login_Check.asp page to do

this and then update the include file statements in every editing page to point to this central Login_Check.asp. Here is a sample of what a central Login_Check.asp page might look like:

```
If Request.Cookies("ADMIN")("login") <> "VALIDLOGIN" Then
    ' redirect user to the login page
        Response.Redirect
    "/fpbible/OPD2002_interface/login.asp"
End If
```

Caution

If you create a central Login_Check.asp page, you will need use an absolute file reference for the redirection URL as indicated in the example code provided (although the actual URL will vary). In this circumstance a relative URL would be interpreted as relative to the original editing page that called the login check, not relative to the Login_Check.asp page itself as you might assume.

Step 2: Distinguishing user login from admin login

Your next challenge is to customize the login to accommodate our dual role model — users who can edit their own pages and admins who can edit any record. This will require some alteration of your initial login scheme. You need to query the user table in such a way as to get back the roleid and userid records for the user who is authenticating. Assuming that they provide us a valid user name and password, you can then redirect them based on their user record. Users with a roleid of 0 (for user level) will be redirected to a special edit form that preloads their user information based on the userid, which you will pass along with the redirect. Users with a roleid of 1 (admins), will be redirected as per our initial example.

Here are the changes you need to make to the login page:

✦ The main change you need to make is to your SQL query. In addition to returning the count function, you now need it to return the userid and roleid from the Users table. In order to do this, you will have to create a specialized SQL statement for dealing with *aggregated results*. You create the statement by adding all of the fields you want to return to a GROUP BY clause and then replacing the WHERE clause with an equivalent HAVING clause that works with GROUP BY. To make a long story, short, the new SQL should look like this:

```
SELECT userid, roleid, Count(userid) FROM Users GROUP BY
userid, username, password, roleid HAVING
username='::login::' AND password='::password::'
```

(By the way, creating difficult SQL like this is much easier done in Access than by hand.)

Note

You have probably realized that in this version of the query, you don't really need the count function at all. You might just as easily return the userid and roleid and just check to see if you got back a record from the database to determine that the login was valid.

✦ The other change you need to make is to customize your redirection, so that non-admins are redirected to a page that enables them to edit their record directly and admins are redirected to the complete database editing environment. The new redirect looks like this (note the addition of another error flag, `HasInvalidRoleId`, which like `HasValidLogin` described above, can be used to flag the need for an error message):

```
If (Fp_FieldVal(fp_rs,"roleid")=0) Then
     Response.Redirect "user_start_page.htm"
Else If (Fp_FieldVal(fp_rs,"roleid")=1) Then
     Response.Redirect "admin_start_page.htm"
Else
     HasInvalidRoleId=true
End If
```

This section has illustrated one method for beefing up the user authentication capabilities provided by the DIW. Recognize, that this is still not high level security — it does, however, add some flexibility to create multiple users and even multiple user-types. In the next section, we take on another limitation of the DIW and show you how to build a database-generated select list.

Adding a database-generated select menu inside a FrontPage database region

Here's the goal: to be able to edit the employee record, including changing department information for the employee. The employee record holds the department id (`deptid`), which is keyed to the `Departments` table. The standard practice for building a form like this is to use a drop-down menu of available options, so that the user can select a friendly department name, like "Human Resources," and then when the data is submitted, the form sends the appropriate id.

Here's the problem. You can build a nice select list using the Database Results Wizard, as described in the previous chapter. But, you cannot insert this select list into the Database Results Region that contains the rest of the employee information. You cannot nest Database Results Regions. Period.

The solution requires a bit of fancy footwork to get around these limitations. The actual custom code required is relatively minimal, but the conceptual model is definitely of the "long way round" school of design — we only recommend this to those who need it. And even then, you should first have a good reason to abandon the DIW altogether and create a custom ASP solution, which in this case would be far simpler to implement. But, for those who are set on doing it the FrontPage way, here are the steps:

The solution consists of four basic elements:

✦ A subroutine to build the department list as the data is being assembled in the database results region — and a variable to hold the HTML string that is being assembled

✦ A call to the subroutine with each set of data to add to the Select string

✦ A function that returns the assembled select item and selects the current value

✦ A call to that function from within the second Database Results Region

Here are the steps you can follow to generate the workaround:

1. Open the `edit.asp` page for the `Employee` table. You will notice the purple warning about not tampering with this form in the Database Results Wizard. Don't panic. It is OK to edit the HTML inside the form, just not the Results Wizard portions (which is what would happen if you opened it in the DRW).

2. Insert the cursor above this purple text warning. Now create a Database Results Region that uses the `Department` table and includes both the `deptid` and `deptname` field values. Create it as a list with minimal HTML — line breaks, no divider lines, and no field names is about the best you can do.

3. Switch to HTML view. Because you are about to delete the column values but want the code, what you want to do next is preserve the ASP code that is inserted in each of the two column values. One method would be to copy both items into the clipboard. In case you lose them, the ASP looks like this:

```
<%= FP_FieldVal(fp_rs,"deptid") %>
<%= FP_FieldVal(fp_rs,"deptname") %>
```

4. Once you have a copy of the two snippets of ASP code stashed away, switch back to Normal view and delete the two column values leaving you with an empty database region. (You can delete these from HTML view, but I find it much easier not to disturb the database region code this way, which causes FrontPage to restore everything back to its original state.)

5. Back in HTML view, find the space between the `<DatabaseRegionStart endspan>` and the `<DatabaseRegionEnd startspan>` tags. This can take some hunting — but basically, the database region consists of two sets of tags — a `RegionStart` that has a `startspan` and `endspan` set of tags, and a `DatabaseRegionEnd` with its own `startspan` and `endspan`. The only place FrontPage will let you make changes is between these two sets of tags. If you are unsure whether you have found the right spot, try making a small change and switching back to Normal view. If FrontPage does not complain, you are OK.

6. Once you find FrontPage's "sweet spot" so to speak, insert the following code:

```
<% addSelectOption
FP_FieldVal(fp_rs,"deptid"),FP_FieldVal(fp_rs,"deptname") %>
```

Note that the two parameters passed to your `addSelectOption` subroutine are the variables you copied earlier, minus the ASP tags. To be safe, you can paste these function calls rather than type them.

7. Still in HTML view, move to the top of the page, above the `<html>` tag, and insert the following block of ASP code:

```
<%
dim deptsel
dim selopts
dim optvalstart
dim optvalend
optvalstart = "value='"
optvalend = "'"

Sub addSelectOption(val,opttest)
    selopts = selopts + "<option " + optvalstart + val +
optvalend + ">" + opttext
End Sub

Function getSelect(name,selid)
    origopts = optvalstart + selid + optvalend
    newopts = "selected " + optvalstart + selid + optvalend
    selopts = Replace(selopts,origopts,newopts)
    getSelect = "<select name='" + name + "'>" + selopts +
"</select>"
End Function
%>
```

You have created two methods here — the first is a subroutine that builds the options sections of the select form element based on the items found in the database. These are the same regardless of the employee. This is the subroutine you call from within the `Departments DatabaseResults` region. The second method is a function that will be called from within the `Employee DatabaseResults` region (which we are getting to) and it will make it possible to customize the name of the element. So, you can use this on a page that displays multiple employee records and a select list for each record if you want to — as well as selecting the correct option for the given employee.

8. The next step, then, is to make the function call. Switch back to Normal view, and locate the `deptid` field. (You can change the name to `Dept`, BTW). Again, we are going to delete the field, but make use of the ASP code that inserts the field value, so preserve that if you want and then delete the field. The code should look like this:

```
<%= FP_FieldHTML(fp_rs,"deptid") %>
```

(You will notice that this line is built using a slightly different FP function call — `FP_FieldHTML` rather than `FP_FieldVal`.)

9. Switch back to HTML view, and where you removed the `dept` field, add the following ASP block:

```
<%= getSelect("deptid",FP_FieldHTML(fp_rs,"deptid")) %>
```

10. Save and test the results. You should have a page that resembles Figure 21-11.

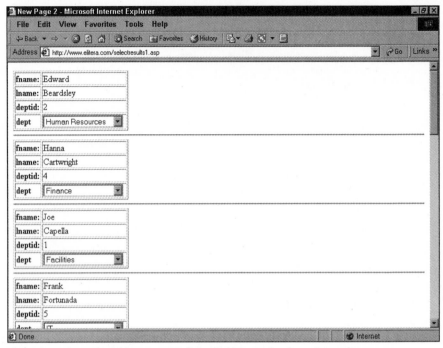

Figure 21-11: A drop-down menu inserted into a database input form

This workaround is useful in its own right. But the mechanism it uses to get around the limitations of the Database Results Region has even wider implications. While we are on the topic, let me give you one last example (if your head is not already spinning from the contortions of this last workaround).

Passing data to a JavaScript object via ASP

Caution   The example described in this section is intended for relatively advanced developers. Proceed at your own risk.

A favorite trick of server-side programmers is to pass information from a server-side programming language like ASP to a client-side programming language like JavaScript. You can use this to create a client-side database application that can change the view of data without having to requery the database server. For example, with data in JavaScript objects, you can build dynamic select menus — when you select an item from the first menu, it dynamically builds the second submenu with an appropriate set of items. To illustrate this principle, we'll build a simple example using departments as the first level menu and employees as the second.

The key to this is writing the data on the server side into custom JavaScript objects that are then processed by the browser. The method for doing this is similar to the one you used in the previous example — first use some basic ASP to create the list of database values you need and then insert those into the appropriate JavaScript to be processed by the browser. This example gets a bit heavy on the code, and we are going to gloss over some of the finer points, but bear with us, it's not too bad:

1. Create a bare-bones `Departments` table results region including `deptid` and `deptname`. Using the method detailed in the previous section, remove the column values and replace them with the following block of ASP code:

```
<%
If Not StrComp(aspDept,"")=0 Then
    AspDept = aspDept + ","
End If
AspDept = aspDept + "new oDept('" +
FP_FieldVal(fp_rs,"deptid") + "','" +
FP_FieldVal(fp_rs,"deptname") + "')"
%>
```

Here you are simply creating a list of `Department` objects that you are going to pass to the JavaScript momentarily. The only tricky part about this is the placement of commas in the list, which is what the initial conditional clause is taking care of.

2. Create a similar `DatabaseResults` region for the `Employee` table, including `eeid`, `deptid`, `lname`, and `fname` fields. Replace the column values with this ASP:

```
<%
If Not StrComp(aspEE,"")=0 Then
    AspEE = aspEE+ ","
End If
AspEE = aspEE + "new oEE('" + FP_FieldVale(fp_rs,"eeid") +
"','" + FP_FieldVale(fp_rs,"lname,") + "," +
"FP_FieldVal(fp_rs,"fname") + "')"
%>
```

3. In HTML view, somewhere after the last database region and before the end of the HTML page, insert a block of JavaScript that looks like this:

```
<script>
<!--//
function oDept(id,name)
{
    this.id=id;
    this.name=name;
}
function oEE(id,deptid,name)
```

```
{
     this.id=id;
     this.deptid=deptid;
     this.name=name;
}
aDept = new Array(
<% = aspDept %>
);
aEE = new Array(
<%= aspEE %>
);

//-->
</script>
```

That last step warrants some explanation. The first half of the code consists of two custom object constructors, oDept and oEE. In JavaScript, you can define an object and assign it properties as illustrated here, much in the same way you would write a standard function. Once you have instantiated your custom object, you can reference its properties just as you would reference standard JavaScript objects. For instance if you created an oEmployee object variable named Fred, you could access Fred.id, Fred.deptid, and Fred.name either to set or to retrieve these values.

The second half of the code performs the magic of passing the data accumulated in the ASP variables to JavaScript arrays. Each of the arrays, aDept, and aEE, consists of a list of oDept and oEE objects respectively, and each of the objects is constructed with the data from the database. The net result is an array of department records and an array of employee records available for your use in JavaScript.

At this point you could do any of a number of things with this data. What we want to do now is build dynamic menu items. To do this involves pure JavaScript. We will leave you to investigate the details, but essentially, a JavaScript function is called by the onload event to build the first menu item. This menu contains an onSelect handler that in turn builds the submenu based on the id (in this case deptid) selected.

Here are the main functions (the complete working page, named asp2js.asp, is available on the Book's Web site. See the Preface for details on downloading files from this site):

✦ BuildSelect(): The meat of the operation

✦ InitPrimarySelector(): Called when the page loads

✦ UpdateSecondarySelector(): Called when an item is selected in the primary list

The final result is illustrated in Figure 21-12.

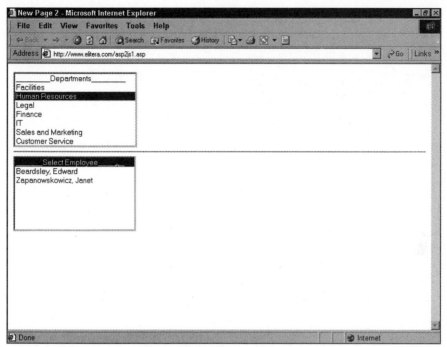

Figure 21-12: Building dynamic select lists using ASP and custom JavaScript objects

Updating multiple tables in a single form

Your database is designed to permit a given employee to have more than one telephone number. Each phone record contains an employee id number (eeid) that is keyed to a record in the Employee table.

You are going to replace the default edit.asp with a more sophisticated form so that the admin or user can edit either the employee information or any of the employee's phone numbers in a single form. This is particularly important for your user interface—because the employee who has to update his or her information does not know about or care about the concept of a database table. They know they have some personal information and a list of phone numbers that they want to make sure are accurate. Putting these together on the same form for editing is therefore more consistent from the user's point of view.

There are a number of ways to build this interface, some more sophisticated than others. Your goal in this application is to simplify the user's task without unduly complicating your development task. For that reason, you will build what amounts to several separate forms within the same page. Each will have its own Submit button. This is not as elegant as a single Update button for the entire form page, but significantly easier to handle—and leverages more of the work the DIW has already done for us.

Our steps:

1. Start by making a copy of the existing edit form for the employee table. You will add your phone information to the end of it.

2. Run the DRW and create a table record for phones that returns the pertinent information. This query returns all of the phone numbers associated with an `employeeid` number.

3. Edit the table to create a unique form element with Update and Delete buttons for each item. Add the `phoneid` to a hidden field for each element. Link the Update and Delete buttons to the existing pages for these functions.

Tip

An alternative method of passing the `phoneid` to delete and update pages is to give each button the name and value of the `phoneid`. This saves you having to create a hidden field.

4. Create an Add button at the bottom of the form, which links to the existing `new.asp` for adding new phone records. Reconfigure the page to return to the main editing page when it is finished. (Alternately, you could embed this form into the editing page as well.)

Beyond the Database Interface Wizard

If you have been following through the examples in this chapter, you may have begun to notice a certain pattern — you used the wizard to create a results page and then deleted all but the bare framework of it. At a certain point, you may decide that it is simply easier to start from scratch to build your application.

If so, we recommend you first consider building your database application using customized data input pages built with the Database Results Wizard. This approach would provide considerably more flexibility than using the Database Interface Wizard (whose strength is the ability to generate a lot of functionality with a minimum of effort on your part).

Summary

This chapter has been all about creating a usable Web-based database application. You began by learning what the main components of such an application are and how the new Database Interface Wizard simplifies the task of creating such an application. You practiced using the wizard by creating a simple editing interface for FrontPage's sample Northwind database. Then, we tackled some of the limitations of this basic application. Using the custom telephone directory example first started in the previous chapter, you learned how to add support for multi-table databases to your application, how to consolidate the login and interface in this case. Next, you developed an alternative login method that uses the database rather than a text file to maintain a list of users and their passwords. In addition, you added the ability to support multiple user roles to the login. Finally, you worked out some advanced techniques for creating dynamic select lists using the Database Results Wizard. With the database techniques you have learned in this and the previous chapter, you are well on your way to being able to create real-world database applications in FrontPage.

✦   ✦   ✦

Advanced Topics

Developing Custom FrontPage Solutions

This chapter offers an overview of the many ways that you can customize FrontPage to suit your needs. The first half of the chapter focuses on relatively simple, non-programming customizations: customizing the FrontPage environment, creating themes and templates, and using macros. The last half of the chapter is aimed more at developers: using Visual Basic Editor (VBE) to create FrontPage macros and using Visual Basic to create design-time controls and wizards (with a brief glance at add-ins). The development section is designed to explore the basic possibilities for customization. A full-scale discussion of programming is beyond the scope of this book.

This chapter in its entirety is not for everyone. If you are a novice FrontPage user, we recommend that you read this chapter's initial section on creating your own templates and themes. These are easy to do and don't require programming skills. You may also want to look over the sections on macros, design-time controls, wizards, and add-ins, just to familiarize yourself with the terminology. Even if you are unlikely to create any of these yourself, understanding what they are and how they work is helpful, in the event that you use controls that someone else has created.

On the other hand, this chapter is highly practical. It does not try to give you a full-blown course in programming. This chapter is for you if you are the kind of person who says, "Gee, FrontPage is a swell Web development tool, but if only it could do X . . ." or, "I have done these same tedious commands 20 times in the last week. I sure wish I could automate this!" If this doesn't describe you, well, maybe this chapter will give you a spark of inspiration!

Customizing the FrontPage Work Space

FrontPage 2002, like the other Office applications, enables you to modify the commands available on the menus and toolbars. You can even create your own toolbars. This section describes the basic toolbar- and menu-customization features. Later in the chapter, after you learn how to create macros, you find out how to add your macros to a custom toolbar by using the methods outlined here.

Using the Customize dialog box

All of the FrontPage customization features are accessible from the Customize dialog box. To open this dialog box, select Tools ➪ Customize (see Figure 22-1).

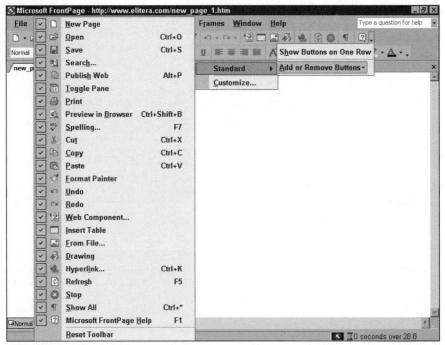

Figure 22-1: The Customize dialog box enables you to create your personal FrontPage interface.

Customizing toolbars

You can customize toolbars by using either of two methods:

    ✦ Use the Customize dialog box.

    ✦ Use the Add or Remove Buttons option available on each toolbar (this option is not available on custom toolbars).

To access the Add or Remove Buttons option, click the small downward-pointing arrow at the right end of a toolbar. This brings up a list of the current buttons, as shown in Figure 22-2. To remove a button, deselect it from the list. To add it back, select it.

You can also access the Customize dialog box from this option menu by selecting Customize, which is the last item on the list.

Figure 22-2: Adding or removing buttons from a toolbar

Moving command items

To move a command from one toolbar to another, press Alt+Ctrl and drag the toolbar command to a new toolbar. If you release the Alt and Ctrl keys and drop the command anywhere other than on another toolbar, it deletes the command from the original toolbar. If you drop it accidentally, you can always add it back by using the Add or Remove Buttons menu, as previously described.

Creating toolbars

Using the Toolbars tab, you can designate which toolbars you want to have visible. To show a particular toolbar, simply select it to check the box next to its name. To hide the toolbar, select it again to uncheck the box.

The Toolbars tab has four buttons:

✦ **New:** Adds a custom toolbar to the list

✦ **Rename:** Changes the name of a custom toolbar that you have added by using the New button

✦ **Delete:** Deletes a custom toolbar that you have added by using the New button

✦ **Reset:** Resets a standard toolbar to its default state if you have made changes to it

When you select one of the built-in toolbars, the only other function available to you, besides the New button, is the Reset button. The other buttons are reserved for any custom toolbars that you create.

As an example, here's how to create a new toolbar:

1. Click the New button and type the name of the new toolbar; call it **Scripting**, because your plan is to add the buttons needed to access the macro functionality that you will use repeatedly later in this chapter.

2. Click OK to create your Scripting toolbar (see Figure 22-3). This toolbar isn't much to look at yet, but in the next section, you learn how to add commands to it.

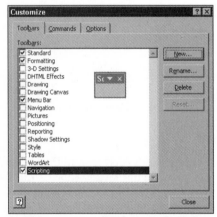

Figure 22-3: Your new custom Scripting toolbar without any commands added yet

Opening the Customize menu performs a bit of magic on the FrontPage interface itself. Unlike most dialog boxes, when you open the Customize dialog box, you can still access menu lists. And, when you do so, a strange and marvelous thing happens: If you drag an item from a menu item, a menu list name (File, Edit, View, and so on), or a toolbar item, you can move it to another location and drop it into place.

The Commands tab

The Commands tab enables you to customize menus and toolbars by adding and deleting commands. To access the Commands tab, select Tools ⇨ Customize and click the Commands tab, illustrated in Figure 22-4. This tab lists all the commands that are available to be added to or removed from toolbars or menu lists. For example, if you select the Tools item in the Categories list on the left side, the list of current commands for Tools appears on the right.

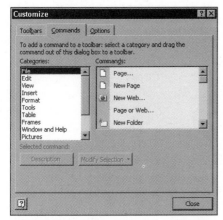

Figure 22-4: The Commands tab in the Customize dialog box

Scroll down the list of commands on the Tools menu until you come to Macros. Click and drag this item onto your Scripting toolbar. Repeat this procedure for Visual Basic Editor and Microsoft Script Editor. Now you have your own toolbar as shown in Figure 22-5. You can hide or view it by using the standard View ➪ Toolbars mechanism. You can even dock and undock your toolbar.

Figure 22-5: Your custom Scripting toolbar with macros added

To remove your toolbar, simply return to the Toolbars tab, select the toolbar that you want to delete, and click the Delete button.

Adding items to menus

As an example, suppose that you have used earlier versions of FrontPage and are accustomed to inserting scripts via the Insert ➪ Advanced menu item. (See Chapter 18 for details on how to insert scripts in FrontPage 2002.) Or maybe you are just tired of hunting for the Microsoft Scripting Editor, buried under Macros of all places, each time you want to edit your scripts. You decide to take matters into your own hands and add an Advanced Scripting menu item to the Insert menu. Do the following:

1. Select Tools ➪ Customize to open the Customize dialog box. Click the Commands tab and select Tools from the Categories list.

2. Scroll down the Commands list to locate the Microsoft Script Editor command. Drag this item to the FrontPage menu bar and pause over the Insert menu item, keeping your mouse button depressed the entire time. The Insert menu expands.

3. Drag the Script command down the Insert menu until you have positioned the MSE command where you want it. Drop it into the menu by releasing the mouse button, as shown in Figure 22-6.

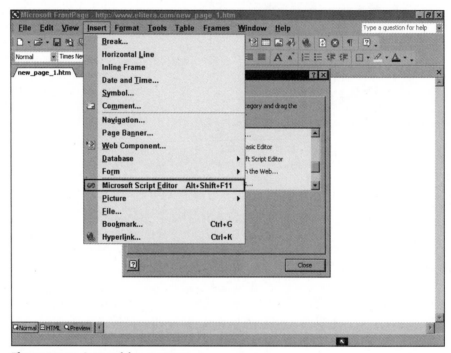

Figure 22-6: Customizing a menu

To change the name of this new item from its default to "Advanced Scripting" (or whatever makes you happy), right-click it and type a new name in the Name Property textbox. To define a shortcut key, place an ampersand (&) in front of the shortcut character. For example, to designate the letter *C* as the shortcut key for a command called My Command, give its name as **My &Command**. Shortcut-key characters are underlined in the menu bar. The command can now be executed by pressing the Alt key and the shortcut key simultaneously.

To remove this new item, right-click it and select Delete.

Tip If you accidentally do something drastic, like, for instance, delete the Tools menu from FrontPage, you can undo the damage by selecting the deleted Menu item from the list in the Toolbars tab and then clicking the Reset button.

Using the Commands option menu

As described in the previous example, if you right-click an item, you see the option menu list, shown in Figure 22-7. This is the same menu accessed when you select an item in the Commands toolbar and click the Modify button. Use this menu to remove, rename, or designate a new icon for an item.

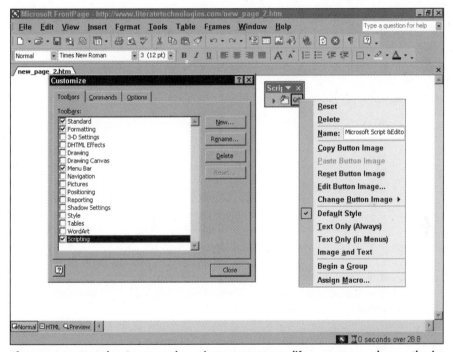

Figure 22-7: Use the Commands option menu to modify, remove, or change the icon for a toolbar or menu item.

The Options tab

The Options tab of the Customize dialog box (see Figure 22-8) contains miscellaneous options that you can control, including the following miscellaneous customization options:

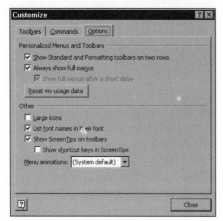

Figure 22-8: The Options tab of the Customize dialog box

✦ **Personalized Menus and Toolbars:**

- **Show Standard and Formatting toolbars on two rows:** Clear this check-box to cause the two primary FrontPage toolbars to occupy a single row. This is useful for conserving space if you have a large enough monitor. Otherwise, you have to scroll the single row to access all toolbar items.

- **Always show full menus:** Clear the checkbox to limit menu lists to recently used commands.

- **Show full menus after a short delay:** Works in conjunction with the previous option to minimize menu clutter. When checked, this option shows you all menu items if you don't select one of the recently used items.

- **Reset my usage data:** Wipes out FrontPage's memory of your recently used commands, enabling you to reset which menu items appear by default.

✦ **Other:**

- **Large icons:** Makes the toolbar icons bigger.

- **List font names in their font:** Causes each font name in the Fonts menu list to display using that font's typeface.

- **Show ScreenTips on toolbars:** Turns on ScreenTips, the little yellow boxes that show up when you place the cursor over an item on the toolbar.

- **Show shortcut keys in ScreenTips:** Adds to the ScreenTip a reminder about a command's shortcut key.

- **Menu animations (System Default, Random, Unfold, Slide, Fade):** Enables you to control how menu lists appear. Select None to have them appear as they have always done—that is, all at once. Select Unfold to have the menu appear from top to bottom. Select Slide to have the menu appear from top to bottom and from left to right. Select Random to enable FrontPage to select at random which type of animation to use each time you access a menu list.

Adding custom menu items

To add a custom menu item to the main menu bar, select Tools ➪ Customize and select the command that you want to add. This can either be an existing command or a custom menu item. To add a custom item, select Macros from the Categories list and select the Custom Menu Item command.

You can add menu commands to any existing submenu. You can even add a Menu command to the menu bar.

You can delete a default menu item from the menu bar. If you do this, and then want to undo the delete, select the Toolbars tab of the Customize dialog box, select Menu Bar, and click the Reset button. If you really get stuck and accidentally delete the Tools menu and the Insert menus, you can always get back to the Customize dialog box by right-clicking the menu bar. You cannot remove the menu bar.

Creating Custom Templates and Themes

Creating custom templates requires no programming. It is as simple as creating an HTML page and converting it to the template format. FrontPage recognizes three template types:

- ✦ **Page:** A single page template, located in the Pages subfolder of the FrontPage main folder
- ✦ **Frame set:** A frame set and all frames, located in the Frames subfolder of the FrontPage main folder
- ✦ **Web:** A collection of interconnected pages, stored in the Webs subfolder of the FrontPage main folder

Creating a page template

To create a page template:

1. Create the HTML page. If you have not yet saved the file, select File ➪ Save. Otherwise, select File ➪ Save As.

2. Select FrontPage Template (.tem) from the Save As Type drop-down menu.

3. Enter a name for the template file and click the Save button, which opens the Save As Template dialog box (see Figure 22-9). Enter a title, name, and description for the template. Click the Browse button if you want to select the title and name from a list of existing templates.

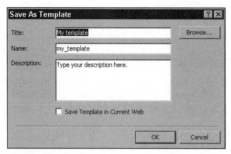

Figure 22-9: The Save As Template dialog box

4. Click OK to save your template.

Creating a frame set or style sheet template

You create a frame set or style sheet template much as you do a page template:

1. Define the layout of the frame set or the style sheet styles.

2. Select File ➪ Save or File ➪ Save As, and select FrontPage Template (.tem) from the Save As Type drop-down list.

3. Complete the template information, as described in the previous section for a page template. Your new frame set template appears in the Frames Pages tab of the New Page dialog box. Your new style sheet template appears in the Style Sheets tab of the New Page dialog box.

Creating shared templates

In FrontPage, you can create a template to be shared among all authors of a given Web. To do this, check the Save Template in Current Web option when you create your template. FrontPage creates a hidden folder, called _sharedtemplates, and stores your shared template there.

Note   Unfortunately, you can't share a template across multiple Webs.

Editing templates

To edit an existing template, you must open the existing template as a new page, edit the page, and resave it as a template with the same name as the existing template. The steps are as follows:

1. Select File ➪ New ➪ Page.

2. Select the template to edit from the General, Frames Pages, or StyleSheets tab. Click OK to open a new page using the selected template.

3. Make changes to the template in the new pages.

4. Select File ➪ Save As and select FrontPage Template (.tem) from the Save As Type drop-down list.

5. Resave the template using its existing name.

Deleting shared templates

To delete a shared template, first show hidden folders in your Web by selecting Tools ➪ Web Settings and checking the Show Documents in Hidden Directories option in the Advanced tab. Switch to Folders view, select the _sharedtemplates folder, select the template to delete, and select Edit ➪ Delete, or right-click the template and select Delete from the options menu.

Creating Web templates

You can create Web templates manually or, if you are using the Microsoft Personal Web Server, you can use the Web Template Maker utility (webtmpl.exe) that is part of the FrontPage Software Development Kit (SDK).

To create a Web template manually:

1. Create a folder called myweb.tem, where myweb is the name of the Web template, and place this folder in the Webs subfolder, located in the main FrontPage folder (\Program Files\Microsoft FrontPage, by default).

2. Create the Web to be used as the basis for the template.

3. Locate the Web files and copy to the myweb.tem folder. If your Web contains files in private or images subfolders, these must be copied as well.

4. Create a myweb.inf file, as described in the next section.

To create a Web template using the webtmpl.exe utility, follow these steps:

1. Launch the utility.

2. Select the Web to use from the available Webs list.

3. Indicate template information.

4. Click Make Web Template.

The template INF file

When you create a template, FrontPage saves all the necessary files in the appropriate template directory. In addition, it creates an INF file for the template. The INF file is simply a standard Windows INI format text file that stores configuration information about the template. This file can have several sections:

✦ `Info`: Contains information on the templates title, description, theme, and any shared borders.

✦ `FileList`: Enables you to map files in a template directory to explicit URLs within the Web that is created. This is the only way to create a Web template with subdirectories.

✦ `MetaInfo`: Store meta information variables that can be used in the Web, typically in conjunction with the substitution component.

✦ `TaskList`: Store information about initial tasks for your Web template, using the `TaskList` section of the INF file. A task has six attributes: `TaskName`, `Priority` (1–3), `CreatedBy`, `URL`, `Cookie`, and `Comment`.

Here, by way of example, is an excerpt from the INF file that accompanies the FrontPage Project Web template. Notice that the contents are divided into two sections — `info` and `FileList`:

```
[info]
title=Project Web
description=Create a web for a project containing a list of
members, a schedule, status, an archive and discussions.
structure=project.map
border=tlb
theme=axis 111
[FileList]
archive.htm=
contact.htm=
discuss.htm=
```

For more information on the format of the INF file, consult the FrontPage SDK.

Working with Macros

In the computer-programming world, a macro is a shortcut, a way to encapsulate a set of tasks or commands into a single step. In FrontPage, you can create timesaving macros by using the Visual Basic for Applications Editor (VBE). You can create macros to automate tasks that you perform in Webs or tasks associated with individual Web pages.

The practical details of how you create a macro using VBE are discussed in a moment, but first a word on how you invoke a macro after you have one. To run an existing macro, select Tools ➪ Macro ➪ Macros to open the Macro dialog box (which looks similar to the one shown in Figure 22-10), which lists all existing macros. To run a particular macro, either double-click it or select it and click the Run button.

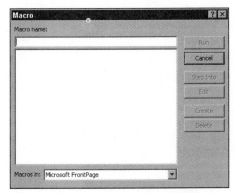

Figure 22-10: The Macro dialog box

Creating and editing macros

You use the Visual Basic Editor (VBE) to create a macro. You access VBE in either of two ways:

✦ Select Tools ➪ Macro ➪ Macros, select a macro, and click Edit.

✦ Select Tools ➪ Macro ➪ Visual Basic Editor to open the editor directly.

FrontPage 2002 includes Visual Basic Editor for creating FrontPage macros. These macros are intended for use when designing Web pages or administering Web sites. They are not part of the Web pages viewed by users. For information on programming that can be added to Web pages, such as JavaScript, DHTML, and ASP, refer to Chapters 18 and 19.

Note   One way to keep this straight is to remember that Microsoft Script Editor is designed for editing scripts that will affect the way your Web pages work in the browser; Visual Basic for Applications Editor is used to change the way FrontPage itself works.

Exploring the FrontPage object model

Before starting to create your own macros in FrontPage, it is helpful to understand how to work with the various elements in FrontPage. FrontPage exposes three object models that developers can use in their macros:

✦ **Application object model:** The top level of the FrontPage programming model. Provides access to add-ins, system information, command bars, and the FrontPage `Application` object, which contains a pointer to Webs and the Web object model.

✦ **Web object model:** This set of objects enables macros to operate on FrontPage Webs and the elements contained in Webs — including folders, navigation nodes, and themes.

✦ **FrontPage Document Object Model:** Parallels the DHTML Document Object Model (discussed in Chapter 18). It exposes design-time document objects within FrontPage.

These three object models are contained in two class libraries, `FrontPage` and `FrontPage_Editor`, which you can peruse by using VBE. To browse these libraries, open VBE and select View ⇨ Object Browser. VBE's Object Browser window provides a brief description of each class, its methods, and its properties, as shown in Figure 22-11.

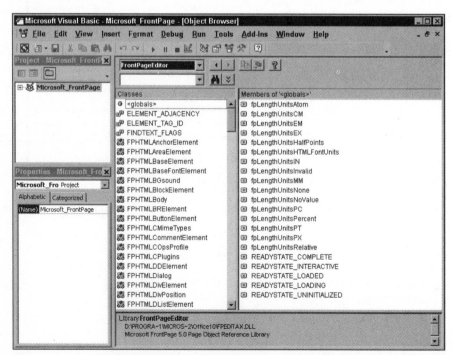

Figure 22-11: Visual Basic Editor's Object Browser, showing the FrontPage_Editor library

A complete description of the FrontPage programmable interfaces is beyond the scope of this book. The tutorials that follow illustrate two simple macros, one demonstrating how to interact with Webs, and the other showing how to use a macro to make changes to a Web page. The discussion assumes that you are familiar enough with VB programming — perhaps you have created macros in Visual Basic for Applications before — to be able to use VBE.

Tutorial 22-1: Creating a Web Switcher macro

A great feature of FrontPage is that you can have multiple Webs open simultaneously. Unfortunately, no list of the open Webs is maintained. In this tutorial, you create a simple macro that enables you to switch among open Webs. This macro does not do all that it might, but it does serve to illustrate some of the basic principles of macro creation within the Web object model.

Step 1: Create the macro routine and user form

The goal is to create a macro that, when run, displays a form containing a list box control that lists the names of the currently open Webs. When the user double-clicks one of the Webs, it is activated.

1. Open the Macro dialog box by selecting Tools ➪ Macro ➪ Macros. Type the name you want to give your macro (in this case **Web Picker**) in the Macro name field. Click the Create button to open Visual Basic Editor (VBE). You will note that FrontPage has automatically created a new subroutine in the main FrontPage module. Alternatively, you can open VBE directly by selecting Tools ➪ Macro ➪ Visual Basic Editor. In this case, you will need to create the subroutine yourself by typing Public Sub WebPicker() and hitting Enter. VBE automatically adds the End Sub line for you.

2. Next you need to create the user form. With VBE open, select Insert ➪ UserForm to create a new default UserForm object. In the Properties sheet for this form, change the name to frmWebPicker, enter **Web Picker** for the caption, and adjust the size as shown in Figure 22-12. You should make your form wide enough to accommodate full Web title (refer to Figure 22-13 below for an example).

3. Add a list box and command button control. Open the toolbox control by selecting View ➪ Toolbox or by clicking the toolbox icon in the toolbar. Add a label element, name it lblWebPicker, and enter **Available Webs:** as the caption. Select a list box control and add it to the user form element. Name the list box lstWebList. Add a command button control, name it cbCancel, and set its caption to **Cancel** (compare with Figure 22-12).

4. Script the button. The Cancel button has a simple role: when clicked, it hides the form element. To add the event script, double-click the Command button and enter the following code in its Click function:

```
Private Sub cbCancel_Click()
    frmWebPicker.Hide
  lstWebList.Clear
End Sub
```

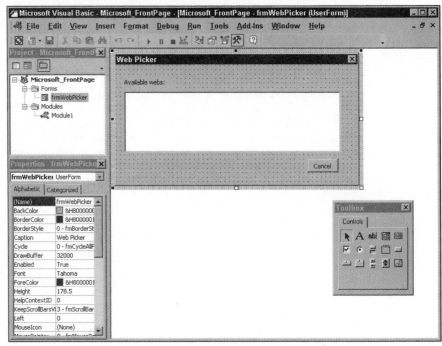

Figure 22-12: Creating the Web Picker user form

5. Script the double-click event for the list box. The list box contains a list of the names of Webs currently open in the FrontPage application (that code is examined momentarily). When the user double-clicks an item in the list box, it should open the Web that has the corresponding name. To add a double-click event, select the list box name (for example, lstWebList) from the object list on the left side of the code window. Then, select Double-Click from the event list on the right. VB automatically creates the correct function syntax. You simply need to supply the code. Use the following:

```
Private Sub lstWebList_DblClick(ByVal Cancel As _
MSForms.ReturnBoolean)
    ' WebPicker will only activate
    ' a web after it is closed.
    Dim pickerIndex As Integer
    pickerIndex = lstWebList.ListIndex
    lstWebList.Clear
    Unload frmWebPicker
    Application.Webs.Item(pickerIndex).Activate
End Sub
```

This function gets the index number of the selected item in the WebPicker list and uses that to select and activate the appropriate Web. Note that the subroutine first closes the WebPicker before activating the selected Web.

This code doesn't add an error-checking routine to handle the case when the user tries to run this macro without any Webs open. For an example of such error handling, see the next tutorial.

You have now completed the form, but how do you get it to show up in FrontPage? That is the task for the next section of the tutorial.

Step 2: Create the macro procedure

For your macro to work properly, you need to create a function in a FrontPage module that instantiates the form and populates it with a list of the names of the open Webs:

1. Get the collection of open Webs — much as you did in the earlier code. Use the Web collection, which is a property of the Application object — the default FrontPage object (which means that you don't need to identify it explicitly; in essence, however, the object Application.Webs is identical to saying Webs).

2. Loop through the Webs collection, extracting the title of each Web and adding it to the list box. Then, instantiate the form. The function, in its entirety, is shown here:

```
Public Sub WebPicker()
    Dim fp_Webs As Webs
    Dim fp_OpenWeb As Web
    Dim fp_WebList As String
    fp_WebList = ''
    Set fp_Webs = Webs

    For Each fp_OpenWeb In fp_Webs
        frmWebPicker.lstWebList.AddItem (fp_OpenWeb.Title)
    Next
    frmWebPicker.Show
End Sub
```

3. Save your work in VBE. FrontPage automatically adds a new WebPicker item to the list of available macros in the Macros dialog box. To test your new macro, first open three or four Webs and run the macro by selecting Tools ⇨ Macro ⇨ Macros and either double-clicking the WebPicker item or by selecting it and clicking the Run button. Figure 22-13 shows the Web Picker form that you created. (For easy access to your macros read the next tutorial for directions on how to add a macro to a custom toolbar.)

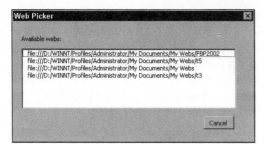

Figure 22-13: The Web Picker macro in action

Tutorial 22-2: Creating a Keyword meta tag macro

This tutorial demonstrates one basic method of handling the editing of HTML within a Web page using a macro. This macro supports the simple entry and editing of `<meta>` tag keywords, which are commonly used by search engines to index pages. The tutorial also explains how to add this macro to a custom toolbar, for easy access.

1. Open FrontPage and access VBE by selecting Tools ➪ Macro ➪ Visual Basic Editor. In the Editor, select Insert ➪ Procedure, enter **EditKeywords** as the Name, choose Sub for Type, and choose Public for Scope. Click OK to create the basic subroutine block:

```
Public Sub EditKeywords()
End Sub
```

2. To work with the HTML of a FrontPage Web page, you use the FrontPage Document Object Model (DOM). The first step is to isolate the `<head>` object in the open page. To do this, use the collection of `all` elements in the `ActiveDocument`:

```
For Each oHTMLTag In ActiveDocument.all
    If StrComp(UCase(oHTMLTag.tagName), "HEAD") = 0 Then
        Set oHeadTag = oHTMLTag
'remove message box after testing
        MsgBox ("Current Header: " & oHeadTag.innerHTML)
Exit For
    End If
Next
```

The `For` loop checks each tag element in the active document until it finds one that has a tag name that matches `head`. Note that the function first changes the tag names to uppercase, so it will match lowercase tag names as well. It then saves that element and exits the loop, after displaying the contents of the header tag to demonstrate that you found the right one.

Tip

For details on the FrontPage DOM, open VBE and select View ➪ Object Browser. This is a good reference source for all the supported object classes and their methods and properties.

3. Add an input box to collect the keywords to add to the `<meta>` tag:

```
sKeywords = InputBox("Enter a comma-separated list of_
keywords:",
"Add Keywords")
sKeyWordTag = "<meta name=""keywords"" content="""_
& sKeywords & """>"
```

The first line presents the user with an input dialog box and stores the input in the string variable sKeywords. Note that this code assumes that the user correctly inputs the keywords. The second line takes the input and creates the `<meta>` tag that you plan to insert. This input box in action is shown in Figure 22-14.

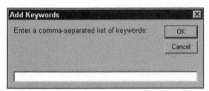

Figure 22-14: A standard Visual Basic input box for collecting keywords

4. Collecting keywords is fine, but you really want to add them to a keyword `<meta>` tag and then add the tag to the page. The goal is to add this tag at the end of any existing `<meta>` tags, which typically are placed before the `<title>` tag. If no `<meta>` tags are in the current document, then you place this tag at the beginning of the `<head>` element.

You really don't need precise placement of the keyword `<meta>` tag, as long as it is somewhere in the `<head>` tag. The motive for placement is simply to try to create cleaner HTML.

This step has two keys:

- **Use of the children collection of the** `<head>` **tag:** The `<head>` tag also has an all collection, but using the children collection is better, because it returns only the tags that are direct children of the named tag. The all collection returns every tag, even if the tag is two or three levels deep in the tag structure.

- **Use of the** innerHTML **property of the** `<head>` **tag object:** In the FrontPage DOM, tags have two HTML string properties: innerHTML and outerHTML. InnerHTML refers to the text between the beginning and ending tags. OuterHTML refers to InnerHTML plus the tags themselves.

The following code loops through the children of the `<head>` tag, each time adding back the HTML of the current tag to the new head element. When the loop finds a `<meta>` tag, it sets a True/False flag to True. When the next tag that isn't a `<meta>` tag is encountered, it adds in the keyword tag and then finishes out the loop. If the loop never encounters a ⟨meta⟩ tag, it places the keyword tag at the beginning of the ⟨head⟩ tag. If the loop never encounters anything after the ⟨meta⟩ tag, it places the new tag at the end of the ⟨head⟩ tag.

```
For Each oChildTag In oHeadTag.Children
    If StrComp(UCase(oChildTag.tagName), "META") = 0 Then
        hasMeta = True
        newInnerHTML = newInnerHTML & oChildTag.outerHTML
    Else
        If hasMeta = True Then
            'we have come to the end of the meta tags
            oHeadTag.innerHTML = newInnerHTML _
& newMetaTag
            hasMetaNew = True
        End If
    End If
Next
If hasMetaNew = False Then
    oHeadTag.innerHTML = newMetaTag & newInnerHTML
Else
    If hasMeta = False Then
        oHeadTag.innerHTML = newInnerHTML & newMetaTag
    End If
End If
```

For some reason, the DOM wants to add an extra CRLF to each tag as it is added back to the head element. The following code can be added to correct the problem, if you encounter it:

```
oHeadTag.innerHTML = Replace(newInnerHTML, Chr(10) _
& Chr(13), Chr(10))
```

Note that you should use the Replace function for all three of the statements that set the oHeadTag.innerHTML at the end of this subroutine.

5. This macro adds keywords nicely to any Web page that does not already have them. Unfortunately, it doesn't yet recognize pages that already have keywords. Until you fix this, the macro adds new keyword tags to the header of the page each time that the script is rerun.

The fix requires two additions to your code. First, you need to check before you show the user the Keyword input box. If a keyword tag already exists, you want to load in the existing keywords and allow the user to edit them. Then, you want to replace the existing keyword tag with your new one. If no keyword tag exists, then you let the user add a new one. The following code performs this check:

```
For Each oChildTag In oHeadTag.Children
    If StrComp(UCase(oChildTag.tagName), "META") = 0 Then
        If
StrComp(UCase(oChildTag.getAttribute("name")),_
 "KEYWORDS") = 0 Then
```

```
                    sKeyword = oChildTag.getAttribute("content")
                    sKeyword = InputBox("Enter comma-separated _
list of keywords:", "Edit Keywords", sKeyword)
                    oChildTag.setAttribute "content", sKeyword
                    isDirty = True
                End If
            End If
        Next
```

The key here is the use of another property of the `Tag` element object: `getAttribute` and `setAttribute`. These enable you to identify keyword `<meta>` tags and then put their current content in the input box for editing.

Notice that another flag, `IsDirty`, also is set, indicating that the page has already been edited. You need to add a check for this before you start adding the code that adds a new keyword tag. To do this, you add the following code around the block of code discussed in Step 4:

```
If Not IsDirty Then
....code...
End If
```

Now you have a functional macro. You can use it to add keywords quickly to your Web pages. (Now, if only you had a feature to add the keywords to every page . . .)

6. This keyword macro isn't meant to provide comprehensive error checking, but one error that is important to check for is that you actually have an active document to work with. Presently, if you try to run this macro with no open document, FrontPage returns an Operation Failed message. This isn't particularly informative to the user, and if you try to run the macro from within VBE, it does not even run.

   A better solution is to trap for errors yourself, and then return a more informative message to the user. To do this, first add an `On Error Resume Next` statement near the beginning of the subroutine. This ensures that the program will carry on, even after an error is encountered. Trapping any errors and reporting them back is your responsibility.

   For now, you'll do this when you first begin to work with the `ActiveDocument` element. If no active document exists, you need to stop the macro and alert the user. Here is the code that traps an error:

```
If Err.Number > 0 Then
        MsgBox ("You must open a Web page document before
using this macro.")
        End
    End If
```

   Place this code right after the beginning of the `For` loop that identifies the all collection of the `ActiveDocument` element. This line fails if no `ActiveDocument` element is present. Now, try it by closing all documents.

7. Now that you have this timesaving macro, you can use the following steps to access it with a single click of a button, rather than selecting Tools ➪ Macro ➪ Macros, choosing the correct Macro, and then clicking the Run button:

- Select Tools ➪ Customize and click the Commands tab. Scroll through the Categories list and select Macros. Drag the Custom Button icon from the Commands list to the location on the toolbar where you want the custom button to appear. (Alternatively, drag the Custom Menu Item from the Commands list and drop it on a menu.)

- Right-click the custom button to bring up its Options menu. Change the name of the button to **&Keywords**, select a new button icon (the key works nicely, I think), select Assign Macro from the options, and choose the EditKeywords macro. Click OK to close the Customize dialog box. Now, you can access your favorite macros with a single click.

If you are new to programming, writing some simple macros is a great way to get started. If you are looking for an even greater development challenge, you can try your hand at writing your own custom Web components and Wizards, as described in the next section.

Web Components and Wizards

In the next several sections, we introduce and briefly explore some of the more heavy-duty forms of customization that are possible in FrontPage. This section discusses the creation of custom Web components and wizards and walks you through the creation of a simple FrontPage wizard. The next section discusses Design-Time Controls (DTC) and Add-ins, with an example of a simple DTC.

Creating custom Web components

The FrontPage Web components, formerly known as Web bots, have been a staple of the FrontPage tool since its early days. You can build your own Web components to add to FrontPage, if you want. If you are interested in trying your hand at designing a custom Web component, check out the FrontPage SDK where you will find programming details and several examples.

Note   As of the writing of this book, Microsoft had not yet updated the SDK for FrontPage 2002. In addition, a few of the examples in the SDK were lifted from the FrontPage 98 SDK and never updated.

Creating custom wizards

In the Windows world, a wizard refers to an application that helps you perform a particular task by walking you through a series of simple steps. FrontPage comes with numerous wizards that can simplify the task of creating a new Web page or a new Web.

You can also create your own wizards. This is particularly useful if you find yourself repeatedly creating the same type of page, or set of pages, with some minor modifications. Of course, you can also create your own wizard just to prove that you are a wizard yourself.

FrontPage supports two kinds of wizards:

✦ **Page wizards:** Create a single Web page. These wizards are accessed when you select File ➪ New ➪ Page. An example is the Form Page Wizard.

✦ **Web wizards:** Create a multipage Web. These wizards are accessed when you select File ➪ New ➪ Web. Examples include the Corporate Presence Wizard and the Discussion Web Wizard.

Creating your own wizards involves real programming, and it is not for everyone. However, the FrontPage SDK includes some examples and code libraries that you can use to get you started. This section illustrates the process of creating a wizard by extending one of the examples found in the SDK.

To create your own wizard, you need to have Visual Basic 5 or greater (the current version at the time of this writing is 6 and on its way to being replaced by the .NET framework tools). Unfortunately, you can't use the Visual Basic Editor that comes with FrontPage. The FrontPage Web wizards are standalone executables, which VBE is not capable of generating.

The FrontPage SDK

The FrontPage SDK includes the following sample wizards, including both compiled versions and source code for Visual Basic:

✦ **Hello Wizard:** A simple page wizard

✦ **Calendar Wizard:** A more sophisticated page wizard that produces a calendar page

✦ **Hello Web Wizard:** A simple Web wizard

✦ **Real Estate Wizard:** A more advanced Web wizard that produces a real estate Web

In addition to these samples, the SDK provides three Visual Basic modules. All three of these modules contain legacy code. Although this code is still supported in FrontPage 2002, some of the language used in these examples has been superceded by the object model, discussed earlier in this chapter.

✦ `Botgen.bas`: Procedures related to creating FrontPage Components

✦ `HTMLgen.bas`: Procedures for creating HTML text

✦ `Wizutil.bas`: Procedures for initializing FrontPage Webs and Web pages

The SDK also includes a Word document, FPDevkit.doc, which provides detailed instructions on creating wizards..

Note These items have not been updated in the current FrontPage SDK.

Using the Hello Wizard

Using the example wizard source files and utility files provided in the SDK greatly simplifies the task of creating a FrontPage wizard. To illustrate how easy it is to create a customized wizard, you will make some minor modifications to the Hello Wizard, a simple wizard written in Visual Basic that is part of the SDK, to create a Contact Page Wizard.

Caution This example assumes that you have a basic familiarity with Visual Basic. If you are looking for a good beginner's book on Visual Basic programming, take a look at John Smiley's *Learn to Program with Visual Basic 6*. For a more thorough reference check out the *Visual Basic 6 Bible* by Eric A. Smith.

Start Visual Basic and open the Hello Wizard project file, hello.vbp. The project file consists of a form, hello.frm, and a programming module, wizutil.bas. Open the form, as shown in Figure 22-15. In general, wizard forms consist of a single form object and multiple frame objects that comprise the wizard panels. The Hello Wizard contains three frames. You can see them all if you increase the size of the form and then move the frames so that they are not on top of one another.

The first screen simply introduces the Hello Wizard. The second screen takes useful (or potentially useful) information from the user and turns it into Web page content. The third screen identifies the name and location of the page to be created.

Editing the wizard form

To explore the Hello Wizard, you will make a few simple changes to the wizard form. To that end, you will add a panel to the wizard to collect contact information to put into your Web page. This panel enables users to enter their name, telephone number, and e-mail address, with an option to hyperlink their e-mail address automatically.

Step 1: Add a new Frame control and input controls

With the sample wizard project open in Visual Basic, add a new Frame control similar to the existing ones and then add some input controls to collect contact information. For our example, we will add name, phone, and e-mail labels; setting their names to lblName, lblPhone, and lblEmail, respectively. Next, add textbox controls for each, as well; and name them txtName, txtPhone, and txtEmail. Add an inner frame control to the main frame control and enter **E-mail Hyperlink** as its caption. Add two option buttons to this inner control with **Yes** and **No** captions. Set the default value of the Yes button to True and the No button to False.

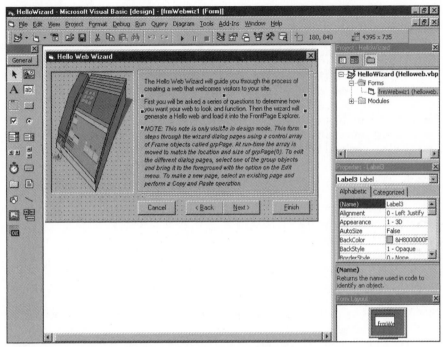

Figure 22-15: Editing the Hello Wizard in Visual Basic

Step 2: Adjust the existing Wizard code

You need to change the name of the new frame control so that it appears in the right order in the wizard (after the greeting frame and before the URL frame). To do this, you need to adjust the indexes on the grpPage array that constitutes the collection of frame elements. Select the last frame, originally grpPage(2) and change its Index property to 3. Rename the new frame that you just created to grpPage and set its Index property to 2.

You now need to make a few minor code adjustments to accommodate your new panel. Double-click the form to open its code page. Select the Form object and go to the Form_Load subroutine. This procedure is called when the form is loaded. It contains a variable, maxpage, that is set to 2. Change it so that maxpage is set to 3.

While you are in the Form_Load subroutine, you need to comment out a conditional statement that does not work properly in FrontPage 2002. The section to remove contains the following code:

```
If Len(WizardPageURL) > 0 Then
    ' do not include the page/url dialog
    maxpage = 1
    txtURL = WizardPageURL
End If
```

You can delete these lines completely or comment them out by placing a single quotation mark (') in front of each.

Step 3: Update the HTML output

The last step is to revise the output generated when the user clicks the Finish button at the end of the wizard. When this happens, the wizard calls a subroutine, `GeneratePage`, whose job it is to create the new HTML page. Select `General` from the object list in the form code page and select `GeneratePage` from the procedure list. This routine creates the file through several `Print` statements to a newly created file. You can edit this page in any way that you like. At a minimum, you need to add some `Print` statements that use the new inputs that you have added to the wizard.

The following code creates a contact page and adds the user's input from the controls you created in Step 1:

```
Print #fn, "<B>Name:</B> " & txtName.Text & "<P>"
Print #fn, "<B>Phone:</B> " & txtPhone.Text & "<P>"
If optEmail(0) Then
    Print #fn, "<A HREF=""mailto:" & txtEmail.Text & """>"
End If
Print #fn, "<B>Email:</B> " & txtEmail.Text & "<P>"
If optEmail(0) Then
    Print #fn, "</A>"
End If
```

After you make these changes, save and recompile the wizard code as `contact.exe` and place it in a folder named `contact.wiz`. Place this folder in the Pages subfolder within the FrontPage main folder.

Note　You may notice that the method the Hello Wizard uses to generate HTML is not the most efficient. To see an example of a more efficient method, look at the more sophisticated SDK samples, the Calendar Page Wizard and the Real Estate Web Wizard.

To test your wizard, open FrontPage and select File ➪ New ➪ Page. You should see a new wizard, Contact Wizard, listed, as shown in Figure 22-16.

Double-click it to start the wizard and complete the information as illustrated in Figure 22-17.

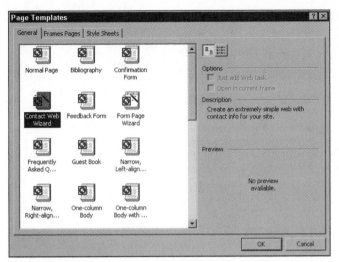

Figure 22-16: Our new Contact Wizard listed among the other new page templates

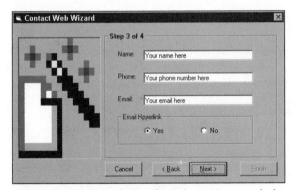

Figure 22-17: Completing the information needed to generate the Contact Wizard Web pages

And voila! You get an instant Web page like the one in Figure 22-18. (Perhaps it could use a bit more work?)

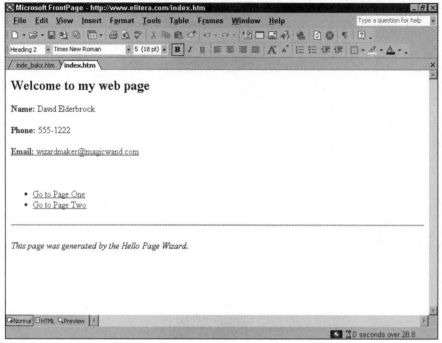

Figure 22-18: The results of your Contact Wizard

Design-Time Controls and Add-Ins

A design-time control (DTC) is an ActiveX control inserted into FrontPage that enables simplified development of some aspect of a Web page. In essence, DTCs work much like the FrontPage components. The main difference is that the FrontPage components are designed exclusively for use by FrontPage, whereas DTCs are intended more as general-purpose tools and are built by using the same ActiveX standards that apply to run-time ActiveX controls.

Basically, a DTC presents the Web page designer with a list of properties that he or she can configure for the control. The control itself produces HTML text that is added to the page at run time, for example, when the page is viewed by a browser. Viewers never see the control, only the text that it generated (or, more precisely, they see the HTML page generated by the text that was generated by the DTC).

If the DTC option is disabled, you probably don't have any controls registered yet. (It can also mean that you don't have a server-based Web open.)

Using Design-Time Controls

To add an existing DTC to your Web page, follow these steps (see the next section, "Creating Design-Time Controls," to find out how to make and register your own DTCs):

1. Open the Web page into which you want to insert the control, and locate the cursor at the desired location.

2. Select Insert ➪ Web Components ➪ Advanced and select Design-Time Control from the list of available components. This opens the Insert Design-Time Control dialog box.

3. If the control that you want to use is listed in this dialog box, select it and click OK to add it to the page.

4. If the control is not listed, click the Customize button to see a list of all registered controls. Check the item that you want to add to the Insert list and click OK to return to the Insert Design-Time Control dialog box. Select the DTC and click OK to add it to the page. Note that you can remove items from the list by unchecking a checked item in the Customize dialog box.

Creating Design-Time Controls

DTCs can't be created in VBE, the macro development tool discussed in the previous examples, because VBE is not capable of creating executable code. You can create DTCs in any programming language capable of creating COM objects (aka ActiveX controls). To follow the next tutorial, you need two things: the DTC SDK, available for download from Microsoft's Web site, and Visual Basic.

To create a DTC, you can use the version 6 SDK that accompanies Visual Studio 6. The SDK is also available (as of this writing) from Microsoft's Web site in the Microsoft Interdev download area (`http://msdn.microsoft.com/vinterdev/downloads/samples.asp`).

Tutorial 22-3: Creating an ASP DTC

In this tutorial, you are going to generate a control that is a simple illustration of the method used to create a DTC. The goal is to create an easy way to insert simple ASP code into your Web page without invoking Microsoft Script Editor.

1. Download and install the SDK, if you don't already have it. The SDK includes the Type Library `webdc.tlb`, samples and documentation, and a utility, `Regsvrdc.exe`, for registering your control as a DTC. The SDK is available from Microsoft's Web site as described above.

2. Create a new DTC project. Start Visual Basic and create an ActiveX control project by selecting File ➪ New Project and selecting the Active X control in the New tab. Select Project ➪ Project1 Properties from the menu bar and rename the project `SimpleASP`.

VB has automatically created a `UserControl` object for you. This control has no real functionality in a DTC. It is, however, displayed in the Normal view of FrontPage when you insert the DTC into a Web page. It is not displayed when the page is viewed in a browser.

Select the UserControl object and change its Name property to `ASPDTC`. Add a Label control and change its caption to `ASPDTC`. You can change other properties if you like to make the control more aesthetically pleasing (or not, it's up to you). For example, see Figure 22-19.

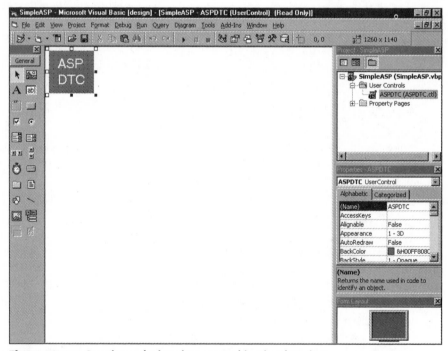

Figure 22-19: Creating a design-time control in Visual Basic 6

3. Add a reference to the DTC Type Library. This step converts your ActiveX control from a standard control to a DTC. To do this, select Project ➪ References from the menu bar. If you have not yet added the DTC Type

Library to VB's list, select Browse and locate the `webdc.tlb` file. The SDK installation puts it in `\Samples\VB\Common` folder in the installation directory that you selected. Select Open to add a reference to the Microsoft Web Design-Time Control Type Library in the list. Click this item to select it, and click OK to return to your control.

Note that after this Type Library is loaded, it remains in the list, but you still have to select it each time that you create a new DTC.

4. Next, you create a Properties dialog box that is accessed by double-clicking the DTC UserControl. To create this interface, you use the ActiveX Control Interface Wizard. Select Add-Ins from the menu. If VB ActiveX Control Interface Wizard is listed as one of the loaded add-ins, select it. If it is not, select Add-Ins Manager and select the Wizard from the list. Click OK to return and then select the add-in.

The first screen of the Wizard is informational only, so click Next to begin using the wizard. In the Select Interface Members screen, remove all members from the Selected Names list by clicking the Remove All button (indicated by double left-pointing arrows, <<). Click Next.

In the Create Custom Interface Members screen, click New. Enter **AspCode** in the Name textbox and select Property (the default) from the Type options. Click OK to return to the wizard. Continue to the next screen.

In the Set Mapping screen, select UserControl in the Control list in the Maps To section. Click Next. In the Set Attributes screen, select String as the Data Type and add

```
= ""Put ASP code here!""
```

as the default value (note the double set of quotation marks to avoid syntax problems later on). Click Finish to complete the wizard. Click Close to close the summary information provided by the wizard.

5. Select Project ➪ Add Property Page and double-click the VB Property Page Wizard. Click Add and enter `ppgAspCode` as the name of the Property Page. Click OK and then click Next. Select the custom property, `AspCode`, from the list of available properties to place on this page, and then click the single right arrow (>) to add it to the Property Page. Click Finish to complete the wizard.

You can edit the layout of the Property Page (see Figure 22-20) by clicking the `ppgAspCode` form. You may want to enlarge the textbox area for inputting ASP code, and edit the label caption and the Property Page caption (which becomes the tab label).

6. Select Tools ➪ Procedure Attributes. Select the `AspCode` property from the Name list and click the Advanced button. Choose `ppgAspCode` from the Use This Page in Property Browser list. Click OK to close the dialog box.

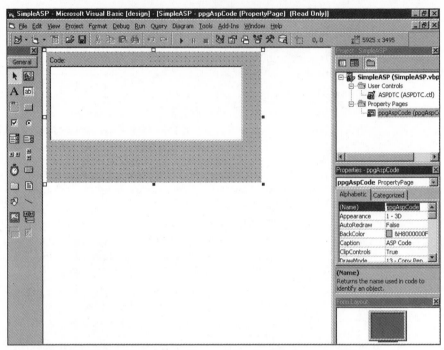

Figure 22-20: Editing the Property Page of the design-time control

7. Code the Text procedure. Open the code window for the UserControl. Add the following line to the general declarations section at the top of the code:

```
Implements IProvideRuntimeText
```

Select the `IProvideRuntimeText` item from the object list and add the following to the `IProvideRuntimeText_GetRuntimeText()` function:

```
Private Function IProvideRuntimeText_GetRuntimeText() As
String
Dim sDTCStr As String
Dim sCRLF As String
sCRLF = Chr$(13)
sDTCStr = "<% " & m_AspCode & " %>" & sCRLF
IProvideRuntimeText_GetRuntimeText = sDTCStr
End Function
```

8. Register the control and the DTC. To do this, save the project. Select File ➪ Make SimpleASP.ocx to compile the control. Open a DOS window and change to the directory in which you saved the OCX files. Register the control by issuing the following command at the DOS prompt:

```
Regsvr32 SimpleASP.ocx
```

`Regsvr32` should return a message box indicating "DLLRegisterService in SimpleASP.ocx succeeded."

At this point, you can adjust the default name of the control using the Registry.

This command registers the control as an ActiveX control. In addition, you need to register your control as a DTC. To do this, you need to use the tool provided in the version 6 SDK. To use this DOS command, change directories to the folder in which this executable is stored and issue the following command at the DOS prompt:

`regsvrdc SimpleASP.ASPDTC`

This command should respond with a DOS response: "Successfully registered SimpleASP.ASPDTC." (See Figure 22-21.)

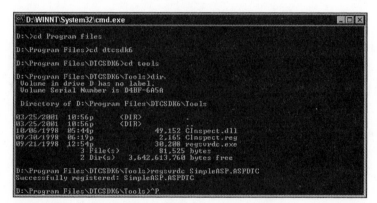

Figure 22-21: Registering a DTC is a two-step process. This DOS window shows the results of registering the control as a DTC.

9. Test the control.

Open FrontPage, and open a new Web page. Select Insert ➪ Web ComponentsSelect Advanced Controls from the Component type list; then select Design Time Control. In the Design-Time Control dialog box, select Customize. SimpleASP.ASPDTC should appear in the list of registered DTCs (see Figure 22-22). Select it to check the box next to it, and click OK to add it to the list of loaded controls.

Select your new DTC in the Design-Time Control dialog box and click OK to insert the control into your Web page. This inserts the UserControl interface as you designed it. Double-click the user control to open the Property page (Figure 22-23) with the default text. You can leave it as is or insert some other valid ASP code.

Figure 22-22: Adding your new DTC to FrontPage

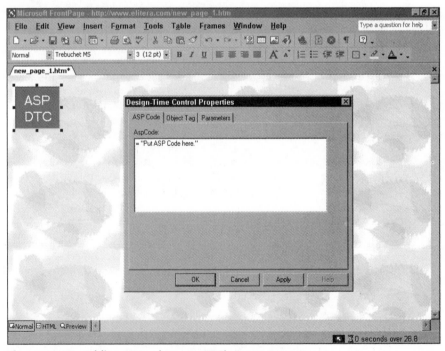

Figure 22-23: Adding ASP using your DTC's Property page

10. Save the page to a folder that has permissions set to run ASP code (see Chapter 18 for details on how to set up a folder to run ASP). Test the page by previewing it in a browser.

Using Add-ins

Add-ins, a new feature that first appeared in FrontPage 2000, are programs, typically supplied by third-party developers, that extend the capabilities of FrontPage. You can also write your own custom add-ins, using Visual Basic or Visual C++. Creation of add-ins is beyond the scope of this book, but if you are curious, Visual Basic includes both an Add-in template and documentation on this topic.

Most users will encounter add-ins only when installing and using a commercially developed add-in. The remainder of this section explains how to add and remove add-ins in FrontPage 2002.

To add a new add-in to FrontPage, select Tools ➪ Add-ins. Click the Add button and locate the Add-in executable. To remove an add-in form the list, select the add-in in the Add-ins dialog box and click the Remove button.

Summary

This chapter has looked at a variety of ways to customize FrontPage. We began by looking at some simple ways to customize the FrontPage work environment using the Customize dialog box. Next you learned out to create custom templates and themes, We also introduced some more sophisticated means of extending FrontPage. You learned to write some simple macros using Visual Basic for Application. We also took a brief look at some serious programming tasks: developing custom Web components, Wizards and Design-Time controls

The last two chapters of the book take us on a tour of the server-side of the FrontPage world. Chapter 23 discusses basic Web server-related topics, focusing on the details of the FrontPage Server Extensions. In the last chapter we introduce the newly released SharePoint Team Services server environment and show how you can use FrontPage in conjunction with this exciting new technology.

✦　　✦　　✦

Web Server Administration

This chapter explains how FrontPage interacts with Web servers. The focus of attention is on FrontPage Server Extensions (FPSE) — what they do, how they do it, and how you install and configure them using Microsoft Personal Web Server (PWS) and Internet Information Server (IIS). The chapter also describes the FrontPage security model and how it integrates with Windows NT security.

This chapter, and the next which covers the new SharePoint technologies, are intended for those who have the job of setting up and maintaining Web servers to work with FrontPage. This chapter will be of interest as well to anyone who wants to set up a local Web server with FrontPage Server Extensions or who is trying to figure out which hosting service to use. See Chapter 3 for detailed information on how to publish Webs and Web pages to a Web server with FrontPage.

Overview of the Microsoft Web Server Scene

As if it is not confusing enough trying to keep track of which browsers support which Web authoring features in FrontPage, you are now faced with the task of determining which features work with which versions of Microsoft (or non-Microsoft) Web servers. Here, at a high level, are some of the major considerations:

✦ You can use FrontPage to publish content to non-Microsoft Web servers, but you will be limited to using FrontPage as a plain-vanilla Web page authoring tool. You will not be able to use any of its built-in components.

✦ All Microsoft Web servers, including Internet Information Server 4.0 and 5.0 as well as Personal Web Server (PWS), come with FrontPage Server Extensions installed. However, you need to check which version of the extensions are installed in order to determine which of the features in FrontPage 2002 will be enabled. FrontPage 2002 is backwards-compatible with previous versions of the FPSE, but of course, the older server extensions do not support the newest features. In addition, FPSE are available for non-Microsoft servers.

✦ The new SharePoint Team Services (STS) Web site has its own server extensions, which are really FPSE plus additional functionality (see Chapter 24 for the scoop on STS). These extensions run only on Windows 2000, either the Professional or Server editions.

The remainder of this chapter discusses the server-related issues focused on the FrontPage Server Extensions. In the next chapter, we discuss the SharePoint server and its features.

FrontPage Server Extensions

For FrontPage to manage Webs, permit Web page authoring, and provide the enhanced Web page component functionality, it needs some means of communicating with a Web server. If you have read Chapter 3 on publishing FrontPage Webs, you realize that FrontPage is capable of sending Web pages to any server that is using standard FTP protocols. In this scenario, however, FrontPage functionality is limited to standard Web page authoring. To take advantage of the enhanced FrontPage features, you need to install and configure FrontPage Server Extensions on your Web server.

The following section provides a quick tour of FPSE. The information presented here is largely excerpted from Microsoft's FrontPage Server Extension Resource Kit (SERK). If you are planning to install and use FPSE, you should obtain the current copy of the SERK and read it carefully. The current version of the SERK is available from Microsoft's Web site at `http://officeupdate.microsoft.com/frontpage/wpp/serk/`.

Exploring server extensions

FPSE is a set of lightweight executable programs that are added to the Web server to enable the FrontPage application to communicate with the Web server. FrontPage Server Extensions come in two basic varieties: the versions designed for Windows platforms are written as Dynamic Link Libraries (DLLs); the UNIX versions are written as standard C program-executable CGI applications. When you install FPSE on your Web server, the installation creates a Root FrontPage Web on each virtual server managed by the Web server, and then installs these executables (as well as administrative information) in that Web. Each subsequent Web (or subweb) that you create in turn creates a separate stub copy of these applications in the new Web.

The installation process creates several administrative folders in each Web, all having names that begin with _vti. The most significant folders and their content are identified as follows:

Note As of the FrontPage 2000 Server Extensions, the stubbed executables are no longer copied into each Web, but rather exist only at the root Web level.

✦ **_vti_bin:** Contains the main FPSE executables that perform key FrontPage functions.

✦ **Web Page Authoring (**author.dll/author.exe**):** Keeps track of the location, hyperlinks, and other aspects of Web pages.

✦ **Web Administration (**admin.dll/admin.exe**):** Handles user permissions and passwords.

✦ **FrontPage Components (**shtml.dll/shtml.exe**):** Provides run-time functionality to the Web page, substituting the component tags with valid HTML. In IIS, these executables are written as ISAPI DLLs and are stored, by default, in \Common Files\Microsoft Shared\Web Server Extensions\40\isapi (or \50 for IIS 5.0)

✦ **_vti_cnf:** Contains configuration files, one per Web page, containing information that FrontPage uses for file management and other tasks. These files have identical names to the Web pages that they describe.

✦ **_vti_pvt:** Contains miscellaneous files that FrontPage uses to manage Web and file operations.

Note Are you curious about why all of these folders start with _vti? Before Microsoft acquired FrontPage, it was a product developed by Vermeer Technologies, Inc. The company has long since been absorbed into the Microsoft juggernaut, but VTI has left its stamp on the FPSE naming conventions.

Communicating with the server

The FrontPage client communicates with a server via standard HTTP POST requests sent to the extension executables. Because all communication takes place via standard HTTP protocols, FrontPage is able to work across a firewall. So, for example, you can develop content inside the company firewall and publish it to a public Web server, or you can work on your company intranet from home (provided the firewall permits HTTP traffic). (See "FrontPage Security," later in the chapter, for more information on this topic.)

Supported platforms and servers

Because FrontPage Server Extensions are standard CGI programs, they work with any Web server that supports the CGI standard (which means virtually all Web servers). When you install a Microsoft Web server, such as PWS or IIS, FPSE is automatically installed. On other platforms and/or servers, you must install FPSE manually. Two flavors of FPSE exist: Those that run on Windows operating systems are DLLs, and the UNIX varieties are standard C executables. Table 23-1 shows the list of supported platforms and servers for UNIX.

Table 23-1
Supported UNIX Servers (from the FP 2000 SERK)

Operating Systems	Web Servers
Digital UNIX 3.2c, 4.0 (Alpha)	Apache 1.2.6, 1.3.3
BSD/OS 3.1, 4.0 (Intel x86)	NCSA 1.5.2 (but not 1.5a or 1.5.1)
Linux 2.0.34 (MIPS) (Alpha)	Netscape Enterprise Server 3.x, 3.5.1
Linux 4.1, 5.0 (Red Hat Software) (Intel x86)	Netscape FastTrack 2.0, 3.0.1
HP/UX 10.2, 11.0 (PA-RISC)	Stronghold
IRIX 6.2, 6.3 (Silicon Graphics)	
Solaris 2.5.1, 2.6 (SPARC)	
Solaris 2.6 (Intel x86)	
AIX 4.x (RS6000, PowerPC)	
SCO OpenServer5.0 (Intel x86)	
SCO UnixWare 7 (Intel x86)	

Table 23-2 shows the list of supported platforms and servers for Windows.

Table 23-2
Supported Windows Servers (from the FP 2000 SERK)

Operating Systems	Web Servers
Windows 2000 Professional/ Server/Advanced Server	Internet Information Services (IIS) 3.0 and later, including IIS 5.0.
Windows NT Server/Workstation	Microsoft Peer Web Services (Windows NT Workstation)
Windows 98/95	Microsoft Personal Web Server 2.0, 4.0 (Windows 95/98)
	FrontPage Personal Web Server
	Netscape Enterprise 3.x, 3.5.1
	Netscape FastTrack 2.0, 3.0.1
	O'Reilly WebSite Pro 2.0

Supported features

Many of FrontPage's Web management and Web page authoring features require the presence of FPSE to function. These features are unavailable to FrontPage users who don't have access to a Web server with FPSE installed. The following are the principal FrontPage Web features that require the server extensions:

✦ **Hyperlink mapping:** Provides graphical mapping of all hyperlinks on a given Web page.

✦ **Full text indexing:** Enables the search engine functionality.

✦ **Persistent structure:** The structure of Webs is related to, but distinct from, the Web server file system structure.

✦ **Web themes:** Associates a set of graphical images, buttons, backgrounds, banners, and so on, with a Web.

✦ **Task list:** Maintains the tasks to be performed for a Web.

✦ **Security settings:** Enable separate Webs to be configured for use by different users or groups.

✦ **FrontPage components:** Includes, but is not limited to, the Search Form handler, the e-mail handler, the Discussion Form handler, and the Database Form handler.

Installing FrontPage Server Extensions

Several ways exist to install FPSE. When you install FrontPage, you can install or upgrade your Web server's server extensions automatically. You can also install FPSE if you subsequently install either PWS or IIS. In this case, too, FPSE is added automatically during installation of the server. The last alternative is to download the latest version of FPSE from Microsoft's Web site.

Note   As of this book's writing, you can obtain the FPSE 2002 from: `http://msdn.microsoft.com/workshop/languages/fp/2002/fpse02win.asp`.

Using older versions of the extensions

FrontPage 2002 can be used with a Web server that has an older version of FPSE. The most likely scenario is one in which you don't control the server that you use to host your Web site. In this case, FrontPage works compatibly with the older version of FPSE, but you can't use the newer features of FrontPage 2002 that depend on the FrontPage 2002 Server Extensions. Likewise, you can use an older version of FrontPage with a Web server that has the latest server extensions, although you will only have the functionality available to you that exists in that version of FrontPage.

Converting disk-based Webs

In most cases, you install FrontPage and FPSE after you install your Web server. However, you may have previously used FrontPage without a server, by creating disk-based Webs. If you do bring up a server, you can convert your disk-based Webs to server-based Webs. The basic procedure is as follows:

1. Open the disk-based Web that you want to convert.

2. Select File ➪ Publish Web.

3. In the Publish Destination dialog box, enter the URL of your new server as the destination or use the Browse button to locate the server.

4. Use the Publish Web dialog box to publish all or part of the disk-based Web to your server. For details on publishing Webs, see Chapter 3.

Administering FrontPage Server Extensions

After you install FPSE and have FrontPage configured and running, FPSE requires very little maintenance. In fact, FPSE includes utilities for installing, updating, removing, and checking the server extensions in both the root Web and all subwebs.

This section describes several of the most commonly encountered methods of administering FPSE.

The FrontPage MMC snap-in

Previous versions of FrontPage used an administrative utility called `fpsrvwin`. Starting with FrontPage 2000 and continuing with FrontPage 2002, this utility has been replaced by a FrontPage snap-in to the Microsoft Management Console (MMC).

MMC is a *shell* application intended to provide a consistent interface for administration of Windows services. Administration programs are written as *snap-ins* to MMC, meaning that their functionality gets added to the MMC shell. When you start an MMC snap-in, it loads into MMC.

You may interact with the FrontPage snap-in as a standalone utility if you are using FrontPage with a Windows 95/98 Web server or with a non-IIS server on Windows NT. If you are using Microsoft IIS 4, the FrontPage snap-in simply adds its functionality to the existing IIS snap-in, and you access it by starting the IIS snap-in.

Using the FrontPage snap-in

This section describes the basic procedure for accessing the FrontPage snap-in functionality for an IIS server. Some of the operations that you can perform by using the FrontPage snap-in are listed in the next section.

To access the FrontPage snap-in, start Internet Service Manager. MMC starts, as shown in Figure 23-1.

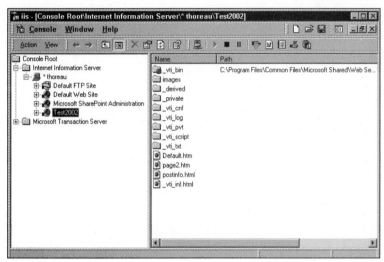

Figure 23-1: The default view of Microsoft Management Console with the IIS snap-in

MMC shows a tree directory of the Webs and folders in the Web server's document directory. To perform a FrontPage-related task, select a Web or folder, select Action ⇨ All Tasks from the toolbar at the top of MMC, and then select the desired task. Alternatively, as shown in Figure 23-2, you can right-click an item in MMC, select All Tasks, and then choose from among the available tasks.

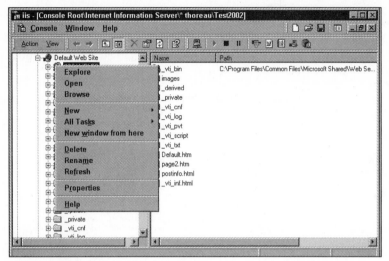

Figure 23-2: Accessing the task list in the IIS MMC

FrontPage snap-in tasks

The tasks you can perform on a particular Web or folder in MMC depend on the item. This section provides a list of the major tasks available from the FrontPage snap-in:

✦ **Configure server extensions:** You can add server extensions to a virtual server or subweb. Select Task ➪ Configure Server Extensions.

✦ **Remove server extensions:** You can remove server extensions from a Web or subweb by selecting Task ➪ Remove Server Extensions.

✦ **Check and fix server extensions:** Occasionally, FrontPage gets out of synch with the files in a Web. Use this function to find and repair the problem. This function can also be used to check on the permission settings on the files in a Web. Select Task ➪ Check Server Extensions.

✦ **Upgrade server extensions:** If a FrontPage upgrade is available, select Task ➪ Upgrade Extensions.

✦ **Create a subweb:** Select New ➪ Server Extensions Web.

✦ **Delete a subweb:** Select Task ➪ Delete Publishing Web to delete both the Web and its content.

✦ **Add an administrator to a Web or subweb:** Select New ➪ Server Extensions Administrator.

✦ **Convert folders and subwebs:** You can convert folders to subwebs and vice versa. Select either Task ➪ Convert Directory to Web or Task ➪ Convert Web to Directory, as relevant.

✦ **Open a Web in FrontPage:** If FrontPage is available on the Web server, you can use this task to launch a Web. Select Task ➪ Open Web in FrontPage.

Setting Web properties

In addition to the FrontPage functions available via the Task menu, you can set a variety of Web properties by using the Properties menu. To access the Properties dialog box for a Web or subweb, select the item and click Action ➪ Properties, or right-click the item and select Properties from the option menu. Select the Server Extensions tab, which will have slightly different options, depending on whether you are working with a Web or subweb (or IIS 4.0 or 5.0). Figure 23-3 shows a sample from a version 4.0 Web.

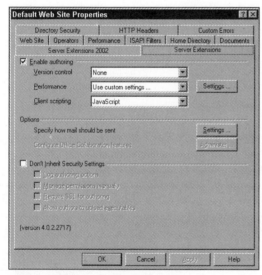

Figure 23-3: The FrontPage Server Extensions tab in the MMC Properties dialog box

Available options include:

✦ **Enable Authoring:** Uncheck this item to disable authoring from a Web.

✦ **Version Control:** Select an available version control utility from the drop-down list.

✦ **Performance:** Choose a performance selection from the drop-down list or click the Settings button to configure manually.

✦ **Client Scripting:** Select a default client scripting language (JavaScript or VBScript).

✦ **Specify how mail should be sent:** Click Settings to enable e-mail on this Web or subweb.

✦ **Configure Office Collaboration features**: This option is enabled only if you have Office Web Server Extensions (superceded by SharePoint Team Services in Office XP) installed.

✦ **Don't Inherit Security Settings:** By default, subwebs inherit security settings from the parent Web. Check "Don't Inherit Security Settings" to configure settings separately for a Web or subweb. Security settings that you can configure include:

- Log authoring actions

- Manage permissions manually

- Require SSL for authoring

- Allow authors to upload executables

Note   Server extension options may vary depending on whether you are on Web or a subweb and on the version of IIS you are running.

Other Administrative Tools

If you are running a server that can't use MMC, you can use three other mechanisms to perform administrative tasks (detailed descriptions are available in the SERK):

✦ Fpsrvadm **utility:** For local, command-line functions; the main application for administering FPSE. It is a command-line program on both UNIX and Windows NT. Use this utility to install, update, remove, and repair server extensions on FrontPage Webs. For specifics on the command-line operations and options available for fpsrvadm, consult the SERK.

✦ Fpremadm **utility:** Enables remote access to Windows servers. Like the fpsrvadm utility, fpremadm is used to install, update, remove, and repair FPSE; and it is intended specifically for remote administration of FPSE in a Windows environment. (If you need to be able to perform remote administration of a non-Windows server, you can use HTML Administration Forms, described next.) For details on the command-line operations and options available for fpremadm, consult the SERK. To use fpremadm, you must first enable HTML Administration Forms, because both use the same CGI (or DLL) applications.

✦ **HTML Administrative Forms:** Enable remote access to Web server administration via a Web browser. For security reasons, these forms are not installed by default. You should read and understand the security implications in the SERK before electing to install and use these forms. For details on installing and using HTML Administration Forms, consult the SERK.

FrontPage Security

The issue of security is one of the main reasons for hesitation by companies considering whether to add FPSE to their Web servers, especially for use in Internet applications. As in most security-related matters, the key question that you need to ask is whether FrontPage is secure enough. The fact that it seamlessly updates files between FrontPage and the Web server is a large bonus. However, the ease with which this can be done is accomplished only by means of some openness in the flow of data.

One advantage of having FrontPage transfer files via HTTP is that FrontPage works with a secure server using Secure Socket Layers (SSL) to encrypt all content. In this case, not only is the content between Web server and users encrypted, but the same is true for content passed between the FrontPage client and the Web server.

Windows NT security

If you are using IIS on Windows NT, FrontPage uses NTFS Access Control Lists (ACLs) as the basis for setting permissions. Users can't be created in FrontPage. You add users to a FrontPage Web by selecting them from a list of valid NT users. When the user initiates an action that requires permission, FrontPage sends the user name and password that the user logged in with.

If you are using Microsoft PWS 4, you can't set permissions for your Webs. All users on the network — whether an intranet or the Internet — can browse your Webs. Authoring and administering Webs must be performed from the computer that is running the Web server. Thus, PWS 4 isn't a good option if you are working on a development site that you don't want to be accessible for general viewing.

Note Earlier versions of PWS are capable of working with user lists if they are connected to a network server that can provide a list of valid users.

UNIX and Non-IIS security

The standard means of maintaining security on a Web server is through the use of ACLs. Typically, these ACLs are maintained separately from the list of user accounts on the system. For most non-IIS servers, FrontPage uses this ACL mechanism to create and authenticate users, authors, and administrators. The steps required to add and remove users, set user permission levels, and change passwords are described in "FrontPage User Administration" below.

Using FrontPage with a proxy server

Many networks use a firewall to protect internal information from the prying eyes of the outside world. A *firewall* is a generic term for any mechanism — whether hardware, software, or both — that restricts the flow of bytes (sometimes referred to as network traffic) across a network. How firewalls do this varies, but one common method is to filter out certain protocols while allowing other protocols through. For example, a firewall might permit outward-bound Web traffic, but prohibit FTP or Telnet. Another example is the case in which the firewall permits outbound traffic only to a specific list of destinations.

In most cases, networks that have a firewall in place also use proxy servers to enable basic network services, such as HTTP, without compromising the security of their network. In this case, all requests go to the proxy server, which determines whether to let the requests through. It then collects any responses and returns those to the requestor.

If you are working with a proxy server, you need to instruct FrontPage to use it. To configure FrontPage to work with a proxy server, select Tools ➪ Options and click the Proxy Settings button in the General tab as shown in Figure 23-4.

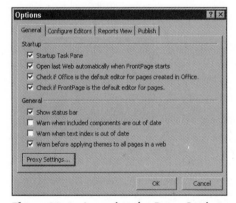

Figure 23-4: Accessing the Proxy Settings button in the Options dialog box

Clicking the Proxy Settings button opens the Internet Explorer Internet Properties dialog box, in which general information about network connections is kept. If you are accessing your Web server via a LAN, click the LAN Settings button. If you access your Web server via a dial-up account (in this scenario, you most likely are outside the firewall and the server is inside), click the Settings button in the Dial-Up Settings section.

In the LAN Settings dialog box, shown in Figure 23-5, check the Use a Proxy Server option and type the complete domain name or IP number of the proxy server. Include the port number (the default for HTTP services is 80).

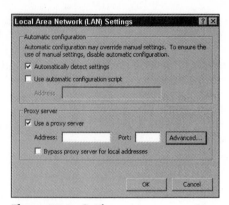

Figure 23-5: Setting a proxy server to use with FrontPage

If you need to configure the proxy server for multiple services, click the Advanced button.

FrontPage User Administration

FrontPage includes tools for configuring user levels in FrontPage Webs at either the root Web level or the level of individual subwebs. In either scenario, you can set three levels of control:

✦ **Browse this Web:** Allows users to view Web pages

✦ **Author and Browse this Web:** Allows users to create, edit, and delete as well as view pages

✦ **Administer, author, and browse this Web:** Allows users to change settings, add new Webs, and perform other administrative tasks, in addition to having full author and browse capabilities

Note   For IIS Web servers running on Windows NT, NT administrators are given FrontPage administrator access by default.

To control permissions, you must either have administrator-level authority or use a site with no active access controls in place. Using FrontPage, you can add new users, add new groups, and modify or delete either users or groups.

Adding users and groups

If you are using PWS 4, your security option is disabled. Likewise, if you do not have a server-based Web open, security is turned off.

In FrontPage, select Tools ➪ Server ➪ Permissions to display the Permissions dialog box. The tabs on this dialog box vary, depending on whether you are in the current Web. The Permission dialog box for a Root Web is shown in Figure 23-6.

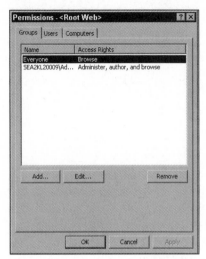

Figure 23-6: Setting permissions for the root Web

The permissions for the root Web has three tabs:

✦ **Groups:** Lists the names and access rights of any existing groups

✦ **Users:** Defines a list of users who have access to the Web server and can make changes on it

✦ **Computers:** Defines who can and cannot use the service, by referring to the IP number, domain name, or the computer used to access the Web

Within each tab, you can add, modify, and delete entries. Users and groups can be granted permission to browse the Web; to browse and author Web pages; or to browse, author, and administer the Web. Access to a Web can be restricted by using either or both users and groups.

To add a user or group, select the appropriate tab, click the Add button, choose a server or domain from the Obtain List From pull-down menu, and then add one or more groups from the Names list to the Add Names list. For each set of groups that you add, you can select the level of access that you want to assign to them. Designate whether all users or only specified users have browse access to the Web. If you don't grant browse access to all users, users will be asked to enter a user name and password when they browse the Web site (see Figure 23-7).

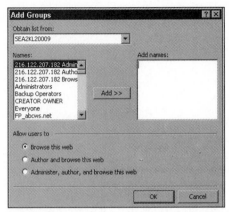

Figure 23-7: Group authentication dialog box in FrontPage

When you are satisfied with your additions, click OK to complete the task.

Editing an existing user or group

After you add a user or group to FrontPage, you can modify their permission level. Open the Permissions dialog box by selecting Tools ⇨ Server ⇨ Permissions and then select the user or group from the appropriate tab. Select Edit and then select a new user level from the dialog box provided. Click OK.

Deleting a user or group

To delete a user or group, open the Permissions tab and select the user or group to be deleted. Click Remove.

Note   Before you click Remove, make sure that you want to remove the group or user, because FrontPage does not prompt you to confirm this option.

Limiting access to specific computers

In addition to being able to specify certain users who have permission to author and administer FrontPage, you can restrict access based on individual computers or on a group of computers. To do this, use the computer's IP number. In the Permissions dialog box, select the Computers tab and click Add. Using the Add Computer dialog box, shown in Figure 23-8, you can specify individual computers by IP, or a range of computers by using wildcard characters.

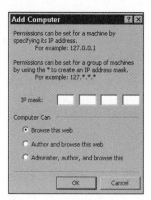

Figure 23-8: Restricting access by computer

Working with subweb permissions

Subwebs have a slightly different interface. When you select Tools ➪ Server ➪ Permissions for a subweb, it displays an initial Settings tab, shown in Figure 23-9. This additional tab enables the current Web to either use the same password system as the parent Web (the default) or keep a list of distinct users on a per-Web basis. If you elect to use the same user names and passwords as the parent Web, you can view but not modify users and groups in the additional tabs.

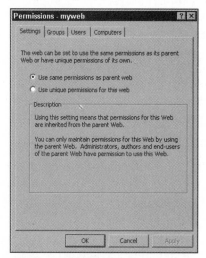

Figure 23-9: For a FrontPage subweb, you can elect to use the same permissions in effect for the root or parent Web, or create an independent set of users and groups.

To enable the buttons for adding, editing, and removing users, you should select the Use Unique Permissions for this Web option.

Changing your password

If you are using IIS on Windows NT, you don't have access to change your password by using FrontPage. Users and passwords can be administered from the standard user account administrative tool only.

If you are using FPSE with UNIX or with a non-IIS (and non-PWS) server, you can change the password that was initially created for you.

To change your password, select Tools ➪ Server ➪ Change Password (see Figure 23-10). In the Change Password dialog box, type the current password in the Old Password box. Type the new password twice — once in the New Password box and again in the Confirm Password box. Click OK. If you accurately typed the same password twice, your new password is effective. Note that if passwords are not in effect on the current Web, the Change Password menu item is unavailable.

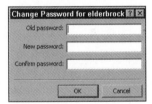

Figure23-10: Changing a password in FrontPage 2002

Summary

This chapter has offered an overview of the configuration and administration of FrontPage Web servers using FrontPage Server Extensions. The chapter has explained how FrontPage works with Web servers, with an emphasis on the two Microsoft servers, Personal Web Server and Internet Information Server. The chapter provides enough information to help you manage your FrontPage Webs at the server. This chapter doesn't claim to provide a complete course on Web server administration.

✦　　✦　　✦

SharePoint Team Services Sites

This chapter introduces the SharePoint Team Services
Web site, which is a new feature of the Office XP suite of
applications. After a brief description of the SharePoint Team
Services Web and its main features, we discuss how to use the
STS, how to customize it using either a Web browser and/or
FrontPage, and how to setup and maintain an STS Web server.

New Feature   SharePoint Team Services is an expanded and repackaged
version of the Office Web Server that shipped with Office
2000. It incorporates new functionality and a new focus on
creating workgroup team collaboration sites quickly and
easily.

Introducing SharePoint Team Services

SharePoint Team Services is a collaborative Web site space
that allows teams to create and share information, conduct
discussions, and manage project activities. It is designed to be
easy to use and easy to administer using a Web browser. Out
of the box, SharePoint Team Services provides a fully functional team Web site, which can be further customized using a
combination of the SharePoint customization features and
FrontPage 2002.

The SharePoint Team Services runs on Windows 2000. It is
similar to the FrontPage Server Extensions in architecture and
includes all of the FPSE features in addition to its own set of
workgroup features. STS also includes a database component,
which can be installed on an existing Microsoft SQL Server
database or using the MSDE database component that comes
with STS.

What can you do with a SharePoint Team Services Web site?

The feature set of STS is designed with three basic categories of users in mind:

✦ **Site users and contributors:** These are team members who will use the site to view and post information, participate in discussions and surveys, and use site personalization features to suit their needs.

✦ **Site designers:** These are team members who have the role of developing and maintaining the structure and overall look and feel of the site. Customizers may create new discussions areas or document libraries, add new surveys, or make changes to the template design of the site.

✦ **Site Administrators:** These are team members who will maintain user's information, create subwebs, and track the health of the site.

The list of major features that SharePoint provides has been divided into these three categories. In the sections that follow, we discuss each of these features in more detail.

User features

SharePoint Team Services sites are envisioned as places where users can collaborate on projects. The emphasis here is on scheduling meetings and tasks, sharing and discussing documents, conducting discussions, and keeping up-to-date with information that has been added to the site. The complete list of user features, includes the capability to:

✦ View and post announcements, events, and tasks

✦ Share documents in document libraries

✦ Discuss documents by inserting or appending comments

✦ Conduct threaded discussions in the discussion boards

✦ Create and maintain various types of lists, including links and contacts

✦ Create surveys

✦ Integrate content with Microsoft Office XP applications

✦ Filter and sort list results

✦ Create custom views of site content

✦ Subscribe to pages to receive notification of updates

Designer features

As you have no doubt realized, much of the content of a SharePoint Team Services site is maintained by the users themselves. In addition, though, the STS site provides a number of capabilities to simply the design and organization of the user content. Using the Web-based site interface, you can

✦ Create new instances of all the major content types

✦ Create your own custom lists

✦ Customize the information columns associated with each type of list

✦ Define workflow rules for document libraries

✦ Create and edit list forms and view styles

✦ Modify site themes and/or styles

Administrator features

Finally, site administration and configuration is performed via a Web-based interface as well. This interface can be used for both local and remote administrative tasks. Using the SharePoint Web interface, site administrators can

✦ Create and manage subwebs

✦ Manage users and user roles

✦ Monitor server health

✦ Implement version control

A Quick Tour of a SharePoint Team Services Site

In this section, we describe all of the major features of the standard, out-of-the-box, SharePoint Team Service site. In the next section, we show you how you can customize and even create your own site components using FrontPage.

To participate in an STS site, you must be added as a member of the site, unless the site permits anonymous browsing (and under any circumstances, you will need to be a user in order to contribute content to the site). You can be added as a user either by a system administrator who creates a user account for you, or by e-mail invitation. If you are invited to join, the e-mail you receive will indicate your user name and a temporary password — which you should change when you first access the site — and links to the site and to the password modification page. (See the section, "Administering a SharePoint Site" later in the chapter for how to add or invite users.)

The home page

The default STS home page provides highlighted content and links to additional content in several areas of the site (see Figure 24-1). This includes:

✦ **Announcements:** A time-sensitive list of items with headlines and descriptions

✦ **Events:** A list of meetings and other scheduled activities

✦ **Shared Documents:** A pre-defined document library (you can add as many more document libraries as you like)

✦ **Links:** A list of links to other content, Web sites, etc.

✦ **Search:** An indexed full-text search of all site content

In addition, the home page contains two navigation elements built using Link Bar components: a top-level navigation bar with links to the main content areas, and a list of Quick Launch items which may come from anywhere on the site.

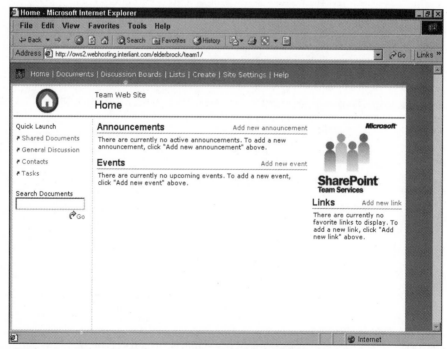

Figure 24-1: The default home page for a SharePoint Team Services Web

The main site navigation bar includes links to the following:

✦ **Documents:** This is the main contents page for all document libraries.

✦ **Discussion Boards:** This is the main contents page for all discussion boards you set up on the site. This section is empty by default.

✦ **Lists:** This is the main content page for all lists on the site. As we noted in passing above, STS comes with several lists pre-defined: announcements, events, links, contacts, and tasks. All lists share a core set of functionality, but can have unique fields of information. You can create additional instances of these pre-defined lists or you can create a custom list type for your own purposes.

Note   Although, not technically a list, any survey you create is also linked to the main List page.

✦ **Create:** This is a centralized index of all the page creation capabilities on the site: Custom List, Document Library, Survey, Discussion Board, Links, Announcements, Contacts, Events, Tasks, and Import Spreadsheet. Most of these elements are accessible elsewhere on the site as well.

Note   The one item with no other means of access (at least until you create one) is the Survey tool.

✦ **Site Settings:** This is a centralized index of site customization and administration tools. It consists of four main sections, each of which contains multiple subsections (which we will discuss a bit later): Web Settings, Web Administration, User Information, and Modify Site Content. The last item, provides links to the customization features for each element on the site, whether a pre-built element or one that you have created. Some, but not all, of the customization functions can be performed from within FrontPage as well. The Administration functions can also be performed using the site HTML Administration tool, which installs on the server (assuming that you have access to the server). These functions make possible a more delegated responsibility for design and administrative tasks.

In the following sections, we examine the main content areas of the STS site in more detail. As we go, you will begin to notice that many of the features share the same core functionality. After we have described a function once, we will only mention it in passing for subsequent elements — and focus on feature-specific functionality.

Working with Documents

Document libraries are collections of documents, which can be of any type, although of course all Office XP applications are designed specifically to integrate with the document library functionality.

The default view of a document library, as illustrated in Figure 24-2, shows a list of available documents. The document name and an icon indicating its format link to the actual document. You can also edit the document's properties, assuming that you have the privileges to do so.

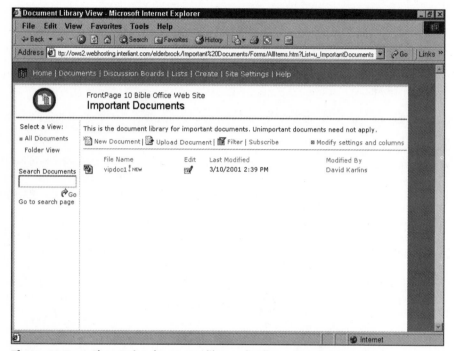

Figure 24-2: A SharePoint document library displays a list of documents.

Adding documents to a library

You add a document to the library in one of two ways: using either New Document or Upload Document links. When a document library is created, it is associated with a default document template. Use the New Document link to create a new document with that template. Click on New Document to open a copy of the template in the appropriate Office application (note that you must have Office XP installed for this to work). When you have created your new document, save it as usual and it is added to the library and the library list is updated.

Note   You can also open the site in FrontPage and add documents to the library as you normally would in FrontPage.

You can also use the Upload Document link to select any existing document you have access to from your computer (you are not limited to Office XP documents here) and add it to the document library. Click Upload Document to go to the upload page (Figure 24-3). Click the upload Browse button to locate the file. Then click the Save and Close button — which is above the form and easy to miss if you have become accustomed to submit buttons at the end of forms — and the file will be added to the document library and the list updated.

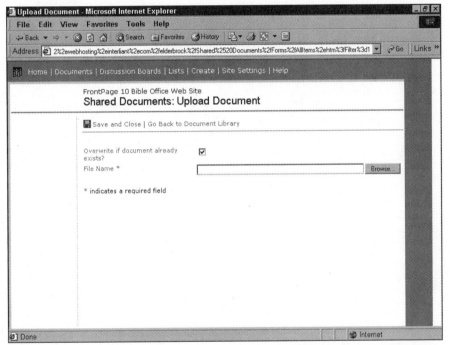

Figure 24-3: You can upload documents from your desktop to the SharePoint site.

Once a document has been added you can edit its properties. The default properties for documents consist of the file name and a title. Click the document's edit icon in the document library list to edit its properties. In addition to editing the document properties, this page offers the following features:

✦ **Delete:** Use this link to remove a document from the library.

✦ **Send for Review:** Send the document via e-mail to a reviewer (requires Office XP installed).

✦ **Discuss:** This feature enables threaded comments about a document to be embedded within the document or associated with it. It requires Internet Explorer 5.0 or greater. (More on this feature in a moment.)

Customizing document library views

As a site user, you can customize the view of any document library to your liking in a variety of ways. These include:

✦ **Sorting:** Click on any field header to re-sort the data by that field. Click a second time to sort on the same field in the opposite order (either ascending or descending).

✦ **Filtering:** This is equivalent to the filtering mechanism available in the FrontPage 2002 reports. Click on the Filter link to show the Filter criteria drop-down lists for all fields that can be filtered. A sample filter list is illustrated in Figure 24-4. Select an item from the list to show only items that match these criteria.

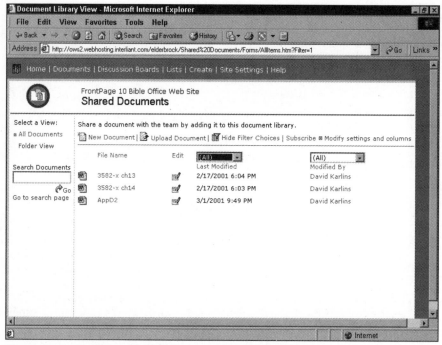

Figure 24-4: Working with filter lists on a SharePoint Web

✦ **Selecting a View:** Each type of content in STS has its own set pre-defined views. In the case of a document library, there is a list view (the default) and folder view (shown in Figure 24-5). You can select your preferred view from the list in the left-hand margin of the document list view page.

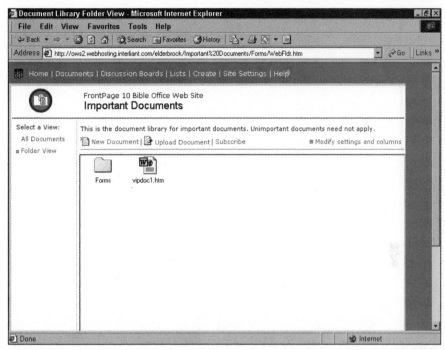

Figure 24-5: You can view a document library in folder view as well as in list view.

Note It is also possible to define custom views using the "Modify settings and columns" page.

Subscribing to documents

To subscribe to a document library (or other STS content) means to sign up to receive notification when content in the library changes. Use the Subscription link on the main document list page to configure your subscription. To subscribe to a document library, select from the following options (shown in Figure 24-6):

✦ **Notify me when:** Options are to be notified when any change occurs, only when pages are updated, only when they are added, or only when they are deleted.

✦ **E-mail address:** Here you type the address where you want notification to go.

✦ **Time:** Options are when a change occurs, once a day, or once a week.

Tip Once you have subscribed to one or more content areas, use the Site Settings page to manage your subscriptions. Click on Site Settings, and under the User Information section, click Edit My Information. Then click the Manage personal subscriptions link.

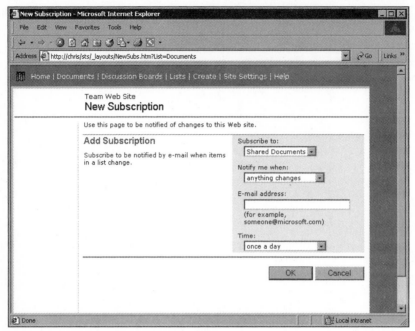

Figure 24-6: Subscribing to STS content

Adding a new document library

Having a shared document library is nice. So nice, that you will probably want to create more libraries for different people, or purposes, or document types. Whatever the reason, creating additional document libraries is quite easy.

Note   You can also create new document libraries using FrontPage 2002. From the File menu select New ➪ Document Library. See section, "Customizing a SharePoint Site in FrontPage" for details.

To create a new document library:

1. Open the main Documents page by clicking on the top navigation link

2. Click the New Document Library link to open the New Document Library form.

3. Indicate a name and optionally a description for this document library. Choose a document template type from the list of available types — or choose none if you do not want to associate a particular template with this library. Indicate whether you want this library added to the Quick Launch bar on the home page.

4. Click the Create button. STS adds your library with the appropriate icon to the main Documents list.

To edit or delete a document library, select the "Modify settings and columns" link on the main contents view page for the library. Under General Settings choose "Change general settings" to edit the information, or "Delete this document library" to delete it.

Caution Deleting a document library deletes all of its contents as well.

Discussing documents

One of the most interesting collaboration features of the STS is the ability to mark up documents by inserting or appending comments to them. There are actually two ways to initiate a discussion about a document, either from within a document library, as we will discuss in this section, or from the Discussion Board section of the site, as we describe in the next section, "Working with discussion boards."

You can use the discuss documents feature from within any Microsoft Office XP application, or you can use Internet Explorer 5.0 or later to discuss Web documents. For our part, we will focus on discussing Web documents, which have the advantage of not requiring anything other than a Web browser to participate in the discussion.

To initiate a discussion of a Web page document in your STS site, locate the document in its document library and click on its title to open it in Internet Explorer. With the document open, click the Discuss button in the far right of the Standard toolbar in Internet Explorer. This opens the Discussion toolbar at the bottom of the Web browser window, shown in Figure 24-7.

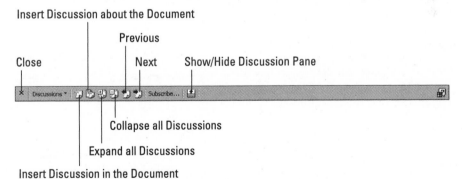

Figure 24-7: The document discussion toolbar

Adding and Replying to Discussion Text

The Discussion toolbar enables you to add two kinds of comments to the Web document. First, you can insert discussion text into the document. To do this, either click the Insert Discussion in the Document icon or select Insert in the Document from the Discussion Drop-down menu in the toolbar. This places a discussion icon in the page as illustrated in Figure 24-8. Double-clicking this icon opens the Enter Discussion Text dialog box. Enter a subject and discussion text in the fields provided, and click OK to add your discussion text to the Web page (this may take a few seconds to update.)

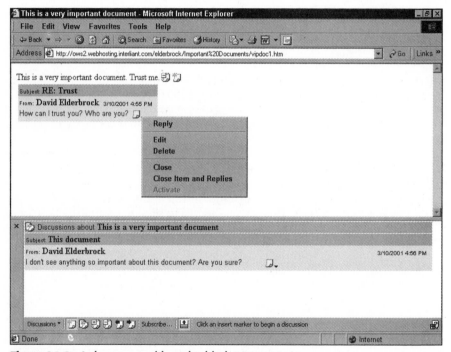

Figure 24-8: A document with embedded comments

If you prefer to create a discussion item that resides in a separate document "pane" and is not directly attached to the document text, use the Insert Discussion about the Document icon or select Insert about the Document from the Discussion Drop-down list. The only difference between these two kinds of comments is their relationship to the page.

Discussion Text Options

Once you have entered one or more discussion items, you can perform other actions related to these comments using the icon associated with each discussion text. Click the icon to reveal a menu of actions. Available options include:

✦ **Reply:** Select this to add a follow-up discussion item that will be associated with the main item, much like a threaded discussion.

✦ **Edit:** Use this option to edit discussion text for items you have submitted.

✦ **Delete:** Use this option to delete discussion text that you have submitted.

✦ **Close:** Closing a discussion item hides it from view in cases when you do not intend to re-open the item (you might think of it as archiving a no-longer-needed discussion comment).

✦ **Close Item and Replies:** Much like close, except that it hides both a discussion item and all of its replies (selecting close on the item only closes it and leaves its replies visible).

✦ **Activate:** This option is only available for closed items and enables you to re-activate them.

The business about closing discussion text items bears a bit of explanation, because it is not entirely self-evident. First some context: If you want to remove one or more discussion items from view temporarily, you should use the Expand all Discussion and Collapse all Discussions icons in the Discussion toolbar. These act as toggle switches, enabling you to show and hide discussion text that has been inserted into the document. Similarly, you can show and hide the Discussion pane that houses discussion items about the document by clicking the Show/Hide Discussion Pane icon in the Discussion toolbar.

These options enable you to manage your view of the document and its associated discussion items. So what of Close? Close is used when you want to "retire" a discussion item, at least semi-permanently. You can bring a closed discussion item out of early retirement, if need be, but it is a bit more work. Select Discussion Options from the Discussion toolbar to open the Discussion Options toolbar. Check the Show Closed Discussions checkbox.

Note   The Discussion Options dialog box also contains options for configuring the discussion fields to display for each discussion item and selecting a Discussion server should you have more than one STS site at your disposal.

Even after you check the Show Closed Discussions checkbox, all "closed" items continues to be treated differently — shown with lighter background and text colors to signify their tenuous presence in the discussion. If you want to revive a closed item fully, use the Activate option in the menu of actions to re-activate the discussion item.

Subscribing to a Discussion Document

Finally, note that you can use the Subscribe button on the Discussion toolbar to subscribe to a particular document, just as you can from the site itself. Clicking this button opens the Document Subscription dialog box, shown in Figure 24-9.

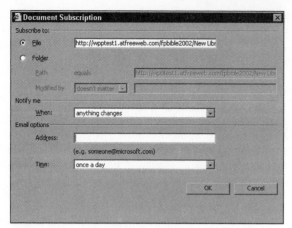

Figure 24-9: Use the Document Subscription dialog box from Internet Explorer to subscribe to a Web document and/or its document library.

Using the Document Subscription dialog box, you can specify a number of options related to when and how and under what conditions you would like to be notified about changes to the designated file or folder. Using this dialog box, you can:

✦ Request to receive notification about a particular file or folder (you can designate these specifically if you like, but given that you have to type in URLs manually, you are more likely to work with the defaults, which correspond to the current document).

✦ Request to be notified when the file is changed by anyone ("doesn't matter") or by someone whose username contains a designated text string

✦ Request to be notified under specific conditions: when anything changes, a new document is created, modified, deleted, or moved, or only when discussion items are added or removed

✦ Designate an email address where you would like to be notified

✦ Indicate how often you would like to be notified: each time a change occurs, once a day, or once a week.

Note that many of the option available here, you can also configure using the Subscription options on the STS site itself. In general, one of the hallmarks of the SharePoint Team Services approach is to create flexible ways for teams to work and communicate. In the next section, we look at the discussion board functions built into the STS site.

Working with discussion boards

A discussion board, as everyone probably already knows, is a space where users can post messages and reply to posted messages. Messages are presented in what STS calls *newsgroup-style*, or *threaded* fashion, so that it is easy to see which message are replies to which other messages.

STS installs with a default discussion board called General Discussion. As with document libraries discussed above, you can add messages to this discussion, customize your view of a discussion board list, subscribe to a discussion, and create new discussion boards. The main functions of discussion boards are as follows:

✦ **To add a message to a discussion:** Open the discussion board to its main view page and click the New Discussion link at the top of the discussion list. Provide a subject and some text for your discussion message. The text, curiously enough, is optional. Click the Save and Close link at the top of the form to return to the main page. Your message should be added to the list.

✦ **To reply to a message:** Click on the linked message subject to view the complete message. Click the Reply link at the top of the form. Complete the reply form. Click Save and Close to return to the main discussion list. Your reply will be listed underneath the original message.

✦ **To edit or delete a message:** Click on the linked message subject to view the complete message. Click the Edit link to make changes to the message or the Delete link to remove it. You must have the appropriate permissions to edit or delete a message.

✦ **To sort and filter messages:** You can sort and filter discussion messages just as you can for documents, as we described in the section "Customizing document library views."

✦ **To change discussion views:** Discussions have two pre-defined views: Summary (the default), which lists only the subject line, author, and modification time for each message; and Expanded (see Figure 24-10), which shows the body of each message as well. To change the view, select either Summary or Expanded from the list in the left-hand margin of the discussion list page.

✦ **To subscribe to a discussion:** You can subscribe to a discussion board as described in the section "Subscribing to documents."

✦ **To create a new discussion:** Click the New Discussion link in the main list of discussion boards. Indicate a new name and optionally a description for your discussion board. Indicate whether you want this board added to the home page Quick Launch link bar.

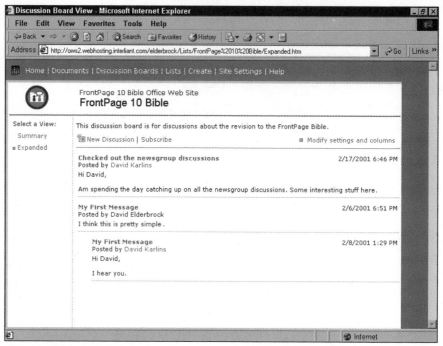

Figure 24-10: Expanded view of the General Discussion board

✦ **To edit or delete a discussion:** Select "Modify settings and columns" from the main list page of the discussion board and select either "Change general settings" or "Delete this discussion board."

✦ **To discuss documents:** The Discussion Board main contents list includes a link that enables you to access a document for discussion, as described in the section "Discussing documents." To access a document from this link, however, you must indicate its URL by typing the address, which makes it somewhat more cumbersome to use than the same mechanism attached to a document library.

Note   You can create a new discussion board in FrontPage 2002 as well, although oddly this function is accessed via the File menu by selecting New ➪ Lists.

Working with lists

In an STS site, a *list* is a generic term for any entity that contains structured (i.e., field-oriented) content that you want to be able to create, view, and manage. In effect, it provides the ability to create simple database applications with a minimum of effort.

STS sites come with five pre-defined list types:

✦ **Announcements:** Consists of a title, body text, and an expiration date. Announcements appear on the home page of the default STS site. You can also access announcements from their own list view page. Announcement lists have only one pre-defined view.

✦ **Events:** Lists scheduled events with Title, Event Date, End Date, Description, and Location fields. Events are also listed on the STS home page as well as being accessible from their own list view page. Events have several pre-defined views: All events, Today's events, My events, Upcoming events, and Calendar view.

✦ **Links:** Lists Web page links including URLs, descriptions, and comments. Links have only one pre-defined view.

✦ **Contacts:** Lists addresses with all the fields you would expect for contacts. You can view All contacts or My contacts. In addition to the standard list export feature (described below), you can also import contacts from your Outlook XP address book.

✦ **Tasks:** A list of to-dos with all of the basic Task fields, including status, priority, assigned to, percent complete, etc. Options include View all tasks, My tasks, Active tasks, By assigned to.

You can use these lists as they are, add additional lists of the same types, customize the columns of information for these lists — including changing the contents of drop-down choice lists — or create your own custom list types. We discuss customizing lists in the next major section, "Customizing a SharePoint Site."

Adding content to a list

Adding content to any list is the same for each. From the main list page, click the New Item link from the top menu. Complete the field information and click the Save and Close link at the top of the form.

Customizing list views

As with discussion boards and document libraries, you can sort and filter all list contents as described earlier. Depending on the list type, a list may also have multiple pre-defined views, indicated in the left-hand margin of the main list page.

Exporting lists

One feature that is specific to lists is the ability to export list content to a spreadsheet. This requires a *SharePoint compatible spreadsheet* (which means Excel 2002). To export the list, click the Export list item in the top menu of the main list page.

Creating surveys

The STS site has the ability to create multiquestion surveys with a variety of question types. This function is something of an anomaly. It is not a pre-defined feature like the document library and discussion board. Nor is it exactly a list, though once you have created a survey, its main link is accessed from the Lists page. The trickiest part about surveys is trying to find the link to create one.

Adding a survey

To create a survey from within the STS site, go to the Create page and click the Survey item. The first step is to give your survey a name, and optionally a description. Indicate whether the survey should appear in the Quick Launch link bar. Specify whether to include user names in survey results and whether to accept multiple responses from a user. Then proceed to add questions to your survey.

Adding a survey question

On the Add Question page, first type a question as shown in Figure 24-11. Note that STS will prevent you from asking the identical question more than once. Next, select the type of answer you want to associate with this question.

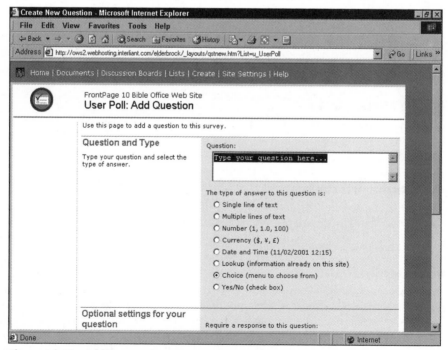

Figure 24-11: Adding questions to a survey

Your question can have one of the following types of responses:

✦ **Single line of text:** A standard text box input

✦ **Multiple lines of text:** A scrolling text box (or text area)

✦ **Number:** A generic number field (e.g., 1, 1.0, 100), with appropriate validation options

✦ **Currency:** Specialized number field (e.g., $, ¥, £), with appropriate validation for currency

✦ **Date and Time:** With special date and time formatting options (e.g., 11/02/2001 12:15)

✦ **Lookup:** A field from a site list or other content that you specify to use as the basis for a choice list

✦ **Choice:** A list of choices and a default selection that you provide

✦ **Yes/No:** A checkbox to indicate the default option

Your selection of an answer type determines the data type of the response as well as the type of form field used to display response options. It also changes the options available in the next section of this page, the Optional Settings for the question. Typical options include whether an answer is required, validation options, and a default value for the answer. Click OK when you have finished configuring your first question.

A mild surprise — adding additional questions

You probably expect that, having created the first question of your survey, you could now repeat the process for any additional questions you might like. If that is what you are expecting, you are in for a surprise, because STS ends the survey creation after the first question.

Instead, you will find yourself in the Customization page for your survey (shown in Figure 24-12). This page has two sections: The General Settings section enables you to modify the general survey information or delete the survey entirely. The Questions section enables you to modify existing questions, add additional questions, and change the order of questions.

To modify a question, click on the hyperlinked question in the list of available questions. Make changes to the question as described in the section "Adding a survey question." Click OK to return to the Customization page.

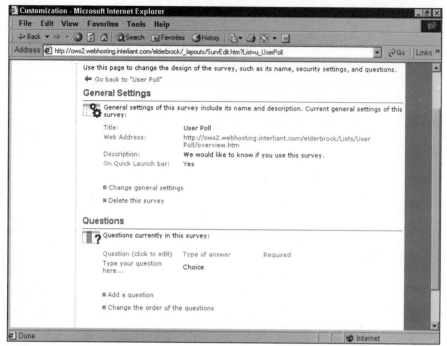

Figure 24-12: The survey page provides the ability to change general settings and add questions to your survey.

To add a question, click the Add a Question link and proceed as above. Each time you finish a question, you will be returned to this list, where you can click on the "Add a question" link again to add additional questions.

Once you have more than one question, you can reorder them. Click on the "Change the order of the questions" link and select the order you desire.

Responding to a survey

Once you have created a survey, it is available from the Lists page (and from the Quick Launch list on the home page if you selected this option). Click the "Respond to this survey" link in the top menu to complete the survey. Click the Save and Close button on the survey page when you are finished.

Customizing survey views

Surveys do not have sort and filter options enabled. They do, however, have several pre-defined views. The default view for surveys displays an overview of the survey, including the number of respondents. Other pre-defined views include

"Graphical summary" and "All responses." Graphical summary shows a breakdown of responses per question (see Figure 24-13). All responses shows a list of each response, linked to the response details.

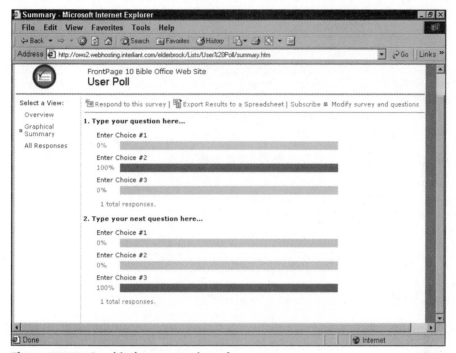

Figure 24-13: Graphical summary view of a survey

Modifying a survey response

From the All Reponses list, you can click on a response to edit it (if you have the proper permissions). This is handy if, for example, you notice that your responses differ from those of the CEO.

Subscribing to a survey

As with other content types, you can subscribe to a survey to be notified anytime the content changes. See the discussion in the section "Subscribing to documents" for more details.

Exporting results

As with other types of lists, you can export the survey results to a spreadsheet. This option is not available from the All Responses view.

Customizing a SharePoint Site

We have already discussed two forms of site customization: the ability to add new content items (the functions centralized in the Create section of the site); and the ability to change the way that content is displayed by changing views, and sorting and filtering list information.

This section identifies additional means of customizing site content. First, we look at some additional customization you can perform from the STS site itself. Then we turn to FrontPage, and examine how FrontPage interacts with an STS site. We will find that it replicates in slightly different format, most of the customization features already described and adds a few of its own.

Modifying the home page layout

When you create your SharePoint Team Services site, a default home page is created for you. You also have the ability to edit the layout of this page, using a special Web-based design tool that is part of STS.

Note   In our opinion, the interface used to modify the home page layout is one of the coolest features about STS (second only to the ability to create lookup lists of site content in a survey). You have to check it out!

To modify the home page layout from the STS site:

1. Select Site Settings.

2. In the Web Site Settings section, select Customize home page layout.

3. The Home Page Layout page, as shown in Figure 24-14, shows three columns of information. On the left is a column of available content areas. The other two columns show the existing content displayed in the center and right columns of your home page. To add an item to the home page, drag and drop the item from the available list into one of the other columns. To remove an item, drag it back to the available list.

Note   You may notice that you are not really customizing the home page layout at all, because that is fixed. You are modifying the content displayed. But who are we to quibble?

4. Click the Save button (at the bottom of the page) to record your changes.

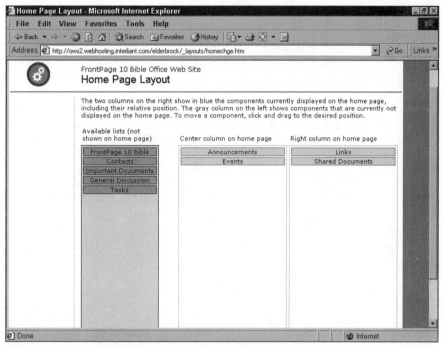

Figure 24-14: Modifying the STS home page layout

Adding a template to a document library

In our discussion of the document library, we mentioned the fact that you can associate a default template with a given library. The STS site comes with a pre-defined list of generic (i.e., blank) Office document templates, but you can easily add your own.

1. First, create the template in your favorite Office XP application.

2. Next, add the template to your Web site. The easiest way to do this is to use FrontPage to import the template. Alternately, you can create a special document library for templates and upload it the file to this document library.

3. Open the document library in question, and click the "Modify settings and columns" link.

4. Click the "Modify general settings" link

5. In the document template section, type the URL of the template. This template will be used each time a user clicks on the New Document link in this document library.

Note
You can also edit the existing template in the General Settings section of the Modify Settings page. Click the Change General Settings link that follows the URL of the current template as indicated in the General Settings section.

Modifying list columns

Many of the content types in the STS site have the option to enable you to change column information for that item. You can edit existing columns, add new columns, and reorder columns.

To modify list columns, open a given list page and click the "Modify settings and columns" link on the far right of the top menu bar. In the Columns section of this page, as shown in Figure 24-15, you can do any of the following:

✦ **Modify existing columns:** Click the column name to open a form for editing column information. Column types of existing columns are fixed. You can change the name, description, and various options about the column, including whether it is required or not.

✦ **Add a new column:** Click the "Add a new column" link to open the Add Column form. Add a name, description, and select a column data type. Depending on your selection, the optional settings will vary. Make your optional setting selections, and click OK to save your changes.

✦ **Delete columns:** You cannot delete default columns of pre-defined lists. You can, however, delete columns you have added. In the edit form, click the Delete button at the bottom of the form to delete the column.

✦ **Reorder columns:** Click the "Change the order of the fields" link and select the new sort order. Click OK to record your changes.

Creating a custom view

You can add your own custom views to the pre-defined views the STS site defines for each content type. To create a custom view, select the "Modify settings and columns" link from the list page. In the View section (see Figure 24-16), click "Create a new view" to open the Create View form.

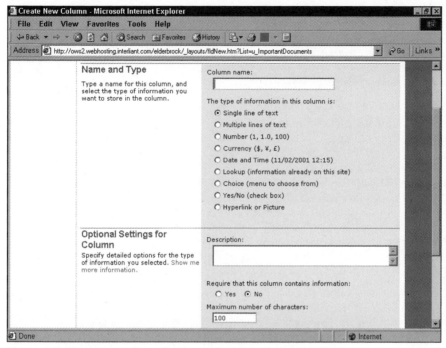

Figure 24-15: Customizing columns and settings for your STS site

This form is not as daunting as it may look at first glance. After naming your view and deciding whether to make this the default view, you can define four aspects of your custom view:

✦ **Columns:** You can determine which columns to include and in what order.

✦ **Sort:** You can define up to two fields to sort on, and designate whether the default sort should be ascending or descending for each.

✦ **Filter:** You can define default filters for the view, or accept the default of unfiltered.

✦ **Item limit:** You can designate a limit to the number of items that display. You can show information in pages of this number; or you can set this as an absolute limit.

Click OK to record your new view.

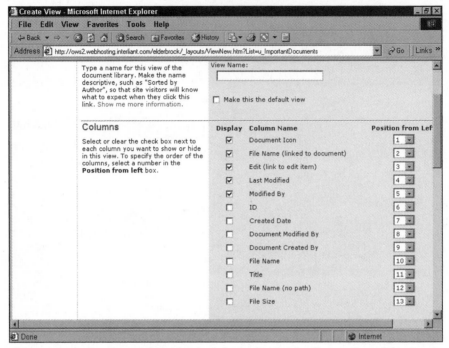

Figure 24-16: Creating custom views of site content — the first section of the Create View form

Note This is not a private view. It is available to all users.

Customizing a SharePoint Site in FrontPage

SharePoint Team Services is designed as a stand-alone Web site. You do not need FrontPage to set up or maintain the site. However, FrontPage 2002 has a number of integration points with SharePoint Team Services that make it a convenient tool for customizing and extending an STS site. Because, after all, this is a book about FrontPage, it seems only fitting that we describe the major ways you can use FrontPage in conjunction with STS. Some of the functionality is redundant with the features of STS described earlier in the chapter, so we will try not to cover those topics in mind-numbing detail. Check back to the earlier discussion for details.

Customizing the site design

From FrontPage's perspective, an STS Web site looks very much like a standard Web site. More accurately, it looks very much like a Web site that uses FrontPage extensions. You open an STS just as you would any other Web. Once opened you will notice (see Figure 24-17) that FrontPage recognizes the various types of content elements in the site and gives each an appropriate icon in the folder list. We will see in a moment that FrontPage also associates a special set of property dialog boxes with these elements. In other regards, however, the STS site looks very familiar. If you open the home page, `default.htm`, you will notice that it has some special regions defined — very much like those you have seen when using FrontPage components.

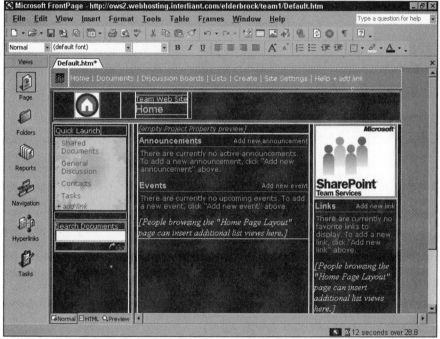

Figure 24-17: An STS Web site as seen from FrontPage — with new theme applied

Just as with other FrontPage Web components, you need to leave these special regions alone. Otherwise, you can edit the pages in an STS site just as you would a page in any regular FrontPage Web site — change page layout, add graphics or other components, etc. You can also apply a standard FrontPage theme to an STS site. You do this just as you normally would: With the home page open, select Format ➪ Theme and choose a theme to apply. But note that if you add a theme, you must check the option to apply the theme using Cascading Style Sheets (CSS).

Modifying site navigation

If you look at the home page of an STS site in FrontPage, you will notice that there are several regions that you can edit. In the first place, there are the two link bar navigational elements: the top-level navigation and the Quick Launch navigation.

To add a link to either of the link bar navigational elements: Click the "+ add link" link to open the Add to Link Bar dialog box (see Figure 24-18). Select an item to add to the link, designate the descriptive text for the link, and click OK. Note that this is functionally equivalent to checking the option to add an item to the link bar when you create it in STS.

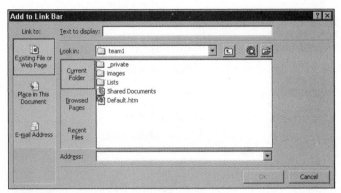

Figure 24-18: Add to Link Bar dialog box

You can also open the Link Bar Properties dialog box for these elements and make changes either to the links or the link bar style. Double-click the Link Bar component on the home page to open its Property dialog box. In the General tab you can add, modify, remove, and reorder links. In the Style tab (see Figure 24-19) you can define a new style for the link bar, if you don't want it to inherit its style from a theme. For more information on working with Link Bar components, see Chapter 9.

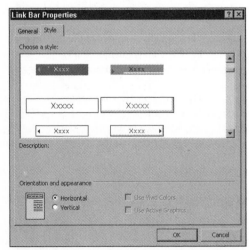

Figure 24-19: Modifying link bar styles in FrontPage

Editing List View component properties

Also on the home page are several List View components. These are same components found in FrontPage's Web component list by selecting Insert ➪ Web Component, and selecting List View.

Double-clicking on a List View item opens the List View Properties dialog box (see Figure 24-20). From here, you can take the following actions:

✦ Click the Lists button to choose a list to display.

✦ Click the Fields button to select fields to display in this view.

✦ Click the Sort button to define default sort order.

✦ Click the Filter button to define default filter criteria.

✦ Click the Options button to define a List View style, select a toolbar type, and display options.

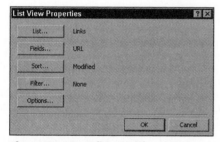

Figure 24-20: Editing in the List View Properties dialog box

Experimenting with the STS home page gives you some taste for the kinds of customization you can make to existing site components (we will explore some more a bit later). But now, let's look at how you can use FrontPage to create site pages.

 Note For the record, the default STS home page also has two inconspicuous Project Property components located in the page banner and at the top of the middle column. Double-click these components to select either the Project Title or Description to display there. By default, the Title displays in the banner header and the description displays in the middle column.

Creating site pages in FrontPage

If you recall, the STS site has a special section called "Create" which collects all of the various site tools for creating new content elements. You can use FrontPage to create all of these elements as well, although the mechanism for doing so is a bit different.

Tip   FrontPage 2002 includes a new Web template that enables you create a complete STS Web site with a single click.

FrontPage lists the special STS items under the File ➪ New menu. The three items listed there are:

✦ **Document Library:** Including a library with auto-backup and another with expiration

✦ **Lists:** Including all of the standard lists as well as Discussion Boards

✦ **Survey:** A standard survey element

All three menu items also include a special wizard that walks you through the steps of creating these elements. The wizard generates the same elements you could create on the site itself, so we will describe each one only briefly.

Creating a new document library

To start the Document Library wizard, select File ➪ New ➪ Document Library.

1. Give the document library a name and description.

2. Designate a template (note that using the wizard enables you to browse for the template in contrast to the STS site creation tool, which requires you to type in the URL.

3. Define the document fields by adding, modifying, or removing items from the preset list. You cannot delete or modify pre-existing fields, besides the Title field.

4. The last step allows you to establish workflow rules to associate with your document library. This is not a feature that is currently available from the site itself, so if you are interested in establishing workflow rules, you should plan to create, or edit, document libraries in FrontPage (at least for the time being). The Rules setup launches a separate Rules Wizard, which bears its own discussion in the next section.

Note   You can add rules to an existing document library from the Rules tab of the library's properties dialog box.

5. When you are ready, click Finish to generate the set of document library files. These include all the forms and views necessary to operate the document library.

Associating rules with a document library

A *rule* is a statement about what, if any, actions to perform under certain conditions in the document library. A typical rule might stipulate that any time a document authored by Jack is added to the document library it should be sent to Jill for approval. You can create rules based on some standard rule templates, or you can create a rule from scratch. Either way the process is essentially the same.

You access the Rules Wizard either when creating a document library, as noted above, or by right-clicking the document library, selecting its Properties dialog box, and clicking the Rules tab.

In the Rules tab (see Figure 24-21), click the Add button to start the Rules Wizard. In the first screen, designate whether you want to work from a rule template or create your own. If you choose to use a template, select the template you want from the list in this screen. If you are going to roll your own, start by indicating the event that should trigger the rule. You can also provide a description for your rule.

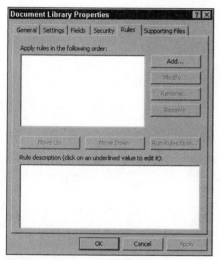

Figure 24-21: Use the Rules Wizard from the Document Library Properties dialog to define rules to be associated with a document library.

The next step is to select the conditions under which the rule should operate. You will notice as you select an item that it is added to the Rule description that is being created in the bottom half of the wizard, as illustrated in Figure 24-22. Some of the words in this description are highlighted. These require you to specify a value. To do so, click on the underlined item to open a value dialog box appropriate to the kind of information required (text, numbers, dates, etc.).

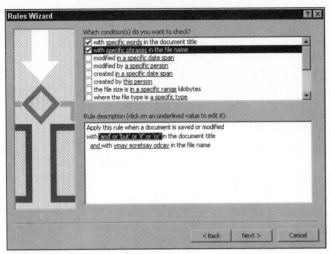

Figure 24-22: Selecting Rule conditions and adding a description

After identifying any conditions for the rule, the next step is to select the action to be performed, again specifying any necessary values. Finally, you can define exception circumstances under which the rule should not be applied.

The rules you create do not constitute full-fledged *workflow*, since you can really only trigger a single set of actions to occur. But this mechanism does provide you some ability to automate the review of documents within the document library.

Creating a new list

Select File ➪ New ➪ List to select the type of list you would like to create. By now, assuming you have been following along, you are probably tired of hearing that you can create default lists for announcements, events, contacts, tasks, and links. (At least we varied the order!) You can also create a custom list, which would really better be termed a generic list, since it isn't custom until you edit its properties and customize it. A better option is to use the List Wizard, since it enables you define the list and security options all in a few wizardly screens. The steps to use the List Wizard are:

1. Name and describe your list.

2. Add, modify, remove, or reorder fields — only the Title field can be modified from the pre-defined fields.

3. Specify who can read and/or write whose list items or modify columns and settings.

That's it. Now you have a new custom list ready to go.

Creating a new survey

Of all the FrontPage page creation tools, the Survey tool is probably the most substantially better than the STS site capabilities, because you can use it define all of your questions in one pass. You create a new survey by selecting File ⇨ New ⇨ Survey. You can create an empty survey and then edit its properties, or use the Survey Wizard and finish the job immediately. Here are the steps:

1. Give your survey a name and description

2. Add Questions to the survey. To add a question, click the Add button (see Figure 24-23), type your question, select a response type, and click Next.

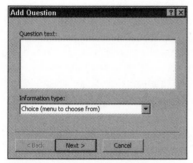

Figure 24-23: Adding a survey question using FrontPage's Survey Wizard

3. The next screen you see depends on what response type you selected. (Just as in the STS site, the options change to reflect the answer type.) Select the appropriate options and click OK.

4. Now you are ready to define the next question. As you accumulate questions, you can reorder them on the main list screen.

5. In the final screen stipulate the permission levels necessary for various survey-related tasks. Indicate which items users can read, which write, and who has the ability to customize the survey using the "Modify settings and columns" link.

6. Also in the last screen, you should indicate whether to show user names in the results page and whether a user should be allowed to submit multiple responses.

Editing properties of existing elements

Once you have created new elements in your site, whether you created them in FrontPage or on the site itself, you can use FrontPage to edit the properties of these elements. Earlier in this section, we indicated that you can edit List View and Link Bar properties. In this section, we will call attention to additional customization you can perform in FrontPage.

Tip   If you have made changes directly to your STS site, it is a good idea to recalculate hyperlinks in FrontPage before using it to update site elements. To recalculate hyperlinks in FrontPage, select Tools ➪ Recalculate Hyperlinks.

Document Library Views

The Document Library View component is very similar in concept to the List component, except that it applies to, you guessed it, document libraries. To insert a Document Library View component onto a page of your STS site, open the page, select Insert ➪ Web Components and select the Document Library View component. The component, as seen in Figure 24-24, first prompts you to specify a document library (if you have more than one).

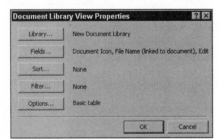

Figure 24-24: The Document Library View Properties component in FrontPage 2002

Then it displays the Document Library View Properties dialog, where you can take the following actions:

✦ Click the Library button to select the library to view (in case you changed your mind).

✦ Click the Fields button to select fields to display in the view.

✦ Click Sort to define a default sort order.

✦ Click Filter to define default filtering criteria.

✦ Click Options to select from a variety of document library specific options.

Note   You will notice that this functionality is equivalent to using the STS site's "Modify settings and columns" page.

Working with list forms and list fields

We have discussed how to create STS pages and how to modify content views in FrontPage. The last item to consider is how to modify the list forms (the equivalent of editing columns using the site tools).

The easiest way to demonstrate the use of the List Form and List Field components is to work from an existing item. Open one of the forms associated with a list: the View form (`DispForm.htm` or `AllItems.htm`), the Edit form (`EditForm.htm`), or the Add Item form (`NewForm.htm`).

Note   By the way, the complete name of the List Form component is the List or Document Library Form component — signifying that you can use this to alter the document library forms as well (also, surveys count as lists in this regard).

With the form page open, double-click the form component to open its List or Document Library Form dialog box. The dialog box gives you the option of selecting a content element from the site to designate a form for and a choice of three types of forms: view forms, edit forms, and new item forms. In fact, you are unlikely to change any of these options for a given form, because doing so would effectively create a different form. But it is good to know that the dialog box exists, because it is the same dialog box you use when creating a List Form page from scratch.

Adding a List form

To add a custom List form:

1. Open the page you want to add the List form to.

2. Select Insert ➪ Form ➪ List Form.

3. Configure the List form, selecting a content item to use in the form, designating the type of form, and electing to include a standard toolbar if you choose. (Note that the "standard toolbars" vary from form to form and from content type to content type.)

Customizing list fields

In addition to using the List Form dialog box to configure the List form in your Web page, you can also use a separate page mode called Layout Customization. To switch your page from Live Data view to Layout Customization view, right click the List form component, and select Layout Customization View. In this view, you can:

✦ **Move field elements:** You can drag and drop field elements within the List form component boundaries (this is similar to using the Database Results regions as described in Chapter 20).

✦ **Insert, modify or delete field elements:** To insert a new field element, right click the List form component and select List Field from the options menu. Select an available field from the List Field Properties dialog box. To modify a field element, double-click it to open the List Field Properties dialog box and select your options. You can also delete field elements — note that this only removes the element from the page, not from the STS database where the information resides.

✦ **Edit other page elements:** You can also make changes to the formatting and content outside of the List Form component.

This is all very nice, but there is a catch — if you open the page in Layout Customization view and make any of the changes described above, you cannot switch the page back to Live Data view. Ever. If you do, FrontPage reverts the page to its default appearance. It does not matter whether you save your changes first, or close the file and open it next week. If you switch back to Live Data view, it reverts back to its original status.

Administering a SharePoint Site

In the final sections of this chapter, we briefly touch on some of the administrative issues related to setting up and maintaining a SharePoint Team Services site. Complete coverage of these topics is beyond the scope of this book, but it is worth noting how Microsoft is evolving the original FrontPage Server Extension model to this new technology.

Overview of STS administration

The SharePoint Team Services technology implements several different levels of administrative control:

✦ **Server Administration:** The SharePoint server administration pages enable a server administrator to view information about the server, specify default settings for each virtual server, and manage users and user roles for the server.

✦ **Virtual Server Administration:** Provides server administration features for an individual virtual server; enabling an administrator to upgrade or uninstall server extensions, and configure settings for an individual server

✦ **Site Administration:** Site administration tasks are specific to a particular Web site. A site administrator can manage users and user roles, configure discussion and subscription settings, configure usage analysis, check on the server health, and create and manage subwebs. The tasks of the site administrator are largely performed using the Site Administration pages, although some site administration tasks can be performed using FrontPage as well.

In this section, we focus on the tasks performed by the site administrator. We discuss each of the major areas that a site administrator is concerned with, indicating, where appropriate, how FrontPage can be used to perform these tasks.

Managing users and roles

The site administrator is responsible for creating and managing user accounts on the site, including assigning users to appropriate roles.

Adding a user

To add a user:

1. Click on the Site Settings link on the STS site.

2. Under Web Administration, click on the Manage Users link

3. As illustrated in Figure 24-25, this page shows a list of current users and their assigned roles.

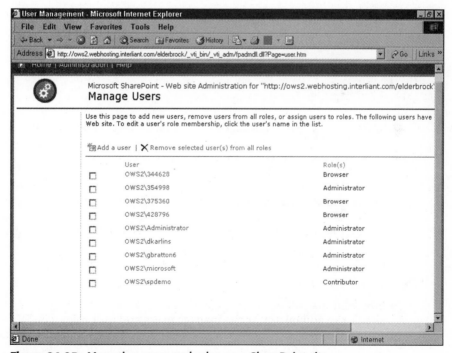

Figure 24-25: Managing users and roles on a SharePoint site

4. Click on the "Add a user" link in the menu list at the top of the page.

5.,In the Add User form, you can add one of two kinds of users. "Non-domain" users do not have an existing user account on the network domain. For these users you must create a user name and assign a password. "Domain" users have an existing account and you simply add them to the list of site users without any additional information.

6. Select one or more roles for the user. The default site defines five roles, which we discuss in the next section. After making your selection, click the Add User button to record the new user information.

Deleting a user

To delete a user:

1. If the user is a domain account, deleting them from all roles effectively deletes them from the site. You can do this by selecting the user(s) you want to remove in the list of users mentioned in the previous section, and clicking "Remove selected user(s) from all roles." A site administrator cannot delete the user's domain account.

2. If the user is a non-domain account, removing their roles does not delete them as a user. To do this, you need to use the Site Administration tool to delete the user.

Inviting users

The alternate way to add a user to an STS site is through inviting them via e-mail to join the site. Sending an invitation to a user adds them as a user. It also sends them notification of their user name and an initial password (which they should change).

To send an invitation to one or more new users, click the Site Settings link, and click the Send an Invitation link in the Web Administration section. Sending an invitation is a three step process: first identify one or more e-mail addresses to send to; next specify an account name and the user's full name (see Figure 24-26); finally, optionally add a custom message and set the user's initial role. Note that if you send multiple invitations at one time, you must set all invitees to the same role. Once the user accounts have been created, of course, you can always edit their roles individually.

Modifying user roles

To modify an existing user's role(s), click on the Site Settings link and click Manage Users. Click on the user in the list of available users. In the Edit User Role Membership form designate the user's new role(s). Click Submit to record your changes.

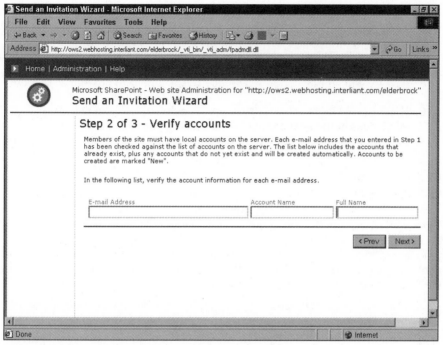

Figure 24-26: Inviting a new user to visit the STS site

Defining user roles

The STS site installs with five pre-defined user roles:

✦ **Browser:** This role can view pages in the Web site.

✦ **Contributor:** Includes all the browser rights, as well as the ability to create lists, participate in document discussions, and subscribe to documents or folders.

✦ **Author:** Includes all Contributor rights as well as the ability to create site pages, edit tasks, and author lists.

✦ **Advanced Author:** Includes all Author rights and adds the ability to author pages in FrontPage.

✦ **Administrator:** Includes all available rights to manage content and users.

If these roles don't meet your needs, you can create your own. To define a new user role, click the Manage Roles link in the Site Administration page. Here you can edit or delete existing roles and add new ones.

To add a new role, click the "Add a role" button in the menu, enter a role name and description in the form provided. Select the rights that you want to apply to this new role. The list of available rights, too long to reproduce in its entirety here, is divided into three sections:

- ✦ **Web Design rights:** Rights pertaining to the ability to customize the site
- ✦ **Team Contributor rights:** Rights pertaining to the ability to add content to the site
- ✦ **Web Administration rights:** Rights pertaining to the ability to configure and manage the site

Controlling access levels

You can decide whether to allow anonymous access to your SharePoint team services Web site and grant access levels to anonymous users. By default, anonymous access is granted at the browser level on an STS site. To make changes to this, click the Site Settings link, and go to the Site Administration page. Click the "Change anonymous access settings" link. Turn access on or off. If you enable access, define the role assigned to anonymous users.

Changing the permission on document libraries and lists

In addition to assigning user roles and access levels, you can also configure individual lists and document libraries with specific security settings. There are two ways to do this. On the site itself, select the "Modify settings and columns" link for a given list or library. In the Security section, configure the following permissions:

- ✦ **Read access:** Users are granted access to all items or only their own items.
- ✦ **Edit access:** Users are granted access to all items, only their own, or none.
- ✦ **Design access:** Specifies who can modify columns in the list — either everyone or only the creator.

Note   Document Libraries only provide Design access options.

Alternately, you can set the same set of permissions in FrontPage. Open the Web in FrontPage, and in the Folder list, right-click the list folder in question and select its Properties option. Click the Security tab, and proceed as above.

Managing document discussions

As described earlier in the chapter, the document discussion feature enables users to add comments to a document, either by inserting them directly into the document or attaching them to the document. Using the Web Discussions and Subscriptions section of the Site Administration page, you can configure options regarding the operation of this feature on your site, including whether to permit document discussions at all. The following is a list of configuration options for Web document discussions:

✦ Enable or disable document discussions.

✦ Specify whether documents anywhere on the Internet or only those on the local team Web site can be discussed.

✦ Designate a time limit to store document discussions by selecting the "Automatically delete stored discussions after" checkbox and typing the number of days to retain discussion data.

✦ View a list of document discussions and individual discussions.

✦ Delete a Web document discussion by checking the box next to it in the list of discussions and clicking Delete.

Managing subscriptions

You can control various aspects of site subscriptions from the Web Discussions and Subscriptions section of the Site Administration page. Options include:

✦ **Enable or Disable Subscriptions:** Specify whether to allow users to subscribe to documents

✦ **Subscription Restrictions:** Specify whether users can subscribe to documents and folders or just to documents.

Configuring subscriptions for documents only will prevent users from being notified when new documents are added to the site.

✦ **Notification Recurrence:** Specify when team Web site members will be notified of changes to subscribed items. Set a time in minutes for immediate notifications, a time of day to send daily notifications, and a weekday and time for weekly updates.

✦ **Mail Settings:** Designate the From and Reply To e-mail addresses for notifications.

Managing subwebs

For FrontPage users, the notion of Webs and subwebs is very familiar. STS provides administrative ability to create and manage subwebs. Alternately you can use FrontPage 2002 to create and manage subwebs on your STS site.

To manage subwebs using the Site Administration page, click the Site Settings link in the main navigation list and click Go to Site Administration in the Web Administration section.

Note You can also use the Create a Subweb link in the Web Administration list to create a subweb. For other subweb-related tasks, use the Site Administration page.

Adding a subweb

To add a subweb to the current Web, do the following (see Figure 24-27):

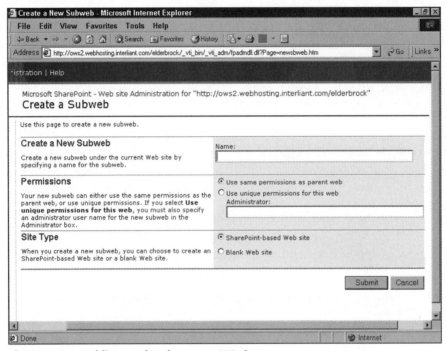

Figure 24-27: Adding a subweb to your STS site

1. Type a name for the new subweb in the space provided.

2. Set the permissions on the new subweb. A subweb can either inherit permissions from its parent (the current Web), or you can assign unique permissions. If you choose to assign unique permissions, you must provide a valid Administrator user name. If you choose to have the subweb inherit user permissions, the subweb will not have the normal user configuration options available to its administrator.

 Note If you change your mind about permissions, you can use the Change Subweb permissions link on the Site Administration page to modify your selection.

3. Choose whether you want the site created as a Microsoft SharePoint Team Services Web site or as a blank Web site. Choosing the blank Web means that the new subweb will have the FrontPage Server Extensions installed, but will not be able to use any of the SharePoint specific functionality.

Merge a subweb

Merging a subweb is a fancy way of saying that you want to convert the subweb to a folder in the parent Web. To merge a Web, click the Merge subweb option on the Site Administration page and select the subweb to merge.

When merging subwebs, you cannot merge any SharePoint-specific contents, such as lists and document libraries. In order to merge the subwebs, you must first remove the contents of these items. After you have merged the Webs, you can re-enter any list contents.

Delete a subweb

To delete a subweb, click the Delete subweb option on the Site Administration page and select the subweb to delete from the drop-down menu of available subwebs.

Administering usage settings

As described in Chapter 3 on publishing FrontPage Webs, FrontPage 2002 contains a set of Web site usage analysis reports that provide valuable information about who is using what parts of your site.

The STS Site Administration pages let you configure how usage logs are kept and how they are managed. To configure usage options, use the Configure Usage Analysis Settings section of the Site Administration page. Here you can set the following options:

✦ **Enable or disable logging**

✦ **Recurrence:** If you enable logging, specify how often you want to process the usage log file.

✦ **Additional Usage:** Set a time period to keep usage data, choose whether to process information in 24 hour increments, and optionally set an e-mail address for notification of complete usage analysis.

Checking server health

The Server Health Check feature lets you ascertain that the SharePoint database, security features, and other supporting file are in good working order. The Server Health Check performs the following checks and makes repairs when it detects a problem:

✦ **Synchronize database:** Ensures that database information matches the site file system.

✦ **Verify existence of Webs:** Ensures that all subwebs are present.

✦ **Check roles configuration:** Ensures that user role settings are correct.

✦ **Tighten security:** Ensures that all the necessary team Web site files and directories are present and that only users with the proper permissions have access to them.

✦ **Check anonymous authoring:** Checks anonymous user access rights to ensure that anonymous users don't have permission to modify content.

Setting Server Health Check options

In the Server Health section of the Site Administration page, you can set the following options:

✦ **Enable or disable server health checking**

✦ **Recurrence:** If checking is enabled, specify how often to perform checks.

Running a Server Health Check

In addition to setting automated health checks, you can run a Server Health Check manually using the "Check server health" option on the Site Administration page. Select the Detect and/or Repair checkboxes to enable the actions that you want the Server Health Check to complete. Click OK to run the health check.

Summary

This chapter provides an overview of Microsoft's new SharePoint Team Services. We have discussed the major features of the STS site, including user services, site design options and server administration. We have explored a number of ways teams can use an STS to communicate easily and effectively—through the use of custom lists, document libraries, discussions, and surveys. You have learned a number of ways to customize and extend the basic STS site using either the STS server's Web based design capabilities or FrontPage. We have seen that even though the SharePoint server is not directly related to FrontPage (neither needs the other in order to work), they do have a close kinship. You have learned a number of ways you can use FrontPage to customize your SharePoint site, and, in turn, extend FrontPage's capabilities by installing and using the SharePoint Server Extensions.

✦   ✦   ✦

Installing FrontPage

FrontPage 2002 is a member of the Microsoft Office XP suite of business applications. This appendix describes the basic system requirements and installation procedures for installing FrontPage as part of the Microsoft Office XP installation.

Installing FrontPage

Installing FrontPage is a straightforward process, assuming that you have the proper system requirements and environment. This guide provides the technical requirements and a general description of the installation process.

Recommended system requirements

The recommended system for Microsoft Office XP Professional with Microsoft FrontPage is Microsoft® Windows® 2000 Professional on a computer with a Pentium III processor and 128MB of RAM.

Minimum system requirements

Operating system: Microsoft Windows 98®, Windows 98 Second Edition, Windows Me®, Windows NT® 4.0 with Service Pack 6 or later, or Windows 2000. On systems running Windows NT 4.0 with Service Pack 6, the version of Internet Explorer must be upgraded to at least 4.01 with Service Pack 1.

Random Access Memory: RAM requirements depend upon the operating system used, plus an additional 8MB of RAM for each Office application running simultaneously: for Windows 98 and Windows 98 Second Edition, 24MB of RAM for the operating system; for Windows Me, 32MB of RAM for the operating system; for Windows NT Workstation or Server 4.0, 32MB of RAM for the operating system; for Windows 2000 Professional, 64MB of RAM for the operating system. Operating system RAM requirements assume default Windows installations, and running additional utilities or applications may require additional RAM.

Storage requirements: Hard-disk space requirements will vary depending on configuration. Customers with Windows 2000 will require 115MB of available hard-disk space for the default configuration of Office Professional with FrontPage Corporate Preview. Customers without Windows 2000, Windows Me, or Office 2000 SR1 will require an extra 50MB of hard-disk space for the Office System Pack. Custom installation choices may require more or less hard-disk space. A CD-ROM drive is required for installation.

Monitor: Super VGA (800 × 600) or higher-resolution monitor; 256 colors or more required.

Pointing device: Microsoft Mouse, Microsoft® IntelliMouse®, or compatible pointing device.

Processor: Pentium 133MHz or higher processor.

Additional Requirements

These requirements pertain to some of the special features available for FrontPage 2002.

Multimedia computer: For sound and multimedia effects.

Speech recognition: Pentium II 140MHz or higher processor, 128 MB RAM, microphone and audio output device.

E-mail features: Requires the presence of Microsoft Exchange, Internet SMTP/POP3, IMAP4, or other MAPI-compliant messaging software.

Microsoft SharePoint Team Services: Pentium 200-MHz or higher processor, Windows 2000 with IIS 5.0, 128 MB RAM, 70 MB hard disk space, Microsoft Data Engine (MSDE) or Microsoft SQL Server 7.0. (MSDE automatically installs with the SharePoint server if no other database is available.)

Installation

1. Back up all vital data files.

2. Close all applications running on your system. If you are running Windows NT or Windows 2000, you need to be logged on to the computer as an administrator.

3. Insert the CD, and follow the on-screen instructions. If you are running a previous version of Office XP (for example a pre-release version), you will be prompted at the beginning of the installation to remove previous versions in order for setup to continue. Click OK at this prompt to continue the Microsoft Office XP installation.

4. If you install on a computer that does not have Office 2000 SR1 or Windows 2000 or later, you will be prompted to install the Office System Files Update. You will need to restart your computer after this installation.

5. After restart, Office Setup will automatically re-launch to guide you through the installation of the Microsoft Office XP applications, including FrontPage 2002.

6. Continue following the on-screen instructions, configuring Office XP according to your needs.

✦　　✦　　✦

What's New in Version 2002

This appendix describes some of the new features available in FrontPage 2002. This includes features such as ease-of-use, graphics handling, dynamic content, and site administration, to name a few. The tables in this appendix list the new features as well as what's been updated from earlier versions.

What's New in FrontPage 2002

FrontPage 2002 is a member of the Microsoft Office XP suite of business applications. The following tables list new, updated, and enhanced features of FrontPage 2002.

Ease-of-use

Table B-1 describes a list of features that make FrontPage 2002 even easier to use than its earlier versions.

Table B-1 Ease-of-Use Features		
Status	**Feature**	**Description**
New	Page Tabs	Enables quick access to multiple open Web pages
Updated	Navigation Pane	Alternates between Folder List and Navigation Pane while keeping a Web page open for editing

Continued

	Table B-1 *(continued)*	
Status	**Feature**	**Description**
New	Table Editing	Table Autoformat enables users to select a table style; Table Fill works like a spreadsheet to allow you to repeat contents in table cells; Table Split enables you to split a table at any location.
New	Hyperlink CSS Formatting	Removes underlining and other hyperlink formatting options
New	Border Drop-Down Tool Button	Simplifies the creation of border formatting
New	Task Pane	A Microsoft Office innovation that provides sidebar-style access to commands such as New Page, New Web, Templates, Clip Art, Search, and the Office Clipboard
New	Office Clip Board	Enables you to cut and copy multiple items, preview clipboard contents, and preserve formatting options
Updated	Find and Replace	A new interface for searching within or across Webs

Graphics

Table B-2 describes new and updated features for graphics handling in FrontPage 2002.

	Table B-2 FrontPage Graphics Features	
Status	**Feature**	**Description**
New	Photo Gallery	Enables users to display a collection of images in a variety of layouts
New	Drawing tools	Autoshapes, drop shadows, Word Art, and text boxes
Updated	Themes	More and updated themes
Updated	Clip-art	FrontPage includes a bonus CD with over 25,000 pieces of clip art

Dynamic content

Table B-3 describes special features for working with dynamic Web content.

Table B-3
New Features for Dynamic Web Content

Status	Feature	Description
New	Automatic Web Content	Add MSNBC headlines and weather, MSN search, Expedia maps, and bCentral small business tools to your Web site
New	Browser Editable Lists	SharePoint technology that enables the creation of announcements, events, tasks, and contacts
New	Discussion Boards	SharePoint technology that enables the creation of threaded discussion forums
New	Surveys	SharePoint technology that enables users to insert online surveys using the Survey Wizard and/or templates. Includes responses and graphs of results

Technology and components

Table B-4 describes new and enhanced FrontPage 2002 components.

Table B-4
Enhanced FrontPage 2002 Components

Status	Feature	Description
New	Link Bars	Create a navigation bar using the Link Bars wizard
New	Web Components	New FrontPage 2002 components include Photo Gallery, Link Bars, Top 10 Lists, List Views, Save to Database, and Automatic Web Content
New	Inline Frames	Support for HTML 4.0 inline frames specification
Updated	Speech Recognition	Automate common tasks with spoken commands
Updated	Handwriting Recognition	Use handwriting recognition to execute common tasks
Updated	Shared Border	In FrontPage 2002, users can apply background colors or images to shared borders

Site administration

Table B-5 describes enhanced FrontPage 2002 site administration features.

Table B-5
FrontPage 2002 Web Site Administration Features

Status	Feature	Description
New	Usage Analysis	Get on-demand reports indicating Web site usage with FrontPage 2002 server extensions
New	Top 10 Lists	Add to any page a list of the ten most frequently accessed pages, and so on, on a given Web site
Updated	Reporting	Autofilter results and export to HTML or Excel
Updated	Permissions	Grant access to individuals and groups based on roles

HTML and programming language editing

Table B-6 describes new and enhanced features for HTML and program editing.

Table B-6
HTML and Code Editing Features

Status	Feature	Description
New	Paste Formatting Options	Keep source formatting or use destination styles
New	XML Formatting	Apply XML formatting rules to an HTML page
Updated	ASP Source Code Preservation	Open all ASP pages in Normal view and leave ASP code undisturbed
Updated	HTML Reformatting	Reformat imported Web pages

Publishing

Table B-7 describes new and updated features for publishing your Web site.

Table B-7 Web Site Publishing Features		
Status	**Feature**	**Description**
Updated	Publishing Dialog Box	View source and destination files; select files to publish or exclude; drag and drop files in either direction
New	Single Page Publishing	Publish a selected page on demand
New	Publishing Log Files	Report on publishing history
Updated	Publishing Performance	Speed reported increased 2–3 times
New	Background Publishing	Continue working while your Web site publishes
Updated	FTP Support	Updated interface to simplify publishing of Web pages via FTP

Productivity and teamwork

Table B-8 describes enhanced productivity features.

Table B-8 Productivity Features		
Status	**Feature**	**Description**
New	Microsoft SharePoint	Discussions and submissions; integration with FrontPage Document Library
Updated	Language and International Support	FrontPage 2002 is available in 26 languages (11 new in 2002)
New	Unicode Support	Improves ability to create Web sites in multiple languages

E-commerce

Table B-9 describes new features for enhancing e-commerce capabilities using
FrontPage 2002.

<table>
<tr><td colspan="3" align="center">Table B-9
E-Commerce Features</td></tr>
<tr><td>*Status*</td><td>*Feature*</td><td>*Description*</td></tr>
<tr><td>New</td><td>bCentral Commerce Manager Add-in</td><td>Subscription service for adding e-commerce capabilities, including a product catalog and shopping cart</td></tr>
<tr><td>New</td><td>Auctions</td><td>An additional feature offering of the bCentral Commerce Manager</td></tr>
<tr><td>New</td><td>Database Interface Wizard</td><td>Simplifies the process of creating forms and pages necessary for viewing and editing database records</td></tr>
<tr><td>Updated</td><td>Forms</td><td>FrontPage 2002 includes new field elements — group boxes and advanced buttons, and a file upload capability</td></tr>
</table>

✦ ✦ ✦

Index of FrontPage Templates

Use this appendix as a handy reminder of the page templates, frame page templates, style sheet templates, and Web templates available in FrontPage.

FrontPage Templates

This appendix provides a list of the templates included with FrontPage.

General page templates

The following templates shown in Table C-1 are accessible from the General tab of the Page Templates dialog box.

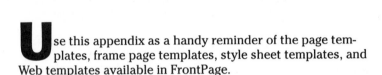

Table C-1 Page Templates	
Template	**Description**
Normal Page	A blank HTML page
Bibliography	A list of bibliographic entries
Confirmation Form	Acknowledges receipt of user input from discussion, form results, or registration pages
Feedback Form	Enables users to submit comments about your Web site, products, or organization
Form Page Wizard	Walks you through the creation of a custom forms page

Continued

Table C-1 *(continued)*

Template	*Description*
Frequently Asked Questions	A table of contents at the top of the page, followed by questions and answers
Guest Book	A simple form enabling visitors to leave their comments in a public log
Narrow, Left-Aligned Body	Narrow column of text on the left, image on the right
Narrow, Right-Aligned Body	Narrow column of text on the right, image on the left
One-Column Body	Centered body of text
One-Column Body with Contents and Sidebar	Sidebar navigation on the left, second sidebar on the right
One-Column Body with Contents on Left	Table of contents on the left
One-Column Body with Contents on Rights	Table of contents on the right
One-Column Body with Staggered Sidebar	Two-column staggered sidebar on the left
One-Column Body with Two Sidebars	Two-column staggered sidebar on the left, plus a sidebar on the right
One-Column Body with Two-Column Sidebar	Two-column sidebar on the right
Photo Gallery	A page to display your photos in one of four layout styles (horizontal, montage, slide show and vertical)
Search Page	A keyword search of all documents in your Web
Table of Contents	Outline-formatted links to pages in your Web
Three-Column Body	Three vertical columns
Two-Column Body	Two vertical columns
Tow-Column Body with Contents and Sidebar	Two columns of body text in the middle, sidebars on left and right
Two-Column Body with Contents on Left	Two columns of text with a sidebar on the left
Two-Column Staggered Body	Two vertical columns with contents staggered
Two-Column Staggered Body with Contents and Sidebar	Two vertical columns with staggered content and sidebars on the left and right

Template	Description
User Registration	User registration (user name and password) for a protected Web; only useful in the root Web
Wide Body with Headings	Single column of indented body text with headings

Frames pages templates

The templates shown in Table C-2 are accessible from the Frames Pages tab of the Page Templates dialog box.

Table C-2 Frames Pages	
Templates	**Description**
Banner and Contents	Three frames: banner top frame, table of contents side frame on the left, and a large, main frame
Contents	Two frames: table of contents side frame on the left and a large, main frame
Footer	Two frames: main frame on top, with a footer underneath. Hyperlinks in the footer update the main frame.
Footnotes	Two frames: main frame on top, with a footer underneath, but the footnote frame is taller and hyperlinks in the main frame update the footnotes
Header	Two frames: navigation header and main frame underneath it. Hyperlinks in the header update the main frame.
Header, Footer, and Contents	Four frames: header frame, footer frame, left side frame for table of contents, and a main frame
Horizontal Split	Two equally sized top and bottom frames
Nested Hierarchy	Three frames: a side frame that runs the entire vertical length of the frame, and a banner frame on top of a larger, main frame. Hyperlinks in the side frame update the banner frame.
Top-Down Hierarchy	Three frames: a narrow top frame, a wider middle frame, and a main frame. Hyperlinks in the top frame update the middle frame.
Vertical Split	Two equally sized left and right frames

Style sheets templates

The templates shown in Table C-3 are accessible from the Style Sheets tab of the Page Templates dialog box.

Table C-3 Style Sheets	
Style Sheet	**Description**
Normal Style Sheet	A blank cascading style sheet
Arcs	Brown Verdana text, brown Times New Roman headers, pale yellow background
Bars	Arial text, Times New Roman Headers, and light olive background
Blocks	Bookman Old Style text and headers, red hyperlinks, and silver background
Blueprint	Century Gothic text and headers, purple hyperlinks, and bright yellow background
Capsules	Arial text and headers, red-orange hyperlinks, and light green background
Downtown	Yellow Garamond text, Verdana headers, orange hyperlinks, and royal blue background
Expedition	Book Antiqua text and headers, peach background
Highway	White Verdana text, Verdana headers, orange hyperlinks, and a black background
Neon	Neon green Verdana text and headers, chartreuse hyperlinks, and a black background
Poetic	Purple Book Antiqua text, Book Antiqua headers, and a white background
Street	Navy Verdana text, Comic Sans MS headers, and a light cyan background
Sweets	Dark blue Arial text, Arial Rounded MT Bold headers, and a pale yellow background

Web templates

The templates shown in Table C-4 are accessible from the Web Sites tab of the Web Site Templates dialog box.

Table C-4
Web Templates and Wizards

Template or Wizard	Description
One Page Web	One blank page
Corporate Presence Wizard	Walks you through the process of creating a corporate site. Includes a home page, What's New, Product/Services, a table of contents, a feedback form, and a search form
Customer Support Web	Includes What's New, Products, FAQ, Service Request, Suggestions, Catalogs, Manuals, Support Forum, Contact, and Search
Database Interface Wizard	Creates a Web site that connects to a database to view, add, update, or delete database records
Discussion Web Wizard	Creates a threaded discussion group with table of contents and search
Empty Web	A new web with nothing in it
Import Web Wizard	Creates a new Web and adds content from an external source
Personal Web	Includes a home page, an About Me page, Interests, Favorites, a Photo Gallery, and Feedback
Project Web	Includes a home page, Members, Schedule, Archive, Search, Discussions, Contact Information
SharePoint-Based Team contact	Creates a team events calendar, document library, task list, Web Sitelist, announcements, discussions and search. Requires a SharePoint-enabled server

✦   ✦   ✦

Best FrontPage Add-ins and Resources

Because Microsoft FrontPage has such a vast user base, there is a large market for the development of sophisticated add-in tools. FrontPage 2002 takes new steps in integrating these additional programs right into the FrontPage interface.

FrontPage Add-ins

When you purchase and install a FrontPage add-in program, that program becomes available when you select Insert ➪ Web Component ➪ Additional Components. Figure D-1 shows the Insert Web Component dialog box displaying additional components.

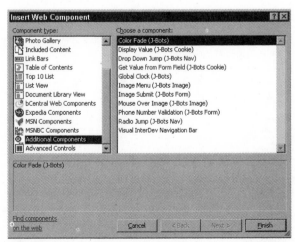

Figure D-1: Available add-in programs are displayed in the Component type list of the Insert Web Component dialog box.

As FrontPage has evolved, three particular add-ins have stuck around, improved, and become more stable and useful. In fact, these add-ins are actually valuable full-fledged programs in their own right. These products have an update schedule that runs parallel to that of FrontPage, and the publishers were cool enough to provide us with pre-release versions of the updated editions of all these programs for FrontPage 2002 in time to test and review them:

+ FrontLook Version 3 includes many presentation and animation tools to enhance your FrontPage site.

+ J-Bots Plus 2002 provides program applets to process form data, insert JavaScript applets, and manage cookie data, and other features.

+ StoreFront 5.0 is the most accessible, integratable e-commerce solution for FrontPage Webs.

This appendix describes the features of these programs in more detail. For updated links to FrontPage resources, visit www.ppinet.com/resource.htm.

Upgrading add-ins

FrontPage 2002 handles add-ins very differently than it's predecessors. Our best information indicates that add-ins developed for previous versions of FrontPage will not mesh smoothly with FrontPage 2002. This is because the file locations for add-ins have changed, and the way add-in features are made available in FrontPage (through the Insert Web Component dialog box) is new.

Only add-ins developed specifically for FrontPage 2002 are guaranteed to work with FrontPage 2002.

Configuring add-ins

You can attach or remove add-ins in the COM Add-Ins dialog box, shown in Figure D-2. To access this dialog box, choose Tools ➪ Add-Ins.

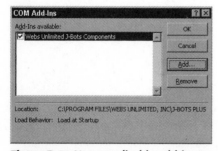

Figure D-2: You can disable add-ins, or re-attach them to FrontPage, in the COM Add-Ins dialog box.

The COM Add-Ins dialog box displays all installed add-ins, and enables you to define whether or not they will be opened along with FrontPage when you launch the program.

Use the checkboxes with each product to elect to load (or not load) the add-in. Use the Add button in the COM Add-Ins dialog box to add new add-in programs, and use the Remove button to *permanently* remove them. Removed programs will no longer be available in FrontPage until you reinstall them using the install features provided by the add-in publisher.

FrontLook

FrontLook provides additional themes, artwork, and theme editing tools that allow you to improve the look of your FrontPage Web site. Series 3 is not exactly an update, it's more like "episode 3" in a series of applets, themes, and Web art that supplement the (rather skimpy) graphical elements that come with FrontPage.

The latest in the series, FrontLook Series 3, has 2 mega applets, over 30 new themes and over 300 pieces of Web art. The scroller applet supports multiple columns with different fonts, text styles, colors, hyperlinking, and sound triggers. The presentation applet supports banners and image presentations, eye-candy image transitions, hyperlinking, and status bar support.

FrontLook basically consists of three elements:

✦ A large set of themes

✦ A large set of clip art

✦ Customizable Java applets for interactive and animated presentations

Unlike other add-ins, FrontLook's features are more integrated into FrontPage itself. Themes are added to your existing list of (FrontPage) themes, clip art is added to your library of clip art, and the customizable Java applets are accessed not from a separate toolbar or the Insert Web Component dialog box, but instead from a special FrontLook menu that is added to the FrontPage menu bar, like the one shown in Figure D-3.

Figure D-3: Choosing a Presentation Applet from the FrontLook menu

Note   When you create animations with FrontLook, you generate Java (class) files. These files are stored in a folder called `_FrontLook` that is added to your Web.

Another new feature of FrontLook is the FrontLook Theme Chameleon. In a nutshell, the Chameleon lets you change the coloring of a theme in a matter of a few clicks. We like the Theme Chameleon because it is extremely fast and you don't need any external graphic products to modify an existing theme.

J-Bots Plus 2002

J-Bots Plus offers 50 handy additions to FrontPage. These features work by generating JavaScript applets that are embedded in your page. Because J-Bots animation and interactivity is based on JavaScript, instead of Microsoft's relatively proprietary DHTML, J-Bots features are more widely supported than FrontPage's DHTML effects.

Like all add-ins, J-Bots features are available from the Insert Web Component dialog box (choose Additional Components). However, J-Bots also comes with a handy custom toolbar, shown in Figure D-4.

Figure D-4: J-Bots add-in applets can be constructed from a custom menu.

Some of the main features of J-Bots include the following:

✦ **Image Components:** Provide effects that can be applied to images.

✦ **Drop Down Image Menu:** Enables your visitor to select from a drop-down menu of images and have the image displayed on the page.

✦ **Flowing Menu:** A text or image menu with URL links flows from an image when hovered over with the visitor's mouse.

✦ **Image Graph:** Charts numeric data.

✦ **Image Menu:** Enables visitors to view images by hovering the mouse over a text-based menu of images.

✦ **Image Preloader:** Preloads image files into the browser's cache.

✦ **Image Status:** Shows a message in the status bar of the visitor's browser when the cursor is moved over the image area.

✦ **Mouse Over Image:** Changes an initial image to another when the mouse cursor is moved over the initial image.

✦ **Random Images:** Displays images from a list of images randomly, with unlimited URLs.

✦ **Form Components:** Adds features to FrontPage forms, such as telephone number validation, credit card number validation, and the use of an image for a Submit button.

✦ **Cookie Components:** Enables you to use cookies to track and display visitor information on Web sites, and utilize cookie data in your page.

One of our favorite J-Bots is the one that generates a navigation drop-down menu. This is one of the most requested "missing" tools in FrontPage — the ability to create a drop-down menu that acts as a jump menu for links.

StoreFront 5

StoreFront 5 provides the most accessible way for FrontPage developers to create e-commerce sites. While any kind of overview of the possibilities and pitfalls of diving into e-commerce is way beyond the scope of this appendix, if you have the product, the marketing, and the distribution end together, you can use your FrontPage skills to generate a full-fledged e-commerce site for a small or medium-sized business.

Tip

In our pre-release version of FrontPage, we tended to lose the StoreFront menu. Periodically, when we launched FrontPage, our StoreFront menu simply disappeared. A helpful article at the StoreFront knowledge base told us to use Tools ⇨ Add-Ins, and remove StoreFront. Then, you must reinstall StoreFront. To do that, browse to the `StoreFront.tem` folder on the hard drive (this path is usually `C:\program files\microsoft office\templates\1033\webs\storefront.tem`) and select `StoreFront.dll`. Click OK. StoreFront 5 should now be listed as an available add-in; Click OK to exit the Add-Ins menu and the toolbar should load. If the toolbar still does not load, press Ctrl+Alt+Del and select End Task on all instances of FrontPage that are running and restart the application.

StoreFront is a powerful and complex program — more or less equivalent in complexity to using FrontPage's database features. You really want to be comfortable with the material in Part VI of this book ("Connecting Databases to the Web") before you begin to install and configure StoreFront. If you *are* comfortable defining and connecting Web databases with FrontPage, however, you'll find that StoreFront has an impressive array of options, from sales tax calculations to suggesting client's preferred purchases.

StoreFront features

Key features of StoreFront 5 include the following:

✦ The capability to sell an unlimited number of products

✦ The capability (and need to) utilize either a Microsoft Access or Microsoft SQL Server (AE Version) database

✦ Customer management with login

✦ Currency conversion services via OANDA

✦ Save for Later/Saved Cart

✦ Sale features, including sale price by product, store-side discounting, and free shipping by order total

Figuring taxes

StoreFront comes with features that calculate taxes and do currency conversions. Supported features include:

✦ Two-tier tax capability for countries with VAT or other multilevel tax structures

✦ One-click support for all Windows currency types

StoreFront interacts with other products

The folks at StoreFront have put together working relationships with many vendors like shippers and electronic payment companies. The following other products are supported in StoreFront.

✦ Support for product-, value-, or carrier-based shipping

✦ Real-time shipping rates for UPS, FedEx, and USPS

✦ Capabilities for electronic checks, purchase orders, COD, credit cards, and telephone/fax

✦ Built-in support for online transaction processing services, including the following: CyberCash, VeriSign Payflow Pro, Cardservice International LinkPoint API, Authorize.Net, Planet Payment, Merchant OnLine, SurePay, SecurePay, Internet Cash, Charge Solutions, Approve.Net, PsiGate, and Quick Commerce

Inventory and reporting features

StoreFront automatically generates e-mail confirmation for sales and connects with affiliate programs. Other reporting features include:

✦ Credit card data encoded for security

✦ E-mail order notification to customer and merchant

✦ Affiliate partner program

✦ Detailed sales reports, invoices, and sales summaries

Note Storefront also just recently released a new feature for their product. This is called the StoreFront Theme Builder. The Theme Design Collection includes ten professional Web store themes and a theme publisher.

Other Add-ins

In addition to the established add-ins we've been able to test ourselves, a growing number of vendors are offering add-ins for FrontPage Web developers. These add-ins fall into three general categories: e-commerce solutions, scripted plug-ins, and graphics.

We'll continue to test these products and make them available at the resources page of ppinet (www.ppinet.com).

Along with these categories of add-ins, you can find many link and banner exchange vendors on the Web. Some offer to broker link trades between your site and others. Alternatively, some of these programs hook you up with other affiliated programs. These affiliated programs are worth exploring as a way to bring small streams of income into your site.

✦   ✦   ✦

Index

Continued

TK
5105.8885
.M53
E433

2001